the Pacific Crest Trail

Volume 2: Oregon & Washington

Jeffrey P. Schaffer
Andy Selters

Maps drawn by
Jeffrey P. Schaffer and Kenneth R. Ng

Acknowledgments

During the summer of 1973, Jeff Schaffer mapped all of the Oregon PCT and some of the Washington PCT: Columbia River to White Pass and Stevens Pass to Rainy Pass. Bev and Fred Hartline mapped the rest of the Washington PCT: White Pass to Stevens Pass and Rainy Pass to Manning Provincial Park. Both parties went back in the summers of '75 and '76, and Schaffer went back in '78, '82 and '85, most of these excursions being for the purpose of mapping newly built PCT segments. Along such trips Schaffer would try to spot check as many roads, trailheads, trail segments and resorts as possible. The Hartlines moved away from the area, so in 1985 Schaffer asked Andy Selters, a professional alpine guide operating out of Bellingham, Washington, to become a co-author. Selters remapped and rewrote the PCT description from White Pass to Stevens Pass.

If one has only a very limited time to do field work on the PCT, he must know what stretches need to be mapped or field-checked. For this information we have relied on the U.S. Forest Service, the National Park Service, the Bureau of Land Management and our readers. We don't have the space to acknowledge all those who helped us in previous editions, but we can acknowledge a few of those who helped with the current edition. Arranged by governmental agency, from south to north, these folks are: Jack Darnall (Klamath N.F.); Phil Akerman, John Czemerys and Margaret Holman (Rogue River N.F.); William Deese (Winema N.F.); James Wieman (Umpqua N.F.); Walter Schloer (Deschutes N.F.); Howard Rondthaler—who has always been very helpful and very critical (Mt. Hood N.F.); Donald Smith (Wenatchee N.F.); and Gail Ross (Manning Provincial Park). Among those in the private sector who who wrote us were Dan Atkinson, Jan Benson, Richard Greve and Ed Patterson. John Larsen of Tualatin, Oregon, deserves special mention, for over the years he has supplied us with every bit of PCT information he's come across.

Once we knew where to hike and what to verify, we were often faced with the problem—as many PCT hikers are—of arranging a shuttle service. At times Ken Ng provided Schaffer with extensive shuttle service and also recorded data on roads, campgrounds, available services and anything else he saw. In like manner Jeff MacDonald and Margaret Wilson provided shuttle service for Selters. Jill Fugate also provided such service, and on top of that, she reviewed Andy's manuscript.

Finally, credit must be given to Thomas Winnett, publisher of Wilderness Press, who conceived the idea of a *detailed* PCT guidebook, and who, despite the many problems of cost and production, strove for increasingly higher guidebook standards while other publishers settled for less. Without him, this book never would have become the "PCT hikers' bible" that it is today.

Jeffrey P. Schaffer
Hercules, California

Andy Selters
Bellingham, Washington

May 1986

First edition 1974
Second edition 1976
Third edition 1979
FOURTH EDITION 1986
Copyright © 1974, 1976, 1979, 1986 by Jeffrey P. Schaffer and Andy Selters

Library of Congress Card Catalog Number 85-041030
International Standard Book Number 0-89997-060-5

All photos by Jeffrey P. Schaffer except as noted
Cover photo: **Mt. Jefferson from Scout Lake**
Title-page photo: **Glacier Peak from the north**

Wilderness Press, 2440 Bancroft Way, Berkeley CA 94704

Library of Congress Cataloging-in-Publication Data

Schaffer, Jeffrey P.
  The Pacific Crest Trail.

  Bibliography: p.
  Includes index.
  1. Hiking--Pacific States--Guide-books. 2. Hiking--
Pacific Crest Trail--Guide-books. 3. Pacific States--
Description and travel--1981-   --Guide-books.
4. Pacific Crest Trail--Guide-books. I. Selters,
Andrew. II. Title.
GV199.42.P3S33 1986   917.9'043   85-41030
ISBN 0-89997-060-5 (v. 2)

Contents

Introductory Chapters

Trail Chapters

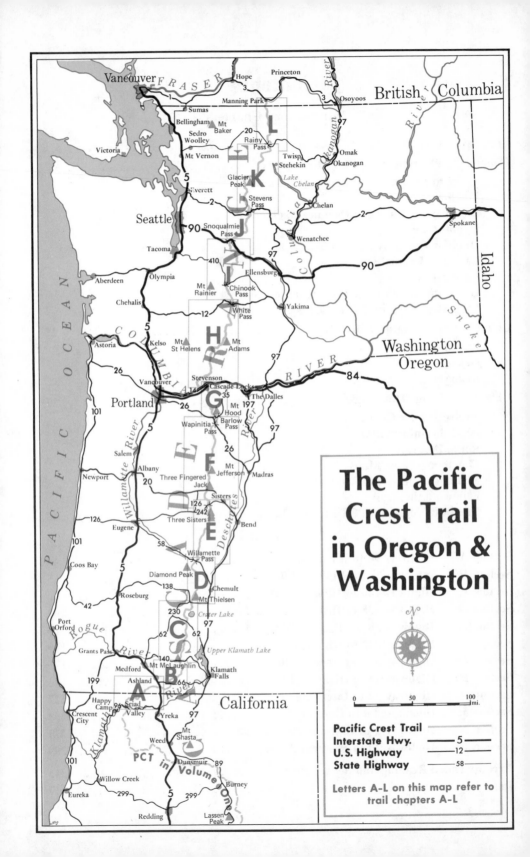

The Pacific Crest Trail in Oregon & Washington

Pacific Crest Trail
Interstate Hwy. — 5 —
U.S. Highway — 12 —
State Highway — 58 —

Letters A-L on this map refer to trail chapters A-L

0   50   100 mi.

Chapter 1: History of the PCT

The first proposal for the creation of a Pacific Crest Trail that we have been able to discover is contained in the book *Pacific Crest Trails,* by Joseph T. Hazard (Superior Publishing Co.). He says that in 1926 he was just ending a business interview with a Miss Catherine Montgomery at the Western Washington College of Education in Bellingham when she said,

"Do you know what I've been thinking about, Mr. Hazard, for the last twenty minutes?

"Just what have you in mind, Miss Montgomery?

"A high trail winding down the heights of our western mountains with mile markers and shelter huts—like those pictures I'll show you of the 'Long Trail of the Appalachians'—from the Canadian Border to the Mexican Boundary Line!"

To go back six years in time, the Forest Service had by 1920 routed and posted a trail from Mt. Hood to Crater Lake in Oregon, named the Oregon Skyline Trail, and with hindsight we can say that it was the first link in the PCT.

Hazard says that on that very night, he conveyed Miss Montgomery's suggestion to the Mt. Baker Club of Bellingham, which was enthusiastic about it. He says that soon a number of other mountain clubs and outdoor organizations in the Pacific Northwest adopted the idea and set about promoting it. Then, in 1928, Fred W. Cleator became Supervisor of Recreation for Region 6 (Oregon and Washington) of the U.S. Forest Service. Cleator proclaimed and began to develop the the Cascade Crest Trail, a route down the spine of Washington from Canada to the Columbia River. Later he extended the Oregon Skyline Trail at both ends so that it too traversed a whole state. In 1937 Region 6 of the Forest Service developed a design for PCT trail markers and posted them from the Canadian border to the California border.

But the Forest Service's Region 5 (California) did not follow his lead, and it remained for a private person to provide the real spark not only for a California segment of the PCT but indeed for the PCT itself. In the early Thirties the idea of a Pacific Crest Trail entered the mind of Clinton C. Clarke of Pasadena, California, who was then chairman of the Executive Committee of the Mountain League of Los Angeles County. "In March 1932," wrote Clarke in *The Pacific Crest Trailway,* he "proposed to the United States Forest and National Park Services the project of a continuous wilderness trail across the United States from Canada to Mexico. . . . The plan was to build a trail along the summit divides of the mountain ranges of these states, traversing the best scenic areas and maintaining an absolute wilderness character."

The proposal included formation of additional Mountain Leagues in Seattle, Portland and San Francisco by representatives of youth organizations and hiking and mountaineering clubs similar to the one in Los Angeles. These Mountain Leagues would then take the lead in promoting the extension of the John Muir Trail northward and southward to complete a pathway from border to border. When it became evident that more than Mountain Leagues were needed for such a major undertaking, Clarke took the lead in forming the Pacific Crest Trail System Conference, with representatives from the three Pacific Coast states. He served as its President for 25 years.

As early as January 1935 Clarke published a handbook-guide to the PCT giving the route in rather sketchy terms ("the Trail goes east of Heart Lake, then south across granite fields to the junction of Piute and Evolution Creeks"—this covers about 9 miles).

In the summer of 1935—and again the next 3 summers—groups of boys under the sponsorship of the YMCA explored the PCT route in relays, proceeding from Mexico on June 15, 1935, to Canada on August 12, 1938. This exploration was under the guidance of a YMCA secretary, Warren L. Rogers, who served as Executive Secretary of the Pacific Crest Trail System Conference (1932–1957) and who continues his interest in the PCT by publishing new information on the trail and conducting trip-planning seminars about it.

During World War II, the Pacific Crest Trail was generally ignored and its completion remained in a state of limbo until the 1960s, when backpacking began to appeal to large numbers of people. In 1965 the Bureau of Outdoor Recreation, a Federal agency, appointed a commission to make a nationwide trails study. The commission, noting that walking for pleasure was second only to driving for pleasure as the most popular recreation in America, recommended establishing a national system of trails, of two kinds: long National Scenic Trails in the hinterlands and shorter National Recreation Trails in and near metropolitan areas. The commission recommended that Congress establish four Scenic Trails: the already existing Appalachian Trail, the partly existing Pacific Crest Trail, a Potomac Heritage Trail and a Continental Divide Trail. Congress responded by passing, in 1968, the National Trails System Act, which set the framework for a system of trails and specifically made the Appalachian and the Pacific Crest trails the first two National Scenic Trails.

Meanwhile, in California, the Forest Service in 1965 had held a series of meetings about a route for the PCT in the state. These meetings involved people from the Forest Service, the Park Service, the State Division of Parks and Beaches, and other government bodies charged with responsibility over areas where the trail might go. These people decided that so much time had elapsed since Clarke had drawn his route that they should essentially start all over. Of course, it was pretty obvious that segments like the John Muir Trail would not be overlooked in choosing a new route through California. By the end of 1965 a proposed route had been drawn onto maps. (We don't say "mapped," for that would imply that someone actually had covered the route in the field.)

When Congress, in the 1968 law, created a citizens Advisory Council for the PCT, it was the route devised in 1965 which the Forest Service presented to the council as a "first draft" of a final PCT route. This body of citizens was to decide all the details of the final route; the Forest Service said it would adopt whatever the citizens wanted. The Advisory Council was also to concern itself with standards for the physical nature of the trail, markers to be erected along the trail, and the administration of the trail and its use.

In 1972 the Advisory Council agreed upon a route, and the Forest Service put it onto maps for internal use. Since much of the agreed-upon route in California, southern Oregon and southern Washington was cross-country, these maps were sent to the various national forests along the route, for them to mark a temporary route in the places where no trail existed along the final PCT route. This they did—but not always after field work. The result was that the maps made available to the public in June 1972 showing the final proposed route and the temporary detours did not correspond to what was on the ground in many places. A common flaw was that the Forest Service showed a temporary or permanent PCT segment following a trail taken off a pre-existing Forest Service map when in fact there *was no trail* where it was shown on that map in the first place.

Perfect or not, the final proposed route was sent to Washington for publication in the Federal Register, the next step toward its becoming official. A verbal description of the route was also published in the Federal Register on January 30, 1973. But the material in the register did not give a center line which could be precisely and unambiguously followed; it was only a *route,* and the details in many places remained to be settled. Furthermore, much private land along the route remained to be acquired, or at least an easement secured for using it.

A portion of the Federal Register describing the PCT is reproduced below together with one of the register's PCT maps.

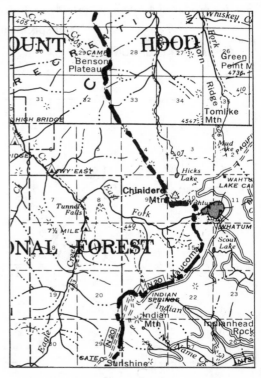

OREGON

At the south end of the Bridge of the Gods is the community of Cascade Locks, elevation 100 feet. This is the lowest elevation on the Pacific Crest Trail between the Canadian border and the Mexican border. A quarter of a mile south of the Bridge of the Gods, the Trail enters the Mt. Hood National Forest and ascends the rugged south side of the Columbia Gorge and quickly attains an elevation of 4,000 feet on Benson Plateau. It continues south, past Chinidere Mountain and Wahtum Lake, traversing the slopes high above Eagle Creek, the West Fork of Hood River and Lost Lake. The Trail then descends gently into Lolo Pass, crosses Forest Road N12 and ascends Bald Mountain where it is joined by Timberline Trail on Mt. Hood. Traversing Mt. Hood, the Trail then descends into the Muddy Fork, passes beneath Ramona Falls, and crosses the main fork of the Sandy River. Two miles south of the Sandy River, the Trail enters Mt. Hood Wilderness near Paradise Park at an elevation of 6,000 feet. It descends and crosses Zigzag Canyon, leaves the Mt. Hood Wilderness, and turns easterly to regain 1,000 feet in elevation and crosses just north of Timberline Lodge and the Mt. Hood Ski Area. It

At the time of the Register's publication, the Pacific Crest Trail was more or less continuous from Canada's Manning Park to Highway 140 near Lake of the Woods in southern Oregon. However, southwest from that highway, the 73-mile PCT route to the California border was *entirely* along roads. (Before the Register's publication of a route, the PCT route coincided with the old Oregon Skyline route, which headed south 40 miles from Highway 140 near Lake of the Woods over to the California border. Only 5 miles of trail existed along this older route.)

Of great importance, then, was the construction of PCT to replace the 73-mile temporary route. In 1973 the PCT in the southern Sky Lakes Area was relocated so that it ended on Highway 140 near Fish Lake. Then, from 1974 until 1978, the trail was built southwest toward Interstate 5. During this time, another stretch of trail was built northeast from Seiad Valley toward Interstate 5. However, as late as 1985 private property stood in the way, and 3½ miles of route were still along roads.

Likewise, private property prevented the PCT in Washington from extending its last few miles south to the Columbia River. Its predecessor, the Cascade Crest Trail, had in fact been completed to the river in 1935, seven years after work on it had begun. However, that old trail ended 12½ miles east of a suitable river crossing, namely, the Bridge of the Gods. Likewise, the Oregon Skyline Trail ended not at a river crossing but rather at a trailhead 3 miles east of the bridge. An Oregon route to that bridge was built in 1974, but its Washington counterpart, across lands outside the National Forest, was not completed until 1984. This Washington stretch, making a roundabout route, takes 44 miles to reach Big Huckleberry Mountain; the old Cascade Crest Trail reached it in 20½ miles.

During the 1970s the existing PCT also underwent changes. In May 1971 the Forest Service produced a *Pacific Crest Trail Guide for Location, Design, and Management,*

Trail specifications, steep slope (from F. S. *PCT Guide*)

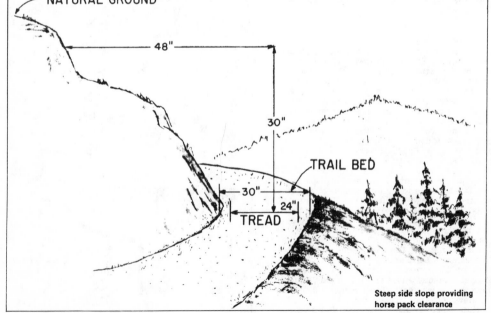

NATURAL GROUND

48"

30"

TRAIL BED

30"

24"

TREAD

Steep side slope providing
horse pack clearance

which stipulated specific characteristics of the final trail. Perhaps the two most significant ones were that the trail should stay close to the crest and that its grade should not exceed 15 percent (a 15-foot rise for 100 horizontal feet). The old Cascade Crest and Oregon Skyline trails veered away from the crest in places, and in many places they were too steep.

In order to reduce the steepness, the trail had to either go around ridges rather than over them, or else it had to have switchbacks added to reduce the grade. Both changes led to increases in the PCT's overall length. The best example of such lengthening is along a stretch from Highway 138 north past Mt. Thielsen to Windigo Pass. Originally 24½ miles long, it was stretched to 30¼ miles by 1977, an increase of 23 percent. North of Windigo Pass a new section of PCT was built because the old Oregon Skyline Trail veered too far east from the crest. This change also increased the overall PCT route length, replacing a 21-mile stretch with a winding, 30½-mile one, an increase of 45 percent! However, not all realignments are longer. For example, in the Goat Rocks Wilderness, minor trail relocations in 1974 and 1978 both led to a small reduction of the PCT's length, as did a relocation in the northern Sky Lakes Wilderness.

The PCT has also been relocated to avoid wet areas. One such area that gave hikers mosquito bites and muddy boots was a short stretch south from southern Washington's Sawtooth Huckleberry Field. The trail was rerouted along slopes above the area's boggy flats.

Publicity about the PCT, especially through Eric Ryback's popular, if inaccurate account, inspired new waves of backpackers to trek along the route. Some parts of the route, however, were overused, and therefore had to be relocated. One such area was the Twin Lakes area, just north of Oregon's Wapinitia Pass. In Crater Lake National Park, a trail stretch was relocated for a similar reason. The Park's most scenic stretch crossed the Pumice Desert and gave the hiker views of both the Crater Lake rim and Mt. Thielsen. Decision makers, however, felt that hordes of hikers would trample the "desert's" fragile wildflowers into ruin—not very likely. Right or wrong, they relocated the trail to conform with the rest of the park's PCT—an essentially viewless, mosquito-infested traverse through a lodgepole forest.

To the consternation of PCT hikers, the decision makers did *not* relocate the stretch of Crater Lake PCT that circumvents Crater Lake. This route, along abandoned roads, stays several miles away from the lake's view-packed rim, and therefore backpackers rarely take it. Surely, if any stretch of PCT deserves to be relocated, it is this stretch, which should be rebuilt so that it *at least* touches or approaches the rim in several places.

After new sections of the PCT were built and many others rebuilt or relocated, the Forest Service turned its attention to trailhead parking lots. Most PCT hikers, after all, do short stretches such as the 12 sections (A–L) found in this book and virtually all of them park their cars near the PCT. In 1977 and '78, the Forest Service constructed several large lots, just off the PCT and major roads, to fill the need. In the 1980s, most work was in the form of new trail construction in southern California. We hope the PCT will be completed, so it exists as one continuous filament threading its way along the tops of mountain ranges from Mexico to Canada.

The trail's place in history is certainly minor when compared with today's world events, but generations from now, future historians may ponder its significance. During the middle of the 19th century, pioneer trails were blazed across the continent to open up new lands and resources for a growing, young America. About a century later, trails of another kind appeared, which we now call National Scenic Trails. These are about as long as the pioneer trails, but unlike them, they serve no economic purpose. At trail's end no fertile valleys, no gold mines, no thriving ports are reached. The Pacific Crest Trail, like the other National Scenic Trails, is not a corridor to an economic end but rather is a process for individual change and growth. Although the trail's end is a desirable goal, it is not a necessary one, for the traveler is enriched in a nonmaterial sense with every step he takes along the way. Clinton Clarke saw the trail as a way to "lead people back to a simpler and more natural life and arouse a love for nature and the outdoors." The trail, then, is a prescription to improve one's understanding of his place in the world. In a way, the trail is like a Norman Rockwell painting. This illustrator painted American land and life not as it was, but rather, as it *should* have been. So, too, the Pacific Crest Trail paints impressions on the hiker's mind, not of a world ravaged by man, but rather of a timeless, largely forgotten world where nature still exists as it was meant to be.

A trail-location drawing (from F.S. *PCT Guide*)

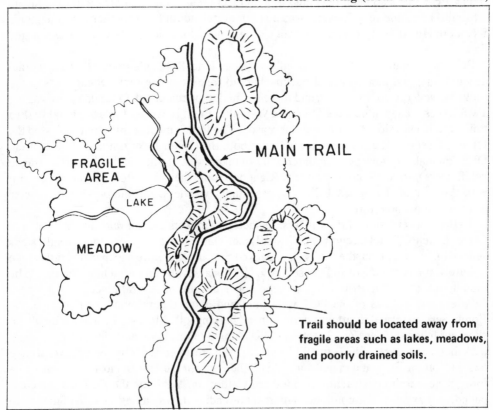

MAIN TRAIL

FRAGILE
AREA

LAKE

MEADOW

Trail should be located away from
fragile areas such as lakes, meadows,
and poorly drained soils.

Chapter 2: Planning Your PCT Hike

What to Expect

Of the thousands of backpackers who will taste wilderness along the Pacific Crest Trail each year, probably a hundred or less will complete the Oregon-Washington section and a few dozen will complete the entire tri-state route. Several hundred may hike either all of Oregon, which takes about 3½ weeks to hike, or all of Washington which, being more rugged, takes a few days more. Probably the vast majority of the trail's travelers will confine their wilderness visit to two weeks or less and therefore will be able to carry all their needs on their backs without having to use resupply points. This guidebook divides the Oregon-Washington PCT into 12 convenient backpack trips (Sections A through L), each starting and ending at a highway. The shortest trip, Section B, is usually done in 2½ to 4 days, while the longest ones, Sections H and K, are usually done in 6 to 12 days.

Some readers will walk the whole trail, Mexico to Canada. This takes 5–6 months to complete if you do 14–17 miles per day *nonstop*. Since most long-distance PCT hikers take layover days and also short side trips to supply points, they usually have to average about 20 miles per day when hiking along the trail. In past editions, we said that we hoped some readers would walk the whole trail in one long season. Some did and some more certainly will. However, for several reasons, we no longer recommend it. Hiking 20 miles a day, you'll be too exhausted to appreciate the scenery. Also, during the first two months and the last month, you are likely to encounter plenty of bad weather, lots of snow-covered ground, or both. These detract from your enjoyment of the scenery as well as impede your progress. Finally, the human body was not meant to carry heavy packs continuously over a rugged 2600-mile distance, and some hikers attempting this feat developed serious bone and ligament problems in their feet and legs.

Those still determined to hike the entire PCT continuously should start in early May (or sooner, if the Sierra Nevada snowpack has been light). The California section takes expert hikers about three months. You should try to complete the hottest part, south of the *southern* Sierra Nevada, by early June. However, you won't want to get into the High Sierra too early, for bad storms occurring as late as mid-June can bring your progress to a halt—or worse. If you're on schedule, you should cross into Oregon in early August and pass through the Sky Lakes Wilderness and the southern Three Sisters Wilderness in mid-to-late August. If you pass through these areas before late July, their seasonally superabundant mosquitoes will drive you almost insane. Perhaps by Labor Day your labor of wilderness love will be celebrated with your entry into Washington. One month later you should hope to consummate your hike, probably under the threat of rapidly deteriorating weather, in British Columbia's Ernest C. Manning Provincial Park.

If you are planning a short stretch and expect to encounter snow, hike from south to north. This way you'll encounter more downhill snow slopes than uphill ones, since snow lingers longer on north slopes—the ones you'll be descending. It's more fun to slide down a snowbank than to climb up one.

If the Cascade Range in Oregon and Washington were a uniform, continuous range, you could expect the snowpack to retreat uniformly northward as the summer wore on, and you could plan a month-long trek north so that you would always have a dry trail yet always have an adequate water source. However, this plan could have an undesired effect if you began at the height of the mosquito season: you'd have a continuous cloud of mosquitoes accompanying you north. The Cascade Range, however, is far from uniform, and often you will find yourself descending a snowbound pass into a warm, soothing, lake-dotted basin. If you are hiking the entire PCT, you are bound to encounter both pleasant and adverse trail conditions. If you want to avoid snow-clad trails, incessant mosquitoes and severe water shortages, then hike the following segments at these recommended times (remembering, of course, that weather patterns vary considerably from year to year).

Seiad Valley, Siskiyou Mountains, southern Oregon: *June through mid-September*
Mt. McLoughlin, Sky Lakes basin, Seven Lakes basin: *mid-July through late August*
Crater Lake: *July*
Mt. Thielsen, Windigo Pass, Diamond Peak: *mid-July through late August*
Three Sisters: *late July through early August*
Mt. Washington, Three Fingered Jack: *late June through mid-July*
Mt. Hood: *late July through mid-August*
Columbia River gorge, southern Washington: *mid-June through early September*
Mt. Adams, Goat Rocks, White Pass, Mt. Rainier, Stampede Pass, Snoqualmie Pass, Stevens Pass: *mid-July through mid-August*
Glacier Peak, North Cascades, Manning Provincial Park: *late July through early August.*

There are, of course, advantages and disadvantages to hiking in any season. In the North Cascades, for example,

- early June will present you with spectacular snow-clad alpine scenery—but also soft-snow walking and a slight avalanche hazard;
- early July will present you with a riotous display of wildflowers—plus sucking mosquitoes and biting flies;
- early August will present you with the best trail conditions—and lots of backpackers;
- early September will present you with fall colors and ripe huckleberries—but also nippy nights and sudden snow storms.

Weather

With the foregoing information plus a scan through the introduction of each of this guide's 12 hiking chapters, you should be forming in your mind a vague idea of where and how long you expect to hike. Let's sharpen that idea by looking at the weather. The warmest temperatures are in mid-July through early August; they can vary from the 90s in southern Oregon to the 70s in the North Cascades. During this period night temperatures for the entire two-state route rarely drop below 50°F—you'll swelter if you're cooped up in a down mummy bag.

In late June, with its long daylight hours, the maximum and minimum temperatures are almost as high as those in midsummer. In addition, you can expect to be plagued with mosquitoes through early August. A *tent is a necessity*—preferably one large enough for you and your friends to prepare meals in. During these warm summer nights, you'll want to sleep *atop* your sleeping bag, and although the mosquitos abate somewhat after dark, without a tent you won't get a mosquito-free sleep until later on in the season when the nights are cooler. Only when the wind picks up (late morning through late afternoon) or when a storm sets in are you afforded partial relief from these cursed insects. In Washington you will also be exposed to at least three species of biting flies—Ouch! But they are slower and easier to swat.

By late August the days have got considerably shorter and the temperatures lower. The evenings and nights in southern Oregon are comfortable but those in northern Washington are nippy, if not freezing. Expect to see morning frost on your tent and prepare for brisk, "autumn" days. Too, there's likely to be a water shortage, particularly in most of Oregon. The national forests may be closed to backpacking or they may require the backpacker to refrain from building campfires and use only a stove. A stove is also useful for boiling stagnant water and for melting snow. An advantage of a hike at this time, however, is that both Oregon and Washington will have a variety of berries ready for picking.

Another consideration is storms. Storm frequency increases northward. Northern California is virtually storm-free from mid-June through early September. In central Oregon the period of good weather is only July through August, and even then occasional storms may be expected. If you visit southern Washington, be prepared for bad weather, even though you might get to hike a week or two at a time in beautiful midsummer weather. Expect bad or threatening weather in northern Washington. It is possible to hike two solid weeks in the North Cascades without receiving a drop of precipitation, but don't count on it—you might just receive a month of rain, as hikers did in the summer of 1978. Here, a tent is necessary to keep out the rain as well as as to keep out the seasonal mosquitoes and flies.

Like storm frequency, lake temperature is influenced by the sun's apparent seasonal migratory pattern. Lakes are generally at their warmest in late July through early August. Also affecting a lake's temperature are its latitude, elevation, size, depth, inflow source and the side of the mountain, if any, that it is on. Below are some representative *maximum* temperatures you can expect to find at certain lakes and rivers, south to north.

Klamath River, northern California	80°F
Emigrant Lake, near Ashland	78
Margurette Lake, Sky Lakes Wilderness	75
Dumbbell Lake, Three Sisters Wilderness	73
Scout Lake, Mt. Jefferson Wilderness	67
Wahtum Lake, northern Oregon	65
Eagle Creek, Columbia River gorge	57

Columbia River	65
Shoe Lake, Goat Rocks Wilderness	65
Pear Lake, Henry M. Jackson Wilderness	63
Lake Janus, Henry M. Jackson Wilderness	72
Mica Lake, Glacier Peak Wilderness	33
Stehekin River, North Cascades National Park	50

After you decide which segment of the PCT you want to do, next comes the question of transportation. Unlike round trips and loop trips, a hike along part of the PCT does not take you back to where you started. So if you take a car and leave it at the trailhead, you have a transportation problem. The solution may be any of several:

● walk back to where you started
● take a bus back to where you started
● hitchhike back to where you started
● arrange for someone to drop you off and pick you up
● arrange with another group to meet halfway along the trail and exchange car keys, or have duplicate sets made in advance.
● take at least 2 people and 2 cars, and leave one car at each end of your trek
● take a bicycle or motorcycle in your vehicle, ride it to your trailhead, and after walking your section pick it up with your vehicle, which you left at the other trailhead.

After you have decided on a solution to the car problem, write it down and put it in your pack. You might forget if your trek is a long one.

Logistics for the Long Distance Backpacker

How can a book describe the psychological factors a person must prepare for . . . the despair, the alienation, the anxiety and especially the pain, both physical and mental, which slices to the very heart of the hiker's volition, which are the real things that must be planned for? No words can transmit those factors, which are more a part of planning than the elementary rituals of food, money and equipment, and how to get them.

—Jim Podlesney, in *Pacific Crest Trail*
Hike Planning Guide, edited by Chuck Long
(Signpost Publications)

The authors agree with that quotation. Furthermore, they do not believe a trail guide is the place for an extensive explanation of basic backpacking techniques, and in any event the PCT end-to-end is no trip for novices. However, the peculiar problems of an *expeditionary* trek do warrant a few pages.

If you are going to be on the trail for more than a couple of weeks, you will want to have supplies waiting for you at one or more places along the route. For this you can mail packages to yourself. Alternatively, you can drive to a place and leave a package with someone, if you are sure that person will be responsible for it. You can also hide caches in the wilderness, if you are willing to carry the heavy load in from the nearest road and carry all the packaging out—and if you trust the wildlife. There are a few towns near the PCT which will perhaps have adequate supplies and equipment—Ashland, Sisters, Cascade Locks, Stevenson and Chelan. However, even those towns may not have an adequate selection of lightweight backpacking food. It is best to depend on post offices. A list of post offices on or near the trail appears on page 15.

SUPPLIES

This discussion of supplies attempts to tell you what you will need, and how best to get it. The discussion relies heavily on the experiences of Ben Schifrin (co-author of Volume 1) during his hike of the entire PCT.

The first thing to know about supplies along the PCT is that they are scarce. Too many young people try to do the PCT without pre-planning their food and other supplies. So they get to a resort and find that there is no white gas, and its store is so limited that they will have to eat the same macaroni and cheese for the next five days. If one wants to go light, the *only* choice is to pre-plan your menus and the rest of your needs, and mail things ahead to yourself.

Food

The main thing to have waiting your arrival at a post office is food. When hiking long-distance on the PCT, food is the main concern. It causes more daydreaming and more bickering than anything else, even sex. As for the bickering, most people hike in groups, and much of the friction in a group is due to different eating habits. Some hikers don't eat breakfast; others won't hike an inch until they've had their steak and eggs. Some people eat every hour; others take the traditional three meal breaks. Many of these problems can be cured if each hiker carries his own food, and suits his own prejudices. This arrangement also allows flexibility in pace and in hiking partners.

As for the daydreaming, it comes to focus on delicious food, and lots of it. Schifrin's first rule is that it won't hurt to take too much, because it will turn out to be too little anyway. He and his two companions ate over 6000 calories a day out of their packs, and still lost weight. The mental stresses, as well as the obvious physical ones, use up energy. So food serves two purposes: to provide fuel, and to bolster morale. Take the things you crave. Most goodies—Hershey bars, beer, double fudgies, fresh cheese, mint cakes—are great energy sources, as well as providing variety and what Schifrin calls a "body con". At the bottom of some horrible ascent, you say to yourself, "You get a double helping of Hershey bar when you get to the top." It's something to sweat for.

Then there's the usual egregious gluttony upon reaching a town (which are so scarce along the Oregon-Washington PCT)—steaks, quarts of ice cream, gallons of chocolate milk, giant shrimp salads. Besides being good for morale and filling you up, these binges can give you a good idea of what's been missing from your diet, namely, whatever you craved and stuffed yourself on. For the next trail segment, correct the deficiency, insofar as you can. And for the whole trek, take a supply of multivitamin pills, just in case your diet is deficient in important vitamins.

The only time people told Schifrin they had brought too much food was when they thought they had brought too much of a *certain item*. One attractive young lady carried only soybeans and powdered milk. She made it—but only after she'd stopped at each ranger station along the route for a few days, and made it with the ranger in exchange for palatable food. Two men, carrying soybeans and something else unpalatably organic, got so sick of this menu that they ripped off a ranger station. (They didn't finish the trail; the ranger caught them two days later, and they went to jail.)

Other hikers seem to think that wild foods are theirs for the taking. Berries— huckleberries in particular—certainly are, but they won't sustain you. Remember that Indians spent most of their waking hours in search of foodstuffs, not just an hour a day.

Besides, if hikers gorged themselves at every berry patch, there would be that much less for other hikers and the wild animals. Sample the berries, don't feast on them. Similarly with trout: don't plan to live off trout—they may not be biting during the time you have free to devote to fishing. View a fresh catch as a bonus, not an essential.

You won't have to rely on "Mother Nature" in Oregon or Washington since, if you're an "average" long-distance PCT hiker, you'll never have to carry more than an 8-day food supply, even on the longest stretches between supply points. Therefore, with careful shopping, you can buy all the food you'll need at your local supermarket rather than buy expensive freeze-dried food. (In California's John Muir Trail section of the PCT, lightweight freeze-dried food is a *must*.) Freeze-dried food, despite its high cost, is preferred by some hikers since, in the Oregon-Washington PCT, using it can cut your pack's weight by 5–15 pounds, depending on how much food you typically eat and how far you are going to hike.

Regardless of whether you carry regular or lightweight food, you will most likely want a balance between cold and hot foods. Cold foods are of course more appropriate for lunch, though we meet hikers who go 100 miles without cooking. Some people refuse to face the dawn without hot drinks. Those who dispense with hot foods to save weight and time may suffer mentally on a freezing evening in the North Cascades. Variety is the key. No matter how much time you spend planning your food, however, you are sure to be dissatisfied, somewhere down the trail, with what you brought or with how much of it you brought. You may find that eventually all freeze-dried dinners taste the same to you. You may find that you can never get a full feeling. You may lose 30 pounds. Or you may find that you brought too much. Just be prepared for such things to happen. Fortunately, you are not totally locked into your planned menus. You can mail back—or abandon—what you can't stand, and buy something else at towns and resorts along the way—although it will not be cheap in such places. You can even ask your contact at home to buy some new food items and mail them to you.

In planning menus, remember that at 5000' elevation, cooking time is double what it is at sea level, and at 7,500' it is triple. So don't bring foods that take long to cook at sea level.

Wood won't always be available, and if you are hiking 15+ miles a day, you'll find neither the time nor the energy to gather wood and start a fire. Anyway, wood is getting too scarce to use, due to the large number of backpackers, so we strongly recommend you bring a stove instead. You should know the rate at which your stove consumes fuel, for you will need lots of it if you do the whole PCT. Cartridge stoves, such as the Bleuet, do not burn as hot as white-gas stoves, particularly when the cartridge is low on fuel, but they do have several advantages: they are very easy to start, and virtually foolproof, and you can mail propane cartridges whereas you can't mail white gas. (Unleaded gasoline, purchased at gas stations, works adequately in white-gas stoves, but be ready for more clogging and shorter stove life.)

Water

Usually you can hike most stretches of the PCT carrying no more than a quart of water. But is it safe to drink? Clear lakes and streams may contain *Giardia lamblia,* a microscopic organism that causes giardiasis. While this disease is usually not life-threatening, it can make you feel absolutely rotten, with diarrhea, cramps, gas and the like. You can guard against giardiasis and similar diseases by boiling your water for 3–5 minutes, although this is time-consuming and can use a lot of fuel. Iodine tablets are easier to carry, but may not be 100% effective. Schaffer doesn't like hot water *or* iodine-tasting water, so he uses a water-filtering device, and it has worked—so far.

Clothing

In planning what clothes to take, realize that rain, and sometimes snow, is possible at any time at any point along the Oregon-Washington PCT. Therefore have good protection against wet and cold, whatever it costs. Remember that cotton clothing is useless when wet. Play it safe and assume there will be a storm. Bring along appropriate clothing and *know* how to keep it—and your sleeping bag—dry.

Boots are the most important piece of clothing. They must be broken in before the trip. Otherwise, they may turn out not to fit, and they will surely give you a crop of blisters. For the entire PCT, it's best to have two pairs of boots in the same size and same style. Mail one pair ahead. Schifrin broke his foot because his two pair were of two different styles, and one pair didn't give his feet the support the other pair had accustomed them to. You might go all the way on just one pair, after one or two resolings, but if you try to make the entire PCT through the North Cascades with the boots you started with, you will be sticking your neck out—and maybe your toes. Treat the boots with Snoseal or another effective compound often, to keep them waterproof and to prevent cracking from heat.

It may not occur to you in advance how tough walking will be on your socks too. One PCT trekker said he wore out one pair every 125 miles on the average, though we think that's a little extreme. Still, you will need replacements. You might start out with a three-day supply of socks—three pairs of heavy wool socks and three (or six, if you wear double inners) pairs of inner socks (polypropylene is preferable). Schaffer has gone 1000+ miles with this combination. If you hope to equal that, you must change socks daily and wash them daily. Note also that clean socks are less likely to give you blisters.

Besides boot soles and socks, you are going to wear out some underwear, shirts and, probably, pants. The less often you wash them, the faster they will wear out, due to rotting. In choosing your clothes to start with, remember that as you hike your waist will get smaller and legs bigger.

Light footwear is very nice to have for fording streams and for comfort in camp. It's damn near heaven to take off those 5-pound boots after a 20-mile day. Tennis shoes are traditional, but gymnastic slippers work almost as well around camp (not in streams), and they weigh only a few ounces. SCUBA diving booties may be the best of the three: they wear well, can be worn in bed, don't absorb water, have great traction, are warmer than down booties, can be worn inside your boots, and can even keep your socks dry in stream fords. But they don't breathe, so wear them with clean feet and socks.

Equipment

Spare no expense. Mistakes and shortcuts in equipment mean lost time, lost money, lost sleep and lost health.

Besides your usual summer backpacking equipment, you may need a tent, skis or snowshoes, an ice ax and a rope. You will need a guidebook with maps—this one. And even if you don't normally carry a camera, PCT trekkers say you'll be sorry if you don't take one on the BIG hike.

Almost all PCT hikers carry a *tent,* and are glad they did. A tent is important for warmth in the snowy parts, and for dryness in all the parts. In Oregon, a tent allows you to sleep by keeping the mosquitoes off you. We recommend a quality 2-man mountain tent—on the large side, or you and your companion may become less than friends.

The question of *skis* versus *snowshoes* for early season in the high mountains remains under debate, and some PCT hikers say they'd rather take their chances without either, considering the cost and the weight. The main advantage of skis, of course, is that you can cover a lot of ground downhill in a hurry—if you know how to ski with a pack. We suspect many of the trekkers who chose snowshoes would have used skis if they had been better cross-country-with-pack skiers. The main disadvantage of skis is that you can't mail them; you have to ship them by Greyhound or some other way.

Many PCT through hikers say an *ice ax* is definitely a necessity, and others say it is at least worth its weight for the many different things it will do. We recommend one for any segment where you expect to be in snow. You should take a *rope* for belaying on steep snow or on ice, and for difficult fords at the height of the snowmelt.

Few hikers are satisfied with the pictures from an "instant" *camera.* We recommend a 35 mm single-lens reflex camera, the best you can afford, and a zoom lens, one that ranges from wide-angle (about 28–35 mm) to short-telephoto (about 90–105 mm). With such a lens you'll be able to capture most of your shots. For the far-away shots, use a teleconverter (either 2x or 3x). Make sure both the zoom lens and the lightweight teleconverter are of high quality, or else you won't be pleased with the quality of your photos. Finally, get a polarizing filter, which reduces haziness, darkens the sky and removes unwanted reflections, such as shimmering lake surfaces. Using a telephoto lens, a teleconverter and a filter all require a fairly "fast" film, as do low-light shots, such as those dramatic sunrises and sunsets every trekker hopes to see. Schaffer prefers films in the ASA 200 range. Films of ASA 100 or less can be too slow, and ASA 400 or more, too grainy.

The cost

You can expect to spend several thousand *dollars* for the whole PCT unless you already have almost all the equipment you will need. Take plenty of money in traveler's checks. You won't be able to resist the food when you are in civilization, and you will find yourself with unforeseen needs for equipment. In addition, you will want to be able to correct some original decisions that you have later found unwise or unworkable, and to do so usually takes money.

MAILING TIPS

You can mail yourself almost any food, clothing or equipment. Before you leave home, you won't know whether you are going to run out of, say, molefoam, but you will have a good idea of your rate of consumption of food, clothing, and fuel for your stove. You can arrange for mailings of quantities of these things, purchased at home, where they are probably cheaper than in the towns along the way.

Address your package to:

>Yourself
>General Delivery
>P.O., state ZIP
>HOLD UNTIL (date)

Also, **boldly** write somewhere on the package: Pacific Crest Trail Hiker. Don't mail perishables. Make your packages strong, sturdy and tight. You are *really* depending on their contents. Have your home contact mail packages at least 24 days before you expect to get them, and even then, pay for the postal service called "Special Handling." Do not seal the packages when you pack them, because you are likely to have second thoughts. You can then write your mail contact and ask him to add certain things to (or take certain things out of) the box that goes to X place, or wherever. Before you leave home, phone the post offices you will be sending mail to, to make sure they will hold your mail for your arrival. They are legally required to hold it only 10 days. Also find out what hours they are open. Remember that if you change your plan, you can pick up a package at a post office and mail some or all of its contents to yourself farther along the route—or you can mail it home.

Post Offices Along or Near the Route
South to North

*= recommended for use

Some stations are seasonal, so check in advance if you're not hiking the PCT from mid-June through mid-September. The best pickup time is weekdays 1–4 p.m.; for ranger stations it is weekday evenings. Typical hours for town post offices are 9–12 and 1–5, Monday through Friday. See appropriate hiking sections for location of each.

*Seiad Valley, CA 96086

*Ashland, OR 97520

*Hyatt Lake Resort
   P.O. Box 447
   Ashland, OR 97520

*Fish Lake Resort
   P.O. Box 40
   Medford, OR 97501

Lake of the Woods Resort, OR 97603

*Crater Lake National Park, OR 97604

*Diamond Lake Lodge, OR 97731

*Cascade Summit, OR 97425

Sisters, OR 97759

*Hoodoo Ski Bowl
   Box 20, Highway 20
   Sisters, OR 97759
   (See page 150: Supplies)

*Olallie Lake Ranger Station
   c/o Clackamas Ranger District
   61431 East Highway 224
   Estacada, OR 97023
   (Not a post office, but its rangers will hold packages from about mid-June through late September.)

Government Camp, OR 97028

*Timberline Lodge, OR 97028

*Cascade Locks, OR 97014

Stevenson, WA 98648

Carson, WA 98610

*White Pass Rural Branch
   Naches, WA 98937

Crystal Mountain, WA 98022

*Snoqualmie Pass, WA 98068

Skykomish, WA 98288

*Stehekin, WA 98852

Chelan, WA 98816
   (An enjoyable 46-mile ferry-boat ride from Stehekin resort to this small city.)

Manning Provincial Park
   British Columbia V0X 1R0
   (Its post office is located at the park's East Gate, which is 10 miles northeast from the PCT trailhead. Write the park for information, if you want to, but don't mail parcels to their out-of-the-way post office.)

Hypothermia

Every year you can read accounts of hikers freezing to death in the mountains. They die of hypothermia, the #1 killer of outdoor recreationists. You too may be exposed to it, particularly if you start hiking the PCT in April in order to do all three states. Because it is so easy to die from hypothermia, we are including the following information, which is endorsed by the Forest Service and by mountain-rescue groups. Read it. It may save your life.

Hypothermia is subnormal body temperature, which is caused outdoors by exposure to cold, usually aggravated by wetness, wind and exhaustion. The moment your body begins to lose heat faster than it produces it, your body makes involuntary adjustments to preserve the normal temperature in its vital organs. Uncontrolled shivering is one way your body attempts to maintain its vital temperature. *If you've begun uncontrolled shivering, you have hypothermia and must act accordingly: seek shelter, insulation and warmth.* Shivering will eventually consume your energy reserves until they are exhausted. When this happens, cold reaches your brain, depriving you of judgment and reasoning power. You will not realize this is happening. You will lose control of your hands. Your internal body temperature is sliding downward. Without treatment, this slide leads to stupor, collapse and death. Learn the four lines of defense against hypothermia.

Your first line of defense: avoid exposure.

1. *Stay dry.* When clothes get wet, they can lose about 90% of their insulating value. Wool loses less; cotton and down lose more. Synthetics are best.

2. *Beware of the wind.* A slight breeze carries heat away from bare skin much faster than still air does. Wind drives cold air under and through clothing. Wind refrigerates wet clothes by evaporating moisture from the surface.

Hypothermia weather moving in, Glacier Peak Wilderness. Particularly in the North Cascades, you can experience day after day of cold, drizzly rain.

3. *Understand cold.* Most hypothermia cases develop in air temperatures between 30 and 50 degrees. Most outdoorsmen simply can't believe such temperatures can be dangerous. They fatally underestimate the danger of being wet at such temperatures. But just jump in a cold lakelet and you'll agree that 50° water is unbearably cold. The cold that kills is cold water running down neck and legs, cold water held against the body by sopping clothes, cold water flushing body heat from the surfaces of the clothes.

Your second line of defense: terminate exposure.

If you cannot stay dry and warm under existing weather conditions, using the clothes you have with you, *terminate exposure.*

1. *Be brave enough* to give up reaching your destination or whatever you had in mind. That one extra mile might be your last.

2. *Get out of the wind and rain.* Build a fire. Concentrate on making your camp or bivouac as secure and comfortable as possible.

3. *Never ignore shivering.* Persistent or violent shivering is clear warning that you are on the verge of hypothermia. *Make camp.*

4. *Forestall exhaustion.* Make camp while you still have a reserve of energy. Allow for the fact that exposure greatly reduces your normal endurance. You may think you are doing fine when the fact that you are exercising is the only thing preventing your going into hypothermia. If exhaustion forces you to stop, however briefly, your rate of body heat production instantly drops by 50% or more; violent, incapacitating shivering may begin immediately; you may slip into hypothermia *in a matter of minutes.*

5. *Appoint a foul-weather leader.* Make the best-protected member of your party responsible for calling a halt before the least-protected member becomes exhausted or goes into violent shivering.

Your third line of defense: detect hypothermia.

If your party is exposed to wind, cold and wetness, *think hypothermia.* Watch yourself and others for hypothermia's symptoms:
1. Uncontrollable fits of shivering.
2. Vague, slow, slurred speech.
3. Memory lapses; incoherence.
4. Immobile, fumbling hands.
5. Frequent stumbling; lurching gait.
6. Drowsiness—to sleep is to die.
7. Apparent exhaustion, such as inability to get up after a rest.

Your fourth and last line of defense: treatment.

The victim may deny he's in trouble. Believe the symptoms, *not* the patient. Even mild symptoms demand immediate drastic treatment.
1. Get the victim out of the wind and rain.
2. Strip off *all* wet clothes.
3. If the patient is only mildly impaired:
   a. Give him warm drinks.
   b. Get him into dry clothes and a warm sleeping bag. Well-wrapped, warm (not hot) rocks or canteens will hasten recovery.

4. If the patient is semiconscious or worse:
    a. Try to keep him awake. Do not give warm drinks.
    b. Leave him stripped. Put him in a sleeping bag with another person (also stripped). If you have a double bag or can zip two together, put the victim between two warmth donors. *Skin to skin contact* is the most effective treatment. Never leave the victim as long as he is alive. To do so is to kill him—it's just that simple!
5. Build a fire to warm the camp.

Other notes on avoiding hypothermia.
    1. Choose rainclothes that are effective against *wind-driven* rain and cover head, neck, body and legs. Gore-Tex and other PTFE laminates are best, but won't last as long as some other materials.
    2. Take woolen clothing for possible hypothermia weather, such as a two-piece woolen underwear set or long wool pants and sweater or shirt. Include a knit wool cap that can protect neck and chin. Cotton underwear is *worse than useless* when wet, as are cotton shirts and pants. As native Americans long ago discovered, one stays warmer in a cold rain when he is stark naked than when he is bundled up in wet clothes. Some folks in the drippy North Cascade forests carry umbrellas.
    3. Carry a stormproof tent with a good rain fly and set it up *before* you need it.
    4. Carry trail food rich in calories, such as nuts, jerky and candy, and keep nibbling during hypothermia weather.
    5. Take a gas stove or a plumber's candle, flammable paste or other reliable fire starter.
    6. Never abandon survival gear under any circumstances. If you didn't bring along the above items, stay put and make the best of it. An all-too-common fatal mistake is for victims to abandon everything so that, unburdened, they can run for help.
    7. "It never happens to me. I'm Joe Athlete." Not always is it the other guy on the trail. It can be you even if you are in fantastic shape and are carrying the proper equipment. Be alert for hypothermia conditions and hypothermia symptoms.

Outdoor Courtesy

Traveling a wild trail, away from centers of civilization, is a unique experience. It brings intimate association with nature—communion with the earth, the forest, the chaparral, the wildlife, the clear sky. A great responsibility accompanies this experience—the obligation to keep the wilderness as you found it. Being considerate of the wilderness rights of others will make the mountain adventures of those who follow equally rewarding.

As a wilderness visitor, you should become familiar with the rules of wilderness courtesy outlined below.

Trails

Never cut switchbacks. This practice breaks down trails and hastens erosion. Take care not to dislodge rocks that might fall on hikers below you. Improve and preserve trails, as by clearing away loose rocks (carefully) and removing branches. Report any trail damage and broken or misplaced signs to a ranger.

Off trail

Restrain the impulse to blaze trees or to build ducks where not essential. Let the next fellow find his way as you did.

Campgrounds

Spread your gear in an already cleared area, and build your fire in a campground stove. Don't disarrange the camp by making hard-to-eradicate ramparts of rock for fireplaces or windbreaks. Rig tents and tarps with line tied to rocks or trees; never put nails in trees. For your campfire, if you must build one, use fallen wood only; do not cut standing trees nor break off branches. Use the campground latrine. Place litter in the litter can or carry it out. Leave the campground cleaner than you found it.

Fire

Fire is a great danger in the mountains; act accordingly. Smoke only in cleared areas along the trail where a sign authorizes it. Report a mountain fire immediately.

Litter

Along the trail, place candy wrappers, raisin boxes, orange peels, etc. in your pocket or pack for later disposal; throw nothing on the trail. Pick up litter you find along the trail or in camp. More than almost anything else, litter detracts from the wilderness scene. Remember, you *can* take it with you.

Noise

Boisterous conduct is out of harmony in a wilderness experience. Be a considerate hiker and camper. Don't ruin another's enjoyment of the wilderness.

Good Samaritanship

Human life and well-being take precedence over everything else—in the wilderness as elsewhere. If a hiker or camper is in trouble, help in any way you can. Indifference is a moral crime. Give comfort or first aid; then hurry to a ranger station for help.

Land-use Regulations

The Oregon-Washington PCT passes through national parks, national forests, Indian land, land administered by the Bureau of Land Management, state land and private land. All these areas have their own regulations, which you ignore only at your risk—risk of physical difficulty as well as possibility of being cited for violations.

On private land, of course, the regulations are what the owner says they are. The same is true on Indian land. In particular, don't build a fire on private land without the owner's written permission. Regulations on U.S. Bureau of Land Management land are not of major consequence for users of this book, since the route passes through only a few miles of it, in Section B. The same is true of state land, in southernmost Washington.

The Forest Service and the Park Service, for good reason, have more regulations. These are not uniform throughout the states, or between the two services. We list below the Forest Service and Park Service regulations that *are* uniform along the trail, plus some that are peculiar to the Park Service. Special regulations in particular places are mentioned in the trail description when it "arrives" at the place.

1. For about a decade *wilderness permits* were required to enter any official wilderness in either Oregon or Washington, but this requirement was dropped by late 1985. Today the only places you'll need a wilderness permit are in the national parks: Crater Lake (Section C), Mt. Rainier (Section I) and North Cascades (Section K). Permits are needed *only* if you will be camping overnight in the backcountry; they aren't needed for day use. Mt. Rainier National Park requires permits only from June 15 through September 30; the other two parks require permits year-round. Personnel at all three parks would like you to pick up a permit in person, which can be very inconvenient. However, they realize the PCT trekker's predicament, and will accept written requests. For North Cascades National Park don't write to the park headquarters but rather to the Skagit District Office, Marblemount, WA 98267.

2. *Campfire permits* also used to be required, but no longer are. Both the Forest Service and the National Park Service discourage campfires and ask that you carry a stove instead. In Mt. Rainier National Park campfires are prohibited at all but the park's lowest backcountry sites, so plan to bring a stove. Except for emergencies you shouldn't make a campfire anywhere along the PCT, since downed wood hosts organisms on which larger animals feed, and as the wood decays, it adds nutrients to the soil.

3. *A fishing license* is required in Oregon for those 14 or older and in Washington for those 15 and older. Both states have a variety of fishing licenses (and fees), based on your age, state of residency and length of fishing excursion. For further information, contact:

Oregon Department of Fish and Wildlife
506 S.W. Mill Street—P.O. Box 59
Portland, OR 97207
(503) 229-5551

or

Washington Department of Game
600 North Capitol Way
Olympia, WA 98504
(206) 753-5700

4. *Destruction,* injury, defacement, removal or disturbance in any manner of any natural feature of public property is prohibited. This includes:

    a. Molesting any animal, picking flowers or other plants;
    b. Cutting, blazing, marking, driving nails in, or otherwise damaging growing trees or standing snags;
    c. Writing, carving or painting of name or other inscription anywhere;
    d. Destruction, defacement or moving of signs.

5. *Collecting specimens* of minerals, plants, animals or historical objects is prohibited without written authorization, obtained in advance, from the Park Service or Forest Service. Permits are not issued for personal collections.

6. *Smoking* is not permitted while traveling through vegetated areas. You may stop and smoke in a safe place.

7. Pack and saddle *animals* have the right-of-way on trails. Hikers should get completely off the trail, on the downhill side if possible, and remain quiet until the stock has passed.

8. It is illegal to cut *switchbacks*.

9. Use *existing campsites* if there are any. If not, camp away from the trail and at least 100 feet from lakes and streams, on mineral soil or unvegetated forest floor—never in meadows or other soft, vegetated spots. Unfortunately, in many popular areas—Jefferson Park, in particular—almost all the good campsites are within 100 feet of water. Until the Forest Service builds or recommends alternate campsites, the hiker will have little choice but to use one of the existing illegal sites.

10. *Construction* of improvements such as rock walls, large fireplaces, bough beds, tables, and rock-and-log stream crossings is prohibited.

11. *Soap* and other pollutants should be kept out of lakes and streams. Use of detergents is not recommended, since they affect the water detrimentally.

12. *Toilets* should be in soft soil away from camps and water. Dig a shallow hole and bury it.

13. You are required to *clean up* your camp before you leave. Tin cans, foil, glass, worn-out or useless gear, and other unburnables must be carried out.

14. *National Parks but not Forests* prohibit dogs and cats on the trail and prohibit carrying or using firearms.

15. *Horses* and other pack or saddle animals should be kept at least 200 feet from any lake, stream or spring, except when watering, loading, unloading, or traveling on established trail routes. Forage may be limited, so you should carry feed. Avoid tying horses to trees at campsites for prolonged periods. Hobble, stake or use a picket line with your stock.

Border Crossing

Most PCT hikers do not cross the U.S./Canada border. In the past, those who did usually crossed it illegally, for dealing with the Customs/Excise and Immigration bureaus of each country was a real quagmire, if not a no-win proposition. Today, legally entering Canada via the PCT is a breeze, but legally entering bureaucratic-minded United States is still a nuisance. Since most trekkers hike north on the PCT (the easier direction of border crossing), we'll first look at that border crossing.

PCT north from U.S. into Canada

If your trek along the PCT will end in Manning Park and you'll then return to the United States by car or other transportation, you're in luck: you won't have to report to Customs. However, if you will be staying in Canada for more than a few days, then you must report to the nearest Canadian Customs office and/or to the Royal Canadian Mounted Police office. For more information about a protracted stay, check at the Manning Park headquarters when you complete your northbound trek along the PCT.

Canadian Customs allows you to bring in personal possessions that you'll need for your brief stay in Canada. Two exceptions are plants and handguns. Rifles and shotguns, other than automatic, are permitted. If you plan to bring any goods to leave in Canada, you'll then have to check with Customs for possible payment of duty and/or tax.

Canadian Immigration requires trekkers to obtain and complete an "Entry to Canada via the Pacific Crest Trail" form. You fill out this simple form *within* two months of the *start* of your trek. Write to:

Canadian Immigration Centre
Huntington, B.C.
Canada V0X 1M0

The Immigration Centre will then stamp and sign the form and return it to you. You must carry this form together with your birth certificate and some other form of identification, such as a driver's license or a passport.

Arriving in Canada on horseback or with a dog compounds your entry problems. If you bring a dog, you must carry a document from a licensed veterinarian which describes the dog and certifies that it has had its shots. Horses crossing the border are subject to inspection.

PCT south from Canada into U.S.

Unlike its Canadian counterpart, U.S. Customs requires all persons entering the United States to report directly to the nearest Customhouse for clearance (Title 19, USC, Section 1459). Customs are at two border towns: Sumas, 68 air miles west of the PCT but 132 road miles west from Rainy Pass; and Oroville, 65 air miles east of the PCT but 121 road miles east from Rainy Pass. The Customs authorities, in their wisdom, perceived that these stations were a bit out of the way for the average PCT hiker, and hence provided a closer site: Marblemount. From Rainy Pass you can now traipse a mere 50 miles west to this settlement, get checked out by a ranger at North Cascades National Park's Skagit District Office, then scurry back to the PCT. This works if you're a U.S. citizen. Trekkers from other countries may still have to report to Sumas. Bon voyage!

And then there's U.S. Immigration. You can be pre-inspected by them. This involves going to a U.S. port of entry (Sumas or Oroville), where you'll get a Form I-94, then head into Canada and start walking south. Upon re-entry into the U.S. on the PCT, you then surrender this form to the office that issued it or else mail it to the office. (No, Immigration hasn't asked the Post Office to install a mail box at Rainy Pass, and no, the Skagit District Office in Marblemount doesn't handle immigration.) All hikers should carry proof of citizenship, such as a birth certificate or passport. Non-U.S. citizens will also need a visa. For them to make a legal entry from Canada, they first must go into the U.S., get pre-inspected, and then head back to the Manning Park trailhead—quite a lot of travel.

For more information on U.S. Customs and/or Immigration, contact:

U.S. Customs Service
Office of District Director
Seattle, WA 98174
(206) 442-1598

North Cascades National Park
Skagit District Office
Marblemount, WA 98267
(206) 873-4590

U.S. Immigration and Naturalization
815 Airport Way, South
Seattle, WA 98134
(206) 442-5956

The information from each agency will probably contradict that from the other two agencies. For more fun and games, contact the U.S. Border Patrol at Oroville and Sumas, then try to maintain your sanity while resolving all the conflicting information you're trying to digest.

Government Administrative Headquarters

General

Regional Forester
  California Region
  630 Sansome Street
  San Francisco, CA 94111
  (415) 556-0122

Regional Forester
  Pacific Northwest Region
  P.O. Box 3623
  Portland, OR 97208
  (503) 221-2971

Bureau of Land Management
  825 N.E. Multnomah
  Portland, OR 97208
  (503) 231-6274

Specific, South to North

Klamath National Forest
  1312 Fairlane Road
  Yreka, CA 96097
  (916) 842-6131

Rogue River National Forest
  Federal Bldg., P.O. Box 520
  Medford, OR 97501
  (503) 776-3600

Winema National Forest
  P.O. Box 1390
  Klamath Falls, OR 97601
  (503) 883-6714

Crater Lake National Park
  P.O. Box 7
  Crater Lake, OR 97604
  (503) 594-2211

Umpqua National Forest
  P.O. Box 1008
  Roseburg, OR 97470
  (503) 672-6601

Deschutes National Forest
  211 N.E. Revere Avenue
  Bend, OR 97701
  (503) 382-6922

Willamette National Forest
  P.O. Box 10607
  Eugene, OR 97440
  (503) 687-6521

Mt. Hood National Forest
  2955 N.W. Division Street
  Gresham, OR 97030
  (503) 666-0771

Gifford Pinchot National Forest
  500 West 12th Street
  Vancouver, WA 98660
  (206) 696-7500

Mt. Baker-Snoqualmie Nat. Forest
  1022 First Avenue
  Seattle, WA 98104
  (206) 442-0170

Mt. Rainier National Park
  Ashford, WA 98304
  (206) 569-2211

Wenatchee National Forest
  301 Yakima Street
  Wenatchee, WA 98801
  (509) 662-4335

North Cascades National Park
  800 State Street
  Sedro Woolley, WA 98284
  (206) 855-1331

Okanogan National Forest
  P.O. Box 950
  Okanogan, WA 98840
  (509) 422-2704

Manning Provincial Park
  Manning Park
  British Columbia, Canada V0X 1R0
  (604) 840-8836

Forgotten Anything?

Here is a checklist of items we feel you should *consider* bringing along. You might prefer to bring other things too.

wallet
keys
watch
travelers checks
wilderness permit
this guidebook
nature guides
pencil and note pad
camera
camera accessories
film
fishing gear
fishing license
mountaineering gear
other special gear
pack
sleeping bag
foam pad or air mattress
ground cloth
tent or tube tent
rain gear (preferably made of
   Gore-Tex)
down vest or down parka
windbreaker and/or sweatshirt
shirts (preferably wool)

pants (preferably wool)
shorts
swimsuit
towel and/or washcloth
underwear (polypropylene)
socks
gaiters
boots and boot laces
camp shoes
wool cap and/or hat
dark glasses
gloves
sewing kit
toilet paper
personal hygiene items
aspirin
prescription medicine
molefoam
first-aid kit
snakebite kit
insect repellent (lots of it)
suntan lotion
lip balm and/or glacier
   cream
toothbrush, toothpaste

flashlight
extra batteries
pocket knife
can opener
food and drink
salt and pepper
stove and fuel
matches in waterproof con-
   tainer
pots, bowls and utensils
Sierra cup
soap: leave it home!
water bottles (½ gallon is sufficient)
several trash bags
stuffsacks for sleeping bag
   and/or bearbagging
50 feet of parachute cord for
   bearbagging
50 feet of parachute cord for
   emergencies (tent lines, pack
   repairs, shoe laces)
100 feet of lightweight nylon
   rope for stream fords and
   risky snow-slope traverse

Chapter 3: PCT Natural History

Introduction

The California section of the Pacific Crest Trail is noted for its great diversity of plants and animals, minerals and rocks, climates and landscapes. The Oregon section of the PCT provides quite a contrast, having the most homogeneous vegetation and landscape of this tri-state route. The Washington section falls between these two extremes. Along the route covered by this volume, certain rocks, plants and animals appear time and time again. The most common entities appear to be

rock: andesite, basalt
flower: lupine
shrub: huckleberry
tree: mountain hemlock, subalpine fir, western white pine
invertebrate: mosquito
fish: trout
amphibian: western toad, tree frog
reptile: garter snake
bird: dark-eyed junco
mammal,
    small: chipmunk, golden-mantled ground squirrel
    large: man, deer.

The average elevation of Oregon's section of PCT is about 5120 feet, whereas Washington's section is about 4550 feet—lower in part because the weathering and erosional processes farther north are more intense (contrast Washington's 4550 to California's 6120). Not only is the average trail elevation different between these two northwest states, so too is the typical terrain that the trail traverses. The Oregon section is flatter, drier, more volcanic and less glaciated than Washington's section. In Oregon, a typical hike is through a mountain-hemlock forest while traversing rolling ridges and crossing lake-bound basins. In Washington, a typical hike is through alternating forests of mountain hemlock and subalpine species while climbing over passes and dropping somewhat into glaciated canyons. Both states, of course, have many distinctive features worth investigating.

Geology

We can thank the existence of western America's mountains for the existence of the Pacific Crest Trail. Without these mountains, we'd have instead the Pacific *Coast* Trail. But why should we have mountains in the first place? The answer lies with plate tectonics—the ceaseless movements of the earth's crust and its associated upper mantle. This composite outer layer is made up of a few giant plates plus more abundant, smaller plates, all interacting with one another. Some movements lead to the formation of mountain ranges, others to ocean basins.

Although plate tectonics has been occurring for several billion years, we need concern ourselves only with the last 50 million or so years. Back then, oceanic plates were diving under continental plates, much as they do today. One oceanic plate, the Farallon plate, was diving east under the continental North American plate, and it was being consumed in the process, particularly in its midsection. By 30 million years ago, the midsection had been totally consumed, leaving a southern part and a northern part. It is the northern part we are interested in, now known as the Juan de Fuca plate. Like the larger Farallon plate, the Juan de Fuca plate continued diving under the North American plate. Also like that plate, it continued drifting north with respect to North America (see illustration).

When one plate dives beneath another, it eventually melts, due to increasing temperature. This typically happens at depths of about 60 to 90 miles. The melt doesn't have the same chemical composition as the plate, for overlying oceanic sediments, laden with water, have been dragged down with the descending plate, and these sediments are incorporated into the melt. The resulting melt, or magma, is relatively light in density, and it works its way up toward the earth's surface. If it reaches the surface, a volcanic eruption occurs, such as the devastating eruption of Mt. St. Helens on May 18, 1980. If it doesn't reach the surface, it solidifies at depth as granitic rock. Erosion over millions of years strips off overlying rocks to expose the granitic rock, which is what we see in the North Cascades.

The continual diving of the Juan de Fuca plate insures continual production of magma, thus guaranteeing a future for the Cascade Range. Note, however, that because the plate is drifting north, so too will the zone of active Cascade volcanoes. In the future new volcanoes will erupt in British Columbia, while old ones in southern Oregon and northern California will cease to erupt.

While the foregoing discourse describes the dynamics of the Cascade Range, it does not describe its history. That history is fairly well known from the mid-Tertiary period onward (see Geologic Time Table on page 28). In the late Eocene and early Miocene epochs, deposits from the ancient Cascade Range reached a thickness of six miles in some places. For such an accumulation to occur, the regional crust must have been relatively stable for some time. By the mid-Miocene, the range experienced folding, faulting and, in the north, intrusion by granitic batholiths, plutons, stocks, and dikes. (These intrusive masses are distinguished by their relative size; a batholith may be tens of miles across, whereas a dike may be only a few feet or a few inches across.) During the mid-Miocene, linear vents east of the Cascades opened and poured forth the very fluid Columbia River basalts, which flooded much of the terrain of southern Washington and northern Oregon. The many flows from the fiery episodes are best seen by the hiker as he descends north toward the Columbia River along the lower half of the Eagle Creek Trail.

Plant fossils collected east of the Cascades indicate the environment was considerably more humid than it is today. From this knowledge the paleobotanist infers that the Cascades were lower in elevation, since there was no evidence of a rain shadow that would have been created if they had been as high as today's crests. One need only drive to have been created if they had been as high as today's crests. One need only drive to Sisters or Wenatchee to notice how much drier the east slopes of today's Cascades are compared to their west slopes.

After the partial flooding of the range by the Columbia River basalts, the earth's internal forces, quite likely due to the interaction between the North American and Juan de Fuca plates, uplifted the range and initiated a series of active volcanoes. Uplift and eruptions continued during the Quaternary, but in this epoch, the higher peaks were subjected to repeated glaciations brought on by changes in the world-wide climatic pattern. Some paleoclimatologists have speculated that the moving plates have rearranged the ocean basins, thereby affecting ocean currents and also major weather patterns, but the influences that initiated the Ice Age (the Pleistocene epoch) are still debated.

The same processes at work in the past are at work today. Volcanoes attempt to grow ever upward, but they are checked by the forces of gravity, weathering and erosion. The

Western North America, about 15 million years ago (left) and today (right). The Juan de Fuca plate (gray) is producing new oceanic crust along its western edge, causing sea-floor spreading (large, dark arrows). This plate is bordered by the Pacific plate on its west and south edges, and by the North American plate on its east edge. Note that in the 15-million-year time lapse, the Juan de Fuca plate has changed its orientation with respect to North America, and that it has migrated considerably eastward and northward while diving under the continent (open arrows). Note that the directions of sea-floor spreading and plate diving are very different. In another 15 million years, the Juan de Fuca plate will all but disappear beneath the North American plate. In the map on the right the stars are major Cascade Range volcanoes and the small rectangle is this chapter's geologic map.

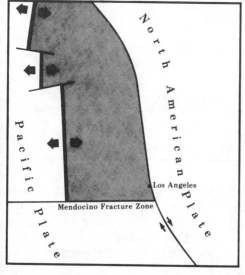
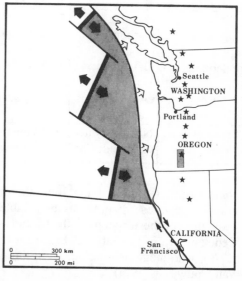

higher a peak grows, the more it is attacked by the icy fingers of glaciers. Gravity pulls loose particles downward; the right snow conditions initiate avalanches; minor eruptions and near-surface intrusions melt snowpacks, thereby creating enormous mudflows. Particularly good examples of the destructive power of such mudflows may be seen in the Mt. St. Helens environs.

The major volcanoes we see today are quite young—definitely late Quaternary. Many of them have erupted in geologically recent times, and there is every reason to believe they will erupt again. The Pacific Crest Trail traverses most of these "dormant" volcanoes, including, south to north: Mt. McLoughlin (9495), Crater Lake (11,500-foot-high Mt. Mazama until 6900 years ago), the Three Sisters (10,358, 10,047, 10,085), Mt. Jefferson (10,497), Mt. Hood (11,235), Mt. Adams (12,276), Mt. Rainier (14,410) and Glacier Peak (10,541). Geologic vignettes of these and other summits are included in our trail descriptions.

GEOLOGIC TIME TABLE				
Era	Period	Epoch	Began (years ago)	Duration (years)
	Quaternary	Holocene	10,000	10,000
		Pleistocene	1,800,000	1,800,000
Cenozoic	Tertiary	Pliocene	5,200,000	3,400,000
		Miocene	21,700,000	16,500,000
		Oligocene	35,000,000	13,300,000
		Eocene	49,000,000	14,000,000
		Paleocene	64,000,000	15,000,000
Mesozoic	Cretaceous	*Numerous*	135,000,000	71,000,000
	Jurassic	*epochs*	195,000,000	60,000,000
	Triassic	*recognized*	225,000,000	30,000,000
Paleozoic	Permian	*Numerous*	280,000,000	55,000,000
	Carboni-ferous		345,000,000	65,000,000
	Devonian	*epochs*	400,000,000	55,000,000
	Silurian		435,000,000	35,000,000
	Ordovician	*recognized*	500,000,000	65,000,000
	Cambrian		600,000,000	100,000,000
Precambrian	No widely accepted time units; oldest known rocks are 3.8 billion years old; Earth's crust solidified 4.6 billion years ago.			

Note: In this Geologic Time Table the durations of Cenozoic epochs differ considerably from those of previous time tables. This major discrepancy is due to a reevaluation of these epochs in the light of isotopic dating and new fossil evidence. The Cenozoic era in this table as based on the work of D.H. Tarling and J.G. Mitchell (1976), who made minor changes in the epoch dates set by W.A. Berggren and J.A. Van Couvering (1974).

During the Ice Age, which has *temporarily* abated, an almost continuous mantle of ice covered the Cascades from Mt. McLoughlin north into Canada. From this mantle, huge fingers of glacier ice extended downcanyon, sometimes for tens of miles and some gave rise to enormous lakes, such as Lake Chelan in the North Cascades. Evidence of large southern glaciers can be found near Crater Lake even though Mt. Mazama, their source, was later blown out of existence. When hikers climb east from Diamond Lake on the Howlock Mountain Trail, about 16 miles north of Crater Lake, they climb up a large lateral moraine left by a Mt. Mazama glacier when it retreated about 10,000 years ago, at the time when most of the Cascades' glaciers melted back.

Today we are living in an interglacial period which could come to an end relatively soon. The hiker trekking along the Pacific Crest Trail today thus sees the Cascade Range in its "atypical" form, for in the last million years most of the range lay under an ice sheet about 95% of the time. So, if you experience chilly, wet weather along your PCT hike, be grateful it isn't worse—20,000 years ago, your hike would have resembled a trek across today's icy Greenland.

Biology

One's first guess about the Pacific Crest Trail—a high adventure rich in magnificent alpine scenery and sweeping panoramas—turns out to be incorrect along some parts of the trail. The real-life trail hike will sometimes seem to consist of enduring many repetitious miles through viewless forests, battling hordes of mosquitoes, or even hiking up to a whole day at a time without reaching fresh water. If you get bogged down in such unpleasant impressions, it may be because you haven't developed an appreciation of the natural history of this remarkable route. There is a great variety of plants and animals, rocks and minerals, landscapes and climates along the PCT, and the more you know about each, the more you will enjoy your trek.

FLORA

A backpacker who has just complete the California section of the PCT might conclude that southern Oregon's forests form a more integrated "neighborhood" of species than California's forests did. Passing through different environments of the Sierra Nevada, he may have noticed the segregation of tree species and concluded that as he ascends toward the range's crest, he passes through a sequence of forests: Douglas-fir, white fir, red fir, mountain hemlock. Near the Oregon border, however, he discovers that these four species—and others—reside together. Certainly, this aggregation would never be seen in the Sierra. The great diversity of environments found within that range has allowed each species to adapt to the environment most suitable for it.

In contrast, the southern Oregon environments—and therefore the plant communities—are not as sharply defined. Still, each plant species is found within a certain elevation range and over a certain geographic area. The general elevation and north-south range of 21 Cascade Range conifers are shown on profiles on the following pages. These species make up virtually all the forest cover you'll pass through on your Oregon-Washington trek. Note how the species vary in distribution, both horizontally and vertically.

South-north profiles of the Cascade Range approximately along the Pacific Crest Trail. Each profile shows the altitudinal and latitudinal range of one or two conifers.

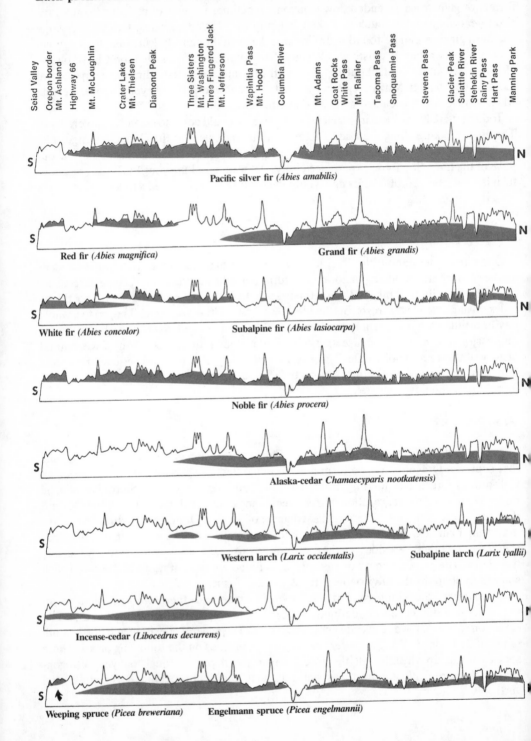

Pacific silver fir (*Abies amabilis*)

Red fir (*Abies magnifica*)   Grand fir (*Abies grandis*)

White fir (*Abies concolor*)   Subalpine fir (*Abies lasiocarpa*)

Noble fir (*Abies procera*)

Alaska-cedar *Chamaecyparis nootkatensis*)

Western larch (*Larix occidentalis*)   Subalpine larch (*Larix lyallii*)

Incense-cedar (*Libocedrus decurrens*)

Weeping spruce (*Picea breweriana*)   Engelmann spruce (*Picea engelmannii*)

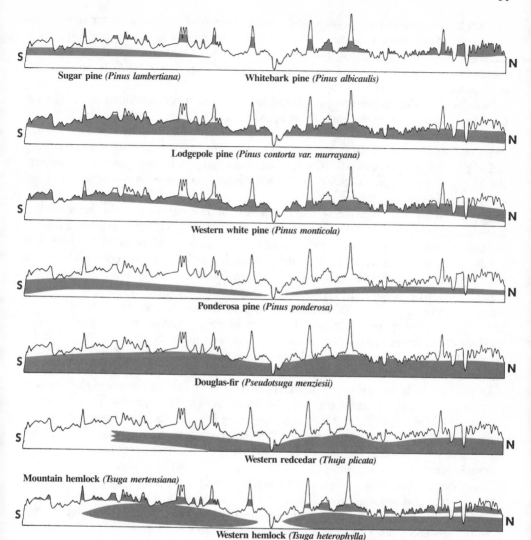

Sugar pine *(Pinus lambertiana)*   Whitebark pine *(Pinus albicaulis)*

Lodgepole pine *(Pinus contorta var. murrayana)*

Western white pine *(Pinus monticola)*

Ponderosa pine *(Pinus ponderosa)*

Douglas-fir *(Pseudotsuga menziesii)*

Western redcedar *(Thuja plicata)*

Mountain hemlock *(Tsuga mertensiana)*

Western hemlock *(Tsuga heterophylla)*

If you've hiked through California's rugged Sierra Nevada, you'll find southern Oregon a much gentler, more uniform landscape. But despite its relatively subdued topography, it still supports a diverse assemblage of plants, and the discerning hiker soon learns what species to expect around the next bend. Ponderosa pines thrive in the drier southern Oregon forests, yet they are nonexistent in the dry pumice soils of the Crater Lake vicinity. Here you'll find lodgepole pines which, ironically, are water-loving trees. These are usually seen growing in boggy soils near lakes, creeks and wet meadows, where they often edge out the mountain hemlocks, which are by far the most common tree you'll see along the PCT in Oregon and Washington. The most suitable habitat for hemlocks appears to be shady north slopes, on which pure stands of tall, straight specimens grow. At lower elevations, mountain hemlocks give way to western hemlocks and Douglas-firs, and, as the environment becomes drier southward and eastward, these two species yield to ponderosa pines. The harder one looks at a forest—even a small piece of it—the more he realizes that this seemingly uniform stand of trees is in fact a complex assemblage of particular plants, animals, soils, rocks and microclimates all influencing each other.

Our trail description commences at Seiad Valley, a man-made ranchland carved from a Douglas-fir forest. Near the end of our odyssey, along Agnes Creek and the Stehekin River, we also encounter a Douglas-fir forest. The two are hardly alike. The Douglas-fir forest of northern California and southern Oregon contains, among other trees, incense-cedar, ponderosa pine, white fir, Oregon oak and madrone. Its counterpart in northern Washington contains, among others, western redcedar, western white pine, grand fir, vine maple and Engelmann spruce.

The two forests vary considerably in the density of their vegetation. Not only does the rain-laden northern forest have a denser stand of taller conifers, but it also has a denser understory. Its huckleberries, thimbleberries, Devil's club and other moisture-loving shrubs are quite a contrast to the stiff, dry manzanita, ceanothus and scrub oaks seen in the southern forest. Wildflowers in the northern forest are more abundant than their counterparts to the south. During rainstorms, they are too abundant, for their thick growth along the trail ensures that you'll be soaked by them from as high as your waist on down. Both forests have quite a number of species in common, but from central Oregon northward, the moisture-oriented species become prominent. Now we find bunchberry dogwood, Oregon grape, Lewis monkey flower and other species growing on the dark, damp forest floor.

In contrast to trees, which are quite specific in their habitat selection, flowers can tolerate a broad range of environments. You'll find, for example, yarrow, a sunflower, at timberline on the slopes of Mt. Hood and also on the Douglas-fir forest floor that borders the southern shore of the Columbia River. Both environments are moist, but the Mt. Hood alpine meadows, at 6000 feet above the bottom of the Columbia River gorge, are a considerably harsher environment.

Some flowers prefer open meadows to shady forests; others prefer dry environments. Thistle, lupine and phlox are found along the sunnier portions of the trail. Growing from crevices among rocks are the aptly named stonecrops, and on the pumice flats too dry for even the lodgepole pines to pioneer, the Newberry knotweed thrives.

In addition to adapting to specific climatic conditions, a plant may also adapt to a specific soil condition. Thus we see on the otherwise barren mica schist slopes of Condrey Mountain, near the southern Oregon border, acre after acre of pink, prostrate pussy paws.

Lastly, a species may have a distribution governed by the presence of other species. Corn lilies thrive in wet meadows, but lodgepoles invade these lands and shade them out. Mountain hemlocks may soon follow and eventually achieve dominance over the lodgepoles. Then the careless camper comes along, lets his campfire escape, and the forest burns. Among the charred stumps of the desolate ruins rises the tall, blazing magenta fireweed, and Nature, once again, strives to transform this landscape back into a mature forest.

From top, left to right: fireweed, paintbrush, tiger lily; Newberry knotweed, corn lily (false hellebore, skunk cabbage), pasqueflower; pearly everlasting, phlox, Sitka valerian

FAUNA

We have seen that plants adapt to a variety of conditions imposed by the environment and by other species. Animals, like plants, are also subject to a variety of conditions, but they have the added advantage of mobility. On a hot summer day, a beetle under a scant forest cover can escape the merciless sun by seeking protection under a loose stone or under a mat of dry needles.

Larger animals, of course, have greater mobility and therefore can better overcome the difficulties of the environment. Amphibians, reptiles, birds and mammals may frequent the trail, but they scamper away when you—the intruder—approach. At popular campsites, however, the animals come out to meet you, or more exactly, to obtain your food. Of course, almost anywhere along the trail you may encounter the ubiquitous mosquito, always looking for a free meal. But in popular campsites you'll meet the robin, the gray jay, the Clark nutcracker, the Townsend and yellow-pine chipmunks, the golden-mantled ground squirrel, and at night, mice and black bears. You may be tempted to feed them, or they may try to help themselves, but please protect them from your food—they will survive better on the "real, organic" food Mother Nature produces. Furthermore, an artificially large population supported by generous summer backpackers may in winter overgraze the vegetation. In the following paragraphs we'll take a closer look at three species.

Mule deer. Two subspecies of this large mammal can be found along much of the Oregon-Washington PCT. Mule deer, like other herbivores, do not eat every type of plant they encounter, but tend to be quite specific in their search for food. Their primary browse is new growth on huckleberry, salal, blackberry, bitterbrush and snowbrush, although they also eat certain grasses and forbs. Together with other herbivores, parasites and saprophytes (organisms feeding on decaying organic matter), they consume a small portion of the 100 billion tons of organic matter produced annually on the earth by plants.

Mule deer face a considerable population problem because some of their predators have disappeared. After the arrival of "civilized" man, the wolves and grizzly bears were exterminated except in some remote areas of northern Washington. In their places, coyotes and black bears have increased in numbers. Coyotes, however, feed principally on rabbits and rodents, and only occasionally attack a fawn or a sick deer. Black bears occasionally kill fawns. The mountain lion, a true specialist in feeding habits, preys mainly on deer and may kill 50 of them a year. This magnificent mammal, unfortunately, has been unjustly persecuted by man, and many deer that are saved from the big cat are lost to starvation and disease. Increasing human population compounds the problem. The expansion of settlements causes the big cats to retreat farther, which leaves them farther from the suburban deer. Forests must be logged to feed this expansion of settlements, and then the logged-over areas sprout an assemblage of shrubs that are a feast for deer. The deer population responds to this new food supply by increasing in number. Then the shrubs mature or the forest grows back, and there is less food for the larger deer population, which is now faced with starvation. Forest fires produce the same feast-followed-by-famine effect.

From top, left to right: Oregon grape, columbine, ligusticum; vanilla-leaf, lupine, eriogonum; yarrow, thistle, beargrass

Golden-mantled ground squirrel. There are two species of these ground squirrels, the Sierra Nevada golden-mantled ground squirrel, which ranges from the southern Sierra north to the Columbia River, and the Cascades golden-mantled ground squirrel, which ranges from the Columbia River north into British Columbia. On the eastern Cascade slopes of Washington, the Cascades golden-mantled ground squirrel lives in the same habitat as the yellow-pine chipmunk, but they have slightly different niches, or roles, to carry out in their pine-and-fir-forest environment. Both have the same food and the same burrowing habits, but the ground squirrel obtains nuts and seeds that have fallen to the forest floor, whereas the chipmunk obtains these morsels by extracting them from their source. The ground squirrel, like its distant cousin the marmot, puts on a thick layer of fat to provide it with enough energy to last through winter hibernation. The chipmunk, like the black bear, only partly hibernates. During the winter, it awakens periodically to feed on the nuts and seeds it has stored in its ground burrow.

Western toad. Every Westerner is familiar with this drab, chunky amphibian. Along the Oregon-Washington PCT, we encounter its subspecies known as the boreal toad. This cold-blooded animal is amazingly adaptable, being found among rock crevices in dry, desolate lava flows as well as in subalpine wildflower gardens in the North Cascades. Its main environmental requirement appears to be the presence of at least one early-summer seasonal pond in which it can breed and lay eggs.

Although you may encounter dozens of boreal toads along a stretch of trail in one day (they occur in clusters), they prefer to actively hop or crawl about at night. Should you bed down near one of their breeding ponds, you may hear the weak chirps (they have no "croaking" vocal sacs) from dozens of males. Moreover, these toads may swarm all over you in their search for meals. Rolling over on one won't give you warts, but later you might feel the puncture, bite or sting of a mosquito, ant or yellow jacket that otherwise would have made a tasty meal for the toad.

mule deer   **ground squirrel**   **western toad**

Chapter 4: Using This Guide

Twelve Hiking Chapters

The bulk of this guide is composed of trail description and accompanying topographic maps of the Pacific Crest Trail. In 12 chapters, Sections A through L, this guide covers the PCT from Highway 96 in northern California to Highway 3 in British Columbia. Readers familiar with this guide's companion volume will note that its Section R is essentially the same as this one's Section A (for an explanation of this duplication, see page 45). We have divided the Oregon-Washington PCT into 12 sections because the vast majority of hikers will be walking only a part of the trail, not all of it. Each section starts and ends at a highway, and often at or near a supply center such as a town, resort or park. All the sections are short enough to make comfortable backpacking trips ranging from about 4 to 12 days for the average backpacker. Each of these sections could be conveniently broken into two or more shorter sections to provide even shorter hikes. However, we've refrained from making a new chapter begin at every road crossing since this would unnecessarily increase the size, weight—and price—of the book. By limiting ourselves to 12 hiking sections, we've kept pre-hike information to a minimum.

Pre-Hike Information

At the beginning of each section you'll find pre-hike information that mentions: 1) the attractions and natural features of that section, 2) the declination setting for your compass, 3) a mileage table between points within that section, 4) supply points on or near the route, 5) wilderness-permit information, if applicable, and 6) special problems. This pre-hike information also includes a map of the entire section.

Features. At the start of each section, an introduction briefly mentions the features—both good and bad—that you'll encounter while hiking through that section. These introductions will help you decide which section or sections are right for you.

Declination. The declination setting for your compass is important if you have to get an accurate reading. Actually, the declination changes very little throughout this whole two-state section, being 17¼°E in northernmost California and increasing to 20°E at trail's end in southernmost British Columbia. Because the magnetic north pole is wandering, the declination is slowly changing. By about the year 2000 A.D., the declinations will have moved only a bit, then giving a range of from about 16½°E to 19¼°E. Since most hikers read their compasses to the nearest 5°, they can set their compasses to the convenient average figure of 18°E and manage fine for this book's two-state stretch.

If your compass does not correct for declination, you'll have to add the appropriate declination to get the true bearing. For example, if your compass indicates that a prominent hill lies along a bearing of 70°, and if the section you're hiking in has a declination of 20°E, then you should add 20°, getting 90° (due east) as the true bearing of that hill. If you can identify that hill on a map, you can find where *you* are on the PCT by adding 180°, getting 270° (due west) in this example. By drawing a line due west from the hill to an intersection of the PCT, you'll determine your position.

Most hikers will agree it's easier to carry a compass with a declination setting than to try and remember if one should add or subtract declination. Regardless of which type of compass you use, you *should not* attempt a major section of the PCT without a thorough understanding of your compass *and* of map interpretation. On a long hike you could be caught in a whiteout and your trail could be buried under snow. Then, your navigation skills, or lack thereof, might determine whether you lived or died. Until you master both map and compass, take only short hikes in good weather.

Mileage Table. Each mileage table lists distances between major points found within its PCT section. Both distances between points and cumulative mileages are given. We list cumulative mileages south to north *and* north to south so that no matter which direction you are hiking the PCT, you can easily determine the mileages you plan to hike. Many of the points listed in the tables are at or near good campsites. If you typically average 17 miles a day—the on-route rate you'll need to complete the tri-state PCT in under 6 months—then you can determine where you should camp to maintain this rate, and you can estimate when you should arrive at certain supply points. Of course, in reality your time schedule may turn out to be quite different from your planned schedule, due to unforeseen circumstances.

At the end of this short chapter we've included a mileage table for the entire Oregon-Washington PCT. By scanning this table's *distances between points,* you can tell at a glance just how long each section is. You can then select one or more of appropriate length, turn to that section's **Introduction,** and see if it sounds appealing. Then read its **Problems** (if any) and see if it still sounds appealing. Of course, you need not start at the beginning of any section, since *every* PCT section is cut by one or more access roads.

Supplies. If you're going to be on the trail for more than two weeks, you'll probably want to stop somewhere to resupply. This pre-trail section mentions the resorts, stores, post offices and towns that are readily accessible to the hiker. In most cases the supply point is just a resort or small store with minimal food supplies and perhaps with a post office. By "minimal" we mean a few odds and ends that typically cater to passing motorists, e.g., beer and potato chips. Therefore, it is best to make your own "CARE" packages and mail them to appropriate post offices. See page 15 for a list of these, their ZIP codes and mailing tips.

Wilderness Permits. In sections C, I and K, you'll pass through a national park. In these you'll need a permit if you camp in their backcountry, and their pre-trail paragraphs tell you where you can write for one or pick one up. Also see page 20 for general information about wilderness permits and page 23 for addresses.

Problems. In every section but B, you can expect early-season snow patches to hinder your progress, while later you can expect pursuing mosquitoes to speed it up. This pre-trail paragraph, not found in every section, mentions these two problems when they are found in superabundance. It also mentions extensive waterless stretches, which are amazingly frequent for such a wet mountain range. After reading about a section's special problems you may decide to reschedule the time you plan to hike through it, or perhaps you may choose a more appealing section.

Section Map. Early editions of the two-volume *Pacific Crest Trail* guides contained only a long sequence of narrow topographic maps. Hikers using them reasonably complained of these maps' "tunnel vision": without a Forest Service map, you couldn't tell what lay more than a few miles east or west of the PCT; you could only look ahead or behind. In response to this problem, we've widened the maps so they are up to 46% wider than in the early editions, thus permitting you to take compass readings on more-distant topographic features. With this expanded lateral coverage you can locate yourself faster and better.

Still, there are instances when you'd like to see miles of lateral coverage, particularly when your trek has gone afoul due to bad weather, injury or other disaster. Then you'll want to know the quickest way out to civilization. Hence we've included section maps to show you the trails, roads, towns and other features you should know about if you must abort your hike. Because we've included these large-area section maps, you should be able to get along entirely without Forest Service maps or any other aids.

Route Description

When you start reading the text of a PCT section, you will notice that a pair of numbers follows each of the more important trail points. For example, at Russell Creek in the Mt. Jefferson Wilderness, this pair is (5520-2.8), which means that you cross this creek at an elevation of 5520 *feet* and at a distance of 2.8 *miles* from your last given point, which in this example is at a junction with the Woodpecker Trail. By studying these figures along the section you are hiking, you can easily determine the distance you'll have to hike from point A to point B, and by noting the elevation changes you get a good idea of how much climbing and descending you'll have to do. Along this guide's *alternate* routes, which are set aside by rows of asterisks, there are occasional second mileage figures, each of which represents the cumulative mileage along the alternate route to that point.

In addition to giving accurate directions, the route description tells you where you can camp, where you can get water, what hazards you should be aware of, how streams and trail condition may change with season, and other useful hiking information. In addition, the description also tells you something about the country you are walking through—the scenery, the geology, the biology, and sometimes a bit of history. We hope this added information will increase your outdoor perception and add to your enjoyment of your trek.

The Topographic Maps

Each hiking section contains all the topographic maps you'll need to hike that part of the Pacific Crest Trail. All these maps are at a scale of 1:50,000, or about 0.8 mile per inch (1 mile per 1¼ inches). Most hikers are acquainted with 7.5′ maps (1:24,000) and 15′ maps (1:62,500). Since our topos are based on these two map sizes, we chose an intermediate scale of 1:50,000 because if 7.5′ maps are reduced any farther, say to 1:62,500, the names and numbers on them become too difficult to read. Yet, if we were to enlarge the 15′ maps to 1:24,000, the size, weight and price of the book would increase by about 25% and the lateral extent of each map would be cut in half. We think the 1:50,000 scale has the best cost:benefit ratio.

Many of this guide's topos show township-and-range sections, which are *usually* square and *usually* measure one mile on a side. Topos with these sections thus have a one-mile grid pattern, which aids in judging distances.

On the topos, the PCT route appears as a solid black line where it exists as trail or a *closed* road and as a dashed black line where it exists as a temporary route along a road. Any alternate route that is set apart in the text by asterisks is also shown on the maps, and it is indicated by an alternating dot-dash black line. Proposed PCT (not yet built or still under construction) has the same symbol as a cross-country route, that is, a dotted black line. A map legend at the end of this chapter lists most of the symbols you'll find on this guide's topographic maps.

Text and Map Cross References

To make this guide as functional as possible, we've tried to place the maps as close as possible to the appropriate columns of trail description, and we've included four reference systems. Perhaps the most obvious system is the one composed of a set of large, bold letters and numbers (**A1, A2,** etc.), which are found at the bottom of each column of route description. These sets identify the appropriate map (Map A1, Map A2, etc.) that shows the section of PCT being described in the column of route description. In most cases, that map is no more than a page or two away.

But what if you see a feature on a map and you want to find where it is mentioned in the text? In that case, turn to the index, which lists entries for both text and maps.

The last two reference systems deal with maps only. Since the Pacific Crest Trail is not an arrow-straight north-south path, neither is the sequence of topo maps that show it. Therefore, along the border of each map we list the maps that touch it. For example, turn to map C3 on page 91. Note that three maps border this map: C1, C2 and C4. The blue tick mark between "see MAP C1" and "see MAP C2" tells you where map C1 ends and map C2 begins. The blue tick mark to the right of "see MAP C4" tells you where the right border of map C4 is. (Its left border is off the page, hence the tick mark lies flat, indicating that the map continues in that direction.) By learning the significance of the topos' tick marks, you should be able to go from map to map with a minimum of orientation problems.

But if you still have problems in determining the location of one map with respect to another, then use our fourth reference system, the large-area section map at the beginning of each hiking chapter. On it all the topo map borders for that chapter are printed in light blue. In like manner, the Oregon-Washington map on page vi shows all the large-area maps for this book's hiking sections, A through L. Thus if you want to hike, say, Sections E through G, you can easily visualize how much of the entire Oregon-Washington stretch you're going to be doing.

Following the Trail

The "Pacific Crest Trail" is usually a trail, though in a few places—notably Goat Rocks' Packwood Glacier and Glacier Peak's Red and Fire Creek passes—it is usually a snowfield. On a clear midsummer's day, the PCT is easy to follow, even if it is a snowfield. However, in early season or in a storm, the trail could be buried under snow. If the snow is a foot or more deep, then the trail's course may become obscure. When this happens, you may have to watch for other visual clues: PCT emblems, posts, blazes and ducks. (A blaze is a place on a tree trunk where someone has carved away a patch or two of bark to leave a conspicuous man-made scar; a duck is an obviously man-made pile of rocks.) Since all these markers can be ephemeral, our route descriptions usually do not emphasize them.

In fact, we're even reluctant to state that a trail junction is "signed," since the sign may disappear in a year or two. Where we mention trail junctions (or road junctions, for that matter), we give the trail's official name and number, if it has both (for example, Jefferson Park Trail 3429). Some trails have only official names or official numbers. Others have neither, and for these we say "trail" instead of "Trail." If a trail once had a trail number but no longer does, we still prefer to state it, since we can fit numbers onto the book's topo maps far easier than lengthy trail names. When the Pacific Crest Trail came into prominence in the early 1970s, it received a lot more hiker use, and consequently it has been kept up very well. With all the signs and markers along it, the PCT can almost be followed without map or guide through Oregon and Washington—if you have good weather and no emergencies.

LEGEND

Heavy-duty road	━━━━━━	PCT route along trails	─────────
Medium-duty road	━ ━ ━ ━	PCT route along roads	─ ─ ─ ─ ─
Improved light-duty road	══════	Authors' alternate route	─··─··─··─
Unimproved dirt road	════════	Proposed PCT	·············
Jeep road or trail	─ ─ ─ ─		
Railroad: single track	┼─┼─┼─┼─┼	Year-round streams	────────
Railroad: multiple track	╪─╪─╪─╪	Seasonal streams	─ ··· ─ ··· ─ ····

Scale of maps, 1:50,000   I   O   I MILE

Oregon-Washington PCT Mileage Table

Mileages:	South to North	Distances between Points	North to South
Highway 96 in Seiad Valley.....................	0.0		1003.3
Section A		64.1	
Interstate 5 near Siskiyou Pass..................	64.1		939.2
Section B		54.0	
Highway 140 near Fish Lake	118.1		885.2
Section C		76.0	
Highway 138 near the Cascade crest............	194.1		809.2
Section D		61.3	
Highway 58 near Willamette Pass	255.4		747.9
Section E		75.7	
Highway 242 at McKenzie Pass.................	331.1		672.2
Section F		112.5	
Highway 35 near Barlow Pass..................	443.6		559.7
Section G		54.4	
Interstate 84 at Bridge of the Gods	498.0		505.3
Walk across Bridge of the Gods		0.5	
Highway 14 at Bridge of the Gods	498.5		504.8
Section H		147.0	
Highway 12 near White Pass	645.5		357.8
Section I		96.5	
Interstate 90 at Snoqualmie Pass	742.0		261.3
Section J		74.5	
Highway 2 at Stevens Pass	816.5		186.8
Section K		117.7	
Highway 20 at Rainy Pass......................	934.2		69.1
Section L		69.1	
Highway 3 in Manning Provincial Park..........	1003.3		0.0

Old and new PCT diamonds plus a duck with post and plastic streamer

12 Trail Chapters

North Sister, from South Matthieu Lake

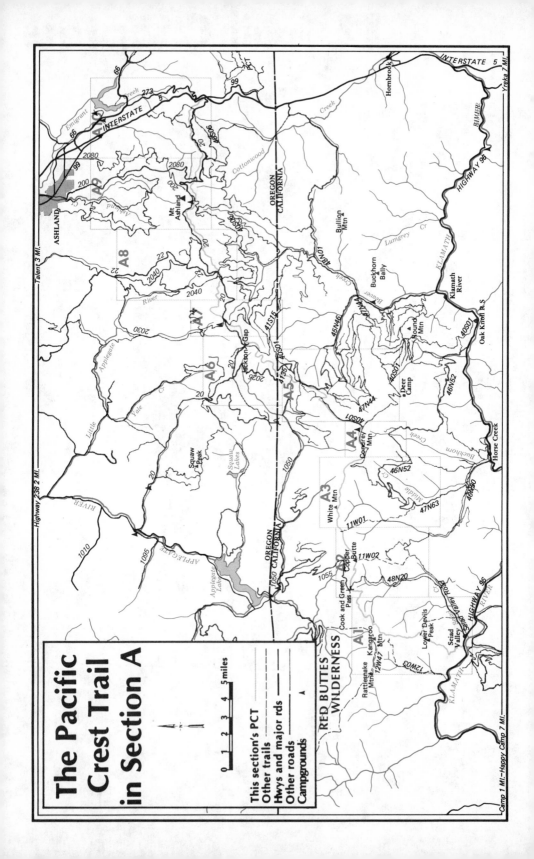

The Pacific Crest Trail in Section A

0 1 2 3 4 5 miles

This section's PCT
Other trails
Hwys and major rds
Other roads
Campgrounds

Section A: Highway 96 in Seiad Valley to Interstate 5 near Siskiyou Pass

Introduction: Pacific Crest Trail hikers who have used the *Volume 1: California* guide will note that its Section R is essentially the same as this volume's Section A. The reason for this duplication is that the Pacific Crest Trail crosses the California-Oregon border in the middle of nowhere, roughly midway between Seiad Valley, on Highway 96, and Ashland, on Interstate 5. Hence hikers wanting to do every foot of California will logicaly continue northeast toward Ashland (or at least to Interstate 5) while those wanting to hike north along every foot of Oregon will logically start near Seiad Valley.

Actually, you can drive to within a short walk of the point where the Pacific Crest Trail enters Oregon. To do this, drive west from Medford, Oregon, on Highway 238, passing through Jacksonville in about 5 miles. The route then goes 7 miles southwest to the tiny community of Ruch, where you leave 238 and head south on a road up the Applegate River. In 6½ miles you'll pass the Star Work Center, then in an additional 2½ miles you'll cross to the east bank of the Applegate River and immediately branch left on Road 20. This road climbs 14½ miles to Silver Fork Gap, located at the east end of Yellowjacket Ridge. From here, Road 20 climbs east to Jackson Gap, but you descend southeast on Road 2025, which winds 4¼ miles to a gap just east of Donomore Peak. Just 40 yards south of this gap the Pacific Crest Trail crosses your road, and if you follow the trail about 200 yards southwest, to where it turns abruptly northeast, you'll be a few feet inside California. By starting north here, you'll save 2–3 days of hiking.

In this guide's Section A, the hiker makes a long traverse east to get over to the Cascade Range. The long traverse west in California, from Burney Falls to Marble Mountain, was quite necessary, though inconveniently long, since a route going north from Burney Falls past Mt. Shasta would be a dry, hot one indeed. Before the Pacific Crest Trail route became final, this sun-drenched corridor was the one most hikers followed to the Oregon Skyline Trail—Oregon's section of the Pacific Crest Trail. Section A's route, almost completely built by late 1978 and due to be completed in 1987, stays remarkably high for most of its length, dropping significantly only at each end. Although high, it has been only mildly glaciated, and because glaciers haven't scoured away the soil, thick forests abound. These, unfortunately, are rampant with logging roads. From Reeves Ranch eastward you are always paralleling one road or another, so you certainly lose the wilderness feeling this high-crest hike is supposed to offer. Views, however, are pleasing enough, and surprisingly few logging operations are seen from the trail. Before early July these roads are an advantage, for signficant stretches of trail are still snowbound. The roads, being more open, are quite easy to follow, though they still have enough snow patches on them to stop motor vehicles. As you progress east on trail or road, you walk across increasingly younger rocks, first late-Paleozoic/early-Mesozoic metamorphic rocks, then mid-Mesozoic granite rocks of the Mt. Ashland area and finally mid-to-late Cenozoic volcanic rocks of the Interstate 5 area.

Declination: 17¼°E

Mileages:

	South to North	Distances between Points	North to South
Highway 96 at Seiad Valley	0.0		64.1
		6.5	
Lower Devils Peak saddle......................	6.5		57.6
		8.8	
Cook and Green Pass...........................	15.3		48.8
		5.3	
Lowdens Cabin site	20.6		43.5
		7.5	
Alex Hole camp entrance	28.1		36.0
		2.3	
Mud Springs spur road.........................	30.4		33.7
		2.4	
Bearground Spring	32.8		31.3
		4.1	
California-Oregon border.......................	36.9		27.2
		4.4	
Sheep Camp Spring	41.3		22.8
		2.3	
Wrangle Gap	43.6		20.5
		9.6	
Grouse Gap	53.2		10.9
		3.8	
Road 2080...................................	57.0		7.1
		7.1	
Interstate 5 near Mt. Ashland Road 20.............	64.1		0.0

Supplies: No supplies are available once you leave Seiad Valley. Along this crest route virtually all roads south will get you down to Highway 96, which has a smattering of hamlets, and virtually all roads north will ultimately channel you down to the Ashland-Medford area. However, we don't think you should descend either direction since you would then be way off route. Even in an emergency situation, you're likely to get help from people driving along the near-crest roads long before you could reach any settlement. If you're continuing through Oregon, you'll want to end Section A in Ashland, and 3 routes to it are described in this chapter. You won't find any more sizable towns within an easy day's walk of the PCT until you reach the Oregon-Washington border area, more than 400 miles beyond this section's end. If you think you'll need a new pack, a camera or a pair of boots, certainly stop in Ashland.

We begin this section at the Seiad Store and post office (1371' elevation, located 46 miles west of Interstate 5 via Highway 96). Walking west along the highway, we immediately cross Seiad Valley Road, which heads northeast up to Horse Tail Falls and beyond to Cook and Green Pass. Wildwood Tavern is soon reached, opposite School House Gulch (1380–0.5), from where the old trail once started. Following the road as it curves west, we quickly reach a newer trailhead for the Lower Devils Peak Lookout Trail 12W04 (1380–0.3). Since it is an exhausting 4400' ascent to potential campsites by the Kangaroo Mountain meadows, one is prudent to start this strenuous trek in the cool shade of the morning.

Under a cover of madrone, Douglas-fir, incense-cedar and Oregon oak, our trail curves west and climbs moderately alongside two sets of powerlines that parallel the highway below.

Momentarily we reach a junction (1600–0.2) with a trail that parallels Highway 96 west for 1.4 miles before ending close to a stream-gaging cable that spans the mighty Klamath River. The PCT was supposed to cross there, rather than on the Highway 96 bridge east of Seiad Valley. However, this plan was abandoned largely because a hiker/equestrian bridge across the broad, flood-prone Klamath proved to be too expensive to justify its construction, and the 1.4-mile trail might ultimately fade into oblivion. For the long-distance PCT trekker, this abandonment may be a blessing in disguise, since that once-proposed route would have inconveniently bypassed Seiad Valley, which is an important resupply point.

From the junction with the Highway 96 trail, our trail heads north into a shaded gully with its accompanying poison oak, and we soon reach a junction with the original Devils Peak Lookout

A1   **A1**

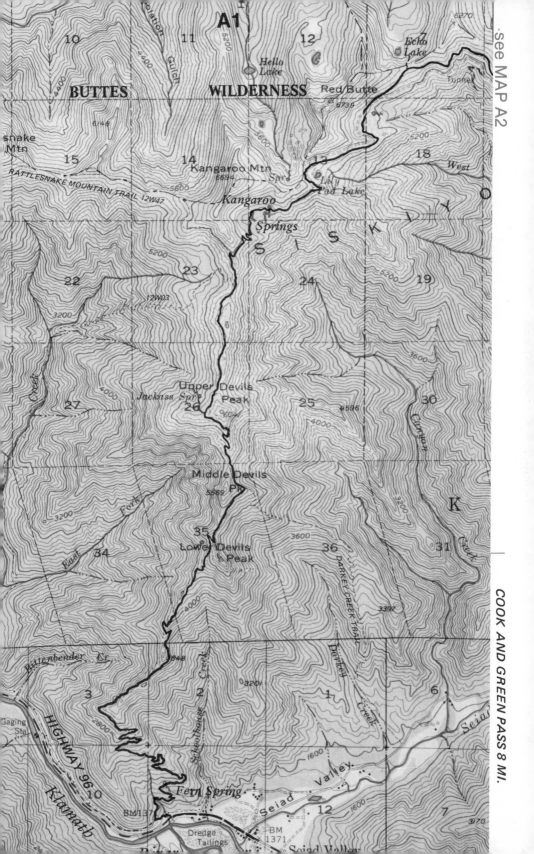

A1

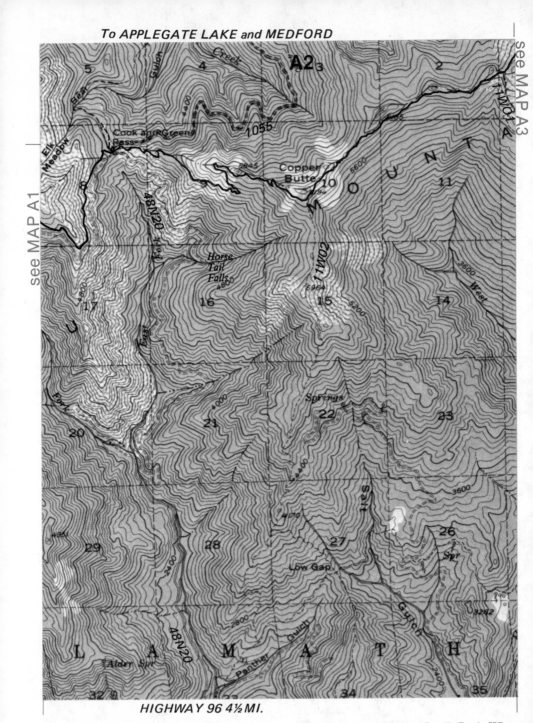

trail, now abandoned. About ¼ mile beyond this junction we reach Fern Spring (1900–0.7), a small seep trickling from a pipe into a concrete cistern. Our well-engineered trail switchbacks up shady, though fly-infested, south-facing slopes, then follows a ridge system northeast up toward Lower Devils Peak. Where the ridge fuses with the peak's flank, we climb up some short switchbacks, then make a final push up to a saddle (5020–4.8) on the Devils Peaks crest. Here you can follow an old, nearly level trail southeast 250 yards along the crest to the

A1   **A1**

remains of Lower Devils Peak Lookout, which was dismantled in 1976. The views you obtain from it are fine, but the many views ahead equal those from the lookout site.

From our crest saddle we head north to the east ridge of Middle Devils Peak and meet the Darkey Creek Trail (5170–0.6), which descends southeast to Seiad Valley. After an initial steep climb up from the east ridge, our trail eases off slightly while ascending the northeast slope to a saddle. Here, and on short switchbacks above it, we can pause for views of snow-capped Mt. Shasta (14,162′) to the east and the Marble Mountain Wilderness to the south. Beyond the switchbacks we reach the western arm of Upper Devils Peak and here we encounter a spur trail (5820–1.0) that descends 330 steep yards past western white pines to a seeping spring amid a cluster of alders. Our trail now makes a traverse north, and along it we observe specimens of the quite rare weeping spruce, with their drooping "Douglas-fir" branches, oversized "hemlock" cones and scaly "lodgepole" bark. Along its open stretches, the trail is seasonally adorned with phlox and wild parsley.

Descending briefly to a saddle, we reach a junction with the faint Portuguese Creek Trail 12W03 (5760–1.2), which descends west, but we climb north up the ridge to a junction with Rattlesnake Mountain Trail 12W47 (5940–0.3), which makes an obvious contour northwest across the slopes. Starting southeast, we mo-

Schaffer at sinkhole

mentarily cross the nearby Devils Peaks crest to leave it for good as we switchback down into a basin at the foot of rusty Kangaroo Mountain. On this descent you may see two moraine-dammed ponds, each having a nearby campsite. Heading north from the switchbacks, we discover a creek that disappears into a sinkhole dissolved from a layer of gray marble that contrasts strongly with the orange, ancient, ultrabasic intrusives of this area. These rocks are likely the northern extension of the rock types one sees along the PCT in the Marble Mountain Wilderness, on the distant southern skyline. Noting that cattle also use our area, we treat its water (see pages 12–13 on polluted water). Heading east, we reach a spring close to our hike's first campsites (5760–0.9).

From this spring—one of the Kangaroo Springs—the trail soon reaches a southeast slope, across which it climbs steadily to the east ridge of Kangaroo Mountain. From this ridge we can gaze down at Lily Pad Lake, with its poor campsites and its hundreds of frogs. Our trail

A1

Weeping spruce and Red Butte

A1

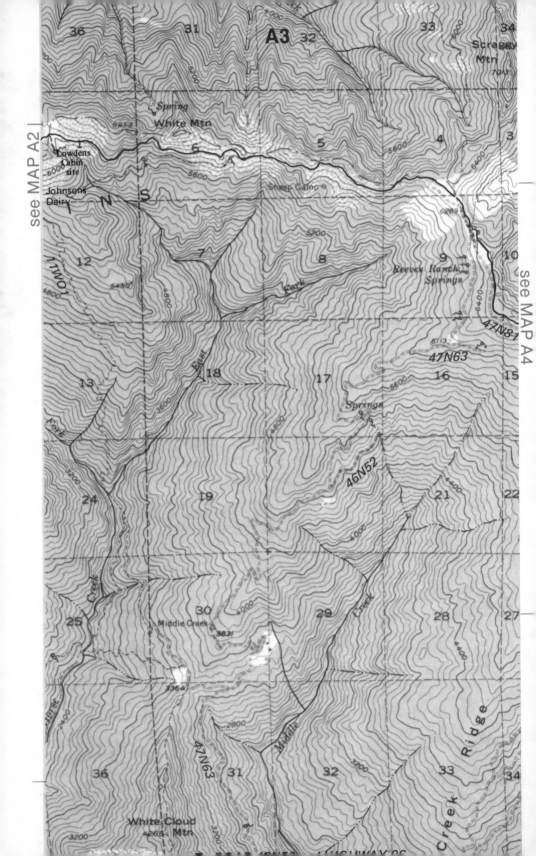

stays high above this lake, arcing northwest over to a narrow ridge, which is part of the Red Buttes Wilderness boundary. At the far end of the ridge we almost reach a closed jeep road, then turn and start a traverse northeast. Immediately, we cross an old trail that descends to Lily Pad Lake, then descend gently east to a ridge that provides views down into the lake's glaciated canyon. From the ridge we circle a shallower, mildly glaciated canyon and cross the jeep road (5710–1.0) which has been staying just above us. The trail has kept below the road to avoid the Chrome King Mine, which lies just southwest of the road crossing. Next we traverse through a stand of timber, then climb past more brush to a junction on a crest saddle (5900–0.5). From it a trail descends northeast toward nearby Echo Lake, whose environs provides camping superior to that at Lily Pad Lake.

Leaving the saddle and the last outcrop of marble we'll encounter on our northbound trek, we make a long, mostly brushy descent, first east and then north, down to Cook and Green Pass (4770–2.5). There is room for at least several hiking parties on the forested, nearly flat crest immediately west of the road that crosses the pass. Get water by going 190 yards along a trail that leads northwest from the pass. Here, along the crest border between the Klamath National Forest to the south and the Rogue River National Forest to the north, a major forest road crosses the pass and descends about 10½ miles to the start of this section's hike, Seiad Store. Our route has been 4 miles longer. By dropping 1.6 miles southeast down this road you can reach water at Horse Tail Falls— not exactly worth the 700-foot loss in elevation. Northbound from Cook and Green Pass, a major USFS road snakes its way about 10 miles down to Hutton Campground, which is situated about a mile from a large reservoir, Applegate Lake.

From this pass we follow an obvious trail, rebuilt in 1976, east up the ridge toward Copper Butte. On it we pass scattered knobcone pines in a vegetative cover that includes manzanita, western serviceberry, tobacco brush and Sadler's oak. Like tombstones, slabs of greenish-gray, foliated mica schist stand erect along the trail and, in the proper light, reflect the sun's rays as glacially polished rocks do. Our trail makes a long switchback up to the crest and enters a stand of white fir, red fir, mountain hemlock, Douglas-fir, ponderosa pine and knobcone pine—a combination we'd never see in the Sierra Nevada, where these trees are altitudin-

ally zoned to a much greater extent. On the north slopes just below the crest, you'll also find the weeping spruce, which we saw earlier.

Rather than struggle to the top of Copper Butte, as the early PCT hikers did on the old trail, we make a slight ascent to its south ridge, on which we meet Trail 11W02 (6080–2.8), which descends south to Low Gap, Salt Gulch and Seiad Valley. In 1976 a logging road was being constructed on the slopes south of us, interfering with the tranquil setting. But Section A is logging country, and you can expect to run into ongoing logging operations as you head east. Our east course now becomes a northeast one and we keep close to the crest, crossing several forested crest saddles before arriving at an open one (6040–2.2), from which the faint Horse Creek Trail 11W01 begins a brushy descent south to Middle Creek Road 46N50. This road descends southeast to the hamlet of Horse Creek on Highway 96. We continue northeast to another saddle (6040–0.3), where you'll find a faint, ducked path heading 130 yards southeast to a small spring with an equally small campsite at the Lowdens Cabin site. It is better to camp at the saddle, where there is more room. Leaving it, we start a contour east and from brushy slopes can identify the spring area, across the meadow south of us, by noting a large log near the forest's edge.

Our brushy contour becomes a forested one before we reach a deep crest saddle and soon after it, in a Douglas-fir forest, encounter specimens of Jeffrey and incense-cedar. Along the south slope of White Mountain we cross somewhat-open slopes again, reach its spur ridge, and then arc east across the upper limits of a meadowy hollow. At its east end is a junction (5950–2.0) with the old PCT, which will lead you to a seep near the hollow's west edge. Late-season hikers will have to descend the hollow a short distance to get their water. Just beyond this junction we reach another saddle and from it we climb east up to a higher crest. We stay close to it on a path that glitters with mica flakes before we eventually curve southeast and descend an open slope. On it we cross, then parallel, a crest road that takes us across a long saddle, passing a *de facto* car-camping area below us, then almost touching the hairpin turn of Road 47N81 (6310–2.4). You can take the lower road branch south ½ mile to the Reeves Ranch Springs, located below the road.

The Pacific Crest Trail parallels the east side of the road's upper branch, climbing first south,

A1, A2   **A2, A3**

Deer on crest near Mud Springs

then east, and eventually traversing the south slopes of Condrey Mountain before descending ¾ mile to a saddle (6630–3.1). On it, a spur road leaves Road 47N81 to descend west-southwest 0.3 mile to a poor campsite beside a trickling spring a few yards farther east. Our roadside trail meets another spur road, this one descending north ¼ mile to the delightful Alex Hole campsite, located near a willow-lined spring. Here, where your far-reaching view north is framed by cliffs of mica schist, your only neighbors may be animals such as deer, chipmunks and mountain bluebirds.

Back on the PCT, we start to parallel climbing Road 47N81, then veer north away from it to climb the main Siskiyou crest. We almost top Peak 7043 before descending into a mountain-hemlock forest. Long-lasting snow patches can make the next mile to the Mud Springs spur road difficult to follow, but then you could take the crest road, just east of us, to the same destination. Just yards away from Road 40S01, the PCT crosses the Mud Springs spur road (6730–2.3), and you can continue northwest 0.2 mile down this road to its end, where there are several very refreshing clear-water springs—a good camping spot.

Past the spur road we have a wonderful, open, near-crest traverse that passes a prominent rock midway in our approach to less imposing, misnamed Big Rock. We descend northeast across its open, gravelly east slope of glistening mica, briefly enter a patch of firs, leave it, and head south back into forest as we descend to a crossing of Road 40S01 (6250–1.6). Our trail now enters an old logging area as it first continues southward, then turns northeast and descends to cross a road immediately north of

Bearground Spring (5930–0.8). As you'll see, this is an area of several springs. In this vicinity—occasionally packed with car campers—you should be able to find a decent campsite, should you need one.

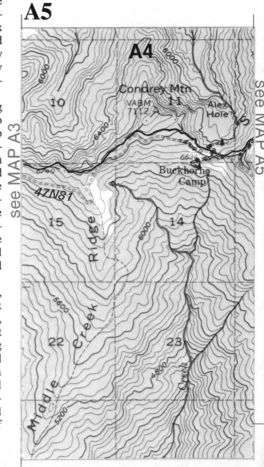

A4, A5

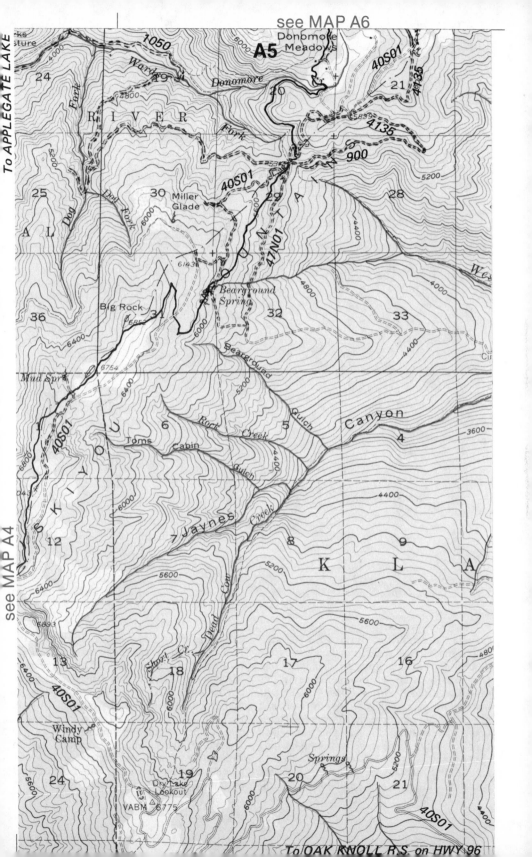

To APPLEGATE LAKE

see MAP A4

A5

Donomore Meadows

40S01

4135

Warm Fork

1050

RIVER Fork

4500

Donomore

4135

900

5200

40S01

30

Miller Glade

29

28

47N01

6143

Bearground Spring

Big Rock

6852

32

33

West

36

Mud Sprs

6754

Bearground

Gulch

Canyon

4400

3600

40S01

6

Rock Creek

5

4

Toms Cabin

Gulch

Jaynes Creek

4400

SKIYOU

12

7

8

9

KLA

5600

5200

6400

6893

Dead Con Cr.

Short Cr.

13

18

17

16

4800

40S01

Windy Camp

Springs

19

20

21

24

Dry Lake Lookout

VABM 6775

40S01

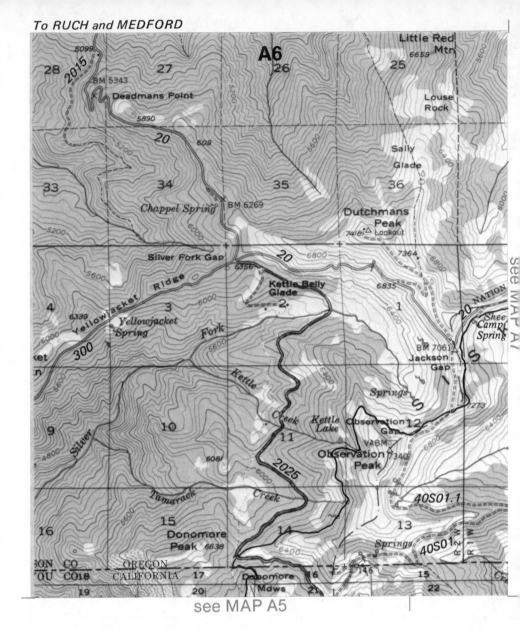

see MAP A5

From the Bearground Spring road you start among shady Shasta red firs and make a steady descent northeast, crossing an abandoned logging road midway to a saddle. Nearing this saddle, you cross narrow Road 40S01 at its hairpin turn, immediately recross the road, and in a couple of minutes reach a 6-way road junction on the saddle (5317–1.3). Our trail, which ends here between the west- and south-heading roads, resumes again between the north- and east-heading roads. However, in 1978 a logging operation had begun and another road—north-

east—was being added at the expense of the PCT. The mess was cleared up and the PCT restored by 1981, but in 1985 the Donomore Meadows PCT stretch experienced more havoc due to logging. And so it goes in the land of timber. The PCT makes a short climb north from the road before embarking on a long traverse that circles clockwise around a knoll to Donomore Creek. This you parallel east to within 100 yards of the Donomore Meadows road, then bridge the creek (5600–1.5) and wind northward up an amorphous ridge that is

A5   **A5**

Wrangle Campground shelter

crisscrossed with misleading cow paths. In ½ mile we cross this road at a point about 80 yards east of a cabin, then parallel a jeep road, immediately below us, which follows the meadow's edge north. At the meadow's upper end, our trail curves east above it, then switchbacks west for a short, sometimes steep ascent northwest into Oregon, and soon veers north up to a logging-road saddle (6210–1.4).

Here we cross wide Road 2025, climb east up a clear-cut crest, then leave it to make a long curving traverse northward to the west ridge (6750–1.6) of twin-topped Observation Peak. Kettle Lake, below us, immediately comes into view as we start an uphill traverse east; if you want to camp at it, then descend directly to it. We climb east to Kettle Creek, then climb north from it high above Kettle Lake before rounding the large northwest ridge of Observation Peak. A southeast traverse through stands of mountain hemlocks—wintery until mid-July—gets us to Observation Gap (7030–1.2), a shallow saddle just west of and above Road 40S01.1. From the gap we go ½ mile on our crest trail, cross Road 40S01.1, traverse around the east slopes of Peak 7273, and then parallel the crest north to Jackson Gap (7040–1.2). Before reaching this gap you'll certainly notice landscape terracing in the Jackson Gap area, done to prevent erosion on the burned-over slopes. Crossing this gap just a few feet above us is broad Road 20, which we'll parallel all the way to the end of Section A.

Before mid-July, snow drifts will probably force you to take this road rather than the PCT.

Leaving the cover of hemlocks and firs, we arc clockwise across the upper slopes of a huge open bowl, soon reaching a spur road (6920–0.3) to Sheep Camp Spring, located 10 yards south on it. Camp space is very limited, and since it lacks tree cover, you will probably greet next morning's sunrise from a very wet sleeping bag. Departing east from the spur road, we gradually descend, with unobstructed views, to a spur ridge, then arc northeast to Wrangle Gap (6496–2.3), reaching it ¼ mile after we cross to the north side of Road 20. Here a spur road descends steeply west to Wrangle Campground—the answer to an exhausted hiker's prayer. This little-used recreation site, nestled among Shasta red firs, has a large stone shelter complete with fireplace, two stoves, tables and even a sink. Get water from a nearby spring or from Wrangle Creek.

From Wrangle Gap the PCT route could have gone east, but instead it makes a long climb north to the end of the Red Mountain ridge and starts to wind southeast up it. It does have the advantage of giving you sweeping panoramas of southern Oregon and its pointed landmark, Mt. McLoughlin—an Ice Age volcano. After crossing the ridge we contour south and then east, leaving Red Mountain's slopes for a winding, moderate descent almost to Siskiyou Gap. In 1985 the permanent PCT dead-ended on a low

A5, A6   A6, A7, A8

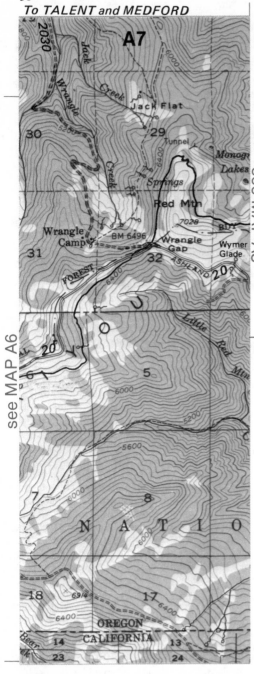

see MAP A6

see MAP A8

To TALENT and MEDFORD

junction (5880–0.8) on forested Long John Saddle.

Road 20 traverses north across the level saddle and a minor logging road descends northeast. Between the two the permanent PCT resumes, paralleling Road 20 north, then climbing northeast through an old logging area. After a mile of hiking we reach a spur ridge and exchange this scarred landscape for a shady forest climb north. From a gully our gradient eases to give us a pleasant stroll northeast to a sunny crest saddle (6710–2.1). On it, our tread almost disappears as it parallels Road 20 for a few yards; then it becomes prominent again and climbs a short ½ mile up to a saddle just north of Siskiyou Peak. From this saddle you'll see chunky Pilot Peak on the eastern skyline—a guiding beacon for early pioneers and for us. If you're continuing through Oregon, you should pass by it in a few days.

Our route now winds ⅓ mile northeast to the main crest, crossing a spur road just 25 yards below its departure from crest-hugging Road 20. We parallel this road northeast, sometimes below it and sometimes above it, to another saddle (7030–1.9) south of the main crest. Here the road bends north to descend, but we first go south briefly before switchbacking to descend northeast to a spur-road junction beside Road 20 (6630–1.0) on expansive Grouse Gap. This spur road will take you 0.2 mile south to a fork, where you branch left for a minute's walk to Grouse Gap Shelter, built in the mid-70s. Rather than use the nearby Mt. Ashland granite, the builders chose to import marble—like that of Marble Mountain—for the shelter's two walls. Although it provides dramatic sunrise views of Mt. Shasta and protection from the elements, it has two disadvantages: it lacks water and it is too visible to car campers. To get water, return to the main spur road and follow it southward ⅓ mile down to a gully, with a spring-fed creeklet.

From Grouse Gap the PCT parallels Road 20 and passes several seeping springs before it gradually drops away from it down to a crossing of Road 40S15 (6480–1.9), which climbs ½ mile back up to this crest road. From their junction, Road 20 contours ½ mile northeast to the Mt. Ashland Ski Area, from which the road is paved. An alternative to camping at Grouse Gap Shelter is to camp at Mt. Ashland Campground, on both sides of Road 20. To reach it, leave the PCT and follow Road 40S15 up to its bend left, about 250 yards, from where you'll see an abandoned logging road that climbs directly

crest (5920–3.8) just west of the actual gap, so the hiker walked a few yards south to Road 20 and followed it east immediately across the sunny gap and then northeast to a 5-way road

upslope to the campground. Water is in the little gully just above the upper tables. From Road 40S15, the PCT contours southeast to the bend and then traverses northeast to an open bowl below the ski area. From this it traverses southeast to a saddle, where we cross Road 20 (6160–1.5). Continuing southeast down-ridge, we follow the PCT down to Road 2080 (6060–0.4).

*　　*　　*　　*

From our ridge you can take a supply route by following Road 2080 north down to Bull Gap (5500–2.8), where you meet old Road 200, which climbs southwest up to the Mt. Ashland Ski Area. Continuing north, take Road 200, which in 3 miles rejoins Road 2080, all the way down to Glenview Drive (2200–8.5) in Ashland. Descend this road north, then descend Fork Street. You quickly reach Pioneer Street and follow it two blocks to C Street. The Ashland Post Office is one block southeast on it, at the corner of First and C streets (1920–1.1). To get back to the PCT, head southwest one block to East Main and walk southeast. It quickly becomes two-way Siskiyou Boulevard (1950–0.3), and you continue southeast on it to Highway 66 (Ashland Street) (2010–1.1). Take this east past the Ashland Shopping Center to

Washington Street, which has the Ashland Ranger Station at its end. Just east of this short street you reach Interstate 5 (1980–1.3–15.1). Since hitchhiking on freeways is legal in Oregon, you can hitchhike up it 9 miles to the Mt. Ashland exit. Alternately, you can continue on Highway 66, then go south up Highway 273 to that exit, about a 12-mile route. This route is described in the opposite direction at the end of this chapter.

*　　*　　*　　*

If you decide against the supply route, then continue east down the forested trail. The PCT stays on or north of the crest, but after 0.7 mile it crosses to its south and in ¼ mile reaches a jeep road that climbs northeast back to the nearby crest. In 1985 the eastbound PCT died out here and the hiker walked a steep 250 yards southwest down the jeep road to Road 20 (5730–1.1). This paved road provides the hiker with almost continual views of Mt. Shasta as he descends east past a saddle (5480–0.5) and a second one (5110–0.8) to a third (4980–0.9). In 1985 the PCT extended southwest from this saddle, only to die out, the right-of-way acquisition still being held up after about 10 years of negotiations. Eastbound, the PCT parallels a crest dirt road for ⅓ mile, then parallels Road 20

A9　　　　A9, A10

Mt. Shasta, from Mt. Ashland Campground

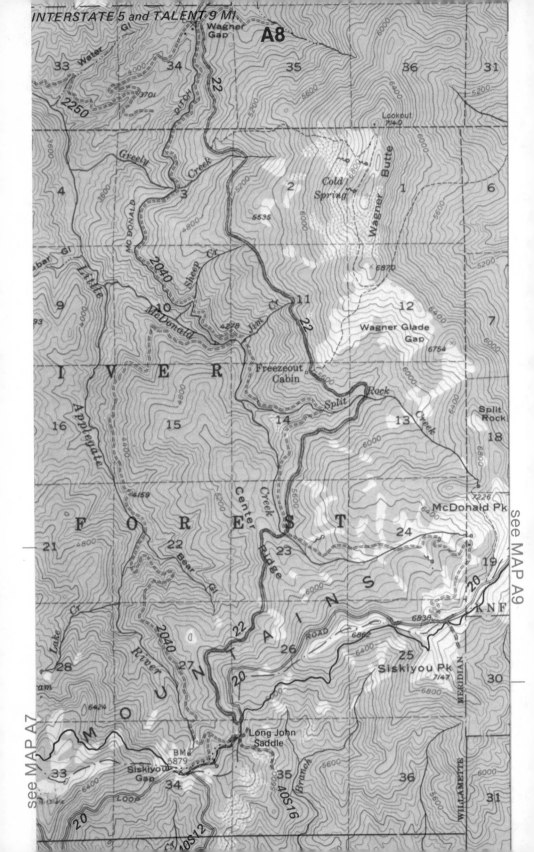

A8

Wagner
Gap

33   34   35   36   31

2250

Water   22

370t

Greely

Creek

Lookout
7140

Cold
Spring

Wagner Butte

4   3   2   1   6

5535

6870

MC DONALD

2040

Sheep Cr

Little

9   10   11   12   7

4278   Jim   Cr   22

McDonald

Wagner Glade
Gap
6754

Freezeout
Cabin

I V E R

Split   Rock

Split
Rock

Applegate

16   15   14   13   18

4159

7226

McDohald Pk

F O R E S T

21   22   23   24   19

4800

Center   Creek   Ridge

Bear   Gl

6838   KNF

2040   22   26

Lake   Cr   27   20   25   30

River   6862   ROAD

6424

M O U N T A I N S

Siskiyou Pk
7147

Long John
Saddle

BM
5879

Siskiyou
Gap
34   35   36   31

20   A0S16   Branch

LOOP

see MAP A9

see MAP A7

MERIDIAN

WILLAMETTE

A0S12

Pilot Rock and distant Mt. Shasta, from PCT above Mt. Ashland Road

as both descend east around ridges and in gullies. Three closely spaced gullies near the end of this descent provide spring-fed water before they coalesce to flow into the East Fork of Cottonwood Creek. Together, they are the first permanent source of water you've seen since the Mt. Ashland springs, about 8.3 miles back, and the last on-route water you'll see until the first spring in Section B, 3.1 miles farther. However, the veteran backpacker will be able to "sniff out" water in a number of gullies below the trail as he continues east.

Because we are on private land, we aren't allowed to deviate from the trail's tread and aren't allowed to camp. Thick brush prevents us from doing either. About 0.4 mile past our last spring-fed gully, we cross a road (4610–2.2) that descends steeply southeast to nearby Road 20, which here turns southeast to cross a broad saddle. Then, after a short, steep descent of our own, we cross a road (4470–0.1) that climbs gently west up to a union with the first road at paved Road 20. Both dirt roads are private—off limits—as is a third road that we parallel east, then momentarily turn south to cross (4360–0.1). Now we parallel this road, staying just above it, dip in and out of a gully with a sometimes flowing freshet, then soon curve away from the road as we glimpse busy, nearby

Interstate 5. Our path ends (4250–0.8) at an abandoned segment of old Highway 99, which we take for 140 yards around a hollow to a fork. Here we go left and descend an old, closed road 150 yards to trail's end on Highway 99. This trailhead is 250 yards north of where Mt. Ashland Road 20 ends at Highway 99 (4240–0.3), and that junction in turn is immediately north of where Interstate 5 crosses over the highway. Here, at the junction of Road 20 and Highway 99, Section A ends. The Mesozoic granitic rocks we've traversed across along the crest of the Siskiyou Mountains are now overlaid by mid-Tertiary, thick, basaltic andesite flows; the Shasta red firs and mountain hemlocks have yielded to Douglas-firs and orange-barked madrones.

If you've hiked the PCT through much or all of California (Volume 1), you may want to celebrate your entry into Oregon by visiting Callahan's Restaurant. Go north on Highway 99 for ⅔ mile to Highway 273 and on it cross under Interstate 5 at its Mt. Ashland exit. The restaurant is just east of it. This ever-popular place, closed on Mondays, serves only dinners, and though it is expensive by backpacker's standards, it is one of the better dining places along or near the entire Pacific Crest Trail. If you've been starving these last few miles, you'll

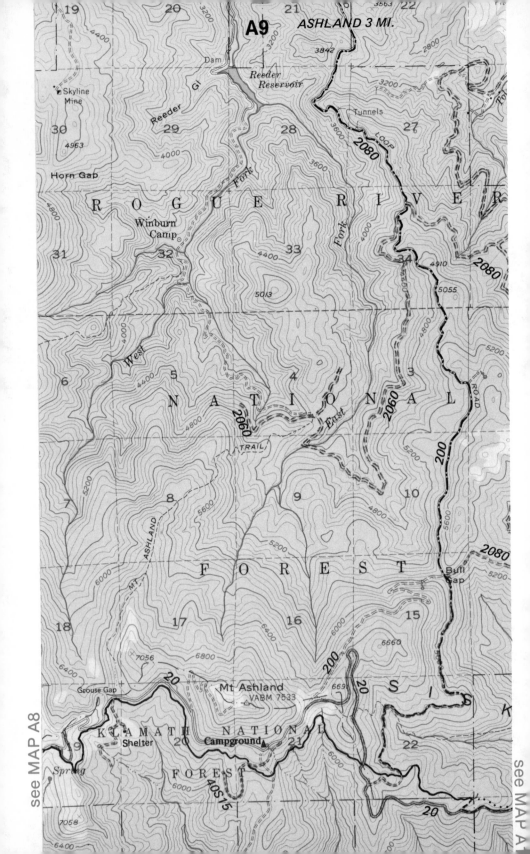

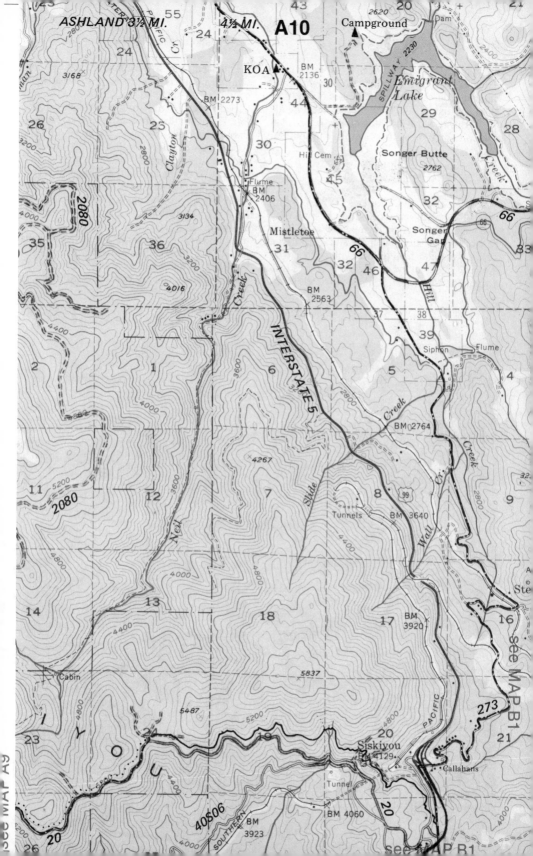

be glad to know that each of their dinners includes all the salad, soup and spaghetti you can eat. You can hitchhike 9 miles down Interstate 5 to the Highway 66 interchange and take the highway west into downtown Ashland to resupply for another stretch of PCT in southern Oregon.

*   *   *   *

Alternately, from Callahan's (3950–0.9 from end of Road 20), you can go down Highway 273 to a junction with Highway 66 (2290–6.7). Just east of it is the shallow upper end of Emigrant Lake, a popular fishing area; the deeper parts are relegated to water skiers, sailors and swimmers. Northwest, Highway 66 leads you to the main entrance to the Emigrant Lake Recreation Area (2150–1.8). Here a paved road heads southeast 0.4 mile up to a lateral dam, then curves north 0.6 mile to a public campground. Past the recreation-area entrance you'll come to fairly expensive but well-equipped Glenyan KOA campground (2140–0.2). It caters to backpackers as well as car campers, and the larger your hiking group, the cheaper your per-person camp fee will be. Continuing northwest on Highway 66, you meet Dead Indian Road (1920–2.6) before your highway turns west and climbs to cross Interstate 5 (1980–0.7–12.9) at the outskirts of Ashland. Some backpackers prefer to celebrate in Ashland rather than at Callahan's, for there are some even better restaurants to choose from. In addition, the

A10   A10

Ashland's Emigrant Lake, along alternate route

The Elizabethan and Bowmer Theatres

Hank Kranzler

more cultured backpackers take in one or more performances of Ashland's Oregon Shakespearean Festival, whose summer season runs from about mid June through late September. If the weather has been dreary or snow patches abundant, then perhaps a Shakespearean comedy will lift your spirits.

A10

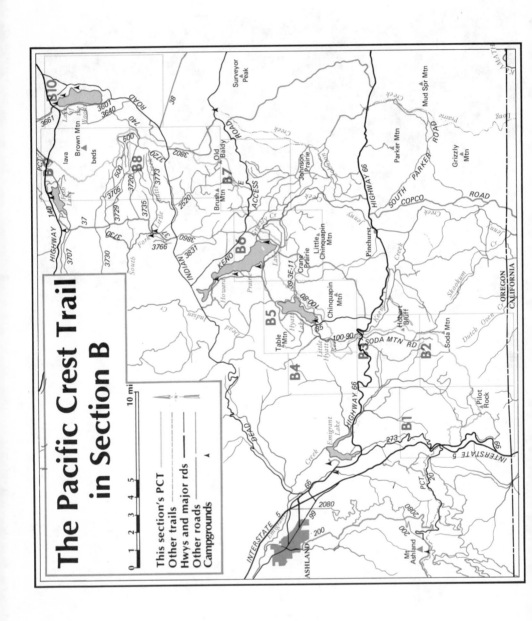

The Pacific Crest Trail
in Section B

This section's PCT ———
Other trails ———
Hwys and major rds ———
Other roads ———
Campgrounds ▲

Section B: Interstate 5 near Siskiyou Pass to Highway 140 near Fish Lake

Introduction: Sections A and C are among the highest stretches of Pacific Crest Trail to be found in either Oregon or Washington. In contrast, Section B, between them, is one of the lowest, and it is certainly the driest, least scenic section to be found in either state. This section abounds with past and present logging projects which the PCT often passes through or skirts around. And if these eyesores don't detract from this section's appeal, the lack of wilderness sensation will: often you are closely paralleling logging roads or jeep roads. Furthermore, although two sizable lakes are approached—Hyatt and Howard Prairie—both are dammed and both lack any alpine or subalpine character. And there is a *notable* lack of drinking water. With such a list of detractions, Section B will certainly be shunned by the masses and its trail will likely be taken only by long-distance hikers passing through to a more scenic section.

Declination: 17¼°E

Mileages:

	South to North	Distances between Points	North to South
Interstate 5 near Mt. Ashland Road 20.............	0.0		54.0
Cross upper Pilot Rock Jeep Road.................	4.6	4.6	49.4
Fenced-in spring	9.6	5.0	44.4
Hobart Bluff spur trail	13.9	4.3	40.1
Highway 66 at Green Springs Summit	17.3	3.4	36.7
Little Hyatt Reservoir	22.1	4.8	31.9
Hyatt Lake Campground spur trail................	23.6	1.5	30.4
Road to Klum Landing Campground...............	31.5	7.9	22.5
Keno Access Road.............................	33.4	1.9	20.6
Dead Indian Road	42.5	9.1	11.5
Highway 140 near Fish Lake	54.0	11.5	0.0

Supplies: If you need major supplies, get them in Ashland before you start hiking this section. Directions to this city are given at the end of the previous section. Since this section is short, the need for supplies will be minimal, and minimal supplies is all you'll find at Hyatt Lake, Howard Prairie Lake, Lake of the Woods and Fish Lake resorts. All but Hyatt Lake Resort are somewhat out of your way, especially Lake of the Woods Resort. Hyatt Lake, Fish Lake and Lake of the Woods resorts conveniently hold packages (see page 15), so the long-distance trekker who is racing against time doesn't have to take a day or two out of his schedule to make a side trip to Ashland.

Problems: In this section you'll have to hike up to 22 miles between on-route water sources. If you intend to do this unattractive hiking section, then try to do it in June, when snow problems are minimal, yet seasonal creeks are flowing.

PCT striking east toward Pilot Rock

Section B's southern starting point is at the junction of Mt. Ashland Road 20 and Highway 99 (4240), this point being immediately north of Interstate 5. To reach it by car, start in Ashland at the Highway 66 exit and drive 9 miles south on I5 up to the Mt. Ashland exit. If you're driving north, note that this exit is 16½ miles past the Highway 96 exit in northern California. From the exit proceed ⅔ mile south on Highway 99 to the Road 20 junction.

From this junction start hiking south up the highway, immediately crossing under noisy Interstate 5. You hike straight for ⅓ mile, then start to curve right. In about 250 more yards you

should see the resumption of PCT tread (0.5–4380), which crosses a gully that runs down the highway's east side. Note that there isn't a large trailhead sign, since this would attract bikers, something the landowners don't want. If you reach a road branching east, you've gone about 120 yards too far.

On the PCT we cross the gully, then momentarily cross the road. On private land we traverse eastward about ¾ mile across Section 28, and then our winding path angles north at a spring (4490–0.9), but quickly switchbacks. On a southward track, we climb moderately up toward a ridge, passing close to another spring,

B1   **B1**

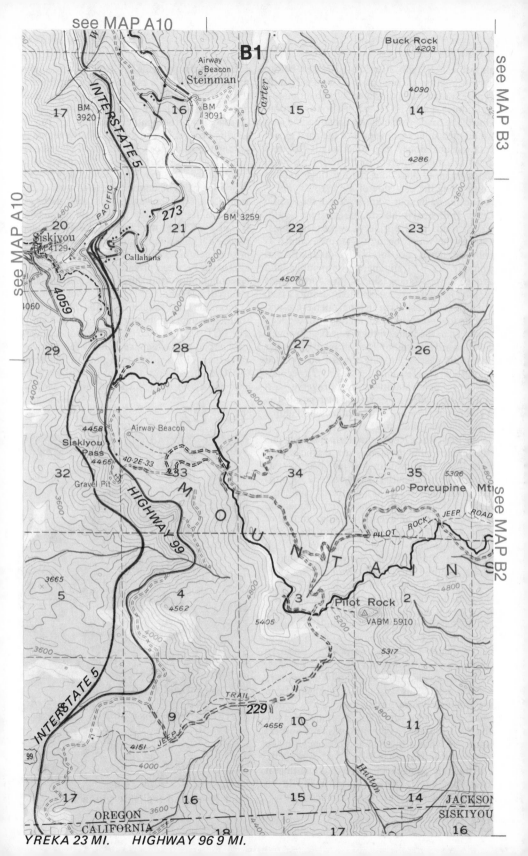

B1

Buck Rock
4203

Airway
Beacon
Steinman

Carter

4090

17   BM
3920   16   BM
3091   15   14

4286

INTERSTATE 5

PACIFIC

273

20   21   BM 3259   22   23

Siskiyou
BM 4129.

4800

Callahans

4507

4060   29   28   27   26

4059   4000

4458   Airway Beacon

Siskiyou
Pass
4466   40-2E-33   33   34   35   5306   Porcupine Mtn
32   4400

Gravel Pit   M   PILOT ROCK   JEEP ROAD

HIGHWAY 99   O   U   5   N   T   see MAP B2

3665   5   4   4562   A   3   Pilot Rock   I   2   N   S
5405   VABM 5910
5317

INTERSTATE 5   TRAIL   229   4656   10   11
9   4151   JEEP
4000

99   17   16   15   14   JACKSON
OREGON   SISKIYOU
CALIFORNIA   18   17   16

almost a half mile after the first, just before leaving Section 28. In Section 33 we wind gently ⅓ mile south up to a crest and, after a moment's walk down a spur ridge, reach a road junction. One of the roads descends to a broad saddle, and we do the same, keeping east of the road as our path, an abandoned jeep road, winds 0.2 mile down to a major intersection (4420–1.3). Here, roads go in all directions, two of them leading south along the east side of a crest.

Starting on lumber-company land, the Pacific Crest Trail begins beside the western southbound road. In 0.2 mile, however, it almost touches the wider, eastern one, then climbs ⅓ mile through a cool forest of Douglas-fir and white fir. As our trail emerges onto public land and southwest-facing slopes, the forest thins rapidly, junipers appear and temperatures rise. We hike southeast across a long, open crest, and past its low point our trail, mixing with old jeep tracks, can become rather vague. However, head toward a cluster of trees, through which our faint trail passes, bearing toward steep-sided Pilot Rock. In a few minutes we cross a secondary crest, bend southwest and traverse to a minor road, which we cross and then parallel as it curves east to a prominent intersection atop a broad saddle (5080–1.7).

The Pilot Rock Jeep Road starts east from this saddle, soon climbing steeply toward the base of Pilot Rock. Our trail makes an obscure start along this road's south edge and after 270 yards (5120–0.2) crosses it for a northeast climb to a nearby volcanic point. If you have the time, you might first make an excursion to the summit of Pilot Rock. The jeep road ends at the rock's base, from which you'll see an obvious chute up to the top. This route is relatively safe and no rope is required. However, acrophobics or careless climbers could get in trouble.

From the volcanic point beyond the Pilot Rock Jeep Road, the PCT goes briefly east along an abandoned road, then descends northeast 180 yards to a trailside outcrop with a summit that provides fair views across the northern landscape. Continuing our northeast descent, we round a ridge in ¼ mile and momentarily reach a crest. This we parallel northeast for a few minutes before turning east across it at a gate (5160–0.9)—the first of many. Immediately, a dramatic volcanic landscape unfolds before us, with a huge blocky pinnacle in the foreground and towering Pilot Rock to the south. The trailside pinnacle is easier to climb than it looks, but due to its exposure, it should be climbed *only* by experienced climbers.

Beyond the pinnacle our trail quickly angles north, then makes a pleasant, winding descent through a Douglas-fir forest to a large gate only a few yards south of a crest saddle (4990–0.7). A road from the southeast climbs up to our saddle, crosses it, and swings west, eventually joining the Pilot Rock Road, which climbs east from Highway 99. Also at this crest is a reappearance of the Pilot Rock Jeep Road, which seems to be quite abandoned west of the saddle. East of it, however, it is in good shape, as we'll see, for we will cross it again and again. Because a barbed-wire fence parallels the jeep road, we'll go through a number of gates. On our next stretch, as on most of Section B, our route alternates between private land—usually lumber companies—and Bureau of Land Management (BLM) land.

From the crest saddle, our trail first descends southeast, then curves northeast over to a gully. The PCT is now routed on an abandoned, overgrown road bed, which we follow a few minutes east, then climb north to a gate at the crest (5020–1.2). A short segment of trail leads us east across north-facing slopes to a road, up

B1, B2

Pilot Rock and trailside pinnacle

B1

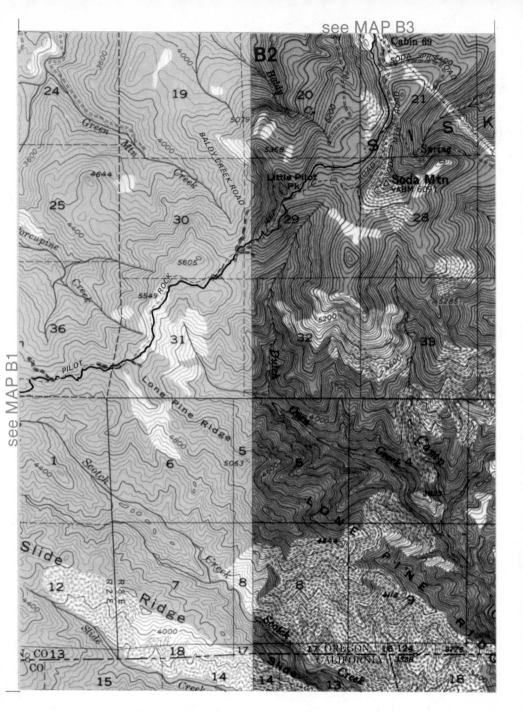

which we walk 65 yards to a minor crest saddle and the trail's resumption, on our left (5040–0.2). This trail segment goes but 110 yards, then we cross the jeep road, pass through a gate and parallel the road east. Twice more we cross the road and pass through a gate, the second time at

a minor road (5270–0.8) that descends southeast.

Our trail now parallels the jeep road northeast, and after ¼ mile it provides us with a half mile of almost continuous views of Mt. Shasta. Pilot Rock, our former guiding beacon, is now

B2

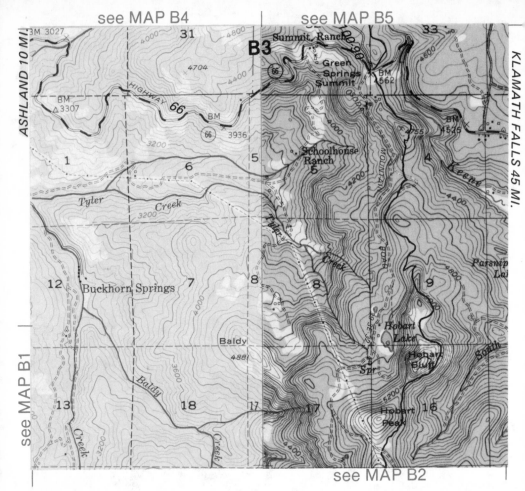

see MAP B2

hidden. Beyond the views our trail enters forest and descends gently east, crossing a broad saddle just before it turns northeast to enter a fenced-in compound with a dilapidated hut beside a very refreshing spring (5290–1.2). This spring, complete with cistern and water faucet, is a full 7.7 miles from the upper spring near the southeast corner of Section 28 (Map B1). Happily, the water situation ahead starts out much better. Since this fenced-in spring is your first reliable water in many miles, you might plan to camp here. The fence keeps out cows—a definite plus—but all the enclosed area is gently sloping—a definite minus.

Still following the jeep road, the PCT descends northeast to a saddle (5140–0.3). The last faint 15 yards of this trail stretch is along the west side of an abandoned, overgrown road—not always apparent to southbound hikers. From the saddle the Baldy Creek Road descends north, another descends east, a third contours northeast, and just above it our jeep road climbs

northeast. The PCT parallels this road's north-west side, twice crosses it, skirts past the south slope (5550–0.9) of unassuming Little Pilot Peak, then dips to the north side of a saddle (5550–0.1). On this saddle you could make a small camp by or on the jeep road. Here you'll see a tiny, man-made pond on an open slope 90 yards north below the PCT. The pond's water should be treated if you drink it.

We continue northeast for a ¼-mile traverse, then bend east for a continuing traverse, passing a seeping spring found between two open slopes. Past the second slope the trail curves northeast and you quickly see a pond and an adjacent spring-fed tub, 80 yards northwest down from the trail (5550–0.8). Before leaving here, tank up, for your next reliable water will be at a spring north of Green Springs Mountain, a dry 8.8 miles away.

Continuing our traverse, we meet an old trail (5560–0.2) that climbs 300 yards to a saddle junction with the Soda Mountain Road. Our

B2   **B2**

companion, the Pilot Rock Jeep Road, ends at this road about 0.3 mile south of the saddle. The PCT stays below the saddle, traversing open slopes that give you views west to Mt. Ashland and all the countryside below you. Beyond the views the trail drops to a shaded saddle (5420–0.6), traverses north along a crest, then drops past powerlines to a crossing of Soda Springs Road (5300–0.5).

Just east of an open saddle, we start north-northeast through a meadow with vegetation that sometimes obscures the trail, but in 100 yards we re-enter forest cover for a shady traverse around Hobart Peak to a long saddle. One-third mile past it we will meet the Hobart Bluff spur trail (5220–0.9), which climbs ⅓ mile to the juniper-capped summit. From it you'll see distant Mt. Shasta to the south-southeast, Soda Mountain to the near south, Pilot Rock behind Hobart Peak to the southwest, Mt. Ashland to the west, the spacious Ashland-Medford Valley to the northwest, and pyramidal Mt. McLoughlin, which we'll see close-up at the start of Section C, to the north-northeast.

From the Hobart Bluff spur trail the PCT traverses through a woodland of pygmy Oregon oaks before emerging on more-open slopes and then curving northwest down into forest cover. This temporarily gives way to a dry-grassland slope, then the PCT descends north-northeast, giving us our last view of the Ashland environs. We climb again and almost top Peak 4755, then descend north-northwest, spying Keene Creek reservoir before we cross Highway 66 at Green Springs Summit (4551–3.4). You can reach the tempting reservoir by hiking ¼ mile northeast along Highway 66, then dropping to the nearby shore. Spots of ground are level enough for camping (no campfires, please).

Immediately east of north-climbing Hyatt Lake Recreation Road 100-90, the PCT climbs gently northeast from Green Springs Summit, then rolls northwest across private land, crossing a one-lane road about 90 yards past a small powerline. If you need water, head 0.2 mile north down the road to private cattleland, leave the road and, staying west of a fence, drop to nearby grass-bordered Keene Creek. Just 0.2 mile past the road crossing on private land, we cross Road 100-90 (4700–1.4) and then climb south-southwest up to a crossing of the Greensprings Mountain Road (4840–0.5). The PCT then continues briefly to the meadow's head, curves north around it, then closely follows the road almost to a saddle. By the

saddle we cross a spur road (4940–0.7) that climbs briefly west from the main road. We then cross immediately north of the actual saddle and descend gently northwest to open slopes with views west. The trail quickly turns northeast and through a shady forest it contours over to a water faucet (4800–0.6) fed by an uphill spring. (Southbound hikers take note: this spring is your last on-route, reliable water until a spring-fed tub of water, 8.8 miles away.)

Beyond the faucet the PCT drops 300 yards to the Greensprings Mountain Road, which we follow northeast for 150 yards, then leave it immediately before this road curves northwest for a moderate descent. Back on trail we descend briefly northeast to jeep tracks beside the Ashland lateral canal (4600–0.5), now a dry gully. It once diverted water from Keene Creek west down to Ashland and thence to the Rogue River, but today Keene Creek flows as it used to, ultimately down to the Klamath River.

The PCT has made a westward diversion of its own—to avoid private property—and it now climbs east to a ridge, drops into a gully, crosses a second ridge, and in a second gully meets a trail (4670–0.9) that climbs northward ¼ mile to Little Hyatt Reservoir. We head east down to the nearby canal, cross it, then follow it momentarily up to the reservoir's dam and adjacent Hyatt Lake Recreation Road 100-90 (4610–0.2). Under ponderosa pines along the reservoir's east shore, you can fish or just stretch out and relax. Swimming is best near the dam, from which you can dive into the tranquil water. It is a great place for a layover day, for it lacks the noise and congestion found at larger Hyatt and Howard Prairie lakes. At Little Hyatt Reservoir you can camp in the *de facto* campground (with toilet) above the east shore.

Moving along, we find the PCT's resumption 25 yards south of where it ended at Road 100-90. The trail first climbs southeast and barely pokes into Section 28's private land—a totally unnecessary intrusion—then it climbs generally northeast past old roads to a road fork (5090–1.5), at which the northbound Hyatt Lake Road branches northwest as Road 100-85 and northeast as Road 100-80. From this fork you can follow steps *over* a fence and then follow a trail north ¼ mile to a campsite that is 80 yards west-southwest of Hyatt Lake Campground's shower rooms. The campsite was specifically established for PCT hikers, but because the trail to it is vague, the authors prefer to take the automobile approach; from the road fork, walk 170

B2, B3, B5, B4   **B4, B5**

Little Hyatt Reservoir

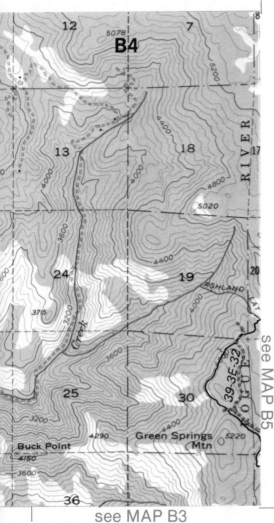

see MAP B5

see MAP B3

yards northeast down to the entrance road, descend another 170 yards to a sign-in, *pay* for a shower, then take the camp's west-climbing road over to the nearby shower rooms. If you don't camp at Little Hyatt Reservoir, you'll almost certainly want to do so at Hyatt Lake Campground. From the campground's north end, a shoreline trail heads west over to the lake's nearby dam, and from its far side, you can walk over to Hyatt Lake Resort, which has a cafe and a limited supply of groceries plus showers and a laundry room. By this route, the resort is a ¾-mile side trip from the road fork.

Back at the road fork, the PCT crosses the Hyatt Lake Road and curves east around the south side of the recreation area's administration building. After 280 trail yards, we reach a spur trail that heads north 140 yards to a drinking fountain—installed for PCT hikers— then continues 100 yards along the building's access road to Road 100-80. The campground entrance road is found 100 yards west on this road. The drinking fountain is your last reliable source of water until Grizzly Creek and its adjacent canal, about 8.5 miles farther.

Beyond the spur trail the PCT climbs east to a usually dry gully, then traverses northeast, crossing gullies and rounding ridges. Our tread stays above usually visible Road 100-80 and snag-tarnished Hyatt Lake. We cross a southeast-climbing road (5100–2.1) then cross east-climbing Wildcat Glades Road 39-3E-11 (5090–0.9). Heading east, we soon cross an older road (5100–0.2) to Wildcat Glades and immediately reach a seeping creek that drains the nearby glades. The water should be all right in early summer, but you may want to treat it later on. You might plan to camp around Wildcat Glades, whose western ¼-mile arm is on BLM land.

Along the seeping creek's north bank, our trail starts upstream but quickly veers north and passes two sets of jeep tracks as it climbs up a ridge. After a switchback our trail swings to the east side of a secondary summit, then in 200 yards approaches the main one (5540–1.0). The scramble up to it (5610) gives you a disappointing view. Now halfway through this book's Section B, we descend northeast along a crest, almost touch a saddle (5310–0.5), then turn east for a long descent. Midway along it a jeep road climbs south across our trail up to a nearby saddle. Just past this road we get a fair view of Mt. McLoughlin and Howard Prairie Lake. Our descent ends when we cross a road (4620–2.0) that climbs southwest to a nearby rock quarry.

At this crossing we are only a few yards south of a major forest road. You can take it 1.6 miles northwest to a spur road that descends ¼ mile to Howard Prairie Lake and the Willow Point Campground. Just off this spur road you'll also find a ranger station. From the spur-road junction you can hike 0.7 mile west up to a paved road, follow it north 1.0 mile, then branch right 0.4 mile down to bustling Howard Prairie Lake Resort, which logically caters more to boating enthusiasts than to backpackers. However, meals and limited supplies can be bought. Howard Prairie Lake, though shallower than Hyatt Lake, is considerably better in appearance, since all the trees were removed before its basin was flooded.

From the quarry-road crossing, the PCT parallels the major forest road east to a quick junction (4620–0.1) with a road that descends an easy ½ mile to Soda Creek before climbing ¾ mile to the Wildcat Glades Road. Water obtained from Soda Creek is certainly better than what you'll find in Grizzly Creek—your next on-route source. Beyond the Soda Creek road, the PCT more or less dies out along a broad, open saddle. At its far end (4620–0.2), where a secondary road starts a climb east, the PCT starts a climb northeast and quickly you'll leave the company of the major forest road.

On the ascent, we get a couple of views down the length of Howard Prairie Lake, but these disappear before our trail's high point, the views being blocked by Douglas-firs, grand firs, sugar pines and incense-cedars. Our easy ascent is

Snag in Hyatt Lake

B5, B6

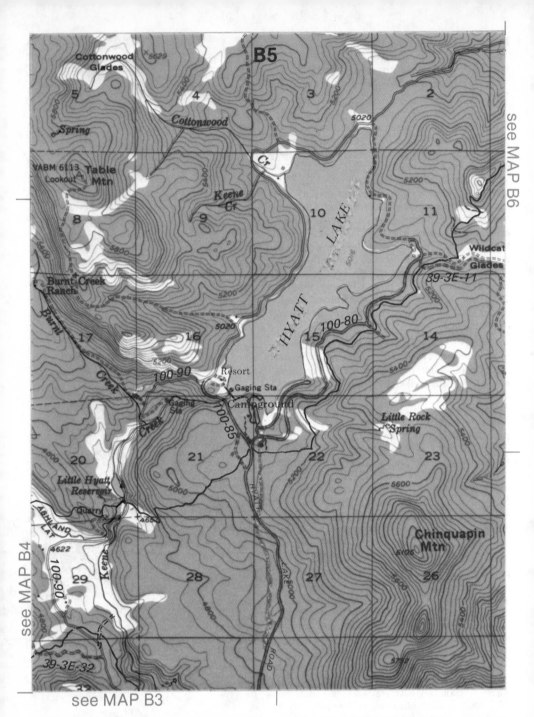

see MAP B6

see MAP B4

see MAP B3

mirrored by an equally easy drop to a crossing of a little-used road (4670–0.9). You can follow this road 250 yards southwest down to the major forest road, then go an equal distance north on that road to the Klum Landing Campground entrance. Like the Little Hyatt Reservoir *de facto* campground, this campground is a good place to spend a layover day. Relax, fish, or perhaps swim out to Howard Prairie Lake's interesting island.

Past the little-used road, the PCT drops northeast to a well-maintained road (4610–0.2) that traverses southwest to the start of the little-used road. Southbound hikers may want to take

B6   **B6**

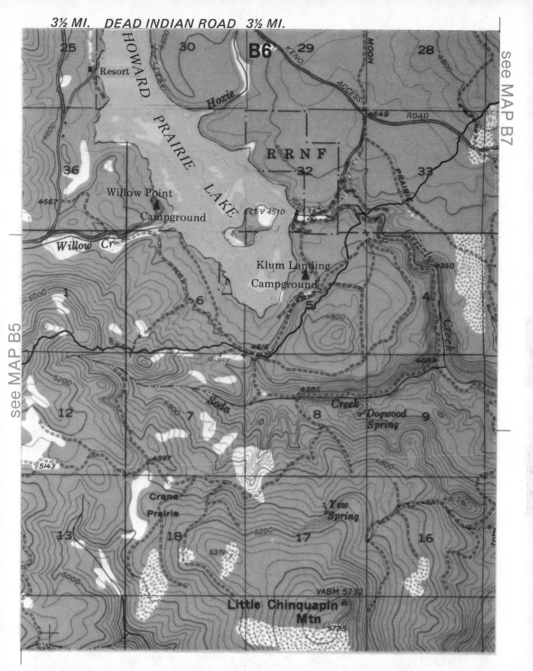

this well-maintained road to the major forest road and thence to Klum Landing Campground. The PCT now heads north through a meadow whose seasonally tall grasses and herbs can hide the tread. Quickly, however, the trail enters forest cover, the tread becomes obvious, and we wind down to a canal, cross it and its maintenance road, then drop in 90 yards to a long bridge over Grizzly Creek (4440–0.5). You *could* camp in this area, which is within BLM boundaries, but all too often you would smell the water in both the canal and the creek. Klum Landing Campground is certainly more desirable, even if it is ⅓ mile off route. You are now 8.5 miles past your last on-route water, near Hyatt Lake, and your next reliable on-route water, northeast below Devils Peak, is a ludicrous 48½ miles away. Fortunately, a near-trail source, with plenty of room for camping, lies only 4.0 miles distant.

B6   **B6**

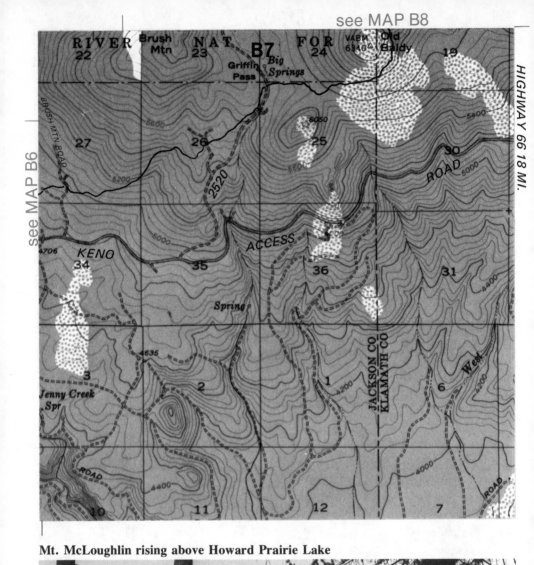

see MAP B6

RIVER 22 Brush Mtn NAT 23 B7 FOR 24 VABM 6346 Old Baldy 19

HIGHWAY 66 18 MI.

Griffin Pass Big Springs

27 26 25 30 ROAD

2520

KENO 4706 34 35 ACCESS 36 31

Spring

JACKSON CO KLAMATH CO

West

3 4635 2 1 4200 6

Jenny Creek Spr

ROAD 4400 4000 ROAD

10 11 12 7

Mt. McLoughlin rising above Howard Prairie Lake

Distant Mt. Shasta, from slopes of Old Baldy

Working toward that goal, we climb east, cross a forgotten road in 160 yards, then continue up to a crossing of the Moon Prairie Road (4580–0.4). The trail now turns northeast and climbs gently to a crossing of paved Keno Access Road (4720–0.8), a major trans-Cascade route for logging trucks bound for Klamath Falls. The PCT continues northeast and climbs to an old road (4790–0.2) whose traffic was pre-empted by the newer logging road. From it we round the northwest corner of a clearcut, pass a minor spur road, then curve east to a bend in the Brush Mountain Road (4960–0.6). Westbound hikers: please note that the last few yards of trail can be hidden by mulleins, thistles and other "weeds" that characteristically spring up in logging areas; therefore, just plow west from the bend.

We initially climb southeast from the bend but gradually curve northeast up through a shady forest of Douglas-fir and grand fir, cross a broad gully, climb to an adjacent ridge and just beyond it reach an old logging road (5480–1.5). This descends 0.3 mile to Griffin Pass Road 2520, which is also our immediate objective. So we continue our moderate climb northeast and soon approach it (5640–0.5). The PCT bends north beside this road, but you should seriously con-sider walking 25 yards over to the road and down it 75 yards to an eastbound spur road. This spur road immediately crosses a creeklet that has been dammed, thus providing the hiker with a pond of fresh water—his last reliable source until the off-route Fish Lake Resort, a long 19.4 miles ahead. Since most long-distance back-packers average 15–20 miles a day, they should plan to camp here one night, then at Fish Lake the following night.

Where the PCT turns north, it parallels Road 2520 up to a crossing (5670–0.2) that is 250 yards short of ill-defined Griffin Pass. Still on BLM land, we parallel the Rogue River National Forest boundary east, immediately cross-ing the seasonal Big Springs creeklet. Don't bother looking for water upstream, since selec-tive logging in that area apparently causes a con-siderable reduction in the springs' output. In ⅓ mile our trail bends southeast for a brief climb to a broad, shady saddle, then it angles northeast for a brief moderate climb to Old Baldy's clear-cut slopes. Our ascent east around this conical landmark is an easy one, and its brushy terrain lets us have plenty of views south across miles of forest to majestic Mt. Shasta.

Chinquapin, tobacco brush and greenleaf manzanita yield to noble fir as our curving trail

B6, B7   **B7**

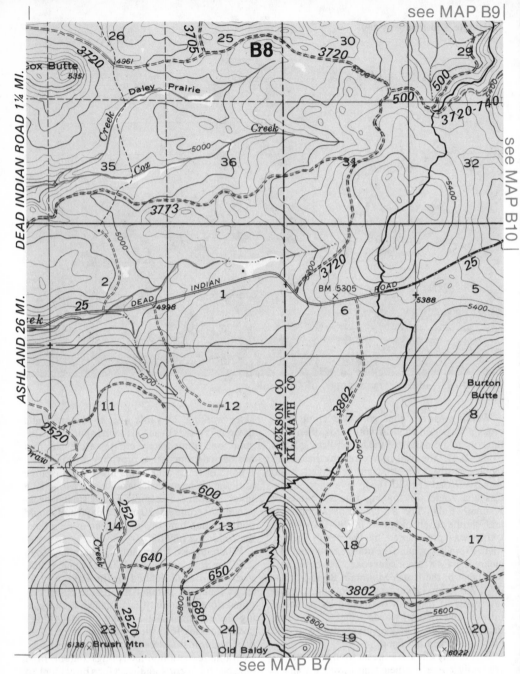

see MAP B10

see MAP B7

climbs to a northeast spur ridge, from which we traverse 140 yards northwest to the Rogue River National Forest boundary (6190–1.7). Before 1972 the Pacific Crest Trail route followed the old Oregon Skyline Trail route—mostly roads in southern Oregon—and it came up a now-abandoned trail to the boundary. In pre-'72 days the "PCT" headed north directly from Shasta rather than making the giant swing west to the Marble Mountains as it does today.

You can scramble south to Old Baldy's nearby summit (6340′) for 360° views. Abandoned by fire lookouts, it is now under the watchful eye of turkey vultures. From it you can see Mt. Shasta (bearing 176°), Yreka (185°), Soda Mountain (217°), Pilot Rock (223°),

Hyatt Reservoir and Mt. Ashland (242°) and Mt. McLoughlin (354°). With these landmarks identified, a careful observer should be able to trace the PCT route over miles of country.

Now within Forest Service land, as we will be almost continually to the Washington border, we start northwest and quickly bend north to descend a pleasant, forested ridge. As we approach a ridge saddle, we come upon a faint spur trail (5880–1.0), which heads 140 yards west to Road 650. Beyond the spur trail, the PCT touches upon the saddle, then switchbacks down the northwest slopes of our ridge, swings east almost to Road 3802, turns north, and quickly crosses a closed road (5390–1.2). We parallel Road 3802, soon cross it (5390–0.3) and then wind north to a crossing of Dead Indian Road (5360–1.9). This crossing is at a point 320 yards east of the road's junction with Road 3802. If you are making a journey that covers hundreds of miles of PCT rather than just Section B, you may want to follow Dead Indian Road over to Lake of the Woods Resort. This alternate route is described at the end of this section.

Northbound, the PCT climbs away from Dead Indian Road, cuts northeast across a broad ridgecrest and then descends through an old logging area to a crossing of Road 740 (5270–1.9). This crossing is about 100 yards south of the road's junction with Road 500, which makes a loop—as our trail does—round the headwaters of South Fork Little Butte Creek. If you've been experiencing water-shortage problems, you'd be better off making a 3¼-mile trek—first north, then west—along Road 500. On it, you're likely to find water at two creek crossings and certainly will find it at a third, where the road crosses the Brown Mountain Trail branch of South Fork Little Butte Creek. From this creek the road climbs ¼ mile north to a broad saddle. Leave the road here and head northeast toward Brown Mountain. You should rejoin the PCT in less than ¼ mile. Here, you'll be about 3.6 trail miles beyond Road 740 and 5.8 trail miles from a junction with Trail 1014 to Fish Lake.

From Road 740 the PCT first contours northeast, then north, paralleling Road 500, which you sometimes see below as you cross an old logging area. Some gullies that you cross may contain water, particularly if you are hiking through in the mosquito-plagued month of June. Finally the trail drops to cross the Brown Mountain Trail branch of South Fork Little

Butte Creek (5180–2.2). The trail was abandoned with the construction of Road 500.

The PCT follows the seasonal creek westward until the stream angles south, then the trail traverses west for ½ mile before turning northwest and dropping 20 feet to a hollow. A 60-foot gain northwest from it takes us to a minor ridge (5210–1.4) to which those taking Road 500 will have climbed. From the ridge our trail continues its long, irregular arc around the lower slopes of Brown Mountain. Although the trail on the map superficially appears to be an easy traverse, careful study of it reveals that it has plenty of ups and downs—some of them steep—as you'll find out. As we traverse the northwest slopes of Brown Mountain, views of Mt. McLoughlin—a dormant volcano—appear and disappear. Nearing Highway 140, we reach a junction with Fish Lake Trail 1014 (4940–5.8).

Unless you are ending your hike at Highway 140, you'll want to visit the Fish Lake environs both for water and for supplies. A layover day wouldn't hurt. Trail 1014 winds ⅓ mile down to a seasonal pond, soon crosses the equally seasonal Cascade Canal, rambles across varied slopes, then treads a stringer separating a youthful upper lava flow from an equally youthful lower one. Next, it descends more or less alongside the lower flow and intersects Road 900 just before that road starts a traverse across the flow. With 1.5 miles between us and the PCT, we wind 100 yards west almost to Fish Lake, turn northeast, and momentarily end at the south tip of Fish Lake Resort's campground. Note the trail's end, for it may not be too obvious, and you'll want to find it later when you return to the PCT. But first, head over to the resort's office and cafe, located just above the boat dock. Food and supplies cater to the beer-drinking fishing crowd, though a beer (or two) will probably sound very tempting after your long, dry haul. Pick up your parcel if you've mailed one to the resort. Get a hot meal and a shower, do some laundry and then perhaps head ⅓ mile west over to the USFS Doe Point Campground.

After your stay at Fish Lake, return via Trail 1014 to the PCT. In 85 yards along the PCT you cross an old, abandoned highway bed, then soon reach broad, straight Highway 140 (4980–0.2). Cascade Canal crosses under Highway 140 about 40 yards west of your crossing. You'll meet the canal just beyond the highway. Don't expect any water flowing in it after midsummer.

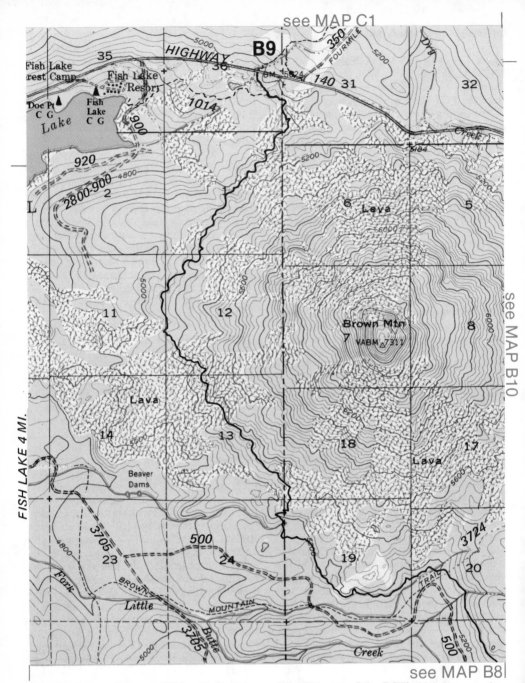

see MAP B10

see MAP B8

Your first near-trail water will be at Freye Lake, ¼ mile off the PCT and 4¾ miles from the highway.

*   *   *   *

Those who take the Lake of the Woods alternate route will reach Highway 140 about 4½ miles east of the PCT's highway crossing. However, rather than traverse west to it, they will climb north to meet it in the popular Sky Lakes Wilderness. By climbing north you pass more than a dozen lakes worth camping at, plus about two dozen trailside ponds—quite a contrast with the virtually waterless Pacific Crest Trail segment to which this is an alternate.

The alternate route begins where the PCT crosses Dead Indian Road. It climbs east ¼ mile from the PCT to the Cascade crest, then descends down to a junction with Lake of the Woods' West Shore Road 3601 (4974–4.7). You could take this road north 3.5 miles to a junction with State Highway 140, from which Mt. McLoughlin Trail 3716 climbs 3.0 miles up a ridge to a crossing of Road 3650, then 1.0 mile up slopes to the PCT. But if you would prefer to take the PCT, rather than Mt. McLoughlin Trail 3716, north from Highway 140, then follow the highway west 3.6 miles. At the junction of the West Shore Road with 140, you can also head east, quickly passing the Lake of the Woods Work Center/Visitor Center, then Billie Creek, and in 250 yards reach a road to the Rye Spur trailhead—see end of chapter.

Disregarding these hiking possibilities, the hungry PCT trekker bears east from the West Shore Road junction, then curves north and passes the Winema National Forest East Side Recreation Residences, along the shore, before reaching the entrance to Sunset Campground (4990–2.2). In summer this is crowded with water skiers, swimmers, campers and fisher-

B8, B10   B10

Mt. McLoughlin and Lake of the Woods early in the morning

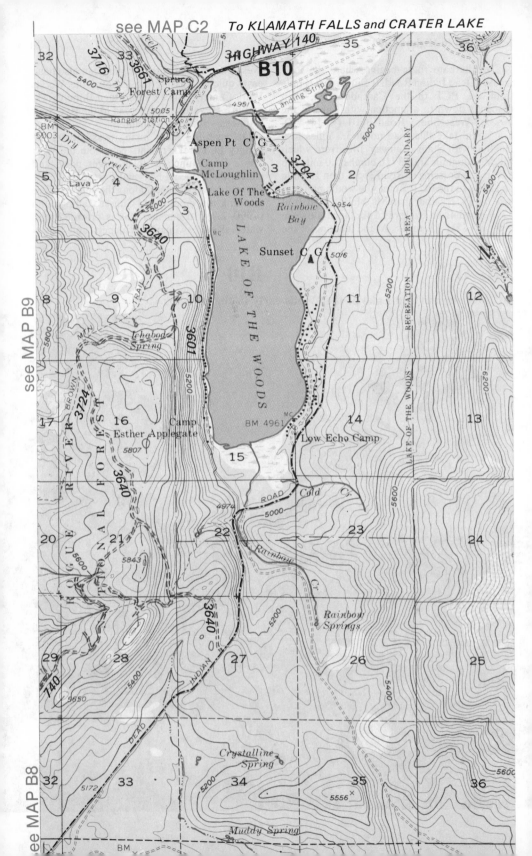

men. You'll find the lake's waters are stocked with Kokanee salmon, rainbow and eastern brook trout, and brown bullhead.

Continuing north, you reach a junction with Road 3704 (4954–1.0), along which you trek northwest to a spur road (5000–0.3) that heads ¼ mile southwest down to the lakeshore and the Lake of the Woods Resort. Here you can restock with enough supplies to last you until Crater Lake Post Office, 52 miles away by this alternate route. The resort also serves good meals and its store has a small post office at which you can pick up goodies you've mailed to yourself.

Back on Road 3704, continue northwest past the entrance to Aspen Point Campground

(4970–0.4), which is also the entrance to a picnic area and a safe swimming area. If you haven't yet taken a dip, do so here. Onward, you reach Highway 140 (4980–0.7), which you then take 0.2 mile west to a pole-line road. Start north, but in 5 yards branch right from it, making a hairpin turn onto a minor road. Follow it 100 yards to the start of Rye Spur Trail 3771 (4990–0.3). Measuring 9.6 miles from the PCT crossing at Dead Indian Road, this alternate route to a Highway 140 trailhead is about 2 miles shorter than the PCT route. A continuation of this alternate route, which is also shorter than the continued PCT route, is described in the early part of Section C.

B10

B10

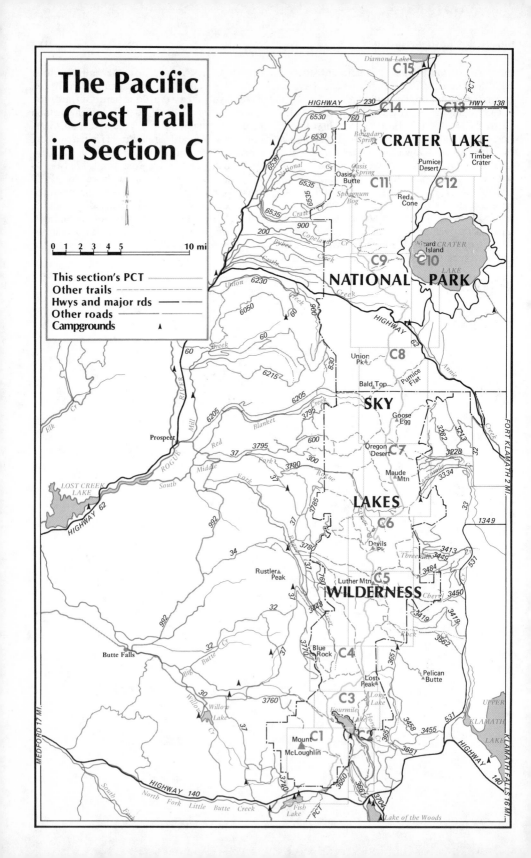

The Pacific Crest Trail in Section C

N

0 1 2 3 4 5   10 mi

This section's PCT
Other trails
Hwys and major rds
Other roads
Campgrounds ▲

Diamond Lake

C15

PCT

HIGHWAY   230

C14

C13

HWY   138

6530

760

Boundary Spring

CRATER LAKE

6530

Pumice Desert

Timber Crater

6530

National

Oasis Spring

6535

Oasis Butte

C11

C12

6535

Sphagnum Bog

Red Cone

6535

Crater

900

200

Copeland

Cr

Dutton

Wizard Island

CRATER

C9

C10

LAKE

Castle

NATIONAL   **PARK**

Union

6230

Creek

900

HIGHWAY   62

6050

60

900

Annie

Creek

60

808

Union Pk

C8

60

6215

Bald Top

Pumice Flat

FORT KLAMATH 2 MI.

Elk

Cr

6205

6205

Blanket

6205

Creek

3795

SKY

Goose Egg

3392

3213

Prospect

Red

3795

600

Oregon Desert

C7

3228

37

Middle

3790

300

Rogue

Maude Mtn

3334

LOST CREEK LAKE

South

Fork

3785

33

LAKES

992

1349

HIGHWAY   62

34

Rogue

3780

C6

Devils Pk

3413

Threemile

3449

Rustler Peak

37

160

Luther Mtn

C5

3484

32

3449

WILDERNESS

Cherry

3450

Butte Falls

32

Cr

3419

Rock

3562

Butte

37

3770

Blue Rock

C4

3651

Pelican Butte

Big

Willow

30

Cr

Lost Peak

Long Lake

3458

3455

531

UPPER KLAMATH LAKE

Willow Lake

37

3760

C3

Fourmile

C2

Honey

3651

MEDFORD 17 MI.

Mount McLoughlin

C1

3650

3651

HIGHWAY   140

KLAMATH FALLS 16 MI.

3740

HIGHWAY   140

South

North

Fork

Little

Butte

Creek

3650

3661

3704

Fish Lake

PCT

Lake of the Woods

Section C: Highway 140 near Fish Lake to Highway 138 near the Cascade crest

Introduction: Both Sections A and B have a paucity of lakes and a surplus of roads, but in Section C the scenery changes and at last the hiker feels he is in a mountain wilderness. In fact, before the mid-1970s the scenery south of Highway 140 was deemed too poor to have a crest trail, and in those days anyone who hiked from northern California to southern Oregon had to follow a route that was almost entirely along roads.

The bulk of Section C is composed of two attractive areas: Sky Lakes Wilderness and inspiring Crater Lake National Park. The number of lakes in the wilderness rivals that in any other mountain area to be found anywhere along the PCT, while the beauty and depth of Crater Lake make it a worldwide attraction.

Unfortunately, the Pacific Crest Trail avoids Crater Lake entirely, and it takes a route the authors find very undesirable. Only equestrians and day hikers take part or all of this essentially viewless route. It is a good stretch to take if one wants to avoid crowds. We have yet to meet any long-distance PCT hiker who has bypassed Crater Lake and preferred the PCT. All have hiked up to the Rim Drive, and most have taken it clockwise for an ever-changing panorama of the lake. This alternate route, plus others in Sky Lakes Wilderness, is described along with the official PCT route.

Declination: 17½°E

Mileages:

	South to North	Distances between Points	North to South
Highway 140 near Fish Lake	0.0		76.0
		4.7	
Mt. McLoughlin Trail, westbound	4.7		71.3
		9.2	
Red Lake Trail (cross the alternate route)	13.9		62.1
		9.6	
Snow Lakes Trail (end of alternate route)	23.5		52.5
		2.4	
Devils Peak/Lee Peak saddle	25.9		50.1
		5.9	
Middle Fork Basin Trail to Ranger Springs	31.8		44.2
		4.6	
Jack Spring spur trail	36.4		39.8
		7.3	
Stuart Falls Trail, northeast end..................	43.7		32.3
		5.2	
Highway 62	48.9		27.1
		6.5	
Lightning Springs Trail..........................	55.4		20.6
		7.9	
Red Cone Spring................................	63.3		12.7
		3.9	
North-rim access road	67.2		8.8
		8.8	
Highway 138 near the Cascade crest...............	76.0		0.0

Supplies: There are no on-route supply points, but an alternate route is described that takes you past the Crater Lake Post Office, which is found in the same building as the park headquarters. This building is about 55½ trail miles north of Fish Lake Resort, in northern Section B, and about 29 miles (via Rim Drive and North Crater Trail) south of Diamond Lake Resort, in southern Section D. Be aware that the post office doesn't like to hold packages longer than one week. Up on the lake's rim you can get meals and limited supplies at the "Rim Village," and meals at Crater Lake Lodge.

Wilderness Permits and Special Restrictions: To camp in the Crater Lake National Park backcountry, you'll need a wilderness permit. It doesn't matter whether you are on foot, horseback or skis, or whether you are entering on a popular summer weekend or in the dead of winter—they are still required. In person, you can get a permit either at the Park Headquarters or at the Rim Village Visitor Center. You can also get a permit in advance by writing to Superintendent, P.O. Box 7, Crater Lake National Park, Crater Lake, OR 97604, or you can phone park personnel at (503) 594-2211.

There are specific camping restrictions at the park. No camping is allowed within one mile of any paved road, nature trail or developed area, and none is allowed within 1½ miles of Sphagnum Bog or Boundary Springs. As in any wilderness area, no camping is allowed in meadows or within 100 feet of any water source. Size of each backcountry party is limited to a maximum of 12 persons and 8 stock.

Problems: Sky Lakes Wilderness is an area of abundant precipitation and abundant lakelets. Both combine to ensure a tremendous mosquito population that will ruin your hike if you're caught without a tent. However, by mid-July the mosquito population begins to drop, and by early August a tent may not be necessary.

Since Crater Lake National Park lacks ponds and lakelets and also has a paucity of flowing streams, you would expect it to also be mosquito-free, right? Sorry, it isn't. This is because the lake's rim receives a yearly average of 48 feet of snowfall and the resulting snowpack provides moist, mosquito-bearing ground through most of July. This same snowpack also can make hiking difficult before mid-July, but in early August, after it has disappeared, drinking water may become scarce. From midsummer onward, the stretch from Red Cone Spring to Section D's Thielsen Creek, a 21-mile stretch, may be dry.

A large trailhead parking lot is provided for those hikers who plan to leave their vehicles along Highway 140. There is a signed road to this lot that begins 0.4 mile east of the PCT's highway crossing. From the sign you go 15 yards north on Fourmile Lake Road 3650, turn left, and parallel the highway west to the nearby lot. From the lot's northwest corner a trail goes 0.2 mile north to the PCT. Don't park at the small space where the PCT crosses the highway, since long-distance backpackers may want to camp there when water is available in the adjacent Cascade Canal.

Our description begins where the PCT starts north from Highway 140 (4980). This point is just 0.2 mile west of the Jackson/Klamath county line and 40 yards east of the Cascade Canal. Just after we start up this trail we cross this seasonally flowing canal, then parallel it northeast to a junction (5100–0.3) with the short trail back to the large trailhead parking lot. Just past this junction the trail almost touches the canal before it angles away and ascends open slopes that provide a view south toward Brown Mountain and its basalt flows. As the PCT

climbs, it enters Sky Lakes Wilderness, where it too crosses lava flows, and then it enters a white-fir forest and continues up to a junction with Mt. McLoughlin Trail 3716 (6110–4.0), in a forest of red firs and mountain hemlocks. Southeast, this heavily used trail descends 1.0 mile to a trailhead at Road 3650, and then its lightly used continuation descends 3.0 miles to the Highway 140/Road 3601 intersection near the Lake of the Woods Work Center/Visitor Center. If you've been hiking the last part of Section B along the lake's west shore, you'll take this trail to regain the PCT.

On the PCT, which briefly doubles as the Mt. McLoughlin Trail, we climb shortly west on an easier grade to the Freye Lake spur trail (6190–0.2), which is just 50 yards past a gully. This ill-defined trail goes ¼ mile over to the shallow, semistagnant lake and its camps.

After an equally short distance west on the PCT (6240–0.2), the Mt. McLoughlin Trail takes its leave, climbing 3½ miles up to the summit of this dormant stratovolcano. The views you get from it are among the best obtained from any peak situated near the tri-

C1   C1

state PCT. If you have good weather, don't pass up the opportunity to climb it. Drop your heavy backpack nearby and take 2 or 3 hours to reach the often snowy summit. On your return you can sometimes use tempting snowfields to speed your descent, but be forewarned that these can lead you astray, as they diverge south-southeast from the east-descending trail.

Leaving the west-climbing Mt. McLoughlin Trail, the PCT quickly tops a ridge, then winds slowly down through the forest, not once offering us a view, and comes to a junction with the Twin Ponds Trail (5840–3.7). This junction lies between two shallow ponds that by late summer are no more than dry, grassy meadows. Small campsites can be found at Summit Lake, 0.4 mile northwest down this trail, but beyond the lake the trail, which is numbered 993, becomes very brushy. To the southeast the trail is numbered 3715, and it winds 2.5 miles to a trailhead at the west end of Fourmile Lake Campground. From the junction our trail starts northeast, quickly veers north past a stagnant pond, climbs steadily up a ridge, and then descends slightly to a junction with Cat Hill Way Trail 992 (6100–1.6). This path climbs 3.6 miles north to a popular trailhead, which also serves more-popular Blue Canyon Trail 982. Southward from our junction you may note the abandoned tread of deteriorating Blue Rock Trail 3737, which can still be followed 2.0 miles, passing Fourmile Lake before ending at the Twin Ponds Trail, along the south shore of Squaw Lake.

Our trail heads north to a gully that is snowbound until late June, then veers east up to a gentle slope before curving northeast and climbing to a broad saddle (6300–1.6). Our route now contours across a slope forested with mountain hemlock, red fir and western white pine. We round a north ridge, descend southeast to another saddle (6240–1.2), then bear northeast down toward a saddle and meet Red Lake Trail 987 (6020–1.1).

*   *   *   *

Some hikers may have taken Section B's alternate route that guides them first to Lake of the Woods Resort for supplies and then north to Highway 140. The following description takes them on an 11.2-mile route north back to the Red Lake Trail junction with the PCT. This stretch, 2.7 miles shorter than the comparable stretch of PCT, provides you with a lower, lake-dotted alternate route from Highway 140.

To reach the trailhead start from the north end of Lake of the Woods' east-shore Road 3704, which ends at Highway 140. Walk 0.2 mile west on the highway, then branch north onto a pole-line road. (If you're eastbound on the highway, you'll find this road about 250 yards east of Billie Creek.) You go but 5 yards north on the road and then branch right, making a hairpin turn onto a minor road. Follow it 100 yards to the trailhead, located just before the pole line. Our mileage begins from here (4990).

Rye Spur Trail 3771 starts west and quickly meets the Billie Creek Nature Trail (5000–0.2), which continues west for a loop around a part of Billie Creek. Our Rye Spur Trail switchbacks steeply northward, then climbs at an easier pace to Road 3633 (5290–0.5). We walk 160 yards northwest up it to the Cascade Canal (5701–0.8). In early summer the canal flows swiftly, but by August it can be bone-dry. The Rye Spur Trail continues climbing northward until it reaches the first of three clustered outcrops (6230–1.2). Here you get some fine views of the scenery from Pelican Butte, to the northeast, across to Mountain Lakes Wilderness, to the southeast. Beyond the outcrops your views disappear, and you hike at a leisurely pace to a recrossing of the Cascade Canal (5730–3.3). This point is but 30 yards down the canal's road from a parking area by Fourmile Lake's dam. Had you hiked north along the canal road to this point, rather than taking the Rye Spur Trail, you'd have saved yourself 0.2 mile distance and about 500 feet of climbing effort. If evening is fast approaching, you can mosey west a short ½ mile to the lake's campground, then on the next day either continue along the alternate route or take Twin Ponds Trail 3715 a rolling 2.5 miles over to the PCT.

Keeping to the alternate route, one walks but 30 yards east down the canal's road to the start of Badger Lake Trail 3759. Just 35 yards up this trail you meet Fourmile Creek Trail 3714, forking right. The Badger Lake Trail visits two of Fourmile Lake's lodgepole-snag bays, presenting us with views of Mt. McLoughlin and its avalanche-prone lower slopes. Now entering Sky Lakes Wilderness, we climb ½ mile to Woodpecker Lake, which is mostly less than chest deep. In ¼ mile we reach more appealing Badger Lake (5910–1.6), with better fishing and swimming than its neighbor. Look for a fairly nice campsite by the lake's northeast edge. Next we pass knee-deep Lilly Pond, then pass a marshy meadow, both of interest to wildflower enthusiasts. Northward, we have a seasonally

C1, C3, C4, B10   **B10, C2, C3**

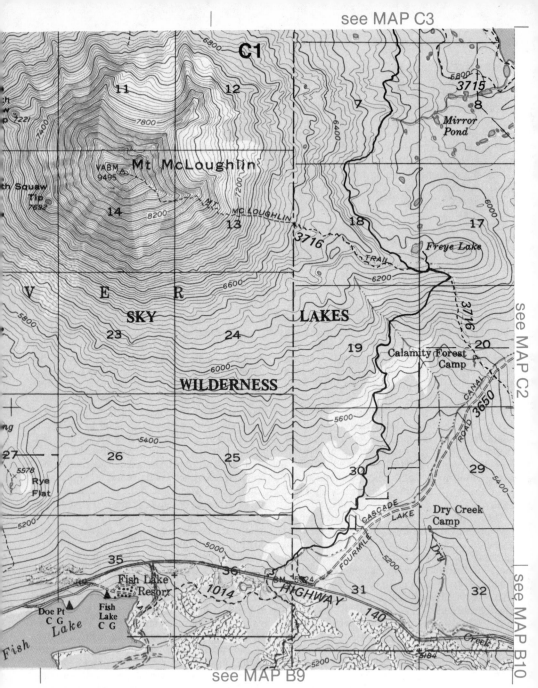

boggy terrain to traverse, and then we climb ½ mile northeast to a junction with Long Lake Trail 3713 (6050–1.7). This winds 0.3 mile east to a junction near the south shore of Long Lake. From it, misnamed Horse Creek Trail 3741 departs south down Long Creek, while a spur trail shoots east to a good south-shore campsite. The lake is quite shallow, though deep enough to support trout and to offer some fair swimming.

Our alternate route, part of the defunct Oregon Skyline Trail, immediately begins a ½-mile easy descent northeast to the west shore of Long Lake, then continues north along it to a junction (6050–0.8) by the lake's north shore. Eastward, a spur trail goes over to Long Lake Camp, spacious enough for group camping. Be aware that mosquitoes can plague the site as late as early August. North of Long Lake our fault-line trail crosses an unnoticeable gentle divide, then descends past a marshy meadow on its way down to a junction with Lost Creek Trail 3712 (6000–1.0). This trail quickly rounds Center Lake, which is knee-deep in its prime but only a grassy meadow in late summer, and then the trail descends 1⅓ easy miles to a switchback in Road 3659 (just off Map C4). Eastward, this road goes 1.3 miles to a main road, 3659, which northward ends in 1.7 miles at Cold Springs Campground. From the Lost Creek Trail junc-

tion Badger Lake Trail 3759 ends and Red Lake Trail 987 begins. We climb over an adjacent ridge and immediately intersect the PCT (6020–0.1–11.2).

*   *   *   *

After the PCT intersects the Red Lake Trail, it makes a quite level, easy traverse north, staying close to a fault-line crest. In about an hour you should reach a junction with the short No Name Trail (6070–2.7).

*   *   *   *

C3, C4

see MAP C3

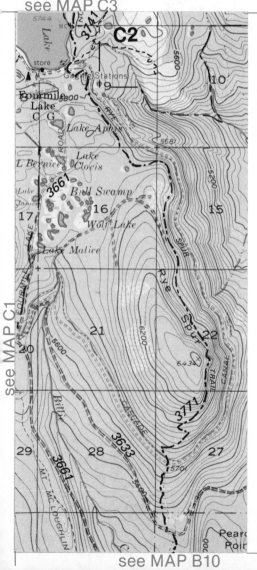

see MAP C1

A more rewarding alternate to this essentially viewless traverse is to continue along the Red Lake Trail, then head up the No Name Trail. Along this route you first make a short, moderate descent to the east end of Blue Canyon Trail 982 (5900–0.2). Westward, you can follow it 0.4 mile to a good spur trail that goes 130 yards north to Island Lake's most abundant campsites. Secluded ones lie above the lake's west shore. Onward, the Red Lake Trail directs us through huckleberry bogs to a junction by the northeast corner of Island Lake (5910–0.5). From an adjacent campsite a *de facto* trail goes 0.4 mile west to very pleasing Dee Lake. You'll find an improved horse camp on the low ridge separating Dee and Island lakes. Dee is an excellent lake for swimming—shallow enough to have warm water, yet deep enough that it isn't an oversized swamp (like the north half of Island Lake, which is mostly less than waist deep).

Beyond Island Lake your boggy, huckleberry-laden route north passes several ponds that are more suited to mosquitoes than to humans, then arrives at large but grassy and extremely shallow Red Lake, with possible camping and fishing. After another ½ mile walk north past the lake, we reach a junction (5870–1.4). Ahead, the Red Lake Trail is abandoned, so we climb east moderately up the No Name Trail to rejoin the PCT (6070–0.7–2.8).

*   *   *   *

From this junction the PCT makes an easy, viewless, uneventful climb northeast to the start of another lake-studded route, the southwest end of Sky Lakes Trail 3762 (6140–1.0).

*   *   *   *

Several optional routes are possible, and they'll add 2–3 miles to your hiking distance as

C4, C5

see MAP B10

Mt. McLoughlin beyond Island Lake

compared to the PCT. We start northeast on the Sky Lakes Trail, which was once part of the now defunct Oregon Skyline Trail. Soon we crest a broad divide, then make a moderate ¼-mile diagonal down a fault escarpment before leveling off near mostly shallow Deer Lake (6070–0.5). Some folks camp here, but far better camping, fishing and swimming lie ahead. Eastward, you arc past a pond to a junction with Cold Springs Trail 3710 (6050–0.4), which winds 2.6 miles over to Cold Springs Campground. Next our trail winds northeast to a junction with Isherwood Trail 3729 (6030–0.3).

The 1.5-mile Isherwood Trail is 0.8 mile longer than the Sky Lakes Trail counterpart, but it passes five lakes and a greater number of campsites. Just a stone's throw over a low ridge the Isherwood Trail comes to Lake Notasha. This lake, with a camp above its east shore, is the deepest of the five lakes, and it is the only one stocked with both rainbow and brook trout. Another low ridge separates Notasha from Elizabeth, which is shallow enough for warm swimming, yet deep enough to sustain trout. Next, you drop to the brink of a fault escarp-

ment along the west shore of Isherwood Lake, one of the few lakes in the wilderness you can dive directly into; for most lakes, you have to wade out to deep water. From a horse camp midway along the escarpment you can walk due west to adjacent, chest-deep Lake Liza, with marginal appeal. Beyond Isherwood the trail winds north to a meadow, then veers east to the north tip of north Heavenly Twin Lake. For isolated camps, look for sites above its west shore. After passing a northeast-shore camp, the Isherwood Trail ends at the Sky Lakes Trail just southwest of shallow Deep Lake.

If you shun the Isherwood Trail, your Sky Lakes Trail soon passes between the Heavenly Twin Lakes, the smaller, deeper southern one being far less attractive than the northern one. Look for secluded camps along the latter's west shore. By these two lakes you reach a junction with misnamed South Rock Creek Trail 3709 (5980–0.3), which traverses 3.1 miles over to Cold Springs Campground.

The Sky Lakes Trail turns north, skirts along the east shore of northern Heavenly Twin Lake, and then meets the northeast end of the Isher-

C5   C5

see MAP C5

C4

Smith Rock
12

Red Lake

JACKSON CO
KLAMATH CO

e Rock

5938

987

Round Lake
13

North Blue Lake Group

Beal Lake

SKY

LAKES

WILDERNESS

TRAIL

Island L

Mud Lake

Dee Lake

Blue Lake
6308

Meadow Lake

Bert L

LOST CR TR

3712

982

ick

South Blue Lake Group

Center Lake

sin
24

19

Pear Lake
20

Carey Lake
20

21

3759

992

Lost Pea
6761

Blue Canyon Lake

Horseshoe Lake

6210

6200

6400

25

6540

30

6200

29

29

28

6449

see MAP C3

see MAP C4

C3

992

30

29

28
6348

Long Lake Camp

3759

Long Lake

SKY

LAKES

WILDERNESS

TRAIL

3713

JACKSON CO
KLAMATH CO

31

3137

32

33

HORSE

LAKE

6400

6589

5800

Cr

Swan
Cr

6000

6200

Lilly Pond

TRAIL

Long

t Lake

993

Squaw Lake

Fourmile Lake

Badger Lake

Woodpecker Lake

BADGER

CREEK

6200

5744

6049

3741

HORSE

Creek

Norris Pond

3715

6

5

4

3

Orris Pond

see MAP C1   see MAP C2

COLD SPR. C.G. and ROAD 3651 ¼ MI.

wood Trail (5980–0.4). From it you continue north past chest-deep "Deep" Lake and its seasonal satellites and reach Wickiup Trail 3728 (6004–0.9). For those who have had their fill of lakes, this trail—2.0 pond-speckled miles through appropriately named Dwarf Lakes Area—provides the first of four routes back to the PCT. Shallow, uninviting Lake Land lies just below the Wickiup Trail's east end. The lake at

best provides some warm swimming; however, you'd be better off visiting Wizzard Lake, a fairly deep lake just 200 yards northeast below Lake Land's outlet. Next we soon pass a knee-deep pond, on the right, then, past a low ridge, two waist-deep lakelets. The south shore of Trapper Lake lies just ahead, and from where you see it you could go 250 yards cross-country southeast to 38-foot-deep Lake Sonya, easily the basin's deepest lake. More likely, you'll want to camp at the east-shore sites of scenic Trapper Lake. By this lake's outlet we meet Cherry Creek Trail 3708 (5940–1.2), which descends 5.2 miles to a trailhead at Road 3450. This road in turn descends 1.9 miles to heavily traveled County Route 531, should you need to vacate the wilderness.

From the upper end of the Cherry Creek Trail, you walk but a minute north along Trapper Lake to its northeast corner, where you'll meet Donna Lake Trail 3734. This 0.9-mile trail makes an initial ascent northeast before curving past Donna and Deep lakes, then climbing back to the Sky Lakes Trail. You can camp at either lake. Donna, being shallow, is a good one for swimming, particularly in early summer, when snow patches still hang around Deep Lake.

The Sky Lakes Trail next climbs briefly west to a ridge junction just above Margurette Lake (6010–0.3). You'll find a couple of camps both north and south of this junction. Starting southwest, Divide Trail 3717 is your second route back to the PCT. It is well-graded, but at 2.6 miles is unnecessarily long. It ends on a saddle immediately west of Luther Mountain. That peak, which is the throat of an old volcano, is well worth climbing. Scramble east up to the summit to get a commanding view of the entire Sky Lakes Area plus an aerial view down Cherry Creek canyon.

Beyond the Divide Trail the Sky Lakes Trail skirts past attractive Margurette Lake. With a prominent cliff for a tapestry and Luther Mountain for a crown, this deep lake reigns as queen of the Sky Lakes. In quick time we pass two lakelets, then meet the northwest end of Donna Lake Trail 3734 (6010–0.4). Ahead, we top out near chilly, unseen Tsuga Lake, just west of the trail, then descend past a lower pair of Snow Lakes, which have a scenic but chilly backdrop. About 200 yards beyond them one could initiate a westward slog through huckleberries to shallow Wind Lake, though only the most determined fisherman will put up with its usual horde of mosquitoes. Our descent ends at nearby, waist-deep Martin Lake, and then we traverse 0.4 mile to a junction with Nannie Creek Trail 3707 (6060–1.3), a 4.2-mile trail that is popular on summer weekends.

Northeastward, we're climbing on Snow Lakes Trail 3739, which makes an exhausting start that abates where it turns southwest (6320–0.4). Ahead, an abandoned but still used segment of the defunct Oregon Skyline Trail climbs rather steeply 1.5 miles to the Devils

Peak/Lee Peak saddle—your third route (and the most direct one) back to the PCT. The Snow Lakes Trail switchbacks up a ridge before switchbacking up to the top of a cliff. On it lie the upper Snow Lakes, which offer scenic, relatively mosquito-free camps. Just 0.2 mile past the southwest lake we end our lake-blessed alternate route as we rejoin the PCT (6670–1.4–7.8).

*   *   *   *

Back where the Sky Lakes Trail departs from the PCT toward the escarpment above Deer Lake, our Pacific Crest Trail heads north-northwest in a forest of lodgepole pines and mountain hemlocks, ascends a gentle slope past several nearby ponds, then reaches an open forest as it approaches a cliff above the Dwarf Lakes Area. Glaciated Pelican Butte (8036) is the prominent summit in the southeast; the more subdued Cherry Peak (6623) is directly east. We can't see the lakes below us, because the area is so forested. Our trail switchbacks slightly up to avoid the cliff, switchbacks slightly down the west side, and soon encounters a 100-yard spur trail (6600–2.5), which takes us to an overlook with a view that encompasses most of the rolling hills to the west. We now switchback several times up to a small summit before descending the ridgeline to a saddle and an intersection of Wickiup Trail 986/3728 (6585–1.0). East, Trail 3728 descends 2.0 miles past more than a dozen stagnant ponds before reaching the Sky Lakes Trail 70 yards south of Lake Land. West, Trail 986 is abandoned. It used to take one through perhaps the best huckleberry fields in all of Sky Lakes Wilderness.

The PCT now takes us northeast up to a ridge where the views east of the Sky Lakes Basin really begin to open up. Along the trail segment that crosses a barren slope of volcanic blocks, you are likely to find, sprouting in the thin volcanic soil, numerous creamy-white western pasqueflowers (also called anemones), which are readily identified by their finely dissected leaves, hairy stems and dozens of stamens. By August their flowers are transformed into balls of silky plumes. Our trail contours north-northeast to the west edge of a saddle and reaches Divide Trail 3717 (6840–1.2). The 2.6-mile Divide Trail strikes due east across the rocky slopes of this peak (7153), makes ten switchbacks down to three presentable ponds, and then winds gradually down to the Sky Lakes Trail junction at Margurette Lake (6010), but

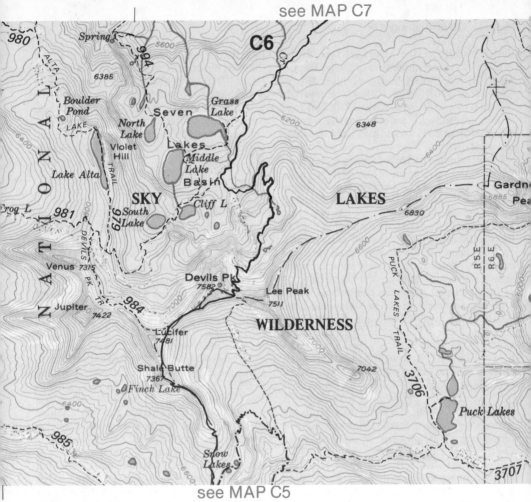

C6

not before passing virtually every body of water in the vicinity. This is quite a lovely side trip to take if you are not in a hurry. Also, if you have the time, climb nearby Luther Mountain for stupendous views of the Sky Lakes Area.

From the Divide Trail saddle we descend moderately to a ridge and follow it north as it gradually levels off to a junction with Hemlock Lake Trail 985 (6600–1.0). This trail is abandoned but followable. Still, most hikers won't want to make the 0.8-mile excursion down to the lake, for the 500-foot-elevation climb back to the PCT is quite a struggle with a heavy pack. After starting up the crest we quickly meet Snow Lakes Trail 3739 (6670–0.2), this junction being the end of the highly recommended alternate route. A 0.2-mile traverse on it takes you over to the first of a pair of Snow Lakes, the environs offering scenic, relatively mosquito-free camps.

C5

C5, C6

Mt. McLoughlin, from PCT on Shale Butte

We climb again, snaking up a ridge, then we obtain views of Mt. McLoughlin, to the south, as we round the west slopes of Shale Butte (7367). Not shale or even slate, it is really a highly fractured andesite-lava flow. Next we traverse the east slope of Lucifer (7481) to a long saddle, on which we meet Devils Peak Trail 984 (7210–1.7). This traverses 1.5 miles northwest to Seven Lakes Trail 981, on which you can go 2.7 miles, first descending past South, Cliff, Middle and Grass lakes, then climbing briefly back to the PCT. On summer weekends the Seven Lakes Basin receives heavy use, and it should be avoided then.

Just 100 yards after you leave the saddle's northeast end you'll spot an abandoned segment of the Devils Peak Trail (7190–0.2). Like Luther Mountain, Devils Peak is the remnants of an old volcano, and its summit views are well worth the effort. The abandoned trail segment makes a ½-mile, no-nonsense climb to the summit, from which you can make an even steeper 300-yard descent to the Devils Peak/Lee Peak saddle. To the north, summit views include some of the Seven Lakes plus a good chunk of the Middle Fork canyon, including Boston Bluff. On the northern horizon is pointed Union Peak, which like our summit and Luther Mountain (2½ miles south of us) is the resistant plug of an eroded volcano. Immediately west of Union Peak you see Mt. Bailey (8363), which like pointed Mt. Thielsen (9182), is a hefty 36 miles away. Mt. Scott (8926) is the easternmost and highest of the Crater Lake environs peaks. On most days you also see Mt. Shasta (14,162), 85 miles due south. Mt. McLoughlin (9495) is the dominating stratovolcano 15 miles to the south-southwest. Try to imagine this landscape, say, 20,000 years ago, when all but the major summits and ridges lay buried under glacier ice, and the glaciers extended east down canyons to the edge of the Klamath Lake basin.

Those who don't visit the summit have a leisurely climb up to the Devils Peak/Lee Peak saddle (7320–0.5). The descent from the saddle is often a snowy one, and it can be impassable to pack and saddle stock even as late as August. Early-summer backpackers generally slide or run down the snowpack until they locate the trail in the mountain-hemlock forest below. Those ascending this north slope on foot will find the climb strenuous but safe. The PCT northbound switchbacks down this slope, crosses a cascading, bubbling creek, and then in ¼ mile passes by a meadow. We cross its outlet creek, switchback downward, recross that creek plus the earlier, cascading creek, and soon arrive at a junction (6250–2.4). Southwest, a trail traverses 0.3 mile over to Seven Lakes Trail 981, along which you can walk 0.1 mile to Cliff Lake. A trail along the lake's east shore leads to a group of very popular campsites (the lake should be avoided on weekends). At the west end of this camping zone, by the edge of a large talus slope, you'll find a small, bedrock cliff that makes a perfect platform for high diving into the lake. No other lake in the wilderness can boast of such a feature.

Beyond the Cliff Lake lateral we head northeast, quickly cross a creek, then make a steepening descent to a junction with Sevenmile Trail 3703 (6130–0.7). Southwest, this trail drops to overused Grass Lake, with its multitude of campsites. If you feel compelled to camp near this lake, try sites along its south shore. Northeast the PCT (a.k.a. Sevenmile Trail) rambles down to a couple of inferior campsites by usually flowing Honeymoon Creek (5980–0.5). Past it we rollercoaster across generally viewless slopes and hear Ranger Springs, unseen below us, as we approach a junction where we leave the Sevenmile Trail (5760–2.1). This trail goes an easy 1.8 miles northeast down to diminutive Sevenmile Marsh Campground, at the end of Road 3334. On weekends the trailhead can be packed.

The PCT descends quickly to a flat, broad saddle, where you'll meet the Middle Fork Basin Trail (5750–0.2), which winds southwest 0.9 mile gradually down to the sonorous, tumultuous Ranger Springs. Northbound, water is scarce, so tank up at these pristine springs unless you plan to visit out-of-the-way Stuart Falls. Bound for Crater Lake we first cross a dry flat and then make an ascent up to a junction with Big Bunchgrass Trail 1089A (6020–1.0). You may not see this trail, since it is officially abandoned. In the past it wound 2.0 miles around Big Bunchgrass—a relatively youthful volcano—to a junction with Trail 1089. On the PCT we reach McKie Camp Trail 1089 (6380–0.9) as we approach a meadowy saddle. This trail goes 3.1 miles down to a junction with Halifax Trail 1088. Solace Cow Camp lies about 90 yards down that trail. Just north from the Halifax Trail junction is a usually flowing creek with an adjacent hikers' camp. Northbound on the McKie Camp Trail one reaches the McKie Camp environs in 1.6 miles, and it too has a usually flowing creek. One can then take the trail 1.9 miles northeast up to the Stuart Falls Trail, reaching it just under ½ mile northwest of

see MAP C6

the PCT. Hikers would take this described route only if they really needed water, for it is quite a bit out of the way. However, the route may appeal to equestrians, since Solace and McKie camps are popular horse camps.

From the saddle between Big Bunchgrass and Maude Mountain the PCT climbs to the latter's west spur, from where it traverses north along west slopes past Ethel and Ruth mountains to a saddle just east of Lone Wolf. We now start east but quickly switchback northwest and descend ½ mile through a snow-harboring fir-and-hemlock forest before curving north to a flat. Here, where others have camped, we spy the Jack Spring spur trail (6190–2.7). It heads west to a low saddle, then from it drops steeply ½ mile northwest to Jack Spring. Due to the steepness of this descent, plus the difficulty some folks

C7   **C7**

have finding bucket-size Jack Spring, you should take this trail only if you *really* need water.

Your route now winds gently down to the Oregon Desert, which holds a reservoir of water, all of it underground. The landscape has been buried in pumice and ash deposited from the final eruptions of Mt. Mazama about 4900 B.C., eruptions that led to the stratovolcano's collapse and the subsequent formation of Crater Lake in the resulting depression. Most of the area's streams were buried under ash and pumice, and the trekker faces water-shortage problems all the way to Thielsen Creek, in Section D, some 47 trail miles away. We traverse the west edge of the "desert," which in reality is an open lodgepole-forest flat, and we pass a wisp of a trail, heading east, about ⅓ mile before we meet abandoned Dry Creek Trail 3701 (6040–2.4), striking southeast. Leaving the "desert" behind, we top a low, adjacent saddle and then meet the south end of Stuart Falls Trail 1078 (6050–0.2).

*   *   *   *

Once the snow melts you won't find any water on or near the PCT all the way north to Highway 62, some 10.8 miles away. And from there you'll have to walk almost a mile east to Annie Spring or ½ mile farther to Mazama Campground. Unless you've got enough water to make this stretch, you are going to have to take the Stuart Falls Trail. In just under ½ mile this trail meets the north end of McKie Camp Trail 1089, which was briefly described earlier. Next we walk an easy 1¼ miles north, then descend moderately northwest to a junction with Lucky Camp Trail 1083 (5420–2.3). Westward this trail passes at least a half dozen springs as it rolls in and out of gullies 1.0 mile over to Red Blanket Falls Trail. That trail, in turn, drops 0.6 mile to Upper Red Blanket Trail 1090, reaching it just above the brink of two-tiered Red Blanket Falls. Trail 1090 then guides the hydrophilic adventurer 0.8 mile back up to the Stuart Falls Trail.

From the Lucky Camp Trail junction the Stuart Falls Trail passes three creeks of various staying power before it crosses always reliable Red Blanket Creek to reach the upper end of the Upper Red Blanket Trail (5360–0.7). (This trail is called *Upper* because it is now just the upper 3.8-mile part of the formerly much longer Red Blanket Trail. A first-rate road, 6205, has supplanted the trail, whisking wilderness travelers to the popular trailhead.)

We now stroll up along Red Blanket Creek to a spur trail which takes us momentarily to Stuart Falls Camp (5450–0.4). This large, flat area near the base of Stuart Falls is for humans only. If you've got stock animals, you must picket them immediately north of the Stuart Falls Trail, not down at the camp. Stuart Falls provides rhapsodic music for campers, a feature that few other southern Cascade campsites have. Next day, tank up on water and start up the Stuart Falls Trail. In about ⅓ mile you enter Crater Lake National Park near a gully with a seasonal creek. From it your route is an old, abandoned road, which faithfully guides you back to the PCT (6290–2.5–5.9).

*   *   *   *

Meanwhile, from the south end of the Stuart Falls Trail, PCT devotees start northeast from the fork. The PCT heads toward the crest, once again thwarting your hopes for water. It climbs north across the lower slopes of the Goose Egg, reaches the crest just beyond it, and then stays very close to it as it descends to a crossing of an old, closed road only a few yards before the trail tread ends at a second old, closed road (6290–5.6). Southwest, the first road descends 2.5 miles to Stuart Falls Camp; northeast, it traverses, as the Pumice Flat Trail, 2.8 monotonous miles to Highway 62.

Already a solid mile within Crater Lake National Park, we head deeper inland, progressing along the second old, closed road. In one mile you may see an abandoned road branching west from ours, but only those with keen orienting abilities will notice it. We ramble onward, gaining slightly in elevation, enter an oval, open flat, then top out at the south end of a long but narrow, open flat (6550–2.4). From this end another closed road—the Union Peak Trail—meanders 1⅔ miles west over to the start of a steep summit trail. Weather permitting, you should not pass up the opportunity to scale this prominent landmark. Drop your heavy pack at the end of the old road and scramble, sometimes using your hands, up to Union Peak's tiny summit.

Onward, the PCT traverses the narrow, open flat, then takes you down through a dense, viewless forest that contains some of the finest specimens of mountain hemlocks you'll find anywhere. Before mid-July this shady stretch can be quite snowbound. Finally we come to a small trailhead parking area along the south side of Highway 62 (6108–2.8). Ahead, your next

C7, C8

C8, C9

C8

S

Union Pk
BM 7698

6507

6560

6379

BM
6291

C

A

1078

6526

Bald Top
6220

Creek

Blanket

CRATER LAKE NATIONAL PARK

5837   127   126   BM 5588   124   123   122   121   120   119
6049   6211   6161

SKY LAKES WILDERNESS

Stuart Falls
Camp

Red

6515

1090

1083

BM 5635

6704

A

Watershed

Divide

6794

Goose
Egg   7125

Rogue
Klamath

SPRINGS

TRAIL

CEDAR

ky Mtn

BM 6042

5029

McKIE   CAMP   TRAIL   1078

1089

Oregon

Pole   Bridge

Bear
Bluff

62

6250

BM 6039

Pumice Flat

Scoria Cone
6627

Goose Nest

7259

3700

6500

6250

6250

6000

on-trail water will be from the Castle Creek headwaters tributaries, at least 1¾ miles away.

The PCT route, which begins as a trail on the other side of the highway, makes a long arc around the lake's west rim, generally staying 2 to 3 miles away from it and 1000 to 2500 feet below it. The route avoids the lake's rim because one of the criteria for the PCT is that it bypass heavily traveled routes—and the Rim Drive surely is one of them. But since we know that you're not going to hike past the lake without seeing it, we'll now describe a road route that takes you up and along the rim before it descends to a reunion with the PCT.

*   *   *   *

From where the PCT crosses Highway 62 at a level stretch 0.8 mile west of the highway's junction with the park's south-rim access road, we start east. In ⅓ mile the highway bends southeast, and we leave it, descending ¼ mile northeast on the old highway's abandoned roadbed. This ends at the base of a gully, up which the Annie Spring Cutoff Trail climbs ½ mile north back to the PCT. Our route heads south-southeast about 300 yards over to the Crater Lake south-rim access road (6010–0.7). This spot is opposite a ranger residence, and it is about midway between Annie Spring and the entrance to Mazama Campground. Since you won't have a legal camping opportunity anywhere along the park's roads, you might as well head 250 yards south to the campground's entrance road, then 0.4 mile on it to the camp-

ground proper. If you've started your day's hike from Stuart Falls by 7 a.m., you'll reach the campground by 3 p.m., even if you've taken in the side trip to Union Peak. By 5 p.m. the campground is often full, though on weekends it can fill much earlier.

Next morning, retrace your steps to where you first met the south-rim access road, and curve 0.1 mile over to a bridge that spans Annie Creek (6010–1.1). You'll see copious Annie Spring—the source of the creek—just upstream from the bridge. Eastbound, we pass Goodbye Creek Picnic Area (6010–0.8), with water, then soon reach a curve north (6040–0.4). From it the Godfrey Glen Trail makes a one-mile loop out to vertical-walled Annie Creek canyon and back. North, we have almost an hour's trek up Munson Valley along the viewless access road, and we pass ranger residences and a gas station just before reaching Crater Lake's Rim Drive (6460–2.2). Still well below the rim we start north, only to meet park headquarters and its post office (6479–0.1). Pick up whatever packages you've mailed to yourself. You can also get information on weather, naturalist programs, wildflower conditions and the like. Here too, you can get a wilderness permit, should you wish to camp in the park's backcountry (such as at Lightning Springs or Red Cone Spring). And you can buy books and pamphlets about the park or the Cascade Range.

From the park headquarters you head north up the Rim Drive, which in ⅔ mile bends south. You wind in and out of a couple gullies and, upon

C9   **C9, C10**

Wizard Island in Crater Lake, from Rim Village

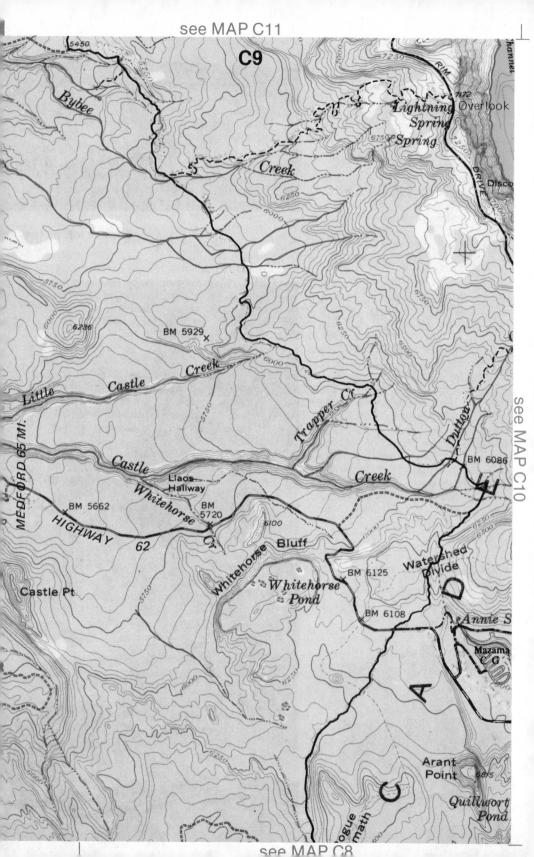

C9

Bybee

Lightning
Spring
Spring

Overlook

RIM

DRIVE

Disco

Creek

BM 5929 ×

6236

5750

6000

Little

Castle

Creek

Trapper Cr.

Dutto

BM 6086

Castle

Creek

Liaos
Hallway

Whitehorse

BM 5662

BM
5720 ×

Cr.

BM 6125

Watershed
Divide

HIGHWAY

62

Whitehorse Bluff

Whitehorse
Pond

BM 6108

Annie S

see MAP C10

Castle Pt

Mazama
C G

Arant
Point

6815

Quillwort
Pond

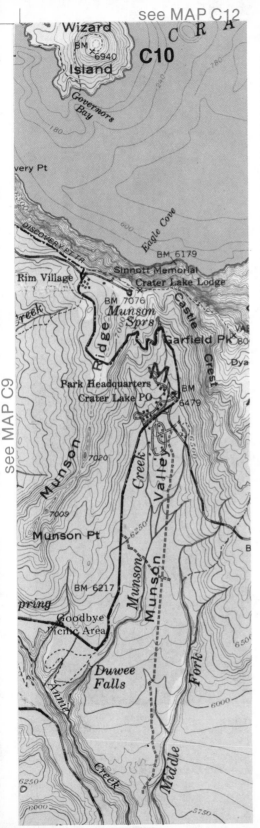

reaching the westernmost one, you have the option of hiking ⅓ mile due north up it to Crater Lake Lodge. Otherwise, head southwest on the Rim Drive up to Munson Ridge, then north ¾ mile to the Rim Village junction (7090–2.7). Just 60 yards before this junction you'll see the top end of the Dutton Creek Trail, which descends rather steeply 2.4 viewless miles to the PCT. If you want to adhere to the PCT as much as possible, take a quick look at Crater Lake and then head down this trail.

Your first view of this 1932-foot-deep lake, like one's first view down into the Grand Canyon, may be one of disbelief—your memory tries to recollect a similar feature. As the deepest lake in the United States and the seventh deepest in the world, Crater Lake is a pristine ultramarine blue on a sunny day, and the 900-foot height of our Rim Village vantage point deepens the color. The lake is also one of the world's youngest, having begun to fill just after the demise of Mt. Mazama and reaching its present level by around 4000 B.C.

Mt. Mazama was a large volcano that was born about ½ million years ago. Over several hundred thousand years it grew, via periodic eruptions, to a large Cascade Range stratovolcano. Fairly late in the Ice Age, perhaps 100,000 years ago, it may have reached an elevation of 11,000–12,000 feet. In size it was larger than Mt. Hood, and perhaps close to the size of Mt. Adams. During glacial times, glaciers extended as far as 17 miles from the mountain's summit. But we know how rapidly a volcano can be destroyed in a cataclysmic eruption, such as the one that decapitated Mt. St. Helens in minutes on May 18, 1980. Mt. Mazama self-destructed about 4900 B.C., only its eruption was about 40 times more voluminous than that of St. Helens. The immediate landscape was buried under tens of feet of ash and pumice; Mt. Rainier, 280 miles to the north, was mantled with 3 inches of it, while southern British Columbia and Alberta received trace amounts.

The eruption took place at night, according to an ancient Klamath Indian legend, and morning's light revealed a huge gaping hole—a caldera—where the mountain had stood. The mountain had died, but there was still enough magma in the bowels of the earth to construct a small volcano—Wizard Island—within perhaps months or years after the catastrophe. A smaller volcano, known as Merriam Cone, also formed, but 500 to 1000 years of precipitation filled the caldera to its present volume, about 4 cubic

C11

Oasis Butte
5685

Watershed Divide

6128

VABM Red
7372

Red Cone Spr
BM 6265

6085

6250

6000

num

Fork

North

5593

BM 5920

Middle Fk

South Fk

VABM
Hillman Pk 8156

Overlook

The Watchman

8056

miles, and in doing so it buried the top of Merriam Cone under 500 feet of water.

From the Rim Village junction one can walk east through the "village," which has a complex with a gift shop, a small grocery store, a cafeteria and a restaurant. Behind this complex are rustic cabins for rent, usually on a daily basis. Just past

the complex is a small Visitor Center, from which stairs drop to the Sinnott Memorial, which provides one of the best views of the lake. Crater Lake Lodge, open only during summer, looms above the end of the Rim Village road, and from it the Garfield Peak Trail climbs 1.7 miles to what Schaffer thinks is the most scenic view of Crater Lake.

C10

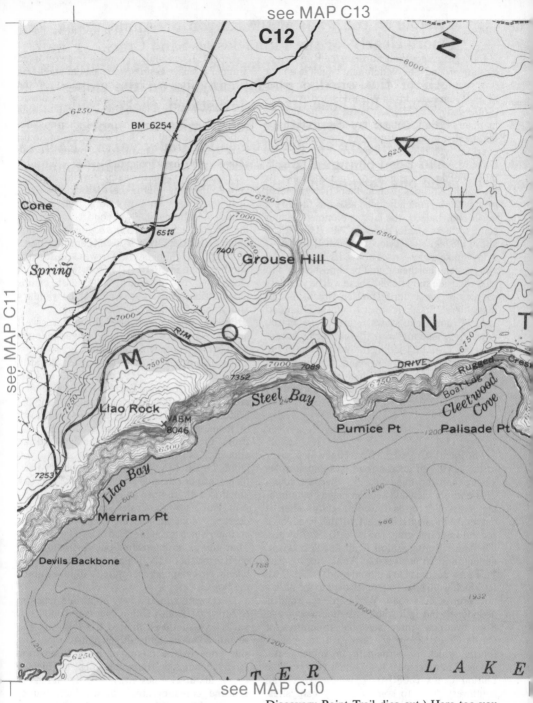

C12

Cone

Spring

6250

BM 6254

6510

6250

6500

7000

6750

7250

7401

Grouse Hill

6500

6250

RIM

M

O

U

N

T

A

6750

7000

7500

7352

7089

DRIVE

Steel Bay

6750

Rugged Ed.

Crest

Llao Rock

VABM
8046

6500

7250

Boat Ldg

Cleetwood
Cove

Pumice Pt

1200

Palisade Pt

7253

Llao Bay

Merriam Pt

Devils Backbone

7200

466

1788

1932

120

6250

1800

1200

W A T E R

L A K E

To resume your journey, hike northwest from the Rim Village junction, taking either the crest-hugging Discovery Point Trail or the saddle-hopping Rim Drive. On the road you reach Discovery Point at your second saddle, and then the Lightning Springs Trail (7172–2.2) at the third. (Here, at the south end of this saddle, the

Discovery Point Trail dies out.) Here too you have a second opportunity to return to the PCT. About ¾ mile down the 4.1-mile Lightning Springs Trail you'll find a short spur trail heading south to campsites among the two Lightning Springs. You'll have more access to water farther down, where the trail—an old road—approaches Bybee Creek.

C10, C9

C9

Lake gazers continue north on the Rim Drive, circling around The Watchman, which is a lava flow that formed on Mt. Mazama's flank about 50,000 years ago. From Wizard Island overlook (7600–1.5), a saddle just north of The Watchman, an often snowbound closed road climbs to that peak's summit. If you like the views at the overlook, you'll love the views from the summit. Onward, we leave the lake views for a couple miles, but do get a glimpse of Diamond Lake, to the north. At times past, glaciers flowing north from Mt. Mazama advanced as far as the lake's north end. Indeed, the lake is dammed behind some of these glacial deposits. Mt. Bailey rises above the lake's west side, while Mt. Thielsen—a day's hike away—rises above its east side. As you descend northeast, you're almost certain to pass roadside snowfields. These will be your last sources of water until Thielsen Creek, though most hikers first head over to closer Diamond Lake. Crater Lake views return as we march down to a junction with the north-rim access road (7253–2.1). Bidding farewell to one of the world's greatest natural wonders, we wind north down the access road, which offers lakeless views until about ¼ mile before we intersect the PCT (6510–2.6–16.4).

*   *   *   *

The Pacific Crest Trail from Highway 62 over to the north-rim access road is about 2 miles longer than the highly scenic alternate route. This entirely viewless section begins by climbing, part of it up a fault-line gully. Then it descends momentarily east to the head of a second fault-line gully (6310–0.8). Southward, the Annie Spring Cutoff Trail heads down it, ending in a flat just west of Annie Spring. The PCT now descends to a closed road (6130–0.6), on which we'll hike 16.9 miles over to the park's north-rim access road. Westward, the road is abandoned but followable; we start northeast. Soon we pass three seasonal tributaries of Castle Creek before we turn west and pass a fourth, which is permanent in some years. About 2 minutes past it we reach very reliable Dutton Creek (6080–0.7), with a spur trail southwest down to some close-by campsites. Here too you'll find the Dutton Creek Trail, which climbs 2.4 fairly hard miles to Crater Lake's Rim Village junction. To take in a bit of Crater Lake scenery, you can hike up this trail, head northwest on either the Discovery Point Trail or Rim Drive, and then descend back to the PCT via the Lightning Springs Trail.

The PCT descends 1¼ miles to two-forked Trapper Creek, passing two seasonal creeks on the way. Trapper Creek flows most of the summer, but later on you'll have to go downstream to find it flowing. Ahead, you ramble about 1¼ miles over to a divide, then make a noticeable descent north to four forks of South Fork Bybee Creek. The first two flow most of the summer and have potential camps; the third flows just as long but is campless; the fourth is vernal. Past the fourth the road briefly rises, then descends ½ mile to lasting Bybee Creek (5860–4.4). Immediately beyond it, an old road, the Lightning Springs Trail, begins a 4.1-mile climb to the Rim Drive. You can camp just north of the trail junction, or you can wind on down to another junction (5610–1.1), from which an old, closed spur road descends ⅓ mile west to camps along a tributary of Bybee Creek. If the tributary is dry, look for water just downstream.

Beyond the spur road the PCT soon turns west and then descends ½ mile to a very abandoned road, which starts west in a small, grassy area. Our route turns north and soon crosses the fairly reliable South (5470–0.9) and Middle (5470–0.2) forks of Copeland Creek. Open, lodgepole-punctuated meadows stretch ¼ mile beyond the Middle Fork, and these, like the meadows north of them, are favorite browsing spots for elk. From the second set of meadows and an adjacent, westbound, abandoned road, you climb 2⅔ miles to a ridge, follow it briefly east, then continue one mile east up gentle slopes to a junction with another abandoned road (6085–4.7). This is now the Crater Springs Trail, which descends moderately a full 3 miles west to the springs, which are at the head of Sphagnum Bog. That area is an interesting one for naturalists, but it is too far off the beaten track for most PCT hikers. No camping is permitted within ½ mile of the bog.

Next, we climb to a very important junction (6240–1.0), from which a spur trail heads 150 yards east-southeast to Red Cone Spring and several adjacent camps. If you plan to avoid any side trips to the Diamond Lake Recreation Area, your next on-trail water will be at Thielsen Creek, about 21 miles away. And if you plan to visit the recreation area, you will have similar water problems. Obviously, one doesn't drop to Diamond Lake to get water, since he could reach Thielsen Creek just as fast. Rather you visit it to resupply and/or enjoy its amenities. Prepare yourself for a long, dry day, unless you are hiking before mid-July, in which case you're likely to encounter trailside snow patches.

C11, C12, C9   C9, C11

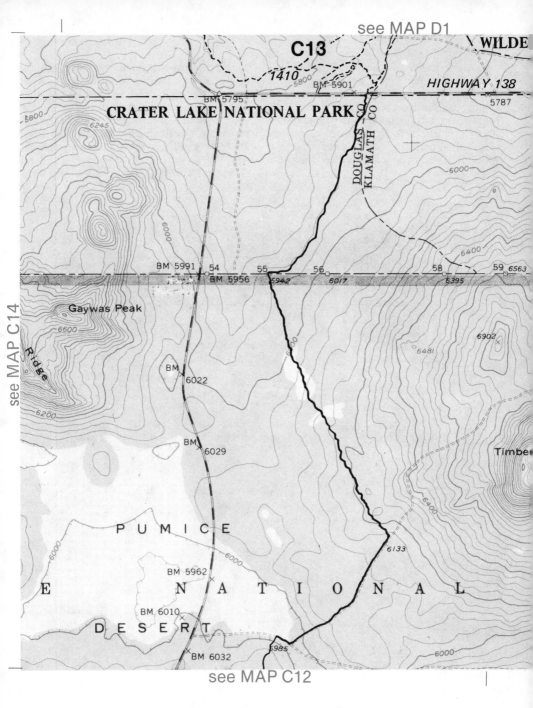

If you find the thought of a long, waterless stretch too distressing, you do have a water-blessed option. And you have to hike a total of only about 14 miles to reach Broken Arrow Campground, above the south shore of Diamond Lake. To take this route, first continue north on the PCT, like other trekkers, down to a junction with the Boundary Springs Trail (6128–0.6).

*   *   *   *

On the alternate route you leave the east-bound PCT adherents as you descend a dry, viewless, monotonous trail north to a junction

C11   **C11, C14**

with the westbound Oasis Butte Trail (5635–4.1). Continue north, then northwest, down to Boundary Springs (5250–1.9), which are so voluminous that you could start, immediately below them, a raft trip down the Rogue River (though fallen trees make such a trip impractical). For many years Crater Lake National Park's north boundary crossed this vicin- ity. No camping is allowed within ½ mile of the springs, so continue north down the Rogue River canyon, leaving the park in about ¾ mile, then presently reach a junction (5080–1.2). From it your Boundary Springs Trail 1057 heads 100 yards north to Road 760, while Rogue River Trail 1034 heads northeast along the river to the road (5070–0.2). If you want to do some

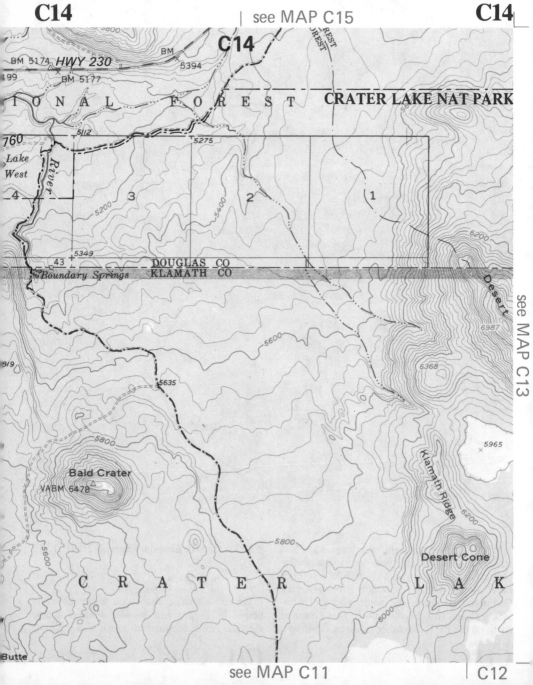

see MAP C13

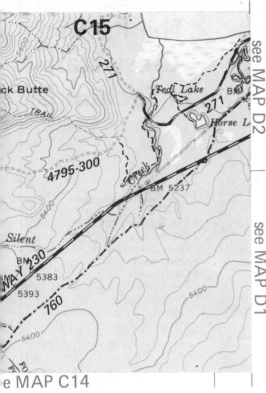

see MAP D2

see MAP D1

e MAP C14

Road 4795, you walk briefly north to a day-use parking area, to the west, and the old Mt. Thielsen Trail, to the east (5190–0.1–14.1). For further instructions see Section D's first alternate route, which also heads north on Road 4795.

*   *   *   *

Hikers hell-bent for punishment ignore the Boundary Springs alternate route and make a generally uphill, usually easy traverse. Most of it is through an open lodgepole-pine forest, and you'll round avalanche-prone Red Cone about 1½ miles before you reach a small trailhead parking area alongside the north-rim access road (6510–3.3). Here, those taking the recommended Rim Drive alternate route rejoin us for a northbound trek.

You begin your viewless, waterless trek by walking east over to the nearby base of Grouse Hill, a huge mass of rhyodacite lava that congealed just before Mt. Mazama erupted and collapsed to create the Crater Lake caldera. Its eruptions, occurring about 6900 years ago, "sandblasted" the top of Grouse Hill, and it is unfortunate that the PCT doesn't traverse that interesting surface.

But it doesn't, so you trod north between road and flow, the two gradually diverging before you reach the Timber Crater Trail. On this closed road you walk 260 yards east to a road fork (5985–2.9) and there branch northeast. We climb gently up toward Timber Crater, and where the road becomes steeper, we branch left, back onto trail tread again (6150–1.3). We climb but ¼ mile northwest before continuing in that direction on a long, viewless, snaking descent to the pre-1980 north boundary of Crater Lake National Park (5942–2.7). From here an old trail heads west ⅓ mile along that boundary line to an abandoned road that goes 1½ miles north to Highway 138, then just beyond that to the North Crater Trail. Short-cutters, take note.

Heading toward Highway 138, the PCT takes a longer way, first striking west along the old boundary, then traversing north-northeast to reach the new boundary immediately before Highway 138 (5920–1.9). This it crosses just 70 yards west of a broad, low crest pass of the Cascade Range. You won't find any parking here, so continue 230 yards from the highway to a junction, from which North Crater Trail 1410 descends ¼ mile northwest to a well-developed trailhead parking area.

camping, take the former trail to Road 760 and follow it west 0.4 mile over to Lake West, which caters to car campers. If you're bound for Diamond Lake, take the latter trail, reach Road 760, and immediately bridge the Rogue River. On 760 you head east, then northeast, to a junction (5390–2.9), from which a short road winds 0.3 mile northwest to busy Highway 230. Northeast, you continue on an abandoned road, whose end is blocked off by a newer section of Highway 230 (5240–2.3). Cross the highway, relocate the abandoned road, and follow it north to the old Highway 230 section (5210–0.3). Southbound hikers: note that this road begins about 100 yards east of Horse Lake. If you reach that lake, you've walked a bit too far. On the unused Highway 230 section you proceed northeast, spying in ⅓ mile the southernmost loop of sprawling Broken Arrow Campground. From here onward you can leave the road at any point and walk over to any of the campground's loops. The old highway section ends in under a mile; then you turn left on old Highway 138 (a.k.a. 4795) and head ¼ mile north to a junction with Road 271 (5205–1.1), which loops around Diamond Lake. Keeping to east-shore

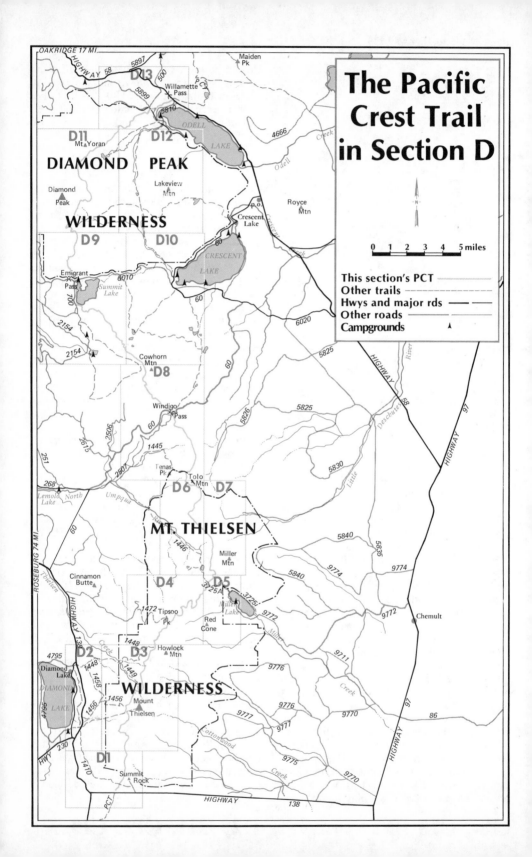

The Pacific Crest Trail in Section D

N

0 1 2 3 4 5 miles

This section's PCT
Other trails
Hwys and major rds
Other roads
Campgrounds ▲

Section D: Highway 138 near the Cascade crest to Highway 58 near Willamette Pass

Introduction: Needle-pointed Mt. Thielsen, approached early on this hike, is this section's star attraction; its terrain is even more spectacular than that seen along the PCT through this section's Diamond Peak Wilderness. Unfortunately, when the Pacific Crest Trail was finally completed through this section around 1977, its route proved to be inferior in esthetics compared with its predecessor, the Oregon Skyline Trail. That trail touched on enjoyable Diamond Lake, which most long-distance PCT hikers visit anyway. It also took you past Maidu Lake, which was one of this section's best camping areas (when mosquitoes weren't biting), and it was an important water source. Now it is almost one mile out of the way. Furthermore, the old trail went past a series of lakes, but this route has been replaced with a nearly lakeless route that remains more faithful to the crest. This new route tends to be snowbound about a month longer than the older route. Finally, whereas the Oregon Skyline Trail came to within ½ mile of the Cascade Summit store and post office at Odell Lake, the Pacific Crest Trail comes only to within 1½ miles of it. Consequently, we will describe the old route as well as the new one.

Despite the foregoing criticisms lodged against this section's Pacific Crest Trail, it is still a good experience. The trail is well-graded and it has interesting, if not dramatic, views of Mt. Thielsen, Sawtooth Ridge, Cowhorn Mountain, Diamond Peak and Mt. Yoran. All are easily accessible to peak baggers, but Mt. Yoran should be left for experienced mountaineers. The only *significant* lake along the official PCT route, Summit Lake, is, like Diamond Lake, a worthy place to spend a layover day.

Declination: 18°E

Mileages:	South to North	Distances between Points	North to South
Highway 138 near the Cascade crest..............	0.0		61.3
		6.2	
Mt. Thielsen Trail.............................	6.2		55.1
		2.2	
Thielsen Creek Trail..........................	8.4		52.9
		3.1	
Howlock Mountain Trail	11.5		49.8
		6.8	
Maidu Lake Trail	18.3		43.0
		6.2	
Tolo Camp......................................	24.5		36.8
		5.9	
Windigo Pass..................................	30.4		30.9
		7.0	
Stagnant pond (6380')..........................	37.4		23.9
		5.7	
Road 6010 near Summit Lake Campground	43.1		18.2
		12.0	
Unnamed lake (6030').........................	55.1		6.2
		3.1	
Midnight Lake.................................	58.2		3.1
		1.5	
Pengra Pass...................................	59.7		1.6
		1.6	
Highway 58 near Willamette Pass................	61.3		0.0

Supplies: Since there are no on-route supply points, most long-distance PCT hikers take one of our alternate routes down to a walk north along Diamond Lake. The store at Diamond Lake Lodge is one of the best to be found anywhere near the PCT. This spacious resort also has a post office, and it serves good meals at reasonable prices.

Near Section D's north end you can leave the PCT at Pengra Pass and descend 1.5 miles to Shelter Cove Resort, which houses the Cascade Summit Post Office. The resort's small store caters to fishermen.

Our section's hike begins at Highway 138 (5920) just 70 yards west of the almost flat watershed divide in this locale of the Cascade Range. Trailhead parking is available just north of Highway 138 and west of the PCT. The short road that goes northeast to the trailhead starts from Highway 138 just 0.5 mile west of the Cascade divide and 0.8 mile east of Crater Lake's north-rim access road.

From Highway 138 the PCT heads northeast 230 yards to a junction with the south end of North Crater Trail 1410 (5910–0.1). Just 3 minutes into our hike, we're faced with a decision—the first of several routes leaving the PCT for the Diamond Lake environs. The North Crater Trail doesn't go to any crater; rather it descends toward Diamond Lake, runs north

above its east shore, then in 9.3 miles ends at the Diamond Lake Corrals, which are situated about ½ mile northeast of Diamond Lake Resort. If you want the quickest, easiest route to Diamond Lake, start along this trail.

*   *   *   *

North Crater Trail 1410 reaches the trailhead parking area in ¼ mile, then continues onward. In 60 yards it reaches an old southwest-descending road that dies out in both directions. Go just 200 yards down this road, then fork right onto a broad path that descends to a gully. From here a snowmobile route climbs northeast, leading eastbound hikers astray. Westward, you cross, in 0.5 mile, an old road, which was

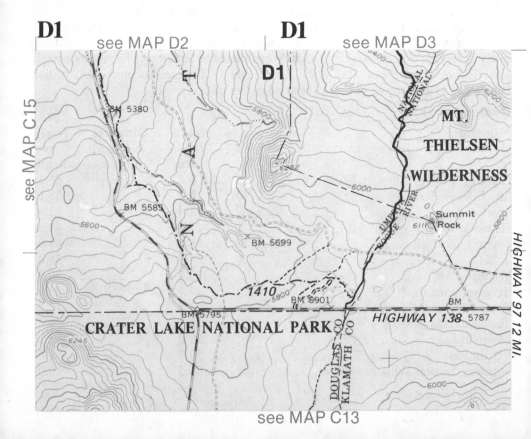

referred to at the end of Section C. Just 0.6 mile later our trail tread joins that road again, where it loops into a gully (5640–1.9). We follow the road ¾ mile down to where it curves west and flattens out. Leave the road and take a trail that starts north along a crest between two gullies. Your route ahead should now be obvious, and you parallel Highway 138 until it diagonals across your path (5275–2.5). Dash across the busy highway and follow a short trail segment over to Highway 230 (5245–0.2). You could continue north along the North Crater Trail, but since that route is largely viewless, you might miss a number of lakeside attractions. Therefore, walk 100 yards west on Highway 230 to a junction with east-shore Road 4795. Just under ½ mile north on it you meet a straight, southeast-heading road—the old Highway 230—along which Section C's Boundary Springs Trail alternate route joins our route (5220–0.5). As in that route we head ¼ mile north to a junction with Diamond Lake's loop Road 271. Anywhere along this last stretch you could have walked west to the east side of nearby Broken Arrow Campground.

In another ¼ mile we pass a day-use parking area, on our left, and the *old* Mt. Thielsen Trail and a private campground on our right, then arrive at South Store (5190–0.5). If you've been living for days out of your pack, you'll certainly welcome this store and its cafe. Just north of the store is the south end of 2-mile-long Diamond Lake Campground, which is sandwiched between the lake and Road 4795. You can drop to it any time you desire. Midway along the lake's east side we reach an intersection (5236–1.4), with the campground's entrance to the west and the Diamond Lake Information Center to the east. From that center a spur trail goes 0.1 mile north to the North Crater Trail, while another goes ¼ mile south to it. Onward, you pass more of the campground, then from its north end you can hop onto a trail that parallels your road and the lakeshore over to Diamond Lake Resort's entrance road (5200–1.2). Head over to the complex (5200–0.3), resupply at its well-stocked general store, pick up your mailed parcels at the post office, and/or enjoy a hearty meal at the restaurant. If you're well-funded, rent a fishing boat and catch a rainbow trout or two, which grow considerably larger here than in the lakes of Sky Lakes Wilderness. Some long-distance hikers may even be desperate enough for civilization's amenities to stay at the resort's lodge.

A Mt. Thielsen pinnacle and distant rim of Crater Lake

View south-southeast from Thielsen's summit

D1, D2

After your stay, however brief or long, start north up the road immediately east of the gas station. This road climbs up to Road 271, reaching it only a minute's walk west of a junction with Road 4795 (5340–0.5). Also at this junction is the entrance road to Diamond Lake Corrals. Walk east to the road's far end, and beside it you'll find a tread (5340–0.1–9.1). Northward, Howlock Mountain Trail 1448 swings east, spinning off Spruce Ridge Trail 1458 (which goes over to Mt. Thielsen Trail 1456) and Thielsen Creek Trail 1449. All take you back to the PCT and will be described in the pages to come. Southward, North Crater Trail 1410 snakes 9.3 miles to the PCT, ending just north of Section D's start, Highway 138.

*   *   *   *

Back at that junction, those taking the mostly viewless, waterless PCT route have an easy climb up to the old, abandoned Summit Rock Road (5935–0.5). This road, which is a ski route in winter, also provides one with a route—albeit inferior—to Diamond Lake. The road curves 4.2 miles over to the new Highway 138, on which one walks 0.4 mile along its shoulder, then follows the defunct Mt. Thielsen Trail 0.5 mile west over to Road 4795, at the lake's southeast corner.

Onward, the PCT climbs gently north for a mile, then the gradient steepens and the trail makes a few open switchbacks up a ridge before it curves northwest around it. We now make a long but comfortable ascent, rounding Mt. Thielsen's southwest ridge before traversing across a glaciated bowl to a trail junction on the peak's west flank. Here we meet the top part of the Mt. Thielsen Trail (7260–5.3), which will now be described east up to the summit. Westward, the still followable but abandoned trail descends 2.8 miles to the new Highway 138, then continues 0.5 mile west to the old highway—Road 4795—meeting it at the lake's southeast corner.

*   *   *   *

The summit of Mt. Thielsen (9182), sometimes called the "Lightning Rod" of the Cascades, is easily accessible and should not be bypassed. When you ascend it, however, leave your pack behind; it has probably one of the steepest trails in existence—more of a climb than a hike. The trail quickly exits above treeline

and then climbs up increasingly loose pumice slopes toward a cleaver, where it seems to veer right (south) around it. This scree slope is the *descent* route. Rather than fight your way up this unstable slope, climb up solid rock along the left

D3
ROSEBURG 77 MI.

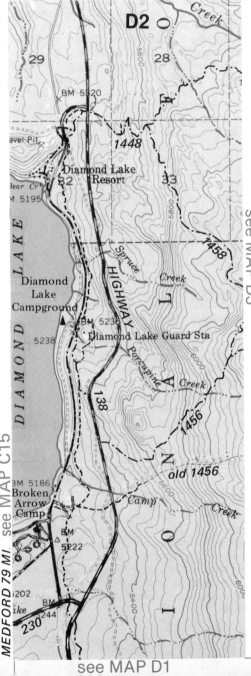

see MAP D1

(north) side of the cleaver and continue up toward the 80-foot-high summit pinnacle, which can be climbed unroped only from its southeast ridge. The near-vertical north and east faces make this last few feet off limits to those with acrophobia.

The view from the summit area is both spectacular and didactic. You can see north 107 miles to Mt. Jefferson (10,497), and south 120 miles to Mt. Shasta (14,162). We can see from the dips, or inclinations, of the strata that Mt.

D3

D3

see MAP D4

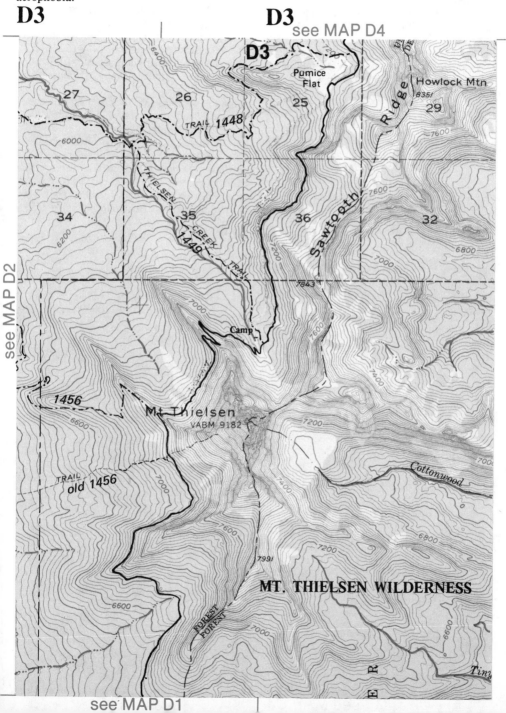

see MAP D2

see MAP D1

Thielsen's summit once lay to the east, and about 1000 feet higher, above what is now a deeply glaciated canyon. Here is a vulcanologist's natural observatory, for the mountain's anatomy is stripped bare. After downclimbing the summit pinnacle, we head south a short way along the ridge and pass some enormous pinnacles clinging to the east wall. Soon we come to an obvious spot, not too far from an isolated scrubby whitebark pine, where nearly everyone begins to descend the scree slope to the trail.

*   *   *   *

From Mt. Thielsen's summit trail the PCT traverses north to the peak's west ridge, on which it meets the new Mt. Thielsen Trail 1456 (7330–0.3).

*   *   *   *

If you want to drop to Diamond Lake for recreation or supplies, but don't want to miss a

foot of the PCT, start down the Mt. Thielsen Trail. This descends at an average gradient of 9¼%, versus 13% for the old Mt. Thielsen Trail. Since the PCT is not supposed to exceed 15%, the old Mt. Thielsen Trail fell within acceptable limits of steepness, and it is unfortunate that the newer, 1¼-mile-longer trail was built. But the new trail's gradient does make for an easy descent, and in under an hour you arrive at a junction with Spruce Ridge Trail 1458 (6240–2.3). You can take either route down to Diamond Lake, but to maximize scenery, why not make a loop?

On the waterless Mt. Thielsen Trail, descend to a trailhead on Highway 138 (5360–1.7). Unfortunately, the trail doesn't continue west to the lakeshore road, as the old trail did, so hike ½ mile north on 138, to where it begins to curve northeast. Drop west about 200 yards cross-country to North Crater Trail 1410. Walk ¼ mile north on it to where it splits, Trail 1410 branching northeast to circle behind a USFS

D3

D3, D2

Cloud-capped Mt. Thielsen, from near Tipsoo Trail junction with PCT

information center. You branch northwest and in ¼ mile reach, along east-shore Road 4795, the entrance to the information center, which is opposite the entrance to Diamond Lake Campground (5236–1.1). Now follow the previous alternate route 1.2 miles north to Diamond Lake

Resort's entrance road, 0.3 mile over to the resort, 0.5 mile up a minor road to Road 271 and momentarily east to nearby Road 4795, then 0.1 mile east through Diamond Lake Corrals to the Howlock Mountain trailhead (5340–2.1–7.2).

Howlock Mountain Trail 1448 heads northeast, joining another trail from the corrals immediately before passing through a horse tunnel under Highway 138 (5360–0.2). From the far side of the tunnel a minor trail heads northward, but you climb southeast up the slopes of a lateral moraine. The glacier that carried this morainal debris originated on the north slopes of Mt. Mazama, a towering volcano that collapsed about 6900 years ago at the site now occupied by Crater Lake. Immediately beyond the crest of the moraine you meet a second minor trail, which heads north down a gully. You then switchback to the crest of a higher moraine and on it meet Spruce Ridge Trail 1458 (5680–1.0), which is the first of three options back to the PCT:

1) The waterless Spruce Ridge Trail 1458 starts along a minor ridge and makes an easy, spruce-free, generally viewless ascent south to the Mt. Thielsen Trail (6240–2.6). Up it, retrace your steps to where you left the PCT, on the west ridge of Mt. Thielsen (7330–2.3–6.1 miles from Diamond Lake Corrals).

2) Continue east on the Howlock Mountain Trail, passing in ⅓ mile the seasonal west fork of Thielsen Creek, later skirting Timothy Meadow, and then ½ mile beyond it reaching Thielsen Creek and adjacent Thielsen Creek Trail 1449 (6040–2.4). Take this moderately climbing trail, which parallels its namesake, back up to the PCT (6960–2.3–5.9). You'll pass a short spur trail over to Thielsen Creek Camp just 100 yards before this junction.

D2

see MAP D7

see MAP D4

D5

3725A

UMPQUA NATIONAL

DOUGLAS CO.

3725A

3725

3725

9772

MILL

Tipsoo

Diam. Point
Campground

Red
Cone

Gifford

CHEMULT 13 MI.

MT. THIELSEN WILDERNESS

22

23

3726

D2, D3

3) From the lower end of the Thielsen Creek Trail, continue east up Howlock Mountain Trail 1448, which can have snow patches in mid-July, but can be waterless by early August. You'll see Howlock Mountain, rising 1000 feet above you, just before you reach the PCT (7320–3.6–7.2).

If you began your alternate route from the southern end of North Crater Trail 1410, your total mileages for these three return routes will be 15.2, 15.0 and 16.3 miles. If you began your alternate route from the upper end of Mt. Thielsen Trail 1456, your total mileages will be 13.3, 13.1 and 14.4 miles.

*   *   *   *

From the Mt. Thielsen Trail 1456 junction the Pacific Crest Trail crosses the open, view-packed northwest slopes to the northwest ridge (7370–1.0). From it we see our next major peak—bulky, snowy Diamond Peak. Our trail now makes long switchbacks down from the ridge, then it descends southeast to Thielsen Creek (6930–1.1). Over this last mile of trail, snow sometimes lingers through late July. Thielsen Creek is your first source of permanent water since Red Cone Spring, 21 miles back. Your next on-route *pure* water is at Summit Lake, a whopping 33 miles ahead, so many hikers stop at out-of-the-way Maidu Lake, a good camping area, only 10.8 miles ahead. Just past the Thielsen Creek crossing you reach Thielsen Creek Trail 1449 (6960–0.1), on which you can descend about 100 yards to a spur trail that leads 100 yards west down to Thielsen Creek Camp. Since this is the first PCT campsite with water since Red Cone Spring, it can be overcrowded.

From the Thielsen Creek area the PCT makes a winding contour 2.7 miles north to an open bowl, Pumice Flat, through which the Oregon Skyline Trail once traversed northeast. The Pacific Crest Trail heads east just above it into a stand of mountain hemlocks. If you are hiking through this area in early season, you might want to camp under a cluster of hemlocks and lodgepoles near the low summit ¼ mile west of you. Early-season water is obtained from the seasonal creek just north of it or from nearby snow patches.

After the PCT heads east into the hemlocks, it quickly starts an ascending, counterclockwise traverse around the bowl. Just past a meadow where the trail turns from north to northwest,

you'll reach a junction (7320–3.1) with well-used Howlock Mountain Trail 1448. The last Diamond Lake alternate route, described earlier, ends here.

The PCT, which can be vague in spots over the last half mile, now makes an obvious climb to a crest saddle (7435–0.4), which lies on a western spur of the ragged, severely glaciated Sawtooth Ridge. Leaving the crest saddle, you may encounter lingering snow banks before you reach your first meadow. The meadows usually have posts through them to help PCT hikers keep on track. Nevertheless, some hikers may be led astray by old Oregon Skyline paths, and as the hiker approaches Tipsoo Peak, he may be confronted with two sets of posts. The correct set is along the upper (northern) tread, and along it you may still see the Cinnamon Butte Trail sign, even though that trail hasn't existed for years. About 50 yards past the abandoned trail, the two treads reunite and in about a minute you reach the high point—in elevation—of the Oregon-Washington PCT (7560–1.3). Tipsoo Peak, due north, is an easy 20-minute climb for peak baggers, and its summit views are second only to Thielsen's for providing an overview of this region.

On the lower south slopes of Tipsoo Peak just north of a broad saddle, the PCT becomes quite plain as it starts a descent northeast. About halfway to a saddle, the PCT bends north across an open gully, then hugs the forested lower slopes of Tipsoo Peak as it continues northeast to that saddle (7300–0.8). Here one can inspect the severely glaciated north face of red-black Tipsoo Peak.

From our saddle hikers used to zip northeast straight down to Maidu Lake, but the route has been changed so that now we make a long, counterclockwise traverse around a flat, volcanic summit. This traverse provides us with three scenic viewpoints that reveal Red Cone and Miller Lake, then the trail veers northwest across the county-line crest to a switchback. The trail then makes a long, winding, viewless descent to the west end of a broad saddle, on which we cross Maidu Lake Trail 3725A (6190–4.3).

Here the Maidu Lake Trail starts north, and it proceeds to cross the county-line saddle, then descends a gully to the south shore of shallow, semi-clear Maidu Lake. Most hikers will want to make the 0.9-mile trek down to this lake's relatively warm waters, for the next PCT campsite with near-water access is the sometimes over-

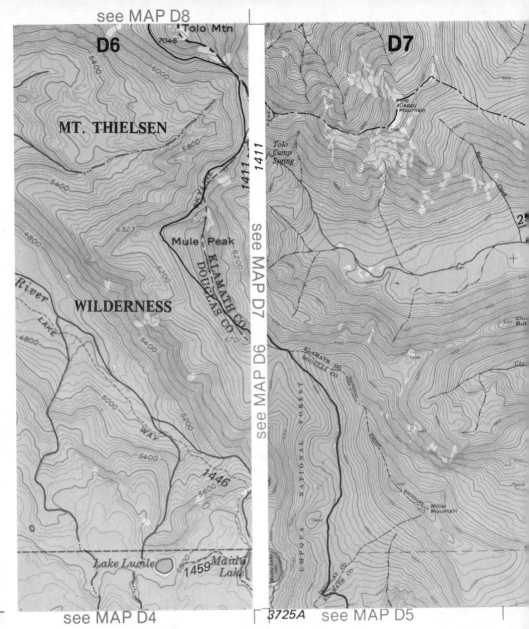

see MAP D8

D6

Tolo Mtn

MT. THIELSEN

Mule Peak

WILDERNESS

River

LAKE

WAY

1446

Lake Lucile

1459

Maidu Lake

see MAP D4

D7

Cappy Mountain

Tolo Camp Spring

KLAMATH CO
DOUGLAS CO

KLAMATH CO
DOUGLAS CO

UMPQUA NATIONAL FOREST

Miller Mountain

see MAP D7

see MAP D6

3725A   see MAP D5

crowded Tolo Camp, 6.2 miles farther. The lake's shore has abundant space for camping, though until early August a tent is necessary to provide refuge from the myriad of mosquitoes.

From the PCT's crossing of the Maidu Lake Trail, you can also start south on this trail, which winds 2.0 miles down to Miller Lake Trail 3725, which you can then follow 0.8 mile south over to the Digit Point Campground. Few hikers will want to make this longer excursion.

The PCT leaves the Maidu Lake Trail, quickly crosses that trail's former tread, and then climbs to a spur-ridge view of Miller Lake. After getting

several views of the lake, we cross the spur ridge and follow it north to a crossing of the main, county-line ridge (6490–1.3). Beyond it we climb gently up to an auxiliary saddle, then in an equal climb we top out at a junction from which the abandoned Oregon Skyline Trail once descended southwest to Maidu Lake. The PCT now contours for ¼ mile, then begins a gradually steepening descent to a crest saddle (6470–2.3).

We now climb up to the long Mule Peak crest, cross it, diagonal northwest down the peak's west slopes, and then diagonal northeast to a

D6, D5

D5, D7, D6

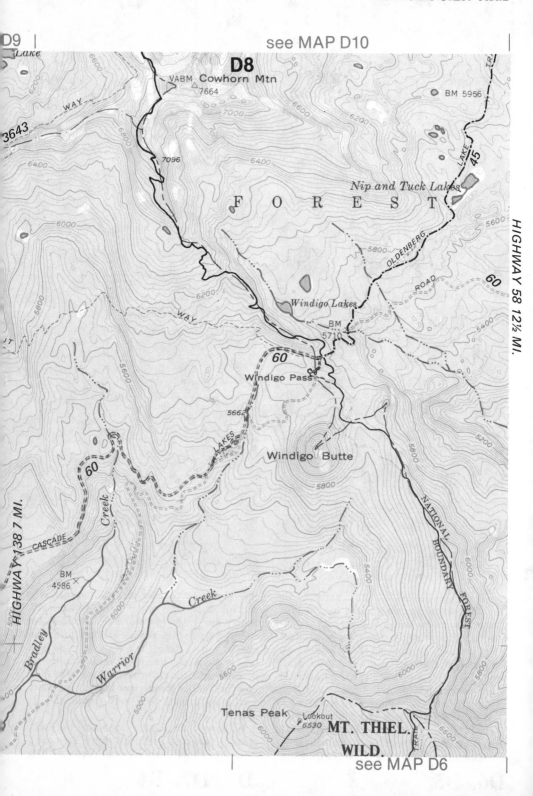

see MAP D10

D8

VABM Cowhorn Mtn
△ 7664

BM 5956

F O R E S T

Nip and Tuck Lakes

Windigo Lakes

BM
5710

60

Windigo Pass

5662

Windigo Butte

National Boundary Forest

see MAP D6

MT. THIEL.

WILD.

Tenas Peak   Lookout
                    6530

HIGHWAY 58 12½ MI.

HIGHWAY 138 7 MI.

CASCADE

BM
4586

Bradley

Warrior

Creek

Creek

LAKES

WAY

WAY

D9

3643

45

60

saddle (6300–1.9). Continuing our crest route, we descend to a second saddle, where lies Tolo Camp (6190–0.7), which has camping space for about six hikers. From the camp, Trail 1411 switchbacks eastward ⅓ mile down to a large spring that has no available camping space. From Tolo Camp there will be no reliable water until Summit Lake, 17.0 miles farther. However, near-trail water and campsites are found at several places north of Windigo Pass.

From the Tolo Camp saddle, we traverse over to another saddle (6235–0.6), then traverse across the south and west slopes of Tolo Mountain to Tenas Trail 1445 (6610–1.3), which starts west down a ridge to the old Cascade Lakes Road. Now outside Mt. Thielsen Wilderness, our trail turns east and descends to the ridgecrest, then follows it for over 2½ miles before swinging west across a broad, low saddle to the lower north slopes of a pyroclastic cone called Windigo Butte (6420). We now descend less than ¼ mile along its north spur, then curve northwest over to a junction with a spur trail (5845–3.7), which goes 250 yards west to a trailhead parking area immediately west of the old Cascade Lakes Road.

Starting north from the junction, our trail quickly drops into a gully, climbs over a low ridge and reaches the new Cascade Lakes Road 60 (5820–0.3) only 140 yards east of Windigo Pass. The old road, which starts by the trail's west side, takes you ¼ mile southwest to the Windigo Pass trailhead parking area, used by north- and south-bound hikers alike.

*   *   *   *

Many hikers still prefer to take the old Oregon Skyline Trail, which closely approaches Odell Lake and which certainly has more lakes at which you can camp. These lakes, of course, have mosquito problems, at least before August, so before then you can choose between mosquitoes on the OST or snow patches on the PCT. If you decide on the Oregon Skyline Trail, then hike northeast down the Cascade Lakes Road to a trailhead (5710–0.7), just 15 yards past a seasonal but obvious creek.

D6, D8

D8

Shallow arm between Nip and Tuck Lakes

12

17

D9

Crater
Butte
6845

16

15

14

Diamond
Rockpile

13

6345

6000

DIAMOND

5600

20

LANE CO
KLAMATH CO

21

22

PEAK

23

Corn

24

FAWN

LAKE

Snell Lake

WAY

WILDERNESS

28

5800

5600

26

Summit

E Ruth Lake

Alpine Lake
mlock Lake

OAD Reflection Lake

25

meda Lake

29

Emigrant
Pass
BM 6500

6010

Forest Camp

27

6500

D   E   S   C

M

700

Summit Lake

5553   SEPT 1956

Emigrant Butte

32

5565

33

34

35

36

6464 Lookout

6000

5600

NATIONAL   BDY

FOREST

5500

5

4

5650

3

2

1

FOREST

amp

8

9

5200

10

11

Windy

Opal Lake

WINDY

6000

5600

ette

4000

River

PASS

6400

4200

5000

Timpanogas
Lake

3643

5200

5400

Forest Camp

Amos

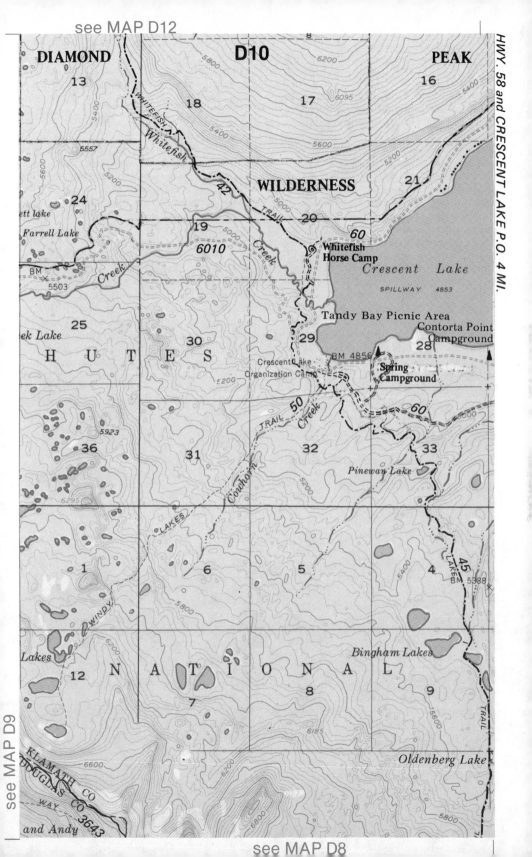

see MAP D12

DIAMOND

D10

PEAK

13

18

17

16

6095

WHITEFISH

5557

Whitefish

21

WILDERNESS

42

TRAIL

20

24

19

60

ett lake

Farrell Lake

6010

Creek

Whitefish
Horse Camp

BM
X
5503

Creek

Crescent   Lake

SPILLWAY 4853

Tandy Bay Picnic Area

25

ek Lake

30

29

BM 4856

Contorta Point
Campground

28

H   U   T   E   S

Crescent Lake
Organization Camp

Spring
Campground

5923

50

60

36

31

TRAIL

32

33

Pinewan Lake

Cowhorn

LAKES

1

6

5

4

45
BM 5388

WINDY

LAKES

Bingham Lakes

12

N   A   T   I   O   N   A   L

8

9

7

Oldenberg Lake

KLAMATH   CO

DOUGLAS   CO 3643

WAY

and Andy

see MAP D9

The trail's name has been changed to Oldenberg Lake Trail 45, and on it we start northeast up the OST, contour across gentle slopes of manzanita and sparse forest cover, then descend slightly to the Nip and Tuck Lakes spur trail (5715–1.7). This heads east-southeast for a level 200 yards to the two lakes, which are only one lake in early summer. The peninsula that juts between the two lobes makes an excellent campsite, and the warm, shallow lake water is very inviting. Our trail heads north-northwest and climbs gently at first, but then it makes a short, somewhat sunny, moderate-to-steep climb up to a ridge (5956–1.0), providing us with only one reward—a view south of Mt. Thielsen. The trail ahead is now downhill almost all the way to Crescent Lake.

We start moderately down and head north to the west shore of Oldenberg Lake (5475–1.3), then north past two of the Bingham Lakes to a junction (5450–1.1) with a west-northwest trail to the third. This third Bingham Lake, at the end of the hundred-yard spur trail, is the largest and perhaps the clearest of all the shallow lakes between Maidu Lake and Crescent Lake. Continuing north along our route, we pass through an "Oregon desert" of sparse lodge-poles, then descend gradually and cross a seasonal creek whose luxuriant green vegetation contrasts vividly with the surrounding sparsely needled lodgepoles. We round a low ridge and then reach the northeast end of murky, man-made Pinewan Lake (5180–2.0), which has a habit of drying up in late summer. Here, and for a short distance west, the trail follows the immigrant road built and used by the Elliot Wagon Train in October 1853.

We go about 100 yards before our trail forks right (northwest) from the road and winds ¼ mile down to a gully. Ahead, it wraps around a minor ridge, then descends ¼ mile to a junction with an abandoned trail (5010–0.7). Ahead, the old Oregon Skyline Trail once wove its way northwest down to an organization camp at Crescent Lake's southwest corner. Today, it goes but 80 yards northwest to a gully, then turns northeast, dying out before reaching close-by Road 60. If you'd walk ¼ mile west on that road, you'd reach Road 260, which descends ½ mile to Crescent Lake's Spring Campground.

From the junction we're now heading west on the Metolius-Windigo Horse Trail. It rapidly reaches the gully, curves around a minor ridge, and then weaves northwest down to a junction

D8, D10   D10

Diamond View Lake reflecting Diamond Peak

Asymmetrical Cowhorn Mountain, viewed from the southwest

(5030–0.9). Northeastward, a spur trail heads 150 yards over to Road 60, then continues just beyond it to a trailhead parking area for the Oldenberg Lake and Windy Lakes trails. Just ¼ mile southeast up Road 60 you'd find Spring Campground's Road 260. Westward, we go about 220 yards before meeting southwest-climbing Windy Lakes Trail 50. Anyone who abandons the high and dry PCT and descends about 4 miles down this trail will join us here.

Onward, our Metolius-Windigo Horse Trail almost touches Road 60 as it traverses from northwest to north over to Summit Lake Road 6010. We cross it, parallel it 100 yards north, walk 100 feet up the road, and then relocate trail tread. In ½ mile we wind down to the boggy environs of Whitefish Creek, then 200 yards past it reach Road 220 (4870–1.4) only 60 yards west of its junction with Road 60. We follow this road north through Whitefish Horse Camp and in ⅓ mile reach a campground loop. Immediately before it is a faucet, which for late-season hikers could be their last reliable water until Diamond View Lake, 5½ miles away. Branch left and locate the Whitefish Creek Trail 42 trailhead along the northwest part of the loop. From the loop's north part the Metolius-Windigo Horse Trail heads northeast.

We start northwest on Trail 42, enter Diamond Lake Wilderness in about ½ mile, and then climb rather gently to a fairly reliable tributary of Whitefish Creek (5080–1.6). The trail remains within hearing distance of White-fish Creek—when it's running—as we climb northwest, then north up to a flat and a linear pond at an intersection with Crater Butte Trail 44 (5770–3.1), four miles due east of Diamond Peak (8744).

From the junction our trail heads north past several shallow, somewhat stagnant ponds before arriving at large but shallow Diamond View Lake (5780–0.7). Photographs are best when the peak is snow-clad, which, unfortunately, is when the lake is mosquito-clad. We pass campsites, then leave the lake behind as we make tracks north through swampy lodgepole flatlands to the headwaters of Trapper Creek. This creek remains unseen and unheard for two miles until the trail reaches slopes above the creek where it cascades north down toward a marsh. In the third mile, the trail reaches the creek and more or less follows it to the marsh, then goes east through a shady mountain-hemlock forest. In order to avoid the creekside's wet ground, the trail generally stays on the lower slopes just south of the creek. We follow the creek as it meanders east past tempting campsites, then cascades northeast down past a small breached dam. Almost immediately after sighting this concrete structure, we reach a trail junction (4870–4.9–21.1), where an access trail continues northeast, but our trail turns north.

The access trail descends 240 yards to the Southern Pacific railroad tracks and crosses them 20 yards west-northwest of a huge, steel overhead signal. Head east across the tracks and

D10   **D12, D13**

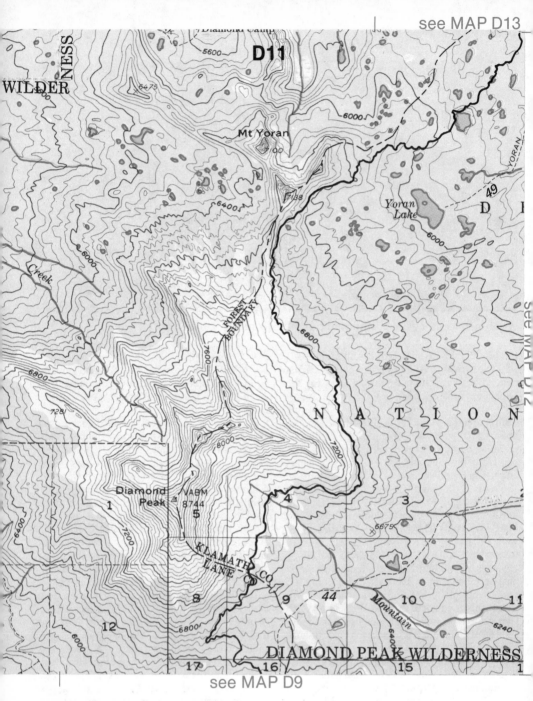

see MAP D9

under the overhead signal to a dirt road that descends 150 yards to Road 5810 along the west shore of Odell Lake (4788). This lake was named for William Holden Odell who, with B. J. Pengra, surveyed the military wagon road up the Middle Fork of the Willamette in 1865. On July 26th Odell climbed a butte and discovered this lake; both butte and lake now bear his name. If you walk ¼ mile northwest on Road 5810, you'll reach the entrance to Trapper Creek Campground. If you walk 250 yards southeast on it, you'll reach the Shelter Cove Resort, which has a small store and, more important, the Cascade Summit Post Office. The store's selection is

D13   **D13**

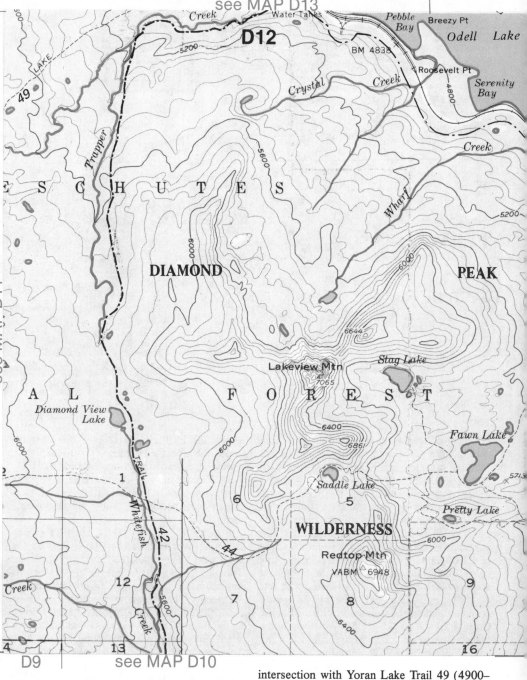

D12

Creek Water Tanks

5200

Pebble Bay Breezy Pt

Odell Lake

BM 4838

Crystal *Creek* Roosevelt Pt

Serenity Bay

49

Trapper

5600

5600

4800

Creek

5200

D E S C H U T E S

Wharf

DIAMOND

6000

6000

PEAK

6644

Lakeview Mtn
7065

Stag Lake

A L

F O R E S T

Diamond View
Lake

6400

Fawn Lake

6000

6000

6861

5713

1

Saddle Lake

5

Pretty Lake

Whitefish

6

WILDERNESS

6000

42

Redtop Mtn

44

VABM △ 6948

9

12

7

8

5600

Creek

Creek

6400

4

13

16

quite limited, so be sure to mail sufficient food and supplies.

After backtracking to the Trail 42 junction (mile 21.1), we curve west 150 yards down to a bridge that crosses Trapper Creek only 35 yards below the breached dam. Leaving this creek behind, we contour the slopes and reach an intersection with Yoran Lake Trail 49 (4900–0.5). This trail goes northeast moderately to steeply 250 yards down to the railroad tracks, from which you follow a dirt road 70 yards to Road 5810. You can follow this road a quarter mile east to the Trapper Creek Campground, then 0.4 mile farther to the Shelter Cove Resort.

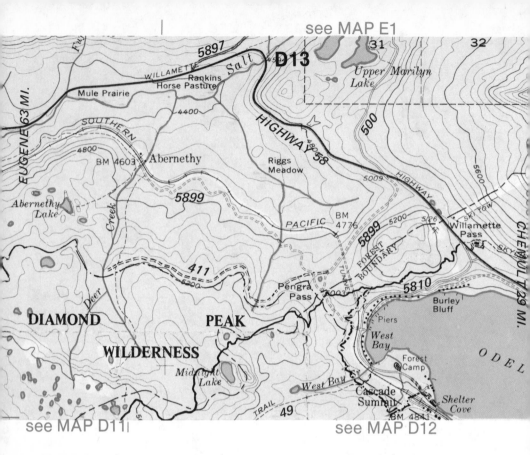

see MAP D11

see MAP D12

North of the trail intersection, our trail parallels the railroad tracks below and passes seasonal creeklets before reaching a spur road (4850–0.7), which climbs northwest 0.4 mile to Pengra Pass. We start along this road from a point 70 yards west of the tracks and follow it up 80 yards around a bend to a resumption of the trail, which branches right and ascends 130 yards northwest to a small creek under the shade of a Douglas-fir forest. Here we find shooting stars, bluebells, bunchberries and Oregon grapes, which are typically associated with this type of forest. Our trail now climbs gently northeast and reaches a junction with the Pacific Crest Trail (5040–0.5–22.8). We now follow that trail eastward 1.1 miles to Section D's end near Highway 58's Willamette Pass.

*   *   *   *

From Windigo Pass on the Cascade Lakes Road, the Pacific Crest Trail begins a 7-mile-longer route to Willamette Pass. It climbs ½ mile, to a crest crossing, from which you could head due north ¼ mile, staying east of the crest as you descend to the southwestern Windigo Lake, about 130 feet below you. Avoiding

water, the PCT closely follows the crest for about one mile, then climbs 400 vertical feet on a winding course to a minor crest saddle (6620–2.3). From here you can traverse 200 yards northwest across relatively flat terrain to a lakelet with acceptable water and a possible campsite.

Beyond the unseen lakelet, the PCT climbs the crest over to a saddle (7100–1.6) by the southwest ridge of pointed Cowhorn Mountain. The short, rewarding climb to the top of this miniature Mt. Thielsen is an obvious though steep one. The trail now descends northwest along the crest, eventually switchbacking down to the edge of a forested bowl that contains a small, somewhat stagnant pond (6380–3.1). This, unfortunately, is the only *permanent* trailside water between Summit Lake, 3.8 miles ahead, and Thielsen Creek, 29 miles behind! It's too bad that PCT hikers must go out of their way to get water or to camp. This relatively new section of the PCT could have easily been routed past springs, creeks and lakes. From the stagnant pond you can head cross-country over the low crest and drop ¼ to ½ mile into the Windy Lakes basin for water and a campsite.

D13, D8

D8, D10, D9

About ½ mile beyond the pond, we start a diagonal descent across a considerable escarpment and soon reach an amorphous terrain on which we cross an imperceptible crest. A little over 3 miles of viewless meandering bring us close to Summit Lake's south shore (5560–4.1), and a short traverse west brings us to Road 700 (5570–0.2), at the lake's southwest corner. This we cross three times as we follow the PCT north along it to a crossing of Road 6010 (5590–1.4). From here you can head 200 yards over to Summit Lake Campground, above the lake's northwest corner. This lake is a good one for a layover day, for, like *large* Cascade Range lakes, it has clear water and relatively few mosquitoes.

From Road 6010 our trail starts northeast, and we enter Diamond Peak Wilderness as we wind northwest past a series of seven ponds and lakelets shown on the map and even more smaller, unmapped ones. After leaving the west shore of the last mapped one (5670–1.1), our trail winds north up a relatively dry stretch to a slope above the south shore of one of the few accessible lakes we'll see (5860–0.9), near which adequate camps can be established. The trail curves down to the lake's east shore, then, in ⅓ mile, crosses a "spring" from an unseen pond only 30 yards from the trail. Continuing north, we wind up to a forested flat across which the Fawn Lake Trail once traversed. Beyond it, we climb north, then northwest easily up to a switchback (6560–2.8), from which we get one of several forthcoming views of stunning, steep-sided Mt. Thielsen. The trail northeast climbs gently-to-moderately across the imperceptible Lane/Klamath county line and levels off in a severely glaciated bowl just east of Diamond Peak. Hikers wishing to climb this peak can scramble west from here up Class 2 rubble slopes.

Leaving the bowl, we traverse east and catch a view in the south of Crater Lake's rim framed between Mt. Thielsen (9182) on the left and Mt. Bailey (8363) on the right. Closer to us, in the southeast, is large Crescent Lake. We round the curving, northeast ridge of Diamond Peak and soon exchange southern views for northern ones. In open breaks in the mountain-hemlock forest, one may see—if weather permits—South Sister (10,358), Middle Sister (10,047), Mt. Washington (7794) and very distant Mt. Jefferson (10,497). Closer by stand two imposing monoliths, Mt. Yoran (7100) and Peak 7138, the latter of which we'll traverse beneath. Before

that northeast traverse, however, our winding course makes a broad arc northward, passing by some reliable creeklets then by tiny tarns before commencing a steady descent past Peak 7138.

Leaving the ridge slopes behind, we descend to lake-and-pond-dotted slopes and arrive above the north shore (6030–7.2) of a green, unnamed lake, near which you could camp. All the lakes and ponds between it and the Rosary Lakes, north of State Highway 58, are less attractive. Not too far beyond it, we see an even larger lake, east of us, through the trees, and the trail descends to within about 100 feet of its northwest corner (5840–0.6). Lack of adequate level ground makes camping at this corner of the lake undesirable, but more-distant shores offer better potential. (Remember that in wilderness areas your camp must be at least 100 feet from the shore.)

Beyond this lake, we descend for 1¼ miles past shallow, mosquito-infested ponds before angling southeast and descending to a broad flat of silver fir, mountain hemlock and western white pine. A bend northward takes us up to a low saddle from which we descend to within 70 yards (5370–2.5) of fairly well hidden Midnight Lake, which has only a poor camping potential. You may wish to stop for water here or at a nearby pond ¼ mile farther along the route. Beyond both bodies of water we cross a saddle, then steadily descend to a closed road at Pengra Pass (5003–1.5), just 80 yards southeast of its junction with Road 5899.

To get food or mailed packages at Shelter Cove Resort (mentioned in the alternate route), follow this road ½ mile southeast, down to Road 5810, then follow it southeast one mile over to the resort. To return to the PCT, either backtrack or else follow the last part of the alternate route—a maintained section of the defunct Oregon Skyline Trail.

At Pengra Pass we leave the wilderness, and then contour east to a junction with the old Oregon Skyline Trail (5040–0.5), at which the alternate route ends. Here you'll also find an old trail that descends steeply south ¼ mile to Road 5810. The PCT now climbs a short ⅓ mile to a small bluff that provides the hiker with the only good view of Odell Lake he'll get along the route. Our trail climbs a few yards beyond the viewpoint, then contours over to a pond, on our right, past which the trail makes a short, switchbacking descent to Highway 58 (5090–1.1), which you reach ¼ mile southeast of Willamette Pass.

D9, D11   **D11, D13**

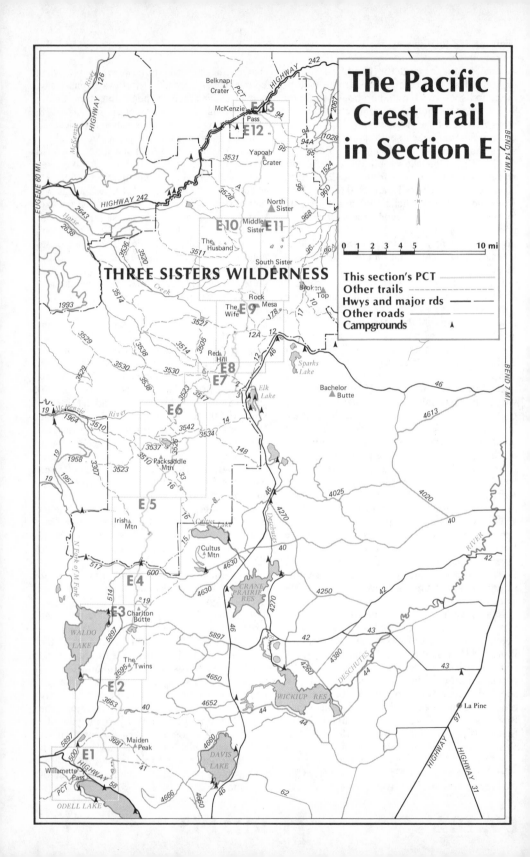

FREE CATALOG

Fill out and mail this card to receive a
free catalog of all Wilderness Press publications.

Our catalog includes:

- books for hikers, backpackers, climbers, skiers,
  bicyclists and other outdoor enthusiasts

- a wide selection of hiking guides to the Western
  states and the Hawaiian Islands

- maps of popular hiking areas in California

- beautiful hardback editions for gifts and personal
  collections

name _____

address _____

city_____ state_____ zip_____

*Please allow 5-6 weeks for delivery. If you need
the catalog sooner, call us and we'll mail 1st class.*
(415) 843-8080

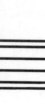

BUSINESS REPLY MAIL

FIRST CLASS   PERMIT NO. 3388   BERKELEY, CA

POSTAGE WILL BE PAID BY ADDRESSEE

WILDERNESS PRESS
2440 BANCROFT WAY
BERKELEY, CA 94704-9885

Section E: Highway 58 near Willamette Pass to Highway 242 at McKenzie Pass

Introduction: In Section E the Pacific Crest Trail traverses across three types of terrain. The first third of this section's PCT traverses across slopes that are deficient in both views and lakes. On the middle third, which starts at Irish Lake, the trail traverses flatter land that is still generally viewless, but is peppered with very enjoyable lakes (once the mosquito population dwindles). On the northern third, the trail skirts around the Three Sisters, and views abound of glacier-draped peaks and spreading, sinister lava flows. Like Section C's Sky Lakes Wilderness, this section's Three Sisters Wilderness, which dominates most of the section, is flooded with weekend hikers. And for good reason—it is very scenic and readily accessible.

Declination: 18¼°E

Mileages:

	South to North	Distances between Points	North to South
Highway 58 near Willamette Pass	0.0		75.7
		2.2	
Lower Rosary Lake	2.2		73.5
		7.0	
Moore Creek Trail to Bobby Lake	9.2		66.5
		7.6	
Charlton Lake Trail	16.8		58.9
		5.6	
Road 600 at Irish Lake	22.4		53.3
		13.4	
Cliff Lake Trail	35.8		39.9
		8.9	
Island Meadow Trail to Elk Lake	44.7		31.0
		5.7	
Camelot Lake	50.4		25.3
		4.4	
North fork of Mesa Creek	54.8		20.9
		10.3	
Glacier Way Trail	65.1		10.6
		3.1	
Minnie Scott Spring	68.2		7.5
		3.4	
South Matthieu Lake	71.6		4.1
		2.7	
Trail to Lava Camp Lake	74.3		1.4
		1.4	
Highway 242 at McKenzie Pass	75.7		0.0

Supplies: No on-route supplies are available, but you can make a 1¼-mile detour over to Elk Lake Lodge, which serves dinners and sells a few goods. Also, there are no nearby post offices, so you just use the one at Shelter Cove Resort in Section D and the Olallie Lake Guard Station in Section F.

Problems: Long-distance PCT hikers seem to agree that the trail's worst concentrations of mosquitos are found either in Sky Lakes Wilderness in Section C or in the lake-and-pond dotted south half of Three Sisters Wilderness. Therefore, bring a tent and plenty of mosquito repellent if you are hiking through this section before August.

The Pacific Crest Trail in Section E begins from Highway 58 about ¼ mile southeast of Willamette Pass and just yards away from a road that peels south-southeast down toward Odell Lake. To reach this highway's PCT trailhead parking lot, go down the highway 200 yards from the PCT to a short Highway Commission road that branches north. This road is about 200 yards northwest of a second road that branches down toward Odell Lake (the two Odell Lake roads quickly unite to become Road 5810). After starting north on the Highway Commission road, you immediately take a short road 150 yards east to the trailhead parking lot. From it, a short trail goes 80 yards north to the PCT.

Starting our hike from Highway 58 (5090), we follow the PCT as it curves east behind the Highway Commission's long cinder-storage building, and then we meet the trailhead-parking spur trail (5130–0.2) immediately past it.

Our trail now climbs steadily east through a forest of Douglas-fir, western white pine and mountain hemlock to a saddle, then curves north and passes a hundred-foot-high rock jumble before reaching the ridge above South Rosary Lake (5730–2.0). This clear lake is deep in early summer, and in this it contrasts strongly with the other lakes its size we've seen so far along our entire route. By late summer, however, the lake level can fall more than twenty feet, due to seepage through the porous volcanic rocks, and leave its eastward drainage channel high and dry. We quickly encounter a very good ridgetop campsite, then curve northward, cross the lake's outlet, and reach an equally good campsite. Now we climb northwest to a campsite near the southwest corner of deep, blue-green Middle Rosary Lake (5830–0.6), which is even more impressive than the south lake because it lies at the base of 400-foot-high Rosary rock. On a weekend, you're likely to see climbers scaling this rock. We walk alongside the lake, then pass by the low dividing ridge between the middle and north lakes, on which is an excellent campsite. We reach shallower North Rosary Lake (5830–0.3), then follow the trail as it climbs west above the lake's north shore before switchbacking east-northeast up to a junction with Maiden Lake Trail 41 (6060–0.6), which descends east-southeast before contouring east toward that lake.

We continue east for 130 yards, then switchback west up to a saddle (6170–0.5), but not before getting one last glance back at Rosary rock and the Rosary lakes, and in the distance,

South (Lower) Rosary Lake

Odell Lake, Odell Butte and Crescent Lake—all lakes owing their existence to glacial excavation. Now we enter the Willamette National Forest and descend steeply to a cove, which we follow north along the east side of a gully. Soon we step across trickling Skyline Creek and reach a meadow with an old horse-camp known as T-M-R Camp (5920–0.4). Continuing down at a lesser gradient, we twice cross the now-bubbling creek, then pass by Douglas Horse Pasture (5520–1.0) east of the creek. We soon reach Bark Table Camp (5480–0.3), then meet Skyline Creek (5460–0.1) and cross it for the last time. After climbing a few yards to a divide, we start down a gully, then parallel unseen Skyline Creek a short way before curving north to Waithere Camp at an intersection with Maiden Peak Trail 3681 (5300–0.5). This trail ascends from the southwest, crosses our trail, then climbs east toward the peak.

We head northeast on the PCT, reach a sign that identifies Mt. Ray (7002) to the northwest, then contour northeast before curving north across wet meadows up to a junction with Bobby Lake Trail 3663 (5440–2.5), which strikes northwest. We turn right (northeast) and start up the trail as it curves quickly up to a triangular

E1   **E1, E2**

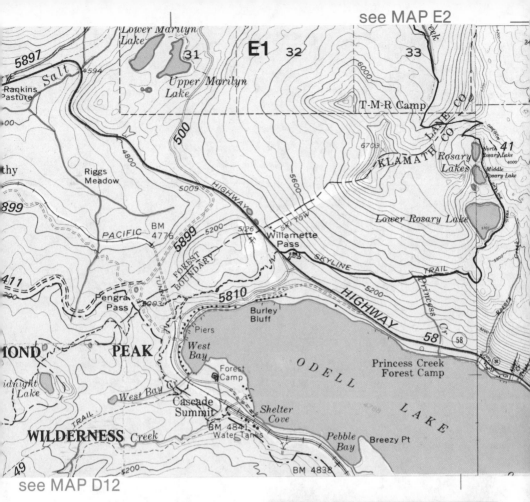

see MAP D12

junction where two forks of the Moore Creek Trail 40 (5470–0.2) branch off from the PCT and merge just east of it. It's best for us now to head east ¼ mile down this trail to a nice campsite at the west end of large, clear Bobby Lake (5408), for our next reliable source of water will be Charlton Lake, about 7⅔ miles farther. It seems ironic that as we progress north into ever thicker, wetter forests, our water sources become spaced farther apart. We had expected drought over the miles of pumice-covered lands around Crater Lake and Mt. Thielsen, but we find it frustrating to be in a dense forest during a drizzling rain and yet have to hike miles to obtain running water to drink. In such areas, ground water percolating through the volcanic-rock structures certainly is the major form of water transport.

Back on the PCT, we now head north past two large ponds, climb northwest to a saddle (5980–1.4), curve northeast gently down from it, and then climb to an intersection with Twin Peaks Trail 3595 (6220–1.3). A viewpoint is supposed

Skyline Creek

E2, E3

see MAP E3

see MAP E1

to be 50 yards southwest down this trail. It isn't. Don't fret, for about a mile north from this junction you can walk 70 yards west across rock slabs and obtain an unobstructed view westward, from Diamond Peak north to Waldo Lake.

After this side trip, the trail shortly starts a gentle descent and begins to cross gullies one after another. You eventually pass above a small pond, then quickly reach a cluster of three ponds (6320–2.4) grouped around the small knob identified on the map as 6362. The route now descends northeast across gullies, reaches the watershed divide by a small pond, then de-

scends west a short distance before curving north toward gentler slopes above Charlton Lake (5692). We head north through a forested flat area, reach the slopes above the lake, and descend to an intersection with Charlton Lake Trail 3570 (5725–2.5), about a hundred yards north of a small pond. The lakeshore is 100 yards southeast; Road **5897** is 150 yards northwest, just beyond a pond. By heading northeast for 0.1 mile, we reach a closed spur road heading southeast to the lake from Road 5897. Then we diagonal north across the road to a broad trail that we follow north about 45 yards to where it

E3

E3

see MAP E2

bends northwest 40 yards to a roadside parking area. From this bend the PCT follows old blazes east-northeast and climbs gently up the divide to a diagonal crossing of Road 5897 (5840–0.6) at a 20° bearing.

Our trail starts north, climbs northwest to the low watershed divide, and then contours north past small ponds and Charlton Butte to a junc-

tion on the right (east) with Lily Lake Trail 19 (5965–1.4), which descends about ¾ mile to that isolated lake. Continuing north, we keep following the divide down a north slope to a small flat, then climb over two low mounds before reaching the southwest arm of shallow Taylor Lake (5550–3.3). Our trail immediately angles away from the lake, heads north past a

E3

E3, E4, E5

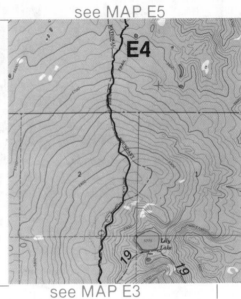

see MAP E5

E4

see MAP E3

Charlton Lake and Gerdine Butte

pond on the left (west), then reaches Road 600 at Irish Lake (5549–0.3). Popular Irish Lake Campground is ¼ mile east on the road.

We can pick up the trail again by going west 25 yards on the road, then north 50 yards along a spur road that takes us to the trailhead. We enter Three Sisters Wilderness as our route heads north above the west shore of Irish Lake then passes west of shallow but clear Riffle Lake (5575–0.8), which has an adequate campsite on its west shore. We now climb a low ridge and descend slightly to a flat with two large lily-pad ponds before climbing up to a higher ridge

(5730–1.2). The lakes and ponds of this area are shallow, and, like those in the Sky Lakes region, they support a superabundant mosquito population from late spring through mid-July.

We pass a number of stagnant ponds and small lakes in rapid succession as we descend to a nice campsite on the east shore of Brahma Lake (5657–0.6), which is distinguished by a forested island. Our route continues north along its shore, contours west, and then climbs moderately up slopes and through a miniature gorge before reaching the northeast corner of clear Jezebel Lake (5855–1.1). A campsite is perched

E5

E5

Riffle Lake

on the low ridge north of this corner. Climbing northwest above the lake, we reach a shady glen, from which a trail once climbed ¼ mile west-southwest to Rock Rim Lake. Our trail rounds a linear ridge descending east, climbs west along its north slope, then angles north to a good campsite beside the outlet of Stormy Lake

(6045–1.0). The towering cliffs of Irish Mountain over a lakeside evening campfire leaves us with a vivid memory of this choice spot.

Leaving this lake behind, we descend to smaller, slightly cloudy Blaze Lake (5950–0.3), then contour northward past an abundance of ponds before the trail descends a ridge to a low

E5

E5, E6

see MAP E6

see MAP E4

E6

Irish Mountain above Stormy Lake

divide just east of open Cougar Flat (5750–2.1). Our route winds down to Lake 5678, then passes smaller water bodies as it follows the ridge northeast down to Tadpole Lake (5340–2.0), perched on a forested saddle, where you may surprise some feeding ring-necked ducks. We traverse the lake's grassy north shore, then descend north to a grassy pond and a junction with the Elk Creek (#3510) and Winopee Lake (#16) trails (5250–0.4). The Elk Creek Trail climbs northwest over a low saddle and descends into the Elk Creek drainage; the Winopee Lake Trail curves south around a knoll before descending to Winopee Lake.

We continue northeast across the lower slopes of Packsaddle Mountain (6144), walk north past a polluted lake to the east, and arrive at a junction with Snowshoe Lake Trail 33 (5250–1.2), which descends east. Now we hike north past Desane Lake and enter the Willamette National Forest again as we cross a flat divide and descend into the Mink Lake Basin, where we meet a junction with Mink Lake Loop Trail 3526 (5160–0.4). This 2.7 mile loop climbs northwest up a low, broad ridge before descending north to Mink Lake, stocked with eastern brook and rainbow trout. From there, the loop winds east, dropping to Porky Lake with more eastern brook, then climbs back to the PCT at the Cliff Lake outlet creek.

Our route follows a string of sparkling lakes that make an appropriate necklace for South Sister. In rapid succession we encounter S Lake (5150), Mac Lake (5100) with rainbow, Merrill Lake (5080) and Horseshoe Lake (5039), a very shallow lake with both rainbow and eastern brook. The trail curves around to the north shore of this lake, then reaches a spur trail (5040–1.5) that bears 0.1 mile north to Moody Lake (5020). We cross the usually dry outlet of Horseshoe Lake, then continue north gently up and around a band of cliffs to a reunion with Mink Lake Loop Trail 3526 (5130–0.8) beside the Cliff Lake outlet creek.

Just 130 yards southeast up a spur trail beside this creek is deep, green, rock-and-alder lined Cliff Lake (5138). The web of trails and the abundance of campsites attest to the popularity

E6   E6

A bedrock peninsula cuts deep into Dumbbell Lake

of this lake. The best campsites are atop the cliff along the lake's northwest shore, but should you be caught in foul weather, you can camp in comfort in the Cliff Lake shelter. Good eastern-brook-trout fishing justifies a stop at this lake, as do good diving rocks near large aspens along the northeast shore. Backtracking from these, we pass beargrass blooming between boulders, and, near the shelter, we avoid stepping on delicate bunchberries and shooting stars that grow on the moist, shady forest floor.

Back at the loop-trail junction, we cross Cliff Lake's outlet creek, walk northwest, then round a pile of large boulders and climb gently to a seasonal creek (5225–0.8). We cross it, hike up a switchback, and then work up northeast to a junction with the Goose Rock (#3542) and Senoj Lake (#3534) trails (5330–0.6). The Goose Rock Trail starts northwest down toward a meadow, then heads west and down to Goose Lake; the 5.6-mile Senoj Lake Trail starts southeast to an unnamed lake, heads east to the divide, then continues as Trail 14 east down to Cascade Lakes Highway 46.

We start north, quickly descend to Reserve Meadow, and head northeast along its edge before curving northwest away from its large, east-end campsite (5320–0.4). We then climb up to relatively deep Island Lake (5438–0.5), which has a patch of grass in its center. From this lake we climb up the trail to a rockpile, contour west past two stagnant ponds, and then hike north until we are just above a 50-yard-long peninsula that juts southwest into Dumbbell Lake (5502–0.7). From this rocky spur you can fish or dive in the lake's warm, clear waters. Our trail now gradually climbs north past many ponds to a low divide (5660–2.2), then descends to a junction with the old Oregon Skyline Trail (5460–0.5), which heads 6.3 miles to Camelot Lake via popular Horse Lake.

From this junction 1½ miles south of Horse Lake, the Pacific Crest Trail branches east. After a few minutes' hiking, we reach an obvious spring seeping from the ground only 10 yards downslope from the trail. This is a good place to obtain water, for the route beyond may be dry until Camelot Lake, 8.8 miles farther. Continuing east, we descend toward Island Meadow, but stay within the forest's edge as we hike southeast along its southern border. We soon reach a bridge across a small, seasoned creek and find a fair trailside campsite above its east bank, 70 yards south of the meadow. Our trail

E6   E6, E7

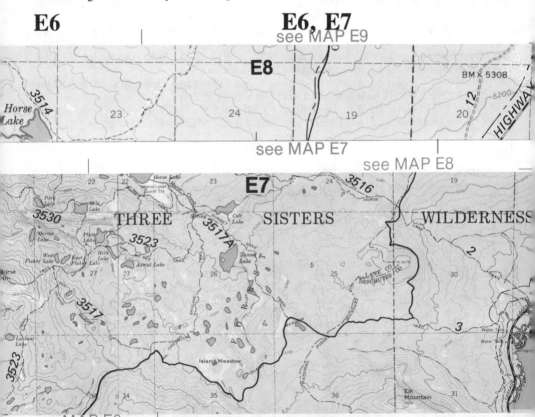

strikes southeast again, but shortly turns and follows a wandering route northeast before descending north to a mile-high meadow across which we traverse north-northeast to a junction with Sunset Lake Trail 3517A (5235–1.9), which passes that lake midway in its descent to the OST. We now go east-southeast on our trail, enter forest and pass a large pond 50 yards south, then snake east over an undetected drainage divide before descending to a junction where the PCT leaves Island Meadow Trail 3/3517 (5250–1.3) and angles north.

The Island Meadow Trail makes a southeast descent 0.9 mile to a trailhead parking area, from which a road descends 270 yards to Cascade Lakes Highway 46. On this you can head south 70 yards to the Elk Lake Lodge entrance. Down at the lakeside lodge, you can obtain dinners plus limited supplies. If you visit the lodge by early July, you'll likely see barn swallows nesting in the rafters above its entrance. Large, 57-foot-deep Elk Lake (4884) offers very good trout fishing and is a nice place for a layover day. Although the lake has no outlet and no permanent inlets, its water stays quite clear because fresh groundwater continues to seep into the lake at about the same rate

that groundwater leaves it. Rather than backtrack up the Island Meadows Trail, you can head north on the road 0.2 mile past its trailhead and start up Horse Lake Trail 2 which takes you 1.6 miles northwest up to the PCT.

Back where the PCT leaves the Island Meadow Trail, the PCT climbs north toward a cinder cone (5676), rounds its eastern half, then heads north to a lesser summit before reaching an intersection on a saddle with Horse Lake Trail 2/3516 (5300–1.3). Following the divide, our trail climbs gently north at first, but steepens as it curves over to the western slope of Koosah Mountain (6520). Here we make a long switchback up to the ridge, then contour to its east slope, where, by stepping a few yards east, we can absorb an eastern panorama from Elk and Hosmer lakes north past conical Bachelor Butte (9065) and deeply glaciated Broken Top (9175) to South Sister (10,358). Although we can't see the Cascade Lakes Highway below, we can hear the rumble of the logging trucks on it.

Hiking northwest, we encounter switchbacks down the north slope, then reach a flat and continue north to a junction at the south shore of placid, shallow Camelot Lake (5995–4.4). Here the OST route heads southwest along the Red

E7

South Sister, from Koosah Mountain (left) and from Wickiup Plain (right)

Hill Trail. The PCT starts northeast, and we follow it to Sisters Mirror Lake (5995–0.2), which in the tranquil morning and evening air is a photographer's delight. The reflected view of South Sister won't last forever, for lodgepoles are invading the open flat, and this lake, stocked with eastern brook trout, is gradually being choked with vegetation. In the meantime, you and the nesting spotted sandpipers can enjoy the lake's serenity. Here, your best "nest" is on top of the rocky bluff along the northwest shore.

Our trail soon leaves the lake and heads due east to a junction with Mirror Lake Trail 20 (5990–0.3), which descends southeast 3.5 miles to the Cascade Lakes Highway. We start on a level hike east-northeast, but quickly begin a short, moderate climb up this Trail 12A segment to a junction with Nash Lake Trail 3527 (6010–0.1), which ascends gently from the west. We hike east up through a forest of lodgepole, with its trailside red heather, then descend to a meadow containing cinquefoil flowers, where our trail, which was once a road, turns northeast toward a gully that has a 50-foot-high lava flow above its east slope. We start up this gully and reach a point where Wickiup Plain Trail 12A (6080–0.7) forks east across the gully and then turns south. A stretch of PCT, from Sisters Mirror Lake to this junction, is due to be replaced by a different stretch in 1986 or '87. We

E9   E9

see MAP E10   see MAP E11

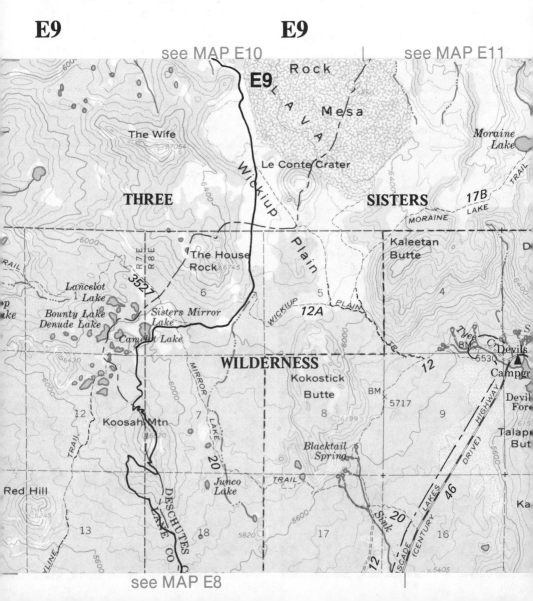

Rock Mesa and Elk Lake, viewed from south slopes of South Sister

continue north on the jeep tracks, pass The House Rock (6745) on our left (west), and reach the partly forested Wickiup Plain.

As we approach Le Conte Crater—a low cinder cone to the northeast—we begin to picture a sequence of events that molded this volcanic landscape. The thick stand of mountain hemlock on the northern half of Le Conte Crater indicates that this cone is at least several thousand years old. An educated guess, based upon comparisons with cones of known ages, is that an eruption took place 6000 to 8000 years ago and built up the cinder cone. Immediately following this eruption came outpourings of fluid, basaltic lava that breached the cone's south rim and flowed south down the gently sloping Wickiup Plain. We see this flow today as the forested, undulating surface south of the cone and off to our right (east). The section of Wickiup Plain over which the trail passes is probably no more than 20,000 years old, for it shows little sign of erosion. We can be quite sure its age is greater than 10,000 years, since it was in existence when the last great Pleistocene glaciers marched down from South Sister and deposited their debris on its eastern side; a conspicuous moraine ends on top of the plain roughly 1½ miles due east of the cone.

Due west from the crater's north base, we meet a trail (6160–1.1) that goes 1.5 miles southeast to the Wickiup Plain Trail. This then goes 1.7 miles to its trailhead on Tyee Creek, which is 0.3 mile west of the Cascade Lakes Highway. This route, starting near Devils Lake Campground, is the fastest way in to the South Sister vicinity.

Just north of Le Conte Crater we see a vast, desolate, steep-sided chaotic jumble appropriately called Rock Mesa. The high point near its east side marks the location of the vent from which dacite lava was extruded 2000 years ago. Because the dacite lava was so viscous, the flow not only solidified before reaching Le Conte Crater but it also solidified halfway down the relatively steep slopes of the Mesa Creek drainage just north of us. It did succeed, however, in covering up any trace of conduit that might have given rise to the older flows of Wickiup Plain.

By now you've probably noticed The Wife (7054)—a conspicuous summit off to the west—and you've probably observed that South Sister (10,358) is a redhead. Should you wish to climb to its summit, strike east from a point just south of Le Conte Crater, then head northeast along the east margin of Rock Mesa. When you reach the peak's lower slope, climb north directly up it and pass between the Clark and Lewis glaciers as you near the summit cone. When you top its rim, you'll find it crowned with a snow-clad lake (10,200) that occupies a crater which may have been active in the last few thousand years. South Sister, with at least three major periods of eruptions, is a geologically complex volcano; its slopes contain over two dozen types of volcanic rocks. This sister is the

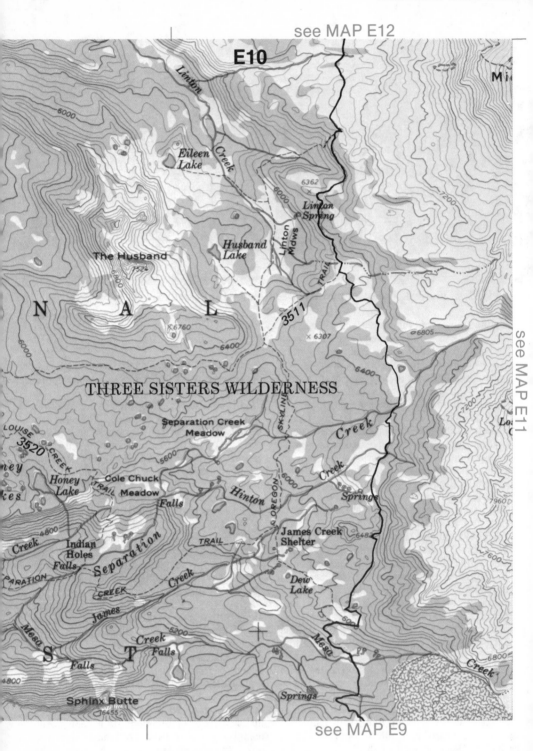

see MAP E12

E10

see MAP E11

see MAP E9

see MAP E12

E11

see MAP E10

THREE SISTERS WILDERNESS

see MAP E9

youngest of the three, and it still retains much of its symmetry because it has been exposed only to late-Pleistocene and Recent glaciation. The latest eruption in the Three Sisters area occurred within the last 200 years.

By the time you finish reading the above discussions, you could have been well on your way to the north end of Wickiup Plain. The posts along the route seem unnecessary since the route is so obvious. Newberry knotweed and scattered grass attest to the dryness of the pumice soil, but plentiful gopher mounds indicate that at least one mammal thrives here. At the north edge of the plain, the trail curves northwest over a low saddle, then descends to a creek (6010–1.2) which passes through a large meadow. In early July this meadow is a continuous field of yellow cinquefoil that contrasts sharply with the wintry chill of deep snow patches on the surrounding forested slopes. We regretfully leave this island of sunshine behind and press onward northwest into the forest and down alongside a small gully. Our trail makes a switchback east and leads us down to the south fork of Mesa Creek. Now we step across it, hike north into a large, grassy meadow, and then reach the north fork of Mesa Creek (5700–0.8). You'll find near-creek campsites both east and west of the meadow. Past the north fork you reach a tributary in 100 yards—a scenic lunch spot.

Leaving the meadow and its sparkling creeks behind, we turn our backs on the frozen "tidal wave" of Rock Mesa and climb northwest up to a junction with the James Creek Trail (5920–0.6), which makes a gentle ascent west before curving north along the old OST route. We ascend east, curve north, and then round a murky lakelet just east of us. Continuing to climb north, our route tends to follow the break in slope between the foot of South Sister, to the east, and the Separation Creek headquarters, to the west. Along our course we pass through numerous small meadows and beside a fine, six-foot-diameter mountain hemlock before we descend slightly to a crossing of Hinton Creek (6320–2.1). After hiking to the other side of a low divide, we descend past a cliff of a high-density, parallel-fractured, shalelike flow. Here we cross Separation Creek (6400–0.5), whose flow, like that of Hinton Creek, has usually sunk beneath the pumice by mid-August.

E11, E9, E10

E12

We now come face-to-face with Middle Sister (10,047), which can be easily climbed up its south or west slope. Continuing north, we follow posts and rock piles across a pumice flat and reach a shallow, clear lakelet (6460–0.4), beside which good campsites can be found. The fragile timberline ecosystem here is very sensitive to human impact, so treat it gently. Beyond, we tread across level bedrock that has a previous glacier's signature etched upon it in the form of striations. The glacier also left souvenirs of its visit: erratic boulders.

Our route north now crosses half a dozen seasonal, step-across creeks as it descends toward Linton Creek and finally bends west down to a meadow at whose north end we meet Foley Ridge Trail 3511 (6270–1.3), which leads south-southwest down a slope. About 25 yards west, at a forested flat, is a justifiably popular campsite. The Husband (7524), off in the west, is the resistant plug of an ancient volcano that once reigned over this area before the Three Sisters matured. Just after we start north again, we reach a tributary of Linton Creek, then 70 yards farther reach a second tributary.

From these seasonal creeks, our trail climbs gradually north through a hemlock forest to where it meets the Linton Meadows Trail (6440–1.7), descending steeply southwest. The PCT ascends moderately northeast to a spring, then angles north to a gentle slope from which we can look south and identify, from east to west; the Mt. Thielsen pinnacle (9182), the Mt. McLoughlin pyramid (9495) and the Diamond Peak massif (8744). We now follow an open, post-lined, undulating pathway north over loose slopes with trailside rose paintbrushes, yellow cinquefoils, pink heathers and white pasqueflowers. Then we cross a rocky meadow, perhaps while being watched by a marmot, and descend to a junction with Obsidian Trail 3528 (6380–2.1), just above Obsidian Creek. This five-mile trail takes you down to Frog Campground by the McKenzie Highway.

We start hiking east moderately up to a slope, then go northeast up to the trickling, 50-foot-high Obsidian Falls, from which we top a small shelf and cross Obsidian Creek. We now tread north on a trail that sounds and feels like glass. It is. The black obsidian is nature's own glass. Our trail, which passes some outstanding camps past the last junction, soon leaves the shelf, descends a ridge, and then turns east and intersects Glacier Way Trail 3528A (6370–1.6). This path descends moderately 0.7 mile to the Obsidian

Rest stop at Scott Trail junction

Trail, which can be followed 3.4 miles to Frog Campground.

An efficient mountaineering party can follow this route up from the campground, climb North and Middle Sisters via the Collier Glacier col, and return to camp late the same day. From the col, Middle Sister (10,047) can be climbed via its north ridge without any special equipment. Likewise, North Sister (10,085) can be climbed via its southwest ridge to the south aréte, but the climb north along this sharp crest requires a safety rope. The view from Middle Sister is particularly instructional, for from it you can compare the degree of glaciation on all Three Sisters. North Sister, the oldest of the three, has suffered repeated ravages from quite a number of glacial advances. South Sister (10,358), the youngest, retains her symmetry, for she hasn't lived long enough to feel the icy tongues cut deep into her body.

Twenty yards east of the Glacier Way intersection, we bridge Glacier Creek, then reach a

E10, E12   **E12**

see MAP F1

SISTERS 13 MI.

MT. WASHINGTON E13

see MAP F1

×5560

WILDERNESS

Dee Wright
Observatory

McKenzie Pass

Snow Shelter

LANE CO

THREE

HIGHWAY 242

EUGENE 77 MI.

5324

BM
5187

Lava Camp Lake
Forest Camp

6582

Black
Crater

5260

SISTERS

WILDERNESS

5600

CRATER
94

5194

see MAP E12

pleasant, hemlock-shaped campsite where Sunshine Shelter once stood. We make a minor climb north over the western spur of Little Brother (7810), then descend slightly to the edge of the steep south slope above White Branch creek (6210–0.9). After climbing along this stream, we eventually descend slightly and cross the trickling creek, which sometimes goes dry by mid-August. Here you can camp above its north bank at a flat called Sawyer Bar.

Our trail bears north 200 yards part way across a basalt flow, then angles east up a ridge of solidified lava to the breached Collier Cone— the obvious source of this flow. Here, mountaineers' paths take off south up to Collier Glacier. We turn north and work our way across several lava ridges before descending north to Minnie Scott Spring (6650–2.2), which is likely to be snowbound through mid-July. You can

E12

camp on the level ground west of the spring. Our trail now makes a curving, counterclockwise descent almost to the Minnie Scott Spring creek, crosses a ridge, descends north to a large, grassy meadow and shortly meets Scott Trail 3551 (6300–0.9).

Descending west to the McKenzie Highway in about five miles, this trail follows the narrow strip of land between the Four in One Cone (6258) basalt flow on its north side and the Collier Cone (7534) basalt flow on its south side. The age of these flows, and of the Yapoah Crater (6737) basalt flow immediately north of us, is about 2600 years. Our route follows the Scott Trail north, which curves northeast and switchbacks up a northwest spur of the Ahalapam Cinder Field. It then curves around the slopes of Yapoah Crater and enters Deschutes National Forest. The crater's lava flow—at least

E12

Views from Dee Wright Observatory: south, the Sisters; north, Mt. Washington and, just barely, Three Fingered Jack

400 years old—extends north to Highway 242 and beyond. Looking north, we can see a row of peaks: Mt. Washington (7794), Three Fingered Jack (7841) and the snowy Mts. Jefferson (10,497) and Hood (11,235).

We now wind along and around ridges of the Yapoah lava flow and are thankful that the rocky trail exists, even when it is covered with snow patches. A cross-country hike across this material would be very exhausting. We reach the edge of the flow and parallel it north on a blocky cinder trail to South Matthieu Lake (6040–2.5) at Scott Pass, from where the Scott Trail (now numbered 95) descends east-southeast toward Trout Creek. If your backpack is a bright red-orange color, you might find that here, as in other places, hummingbirds buzz up to it and try to extract nectar from your alluring "flower."

At this pass, you get one of your best views eastward of central Oregon, which is drier than the west countryside because of the rain shadow cast by the Cascade Range. In beauty, 70-yard-wide South Matthieu Lake is a far cry from North Matthieu Lake, which has long been a favorite camping area. The north lake, however, got too much use, so the section of trail descending to it was closed after a new high route was completed in 1972. Now, unfortunately, the smaller south lake, with windy campsites, must bear the brunt of the backpackers.

We follow the old trail above the north shore of the south lake, then take the new trail around the west slope of Summit 6302 and are rewarded with excellent views below of the Yapoah lava flow, which was deflected northeast around the lower slopes of Belknap Crater. Our trail soon begins a moderate descent and eventually arcs west in its descent to the north end of the blocked-off OST route (5400–2.3). On almost level terrain now, we proceed northwest alongside the flow's edge to where a spur trail (5300–0.4) continues straight ahead but the PCT turns left (west) and climbs up the flow.

Since your next potential source of trailside water is at Coldwater Spring, 11.2 miles distant, you had better head over to Lava Camp Lake first. (Coldwater Spring has been known to go dry in late summer due to over-use.) Follow the spur trail 0.2 mile northwest to the trailhead, parking area and Road 900, which are reached just after a crossing of the seasonal Lava Camp Lake outlet creek. Road 900 goes north 0.1 mile to the McKenzie Highway. We follow Road 900 east 0.4 mile to Lava Camp Lake, where the people and the jays outnumber the six-inch trout, yet water, campsites and good summer swimming are always available. Backtracking to the PCT, we follow its zigzag course west over the blocky lava field and leave the Three Sisters Wilderness as we cross the narrow McKenzie Highway (State 242) (5280–1.1) 500 yards west of the Dee Wright Observatory—a lookout tower well worth visiting for its views. Just 0.2 mile west down this highway is a parking area with a trailhead for those starting their hike north from McKenzie Pass. This pass was named for the river that was explored in 1811 by Donald McKenzie, a member of John Jacob Astor's Pacific Fur Company. It was opened to travel in 1862 when Felix Scott, with a party of 250 men, chopped their way through the forest, building the road for their 106 ox-hauled wagons as they traveled. They crossed the divide by what is known as the Old Scott Trail, two or three miles south of the present road.

Having crossed the highway, we leave Three Sisters Wilderness and enter Mt. Washington Wilderness. Due to the jumbled nature of the lava flow, our trail must take a twisted route over to the small trailhead parking area (5210–0.3), where our section's hike ends.

E12, E13   E13

Male (left) and female (right) red crossbills at Dee Wright Observatory

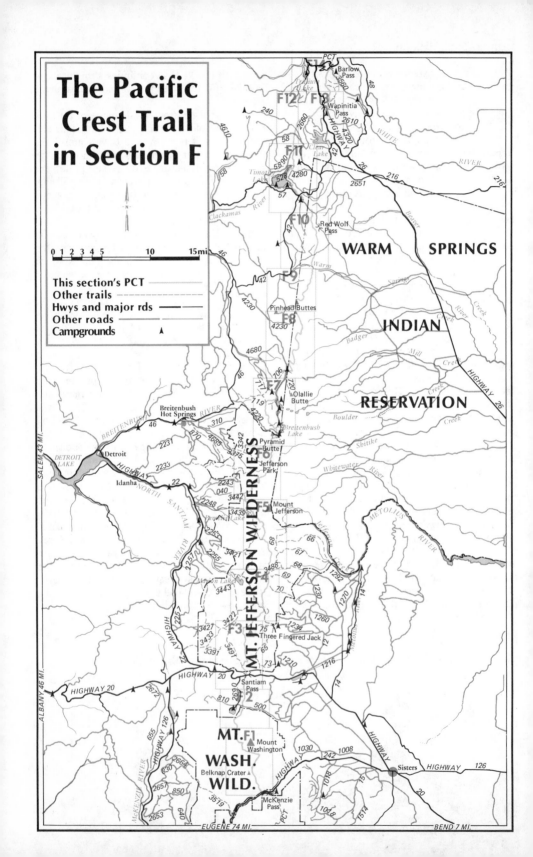

Section F: Highway 242 at McKenzie Pass to Highway 35 near Barlow Pass

Introduction: The terrain crossed in Section F is an approximate mirror image of that crossed in Section E. Starting from Highway 242, you head north across recent lava flows that also made up the last part of Section E. You then pass three major peaks—Mt. Washington, Three Fingered Jack and Mt. Jefferson—just as you passed the Three Sisters. All six peaks are volcanoes in various stages of erosion. Mt. Jefferson, the northernmost, and South Sister, the southernmost, are the two youngest.

North of Mt. Jefferson you hike through the lake-studded Breitenbush Lake-Olallie Lake area, which is a smaller version of the southern Three Sisters Wilderness. Finally, you hike a lengthy stretch across slopes that are deficient in both views and lakes, just as you did in the first third of Section E. Both sections on the average, are fairly scenic, and it is difficult to say which is better. For many, however, Jefferson Park is the scenic high point of the Oregon PCT. But in this spectacular plain (see front cover) you'll find a back-packing crowd to match or exceed that on any other part of the tri-state Pacific Crest Trail.

Declination: 18½°E

Mileages:

	South to North	Distances between Points	North to South
Highway 242 at McKenzie Pass	0.0		112.5
Washington Ponds spur trail	7.3	7.3	105.2
Coldwater Spring.............................	9.7	2.4	102.8
Highway 20 at Santiam Pass	17.1	7.4	95.4
Minto Pass.................................	27.3	10.2	85.2
Rockpile Lake	31.0	3.7	81.5
Start of Pamelia Lake alternate route	37.9	6.9	74.6
Shale Lake.................................	39.7	1.8	72.8
End of Pamelia Lake alternate route..............	44.2	4.5	68.3
Trail north to Scout Lake.......................	50.3	6.1	62.2
Skyline Road 42 near Breitenbush Lake...........	56.9	6.6	55.6
Skyline Road 42 near Olallie Lake Guard Station ...	63.4	6.5	49.1
Jude Lake.................................	67.1	3.7	45.4
Lemiti Creek	73.1	6.0	39.4
Warm Springs River..........................	84.2	11.1	28.3
Miller Trail to Clackamas Lake Campground........	92.7	8.5	19.8
Little Crater Lake Trail	99.5	6.8	13.0
Highway 26 at Wapinitia Pass	107.5	8.0	5.0
Highway 35 near Barlow Pass	112.5	5.0	0.0

Supplies: In the past some hikers have picked up mailed parcels at Santiam Lodge, which is located on Highway 20 less than a mile west of the PCT crossing, and about 140 yards west of Big Lake Road's junction with the highway. The lodge was also a member of the American Youth Hostel, and therefore it provided low-cost rooms and inexpensive meals.

However, in late 1985 the lodge changed ownership, and it is now managed by the Hoodoo Ski Bowl. As of December 1985 the ski-bowl manager stated that PCT hikers may certainly use Hoodoo Ski Bowl as a mail drop, though he didn't have plans at that time to re-open the hostel. This situation may change in the future. Should you plan to drop or mail parcels, first contact the ski bowl. You can phone them by asking for the Sisters (town) operator and then ask for Hoodoo Toll Station #2.

If at some future date you can't use Hoodoo Ski Bowl as a mail drop, then you'll have to resort to the Olallie Lake Guard Station, which is not far beyond this section's halfway point. Just east of the guard station is Olallie Lake Resort, with a somewhat limited supply of food. The guard station, like Santiam Lodge, might stop holding parcels at some future date, and if so that would pose real logistical problems for long-distance trekkers. You might first check with the guard station to be sure they'll hold your parcels. As with the ski bowl, a stamped, self-addressed envelope would be appreciated.

At the end of this section you could hike several miles out of your way down to the town of Government Camp, which has a post office and a moderately well-stocked store.

Our section's PCT begins at a small trailhead parking area just west of ill-defined McKenzie Pass. This trailhead is very easy to find, for it is at a bend in Highway 242 from which the road to the east is very curving but that to the southwest is straight as an arrow.

From the trailhead at the south boundary of the Mt. Washington Wilderness, we make an ascent northwest up the Belknap Crater basalt flows and pass between two forested islands of older, glaciated basalt that stand in a sea of younger basalt. The desolate young basalt flows look as if they had cooled only a few years ago, yet those emanating from Little Belknap (6305) are 2900 years old. The flows seen today on Belknap Crater (6872) and its flanks are mostly 1500–3000 years old. All the flows between

North Sister and Mt. Washington compose a 65-square-mile field that represents the Cascade's greatest post-Pleistocene outpouring of lava. Belknap Crater is an excellent example of a shield volcano, and is quite similar to the shields that the Three Sisters and Mt. Thielsen grew upon.

Our route now takes us up to a junction with a spur trail (6120–2.3) that leads east-northeast up to the summit of Little Belknap. This area we're in looks quite lifeless, yet up here among the rocks you might spot a whistling marmot scurrying for its hole, or even more astounding, you might discover a western toad. Mountain chickadees sing out their name as we enter a strip of forest near Belknap Crater and descend through it to the eastern edge of a fresh-looking

F1   F1
Hiking up the Belknap lava field toward Mt. Washington

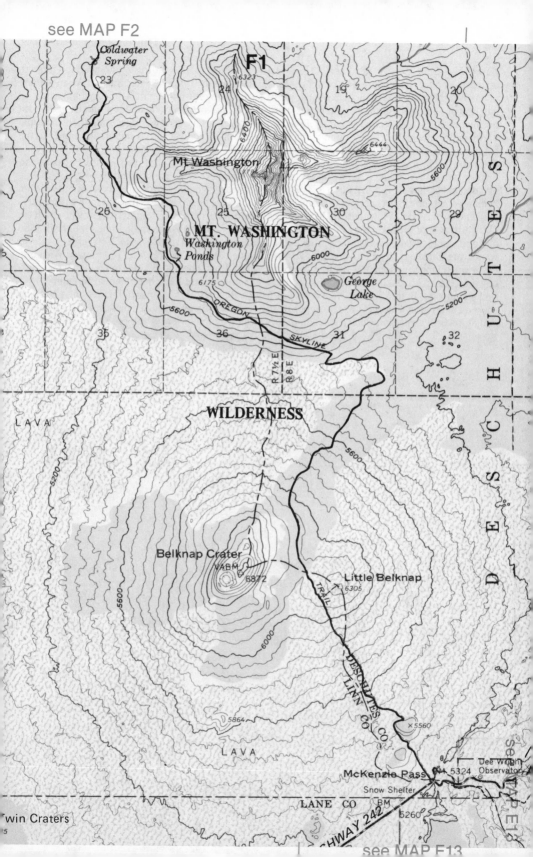

see MAP F2

Coldwater
Spring

23

F1

24

6323

19

20

Mt Washington

6444

5600

26

25

30

29

MT. WASHINGTON

*Washington
Ponds*

6000

35

36

6175

George
Lake

5200

5600

OREGON

31

SKYLINE

R 7½ E

R 8 E

32

WILDERNESS

LAVA

5200

5600

5600

Belknap Crater

VABM
6872

Little Belknap
6305

TRAIL

6000

5600

5864

LAVA

×5560

DESCHUTES CO.

LINN CO.

Dee Wright
Observatory

McKenzie Pass

BM 5324

Snow Shelter

LANE CO.

BM

5260

win Craters

HIGHWAY 242

see MAP F13

D E S C H U T E S

flow (5320–2.5). We first head north, then west up along its edge, which borders the south slope of Mt. Washington. We then switchback northeast and in a couple of minutes switchback west-northwest. From this second you can climb due north rather steeply up fairly open slopes and across minor ridges over to George Lake. If you're on track, you'll reach a steep ridge immediately south of the lake. Some hikers try to avoid unnecessary elevation gain to this ridge by heading north-northeast, hoping to arrive at the east end of the lake. However, if they are just 200 yards east of the lake, they may not see it at all, and could waste lots of time and energy wandering aimlessly. You, however, have been forewarned, and will do better. Follow the ridge down to the lake's east shore, by which you'll find a campsite. Better ones lie above the north shore. Camping at George Lake is superior to that at lower Washington Pond, which in turn is

superior to that at rusty, horse-urine-tainted, seasonally dry Coldwater Spring. When you are ready to return to the PCT (George Lake is good for a layover day), head due south from the east shore, attain a low ridge, and then diagonal south-southwest across undulating slopes to the PCT.

From where the trail switchbacks west-northwest, we climb steadily to the Cascade divide, where our trail levels off. We then traverse northwest for about ¾ mile before curving north for a ⅓-mile stint to a gully in which the easily missed Washington Ponds spur trail starts northeast (5710–2.5). In 200 yards it curves over to shallow, 25-yard-wide lower Washington Pond, beside whose semiclear water desperate hikers have been known to camp.

Beyond this unmarked junction we climb slightly higher through a meadow that affords us an excellent view of the basalt plug that makes

F1   **F1**

see MAP F3

see MAP F1

Mt. Washington, from the southwest

up the steep-walled summit block of Mt. Washington (7794). An ascent of its 500-foot-high south aréte requires a complete set of technical rock-climbing equipment. This extremely glaciated peak probably once stood as high as North Sister at a time when that peak was still undergoing its growing pains.

Our route arcs west and descends moderately alongside the west spur, then descends northward around it to an overused meadow that contains an obvious well (18-inch-diameter pipe) known as Coldwater Spring (5200–2.4). Since this meadow is the only trailside PCT campsite in the Mt. Washington Wilderness that has "fresh" water, it has been overused, so much, in fact, that *it sometimes dries up.* Be prepared. On weekends, as many as two dozen mountaineers

F1

will make this their base camp and then climb up the north spur to the 300-foot-high north aréte of the summit block—the easiest summit route, but still requiring ropes and other equipment. The organic evidence lying profusely around the grassy meadow lets us know that horses use this site too. There may be some question about the water quality of the shallow well. It is, however, our last fresh water on route until Rockpile Lake, about 21.5 miles farther. Less desirable ponds and lakes exist near the trail, and snow patches linger through mid-August on the northwest slope of Three Fingered Jack.

Our route continues its northward descent through a hemlock forest occupied by clicking juncos and drilling red-shafted flickers. We pass by an unmarked climbers' trail (5050–0.5) that ascends east-southeast toward the peak's north spur, then we descend north to a fork with a broad trail (4760–0.9), which continues straight ahead. If you sorely need water, descend this old trail 0.7 mile to the grounds of the Oregon Conference of Seventh Day Adventists. You'll find a water faucet about 60 yards east, by their horse corral. From the grounds you can continue north ¾ mile to the Old Santiam Road, then 250 yards east over to the PCT. Please don't take this route unless you absolutely have to. Onward, the PCT veers right (northeast) and traverses across slopes that are waterless once the snow patches disappear. We leave the Mt. Washington Wilderness just before we reach the old Santiam Wagon Road (4680–2.0). This waterless spot is very popular with car campers on summer weekends and during hunting season.

*   *   *   *

If you plan to stop at the Hoodoo Ski Bowl to pick up your parcels, strike west along this historic road, passing the entrance to the Seventh Day Adventists' Big Lake Youth Camp before you reach the Big Lake Road (4670–0.6). If you need water or a place to stay, trek ½ mile southwest to moderate-sized Big Lake Campground, which unfortunately can be noisy, due to the type of crowd it can attract—powerboat enthusiasts. If you don't need to camp, head north on Big Lake Road 2690, stop at the Hoodoo Ski Bowl (4720–2.2), and then continue north to Santiam Highway (State 20) (4750–1.0). The entrance road to Santiam Lodge lies 140 yards west of this junction. To conclude this supply route, hike east on State 20 back to the PCT (4810–0.7–4.5). If you need

F1, F2, F3

F3

Duffy Butte 3835
Mowich Lake
Forest Camp
North Dixie Lake
South Dixie Lake
Porcupine Peak 6600
LINN CO.
JEFFERSON CO.
Canyon Creek
5600
6572

Duffy Lake 4793
Forest Camp
5375
Little Duffy Lake
3427
3491
3494
Duffy Prairie
OREGON
3433
Ralphs Lake
Toms Lake
6855
Three Fingered Jack
6000

Forest Camp
Santiam Lake
5200

SKYLINE
5602
6000
7696
First Creek Camp

Maxwell Butte
VABM Lookout 6229
5600
Summit Lake
5600
SUMMIT
Martin Lake

Upper Berley Lake
Lower Berley Lake
5200
5722
Booth Lake
R 8 E
R 7 E

5362
5445
Craig Lake
5200
Jack Shelter
3491
5600
180

4800
5406
RAILROAD
ALBANY 76 MI.
5447
APPROXIMATE
Square Lake

Lost Lake
BM 4746
X 5271
MT.
GRADE
22
BM 4357
JEFFERSON
WILDERNESS
19
Douthit Spr
BM 46
potato
4400
Gravel Pit
Hogg Rock
Lodge
BM 4758
HIGHWAY
BM 4711
20

Hoodoo
BM 4631
BIG LAKE ROAD
2690
Creek
25
Circle Lake
26
27
4800
TRAIL
Pass
30

Hoodoo Ski Bowl
JEEP
4800

Three Fingered Jack, northeast face

water, you could continue about ¼ mile east to Douthit Spring, though it has been known to dry up.

*   *   *   *

From the old Santiam Wagon Road the PCT heads northeast through a ghost forest of burned lodgepole snags and past abandoned logging roads on a route that gradually turns north and reaches a hundred-yard-long lily-pad pond (4790–2.0) just west of the trail. This unsightly stretch we have just passed through is easy to follow, despite the junctions. Southbound along it, the hiker at least has open, if not scenic, views of Mt. Washington. Just north of the pond, we climb over a low saddle and into a green forest once again. After traversing north over a gentle, open-forested stretch, we hear the drone of automobiles, then our trail turns northeast and heads for a crossing of the Santiam Highway (State 20) (4810–2.0) about 200 yards west of the national forest boundary at Santiam Pass. This pass was first crossed in 1859 by Andrew Wiley. He explored an old Indian trail up the Santiam River and worked his way farther east each year on his hunting expeditions from the Willamette Valley.

Just 240 yards west of our crossing is a PCT access road that curves 0.2 mile northeast to a parking area at a popular trailhead. We cross the highway and after 200 yards spy the parking area, immediately west. Our trail bears north, curves northwest and enters the Mt. Jefferson Wilderness, then climbs increasingly steep slopes and passes a few stagnant ponds just before a junction with the Santiam Lake Trail 3491 (5200–1.4), which curves northwest around a prominent boulder pile.

*   *   *   *

Because most of the PCT through Mt. Jefferson Wilderness is rather lakeless, one hiker has suggested we mention an alternative, the old Oregon Skyline Trail. Since Schaffer hadn't had the time to map this route, he is basing the following description on USFS topographic maps and mileages. Take Trail 3491 2.1 miles northwest to Lower Berley Lake, then 1.9 miles farther to more attractive Santiam Lake. Just 0.6 mile north of it you reach a junction, where Trail 3491 turns west. Start northeast on Trail 3494, hike north past South and North Dixie Lakes, and in 1.5 miles reach a junction with Trail 3422. Next, in 1.0 mile you

hike northeast past diminutive Alice Lake and average-sized Red Butte Lake to reach a junction by the south shore of fairly large Jorn Lake. Trail 3422 heads past the lake's west shore, but you head east on Trail 3492 about 0.7 mile to Bowerman Lake, then traverse 2.7 miles beyond it to a junction with Trail 3437, which climbs 2.7 miles southeast up to Minto Pass and the PCT. Next you descend 2.0 easy miles on Trail 3437 to a junction on a descending ridge that juts into Marion Lake. Leaving the wilderness' largest lake, you climb 1.6 miles up Trail 3493 to the John Swallow Grave. From this vicinity Trail 3488 climbs 3.7 miles up to the PCT. Keeping to 3493, you quickly pass aptly named Midget Lake, soon cross Whiskey Creek, find Lake of the Woods just beyond it, turn west at Puzzle Creek, and end your 2.7-mile stretch at a junction with Trail 3421 below the crest of Bingham Ridge (just off Map F5). Northeastward, you soon cross the ridge as your Trail 3493 traverses 2.6 miles, passing pint-sized Papoose Lake before reaching a junction with a trail that climbs 1.8 miles southeast to the PCT, on a saddle near the south end of the Cathedral Rocks. From this junction follow the alternate route description found on page 159. Basically, you drop 1.4 miles to the Hunts Cove spur trail, then 3.1 miles to the north shore of Pamelia Lake, from which you climb 0.7 mile north back to the PCT. The total length of this route is 24.6 miles, more or less, versus 25.5 miles for the comparable stretch of PCT.

*   *   *   *

From the Trail 3491 junction with the PCT just 1.4 trail miles north of Highway 20, we climb northeast up to a forested ridge, then follow it north-northwest toward Three Fingered Jack. The trail eventually leaves the ridge and curves northeast across a prominent cliff above Martin Lake, then heads up a small gully and quickly curves north-northwest (6000–2.5). If you are in desperate need of water, you can now head east cross-country, starting from an obvious flat atop the cliff, then follow markers 0.4 mile north down to sparkling Summit Lake (5800), a favorite among mountaineers.

Back on route, we follow the PCT as it switchbacks up to the ridge again, crosses it, and traverses the lower west slope of Three Fingered Jack (7841), which up close has a totally different appearance than when we saw it from a distance: he seems to have considerably more than three fingers. The easiest route to the

F2, F3, F4   **F4, F5, F3**

see MAP F3

highest summit is a Class 3 ascent that starts on a faint trail up its southwest talus slope, then climbs its south ridge. Most of the routes up to the serrated crest require climbing equipment.

Our trail rounds the peak's northwest spur (6390–2.6), turns east toward a snow patch that lasts through mid-August, then curves northeast up to a saddle (6500–0.5) along the Cascade divide. From this vantage point we can observe the remaining structure of an ancient volcano that stands today as a crest called Three Fingered Jack. This peak is composed of remarkably uniform, thin, alternating beds of cinders and flows that dip west about 20°; their *regularity* over such a great thickness indicates a long period of minor eruptions. The reddish-brown, unsorted cinders consist of ash, lapilli,

F3   **F3**

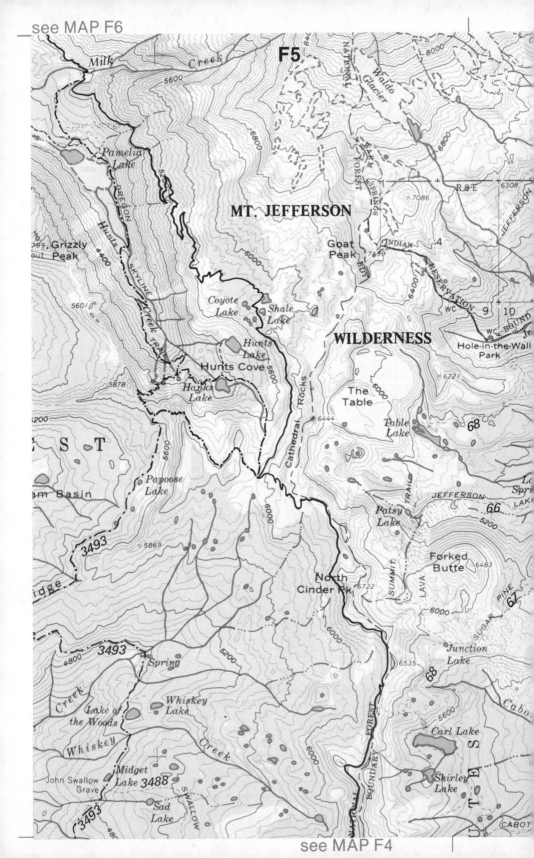

F5

Milk Creek

Pamelia Lake

Grizzly
Peak

MT. JEFFERSON

Waldo Glacier

NATIONAL FOREST

WARM SPRINGS

×7086

R 8 E

Goat
Peak

INDIAN

RESERVATION

WILDERNESS

Hole-in-the-Wall
Park

Coyote
Lake

Shale
Lake

Hunts
Lake

Hunts Cove

Hanks
Lake

×5878

Cathedral Rocks

×6444

The
Table

×6221

Table
Lake

66

S T

Basin

Papoose
Lake

×5869

North
Cinder Pk.

×6722

Patsy
Lake

Forked
Butte
×6483

SUMMIT TRAIL

LAVA

PINE

67

SUGAR

3493

Ridge

3493

Spring

6535

68

Junction
Lake

Creek

Lake of
the Woods

Whiskey
Lake

Whiskey
Creek

SWALLOW

John Swallow
Grave

Midget
Lake 3488

Sad
Lake

3493

BOUNDARY FOREST

Carl Lake

Shirley
Lake

TES

Cabo

CABOT

blocks and bombs that contrast strongly with the brownish-gray andesite flows.

We now descend several switchbacks, soon recross the divide, and then descend northeast along forested slopes to a smattering of stagnant ponds just southwest of an intersection with the Minto Pass Trail 3437 (5350–3.2) at Minto Pass. This trail descends south one-quarter mile to large, green, ten-foot-deep Wasco Lake, whose shores see a lot campers in August once the mosquitoes have left.

The PCT quickly turns north, climbs to a saddle and reaches the Wasco Lake loop trail (#65) (5430–0.5), which descends southeast half a mile to an unnamed lake before curving west to Wasco Lake. We continue north up the divide, switchback as it steepens, and then traverse across to the southeast spur (6210–2.2) of Peak 6488, from where we can look south and see how Three Fingered Jack got its name. Continuing north, we contour to a saddle, then contour across the east slope of Rockpile Mountain (6559) and pass the Two Springs Trail 70, descending southeast, just before we reach a pond and beautiful Rockpile Lake (6250–1.0). This shallow but clear lake had an excellent campsite above its southeast shore and a very good one at its north end, but now camping is prohibited.

Our trail heads north on the rocky slope along the lake's west shore and then descends the divide to a saddle where a trail (6140–0.5) forks right, dropping generally east, soon as Trail 69, toward roads near Abbot Butte. Our route stays

west of the divide and climbs up to a level, open area just east of a breached cinder cone. Although there are no lakes or ponds near us, we nevertheless find that in midsummer this flat is crawling with one-inch toads. Continuing north, we pass a second cone, South Cinder Peak (6746), which is of post-Pleistocene age, as is the other one. We soon reach a saddle and an intersection with unmaintained Swallow Lake Trail 3488 (6300–1.0), which descends two miles southwest to Swallow Lake and two miles northeast to Carl Lake.

The PCT continues north along the west slope of the divide and reaches a saddle (6400–1.2) on a northwest ridge, from where a spur trail climbs west-northwest to a small knoll with a good view of Mt. Jefferson, six miles north of us. Our trail now crosses a snow patch that lingers through late July, then arcs eastward to the divide and descends it to a level section that contains an adequate campsite beside a small, fresh-water pond 50 yards east of the crest. Hiking a few minutes longer, we encounter an unsigned trail (6240–0.9) that descends southeast about a mile to large, emerald Carl Lake (5500), where camping is prohibited.

From the junction we hike once again up the ridge route, then contour across the forested west slopes of North Cinder Peak (6722) to a small, grassy meadow (6240–1.7) that has obviously been camped at, and for a good reason. A hidden, rock-lined pond lies on the other side of a low pile of rocks that borders the meadow. This is a good water hole to stop at if you are passing through late in the summer.

F3, F4

F4, F5

Mt. Jefferson, from escarpment north of North Cinder Peak

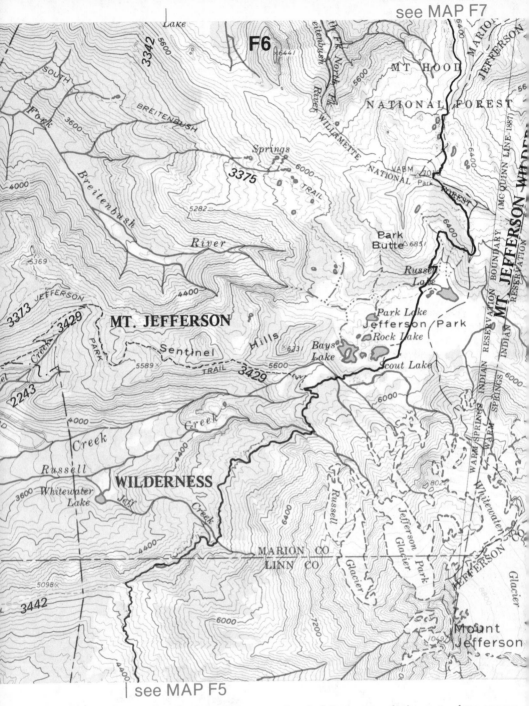

| see MAP F5

After a brief ascent north, we arrive at an escarpment (6340–0.4) where Mt. Jefferson (10,497) towers above us in all its presidential glory. On March 30, 1806, Lewis and Clark saw this snowy peak from the lower Willamette River, and they named it after their president. At the base of its south slope below us lies a bizarre glacio-volcanic landscape. During the last major glacial advance, glaciers cut a deep canyon on each side of the resistant Sugar Pine Ridge, seen in the east. After these disappeared, volcanic eruptions burst forth and constructed Forked Butte (6483), east of North Cinder Peak. This butte was subsequently breached by out-pourings of fluid basaltic andesite that flowed east down the glaciated Jefferson Creek and

F5   **F5**

Cabot Creek canyons. A smaller cone with a crater lake, north of us, also erupted about this time, but it was aborted by nature before any flows poured forth. To its north stands the flat Table, and between it and the ridge of Cathedral Rocks is a large, deep, enigmatic depression that may represent a collapsed flow.

Time, which allowed nature to sculpt this surrealistic art work, now forces us to press onward. We descend northwest, still marveling at the configurations below, then leave the ridge and switchback down to a junction where a faint, unsigned trail (6130–0.7) climbs 100 yards back to the divide before descending into the marvelous basin. After more switchbacking down, we reach a saddle (5910–0.5), from where three variations of the Pacific Crest Trail continue northward.

* * * *

The *oldest route* starts north steeply down the glaciated valley and curves west to shimmering, pure Hanks Lake (5144–1.2). Along its north shore, the Hunts Cove spur trail climbs north up to another gem, Hunts Lake (5236–0.4). It also descends west to a junction with a newer PCT route (5020–0.5–1.7).

* * * *

The *newer route,* which was the standard one through 1972, starts on a contour northwest from the saddle, crosses over a low ridge, then makes a descent to the Trail 3493 junction (5640–1.8), near a saddle, before it switchbacks down to the Hunts Cove spur trail (5020–1.4). The older route joins the newer one here, continues a descent into the glaciated valley and finally arrives at the southeast shore of shallow Pamelia Lake (3884). Paralleling the shore, the route curves west to a junction with the Pamelia Lake Trail 3439 (3970–3.1), which takes us down to many campsites near the lake's deeper end. Early in the season, the lake is high and attractive, but by August, Pamelia is reduced to a putrid puddle dotted with hikers who climb the easy 2.4-mile trail to this lake. Leaving this potential eyesore behind, you can ascend north, then northeast up toward Milk Creek and reach a junction (4320–0.7–7.0) with the newest PCT route.

* * * *

The *newest* PCT *route,* completed in the early '70s, starts on a gentle descent north-northeast from the saddle and heads along the lower slopes of the inspiring Cathedral Rocks, which, judging

Russell Creek

by their color, must have been constructed in the Dark Ages. Our route curves northwest to the crest of a lateral moraine well above sparkling Hunts Lake, then leaves this escarpment and winds north to the west shore of placid Shale Lake (5910–1.8), which is a logical spot to stop for the night. However, camping is now forbidden at this lake and at other nearby lakes, so you might try camping on relatively flat ground east and northeast of Shale Lake. The shale implied by the lake's name is actually basaltic andesite that has become highly fractured along many parallel planes.

Just north of this popular lake, we reach a shallow, seasonally larger lake that in late summer dwindles to a mudhole. Beyond it, our trail drops west to the glaciated escarpment, then oh-so-gently descends it before entering a Douglas-fir forest and reaching a junction with the Oregon Skyline Trail (Old PCT) (4320–4.5), just south of Milk Creek. Those taking one of the alternate routes join us here. We start up the gravelly, bouldery outwash deposits of Milk Creek canyon and pass a lavish display of

F5   **F5**

wildflowers and shrubs before hiking north past a two-person campsite to a crossing of aptly named Milk Creek (4320–0.2). Its silty color is caused by fine volcanic sediments that may in part be glacially ground to create "rock flour." We shall see many more creeks like it as we encounter glacier-clad volcanoes along our journey north.

Beyond this minor torrent we now make tracks northwest across many small, deceptive ridges before we reach the real Woodpecker Ridge and a junction with lightly used Woodpecker Trail 3442 (5040–1.6), which descends west. We head east gently down from the ridge and soon pass a stagnant pond with a fair, but illegal, campsite at its west end. The open forest here is quite choked with an understory of spiraea, corn lily, gooseberry, rhododendron and the ubiquitous huckleberry. You'll easily identify Whitewater Lake, way below you, by its milky color, due to a high influx of fine sediments.

Not much farther along, we pass a small spring, enter a shady forest, and then cross a creeklet whose gully is a channel for periodic avalanches. Two minutes past it we cross Jeff Creek, cross a nearby two-person campsite, and see more evidence of avalanches. After ½ mile of gentle ascending north, our trail ascends east, sometimes moderately, then quickly drops to a ford of milky Russell Creek (5520–2.8). Plan to cross this creek *before 11 a.m.* The afternoon's warmer temperatures greatly increase the snowmelt from the Russell and Jefferson Park glaciers, and that increased flow has swept some hikers on a one-way trip down the gorge immediately below the ford. This diurnal fluctuation is a second characteristic of glacier-fed creeks that we will encounter on our future traverses around major Cascade peaks.

Our trail now curves around a minor, westward-descending ridge with a poor campsite, soon makes a loop around a small, boggy area, then briefly descends to cross the headwaters of a Whitewater Creek tributary. From its north bank we make a minute's walk west to a junction with heavily traveled Jefferson Park Trail 3429 (5640–0.6). Starting from the end of Whitewater Road 1044, this trail—the shortest one into popular Jefferson Park—climbs 3.9 miles to the main branch of Whitewater Creek, then climbs an additional 0.4 mile to our junction.

From this point our PCT/Jefferson Park Trail makes an easy climb east-northeast to ford that

branch (5680–0.4). This crossing can be a wet one, but unlike the ford at Russell Creek, it is always a safe one. We continue our easy ascent in the same general direction, then curve north for a momentary climb to the south rim of beautiful but over-populated Jefferson Park.

Our trail quickly curves northeast (5860–0.5), and at that point a short spur trail descends to the nearby shore of cool, deep, green Scout Lake (5830). Camps rim the lake's shoreline, but like other lakeside camps in Jefferson Park and in *every* wilderness, these are illegal. However, there is no other acceptable camping alternative. You would think that after years of this area's overuse, the Forest Service would build ecologically sound campsites. Funds and/or motivation for such a program have yet to appear.

If you enjoy crowds, camp at Scout Lake. Otherwise, try nearby Bays Lake, more-distant Park Lake, or some dry, nonmeadow spot in between. Beneath hemlocks on the north shore of Scout Lake, you get beautifully framed views across the reflective lake of stately Mt. Jefferson (10,497) with its ermine robe of glaciers. At this lake and the adjacent lakes of Jefferson Park, you might make a strange catch while fishing for trout: Pacific giant salamanders that inhabit these lakes' shady waters.

The PCT turns right (northeast) at the first spur-trail junction, follows blazes past radiating, narrow spur trails, then curves north past a seasonal pond and reaches a spur trail (5930–0.3) that heads west to Scout and Bays lakes. We now hike north-northeast across the open flat of Jefferson Park and obtain impressive views back at the peak all the way to a junction with South Breitenbush Trail 3375 (5870–0.5), which starts west-southwest before descending northwest. Just 30 yards farther, a prominent spur trail branches northeast 250 yards to shallow Russell Lake (5856). Camping is prohibited at this lake, but you might consider camping in this vicinity at a fair distance from the lake. By late season, this lake may be fairly depleted and others in the basin may be completely dry. The PCT turns abruptly northwest at this junction, then quickly descends northeast to a step-across ford of South Fork Breitenbush River (5840–0.1). As you begin your ascent northeast, you can spot an excellent campsite 40 yards southeast just above the other side of the "river." The trail now climbs steeply up a slope and into a glacial cirque, where we again step across the river. Here, a steep shortcut northeast

F5, F6   **F6**

see MAP F9

West
Pinhead Butte
VABM 5577

South
Pinhead Butte
F8

Chinquapin Viewpoint

5337

120

4800

354

4220

4276

4800

4800

4387

4230

4230

480

4391

4480

SKYLINE

BM
4295
4230

Gravel
Pit

Creek

WASCO
CLACKAMAS CO

MOUNT HOOD NATIONAL FOREST

WARM SPRINGS INDIAN RESERVATION BOUNDARY

Cam
Prai

BM
4264
4220

Lemiti
Campground

BM
4207

Lemiti
Butte
4530

140

Slow

Creek

4522 x

Lemiti
Mdw

Lemiti Creek

Trooper Springs

4800

South

4400

Creek

4690

CLACKAMAS CO
MARION CO

4800

5073

4134

S   T

x 4528

BM
4278

4220

Fork

BM
4439

(MC QUINN LINE 1887)

MARION CO
WASCO CO

4800

4800

5200

Olallie

Creek

ROAD

Olallie
Meadow

4400

4989

BM
4508

Olallie Meadow Campground

Brook
Lake

5200

River

4172

Jude Lake

716

Russ
Lake

BLUE LAKE

4800

5200

5200

5200

MARION CO
WASCO CO

Triangle
Lake

706

SKYLINE 4220

4220

BOUNDARY

BM

706

5395

Campground

4400

MARION CO
WASCO CO

see MAP F7

may look more like the trail than the trail itself does. It developed, as so many shortcuts do, when early-season hikers chose to descend straight down the slope rather than follow the buried trail across snow patches. The real trail parallels the trickling river a short way north, then curves and climbs moderately southeast to a spur on the Cascade divide. This is climbed in an arc up to Park Ridge, which is then traversed 70 yards west to a viewpoint (6920–2.0), where you obtain your last look down at justifiably popular Jefferson Park. A short trail climbs 200 yards west up to Peak 7018 for an even better view. In the distance, just east of north, towers magnificent Mt. Hood (11,235), and just to the west of north stands southern Washington's decapitated Mt. St. Helens (8364).

We now descend the trail—or rather, the semipermanent snowfield—toward small, shallow lakes and ponds. As the gradient eases, the trail becomes very obvious as it selects a pond-dotted route north out of the alpine realm and into the hemlock forest. Our path momentarily takes us over a low saddle (6150–2.1), then meanders northeast, giving us some views of locally dominating Pyramid Butte (6095) as we cross many minor gullies and ridges. Views disappear and soon we start through a small flat with a low hill on our left. Here we leave the Mt. Jefferson Wilderness and immediately meet a conspicuous trail—the old Oregon Skyline route—branching right. In 1985 this misleading trail was conspicuously signed THIS IS NOT THE PACIFIC CREST TRAIL. We hope the sign stands for years.

Our trail rambles onward for ⅓ mile, passing a small, volcanic butte of shalelike rocks before it meets a spur trail, which goes 280 yards northeast over to the Breitenbush Lake Campground. This campground, which has a shelter near its south end, lies just within the western limits of the Warm Springs Indian Reservation. It is, however, administered by the U.S. Forest Service. A few paces beyond the spur trail we cross Breitenbush Lake's outlet creek, then immediately reach decrepit Road 4220 (5500–1.6). If you plan to do just a short stretch on the PCT, you can drive east up this road to a trailhead parking area just west of the campground's entrance. However, you'll be gritting your teeth, and if drive onward, over to Horseshoe Lake, you'll swear you'll never do it again (ORV drivers can ignore this warning).

Keeping within Mt. Hood National Forest, we climb a winding trail up to the east shore (5750–0.5) of a shallow lake, curve around to its north shore, and then pass near a smaller, triangular lake. Our trail then traverses the bouldery southwest slope of summit 5975 before winding down to a junction with the old OST route (5510–1.0), now Gibson Trail 708. Starting northwest, we momentarily reach Horseshoe Saddle Trail 712 (5520–0.1), logically, atop a saddle above Horseshoe Lake. You can follow

F6, F7

Mt. Jefferson, from Olallie Lake Resort

F7

Olallie Butte, from Russ Lake

this trail ¾ mile down to its trailhead by Road 4220's Horseshoe Lake Campground.

A short distance northwest along our ridge route, we encounter the Ruddy Hill Trail 714 (5600–0.3), which climbs west. We now contour northward through a thick forest, then climb up to a low knoll before descending slightly to Many Lakes Viewpoint (5660–1.2), which lives up to its description. Mile-long Olallie Lake is the focal point of the basin, and andesitic Olallie Butte (7215) rules above it. ("Olallie" is what the native Indians called the huckleberries.) This volcano has been active in both glacial and postglacial times.

After hiking counterclockwise down the knoll's northern slopes, we reach a dry flat, from which the southbound traveler sees the lofty

F7

see MAP F10

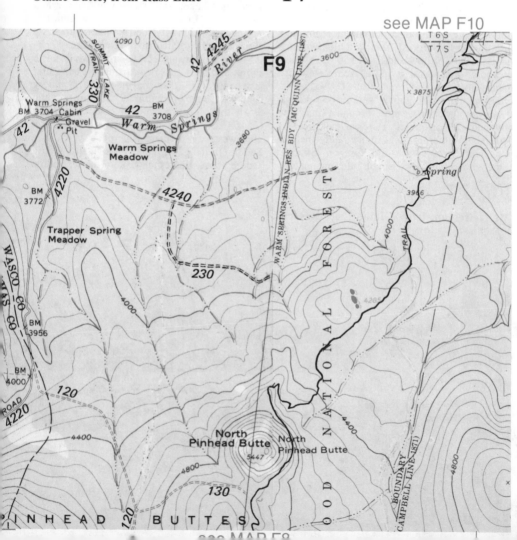

see MAP F9

crown of Mt. Jefferson beckoning him onward. Here our trail crosses a seasonal creek, then descends north steeply alongside it, and veers northwest to a very good campsite at reposeful Upper Lake (5380–0.9). Continuing north, we pass several seasonal ponds and shallow, linear Cigar Lake (5350–0.4), from where a 0.6-mile

trail first winds northeast down to Top Lake (5170), with a good west-shore campsite, then climbs back to a mile-high crest junction with the PCT. Leaving Cigar Lake, the PCT takes an easier, more direct route to that crest junction (5280–0.4), from which Red Lake Trail 719 goes 1¼ miles northwest to Fork Lake.

F7   **F7**

Cooper

Creek

Crater Cr

2660

2

1

58

6

4000

Clear La
Bu

5890

Crater Cr

2

1

ABBOT

VABM 4458

Looko

Little Crater
Meadow

58

Little Crater
Meadow 12

7

11

12

11

500

3600

Little Crater Lake

Forest Camp

ROAD

58

14

13

14

14

13

18

3600

5890

528

(MC QUINN) LINE 1887)

Meditation Point
Campground

23

24

23

23

24

19

Timothy Lake

4280

3600

BM

+Mile
15.8

BM
3522

57

SPILLWAY 3217

528

Gone Creek
Campground

Clackamas R Fk

Oak Grove Fk

BM

Hood View
Campground

25

26

26

26

25

30

26

57

42

Oak Grove

Clackamas Lake
Forest Camp

Guard Station

BM
3346

*Clackamas
Lake*

Fork

Big 31

35

36

42

534

BOUNDARY

35

35

4270

4270

BM
3444

36

230

R 8 E

R 8½ E

BM 3421

BM
3523

ROAD

4270

closed

BM 3468

Stone

The PCT contours north along the divide, curves northeast and crosses it, then follows it east down past a small triangular, semiclear lake (5180–0.9) and arrives at the shore of deep, clear Head Lake (4950–0.7). Here a short spur trail curves eastward 60 yards to the Olallie Lake Forest Service Guard Station beside Skyline Road. For northbound hikers this spur trail is the quickest way to Olallie Lake Resort. A pleasant picnic area separates the resort from the guard station.

From the spur trail, the PCT climbs above the southeast shore of Head Lake, and on it we pass a very good trailside campsite only 50 yards before we reach Skyline Road 4220 (4990–0.1) at a point 20 yards north of its signed 4991-foot divide. *Southbound* hikers can follow the road 100 yards south to a "Y" junction, from where they can follow a spur road 200 yards east to Olallie Lake Resort. It has a limited food selection, as did the store at Odell Lake's Shelter Cove Resort, about 143 miles back. Northward, you can look forward to good, but expensive, meals at Timberline Lodge, 54 miles distant.

From the Skyline Road crossing, the PCT starts northeast, then makes a long, gentle descent north along the lower slopes of Olallie Butte (7215) to an intersection with Olallie Butte Trail 720 (4680–2.2), which descends 220 yards west alongside the southern powerline to Skyline Road. We cross under the three sets of powerlines and parallel the unseen road, going north-northeast until we observe a flat, bushy, open depression on the right (east). Then our trail veers northeast, but a blocked trail continues north. This trail (4570–1.0) is a 230-yard link between the PCT and the old OST (now Lodgepole Trail 706). Our trail now enters Warm Springs Indian Reservation land, and will remain on it almost to Clackamas Lake. We continue northeast on a low ridge, angle north and intersect the Russ Lake Trail 716 (4550–0.3), ascending southeast from Olallie Meadow Campground. This trail continues 0.3 mile southeast past an adequate campsite at Jude Lake to a better one at deeper Russ Lake (4600).

We start north, then ramble northeast to shallow Jude Lake (4600–0.2), which has a good campsite on its northwest shore. Get a good drink of water, for the spring 0.4 mile ahead sometimes dries up by mid-August. You then have a long, dry (though shady) walk around the lower ends of two ridges before you descend to trickling Lemiti Creek (4360–6.0) at the lower end of Lemiti Meadow.

The trail arcs clockwise through the forest around the meadow's northeast fringe to a signed spur trail (4400–0.5) that gently descends 70 yards southwest past a spacious campsite to a five-yard-wide fresh-water hole known as Trooper Springs. On a weekend, you may have to compete with the Scouts as well as with the frogs—your next water will be at a spring 8.3 miles farther.

Our trail continues southeast for 0.1 mile, then turns north and climbs over the low Cascade divide. It more or less follows the divide north through a viewless forest, until South Pinhead Butte (5337), where we reach the trailside Chinquapin Viewpoint (5000–2.8), rather disappointing, but at least it permits us to see over the forest. Better views are just ahead. We contour the butte's slopes northward, cross a saddle (4980–0.8) with an abandoned spur road going west, then reach the southeast slope of North Pinhead Butte (5447), which is the youngest of the three andesite buttes. Looking south, we see Mt. Jefferson once again and are reminded of the beauties of Jefferson Park.

We now descend north to a lava flow, where a signed spur trail (4640–1.4) heads northnortheast 60 yards across it to an open view north of Mt. Hood (11,235) and east of Warm Springs River basin. We then make a switchback, descend back into the depths of the forest and generally follow a gentle ridge route down to a junction with a spur trail (3860–3.3) that descends moderately west-southwest 70 yards to a seeping spring. You may have to treat the water before drinking it. The slopes steepen, and so does our route, which switchbacks down to a dry creek, contours northward, then turns west and makes a crossing of Warm Springs River (3330–2.3), with a campsite nearby. You've also just crossed the 45°N Latitude line and are midway between the Equator and the North Pole. If you hike the entire Pacific Crest Trail, about 2600 miles long when it is completed, you'll cover only 16½° of latitude, going from about 32½° at the Mexican border to about 49° in Manning Park.

We now climb north above a tributary gully and reach a flat, where we meet another signed spur trail (3450–0.4), which heads 70 yards east-southeast to a spring. Camp can be made almost anywhere in this open-forest area. Beyond it we cross a northwest-trending linear meadow that is being invaded by lodgepoles, then we climb gradually increasing slopes up to a junction with Road 4245 (3720–1.0). Traveling southwest along this road, you would reach

F7, F8   **F8, F9, F10**

Little Crater Lake

Skyline Road in 3.4 miles. We walk 17 yards northeast up Road 4245 to a resumption of the trail and follow it north up to the east slope (4240–1.7) of andesitic Summit Butte (4790). Without getting a view anywhere, we make a gentle descent north, pass under a six-cable powerline, cross northwest over Red Wolf Pass (4120–1.4) without noticing it, then reach a jeep road (3990–0.8) that diagonals northeast across our route.

Our trail continues its northward descent and parallels a seasonal creek on our right (east), shortly before intersecting the closed Road 230 (3580–1.3), which, like our trail, heads toward the Clackamas Lake area. We cross this road and roughly parallel it northwest, leaving the Warm Springs Indian Reservation before we reach a junction with Miller Trail 534 (3400–1.9). The Miller Trail makes a moderate descent northwest before contouring west to fairly large, well-maintained Clackamas Lake Campground, 0.3 mile distant. Why it is so popular is a mystery, for nearby Clackamas Lake appears to be little more than a polluted cattle pond, and campground vistas are virtually nonexistent. Could it be the campground's two old-fashioned, muscle-powered water pumps? Judge for yourself. Actually, the lake's water is better than one would first guess, for it is spring-fed. The PCT turns north and proceeds through the forest bordering the meadow's edge to a usually dry crossing of Oak Grove Fork Clackamas River (3350–0.7) shortly before a junction with now

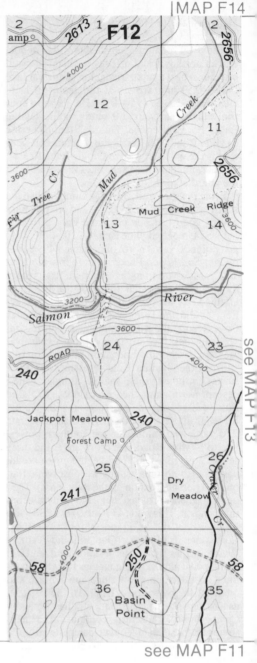

see MAP F14

see MAP F13

see MAP F11

paved Skyline Road 42 (3370–0.2). The PCT crosses this road just 90 yards northeast of the entrance to Joe Graham Horse Camp, which in turn is 200 yards northeast of a junction with Road 57. We start west on the trail and soon see Oak Grove Fork Clackamas River below us on our left (southwest). We momentarily descend to this creek, then climb a little and pass a spring

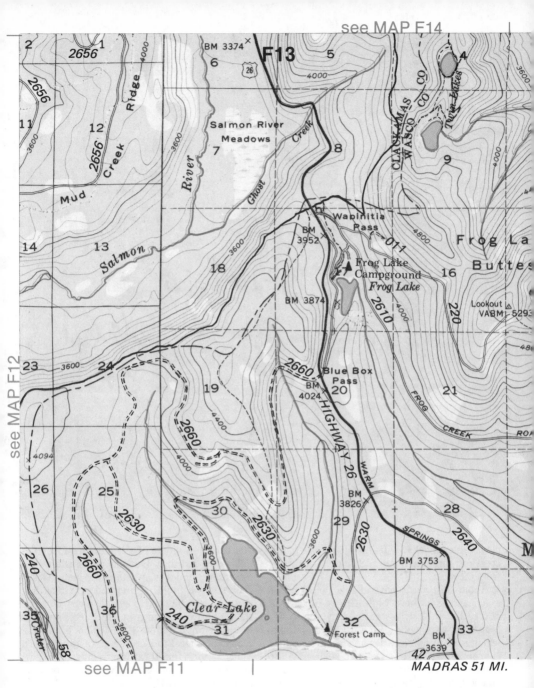

see MAP F12

see MAP F11

MADRAS 51 MI.

⅓ mile before reaching Timothy Trail 528 (3320–1.4), which makes an eight-mile traverse around Timothy Lake (3217), passing campgrounds, picnic areas and creeks before rejoining the PCT near the lake's northeast end.

You can see the lake from this junction, from which the PCT winds gradually down to its unappealing east shore. The shoreline improves as you head north, where you are perhaps tempted to swim across the lake's narrow arm or make an adequate campsite beside it. Farther north, the arm enlarges to a shallow bay that in late summer becomes a swamp, and the trail contours northeast around it, passing several trailside springs, some of them seasonal, a few minutes before you reach a bridge over wide,

F11

F11

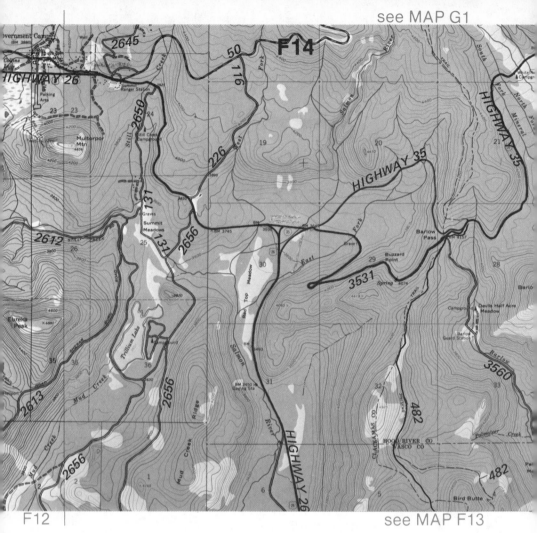

clear Crater Creek (3220–4.3). Just north of this crossing, Timothy Trail 528 rejoins our route from the west.

About 250 yards beyond this junction, we reach another, where Little Crater Lake Trail 500 (3230–0.2) strikes east 220 yards to 45-foot deep, extremely clear Little Crater Lake, which is an oversized artesian spring. Its purity is maintained by a fence that keeps out the cattle. You can camp either back near the trail junction or at pleasant Little Crater Campground, which is just 200 yards east of the lake. Little Crater looks like the ideal swimming hole, but stick your arm down into it—brrrr!—as with most springs, its water stays an almost constant year-round 40°F. We re-enter forest and get back on the PCT.

Our path north to Mt. Hood is now deficient in views, lakes, creeks and hikers, but it is great if you like the solitude of a shady forest, such as this one, that has Douglas-fir, western and mountain hemlocks, western red and Alaska cedars, silver, noble, grand and subalpine firs, and western white and lodgepole pines. Our trail starts northwest, then gradually curves north up to Road 5890 (3360–1.6), which gently descends northeast to a crossing of Crater Creek. We bear north for 30 yards on a diagonal across the road, then continue north up to Abbot Road 58 (3860–1.4), which would lead you back to Little Crater Campground and Skyline Road. Traversing through a forest of mountain hemlock and lodgepole, we next reach Linney Creek Road 240 (3880–0.8). Not far beyond it, we pass through a small campsite (3910–0.2), which has a seeping spring. This could be your last on-trail water until the upper Salmon River, 13.7 miles farther. However, water can be ob-

F11

F11, F12

tained ½ mile off the PCT at the Frog Lake Campground, about 4¾ miles away.

The PCT now climbs north to a saddle (4010–0.5), then makes a long northeast traverse through a beautiful forest with rhododenrons to a junction with Blue Box Trail 483, which strikes south to Clear Lake (3500). In 50 yards you reach U.S. Highway 26 (3910–3.5) at Wapinitia Pass. We used to recommend that hikers should follow this highway 7.7 miles to the post office and village store at Government Camp. While you can still take Highway 26 over to that settlement, you'll find the route noisy—in 1978 it was widened to four lanes to meet the demands of ever-increasing traffic. We now recommend another route that starts from Barlow Pass and is described at the end of this chapter.

Walking 70 yards closer to that pass, we reach a spur trail that goes 40 yards to the Wapinitia Pass PCT trailhead parking lot, beside the busy highway. From the parking lot, Road 2610 curves southeast and after ⅓ mile gives rise to Frog Lake Road 230, branching southwest. Starting on it, you'll come to the entrance to the new Frog Lake Campground, built in 1978. You might plan to camp here, or at least get water at it.

Only 120 yards past the parking-lot trail, the PCT meets southbound Frog Lake Trail 530, which quickly crosses Road 2610, then soon crosses Road 230 and parallels it to the northwest lobe of Frog Lake. Leaving Trail 530, the PCT continues northeast through a solemn forest of western hemlock, curves southeast upward, then makes a switchback north to a near-crest junction (4360–1.2). From here the Twin Lakes trail immediately crosses a crest saddle, visits the two glistening orbs, and then, after a total length of 2¾ miles, rejoins the PCT. This lake loop used to be a part of the PCT, but the easily accessible Twin Lakes became overused and the PCT was rerouted in the mid-70s. Still, many PCT hikers prefer this longer route, if not for its aesthetics, then at least for its water. No reliable water is found until off-route sources near Barlow Pass.

Beyond the near-crest junction, the PCT makes a shady, viewless traverse north to a broad saddle (4450–1.1), then continues northwest to a reunion with the loop trail (4500–0.5). From this junction our route heads north, passes by southeast descending Palmateer View Trail 482 (4550–0.5), then soon hugs the crest for a 1.2-mile descent to an *old* section of Highway 35 at Barlow Pass (4157–1.5). You'll find a

PCT trailhead parking area immediately west of here. Then, as you start to parallel the old highway northeast, you immediately cross Road 3560, descending south. Past it, the PCT soon becomes an abandoned road, which takes the hiker on a minute's walk to this section's end, a crossing of a new section of Highway 35 (4155–0.2). You should be able to find water in a gully about 130 yards east of this crossing. If not, and you're desperate, then start down the following alternate route, which begins 0.2 mile back.

*　　　*　　　*　　　*

Most hikers will continue along Section G's PCT to Timberline Lodge, which serves good, but expensive food, and which also holds parcels mailed to it—for a fee (see Section G: **Supplies**). Long-distance PCT hikers on a shoestring budget may want to have their parcels mailed to Government Camp Post Office, rather than to Timberline Lodge.

You can reach Government Camp by descending west along the old section of Highway 35, now Road 3531. Starting at Barlow Pass, this takes you down past an obvious roadside spring (4074–0.6) to a scenic hairpin turn, then down to a pioneer woman's grave, on your left, about 100 yards before crossing the East Fork Salmon River. Just ⅓ mile west of the crossing, Road 3531 ends at the new section of Highway 35 (3665–1.9).

Continuing west, you soon pass through the large, high-speed interchange of Highways 26 and 35, then follow traffic over to the start of the Timberline Lodge road (3980–2.7), opposite the Summit Ranger Station. Just ¼ mile past it, you fork right and take the Government Camp road through town, reaching Government Camp Post Office (3840–0.8–6.0) just 250 yards past the moderately well-stocked village store.

Now backtrack to the Timberline Lodge road (3980–0.8) and follow it up past the entrance to Alpine Campground (5450–4.5), then up to road's end at giant Timberline Lodge (5940–2.2–13.5). At the north end of the large hikers' parking lot, below the lodge, register at a small hut. You'll find the Pacific Crest Trail making an obvious slice across the slopes just above the lodge. Although you've bypassed part of the PCT by taking this alternate route, you can see from a distance the best part of what you've missed by following the PCT a long half mile eastward to the White River Buried Forest Overlook, described in Section G.

F12, F13, F14

F14, G1

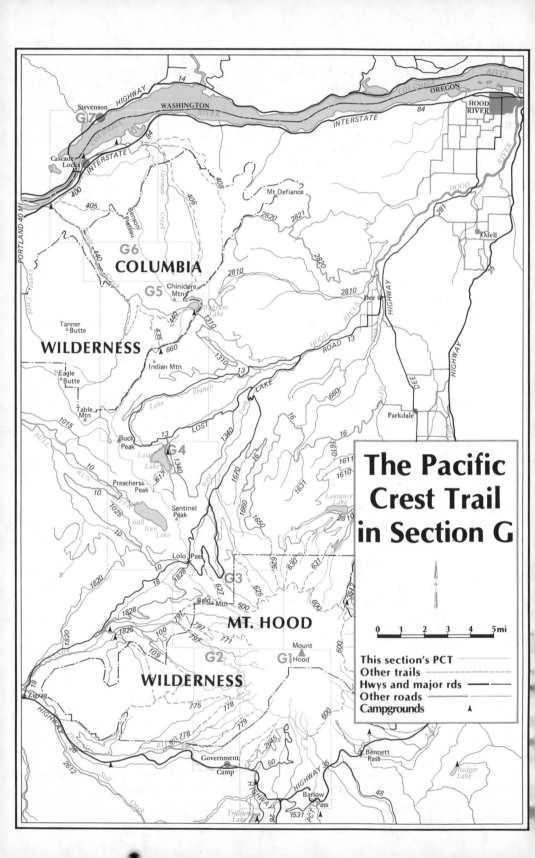

Section G: Highway 35 near Barlow Pass to Interstate 84 at Bridge of the Gods

Introduction: In this short section, the hiker traverses around Oregon's highest and most popular peak, glacier-robed Mt. Hood. If you start your hike at Timberline Lodge, you can traverse around the peak in one long, though relatively easy, 18.7-mile day. However, hiking in the opposite direction requires considerable effort, for in that direction you have a *net* (not total) gain of 2520 feet instead of a net loss.

From Bald Mountain north past Lolo Pass to Wahtum Lake, the scenery is subdued—a typical, forested Oregon Cascade crest. North of Wahtum Lake, the Pacific Crest Trail has the potential to be highly scenic if the route were only slightly relocated. As it now exists, it has a noticeable lack of views, particularly as you're descending into the spectacular Columbia River gorge. We therefore recommend the unusually beautiful, dramatic Eagle Creek Trail as an alternate route, for it abounds in waterfalls within a steep-walled canyon.

Declination: 18¾°E.

Mileages:

	South to North	Distance between Points	North to South
Highway 35 near Barlow Pass	0.0		54.4
		3.6	
Join the Timberline Trail	3.6		50.8
		1.4	
Timberline Lodge	5.0		49.4
		4.6	
Paradise Park Shelter	9.6		44.8
		6.0	
Ramona Falls	15.6		38.8
		5.3	
Leave the Timberline Trail	20.9		33.5
		2.8	
Lolo Pass	23.7		30.7
		4.3	
Huckleberry Mountain Trail	28.0		26.4
		8.2	
Indian Springs Campground	36.2		18.2
		2.6	
Wahtum Lake at Eagle Creek Trail junction	38.8		15.6
		4.8	
Camp Smokey saddle	43.6		10.8
		3.7	
Teakettle Spring	47.3		7.1
		3.0	
Lateral trail to Herman Creek	50.3		4.1
		4.1	
Bridge of the Gods, east end	54.4		0.0

Supplies: This section is short enough so that most hikers don't worry about supplies. However, the long-distance hiker will certainly want to pick up packages he mailed to Timberline Lodge, which lies only five miles into this section's route. In 1978 the lodge charged 25¢ per week for *each* package regardless if it was mailed or dropped off. By 1985 the rate per package had risen to $1.50 per week and $4 per month. Therefore, try to send only one package and not too early. You could avoid this charge by picking up your package at Government Camp, a few miles off the route. An alternate route at the end of

Section F tells you how to reach this small settlement. Timberline Lodge, like other mountain lodges, offers rooms, meals and showers, but it also has a hot pool and a sauna, which can be real treats for the trail-tired trekker.

Half way through your trek you can take the Huckleberry Mountain Trail down to a small store at the north end of Lost Lake. However, few hikers do so.

Finally, at trail's end in Cascade Locks, you can find almost anything you need. If you can't, take the bus west into Portland or east to much closer Hood River.

Section G begins where the PCT diagonals across the east end of a relatively new stretch of Highway 35. This crossing is 40 yards northeast of the new Barlow Pass elevation sign (4161), which in turn is 40 yards northeast of the old stretch of Highway—*now* Road 3531. (The *real* Barlow Pass is ¼ mile southwest of the PCT crossing.) Road 3531 goes ¼ mile southwest to a PCT trailhead parking area—the start of Section F's alternate route that goes to Government Camp. If you must stock up on water, get it at an obvious roadside spring ½ mile southwest past the parking area or in a gully about 130 yards east of where the PCT crosses Highway 35.

From Highway 35 (4155), the PCT starts northeast, but immediately angles west for a climb to the Cascade divide. Ascending north, it stays close to the crest of the divide, then quickly curves northwest over to a gully (4870–2.7) with a campsite and with *usually* flowing water. From this cool forest retreat, our trail methodically climbs over to the slopes of the Salmon River canyon, where we can look west toward Alpine Campground and see a cliff below it of loose hornblende andesite debris. Our trail then climbs northeast up to a junction with Timberline Trail 600 (5340–0.9), which starts a descent east to the White River. This trail, which stays near timberline as it circles Mt. Hood (11,235), offers an alternative 22.7-mile route if you take it counterclockwise to a reunion with the PCT near Bald Mountain. Clockwise, it coincides with the PCT, which starts northwest up a ridge of loose, gravelly debris, and soon ramifies into a number of sandy paths that parallel one another up the ridge.

If you look east at the cliff composed of unsorted volcanic debris that is above the White River, you'll get an idea of the type of sediments you're walking on. These deposits, which are on the south and southwest slopes of Hood, are remnants of a huge debris fan of hornblende andesite that was formed 1700–2000 years ago when a crater was blasted out near the mountain's summit and a plug dome of viscous lava welled up, melting the surrounding ice field. The sudden release of frozen water created devastating mudflows that carried the volcanic debris down to these slopes that the PCT crosses today. Due north of us, we can identify Crater Rock (10,560), which is a remnant of that plug dome. Just north of it, numerous fissures still emit steam and hydrogen-sulfide gas. On clear, windless days the gas emissions from these fumaroles are visible from as far away as Portland. Mt. Hood had minor eruptions during the last century, and we can be sure that it is still alive today.

Our paths eventually merge, and we reach the White River Buried Forest Overlook (5790–0.8), which in 1978 was signed with an incorrect elevation, as many such signs are. If you scrutinize the *lower* mudflow sediments in the canyon's wall opposite you, you should be able to recognize a few buried snags. It was these snags that provided radiocarbon dates for eruptions mentioned in the previous paragraph.

Leaving the overlook, we soon curve northwest away from the canyon views, cross a dry creek bed, then cross the upper Salmon River (5900–0.3), which derives its flow from an arm of the Palmer Glacier. This flow is your first reliable on-route water since a seeping spring just past Linney Creek Road, 13.7 trail miles south. The trail now contours southwest past an ascending dirt road, then quickly reaches a spur trail (5960–0.2)—one of many—that descends to the east side of gigantic Timberline Lodge (5940–0.1). No hiker should pass up the opportunity to inspect this grand structure built by the Works Progress Administration in the late 1930s.

Just east of and below the lodge's parking lot is an even larger lot for backpackers and mountaineers; and at its north end is a small hut

G1   G1

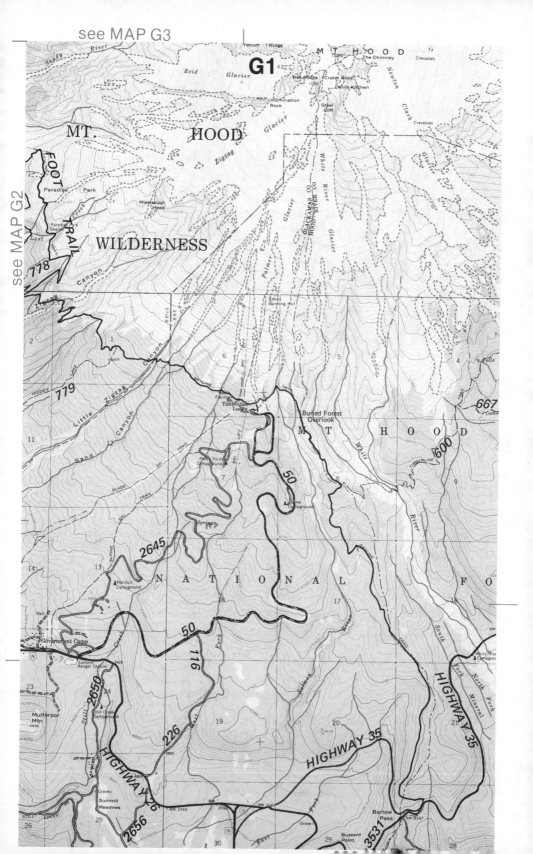

G1

MT HOOD

Yocum Ridge

Reid Glacier

The Chimney
Crevasses

Hot Rocks
Crater Rock
Devils Kitchen
Newton
Clark

Illumination
Rock

Sthel Cliff

Crevasses

Glacier

MT.

HOOD

Zigzag

Glacier

FOOT TRAIL

Paradise
Park

CLACKAMAS CO
HOOD RIVER CO

White River

Glacier

Mississippi
Head

Palmer
Glacier

Paradise Park
Shelter

WILDERNESS

778

Canyon

Silcox Warming Hut

HIDDEN

2

779

TRAIL

Little Zigzag Canyon

667

SKI

SKYLINE

Timberline
Lodge

667

6

5

Falls

UMBR

4

Sand

TRAIL

Buried Forest
Overlook

M T

H O O D

11

Canyon

LIFT

White River

TIMBERLINE

600

GLADE

TRAIL

Pima Point
Campground

7

50

9

8

SKI TRAIL

Alpine
Campground

14

13

ALPINE

Springs

Nanitch
Campground

2645

N A T I O N A L

F O

Well

18

17

15

Government Camp

50

226

226

26

Summit
Ranger Station

116

South Fork Salmon

White River
Campground

BM

23

34

2650

Multorpor
Mtn
4656

Still Creek
Campground

19

Fork

20

Salmon

21

HIGHWAY 35

North Fork Mineral

226

HIGHWAY 35

HIGHWAY 26

2656

Graves
Summit
Meadows

25

BM 3745

3590

BM 360

4410

3500

East

Grave

29

Buzzard
Point

Barlow
Pass

35351

BM 4157

26

30

28

Southbound hiker near the White River Buried Forest Overlook

Mt. Hood's White River Glacier

in which you should register if you plan to hike any farther or if you plan to climb Mt. Hood. Mountaineers who climb Mt. Hood often try to reach its summit by sunrise in order to avoid avalanche hazards generated by warming snow and ice. By early July rockfalls can become a real danger along south-slope routes. Don't attempt to climb the peak unless you are an experienced mountaineer and are familiar with Hood's routes and hazards.

After ascending one of the spur trails or roads from the lodge back to the PCT, we hike west under the ski lift and past a microwave tower (5980–0.2) below us, then gradually descend westward with views south across a rolling topography to lofty Mt. Jefferson (10,497). Several seasonal creeks are crossed before we make a three-yard boulder-hop across silty Little Zigzag creek (5760–0.9), enter Mt. Hood Wilderness, then continue our descent to a junction with Hidden Lake Trail 779 (5680–0.4), which goes southwest down a morainal ridge to Hidden Lake. Our trail continues its rambling descent, then climbs to a narrow ridge from where we get a great view of Mt. Hood and glaciated Zigzag Canyon. We switchback down the steep slope, jump across the silty Zigzag River (4890–1.3), and climb moderately into a tributary canyon, then out of it up to a slope where the PCT (5140–0.5) splits into two routes.

*　　*　　*　　*

G1

The newer horse trail starts west-southwest and switchbacks up to a broad ridge where we intersect Paradise Park Trail 778 (5390–0.4), a footpath that climbs northeast. The horse trail ascends north across the ridge and passes a camping area below us just before it turns northeast and descends to splashing Lost Creek (5390–0.6), which cascades down a cliff just east of us. We cross it and its more reserved tributary, then pass another camping area below us as we make a climb west up to a ridge, top the ridge, and descend once again—this time to a crossing of Rushing Water Creek (5440–0.6) just below its narrow waterfall. After climbing steeply north out of this cliff-bound canyon, we follow a rather direct trail down to a reunion with the foot trail (5400–0.5–2.1).

*　　*　　*　　*

The older foot trail, which is by far the more scenic route, starts northeast and zigzags up the tributary canyon of Zigzag Canyon. If you're wondering about the composition of the loose cliffs—yes, they are part of the debris-fan deposits that originated from the Crater Rock area. Our ascent finally eases off just after gaining access to a ridge and meeting Paradise Park Trail 778 (5740–1.0), a footpath descending west-southwest through an alpine meadow. We now hike over to Lost Creek (5720–0.2), whose banks are ablaze with common and Lewis monkey flowers, lupine, bistort, corn lily, Mariposa lily, yarrow, paintbrush, pasqueflower, aster and eriogonum.

Remembering that campsites must be at least 100 feet from any creek or body of water, we push onward and quickly reach the Paradise Park Shelter (5730–0.1) in an open forest of dwarf hemlock. This ten-foot-square shelter, constructed with andesite blocks from the surrounding lava flow, once had an operable fireplace. Beyond it, our trail makes a slight climb, then contours across more alpine meadows, and perhaps gives us a chance to spot a pair of sparrow hawks before it switchbacks down to a reunion with the PCT horse trail (5400–2.2).

We now make a switchbacking descent and obtain two fantastic views: up toward the glacier-mantled summit above and down upon the mountain's anatomy below, exposed by the incising Sandy River. We get one more view— from a vertical-sided ridge at the end of a 50-yard spur trail—and it is the most revealing of

all: the cliffs of the Sandy River canyon and its tributary canyon are composed of andesite flows and interbedded pyroclastic deposits. As if this flood of magnificent scenery were not enough to satisfy, our trail takes us down to the west side of the ridge where, from a viewpoint, we are saturated with the impressive, naked

G2

see MAP G3

G2

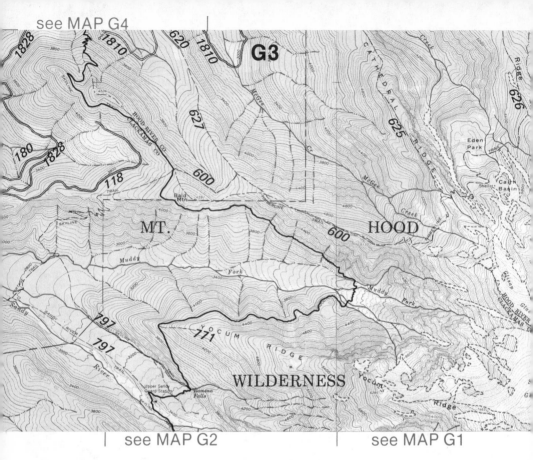

see MAP G2 | see MAP G1

cliffs of Slide Mountain (4872) and of the Rushing Water Creek canyon all around us.

After such a day as this, one is bound to reminisce about his alpine adventure, and a good place to stop and talk it over is at large, flat Scout Camp (3400–3.0) which is beside Rushing Water Creek at the bottom of the switchbacks from the viewpoint. Leaving this forested site, which is closed to camping, we descend the trail northwest 100 yards and arrive at the bouldery, bushy bottom of the Sandy River canyon. We immediately make a log crossing of the three-yard-wide river, which in high runoff expands to fill its 30-yard-wide channel. Continuing northwest downstream on a sandy trail, we wind 270 yards between bushes and over bars to a low cliff of unsorted, poorly bedded sediments of a glacial moraine. Our trail makes a short climb up it and reaches a flat bench (3270–0.3), which is suitable for camping. From it, a steep path climbs about 50 yards east to Upper Sandy Guard Station, which is often locked and unmanned. From the bench, the PCT climbs north to a quick junction with Ramona Falls Loop Trail 797 (3320–0.1), which de-

scends northwest from the rim of a high stream terrace. If you need help or if the weather is terrible, you can abort your trip by descending 1½ miles along this trail to Muddy Fork Road 1825–100, which you take 1½ miles west to Road 1825, then 1½ miles down to Riley Horse Camp, or ¼-mile farther to McNeil Campground. One-fourth mile past this campground, Road 1825 ends at Road 1828, which goes ½ mile southwest to Lolo Pass Road 18. This continues southwest 4¼ miles to the settlement of Zigzag, beside Highway 26.

The Ramona Falls Loop Trail, the Muddy Fork Road and other trails and roads between these and Interstate 84 were ordered closed on November 24, 1976, when James Burns, a Federal judge, issued a final decree. This decision stemmed from a 1973 lawsuit brought against the Mt. Hood National Forest by a coalition of environmentalists who wanted to halt logging operations in Portland's watershed, the Bull Run Reserve. Judge Burns agreed with the environmentalists, but added that a strict interpretation of the legislation that banned logging in the first place—the 1904 Bull Run

Trespass Act—also prevented any kind of trespass. Hence the trails were closed and environmentalists (not to mention the general public) were banned from enjoying the land they sought to preserve. Fortunately, Congress in 1977 drew up and passed the Bull Run Watershed Management Act, which changed the watershed boundaries, and popular trails such as the Ramona Falls Loop Trail and the Eagle Creek Trail were again opened to the public.

Bearing this legal lesson in mind, we start southeast along the loop trail, then follow it east across the broad terrace, which sprouts a dry, open forest, to beautiful Ramona Falls (3460–0.4), splashing down moss-draped rocks. Due to overuse in the past, no camping is allowed within 500 feet of the falls. Just a few yards after we cross the falls' creek, we leave the loop trail, which descends along the creek while we climb high above it to a ridge junction with Yocum Ridge Trail 771 (4000–0.6). During the mid-70s, this trail was extended southeast up to

alpine slopes near the south edge of Sandy Glacier.

The PCT climbs as it leaves this ridge trail, then it levels and traverses in and out of gullies, and drops to a cluster of small campsites (4100–2.0) about 70 yards before the first glacier-fed tributary of Muddy Fork. You may have to wade across the first three tributaries, particularly if you are crossing them on a hot afternoon. Between the second and third fords, you get particularly impressive views up-canyon of a serrated, pinnacle-studded ridge that separates cascading creeks which descend from spreading Sandy Glacier.

Beyond the third ford we make a minute's stroll over to the jump-across fourth ford, which, unlike the others, flows beneath forest cover. Another minute down it, we come to a spur trail (4060–0.4) that immediately crosses the creek to an official, south-bank, four-person campsite. Just past it the PCT leaves the canyon floor, then in ½ mile makes a gentle ascent westward. We

G3

Exposed sediments of Slide Mountain

G3

see MAP G3

HIGHWAY 26 9 MI.

pass several creeklets before we traverse Bald Mountain's south slopes. On these we get unrestricted views of towering Mt. Hood, forested Muddy Fork canyon, and the canyon's east-end, glacier-fed cascades.

Views disappear as we curve north out of Mt. Hood Wilderness, enter forest cover and make a ¼-mile easy descent to a shady-crest junction with the old Oregon Skyline Trail (4270–2.3), climbing from the west. Here, Timberline Trail 600, which has been with us since mile 3.6 of this section's hike, strikes east for a 22.7-mile traverse around Mt. Hood back to that mileage point.

G3   G3

Ramona Falls

From this junction, our route is mostly down-hill to the Columbia River. Descending north-west 50 yards, we reach a junction with Top Spur Trail 785, which starts a westward descent toward Road 1828–118. We continue our forested route northwest to the crest's end (4200–1.4), then start north down a series of switchbacks. The thorny gooseberries, thimble-berries and giant Devil's clubs attest to the cool, moist slope of this forest, which we leave behind as we descend a drier north ridge to a flat clear-ing immediately south of Lolo Pass Road 18 (3420–1.4) at Lolo Pass. A quarter mile west of here, you can find water running down to the road. The north trailhead is about 20 yards southwest along paved Road 18 and 30 yards before this road's junction with paved Road 1828. Immediately east of the PCT, Road 1810 branches southeast from Road 18, taking one 0.4 mile to spring-fed water.

We start northwest from Lolo Pass, quickly cross north under four sets of buzzing power lines, and then glance back northeast at Mt. Hood's deeply glaciated north face. Before the glaciers performed their cosmetic surgery, the peak's summit towered to about 12,000 feet. You soon reach a gully with a trickling creek (3520–0.4), then climb gradually north to the divide, and circle around the east slope of Sentinel Peak (4565). Rejoining the divide, we contour northwest past two low summits before arriving at a junction with Huckleberry Moun-tain Trail 617 (4020–3.9), which descends slightly for 0.3 mile to a trickling creek in the gully below the Preachers/Devils saddle. If you descend this trail farther, you reach Lost Lake (3143–1.7), follow its east shore north to Lost Lake Campground (3160–0.8), then finally reach a small store (3160–0.3–2.8) by the lake's north end. The Oregon Skyline Trail once followed this shoreline route, but the trail segment has since been abandoned.

From the junction we contour 270 yards to a sharp bend in the trail, where a spur trail descends 50 yards to a trickling creek and a small flat called Salvation Spring Camp. Back on route, we continue north to an obvious gully and then switchback up to the Preachers/Devils saddle (4340–0.9). Avoiding sermons from its two summits, we follow a huckleberry-lined path in a forest of hemlock and fir, descend to a saddle, climb north up the ridge above Lost Lake, and then descend west to a notch (4250–1.9). Now, a short, stiff climb north takes us to a saddle and a junction with Buck Peak Trail 615 (4500–0.5), which continues along the ridge up to Buck Peak (4751). We descend north across the west slope of this peak and discover a small spring (4340–0.4) a couple feet below the west edge of the trail. A little farther down the trail, we reach the ridge (4230–0.3) again, then switchback down to a long saddle, from which we can get a glimpse below of Blue Lake (3780) to the southwest. As we arc northeast, we leave Portland's Bull Run Watershed behind for good, and with it the posted *no camping* signs that have bothered us while within that section of the county since Lolo Pass. They don't want fires.

Ahead, we'll flirt with the southeast boundary of Columbia Wilderness for more than 7 miles, as both the PCT and the wilderness boundary parallel an old crestline road northeast. Columbia Wilderness, about 61 square miles in size and containing about 125 miles of trail, was offi-cially created in 1984. Before that date the area had long been a *de facto* wilderness, spared the logger's ax. It's good to know we don't see any clearcutting once we reach Wahtum Lake. We'll

G5

Falls

434

440

600

1600

Wahtum Lake
Guard Sta

Hicks
Lake

406

670

Blue Ridge Camp

Tunnel Falls

Chinidere
Mtn
4673

Wahtum
Lake

670

Falls

East

2000

EAGLE

Fork

TRAIL

Forest Ca

660

3½ Mile Camp

F   O   R   E   S   T

440

Scout
Lake

13

1600

3600

CREEK

3600

4400

COLUMBIA

WILDERNESS

660

4400

1600

435

3200

Indian
Springs

Forest
Camp

W   A

660

Falls

Creek

M

Indian

660

Indian Mtn
Lookout

322

2800

4000

2800

2400

No   Name

Creek

13

2400

Eagle

3200

W   A   U   C   O

4400

13

ROAD

2400

2800

Branch

BRANCH   13

2400

2800

TRAIL

BASE   LINE

3600

LAKE

3600

3600

Sawtooth   Mountain

Creek   Lake

3

2

Laure

223

SKYLINE

Washout

13

Raker Pt

4

3600

13   LOST

2800

Blue
Lake

Buck Pk

8

9

10

Lost Lake Butte

11

Mt. Hood, from one mile north of Buck Peak

certainly see enough of it to the east of us as we make a crestline traverse.

This stretch follows a fairly level crest northeast, contours across the southeast slope of a low, triangular summit, then, just below a saddle, reaches the abandoned Oregon Skyline Trail (4190–2.2), which climbs from the southwest to merge with the PCT. Climbing gently northeast, we quickly reach Larch Mountain Road 322 (4240–0.1), which is momentarily atop the ridge. We locate the trail on the northwest side of the road, parallel it northnortheast and then round the narrow north spur (4400–1.6) of Indian Mountain (4890), from which we see Mts. St. Helens (8364), Rainier (14,410) and Adams (12,276). Then we descend eastward to Indian Springs Campground (4300–0.3), which has few car campers because of the rough, rocky nature of Road 660, which is used to reach it. Unfortunately, this area had to be logged over to remove snags left by a devastating 1920 fire. The camp's spring is just beyond the west end of the camp's road loop, and just beyond it, the brushy, unmaintained Indian Springs Trail 435 starts northwest toward the north spur, follows it, then steeply descends it two miles to Eagle Creek Trail 440.

The PCT recommences at the east end of the loop and parallels the road, first below it, then above it to a saddle, where it leaves the roadside and winds gently down a forested slope, then northeast down to a junction with Eagle Creek Trail 440 (3750–2.6) just above the southwest shore of Wahtum Lake (3732).

*　　　*　　　*　　　*

The hike from Wahtum Lake down to the Columbia River is far more scenic along the Eagle Creek Trail than along the PCT, and is therefore described here as a highly recommended alternate route. From the Wahtum Lake outlet (3740–0.1), which is the East Fork of Eagle Creek, Trail 440 begins as a typical trail, for it descends through a Douglas-fir forest with an understory that includes inconspicuous annuals such as coolwort, false Solomon's seal, queen's cup, bunchberry and vanilla-leaf. In a north-draining canyon, we reach an adequate campsite beside a trickling creek (3300–1.2), then arc westward gently down to a ford of the Indian Springs fork (3040–0.8) of Eagle Creek, which could be tricky to cross in early summer. Along its banks is a very good campsite.

We now begin a descent northwest that takes us past rhododendron, gooseberry, red elderberry, thimbleberry, huckleberry, Devil's club and Oregon grape. Along this cool descent, you may see Indian Springs Trail 435, which climbs two steep miles up to Indian Springs Campground. After reaching a viewpoint (2350–1.6) at the tip of a north spur, our trail turns south and descends past a campsite (1920–1.0) by a shallow gully, crosses seasonal creeklets, and then makes a switchback (1600–0.7) north.

G5　　　　　　　　　　　　**G5**

The slope is now much gentler, and in the near distance we can hear Eagle Creek splashing merrily down its course. In a short distance we reach a rockbound creek (1440–0.5) and pause for a drink. Don't be too surprised if a red-spotted garter snake is climbing up a rock behind you; he needs water too. It is not uncommon to encounter half a dozen of these beneficial snakes in a day's hike along this verdant route. Just beyond this refreshing creek we meet several trails that descend about 50 yards west to 7½ Mile Camp (1380–0.1), complete with a primitive shelter. If you intend to camp before reaching the trailhead, this certainly is a good place to stop at. Before us lies the string of impressive waterfalls that make this last half of the trail so popular.

Our trail gradually descends to the bank of Eagle Creek, and we see a 50-foot cascade (1180–0.7)—not too impressive—but a sample of what's to come. The creek enters a safe, very deep, crystal-clear pool (1120–0.3) that is extremely tempting for an afternoon swim, but the cool water will ensure that you won't stay in for long. Immediately beyond it is a two-stage, 100 foot-high waterfall, sliced into a narrow gorge, which we don't see until we round a vertical cliff, where our precariously exposed trail, blasted from the cliff, heads toward 150-foot-high Tunnel Falls (1120–0.2). This trail is definitely not for the faint-hearted, nor is its ceiling sufficient for those on horseback. The fall, in its grotto of vertical-walled basalt, is spectacular enough to make it the climax of this route, but our sensations of it are heightened even more as we head through a wet tunnel blasted behind the fall about midway up it. Exuberant from the wall of water around us, we leave this grotto of the East Fork in expectation of more high adventure. Below us, Eagle Creek cascades 30 feet down to another layer of this Miocene Columbia River basalt.

Our trail's exposure decreases considerably as we leave the falls' narrow gorge. We soon reach pleasant Blue Grouse Camp (1120–0.3), then continue on to a junction with Eagle Benson Trail 434 (1000–0.5), which climbs steeply up to the PCT. This narrow footpath is not recommended by the authors, who believe it is too narrow to be safely climbed or descended with a heavy pack. In places it is quite easy for you to slip on loose gravel and then fall over a hundred-foot cliff. Just around the corner from this junction, our trail enters another side canyon and bridges a murmuring tributary a hundred yards downstream from its slender, 80-foot-high fall. Unseen above it is the Eagle Benson Trail, which descends near the mossy brink of this graceful fall.

Continuing northwest, we soon enter another side canyon, and this one provides us with Wy East Camp (960–0.5), which is just above the trail. Progressing farther downstream on this trail, we reach a bridge (710–0.7) across Eagle Creek, 20 feet below. A daredevil instinct may urge some to jump from the bridge into the tempting 8-foot-deep pool below, but better judgment takes hold and we pass up the opportunity for another time.

Now above the creek's west bank, we follow the singing creek down to the popular, excellent 4 Mile Camp (680–0.6), also known as the "Tenas Camp." How many campsites do you know of that have a beautiful waterfall near them? We've seen just a few. This one has a two-step, 40-foot fall, and near it, you'll find the dipper, or water ouzel, which is a gray, chunky, water-loving bird that tenaciously clings to the bottoms of swift streams in search of aquatic animal life. The name "dipper" refers to the bird's bobbing motions while standing on land, and, taking that word as a suggestion, we decide to take a dip in the 57°F creek ourselves. After a quick, invigorating frolic in the pools below the lower fall, we stretch out in the afternoon sunlight to thaw out before hiking once again.

Back on the trail, we walk spiritedly north to a bridge (690–0.3) across a 90-foot-deep creek that is only 30 feet wide. A hundred yards downstream from this crossing, the swirling creek has cut, with the aid of churning boulders, deep potholes that would make superb swimming holes were it not for the cool temperature. The six-inch trout don't seem to mind it though. Above the potholes, wispy Loowit Falls emerges from the vegetation to flow silently down the polished rock and into one of the pools.

Continuing downstream, we soon enter another side canyon, bridge a creek 50 feet above it, then pass by massive, vertical-walled flows of this Columbia River basalt. The contact between two flows tends to be a weak point, and both the creek and its tributaries tend to flow along such contacts. The height of a waterfall often represents the thickness of a single flow. The minutes pass by quickly, and before we know it, we cross Tish Creek and arrive at an overlook (500–1.4) above Punch Bowl Falls, which drops 40 feet into a churning cauldron

Along a part of the Eagle Creek Trail below Tunnel Falls

below us. It's hard to judge just how deep this huge pool is, but right beneath the falls a depth of 20 feet wouldn't be much of an exaggeration.

Here our trail starts to climb high above the now-impassable gorge, and we soon see more reasons why horses aren't allowed on the trail. At times, the overhanging walls seem to press us terribly close to the brink of the dead-vertical cliff below us, and we're thankful that the trail crew installed cables along these stretches. We now reach another overlook (520–0.7), where we can look 200 yards upstream to Metlako Falls, whose silvery course plummets another step down into the inaccessible gorge.

Our route gradually begins to descend toward the trailhead, and we leave the threatening,

Eagle Creek gorge just above Loowit Falls

moss-covered cliffs behind as we descend into the realm of a cedar-and-Douglas-fir forest. Alder, maple, dogwood, ocean spray, blackberries, thimbleberries, moss, three species of ferns and dozens of wildflowers harmonize with the conifers on these canyon slopes to create a symphony of nature at her best. All too soon, our verdant route reaches the trailhead (150–1.5), which is by a bridge that spans Eagle Creek. On the creek's west side, you'll find a short, looping nature trail that splits off from climbing, 1.8-mile Wauna View Point Trail 402.

To reach Bridge of the Gods, we take Gorge Trail 400, which starts from the parking area. This trail climbs through a picnic area, crosses the short road up to Eagle Creek Campground (200–0.1), passes between the campground and Interstate 84, then quickly reaches a part of the abandoned, narrow Columbia River 'highway.' On this we curve over to Ruckel Creek (230–0.6), where, on its east bank, Ruckel Creek Trail 405 makes a 5.3-mile climb to the Pacific Crest Trail.

Our shady gorge trail continues northeast, and at times it almost touches Interstate 84. After traversing a few hundred yards across grassy slopes—absolutely miserable in the rain—the trail ends at Moody Avenue opposite the PCT (280–1.9–16.3). From here the PCT route follows a road under nearby Interstate 84, then as a trail again it curves 200 yards over toward the toll booth at the south end of Bridge of the Gods. See the end of this section's PCT description for a list of the available services in Cascade Locks.

*   *   *   *

The Pacific Crest Trail, which is 0.8 mile shorter than the Eagle Creek route, starts a

G7, G5

see MAP G7

H O O D

405B D

G6

31   2800   32   3600   33   34

434

Camp Smokey

Loowit Falls

440   Falls   COLUMBIA   WILDERNESS

4 Mile Camp

Tomli

3600

2000

3200   3200

4380

see MAP G5

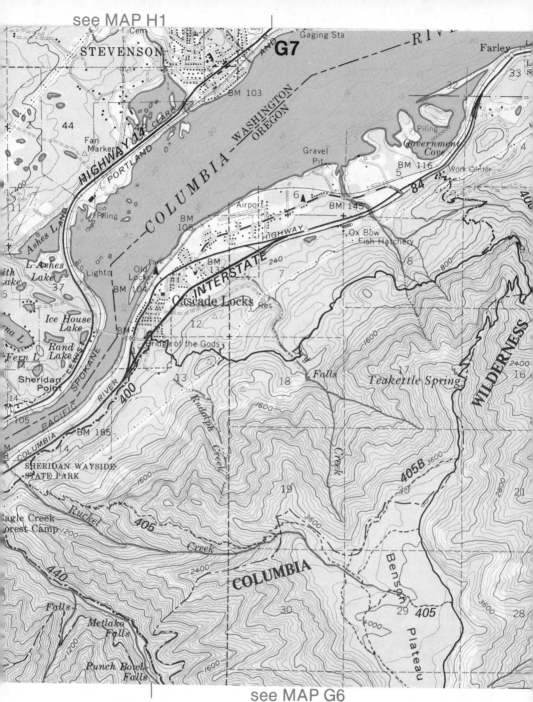

see MAP G6

traverse east along Wahtum Lake's southwest shore. It then meets a lateral trail (3750–0.2) that climbs ⅓ mile up to the Wahtum Lake Campground, atop a saddle. From that saddle Road 1310 descends southeast toward other roads that lead out to the city of Hood River, and crest-hugging Road 660, from Indian Springs

Campground, crosses the saddle and traverses northeast high above Wahtum Lake.

From the lateral-trail junction, the PCT, like Road 670, circles Wahtum Lake, leaving its popular south-shore campsites behind. The trail's gentle, long, counterclockwise climb ends high above the lake at a junction with a ¼-mile-

G5

G5

long spur trail that heads northeast to Road 670. In 200 yards our now-level trail reaches a junction with the Chinidere Mountain Trail (4270–1.8). If you're having good weather, don't pass up this ⅓-mile long, 400-foot ascent to its superb, panoramic summit. From the summit you can see decapitated Mt. Helens rising skyward above the north-northwest horizon, massive Mt. Adams lording over the north-northeast horizon, and graceful Mt. Hood dominating the south-southeast horizon. You also see the Columbia River and Wind River canyons, due north, while closer by, you're surrounded by deep, slightly glaciated canyons.

Leaving the Chinidere Mountain Trail junction, the PCT curves northwest around this miniature mountain to a saddle (4140–0.6), then contours across the southwest slopes of summit 4380 to a crest viewpoint. It then drops to a second saddle (3830–1.4) and traverses to a third saddle (3810–0.8), this one signed *Camp Smokey.* Perhaps someone once smoked too much, for these two saddles and the southwest-facing slopes between them were part of an area burned by a large forest fire. A small campsite is found at the Camp Smokey saddle, but a better one is found 180 yards down the Eagle Benson Trail. You'll find a refreshing spring just 50 yards past the campsite. Beyond the spring, the Eagle Benson Trail, descending to Eagle Creek, is usually unmaintained.

Pushing toward the deep Columbia Gorge, we leave the Camp Smokey saddle and climb up to the southeast edge of spreading Benson Plateau, which is a preglacial land surface that is being slowly devoured by back-cutting tributaries of Herman and Eagle creeks. In a gully on the plateau's southeast edge, we meet lightly used Benson Way Trail 405B (4100–0.5), which starts west but eventually curves north over to the Ruckel Creek Trail.

Staying near the plateau's east edge, the PCT winds north to the Ruckel Creek Trail 405 (4110–0.9), which you can follow west ½ mile to a large campsite. This campsite is the only one between Wahtum Lake and Dry Creek that is suitable for equestrians, so don't be surprised if you find horses at it. Forty yards south of this campsite you'll find a spring in a small meadow. From this campsite you could continue about 4.8 miles down the trail to Gorge Trail 400, which is mentioned at the end of the alternate Eagle Creek Trail route, described earlier.

Beyond the Ruckel Creek Trail junction, the PCT descends gently northwest along the pla-

teau's east edge and it soon meets the abandoned-but-visible Benson Ruckel Trail (3980–0.7), which once traversed west-southwest one mile to the Ruckel Creek Trail. Past this junction the PCT curves northeast and leaves Benson Plateau by the time it arrives at a junction with the *second* Benson Way Trail 405B (3760–0.7). Here you'll find a waterless campsite that will accommodate four persons.

We now hike north along a forested crest and pass another waterless campsite (3680–0.6) just before the trail curves east to begin a descent into the deep Columbia Gorge. Our moderately-to-steeply dropping trail briefly descends the crest, then heads west to a switchback. Immediately past this turn we encounter Teakettle Spring (3360–0.3), which can easily be missed when its sign is gone.

Past the spring our trail switchbacks once again down to the crest, on which it reaches a barren area that gives us revealing views of the giant Columbia Gorge. We can identify the towns of Cascade Locks, Stevenson and Carson, and with the use of this book's maps can mentally sketch the winding route of the PCT up the gorge's north wall. You can also identify large landslides (see the beginning description of Section H). To the west we see an impressive set of cliffs that are composed of the same kind of volcanic rocks that compose our barren area—pyroclastic rocks. These indicate that in preglacial times a volcano may have existed at this site or close by.

From the barren area atop the crest, our trail starts west, turns north, soon crosses the crest, then makes a fairly steep, viewless descent into the deep Columbia Gorge, recrossing the crest—now a ridge—near its lower end. From it, the PCT traverses ⅓ mile west to a junction (1120–3.0) with a 1.8-mile trail that provides a fast way out to the highway, ending at the Columbia Gorge Work Center.

The hiker who intends to cross into Washington should continue along the westbound Pacific Crest Trail. Departing from the lateral trail down to Herman Creek, the PCT continues its traverse across open talus slopes, then enters a cool, mossy forest of Douglas-fir and maple. A creek is soon crossed (960–0.5), just beyond which we pass through a shallow saddle and then round a steep bowl. As our trail reaches a ridge and turns west to leave the bowl, a spur trail heads northwest steeply down the east side of a small gully. The PCT traverses southwest for about a mile, dropping slowly, then turns south and

Bridge of the Gods

southeast. Our trail contours over toward a saddle and joins a power-line road (680–0.7) that climbs up and over it. We head northwest down this road only 70 yards, then branch left on the trail. This segment rollercoasters west ½ mile around the north slopes of a low summit, turns north and descends to Moody Avenue. The Eagle Creek Trail alternate route ends here, opposite the PCT.

Down this dirt road we go 70 yards to its junction with SE Undine Street (240–1.0), where it becomes paved. Moody Avenue immediately crosses under the freeway, and 5 yards west of the freeway's largest pillar, the PCT resumes, curving 200 yards northwest over to the paved loop road that leads up to the Bridge of the Gods (200–0.1). Section G ends here and Section H begins on the other side of the Columbia River, at the bridge-road junction with Washington's Highway 14, 0.5 mile distant. In 1985 it cost 25¢ to walk across Bridge of the Gods.

If you're a long-distance hiker, you'll want to resupply in Cascade Locks. Walk down to the town's nearby thoroughfare, old U.S. Highway 30, which here is known as Wa Na Pa Street. On it you walk 0.4 mile northeast to the Cascade Locks Post Office, which is conveniently located opposite the Columbia Gorge Center, with a general store, a restaurant and other stores. In another 0.4 mile you'll reach a road that heads north to the Cascade Locks Marine Park. It has a campground and nearby, in the visitors center, it has showers. Both are *free* to PCT hikers. One great feature of the park's campground is its roofed cooking area, with tables, under which you can camp and keep dry on those all-too-often rainy days. In this park you can visit the shipping locks, built in 1896, which allowed ships to travel upriver beyond the Columbia River's Cascade Rapids. The town of Cascade Locks was spawned by the resulting commercial activity. Be sure to visit the park's museum before you resume you trek, but don't be taken in by a "serious" explanation for a *natural* Bridge of the Gods—it grossly misinterprets geologic evidence.

If you are waiting for the weather to improve, then you might spend time at the city hall, on Wa Na Pa Street ⅓ mile east of the park entrance. Most of this building is, surprisingly, occupied by an indoor basketball court, but there is also a neat little library tucked away in an upstairs room. Here you can catch up on all the gruesome news you've been missing while out on the trail.

quickly descends to a bridge across perennial, misnamed Dry Creek (720–1.8). Camping is possible here and at other spots along this creek. Immediately beyond it, we encounter a dirt road, which can be followed 0.2 mile up to its end, where you'll see an ideal shower—a 50-foot-high waterfall.

From the dirt road, the PCT starts west and after a few yards passes a spur trail branching

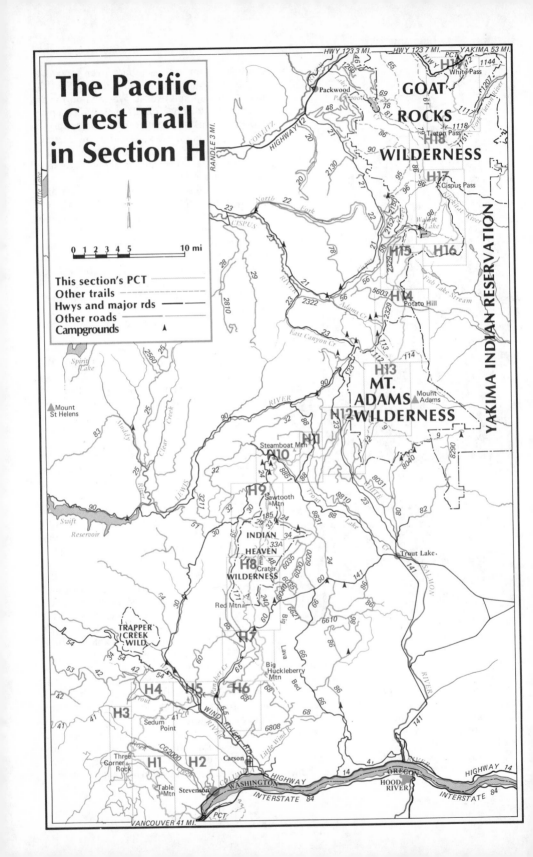

Section H: Highway 14 at Bridge of the Gods to Highway 12 near White Pass

Introduction: Because this is the longest section and because it has the greatest elevation change, it is the most diverse. It starts near the west end of Bridge of the Gods, which at 180 feet elevation is one of the lowest points on the official Pacific Crest Trail (the lowest point—140 feet—is met just one mile southwest from the start of Section H). Near this section's end, the PCT climbs to 7080 feet elevation—its highest elevation in Washington—before it makes a traverse across the upper part of Packwood Glacier.

Between these two extremes we pass through several environments. After starting in a lush, damp Columbia River forest, we climb usually viewless slopes, wind past an extensive, recent lava flow, traverse through a lake-speckled, glaciated lava plateau, and climb to a subalpine forest. We then circle around a major, periodically active volcano, Mt. Adams, traverse high on the walls of deep, glaciated canyons, and finally climb up to an alpine landscape at Packwood Glacier. Along Section H, then, we pass through all of the landforms and vegetation belts that one sees along the PCT from central Oregon to trail's end in southern British Columbia.

Declination: 19°E

Mileages:

	South to North	Distances between Points	North to South
Bridge of the Gods, west end	0.0		147.0
Gillette Lake	3.8	3.8	143.2
Spring near Table Mountain	9.7	5.9	137.3
Spur trail to Three Corner Rock water trough	15.3	5.6	131.7
Rock Creek	20.3	5.0	126.7
Sunset-Hemlock Road 41	26.1	5.8	120.9
Road 43 alongside Trout Creek	30.1	4.0	116.9
Road 65 near Panther Creek Campground	35.5	5.4	111.5
Big Huckleberry Mountain summit trail	44.2	8.7	102.8
Road 60 at Crest Campground	51.0	6.8	96.0
Blue Lake	58.4	7.4	88.6
Bear Lake	61.4	3.0	85.6
Road 24	67.7	6.3	79.3
Road 88	76.5	8.8	70.5
Road 23	82.3	5.8	64.7
Round the Mountain Trail	88.9	6.6	58.1
Killen Creek cascade	97.7	8.8	49.3
Lava Spring	102.7	5.0	44.3
		3.6	

Mileages:	South to North	Distances between Points	North to South
East-west road near Midway site	106.3	11.7	40.7
Walupt Lake Trail	118.0	4.5	29.0
Sheep Lake near Nannie Ridge Trail	122.5	4.5	24.5
Trail 86 to Bypass Camp	127.0	2.1	20.0
Dana May Yelverton Shelter	129.1	6.9	17.9
Tieton Pass	136.0	7.5	11.0
White Pass Chair Lift spur trail	143.5	3.5	3.5
Highway 12 near White Pass	147.0		0.0

Supplies: When Schaffer first mapped Section H in 1973, it was 136½ miles long. You could pick up mailed parcels at Stevenson, early in the hike, and at Midway Guard Station, about two thirds of the way through. Unfortunately for the long-distance hiker, the guard station burned down in 1976 and, with the completion of the last segment of trail in 1984, Stevenson no longer lies along the route. No supplies—mailed parcels or otherwise—can be found along Section H, which today is 10½ miles longer. Only the southern and central High Sierra has a bleaker logistical problem. If you aren't up to such a rigorous hike, you can bypass the first 35½ miles of the PCT, taking an alternate route on roads through the towns of Stevenson and Carson. Doing so will cut 21 miles off Section H's length and will save you about a vertical mile of unnecessary climbing. In Stevenson you should be able to purchase almost anything you'll need, but in Carson you'll find very little. Both towns have post offices, but the Carson Post Office is preferable because, being 4½ miles closer to White Pass, it shortens your walk with a full pack just a little. PCT adherents avoiding these towns will have to resupply at Cascade Locks (end of Section G) and at White Pass (end of Section H). At the pass you can pick up mailed parcels and usually can get a hot meal. Don't expect much else.

Special Restrictions: The Forest Service would like to see you camp at least 200 feet from the Pacific Crest Trail when you are in an official wilderness area. Unfortunately, topographic and/or vegetative constraints often make this impossible. Nevertheless, try to choose a site that will have a minimal impact on the environment and on other trail users. Packers mustn't let their animals graze within 200 feet of lakes, and if they pack in feed, it must be processed so as to prevent seed germination. All these rules apply to *all* of Washington's wilderness areas.

View toward crest, from climb north up the west slopes of Table Mountain

The Cascade crest lies to the east, but the Pacific Crest Trail begins westward, which makes for a very roundabout—and hilly—route. In general terms this 35½-mile route climbs 3300 feet to a ridge, drops 2000 feet to Rock Creek, climbs 1700 feet to Sedum Ridge, drops 2200 feet to Trout Creek, then climbs and drops hundreds of feet as it rolls east to Road 65 near Panther Creek Campground. Your net elevation gain from Bridge of the Gods is a mere 750 feet, yet with a fully laden backpack, you could take three days to do this arduous stretch. However, if you take the most direct route to Road 65, you can reach the PCT near Panther Creek Campground in a mere 14.7 miles. Furthermore, if you start with a light pack and wait until you reach the Carson post office to pick up your mailed parcels, then you have to hike with a full pack only 7.6 miles to reach the PCT. Following this plan, Panther Creek Campground is reached by a relatively easy one-day hike. This short, alternate route will be described first.

*   *   *   *

The alternate route starts north from the west end of Bridge of the Gods toll road (180–0.5, if you're counting the mileage from the end of section G). Our Highway 14 curves past Ashes Lake, then heads northeast to the town of Stevenson (110–2.7), which has stores and cafes, plus the Stevenson Post Office, located at the corner of First and Russell, one block south of the highway. In Stevenson you should be able to buy food, boots, packs and other equipment.

East of Stevenson, our highway climbs rocky bluffs and provides us with scenic views up and down the river. Douglas-fir and maple provide plenty of shade even if you're doing this stretch on a rare sunny afternoon. Our road eventually descends slightly to a junction with the Wind River Road (280–3.4), an "all weather" route we take northeast. It curves over to the sleepy settlement of Carson (450–1.0), which has a post office on the road's east side. This is the last one you'll find until you reach White Pass Village, a very long 119 miles away. If you're doing the whole PCT or at least the Oregon-Washington part, you'll want to mail your heavy packages here rather than carrying them from the Cascade Locks or the Stevenson post office.

The Wind River Road leaves Carson, bends northwest, crosses a bridge spanning the 200-foot-deep Wind River gorge (570–2.5), and reaches a junction (802–2.3), where we turn right and follow the Old State Road briefly east to Panther Creek Road 65 (802–0.1). On this we walk one mile north, then soon begin a winding stretch of road up along Panther Creek to the Pacific Crest Trail (930–2.7–14.7). This trail crosses our road only 230 yards south of Warren Gap Road 6517 and its adjacent Panther Creek Campground. This is a good place to spend the night, for the next near-trail campsite with *good* water is at Blue Lake, about 23 miles farther.

*   *   *   *

From the west end of Bridge of the Gods toll road (180) you head south on Highway 14 past Ice House Lake—an oversized pond—and just 90 yards beyond it reach the PCT trailhead (150–0.2). You'll find limited parking space nearby, but an official trailhead parking area is lacking. Your "trail" at first is along an old powerline road which parallels Highway 14, just below you. Because the roadbed is rather overgrown, the trail sticks to the road's outer edge, which in one short stretch is very exposed—one slip and you'll fall off a vertical cliff to almost certain death. Here, the trail needs a guard rail or needs to be moved to the road's inner edge. The short clifftop stretch soon gives way to safer slopes, and presently you reach a road that climbs briefly up to a nearby cistern, which is your first source of reliable water. You follow the road for 280 yards, angle right from it, then in 110 yards cross a paved road (140–0.8), which climbs from Highway 14 to Wauna Lake.

Leaving most trappings of civilization behind, we climb into a shady, often-fern-floored forest, which covers a hummocky terrain. The stretch of trail shown on Map H1 is highly convoluted, but the map fails to show all the minor ups and downs, which are considerable. You are walking across an extensive area of landslide deposits.

Large and small landslides have descended from both walls of the Columbia Gorge. In part this is due to the steepness of the gorge's walls. However, it is also due to another factor. The volcanic flows and associated volcanic sediments composing the walls belong to two distinct time periods. The lower layers are about 25 million years old, while the upper ones are about 15 million years old. The surface of the lower layers thus had about 10 million years to deeply weather to clay in its warm, humid, preglacial climate before it was buried under a sea of younger deposits. This clay layer is the

H1   **H6, H5, H1**

H2

Steep Cr

Hamilton

Greenleaf Pk

29

Greenleaf Basin

Red Bluff

Creek

Table Mtn

Carpenters Lake

Moffetts Hot Springs

Aldrich Butte

Lookout

Hardy

BEACON ROCK STATE PARK

Hamilton Mtn

Substation

Greenleaf

HWY 14

VANCOUVER 33 MI.

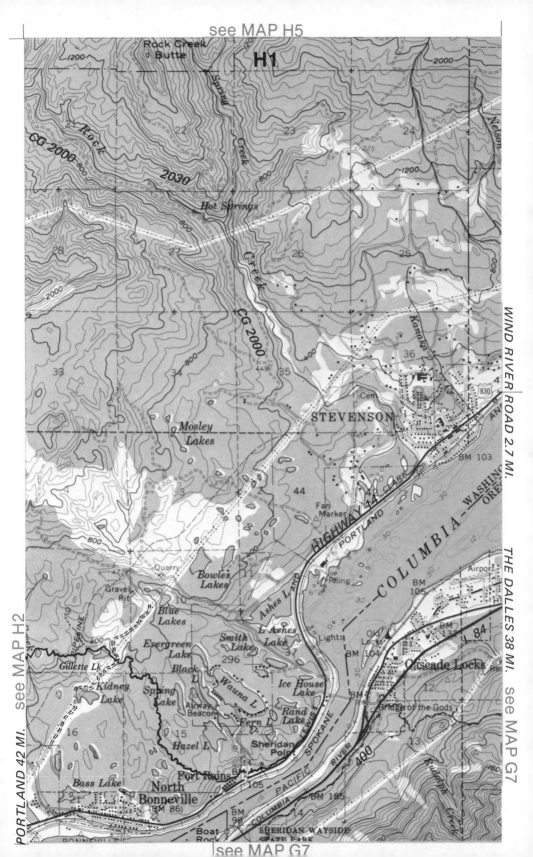

H1

see MAP H2

PORTLAND 42 MI.

WIND RIVER ROAD 2.7 MI.

THE DALLES 38 MI.   see MAP G7

structurally weak element that causes overlying layers to give way, as in the landslides from Table Mountain and the Red Bluffs.

The gorge's north wall is more prone to landslides than is the south wall because the volcanic rocks that compose both walls dip to the south. Naturally, then, rocks tend to slide south along this incline, and resulting landslides push the Columbia River against the south wall. Such landslides can temporarily dam the Columbia River, and such temporary dammings perhaps provided a basis for the Indian legend about the Bridge of the Gods. It is known that certain Oregonian Indians witnessed the eruption of Mt. Mazama 6900 years ago, leaving Crater Lake basin in its aftermath, and it is therefore quite likely that the Multnomah Indians witnessed one or more devastating landslides in the last few millennia.

After about an hour of seemingly aimless wandering—more of it up than down—you temporarily break out of forest cover at a utility road (410–2.5), which serves three sets of Bonneville Dam powerlines. Across this major road the PCT follows an abandoned road down toward Gillette Lake (280–0.3). You'll find a 75-yard spur trail heading east to the lake's northwest shore, which may be your first possible Section H campsite. On private land in a setting that is anything but pristine, the lake is, nevertheless utilitarian, and swimmers will find the water relatively warm.

We re-enter forest and in a couple minutes pass the lake's seasonal inlet creek, then climb for ¼ mile to a "firebreak." From it you follow an old road 70 yards west before leaving it. Eastbound trekkers could be led astray if they miss the PCT tread starting from the east side of the firebreak. On trail tread westbound trekkers make an easy climb to a lily-pad pond before momentarily dropping to a horse bridge across Greenleaf Creek (510–0.9). This is your last totally reliable *on-trail* water source until Rock Creek, 15.5 miles farther. Fortunately, some near-trail water sources are available.

We switchback upward from the creek and get our only views of sprawling Bonneville Dam as we make a short traverse southwest. We then angle northwest to a gully with a seasonal creeklet, ramble west to a second creeklet, then climb north along a third before switchbacking up to a low ridgecrest (1100–1.9). Here, we turn north and parallel a little-used road up Cedar Creek canyon. Along this stretch you can drop to the nearby road, camp along it, and wade through dense vegetation to get water from Cedar Creek.

H1, H2

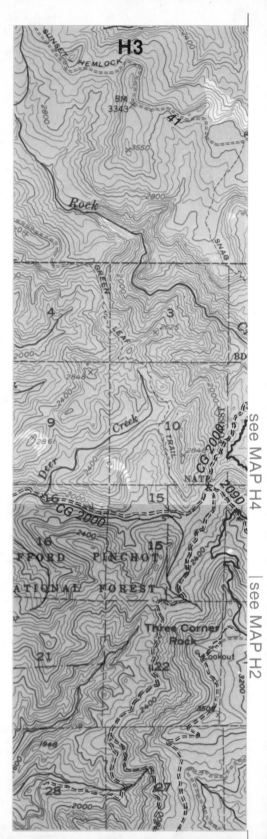

After a crest walk northward, we cross the road (1300–0.6), and then in ⅓ mile recross it. Ahead, the trail unfortunately climbs above the creek's headwaters, leaving you high and dry, so plan accordingly.

In about ⅓ mile our climb north takes us to a creeklet, just beyond which we meet an old trail that climbs very steeply up a minor ridge. On a moderate grade we climb northwest, then southwest up to a larger ridge (1970–1.2), it too having an old trail along it. Now we exchange the Cedar Creek drainage for the larger Hamilton Creek drainage. We drop a bit, quickly emerge from forest cover, then drop some more to avoid steep slopes on the west side of towering Table Mountain. Enjoy the panoramic views while you can, for you still have 1500 feet of climbing ahead. On a hot, muggy summer's day you may be too tired to enjoy anything, particularly with that heavy pack on your back. The earlier in the morning you make this protracted climb out of the Columbia Gorge, the better.

On a shady bench due west of Table Mountain the PCT latches onto an abandoned roadbed which, fortunately, is alder shaded along its first half mile. You'll need the shade, for the gradient averages a stiff 17%. Just before the gradient abates you'll get a view (2480–1.3). Stop and listen for music to your ears—a never-failing creek. Reaching it is another problem. It could use a spur trail down to it, but unfortunately the creek is on private land. Drop your pack and cautiously head downslope, trying to keep slipping and sliding to a minimum. (Equestrians have a real dilemma: horses can't reach this spring-fed creek, and they may not be able to reach Cedar Creek, mentioned earlier. Horses could get heat prostration on a hot summer

afternoon—you may have to walk your horse up this perspiring stretch.)

Onward, in about 140 yards you re-enter forest cover and bend west. Soon you leave the old roadbed, pass under a buzzing powerline, traverse a short stretch of beargrass turf, and then ramble over to a nearby road (2790–0.8). You climb briefly north, then east on a rather steep, very rocky tread across a rubbly open slope that offers fine views south down Hamilton Creek canyon. Mt. Hood also comes into view, poking over the shoulder of multilayered Table Mountain. With a final burst of effort you reach a ridge (3120–0.5) above a powerline saddle. Welcome back to a crest route; you've struggled 11 miles to reach it.

Having put most of the elevation gain behind us, we can enjoy the next stretch, which has views east past Greenleaf Basin and Peak to the Columbia Gorge and south past Table Mountain to Mt. Hood. Typical of a crest route, the PCT climbs to a saddle and crosses it (3400–0.7), giving us our first view of Three Corner Rock—a conspicuous knob to the northwest. The trail climbs briefly, topping out at just over 3400 feet, then makes a minimal descent over to flowery, bushy slopes, immediately beyond which we come to a seep (3370–0.3). It may be dry, so don't count on it.

Next we wind around a ridge, absorbing panoramic views to the south, west and northwest, then submerge in a forest canopy for a descent to a saddle with a crestline road (3020–1.3). This jeep road heads over to Three Corner Rock, and the PCT parallels it in the same direction. Traversing along the PCT we get sporadic views to the north and east, with Mt. Adams and

H2   H2

PCT bridge across Trout Creek

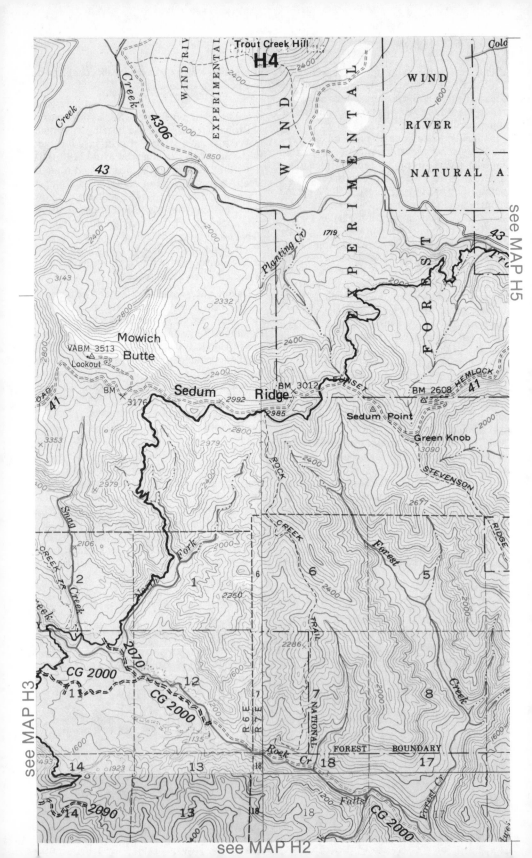

see MAP H5

see MAP H3

see MAP H2

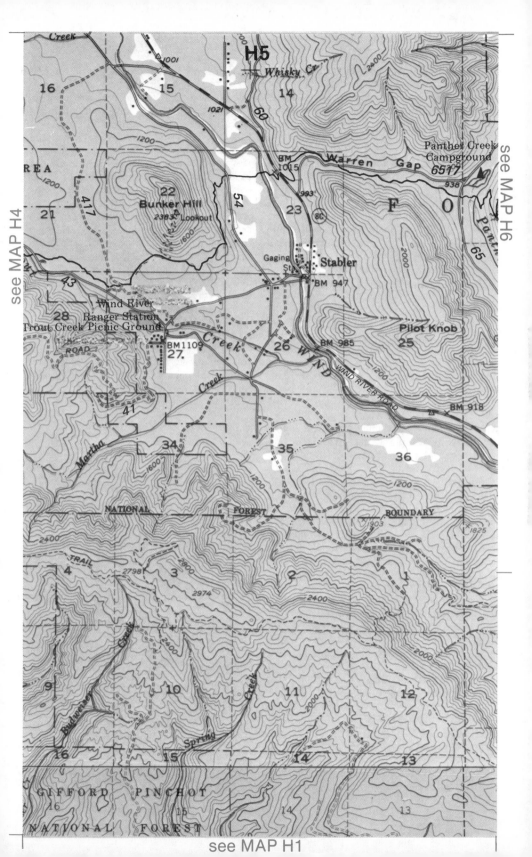

see MAP H4

see MAP H6

see MAP H1

H5

Creek

Whisky Cr.

16

15

14

60

1001

1021

1200

1200

417

REA

21

22
Bunker Hill
2383 Lookout
1600

54

BM
1015

Warren Gap

993

23

8C

Panther Creek
Campground
6517

938

F O

Panth

65

2000

43

Gaging
Sta.

Stabler

BM 947

28
Wind River
Ranger Station
Trout Creek Picnic Ground

ROAD

26

Creek

BM1109

27

Creek

BM 985

WIND

WIND RIVER ROAD

1200

Pilot Knob

25

2000

1200

BM 918

41

34

35

36

Martha

1600

1200

1200

1903

1825

NATIONAL

FOREST

BOUNDARY

2400

TRAIL

4

2798

3
2900

2974

2

2400

2000

Creek

9

10

Creek

11

Spring

12

2400

Budweiser

2000

16

15

14

13

GIFFORD PINCHOT

16

15

14

13

NATIONAL FOREST

clearcuts catching our attention. Views disappear about ¼ mile before our trail touches the jeep road, and ahead we climb, first viewlessly southwest, then viewfully west up to a spur trail (3320–2.0). Your next on-trail water is way down at Rock Creek, a hefty 5.0 miles away. If you really need water, you can gamble and take the narrow, bouldery spur trail ⅓ mile over to a water trough. You'll find it about 30 yards west of the trail at a point just 40 yards before the trail ends at a jeep road. The trough is bathtub size, and when Schaffer visited it, it looked like folks had bathed in it. You'll certainly want to treat the water! The trough, unfortunately, could have sprung a leak, leaving you thirsty and frustrated. If you've hiked as far as the water trough, you might as well scramble up the jeep road to close-by Three Corner Rock for unrestricted views, which include Mts. Hood, Adams, St. Helens and, weather permitting, Rainier.

From the junction we get a few views of unesthetic clearcut slopes as we wind and switchback northward down to a viewless saddle (2360–1.9), which is crossed by Road 2090. Next we skirt east just below a ridgecrest, soon enter a clearcut, then gratefully leave it just before ducking through a crest gap (1980–0.5). After immediately switchbacking west below the gap, we quickly plunge into a deep forest and wander in and out of numerous usually dry gullies before crossing Road 2000 (1720–1.8). If you need to abort your trip, take this well-maintained road 11 miles down to Stevenson. Otherwise, follow the PCT down and across gullies to an ultimate bridging of Rock Creek (1420–0.8). This 5.0-mile stretch from the spur trail has been a well-graded, very steady descent across a generally viewless, intricately complex terrain. Our hats are off to whoever surveyed this route; it must have been a formidable task, particularly with such dense vegetation.

Your water problems are now over, at least until you leave Panther Creek Campground, some 15+ miles ahead. You quickly climb above Rock Creek, traverse east to a junction with the Snag Creek Trail, then in 120 yards reach its namesake, Snag Creek (1470–0.4). Ahead we soon emerge from forest cover, cross a clearcut with crowding, waist-high vegetation (very miserable on a rainy day), then reach Road 2070 (1450–0.3). If you're in need of a campsite, you can head about 250 yards down this rocky road and set up camp along the North Fork of Rock Creek. Otherwise, prepare for a challenging ascent.

H2, H3, H4

At first we have a pleasant stroll through a forest of Douglas-firs, alders and vine maples. The North Fork stays close by for the first ¾ mile, then we enter and leave a prominent gully and climb to a north-trending North Fork tributary. It is usually flowing, but is a problem to reach because the PCT typically stays 100 feet above it on steep, densely vegetated slopes. Finally we cross a seasonal creeklet (2080–1.8), one's last hope for any water until a Trout Creek tributary 7.0 miles away. Switchbacks carry us up to gentler slopes, across which we climb to a lushly vegetated, though dry, gully. Ahead, we climb east to a ridge and then north to the base of steep slopes below crest-hugging Sunset-Hemlock Road 41. Southeast, we climb a short half mile, obtaining poor views before we reach a south-trending ridge (3080–1.8). Next we skirt over to an adjacent crest saddle, then just beyond it have our first good views as the trail skirts the base of a lava cliff. At a second saddle (2985–0.7) we almost touch Road 41, and here you might note the abandoned Sedum Ridge Trail, descending 4 miles to Road 2000, along Rock Creek. We climb once more, topping out at 3130 feet near a viewful, south-trending ridge,

H4

1978 PCT bridge construction at Wind River

and then we descend to Sedum Ridge, where we finally cross Road 41 (2950–0.8).

Leaving the road, the PCT hiker meets what's left of Greenknob Trail 144 in ¼ mile, and on his PCT descent he is likely to see traces of this former trail. The PCT reaches a gully, descends briefly north, turns east around a knifeblade ridge, then drops north through a lush forest to the main ridge (2550–1.0). Here we get our first good view north and see Bunker Hill, to the east, standing alone in a flat-floored valley.

The view disappears and once again we disappear into a lush forest. If you are hiking the

trail on one of those damp misty days so common to this area, you may see a dozen or more rough-skinned newts. The trail quickly reaches gentler slopes and angles northeast down to a viewless saddle (2150–0.7), then continues northeast down into several gullies which often though not always provide water. The trail leaves these gullies and in ⅓ mile crosses a wide, splashing tributary (1210–2.0) of Trout Creek. Now on nearly level ground, we curve east to Trout Creek and cross it on a concrete span built to last as long as the PCT does. This is a good spot to camp. Immediately past the bridge, our

H4

H4, H5

see MAP H7

see MAP H5

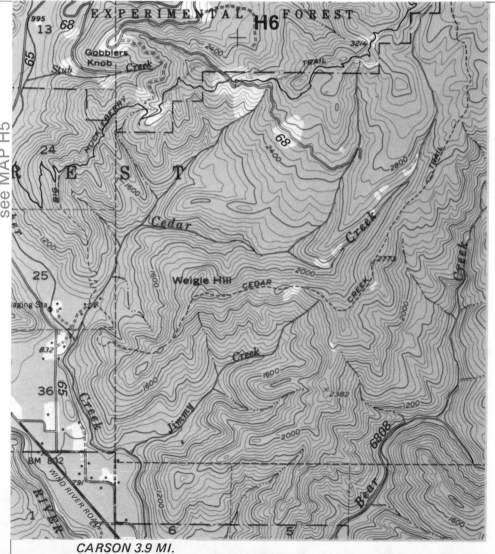

trail crosses Road 43 (1180–0.3), which gently descends 1.3 miles to the Trout Creek Picnic Ground, with a good swimming hole.

From the road we hike 280 yards over to a bend in the trail, and here a faint path heads 75 yards west over to a nearby campsite at the end of a short spur road. Past the campsite, the PCT soon parallels unseen Road 43 southeast to Road 417 (1120–0.8). Walking east 30 yards on this road, we locate the PCT's tread, which follows the road's north edge 120 yards to a road junction (1120–0.1). From here a road goes ½ mile southeast to the Wind River Ranger Station, which is near the picnic ground. Road 417 heads northwest along one edge of a tree farm while our trail heads east along its fenced-in south edge.

We briefly parallel the farm's east edge hiking northward, then in 100 yards angle northeast for a steepening walk up to the Bunker Hill Trail (1210–0.5), which switchbacks up to the summit. The PCT now winds, dips and climbs eastward along the hill's viewless, lower slopes, crosses a crest (1250–0.7), then descends north

H5

H5

see MAP H8

see MAP H6

H9

gradually down to a crossing of Little Soda Springs Road 54 (940–0.8).

East of the road a row of trees bisects a large meadow, and our trail stays along the row's north side as it traverses east. It leaves this meadow just before crossing Wind River (940–0.3) on a major bridge, built in 1978, which is one of the largest bridges to be found along the entire PCT. You could camp in this vicinity, but Panther Creek Campground, less than an hour's walk ahead, is better for logistical reasons.

From this river we climb to busy Wind River Road (1020–0.2) and cross it just 0.2 mile northwest of this road's junction with Warren Gap Road 6517. The PCT starts a climb southeast, almost touches Road 6517, eventually crosses it (1180–0.8) just past Warren Gap, then winds east down to Panther Creek Road 65

H5

Fern-decked path north of Crest C.G.

(930–1.2). The entrance to Panther Creek Campground is just 230 yards up the road, opposite the end of Road 65. You should plan to camp there, for once you leave Panther Creek, you won't have any campsite with *good* water until Blue Lake, 23 miles farther.

From the Panther Creek Road, the PCT winds east 300 yards to Panther Creek and from it we switchback upward, passing two trickling springs long before we reach the westernmost end of a ridge (2100–2.3). Now we largely follow the old Big Huckleberry Trail up to Big Huckleberry Mountain. We start by paralleling a slightly climbing ridge crest northeast to a saddle (2300–1.1), from which a good dirt road starts a northeast descent and a vegetated one starts a southeast traverse. We take the vegetated road and follow it for 300 yards, curving around a brushy wash and then meeting a trail once again just before the road curves south around a ridge. We hike east, up this trail, recross the head of the wash, and wind around two minor ridges before coming to a saddle. This we cross; then, after a ½-mile climb across south slopes, our trail becomes an old road that quickly arrives at a junction with Road 68 (2810–1.3), on a saddle.

The trail continues east from the road, staying just south of the crest as it traverses a logged-out area, then, just before a saddle, curves around the forested south slopes of the ridge, soon returning to the crest. We now stay fairly close to the crest, which narrows to 5 feet in one spot, then descend to a broad, open saddle (3214–1.7). Now we climb, aided by occasional switchbacks, moderately up along the crest to a junction with the old Cascade Crest Trail (4000–2.2) near the summit of Big Huckleberry Mountain. From here we climb steeply for 130 yards up to a junction with the Big Huckleberry Mountain summit trail (4070–0.1), which climbs steeply east 200 yards to the summit.

Our path now eases off, curves northward and descends a "fog drip" ridge route, crosses a saddle ⅓ mile past our last junction, then skirts across slopes that give us views of Mt. Adams before we make a second saddle crossing (3730–1.2). Past it we descend to a gully (3550–0.5), which has a fairly reliable spring. This spring, 10.3 miles beyond Panther Creek, will probably be your last water until the Sheep Lakes, 7.0 miles farther. From this spring we contour northward through a shady forest of Douglas-fir, western hemlock and western white pine, reach a viewless, broad saddle (3580–

H5, H6, H7

0.8), and then wind down toward Road 6801, coming within 150 yards of it (3220–0.8) near an open saddle.

Contouring counterclockwise around Summit 4170, we follow the edge of geologically recent Big Lava Bed, cross one of its western overflow channels—which reveals the detailed intricacies of the flow—and then contour around another summit and cross another channel to the back of the Crest Campground (3490–3.5), which is on the south side of Carson-Guler Road 60.

The campground has a horse corral but no water, so we pick our packs off the tables, put them on our backs and trudge north up the signed Pacific Crest Trail. This moderate ascent up a fern-decked path is really quite nice if you aren't running short of water. We climb to a flat and reach a duck pond (4020–1.9), which is no more than an oversized mud puddle after your arrival frightens the ducks away. Nevertheless, it boasts the name *Sheep Lake*. You can camp near it, if necessary. After climbing northwest through a more open forest, we enter Indian Heaven Wilderness and reach another pond, a 35-yard-wide puddle, Green Lake (4250–1.1), which gets as deep as a foot in early summer and serves as a vital water supply.

When one of the authors (Schaffer) visited this "lake" in late August 1973, it had just been converted into an oversized latrine by an unscrupulous packer and his family who let their eight horses defecate and stomp around in it. Having followed in his tracks for several days, I observed that he always let his horses do this, presumably after the family first got its share of water. I wish I could say that he was the only packer I encountered who had such disgusting trail manners, but in fact, *every* packer I saw camped near water disregarded the 200-foot Forest Service shoreline limit and allowed his animals to graze and defecate right up to the water.

Since you may find Green Lake too polluted to suit your standards, prepare for a dry march and start northwest past a meadow, then reach a junction with Shortcut Trail 171A (4240–0.4), which strikes west-northwest half a mile to a large, stagnant pond and to the Racetrack, which supposedly was used by Indian horsemen. We hike north-northwest through a forest, then climb several long switchbacks up the sunny south slope of Berry Mountain before reaching its crest. The abandoned Cascade Crest Trail, on the shady slopes way below us, led thirsty hikers

past a spring. Our trail provides us with excellent views of Mt. St. Helens (8364) to the northwest, Mt. Adams (12,276) to the northeast and Mt. Hood (11,235) to the south. Upon reaching the north end of linear Berry Mountain, we descend short switchbacks to a saddle (4730–2.9), follow a rambling path down past the seasonal outlet creek of Lake Sebago (4640–0.9), and come to an overlook of a 100-yard-wide stagnant pond beyond which we finally reach the welcome, clear waters of Blue Lake (4630–0.2), nestled at the foot of Gifford Peak (5368). Here you'll find the first good campsites since Panther Creek Campground, 23 miles back. Starting along the lake's east shore, Thomas Lake Trail 111 heads ¼ mile northwest over to an additional good campsite at shallow, circular Lake Sahalee Tyee. Camp at it if the Blue Lake campsites are full.

The Pacific Crest Trail, which barely touches Blue Lake, starts northeast from the lake's southeast corner, then winds north up to a west arm of East Crater. The trail curves northeast around this youthful feature, then angles north for a short drop to a junction with East Crater Trail 48 (4730–1.9), which starts east along a skinny west finger of pleasant Junction Lake. You'll find a good campsite near its southwest shore and a poorer one near its northwest shore.

At the tip of the finger we cross the lake's outlet and meet Lemei Lake Trail 33A (4730–0.1), which climbs east before swinging north past Lemei Lake to Indian Heaven Trail. Whereas the old Cascade Crest Trail skirted along Indian Heaven's mosquito-populated ponds and lakes, the newer Pacific Crest Trail stays on lower slopes just east of and above them. We'll see parts of the old trail as we hike north toward Road 24.

By adhering to the lower slopes, the PCT avoids the bogs that were found along the old CCT, but in early season, snow patches may be quite a problem. One-quarter mile past our crossing of the usually dry Lemei Lake creek, we intersect Indian Heaven Trail 33 (4790–1.0) above Bear Lake's southeast shore. You'll find camps on a low ridge above its southwest shore. Fill your water bottles at this beautiful lake, for the water sources ahead aren't as pure. Our trail next traverses over to a slope (4830–0.4) above the east end of Deer Lake, whose shoreline camps are fewer and poorer than those at Bear Lake.

H7, H8   **H8, H9**

With no more lakes before Road 24, we continue north, pass two seasonal ponds, and just past the second one reach a near-saddle junction with Placid Lake Trail 29 (5030–1.1), which parallels our route 0.2 mile north before branching west. We continue north to a second saddle, then traverse northeast to a third, almost touching the old Cascade Crest Trail at each. At the third (5110–0.6) you can hop on the old CCT and follow it 150 yards down to a campsite by a pleasant, unnamed lakelet. From that lakelet, the Wood Lake Trail heads ½ mile northwest over to its namesake, which is not worth a visit.

Staying high, the PCT contours around the lakelet and soon meets Wood Lake Trail 185 (5150–0.4), which descends ¼ mile southwest to the lakelet and also climbs 200 yards northeast to Saddle 5237 before descending to large Cultus Creek Campground along Road 24.

Our trail now stays close to a well-defined crest, which it eventually crosses and thereby gives us views of massive Mt. Adams and the terrain being logged around it. Just past our crest crossing, the trail heads briefly south, only to switchback north and descend to a crest saddle. At the switchback you'll see a prominent huckleberry field just below you, with berries in season from about mid-August until mid-September. You might sample these if you haven't already made a side trip to huckleberry fields back near Indian Heaven.

From the crest saddle (4850–1.2) a 1.7-mile-long footpath switchbacks almost up to the knife-edge crest of Sawtooth Mountain before switchbacking down to the PCT. From the serrated crest, which can be reached by a short scramble, you get an exhilarating view down its east cliff as well as an unobstructed view of Mt. Adams. On a clear day you also see three other snowy peaks: distant Mt. Hood in the south, bleak Mt. St. Helens in the west-northwest, and distant Mt. Rainier in the north.

The PCT stays low as it traverses north gently down the west slopes of Sawtooth Mountain to a reunion with that summit's footpath (4570–

H9   **H9**

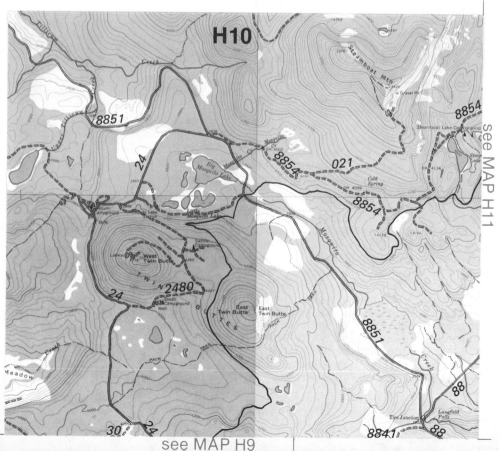

1.4). It then leaves Indian Heaven Wilderness as it descends into the Sawtooth Huckleberry Field, reaches a spur road, and parallels it 60 yards northeast to a signed PCT crossing of Road 24 (4260–1.2). The large berry field at this flat was being harvested by Indians when George B. McClellan's exploration party came through in 1854. Needless to say, it had probably been harvested for countless generations. Roads were built up to it around the turn of the century, and today the Indians have exclusive rghts only to the berries *east* of the road. Frankly, we were hard-pressed to find many bushes on that side, and wondered whether some midnight raiding party of pioneers had transplanted some of the bushes to the west side.

Our trail now descends gently east-northeast, enters forest, and passes above the little developed Surprise Lakes Campground, which is for *Indians* only. Continuing northeast on the 1972 Surprise-Steamboat lakes section of the PCT, we descend to a saddle (4070–1.4), then climb northwest up this well-graded trail and round the west slopes of East Twin Butte (4690). We reach a platform between the two Twin Buttes, which are obvious cinder cones, descend northwest below unseen, dumpy Saddle Campground, switchback northeast, and descend to a crossing of a trickling creek immediately before reaching Road 8851 (3915–2.5) at a junction 35 yards southeast of the west-trending Little Mosquito Lake road. Our trail bears northeast from Road 8851 and quickly reaches the wide, refreshing outlet creek from Big Mosquito Lake (3892).

The PCT leaves the creek and climbs gently east along the upper margin of a sheep-inhabited clearing, then rounds a spur and shortly crosses a dirt road (4090–2.5) that snakes northwest 130 yards up to Road 8854. We continue northeast and descend to a small gully with a seasonal creek, and here the Steamboat Lake spur trail (3980–0.4) climbs north moderately 0.2 mile up to that lake (4022), from which you can then follow an east shoreline road northward. By the time you've reached the lake's northeast corner, this road deteriorates to a log-strewn trail. Then you can take a steep trail northeast up to Road 8854 and small, waterless Steamboat Lake Campground, ¾ mile from the PCT. At the northeast edge of the camp, a ½-mile-long trail descends to a shallow, unnamed lake and then rejoins the PCT at a bend.

From the Steamboat Lake spur-trail junction, the PCT curves counterclockwise from the gully and makes a gentle descent to an outlet creek 70 yards downstream from an unseen, unnamed lake, where it meets the end of the alternate trail (3970–0.8), which climbs west to Steamboat Lake Campground. Here our trail descends first northeast, then east, weaving through a quiet forest down to a junction with Road 88 (3470–1.2). The swath this road cuts through this forest is so oriented that we have an open view directly at Mt. Adams.

H10, H11

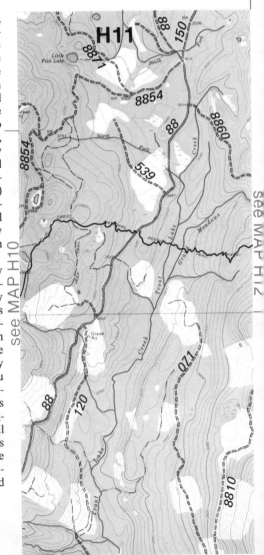

see MAP H10

see MAP H12

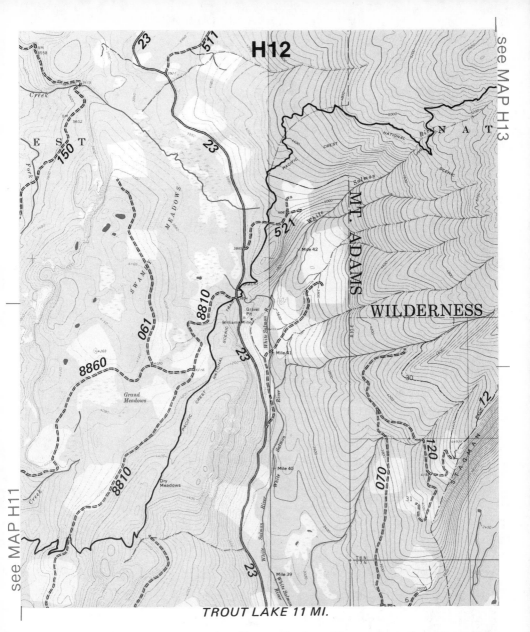

TROUT LAKE 11 MI.

Our trail recommences at a large sign 50 yards northeast up this road, and on it we top a minor ridge before descending to three-yard-wide Trout Lake Creek (3310–0.4). North of the trail at a point 25 yards east of this creek, we see a very good campsite, and 100 yards later we cross the smaller Grand Meadows Creek. Our trail now ascends eastward, steeply at times, but momentarily descends to a tributary before making a final, stiff climb up to Road 8810 (4140–2.1). Continuing east up the slope, we reach the crest (4570–0.6), then begin a gen-erally descending route north-northeast along the ridge down to a trailhead at Road 8810 (3854–2.7). We walk east 50 yards to this road's junction with north-trending Road 23 and a trail-head for the Mt. Adams Wilderness.

Our trail drops to a two-yard-wide creek just east of Road 23, then climbs north around the slopes of a low summit to a crossing of east-trending Road 521 (4020–0.9). After hiking ¼ mile north, we reach a small, good campsite near a bridge over a permanent creek. In the next ¾ mile we cross two usually flowing creeks.

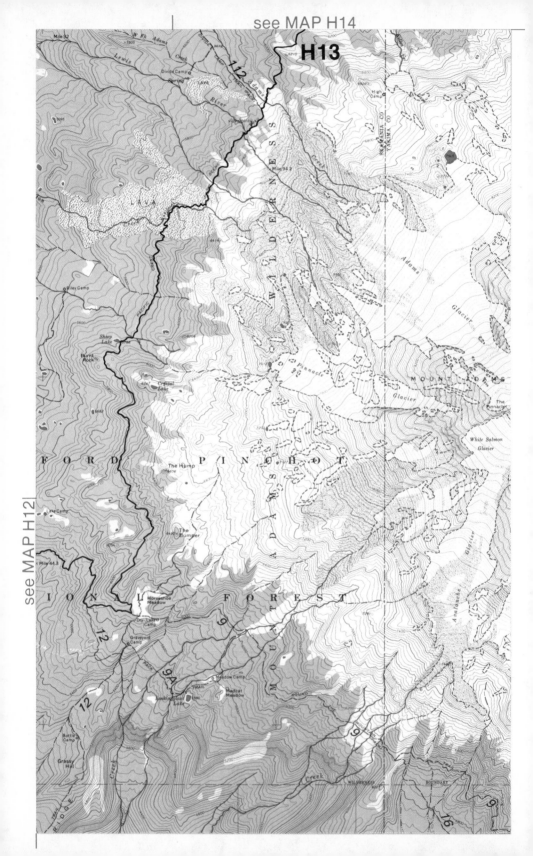

see MAP H12

Mt. Adams and Adams Glacier

see MAP H15

H14

see MAP H13

Now we continue up an increasingly steep trail to the Mt. Adams Wilderness boundary, switchback northeast, traverse east, and finally drop gently to a barely recognizable, often dry creek known as the White Salmon River. About 100 yards past it (4900–2.7) you'll see a spring gushing from thick vegetation 50 yards below the trail. This is your last reliable water until Sheep Lake, 6.5 miles later.

Our trail then switchbacks, crosses the "river" in a shady bowl, switchbacks again, and then makes a long, snaking ascent to a junction with Stagman Ridge Trail 12 (5790–2.5), which starts a descent south. Pressing onward, we climb east up to a junction with Round the Mountain Trail 9 (5900–0.5). This traverses ¼ mile east to dry Dry Lake Camp, then continues 6¼ miles to Timberline Camp, above the end of Road 8040. The easiest and most popular route to the summit of Mt. Adams (12,276) starts there and climbs up the south ridge. You should have no trouble attaining the summit in good weather, for this is the route that mule trains used in the 1930s. Back then, a sulfur claim had been staked out on the summit, but it didn't pay off. This massive andesitic stratovolcano, like the others we've seen, should still be considered active. Its last eruption may have been 1000 to 2000 years ago, and in May 1921 its near-surface magma generated enough heat to initiate a large snow slide that eradicated the forest on the slope below it.

On the high slopes east of our junction with Trail 9, we can see the White Salmon Glacier. Some PCT mountaineers prefer to climb Mt. Adams via that icy route, which starts from our junction and crosses Horseshoe Meadow.

The Pacific Crest Trail climbs northwest around a ridge that separates this glacier from the Pinnacle Glacier, immediately north of it. Our northward, round-the-mountain route is quite a contrast with that of Mt. Hood; it stays at a relatively constant elevation, and where it climbs or descends, it usually does so on a gentle gradient. To the north and northwest, we can often see Goat Rocks and Mt. Rainier. After traversing to a saddle (5950–3.2) just east of Burnt Rock, our trail descends toward 70-yard-wide, 5-foot-deep Sheep Lake (5768–0.3), which is 40 yards northwest of the trail, then reaches milky jump-across Riley Creek (5770–0.2).

Next on our menu, Mutton Creek (5900–1.3) is approached, and we follow it up beside a geologically recent, rather barren lava flow over which we eventually diagonal quite a distance up. Our route then bounds from one wash to the next, crosses milky Lewis River (6060–1.3), and in 200 yards reaches a spur trail that goes 110 yards north to a viewpoint. From it you'll see distant, snowy Mt. Rainier standing above a nearer, clearcut-patched landscape. Our PCT quickly crosses some silty tributaries of West Fork Adams Creek before it curves north-northwest to a junction with Divide Camp Trail 112 (6020–0.3), which descends northwest toward Road 2329. Directly upslope from us is the overpowering, steeply descending Adams Glacier, which appears to be a gigantic frozen waterfall rather than an advancing snowfield. Along our journey north, our glances back toward this massive peak will always single out this prominent feature.

We head northeast across a 330-yard swath of bouldery glacier outwash sediments, then jump across silty Middle Fork Adams Creek. After climbing its bank, our route contours northeast past a 70-yard-wide pond (6110), and in a few minutes we arrive at a junction with Killen Creek Trail 113 (6084–1.4), which starts beside a seasonal creek as it descends northwest toward Road 2329. We contour onward, descend to a large flat through which flows clear Killen Creek, then cross this creek as it reaches a brink (5920–0.8) and cascades merrily down 30 feet to a small meadow and a beautiful campsite nestled under a cluster of subalpine firs.

As we are about to head north away from the mountain, we reflect upon another characteristic of this crescentic trail which distinguishes it from its counterpart on Mt. Hood: this trail stays on the mountain's lower slopes, and we never feel like we've set foot on the mountain itself—the upper slopes don't begin until a "distant" 2000 feet above us. In this respect, the trail resembles those around Mt. Jefferson and the Three Sisters. A short distance from the campsite, our trial meets Highline Trail 114 (5900–0.2), upon which you may find *footprints* leading east toward the Yakima Indian Reservation. About 100 yards along this trail you'll find a shallow lakelet, near which you can camp.

Just north beyond this junction we spy a 70-yard pond a hundred yards northwest of us. It is better to descend 80 feet down the slope to this pond than to continue onward to a second, readily accessible one (5772–0.4) that receives too much impact from packers. The PCT now becomes a rambling, evenly graded pathway

H12, H13   **H13, H14**

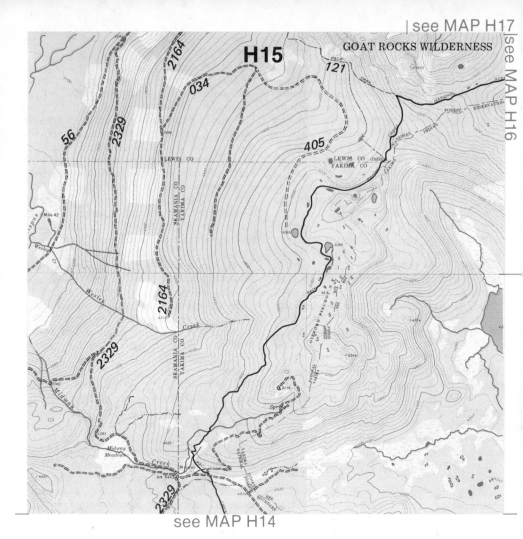

see MAP H14

that descends north-northeast into a subalpine-fir/lodgepole-pine forest whose monotony is broken by an intersection with a trail (5231–2.0), which starts east-northeast toward a junction two miles later with the Highline Trail.

Meeting no traffic other than perhaps chickadees or juncos, we continue northward and eventually reach a sturdy bridge across the 5-yard-wide Muddy Fork (4740–1.6), by which we find a small campsite. Curving northwest, our path soon reaches and then parallels an alder-and-willow-lined silty creek westward to a very good campsite (4590–0.5), nestled between two of this creek's branches. A short distance farther we round the nose of a recent lava flow and head north to the vibrant, crystal-clear waters gushing from trailside Lava Spring (4520–0.3) at the foot of the flow. Since its water is among the best you'll find along the *entire* PCT, you might as

well rest and enjoy it. An American dipper—a drab, chunky bird—may be camped here.

Leaving it, we follow the 40-foot-high edge of the flow a short way, leave Mt. Adams Wilderness, then climb gently through a predominantly lodgepole forest to a small trailhead parking lot a few yards north of paved Road 5603 (4750–1.6). From the lot we walk northeast 50 yards along an old jeep road, then veer north-northeast along a trail that ascends gently toward Potato Hill (5387). Although motorized vehicles are specifically barred from the PCT, they or their tracks are likely to be encountered along this rather unscenic stretch through second-growth forest. We quickly reach the jeep road again and follow its northwest-curving path around Potato Hill, then take this dusty road north-northwest past huckleberries and mountain ash to a junction with Road 115

H14

H14, H15

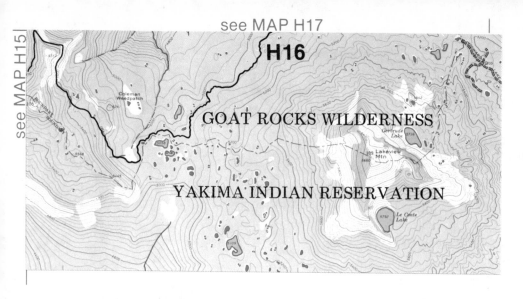

H16

GOAT ROCKS WILDERNESS

YAKIMA INDIAN RESERVATION

(4490–2.0). By walking 0.3 mile west on it, you'll reach the site of Midway Guard Station (which burned down in 1976) beside Road 2329 and Midway Creek. Although you can't pick up mailed packages as you could in the "good old days," you can find ample room to camp. We walk 50 yards up a road, then branch left for a grassy diagonal up a trail to closed Road 655 (4520–0.1), which descends west-southwest 0.1 mile to Road 115. We'll walk across no more roads until at Highway 12 near White Pass, 40½ miles distant.

Our trail starts west-northwest up toward Midway Creek, crosses it (4690–0.4), then climbs up through alternating forested and cleared land toward the crest. As the gradient eases off, we enter forest for good and follow a winding path that takes us past eight stagnant ponds. You could have an adequate campsite at any of them if you're willing to purify the water. After leaving the last pond (5070–2.8), on our left (west), we hike around the west slope of a knoll, descend gently to the west side of a broad saddle, then climb moderately to a switchback (5220–1.6), from which Trail 121 descends to Walupt Lake Horse Camp. Now within Goat Rocks Wilderness, we climb east to a saddle (5450–0.7), and pass two small ponds, on the left. We then climb north to a prominent ridgecrest (5600–0.8), that stands directly south

H15

Mt. Adams, from Sheep Lake campsite

H15, H16

Ives Peak and Cispus River headwaters

H17

YAKIMA INDIAN RESERVATION

GIFFORD PINCHOT NATIONAL FOREST

GOAT ROCK

WILDERNESS

SNOQUALMIE

GOAT

Conrad Glacier

Meade Glacier

Klickitat

Nannie Peak

WALUPT LAKE

of Walupt Lake (3926). North of us we see the glistening summit of Old Snowy Mountain (7930), in the heart of the Goat Rocks country, over whose slopes we must soon climb.

Our route now winds southeastward down auxiliary ridges and enters a forest of mountain hemlock, western white and lodgepole pines, and Alaska yellow cedar. We pass near two undesirable ponds before we cross a trickling creek (5140–1.4) that you shouldn't overlook, for it contains the best water you'll taste for miles. After descending gently eastward, we curve counterclockwise around boggy Coleman Weedpatch to a 50-yard pond (5050–0.5). An old trail east from it goes to a nearby, shallow lake (5058) on a forested, flat saddle immediately within the Yakima Indian Reservation. On the PCT we arc eastward, north of the unseen lake, then follow our easy path northwest through a dense mountain-hemlock forest across the lower slopes of Lakeview Mountain (6660). As we veer east, our forest transforms into an open stand of lodgepoles, and we finally curve southeast to a junction with Walupt Lake Trail 101 (4960–3.4), which goes 4.4 miles to its trailhead at Walupt Lake Campground. You will find several fair-to-good campsites ⅓ to ½ mile down this trail.

Beyond the junction the countryside is quite open, and the topography stretches out below us as we hike the trail up the west slope of a long, north-trending ridge. Fireweed, yarrow, lupine and pearly everlasting proliferate along the trailside before we reach the shady confines of a coniferous forest. We now contour for several miles before reaching the diminutive headwaters

Glacier-striated rocks

of Walupt Creek (5480–3.9). If there were enough level ground here, a primitive campsite by the stream would be nice. Instead, it is better to continue west up toward a saddle where you'll see shallow, clear 130-yard-long Sheep Lake (5710), which has good but open campsites. Just north of it, we meet a junction, with Nannie Ridge Trail 98 (5760–0.6), which descends 4.5 miles to its trailhead at mile-long Walupt Lake.

Our route north through the Goat Rocks country will take us on ridges high above glaciated canyons. Walupt Creek canyon was the first major one we've seen in this wilderness, and the ones north of it are even more

H16, H17

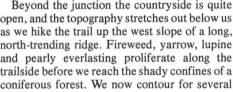

Forty-foot-high "Split Rock" along PCT

H17

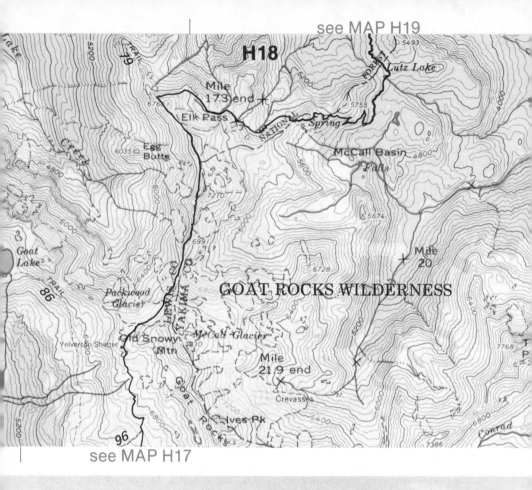

see MAP H19

H18

Lutz Lake

Mile
17.3 end

Elk Pass

Egg
Butte

Spring

McCall Basin
Falls

Goat
Lake

Mile
20

GOAT ROCKS WILDERNESS

Packwood
Glacier

Yelverton Shelter

Old Snowy
Mtn

McCall Glacier

Mile
21.9 end

Crevasses

Ives Pk

Conrad

see MAP H17

Goat Lake and Mt. Rainier

spectacular. From our junction we descend ⅓ mile before diagonaling up a mid-70s stretch of PCT to a crest saddle (6100–1.4). Now in Yakima Indian territory, we traverse north across barren slopes that have snow patches through most of the summer. Our trail steepens as it approaches often snowbound Cispus Pass (6460–0.9), where we leave the Indian reservation.

Our timberline trail drops north and passes by dwarfed specimens of mountain hemlock and subalpine fir as it descends toward the headwaters of the Cispus River. The basin is much smaller than it first appears, and we quickly reach an open campsite beside the easternmost tributary (6130–0.6). The scale of the canyon is put in true perspective when backpackers hike past miniature conifers that are now seen as only 30 feet high instead of as 80, as we originally presupposed. After descending west, we jump across the base of a splashing, 20-foot-high waterfall, then make a winding contour to a junction with Trail 86 (5930–1.6).

This trail goes 0.6 mile west down to Bypass Camp, with wind-shielded sites on both sides of Snowgrass Creek. If you hike to it, you can take Trail 96—the shortest trail into the Goat Rocks area—⅓ mile up to Snowgrass Flat (no camping), then north just beyond it to a junction. From it the Lily Basin Trail passes well-named Alpine Camp in less than ¼ mile, while Trail 96 climbs back to the PCT in ¾ mile, completing a 1.9-mile alternate route.

Leaving the Trail 86 junction, the PCT switchbacks up to a saddle, traverses slopes above Snowgrass Flat, and arrives at the end of the alternate route, Trail 96 (6640–1.2). Forty yards from this junction is 40-foot-high "Split Rock," which broke apart eons ago, for full-sized conifers now grow in the gap between the two halves.

Our route, substantially easier, goes north up a ducked alpine trail that passes a few specimens of pasqueflowers and Rainier gentians. A half mile beyond our junction, we tread across rocks with deep striations, convincing "fingerprints" of past glaciers. Climbing up to the low west ridge of Old Snowy Mountain, we encounter the Dana May Yelverton Shelter (7040–0.9), 12 feet square, which provides plenty of protection from the frequent summer storms (no fires allowed). The six-inch-high junipers here attest to the severity of this environment. Above us lies the realm of rock and ice—the habitat of the alpine mountaineer.

After a moderate 40-yard climb north, we see to the left, just below us, a trailside, two-foot-high windbreak assembled from loose stones at the edge of a permanent snowfield. Upslope 60 yards from this windbreak is a larger, three-foot-high one. Neither gives you much protection if you are caught in a storm, but both shield you from the misty, howling winds that you might encounter at night. Crossing a snowfield takes us to the brink of the severely glaciated, 3000-foot-deep Upper Lake Creek canyon, which will become even more impressive as our northbound trail provides us with even better views down and across it. To the northwest we see perpetually frozen Goat Lake (6450) nestled in a classic glacial cirque at the southeast end of the Johnson Peak ridge. At the brink, ¼ mile beyond the shelter, past hikers used to start a contour northeast across the gentle upper slopes of the Packwood Glacier, rather than climb 550 feet higher to the north shoulder of Old Snowy Mountain (7930). In 1978, the Forest Service blasted a route that more or less follows the one taken by these hikers. When you start across it, you leave the highest PCT point in Washington—7080 feet.

In a way it is unfortunate that the old trail up Old Snowy was abandoned, for from it you had an almost full-circle panorama of the Goat Rocks country. Looking above the canyons to the northwest, you saw the monarch of the Cascade Range—mighty Mt. Rainier (14,410)—ruling above all the other stratovolcanoes. To the south was Mt. Adams (12,276), the crown prince and second highest peak in the range. Off to its west lay the youthful princess, Mt. St. Helens (8364). The Multnomah Indians had a different interpretation. They said a feud developed between Klickitat (Mt. Adams) and Wyeast (Mt. Hood) over the beautiful Squaw Mountain (Mt. St. Helens), who had just moved into the neighborhood. She loved Wyeast, but Klickitat triumphed in a fight, so she had to reside in Klickitat's domain. She refused to bed down with him, however, and after a while, as would be expected, his flames of love for her died, and both volcanoes became dormant. A modern-day account would say she couldn't stand Klickitat any longer, so finally on May 18, 1980, she blew her top. Literally. You'll find traces of Mt. St. Helens' ash along the trail.

The newer PCT cuts rather precariously across the upper part of Packwood Glacier before curving north down to a crest saddle

(6850–1.0). This Egg Butte section of the PCT, constructed with heroic efforts in 1953–54, now continues along the jagged ridge, contours around its "teeth" and provides us with alpine views across the sparkling McCall Glacier toward Tieton Peak (7768), due east of Old Snowy. We reach a small saddle, from which the trail makes a precarious descent across a steep slope as it bypasses summit 7210. You can expect this narrow footpath to be snowbound and hazardous through most of July. Crampons may be required, particularly in early-summer, and equestrians are forced back. Reaching the ridge again, we follow it down to Elk Pass (6680–1.3). Here the windswept whitebark pines stand chest-high at most, and the junipers creep but inches above the frost-wedged rocks.

Despite its foreboding appearance, the pass does have animal life. Excluding invertebrates, the most common wild animals seen are chipmunks and ground squirrels. A sparrow hawk may dive swiftly past you, and if you're lucky, you might even have a weasel dart across your path. As for the mountain goats—well, there's not much chance that you'll see any as long as you adhere to this popular trail. The goats have good reason to fear man.

Pushing toward supplies at White Pass, we first drop northwest from Elk Pass to Coyote Trail 79 (6600–0.3), which continues a ridge descent in the same direction. We turn right and diagonal east across Peak 6768's usually snow-clad north slope, then reach bleak, alpine campsites (6320–0.3) just below the peak's northeast ridge. These do, however, give the hiker a stunning sunset and sunrise as the rays bounce off the Elk Pass snowfield, across from us. If you're hiking south, these are the last campsites you'll see until south of Old Snowy.

Our trail descends east-southeast along the foot of the snowfield, crosses its runoff creek and several others, passes by glacially striated bedrock, and then makes short switchbacks down to a small pond at the foot of another snowfield. By later afternoon the snow fields in this basin are melting at a good rate, as evidenced by the roar of the cascade to the west. From the pond we now climb steeply 200 yards to a saddle (5820–1.3). The PCT formerly dropped east-southeast to wet, meadowy, over-used McCall Basin, but now a newer tread switchbacks east. It almost touches a crest saddle (5580–0.6), on which one could set up an emergency camp, then it switchbacks down to a

H18

H18

Old Snowy Mountain and McCall Glacier

H19

Campground
Leech Lake
4412

White Pass
4470

HIGHWAY 12

Creek

4400

Picnic Area

Knuppenburg Lake

SAND

Millridge

LAKE

4400

5401

Hogback Ridge

5600

6000

6375

Hogback Mtn

6789

Miriam Lake

6000

6717

Shoe Lake

6000

6652

5200

6427

5600

5472

Mile 15

CLEAR

FORK

TRAIL 61

BOUNDARY

5535

Tieton Pass

4800

NORTH

FORK

SKI LIFT

5200

5967

JEEP

TRAIL

Ginnette Lake

Hell Lake
5249

5200

5600

4400

Miriam

4800

5663

6406

5200

Scatter

5723

Creek

4000

4000

GOAT ROCKS WILDERNESS

HIGHWAY 12 7½ Mi.

1207

1117

4800

TRAIL

3600

Fork

North

1118

Mile 15

3320

TIETON

7128

Tieton Meadows

SOUTH

4800

HOGBACK

1144

4000

GOAT ROCKS WILDERNESS

Hidden Spring

SHOE LAKE

Mt. Rainier above the Chimney Rock-Elk Pass crest

junction with the former PCT route (5200–0.5). Ignoring the old trail, we traverse over to a saddle that holds knee-deep Lutz Lake and several small campsites (5100–0.6). Beyond this viewless environment we descend north around the west slope of Peak 5493 to Tieton Pass (4570–1.0). Here by a dry campsite with springs downslope, Clear Fork Trail 61 starts a moderate descent west-northwest on its route north toward U.S. Highway 12. North Fork

Tieton Trail 1118, which at 4.6 miles is the shortest trail approach to this pass, descends east before curving northeast down to the North Fork Tieton Road 1207 at a trailhead near Scatter Creek.

Our trail starts a gentle descent northwest, then gradually makes a winding route north past two stagnant ponds, then crosses east over the divide (4930–1.5) and rounds Peak 5472. We now continue on our viewless path east until we

Mt. Rainier poking above Shoe Lake-Hogback Mountain crest

Shoe Lake—rest here, but don't camp overnight

climb the southeast spur of Peak 6427 and then reach a junction with Trail 1117A (5520–1.8). This goes 290 yards east to Shoe Lake Trail 1117, along which you'll see two or more camps as you descend a brief distance to Hidden Spring, which lies just above a beautiful meadow. On the PCT we climb briefly but rather steeply to Trail 1117 (5680–0.2), down which southbound hikers would drop to Hidden Spring.

From this merger we climb north to an open ridge (6200–0.8), from where a trail descends to clear, cool, shimmering Shoe Lake. Due to overuse, the lake was closed to camping in the late 1970s, but later this ban was lifted. You can camp within 100 feet of the shoreline, but you can't build a fire. Past the open ridge, we make a switchbacking arc up to a saddle (6620–0.7). From it we see Mt. Rainier poke its head above Hogback Ridge while Mt. Adams just manages to lift its crown above Goat Rocks.

The volcanic flows around us here superficially resemble sedimentary rocks, for they have broken along close, evenly spaced horizontal joints to give the illusion of alternating, stepped beds of sandstone and shale. We make one switchback, descend a well-graded trail past a thumb above us and Miriam Lake below, then reach the stepped slope of Hogback Mountain (6789). As we descend its northeast ridge, we obtain views of Mt. Rainier, whose slopes we should set foot upon in a few days' time.

Entering forest once again, we cross a vaguely defined saddle, then climb gently to a junction with the White Pass Chair Lift spur trail (5830–2.5).

Many hikers truck 0.4 mile north up it, then take the lift ($3, one-way, in 1985) down to the White Pass ski lodge (4480), which houses the Continental Cafe, open year-round. From it they can walk east 100 yards past the White Pass Village, with its Nor'wester Restaurant, then in 70 yards reach the Kracker Barrel Grocery and post office at a gas station. Minimal supplies are available here but you can wash your clothes and make a phone call home. A half-mile walk northeast on U.S. Highway 12 takes you to a spur road beside which the PCT crosses the highway.

From the spur-trail junction, the PCT makes a winding descent northeastward to a junction with little-used Hogback Trail 1144 (5400–1.1), which starts on a gentle descent east before curving north. Our trail curves northwest, passes a small, stagnant pond, then reaches green, 100-yard-long Ginnette Lake (5400–0.2). We now leave Goat Rocks Wilderness, get a glimpse of the chair-lift jeep road northwest of us, and then switchback down to a trailhead parking lot 50 yards south of U.S. Highway 12 (old state Highway 14) (4405–2.2). The short road to the trailhead begins just 30 yards east of the road to White Pass Campground.

H19   **H19**

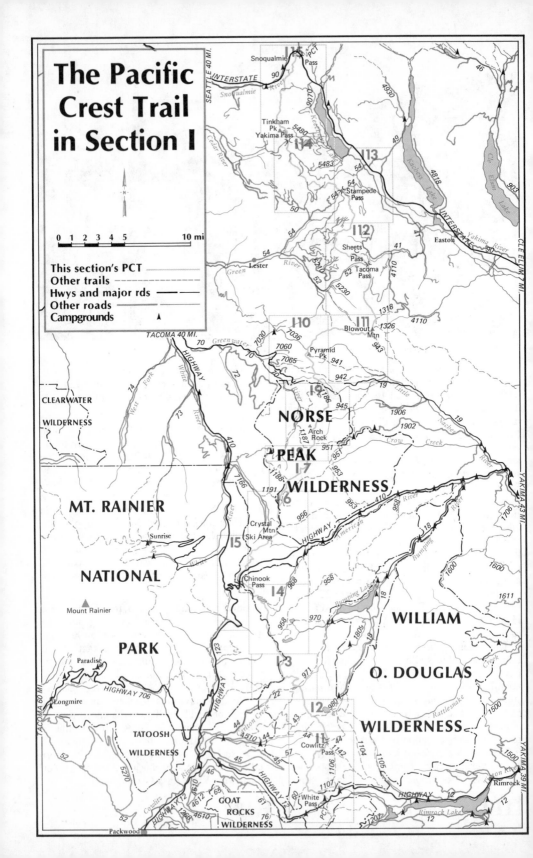

The Pacific Crest Trail in Section I

N

0 1 2 3 4 5   10 mi

This section's PCT ——————
Other trails ----------
Hwys and major rds ——————
Other roads ————
Campgrounds ▲

SEATTLE 40 MI.

Snoqualmie
INTERSTATE
90
Snoqualmie
Pass
PCT
Cedar River
Keechelus Lake
46
4930
49
I14
Tinkham Pk
Yakima Pass
5480
5483
I13
64
4818
Cle Elum Lake
903
Stampede Pass
54
INTERSTATE 90
Yakima River
CLE ELUM 7 MI.
50
54
I12
Sheets Pass
41
Easton
Green River
Lester
54
5240
52
Tacoma Pass
52
4110
5230
1318
I10
7030
7036
7090
7060
I11
Blowout Mtn
1326
943
4110
TACOMA 40 MI.
Greenwater
70
72
7065
Pyramid Pk
941
942
19
Little Naches River
CLEARWATER
WILDERNESS
74
HIGHWAY
White River
73
186
945
19
1906
NORSE
1187
Arch Rock
951
1902
Crow Creek
19
MT. RAINIER
166
PEAK
951 957
I7
953
1188
I6
1191
WILDERNESS
953
410
958
318
966
HIGHWAY
410
1706
Crystal Mtn Ski Area
15
Sunrise
American River
NATIONAL
968
958
Bumping River
1600
1600
Mount Rainier
Chinook Pass
I4
968
958
18
1611
PARK
968
970
Bumping Lake
1805
18
WILLIAM
Paradise
123
971
O. DOUGLAS
HIGHWAY
22
I3
Longmire
HIGHWAY 706
Rattlesnake Creek
1500
TACOMA 60 MI.
5270
44
I2
980
WILDERNESS
1142
Ohanapecosh River
4810
44
44
1104
52
TATOOSH
45
57
Cowlitz Pass
1105
1500
Rimrock
WILDERNESS
46
45
1106
Yakima River
12
YAKIMA 39 MI.
4612
4610
68
1107
1201
HIGHWAY 12
76
White Pass
PCT
HIGHWAY 12
Rimrock Lake
12
52
61
GOAT ROCKS WILDERNESS
Packwood

Section I: Highway 12 near White Pass to Interstate 90 at Snoqualmie Pass

Introduction: Graphic contrasts in land use separate Section I into two very different segments. The southern half is largely a subalpine parkland glistening with lakes cupped in forests and meadows. Long-appreciated, most of this backcountry lies protected within the boundaries of two recently designated (1984) wilderness areas and Mt. Rainier National Park. The northern half, on the other hand, being lower, is totally within the montane forest belt so favored by the lumber industry, and it blisters with a lot of barren earth, some of the most extensively clear-cut land in the West.

Moderate topography characterizes both halves of Section I, and fit border-bound hikers can make good time. From White Pass the trail sloshes through soggy muskeg country, crossing a plateau pocked with pools and lakes. As the Cascade divide rises into a knobby backbone, the trail follows it faithfully, swinging from saddle to subalpine saddle, passing within 12 miles of massive Mt. Rainier. Not quite one third of the way through Section I at Chinook Pass, the broadest of these flower-rich saddles, State Highway 410 crosses the crest.

Halfway through Section I the craggy divide slopes below the subalpine zone, and though fir and hemlock forests dominate here, meadows and crest-top vistas keep the hiking varied and interesting. Still 40 miles from Snoqualmie Pass, the trail enters land shared in a checkerboard pattern by the Forest Service and Burlington Northern railroad. The railroad received title to every other square mile during the railroad subsidies of the 1880s in return for laying tracks across Stampede Pass. Neither owner being fully responsible for the territory, the forests have been mined, and nearly one half of this last stretch goes through clearcuts laced with logging roads and bulldozer tracks. By 1984 most of the Burlington Northern sections that the PCT passes through had been logged and the trail permanently rerouted through them, whereas most of the Forest Service sections were roaded but still holding their forests.

Declination: 19½°E

Mileages:

	South to North	Distances between Points	North to South
Highway 12 near White Pass	0.0		96.5
Buesch Lake	5.8	5.8	90.7
Bumping River ford by Bumping Lake Trail........	12.5	6.7	84.0
Dewey Lake......................................	24.2	11.7	72.3
Highway 410 at Chinook Pass	27.4	3.2	69.1
Sheep Lake	29.6	2.2	66.9
Big Crow Basin Spring near Norse Peak Trail	38.1	8.5	58.4
Arch Rock shelter spur trail	45.2	7.1	51.3
Camp Urich at Government Meadow	50.2	5.0	46.3
Unnamed spring 2.1 mi. n.e. of Windy Gap........	55.0	4.8	41.5
Granite Creek Trail on Blowout Mountain	61.0	6.0	35.5
Sheets Pass	69.0	8.0	27.5
Stampede Pass	78.3	9.3	18.2
Stirrup Creek..................................	83.4	5.1	13.1
Mirror Lake...................................	87.8	4.4	8.7
Lodge Lake	94.7	6.9	1.8
Interstate 90 at Snoqualmie Pass..................	96.5	1.8	0.0

Supplies: Restaurant food, post offices, and the typically minimal foodstuffs can be found at White Pass and Snoqualmie Pass (see page 225). Similar amenities can be found about one third of the way north from White Pass, at Crystal Mountain, a couple miles away from and 1400 feet below the PCT.

Wilderness Permits: No wilderness permits are required along this section, unless you venture some distance west of the PCT into Mt. Rainier National Park (see page 20).

Problems: Mosquitoes can be especially bad in the marshy terrain north of White Pass. On the crest-top route between Government Meadow and Stampede Pass, though, water is scarce, partly because logging has obliterated some springs. By mid-August only one reliable water source can be found for the last 23 miles of this section, and even it is somewhat inconvenient. In early season, snow clinging to north and east slopes between Bumping River and Blowout Mountain can make carrying an ice axe worthwhile.

In some of the logged areas, blowdowns and generally battered soil make following the trail less than easy, although few hikers get off route. The trail crosses many logging roads and follows a few for very short distances. *Most* of these crossings and followings are clearly posted with PCT emblems or diamonds, but a few require a brief search. Finally, active logging operations can temporarily reroute the PCT, in which case hikers follow impromptu signs, blazes and surveyor's tapes. This chapter's maps and prose depict only one detour off the established PCT, a ½-mile diversion north of Government Meadow.

Hikers driving to White Pass will want to turn north off Highway 12 just 0.5 mile northeast of White Pass and park, after 0.2 mile, at the trailhead parking lot near Leech Lake. The PCT crosses Highway 12 only 30 yards east of the Leech Lake PCT trailhead turnoff and passes an old shelter on its way to this parking lot.

Pulverized duff and "trail apples" evince this trail section's popularity with horsemen as we start from the lot (4415–0.2) in a gentle switchbacking climb, crossing a bulldozer track before entering William O. Douglas Wilderness. A staunch conservationist, the late Supreme Court Justice Douglas grew up near

I1

I1

OWLITZ
44

Penoyer
Lake

TRAIL

Tumac Mtr
6340
Lookout

44
5600

Jess Lake

BM 5191

Benchmark Lake

Cowlitz
Pass

Pillar
Lake

5200

Pipe Lake

Long John
Lake

Art Lake
5110

Hill La

Shell
4926

Buesch
Lake
508

WILLIAM O. DOUGLAS

5200

Dumbbell
Lake

SHELLROCK

1142

Cramer Mtn
5992

Cramer
Lake
5225

Otter
Lake

Dancing Lady
Lake

BOUNDARY

57

5569 x

5200

5200

North

CRAMER LAKE TRAIL

1106

BIG PEAK

Spiral Butt

TRAIL

1108

WILDERNESS

4800

4400

NATIONAL

FOREST

4800

4800

5295

Sand Lake

Fork

Dog Lake
4207

Falls

LANTHR CREEK

Shelter

5200

60

5206

OARK MEADOWS

TRAIL

1107

Quarry

Falls
Campground

Cortright
Point
5765

Deer Lake

4400

Falls

Fork

4000

YAKIMA CO
LEWIS CO

White Pass
Campground

South

GOAT ROCKS

Leech
Lake
4412

4800

5843

HOGBACK

1144 Twin Peaks

White Pass

5200

4470

WILDERNESS

HIGHWAY 12

SKI LIFT

Creek

Picnic Area

Knuppenburg
Lake

4400

5200

Ginnette
Lake

JEEP

TRAIL

Hell Lake

Hell

Millridge

5401

5961

Sand Lake

Yakima, and he hiked throughout his life in the lands now named after him, loving the area enough, despite his world travels, to establish his home in Goose Prairie, on the Bumping River. After leveling out in the fir-and-spruce forest, we pass a junction with Dark Meadows Trail 1107 (4780–1.1), which descends east to Dog Lake. Resuming a gradual climb, we skirt a meadow, rise beside and then cross Deer Lake's outlet creek, and next pass a much larger meadow just before reaching Deer Lake (5206–0.9). Here there is an extensive and beaten down camping area.

Ahead, a barely ascending walk north through forest and lupine-rich glades brings us to Sand Lake (5295–0.5) where, from the base of the lake's peninsula, a spur leads south to a renovated shelter that's barely large enough to sleep three. Just beyond this spur a sign points west to Highway 12, along obscure Sand Lake Trail 60. We, however, continue north on an essentially level track, noting the curious spikes of beargrass, and meet Cortright Creek Trail 57 (5520–2.0) coming from the northwest. Not far northeast from here we leave the almost unnoticed divide on a broad, mucky track. A number of similar, abandoned swaths in this area show how heavy use in a soggy soil, especially by loaded horses, turns trails to quagmires.

The brief descent ends at Buesch Lake (5081–1.1), entry point onto the heart of the plateau that caps this part of the gentle divide

between the Cowlitz and Yakima rivers. Andesite lavas erupted in the Pliocene and Pleistocene epochs to form this plateau, and during the cooler Pleistocene, a small ice cap formed over it and helped smooth it out. For half a dozen miles now the trail runs across hummocky flatlands riddled with ponds, puddles, mudholes and muskeg. Patchily forested with droopy hemlocks and pointy subalpine firs, and carpeted with heather, huckleberry and azalea, this area supports only acid-tolerant plants.

A short rerouting, not yet finished in August 1985, will take the PCT farther west from the mapped route near the west shore of Buesch Lake, and proceed northeast past the Dumbbell Lake spur (5130–0.5). From here the PCT continues within 40 yards west of a pleasant campsite at Benchmark Lake. Then, just beyond southeast-branching Shellrock Lake Trail 1142, it crosses Cowlitz Trail 44 (5191–0.9) at a vista of the white hulk of Mt. Rainier. Continuing a muddy, gently rolling course, our trail bends from north to northwest past campsites at Henry Lake (5150–1.2), and soon it intersects Twin Sisters Lakes Trail 980 (4880–1.1).

Imperceptibly descending, the PCT next passes Jug Lake Trail 43 (4670–1.2), which forks southwest, crosses a creeklet near a campsite with a meadow view, and then decidedly drops off the plateau to the outlet of Fish Lake, headwaters of the Bumping River (4100–1.8). Across this creek is a large campsite and a junction with Bumping Lake Trail 971,

I1   **I1, I2, I3**

where our path cuts west to touch the north shore of long, shallow Fish Lake. It promptly leaves the lakeside path and starts working up long switchbacks that take us above Buck Lake, across Crag Lake's outlet, and then back to a spur that drops to Crag Lake itself, where there are some comfortable campsites. As the PCT contours just beyond this spur, it passes a reliable drinkable rill (5170–2.7).

A couple more long, lazy switchbacks have us rising across meadowy slopes verdant with aster, spiraea, blueberry, and corn lily. Marveling at Mts. Rainier, Adams and St. Helens, we then turn north around the Cascade divide and pass Laughingwater Trail 22 (5690–1.6), which drops southwest. Here at the start of a long tour high along the Cascade backbone, you can in good weather look forward to miles of glorious, expansive views; in bad weather you'll find yourself shrouded in clouds, exposed to the brunt of wet westerly storms.

Contouring now, we soon recross the divide to traverse above One Lake, and eventually to Trail 380 (5660–1.6), which descends 0.3 mile to Two Lakes. Next, a quick climb takes us back to the west side, where Mt. Rainier's overwhelming presence hardly lets us notice the many wildflowers at our feet, of which partridge foot is the most common. Along here we meet Cougar Lakes Trail 958A, which heads back over the crest, and we start another long traverse, contouring through forest and meadow across a couple of spur ridges before dropping via abrupt switchbacks to a saddle and Ameri-

can Ridge Trail 958 (5320–2.6), which departs eastward. Just past this junction we come to a campsite, although finding water here would require a bit of a walk downhill. Here we look down the long, forested (and previously glaciated) valley of the American River.

Now the PCT makes a brief climb north to cross a crest saddle, then contours through subalpine-fir groves before winding down to visit Anderson Lake (5340–1.4), just within Mt. Rainier National Park. It has a nice campsite, and you won't need a permit to camp at it. Continuing north, the trail barely climbs as it crosses a seasonal trickle, traverses scree, and rounds a spur ridge. It then arcs down toward Dewey Lake, first meeting Dewey Way Trail 968A, which splits northeast to connect with Trail 968. Just beyond the junction, Dewey Lake's expansive waters and numerous campsites along the shore-hugging PCT invite a pause (5112–1.8).

After rounding Dewey Lake's shore and bridging its inlet, our route passes Dewey Lake Trail 968 (5130–0.5), which branches east to the American River valley, and then our route climbs out of the soggy lake basin, working west through dark forest before emerging onto meadowland. After this it switchbacks and immediately meets the Tipsoo Lake Trail, a day hiker's path that reaches Highway 410 only ⅓ mile south of Chinook Pass. Here is an introduction to some amazingly colorful flora. Paintbrushes, pasque flowers, lupines, avalanche lilies and a galaxy of other blossoms spill over

I3, I4   **I4**

see MAP I3

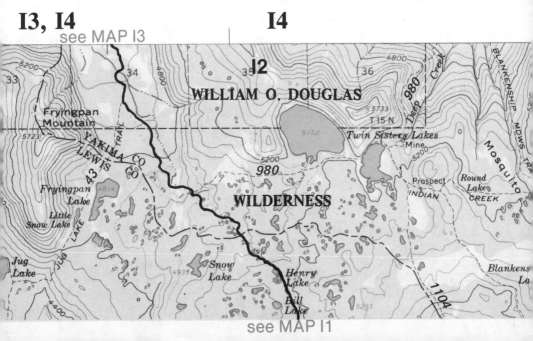

see MAP I1

the PCT as it tops the rise and then descends, first abruptly and then in a long traverse past a tarn, to Highway 410's fairly steady traffic at Chinook Pass (5432–2.7). Water can be found at a picnic area ⅓ mile south from here, but it must be treated. From this pass it's 68 miles east to Yakima, 41 miles northwest to Enumclaw, and 34 miles southwest to Paradise, the starting point for the challenging "standard" route to the top of Mt. Rainier.

Beyond the footbridge over the highway, the PCT turns north onto an old roadbed, crosses a bench and then as a trail approaches traffic as it makes a rising traverse. This steep slope supports a scrubbier flora than that at Chinook Pass proper. Fireweed, huckleberry, manzanita, pearly everlasting and bedraggled Alaska-cedars, hardy plants all, testify to tougher conditions. The gradual ascent turns up a ravine and then steepens into a couple of switchbacks before reaching Sheep Lake (5750–2.2), a popular spot for day hikers and overnighters. After following the lakeshore for a bit, our trail starts upslope, weaving and switchbacking generally northeast across meadowy bowls and

up into ptarmigan and pika country. It then traverses under small crags to Sourdough Gap (6440–1.2). The name of this saddle, as well as other features to the north, recalls the gold and silver prospectors who worked this region until not so long ago.

Admiring Mts. Adams and St. Helens, we can savor here the start of another long stretch of high traverse, which is wonderfully scenic if the weather is good. Skidding down scree off the gap, we come to an unsigned spur at the first switchback, and after another hairpin we settle into a long, gently descending traverse near treeline. Placer Lake comes into view 600 feet below as you approach Bear Gap, where you'll find a major trail plexus (5882–2.1). Here Silver Creek Trail 1192 drops northwest to civilization at Crystal Mountain Ski Area, Hen Skin Lake Trail 1193 starts a traverse southwest, and Bear Gap Trail 967 comes up from Morse Creek and Highway 410 to the east. We, however, take the PCT in a slant across the gap and then contour north, viewing ski lifts and condominiums well below, until we turn southeast on our way around the steep flanks of Pickhandle Point.

I5, I6   I6

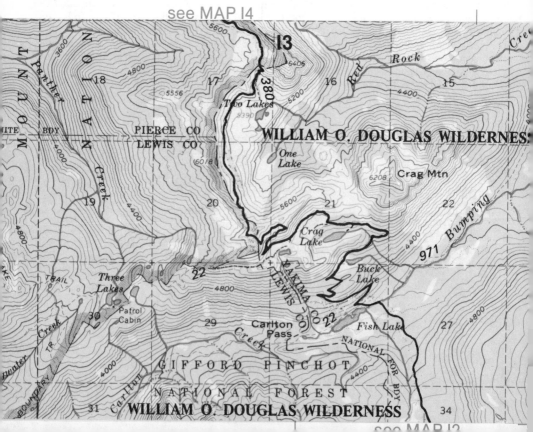

Tarn near Chinook Pass

Next we angle back across the crest at Pickhandle Gap and promptly meet an obscure trail, signed FOG CITY and GOLD HILL, dropping east (6040–1.1). Then we rise along the open south slopes of Crown Point and, at the breathtaking crest between Crown Point and Gold Hill, reach the southern boundary of Norse Peak Wilderness. Here we meet two other trails (6200–0.3). One is unsigned, following the ridgecrest east to Gold Hill, and the other is Union Creek Trail 956, dropping north off the crest 50 yards west of where we gain it. We follow the PCT on a steady climb west and then north around Crown Point, before long coming onto the narrow watershed divide at Blue Bell Pass (6390–0.4).

From this saddle the trail contours north and, as it approaches the spur dividing Pickhandle

I6
Sourdough Gap

I6

and Bullion basins, it intersects an unsigned path. The lower track drops steeply into Bullion Basin, while the upper one climbs to the top of summit 6479. We contour around this summit, which takes us to narrow Bullion Pass. Balancing astride this narrow saddle, we first meet a steep, unsigned trail crossing the ridge, then meet Bullion Basin Trail 1156 (6150–0.9), descending to the west. As the crest rises to a summit again, we ascend along its west flank in a long, meadowy traverse to Scout Pass (6530–1.5). This presents us with a view across Lake Basin's gentle parkland bossed over by one of the area's larger crags.

A gentle descent leads one across the head of Lake Basin, and you pass first an unsigned and eroding trail that beelines down into the basin, then a designated trail (6390–0.6), which descends to excellent camping at Basin Lake, ½ mile below. Next you round the northeast spur of Norse Peak and descend into Big Crow Basin. As you near the bottomland at the head of this basin, you pass 30 feet above a welcome and reliable spring (6290–0.4). Some 40 yards beyond this you meet the junction with Norse Peak Trail 1191, which climbs west, and Crow Lake Way 953, which passes an old shelter ½ mile away on its eastward descent. Next the PCT passes a campsite as it rounds Big Crow

Basin, and then it rises along a bench and back to the crest at forested Barnard Saddle (6150–0.8). After weaving through a couple of small crestline ravines, passing an unsigned track that drops west in the first, it returns to the east side of the divide at Hayden Pass (6150–0.3) and we get a view over Little Crow Basin.

We make a steep slant down into this basin, and then gradually descend across its upper glades and fir forest to a sign, LITTLE CROW BASIN (5930–0.4). Twenty yards before this sign one can drop off the trail 75 yards to an established campsite. In a draw another 100 yards below and south of this site, water trickles much of the summer.

The PCT soon crosses an avalanche gully and continues slanting down out of Little Crow Basin, and then it traverses northeast for some time before making a brief climb up to Martinson Gap (5720–1.4). Beyond this gap the track turns northwest to angle up the slopes of Peak 6373, passing the "ghost trees" of an old burn. Next the trail pivots and arcs around the south and east slopes of 6373, recrosses the crest, and gradually settles onto the broadening Cascade divide, still presenting Mt. Rainier's massive white dome through the scattered and stunted subalpine firs. Along this stretch the trail intersects Arch Rock Way 1187 (5930–2.1)

I6
Lake Basin and Basin Lake

I6, I7, I8

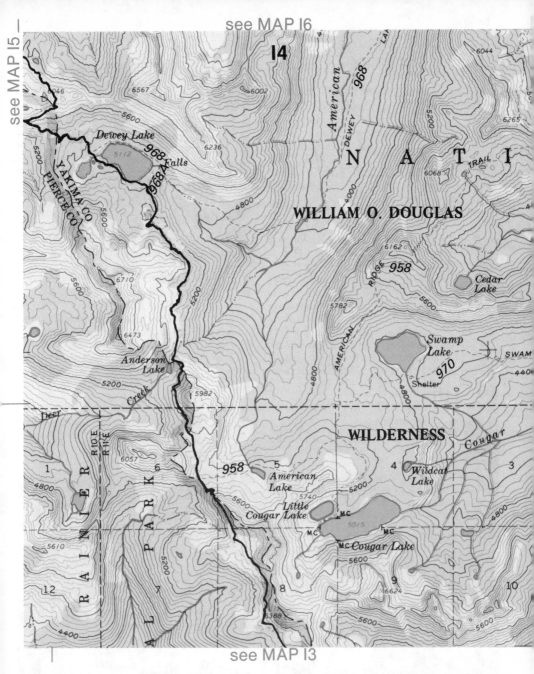

14

N A T I

WILLIAM O. DOUGLAS

Dewey Lake

968 Falls

958

YAKIMA CO
PIERCE CO

Cedar
Lake

958

Swamp
Lake

970

SWAM

Shelter

Anderson
Lake

Creek

Deer

WILDERNESS

Cougar

1

958

5

American
Lake

4

Wildcat
Lake

3

RAINIER

Little
Cougar Lake

MC

12

8

MC Cougar Lake

9

10

which, on its way west to Echo Lake, descends past nearby Saddle Springs. Although these springs are convenient to the PCT user, many years they trickle only into midsummer. However, beyond this junction an unsigned spoor (5700–0.5) drops east ¼ mile to a packer camp known as Morgan Springs, a more enduring water source.

Beyond this path, easy walking for ¼ mile takes us to Cougar Valley Trail (5780–0.3),

which heads east along a spur ridge, and more strolling along the crest brings us to an unsigned trail junction (5920–0.5), at the base of an open rise. We avoid the fork that climbs directly up this broad summit and take the one contouring to the east, passing through more blends of forest and meadow on our way to the spur trail (5760–0.8) to Arch Rock shelter. At the end of this 200-yard-long spur one finds a perennial spring trickling from a pipe, as well as an old four-sided shelter. Camp spots can be found in the forest below.

Beyond the turnoff the PCT descends past the northern access to the shelter, and then it crosses a seasonal branch of South Fork Little Naches River. Well sheltered now under silver fir and western hemlock, the route loses elevation along the broad crest to Louisiana Saddle (5220–1.5), from where obscure Middle Fork Trail 945 traverses east. Our trail continues descending through deep forest to Rods Gap (4820–1.1), from where it abruptly gains back 400 feet. Near the top of this climb a poetic sign warns that the wrath of the ghost of Mike Urich, a trail worker in this area during the '40s and '50s, will fall on anyone who harms the area's trees. One must imagine that Mike's ghost has his hands pretty full trying to catch up with the loggers who've worked not far to the north! After leveling out for a bit, our forest trail gently descends northwest and meets Maggie Way Trail 1186 (4850–1.6), heading west for a deep drop to the Greenwater River. Not much farther northwest our descent takes us out of Norse Peak Wilderness and ends

Shelter at Camp Urich

at perennial Meadow Creek. After fording this we momentarily arrive at Camp Urich (4720–0.8). Here we find a rough shelter with an excellent wood stove, a large camping area, and a privy, all set on the west edge of expansive Government Meadow.

From the shelter we continue north on a broad track, and we promptly come to another Mike

I9, I10

I10

Hikers on an andesite rock outcrop west of Green Pass

Blowout Mountain, viewed from the north

Urich warning and an old wagon wheel. The latter recalls the first wagon train to cross the Cascades east of Puget Sound. In 1853 the party, headed by David Longmire, rested here before starting a rough descent into the Greenwater River canyon. By 1855 a military road was completed through this area, crossing gentle

I10

Mt. Rainier, from above outcrop

Naches Pass, ½ mile to the east. Just beyond this spot the PCT crosses this historic road (4800–0.2), which dirt bikers now know as jeep road 942. A VEHICLES PROHIBITED sign a few yards beyond this track shows us the way up a gentle rise to near the edge of Burlington Northern land. Loggers were sawing trees here in the summer of '85 and a temporary detour had hikers first drop a short distance east on a rough trail to meet a logging road at a sharp turn. They then followed this road uphill for ½ mile, passed an iron gate, and rejoined the established PCT back at the crest, where the road turns southwest (4840–1.1). Eventually the PCT should be rerouted through the new clearcut, and then it will again stay just east of the crest.

Staying on or just west of the crest now, our level trail soon comes to a spur trail, which climbs 0.4 mile to the top of Pyramid Peak—an excellent vantage point. The PCT itself gives excellent vistas of Mt. Rainier as it contours around the peak's steep west slopes to Windy Gap (5200–1.4). Along this saddle it follows a jeep road for 30 yards before branching east off it and starting a long traverse. Eventually the path rounds a spur ridge, then descends for 0.5 mile and passes 20 yards above a delicious spring, where a couple of small camp platforms have been hewn (5180–2.1).

I10

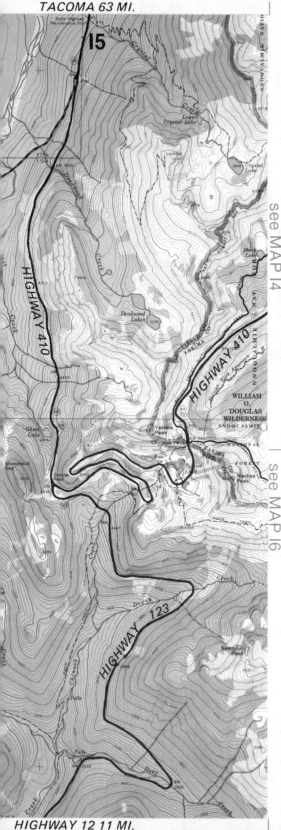

Mostly well shaded by silver firs and Douglas-firs, the PCT continues contouring a couple of hundred feet below the ridgecrest that divides the Little Naches and Green rivers. After some time, though, the crest drops and meets our generally level tread. At this spot (4890–2.4) a dirt road that follows the divide forks, and we cross its branch just below the ridgecrest and continue heading east. A brief climb now introduces a vista south of splintery Goat Rocks, then we have a rollercoaster section of trail, which takes us back to the crest and across the ridgetop road (5000–1.1).

Brushing against wild rhododendrons in the shady fir forest, we rise above the road and then follow the crest into a gentle descent past a dry campsite (in early season water *can* be found downhill from here). The PCT enters brushy terrain thick with huckleberries and invading fir saplings, and coasts along Green Pass (4940–0.5). Next we face the first significant climb in many miles—up the west ridge of Blowout Mountain. We follow a couple of switchbacks and then, viewing Goat Rocks and much of the broad Naches River drainage to the south, we slant up to the ridgecrest, from where the obscure but signed West Fork Bear Creek Trail (5340–1.0) drops off to the south. The PCT continues climbing, switching back once and entering a small stand of subalpine firs, where we meet a sign pointing out obscure Granite Creek Trail 1326 (5480–1.0), bound for Mt. Clifty and Quartz Mountain.

* * * *

A bench on the northeast side of Blowout Mountain cups a marshy pond and contains a spring that, by the beginning of August, provide what can be the only water at all convenient to the PCT for 6 miles to the south and over 17 miles to the north. Granite Creek Trail 1326 is the southern end of a 1.2-mile alternate route that thirsty PCT hikers can take past this oasis, reconnecting with the PCT just north of Blowout Mountain. To do this, turn onto hard-to-follow Trail 1326, traverse east, and descend, first steeply and then more reasonably, to a saddle on the east ridge of Blowout Mountain. Here, 0.4 mile from the PCT, you meet Manastash Ridge Trail 1388. Take this trail north 0.3 mile to the pond and its adjacent campsites. To rejoin the PCT, climb north on eroding 1388 to crest the east-west ridge north of the pond's bench. Turn west here on Blowout Mountain Trail 1318 and

I10, I11

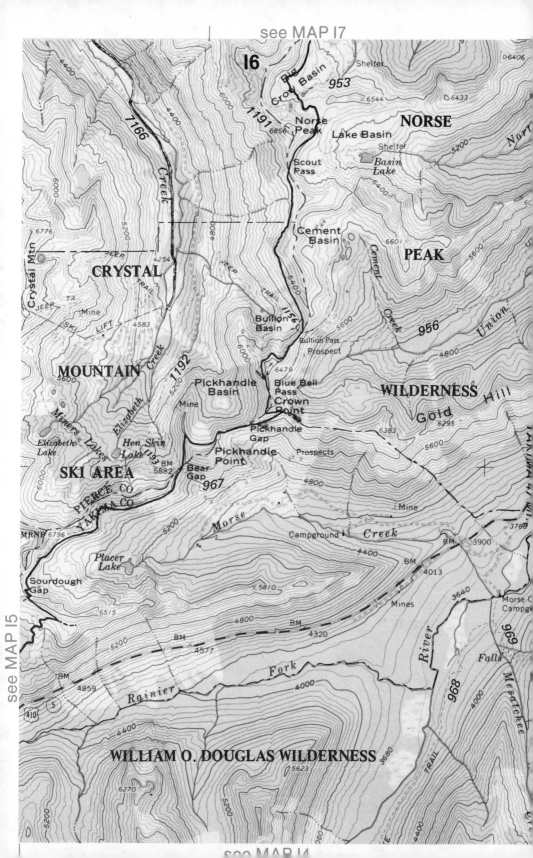

16

Big Crow Basin

953

Shelter

6406

NORSE

1191

Norse Peak
6856

Lake Basin

Shelter

Basin Lake

5200

Norr

6544

6433

7166

Creek

4400

6000

4400

6000

6000

5200

6776

4254

JEEP

CRYSTAL

Crystal Mtn

JEEP
TR

JEEP
TRAIL

Mine

SKI LIFT

4583

MOUNTAIN

5600

6000

Miners Lakes

Elizabeth
Lake

Elizabeth Creek

Hen Skin
Lake

1192

Mine

1113

BM
5882

Bear
Gap

Pickhandle
Basin

Scout
Pass

Cement
Basin

PEAK

6601

Cement Creek

5600

4800

956

Union

Gold Hill

6383

5600

6295

TRAIL WN

+

1156

TRAIL

6400

6000

5600

Bullion
Basin

Bullion Pass
Prospect

6479

Blue Bell
Pass
Crown
Point

Pickhandle
Gap

Pickhandle
Point

Prospects

WILDERNESS

5600

SKI AREA

PIERCE CO.
YAKIMA CO.

967

Prospects

4800

Mine

3788

MRNP 6796

5200

Placer
Lake

Morse

4800

Campground

Creek

4400

BM 3900

BM

4013

Mines

3640

Morse C
Campg

Sourdough
Gap

6515

5200

5810

4800

BM

4320

969

River

Mesatchee

Falls

968

BM

4577

410 5

BM

4859

Rainier

Fork

4000

4000

4000

4000

TRAIL

4400

WILLIAM O. DOUGLAS WILDERNESS

3680

5623

6270

5200

5200

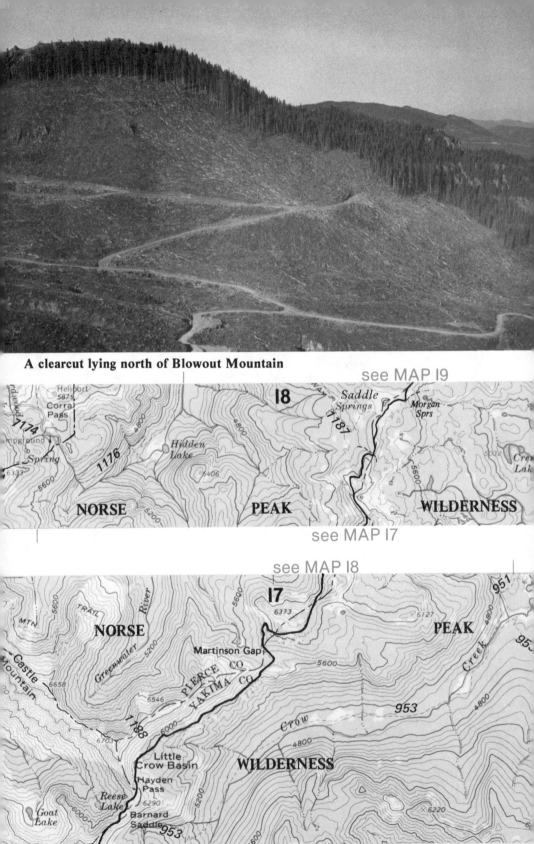

A clearcut lying north of Blowout Mountain

see MAP 19

18

Saddle
Springs

Morgan
Sprs

7174

Helinort

Corral
Pass

1176

Hidden
Lake

Spring

NORSE   PEAK   WILDERNESS

see MAP 17

see MAP 18

17

951

NORSE

Martinson Gap

PEAK

Castle
Mountain

PIERCE CO
YAKIMA CO

953

Little
Crow Basin

Hayden
Pass

Reese
Lake

WILDERNESS

Goat
Lake

Barnard
Saddle   953

see MAP I8

you'll join the PCT in 100 yards. PCT hikers coming from the north, or north-bounders not wanting to hassle route-finding along obscure Trail 1326, can branch off at 1318 and follow this description in reverse to the pond.

*   *   *   *

From the Granite Creek turnoff we climb a bit more to the crest of Blowout Mountain, where we get the most expansive view in some time, once again seeing Mt. Rainier dominating the central Washington hinterlands. Now we follow the trail along a narrow summit ridge, and look

east down to the aforementioned pond, which could be our last water source for a *long* way. We then round the north summit of Blowout Mountain and switchback down through a dense fir forest to Blowout Mountain Trail 1318 (5260–1.1), the northern access to the pond.

North from the junction a steep ridgeline descent ends our hiking through extensive unmarred terrain, as we emerge onto a vast clearcut landscape. One's first reaction might be revulsion at ridge after ridge riddled with roads and shaved down to soil, but PCT hikers might consider that hiking the PCT is more than just a pleasant walk through beautiful scenery—it is a

I11   **I11**

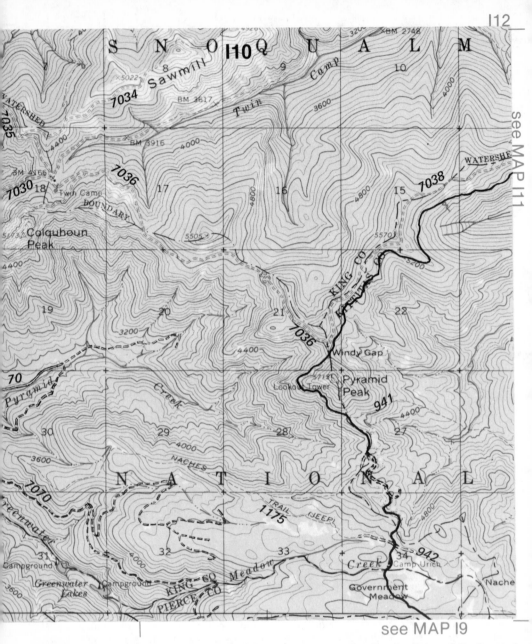

see MAP I11

see MAP I9

coming to know the Pacific Crest, its condition and goings-on. Hikers can see for themselves that much of this clearcut land is *not* regrowing marketable trees, and that the owners have not invested in long-term forestry. Many hikers might contemplate that perhaps their own home was constructed of the exceptional firs and hemlocks that were dragged from these hills.

For quite some time the trail keeps on or near the ridge dividing the Yakima and Green rivers. At first it is barely east of deforested private land, but then it follows the flat but narrow ridge

across a section line back into fully forested government land. Our track eventually emerges from the woods just east of the crest, where one can see the PCT rising around barren Point 4922, ahead, at the end of a logging road. The route barely touches this road, then contours before climbing 50 yards onto the adjacent crest. From this it then switchbacks down, crossing two roads on its way to a major saddle (4400–2.8).

From this saddle we traverse around the east side of Point 4922, then re-enter forest and

I11

I12

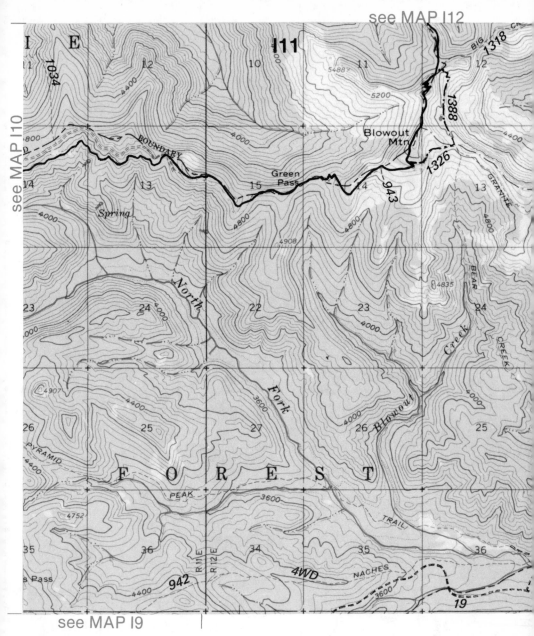

see MAP I10

see MAP I9

make a long, lazily switchbacking descent to Tacoma Pass (3460–2.7). Road 52 crosses this pass, and we jaywalk this logger's thoroughfare to ascend northwest into clearcut land again. Here the trail is not well maintained, but with a little care we follow it in an arc back up to the crest. With Mt. Rainier in full view, we now stride northwest along the divide as we cross one old logging road and then follow another one downhill for 30 yards before crossing it.

Now in forest, we cruise across Sheets Pass (3720–1.4), and then we climb and contour

through pleasant woods to a campsite and a seasonal creek (3860–0.4). This rill might carry water into mid-August of a wet year, but in 1985 it was dry by then. From here the route turns south and climbs around the south ridge of Bearpaw Butte. On the west side of the ridge we start switchbacking in and out of the next clearcut, and we find the trail a bit obscure as we clamber over and squeeze under a number of fallen trees. Forest conifers such as these often fall prey to strong winds, when left without wind-breaking neighbors. As one zigzags uphill,

I12   **I12**

I12

PCT marker on a stump in a clearcut

generally trending northwest, one can spot a stagnant pond about 300 feet below the trail, which the truly desperate might find refreshing.

Our climb takes us to the crest, which we follow across an old log landing, across an old road, and then across another landing. Shortly we drop a few yards south to avoid a ridgetop road and, as we traverse toward Snowshoe Butte, we make the short climb back and cross the ridgetop road where it curves. Next, at the forest border, the trail turns north along the east slope of Snowshoe Butte, but re-enters razed land on the butte's north ridge. A switchbacking descent takes us in and out of this clearcut across one road and then lands us on a second road. We follow this second road for 250 yards downhill (northeast), and then leave it from the same side we entered it on to walk back into the forest onto a broad saddle (4200–3.8) littered with blowdowns.

As we then follow the low crest from here, we branch left (north-northeast) at an unsigned trail junction back into a clearcut and, at the crest of a small knob, turn east onto a bulldozer track. We follow this for 200 yards past an old slash pile and continue east more or less directly up the adjacent ravine, passing a glade of corn lilies before we reach the edge of the clearcut just shy

of a ridgetop. Here the trail is obscure and easy to lose in a tangle of blowdowns, but it turns north and promptly descends through a corner of forest, only to enter another clearcut and continue descending just east of the rounded divide to a pass (4290–2.3), where we view a microwave repeater.

The trail crosses a road at the pass and makes a short climb up the next knob north before starting a descent toward the Stampede Pass weather station, visible ahead. Steep switchbacks bring the trail onto a bulldozer track for 30 yards, then the switchbacks resume and cross a more substantial road. The last switchback takes the trail into dense forest, in which the trail then follows the rolling divide, undulating past one powerline cut, and then another with old log poles. Deep beneath this latter line runs the Northern Pacific railway tunnel.

A short distance farther we cruise behind the weather station, cross its access road (3950–1.8), and then cross another powerline cut. With the maze of human disturbances that could lead one off route in this area, we depend a great deal on the stubby PCT posts that point the way across *almost* every road and powerline cut. We follow the low Cascade divide as it turns west, crossing another road and then another power-

I12   **I12, I13**

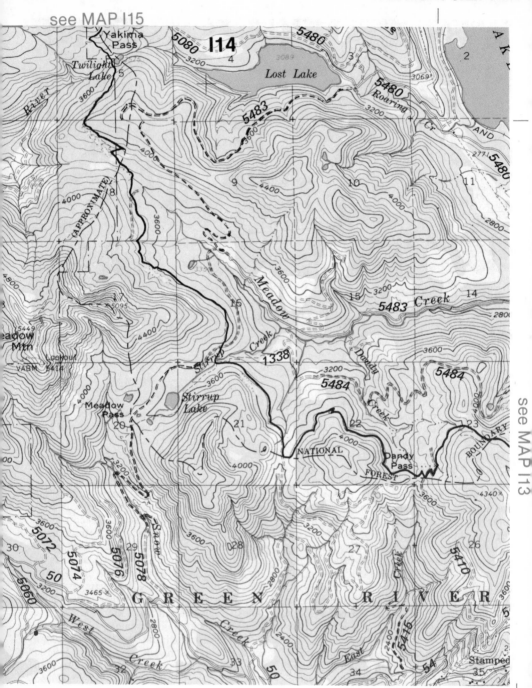

see MAP I15

see MAP I13

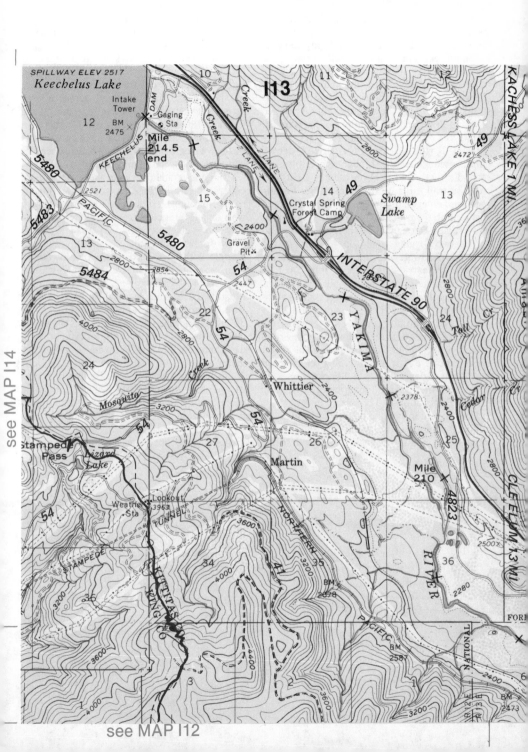

SPILLWAY ELEV 2517
Keechelus Lake

Intake
Tower

I13

12   BM
2475

Mile
214.5
end

Gaging
Sta

Crystal Spring
Forest Camp

14   49

*Swamp
Lake*

13

15

Gravel
Pit

54

22

23   YAKIMA

24   Toll

Whittier

Martin

26

Mile
210

25

Mosquito

27

Stampede
Pass

*Lizard
Lake*

Weather
Sta

Lookout
TUNNEL

34

41

35

36

NATIONAL

STAMPEDE

KITTITAS
KING

PACIFIC

see MAP I14

see MAP I12

line cut, on our way through a regrowing forest of silver fir, Douglas-fir, lodgepole pine, white pine and western hemlock. A gradual descent then drops us onto Stampede Pass Road 212 (3680–1.0), a couple of hundred yards south of the pass proper. About 0.2 mile south down this road lies Lizard Lake, a swampy, fetid pond with a fouled campsite on its south shore. Unpleasant though it may be, next to crackling powerlines and an abandoned auto, any campsite with water near the trail is rare along this stretch of PCT, and the author (Selters) camped here and drank the water, after boiling it for 10 minutes or more, without any ill effects.

From Road 212 the PCT strikes steeply uphill, switchbacking through the adolescent second-growth forest. Soon after it crests the rise, the trail turns north, parallel to a logging road, and enters a more recent clearcut. After a slight climb the trail cuts west across the divide and cruises through huckleberry prairies and across two logging roads on its way to the forested headwater ravine of Dandy Creek, which might carry water through July. The trail barely descends into the ravine before contouring south out of it, and then it slants southwest down through thick fireweed and other pioneers of clearcuts. It crosses a logging road and then empties onto and follows the same road to a hairpin (3840–2.1), where a rill might trickle into late August. Dropping off the road here, the trail descends gradually, switchbacking across another logging road before reaching Dandy Pass (3680–0.3).

Here we enter forested public land and circle halfway around a hill under the shade of a magnificent forest of giant old-growth hemlocks. This mile-long arc is a now-rare glimpse at the quality of tree for which the Pacific Northwest is famous, and with which the lumber industry made its killing. Eventually we cross the section line and enter brushy country again just shy of a saddle. Here we turn north and skirt the saddle to cross and then parallel a logging road, and in a few minutes we come to a creek (3600–1.9), which probably cascades year-round. A rough, rocky traverse north from here, paralleling and then dropping across a road, brings us to an even more certain stream, Stirrup Creek (3480–0.8). Along the south bank of this stream Meadow Creek Trail 1338 runs ½ mile through a clearcut up to Stirrup Lake, where one can find a pleasant campsite.

Climbing gradually from here among tall cedars, the trail crosses a well-graded logging road and rounds a ridge, and then strikes northwest on a level traverse, eventually crossing the corner of a clearcut on a rocky tread. As we re-enter forest along this swath's border, we grapple with a 70-yard tangle of blowdowns, then cross a road, but soon we're rewarded, before late August anyway, by the dribbling of Meadow Creek's headwaters (3660–2.1). From here we work up a couple of hairpins, gaining 350 feet to a ridgeline that overlooks the mostly clearcut headwaters of North Fork Cedar River, a major feeder into Seattle's water supply. At the valley's head we see Yakima Pass cupping Twilight Lake, which, at the bottom of a massacred amphitheater, looks like a forlorn island of natural beauty trying to hide behind a relict forest curtain. We slant down to the pass, crossing a logging road en route, and skirt Twilight Lake on its west shore (3575–1.4).

I13, I14
Lizard Lake and Mt. Rainier

I14

Mt. Rainier, from Dandy Pass

Campsites can be found in the scant trees on the east shore.

From the pass—part of an old Indian route—we strike northwest directly uphill, cross a road, and then cut northeast to ford the creek that issues from Mirror Lake. Just beyond this first ford the PCT turns across the end of a logging road and then climbs steeply to cross and recross the outlet creek on our way to Mirror Lake (4195–0.9). Suddenly we've entered a refuge of undisturbed mountain landscape; craggy Tinkham Peak looks over the sapphire waters that periodically ripple with feeding trout, and the rimming fir forest invites secluded access to a scenic swim, in warm weather anyway.

After passing a number of campsites on our way around the east shore of the lake, we exit the lake basin and meet Mirror Lake Trail 1302 (4220–0.4), coming up from the Lost Lake trailhead only a mile to the southeast. Here the PCT merges with Twin Lakes Trail 1303, continuing north for a bit and then climbing some steep hairpins to a spur of Tinkham Peak. Trail 1303, here signed as Cold Creek Trail, drops north from our route (4500–0.5), which goes west on a hillside, below andesite bluffs. Soon we cross a small creek on our way down to a soggy bowl with a couple of tiny ponds and a rug of marsh marigolds. Next we turn north and pass unmaintained Garren Ridge Trail 1018, which climbs west, and then we start a very steep, rocky climb of our own as we traverse on the slopes of Silver Peak. This climb takes us to a tiny side valley, behind a knob, from where we make a steep, then a moderate, traversing

descent among silver firs to a perennial creek (3900–2.5).

After crossing this creek we continue north, soon entering a clearcut that allows a view of Chair Peak and its satellites across the gash of the Snoqualmie River valley, and then we descend to and follow Olallie Creek. We cross a road and then a feeder of Olallie Creek, and finally cross to the east bank of Olallie Creek itself (3620–0.8). Along the creek we pass through a patch of forest and then break back into logged land, hearing the roar of Interstate 90 some 1400 feet below. Soon we follow a logging road a few yards north before descending from it, and then we traverse under powerlines and drop onto the powerline access road (3350–0.7). This we follow west downhill for 0.4 mile, past a spur road climbing east, and then we drop beside Rockdale Creek, which tumbles under a canopy of maples and firs. Across the creek we turn north under powerlines, proceed across talus slopes dotted with vine maple, and then enter deep fir-and-cedar forest for a long, flat traverse.

Eventually the steep slope we traverse levels into a bench, and the path skirts a small pond where an unsigned track branches northwest. Quickly, our trail then comes to a sign pointing out a 100-yard spur to Lodge Lake (3180–2.0). Down this spur one finds the lake's campsites, some close to the PCT, although a number, popular with overnighters, are set around the shallow, muskeg-rich lake. The PCT rises as it rounds Lodge Lake's bowl, then traverses slopes up past a creek ford to cross a forested saddle and enter a swale holding Beaver Lake (3480–

Peaks north of Snoqualmie Pass, l. to r.: Snoqualmie Mountain, Guye Peak and Red Mountain

0.8). Here the trail passes under one of the newer ski lifts of the Snoqualmie Pass ski area before starting a long, descending arc down the groomed ski slopes. The trail slowly curves far to the west, presenting views of Interstate 90 and the complex of cute buildings at Snoqualmie Pass below the craggy peaks across the valley. The latter promise a more ruggedly scenic and pristine section of PCT to the north. A final switchback ends by a huge parking flat at the northwest end of Snoqualmie Pass (3030–1.0). In the village ⅓ mile to the southeast one can find two restaurants, a burger stand, and a post office. From the other side of I-90's closest underpass, the northbound PCT starts for Stevens Pass.

I15

I15

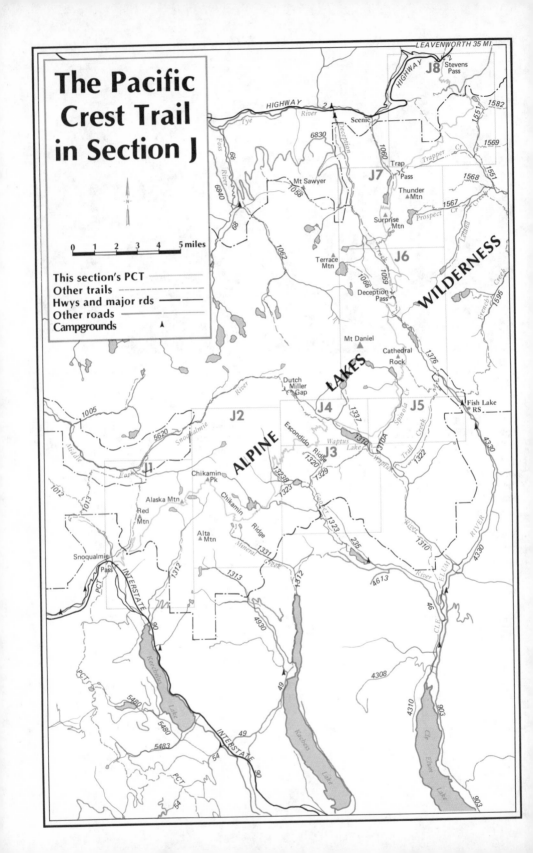

The Pacific Crest Trail in Section J

↑
N

0 1 2 3 4 5 miles

This section's PCT ———
Other trails - - - -
Hwys and major rds ——
Other roads —
Campgrounds ▲

LEAVENWORTH 35 MI.

Stevens Pass

J8

HIGHWAY 2

Scenic

6830

Trap Pass

J7

Mt Sawyer

T058

Thunder Mtn

Surprise Mtn

Terrace Mtn

J6

Deception Pass

WILDERNESS

Mt Daniel

Cathedral Rock

LAKES

Dutch Miller Gap

J4

Fish Lake RS

J2

J5

ALPINE

Escondido Ridge

Waptus Lake

J3

Chikamin Pk

J1

Alaska Mtn

Red Mtn

Chikamin Ridge

Alta Mtn

Snoqualmie Pass

INTERSTATE 90

Keechelus Lake

Mineral Creek

Kachess Lake

Cle Elum Lake

INTERSTATE 90

Section J: Interstate 90 at Snoqualmie Pass to Highway 2 at Stevens Pass

Introduction: From high traverses along craggy crests, to meadowland tours past swimmable lakes, to forest walks near churning rivers, Section J bisects a spectacular variety of Cascade backcountry, making for a classic week-long backpack. This is the land of Alpine Lakes Wilderness, an area that was so designated after one of the 70s' most bitter wilderness battles.

From Snoqualmie Pass the PCT climbs directly to the crest-top crags and boldly traverses right among them. Confronted by Chikamin Peak and brutal Lemah Mountain it relinquishes the divide, swerving east to where summer storms generally dissipate into clear skies. On this stretch the route dips into and climbs out of two major watersheds, Lemah Creek and the Waptus River. It then works back to and weaves along the descending divide, visiting a number of memorably scenic lake basins on its way to Stevens Pass. In all, Section J will challenge your legs, lift your spirits, and probably confirm your reasons for backpacking.

Declination: 19½°E

Mileages:

	South to North	Distances between Points	North to South
Interstate 90 at Snoqualmie Pass	0.0		74.5
		7.0	
Ridge Lake and Gravel Lake	7.0		67.5
		8.2	
Park Lakes campsites	15.2		59.3
		6.5	
Lemah Creek	21.7		52.8
		9.8	
Waptus Burn Trail	31.5		43.0
		4.8	
Waptus River	36.3		38.2
		7.7	
Deep Lake	44.0		30.5
		3.2	
Cathedral Pass	47.2		27.3
		5.3	
Deception Pass	52.5		22.0
		3.4	
Deception Lakes outlet creek	55.9		18.6
		4.0	
Glacier Lake campsite	59.9		14.6
		6.5	
Hope Lake	66.4		8.1
		3.8	
Lake Susan Jane	70.2		4.3
		4.3	
Highway 2 at Stevens Pass	74.5		0.0

Supplies: Two restaurants, a burger stand and a post office are found at Snoqualmie Pass, where Greyhound offers daily bus service from the east or west. No supplies are available along the route, nor at Stevens Pass. The closest town and post office to Stevens Pass is Skykomish, about 14 miles to the west.

Wilderness Permits: None are required along this section, but the Forest Service asks that all hikers self-register at the post just beyond the Snoqualmie Pass trailhead.

Problems: Snow typically lingers through mid-August on some of the steep traverses during the first 15 miles, making for some treacherous gully crossings.

Snoqualmie Pass, at 3127 feet, is the lowest gap in the Washington Cascades. Its name comes from the local Indian term for the moon, which the natives' legends held to be the life source of their tribe. Hikers starting from here should turn off I-90 at the westernmost turnoff, signed ALPENTAL ROAD. The first right on the north side of the freeway branches right again to the trailhead parking lot. The actual PCT heads up the roadcut from the Alpental overpass and in 100 yards merges with the trail coming from this lot.

Embarking east from the parking lot, we promptly meet trails coming from the equestrian lot to the north and from the highway, and then reach the trail register. With fir and hemlock above us, and bunchberry, spring beauty, huckleberry and devil's club at our feet, we cross an abandoned road and before long start climbing three long, well-graded switchbacks. They lift us around a ridge away from the freeway noise and into the valley of Commonwealth Creek. As we traverse above this valley's floor, we cross a tributary right below a spraying waterfall, and then we come to Red Mountain

Trail 1033 (3820–2.7). Heading up Commonwealth Creek, this is the old Cascade Crest Trail, and it used to keep PCT hikers west of the divide until they reached Dutch Miller Gap. From the junction we resume climbing on the newer PCT, heading for high country that was seldom visited before the completion of this PCT segment in 1978.

To the west and north, Chair Peak, Snoqualmie Mountain, Red Mountain and other summits already hint at the alpine terrain awaiting as we next switchback south. Returning into deeper forest, we continue climbing steadily on another switchback leg, up to the divide between the Snoqualmie and Yakima rivers. Along here we glimpse Kachess Lake, to the southeast, then immediately angle back onto the west flank of the steepening divide and continue our ascent.

Before long the route emerges onto talus, and the high country opens up all around us. Besides the craggy, multicolored peaks to the west, Mt. Rainier rises like a huge apparition to the south. Even if bad weather obscures this view, we can still find our spirits lifted by brilliant pockets of paintbrush, columbine, spiraea, valerian, tiger

J1   **J1**

Red Mountain, from PCT in Commonwealth Basin

Mt. Rainier, from above Commonwealth Basin

lily, and other flowers. The PCT continues rising gradually, with dwarfed mountain hemlocks clinging to trailside craglets, while more peaks come into view to the north, including Mt. Thompson and distant Mt. Stuart. We cross to the east side of the crest (5440–3.2), from where level hiking shows us Chikamin Ridge at the head of Gold Creek Valley, and Alta Mountain and some amazing cliffs of Rampart Ridge draw our eye across the valley.

Water might seep from late snow patches on this trail, but otherwise this airy section, often

just a ledge blasted from the rocky crest, is fairly dry. Soon the trail rounds a narrow spur ridge well above glistening Alaska Lake, and then it cuts down to the crest saddle (5270–1.1) between Ridge and Gravel lakes. Campsites away from the west shore of Gravel Lake, the northwestern of the two lakes, are the last sites until Park Lakes, 8.2 miles distant. Camping is not allowed at well-worn Ridge Lake.

From the north side of Ridge Lake our trail takes off on a talus traverse around the rim of the cirque holding Alaska Lake, and then climbs

J1   **J1**

PCT, outlying fir and Snoqualmie Mountain

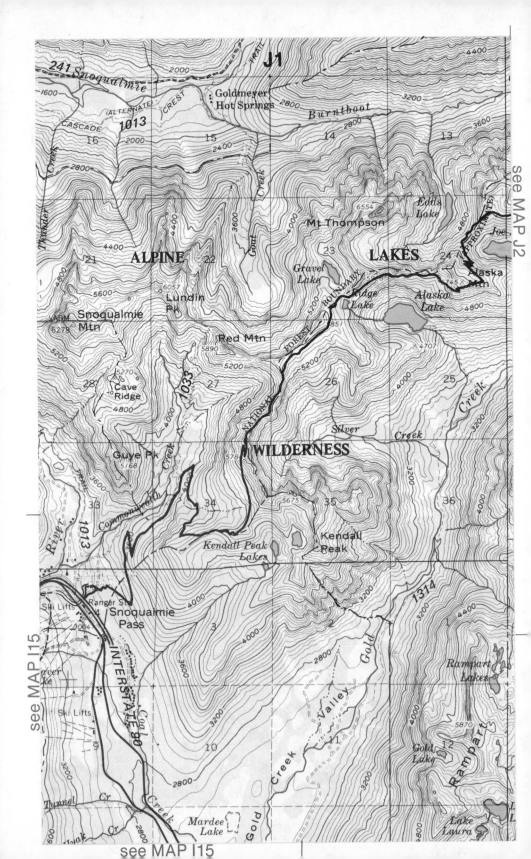

see MAP J2

see MAP I15

see MAP I15

241 Snoqualmie

J1

1013

CASCADE

(ALTERNATE)

CREST

16

15

14

13

Goldmeyer
Hot Springs

Burntboot

Eolis
Lake

Mt Thompson

Joe

ALPINE

21

22

23

LAKES

24

Gravel
Lake

Alaska
Mtn

Lundin
Pk

Ridge
Lake

Alaska
Lake

6057

BOUNDARY

Snoqualmie
Mtn

6278

Red Mtn

5890

FOREST

26

25

Creek

28

27

Cave
Ridge

1033

NATIONAL

Silver   Creek

Guye Pk
5168

WILDERNESS

33

34

35

36

Commonwealth

Creek

Kendall
Peak

Kendall Peak
Lakes

1314

Ranger Sta
Ski Lifts

Snoqualmie
Pass

3

Rampart
Lakes

River

1013

INTERSTATE 90

Coulo

Ski Lifts

9

10

11

Gold

Valley

Gold
Lake

5870

Rampart

Tunnel   Cr

Cr

Creek

Gold Creek

Mardee
Lake

Lake
Laura

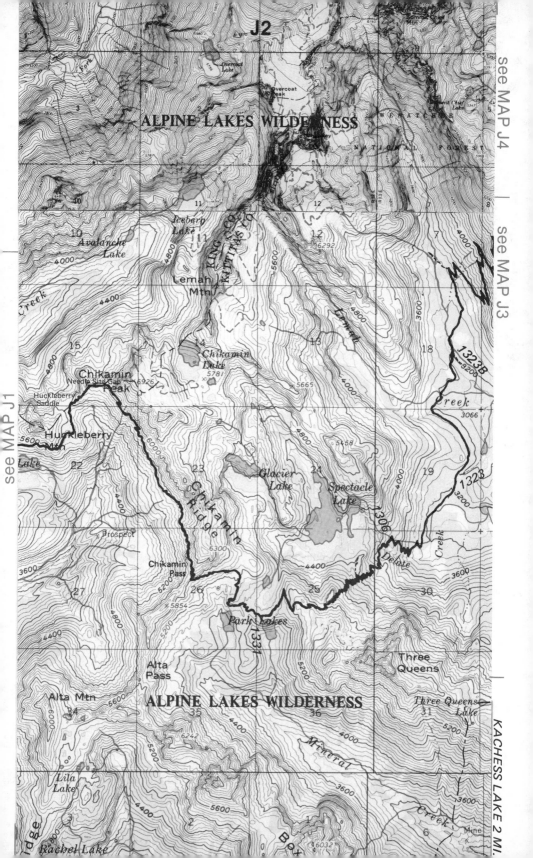

see MAP J4

see MAP J3

see MAP J1

KACHESS LAKE 2 MI.

ALPINE LAKES WILDERNESS

Overcoat
Lake

Overcoat
Peak

Summit Creek
Mtn

WENATCHEE

NATIONAL   FOREST

Iceberg
Lake

Avalanche
Lake

Leman
Mtn

KING CO
KITTITAS CO

Leman

Chikamin
Lake

Chikamin
Peak

Needle Site Gap

Huckleberry
Saddle

Huckleberry
Mtn

Lake

Chikamin
Ridge

Glacier
Lake

Spectacle
Lake

1323B

Creek

1323

Prospect

Chikamin
Pass

Delate

Creek

Three
Queens

Three Queens
Lake

Alta
Pass

Alta Mtn

ALPINE LAKES WILDERNESS

Park Lakes

1331

Mineral

Lila
Lake

Rachel Lake

Box

Creek

Mine

Looking over Ridge Lake toward distant Mt. Stuart

some as it rounds the sharp east ridge of Alaska Mountain. Next, steep switchbacks that hold snow into August take us down the north slope of this peak, and then a traverse leads us to a narrow, forested saddle (5030–2.2), between Joe and Edds lakes. These lakes lie, respectively, 400 feet below us to the east and 800 feet below us to the west.

We slant off the saddle into a meadowy ravine, and then rise across the open, rocky south flank of Huckleberry Mountain. As we turn north around the east side of this peak, which is a summer pasture for wary mountain goats, we enter a beautiful hanging vale. Here, with a full view of Mt. Rainier, we meet a stream that cascades among rock slabs and heather gardens. At the head of this ravine you'll pass a couple of small pools before coming to the crest at Huckleberry Saddle (5560–1.5), which is a broad pass with a fragile carpet of bilberries. This scenic gap has remained nearly pristine largely because the Forest Service prohibits camping at it.

Short switchbacks among dwarfed hemlocks take us above the saddle, allowing one to view Mt. Index and the Olympic Mountains in the distant northwest. This climb then leads to a traverse below the tip of a crag to Needle Sight Gap (5930–0.6). After a glimpse through this

notch beyond the Burntboot drainage to distant Glacier Peak, we turn southeast for a long alpine traverse along the meadowy and rocky southwest face of Chikamin Ridge. Whole platoons of marmots may whistle loudly and then scurry from our approaches as we make our way across this headwall of Gold Creek, from which we can admire the placed sheen of Joe Lake, the twin thumbs of Huckleberry Mountain and Mt. Thompson, and the miragelike dome of Mt. Rainier. On the way the trail crosses a few steep chutes that usually shelter slippery tongues of snow well into midseason.

After climbing gently on the last third of this traverse, we reach Chikamin Pass (5780–2.5), where we can look across Park Lakes' basin to Three Queens, Box Ridge and, in the distant northeast, the granite pyramid of Mt. Stuart. Now we brake down a couple of switchbacks into the lake basin, where mosquitoes swarm in the subalpine meadows much more thickly than at the breezy crests we leave. Once on gentler ground the route passes campsites, then southbound Mineral Creek Trail 1331, and finally an access spur (4960–1.4) that leads to more campsites. Weaving through this hummocky plateau, which actually straddles the divide between Mineral Creek and Delate Creek, we follow the PCT generally east and then north-

J1, J2

J2

east around the bowl of the northernmost Park Lake. The lake behind us, we climb a pair of switchbacks to pass some ponds and gain a northwest spur of Three Queens (5350–0.8). Here you can look north over turquoise Spectacle Lake to the spiny metamorphic fangs, hanging glaciers, and alpine waterfalls of Lemah Mountain. The rolling Wenatchee Mountains rise in the more distant east.

Now we start a bone-jarring 2000-foot descent, twisting and pounding down literally scores of tight switchbacks—hairpins that continue from a chute on the east side of a knob down to the runout of Three Queens' avalanche slopes. As the trail drops into thicker forest we pass Spectacle Lake Trail 1306 (4440–1.6), which forks north, and below this we walk on a sturdy bridge across roaring Delate Creek (3920–1.2). Just beyond, we find the old, steeper Spectacle Lake Trail, branching up the drainage, and then find a small campsite (3800–0.3). The last series of switchbacks finally drops us onto a bottomland forest with fern glades, and we later cruise past eastbound Pete Lake Trail 1323 (3210–1.8).

Northbound, the PCT rounds a small knob and then gently descends northwest to the trunk stream of Lemah Creek (3200–0.8), where there

are many sandy-gravelly campsites. From here the trail continues north, rising over a small moraine and then dropping to cross a bridge over North Fork Lemah Creek. Immediately after climbing out of this stream's ravine, our trail meets Lemah Meadow Trail 1323B (3210–0.7) which climbs northwest from Pete Lake. The PCT continues north past a couple of campsites (3240–0.1), gradually leaving Lemah Creek, then passes through forest and meadow and across a freshet. It then comes to a switchback (3370–0.7), from where an access spur descends ¼ mile to more campsites back at Lemah Creek's north fork. Here the PCT embarks on a 2200-foot climb to the top of Escondido Ridge, a climb best started early in the morning if it's to be a warm day.

Not far into this climb we cross a couple of seasonal streams, but beyond these we must count on vistas through the cedar, hemlock, and vine-maple forest to inspire us on. Brief though they are, these impressive alpine views of Lemah Mountain, Chikamin Ridge and Three Queens broaden with every switchback. Eventually the montane forest wanes, and smaller mountain hemlocks and subalpine firs spread around us as we turn up a ravine into a secluded cirque with a chilly tarn (5520–5.3). Camping is

J2   J2, J3

View across Joe Lake toward Alta Mountain and the Three Queens

Three Queens and Alta Mountain

prohibited here, but after we switchback once more and contour southeast 0.3 mile through subalpine parkland we come to some designated campsites.

Continuing around point 5984, we reach another cirque, where camping is also prohibited, and we cross the inlet (5300–1.3) of the lowest of a chain of crystalline tarns before starting a gradually rising traverse across the next ridge. From the top of this ridge the PCT arcs around a sheltered vale, jumping its creek and passing a campsite a few hundred yards farther southeast. Next we exit this meadowy glen and emerge onto the edge of Escondido Ridge, where we have a view over Waptus Lake and beyond to ever-closer Mt. Stuart. Not far along the ridge we find Waptus Burn Trail 1329C (5180–1.7), which continues down the ridge, whereas we switchback down and begin a 2200-foot descent to the Waptus River.

A grand alpine panorama oversees our well-graded switchbacks. Across the valley long waterfalls drain the lofty Mt. Daniel-Mt. Hinman massif, and at the valley's head, the impressive sedimentary slabs of Bear's Breast Mountain thrust skyward. As we stomp down the first switchbacks, pointy subalpine firs give way to open brush (a scar from the 1929 Waptus Burn fire), then we traverse north to the main bank of switchbacks, the last three touching a cascading stream.

Western redcedar droops over us as we empty onto the broad valley floor and come to a campsite at northwest-bound Dutch Miller Gap Trail 1362, but we don't find water until 0.1 mile later, at the Waptus River (3020–4.8). A girdered bridge gets us across this cold torrent, and we turn downstream alongside a *roche moutonnée,* a "dome" of rock that stood fast even though it was overridden by the glaciers that filled this valley. The PCT then winds northeast past a connection to the Dutch Miller Gap Trail and continues under Douglas-firs that rise above a carpet of ferns and vanilla leaf. As we start rising off the valley floor, we cross Spade Creek and meet Waptus River Trail 1310 (3070–0.8). This trail comes up from campsites ¾ mile away at Waptus Lake, and ultimately from the Cle Elum River, about 12 miles away.

Our trail proceeds on a gently rising traverse above the valley, well shaded under spruce, fir, and cedar boughs, but we get occasional blue glints of large Waptus Lake below. On the way our path crosses a couple of fairly reliable streams. Between them Spade Lake Trail 1337 climbs north, and at the second one there is a campsite (3400–1.5). Eventually our trail turns north into the Spinola Creek valley and meets Spinola Creek Trail 1310A (3440–1.1), which climbs about one mile from the outlet of Waptus Lake. Through alternating patches of forest, meadow and talus, our trail steepens some and

J3, J4   **J4, J5**

see MAP J6

ALPINE   J4   LAKES

see MAP J2

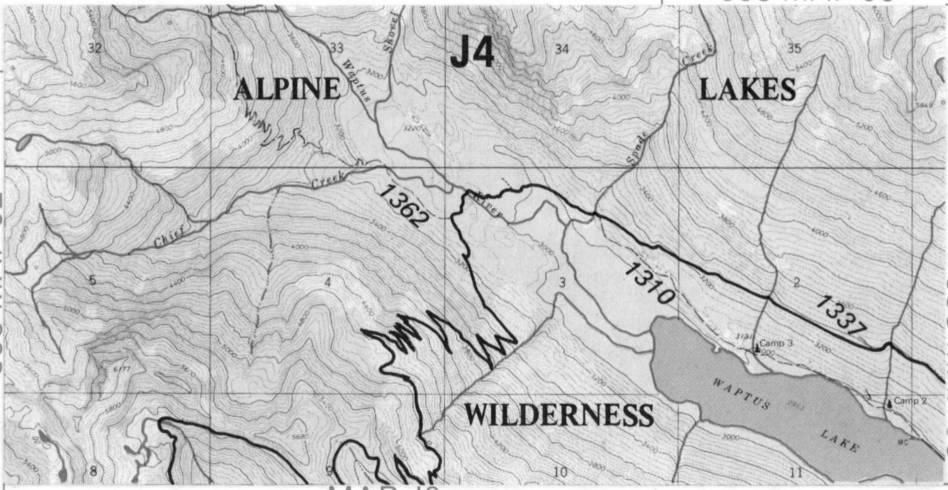

1362

1310

1337

see MAP J5

WILDERNESS

Camp 3

WAPTUS LAKE

Camp 2

see MAP J3

see MAP J4   J5

J3

Waptus Lake Camp 1

Escondido Lake   1329C   1329

1320   WAPTUS PASS TRAIL   Quick Creek   1310

ESCONDIDO TRAIL

Waptus Pass

ALPINE   1329   LAKES

1323   1309

Pete Lake

Lemah Cr

WILDERNESS

Island Mtn   1323   1317

Delate   Creek

Chikamin   Ridge   1309

Tired   Creek   Polallie

Diamond Lake

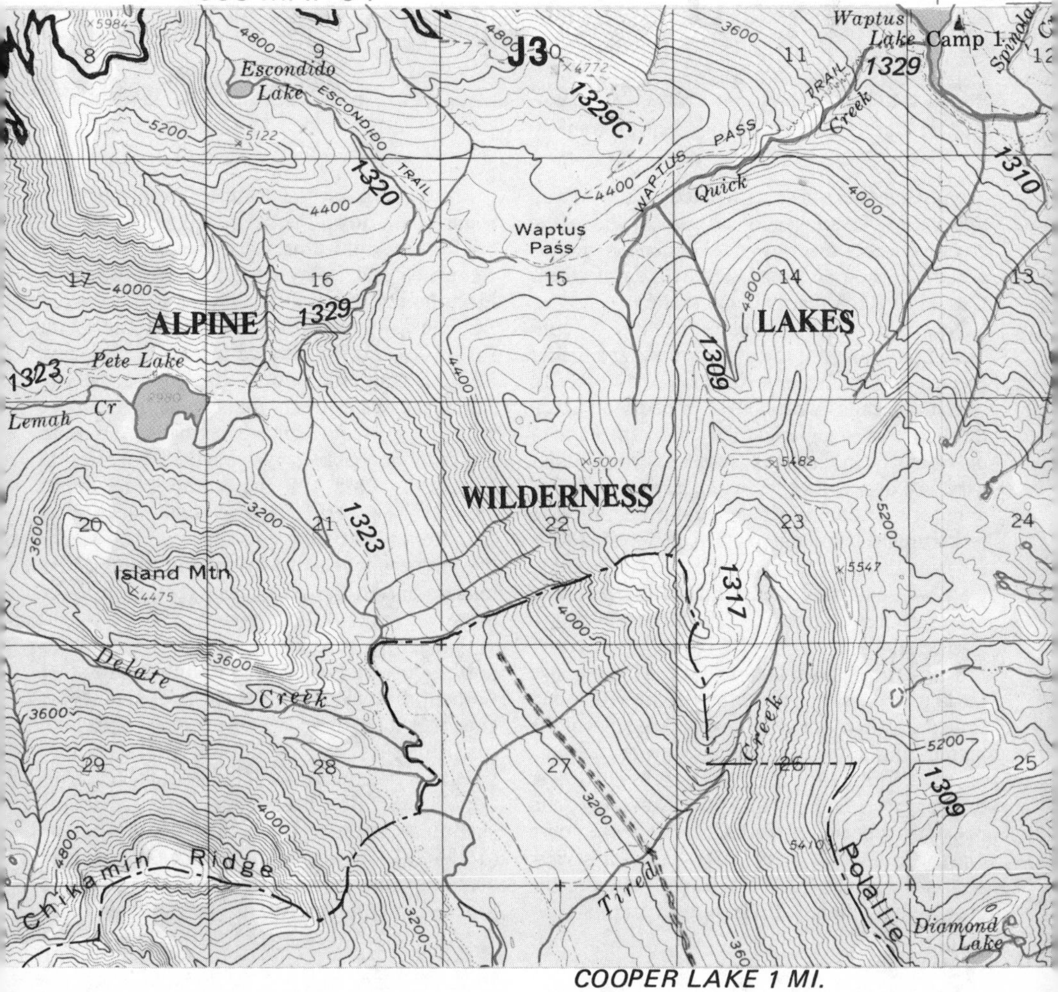

COOPER LAKE 1 MI.

Box Ridge, from the Park Lakes basin

even switchbacks in several places as it works up this valley, keeping some distance above the creek. A second series of switchbacks gets us around a knob and onto a bench, from where Cathedral Rock marks our direction.

Now in a meadowy subalpine realm, we continue north, and not long after crossing a feeder creek meet Lake Vicente Trail 1365 (4440–3.8), which ascends west. We immediately turn through a small gap and then follow the bank of now-quiet Spinola Creek, soon crossing another tributary at a campsite. A bit farther north we approach Deep Lake's indigo surface, only to fork from the lake's campsite access trail (4400–0.5) and turn east to wade its ankle-deep outlet. Now we head for the east side of Deep Lake's basin, to the start of a 1200-foot climb to Cathedral Pass.

Well-graded switchbacks take us far above the lake to the scraggly outliers of the subalpine-fir forest, where we get a new perspective of the alpine bluffs of Mt. Daniel. From the last hairpin, Trail 1375 (5560–3.0) forks northwest to Peggys Pond. Under the towering and resistant andesite of Cathedral Rock, we top a crest at Cathedral Pass (5610–0.2) for a view across the upper Cle Elum River valley to the gray alpine uplands of Granite Mountain.

From the pass, the Rainier View spur trail heads south down the ridge, while we descend briefly east onto a parkland bench with a few campsites and a few small tarns (5460–0.1). From here Cathedral Rock Trail 1345, the old PCT, drops south 2000 feet to the Cle Elum River. The Forest Service warns that the new PCT, in continuing north high above the Cle Elum, crosses a stream that can be treacherous at high water, and suggests taking the old route and climbing back up to rejoin the newer trail at Deception Pass. In the author's (Selters') opinion, however, for the average backpacker the stream crossing in question is rarely dangerous enough to warrant the lengthy 9½-mile detour. Still, we've drawn it on Map J6 for those who may want to take it.

Wandering around hillocks as it continues north, our trail proceeds in the shadow of Cathedral Rock along the edge of the scenic bench. It then starts twisting down a ridgeline, steepening as it goes until it traverses into montane forest, where we find a couple of longer switchbacks. These end at a bench that has shady campsites at a junction of two streams (4600–2.0). North from this bench the trail continues descending steadily across slopes forested in complex patches of mountain hem-

J5, J6   **J6**

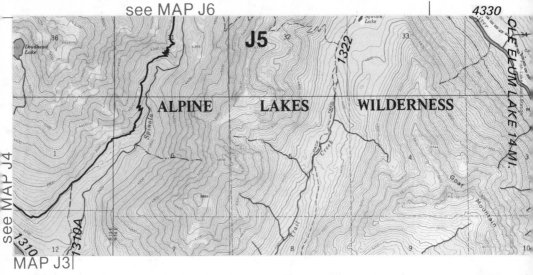

see MAP J6

lock and subalpine fir, then redcedar, Douglas-fir and alder. The route crosses one creek, and then comes to a second, which is the one the Forest Service warned of (3770–1.4). This stream, which drains Mt. Daniel's northeast slopes, is swift and cold, and you'll want to wear shoes or boots to cross its stony bed. However, the current is not capable of carrying a person away. Before the sun gets high or on a cloudy day the ford won't be more than a shin-deep swash for a few short strides.

From this ford the trail ascends steadily across avalanche swaths and two or three more streams. The last, where the trail turns east at the head of the Cle Elum drainage, will likely require another, less vigorous footbath (4180–

J6

Lemah Mountain, from Escondido Ridge

see MAP J7

J6

ALPINE   LAKES   WILDERNESS

NATIONAL FOREST

1.0). The gradual climb turns north again in a
forest of unusually large subalpine firs and tops
out at Deception Pass (4470–0.8). A number of
trail options confront the hiker here: the old PCT
(now Trail 1376) comes up from the Cle Elum
River and Hyas Lake; Marmot Lake Trail 1066
branches west; and Trail 1059 forks north for
Deception Creek, meeting Highway 2 six miles
east of Skykomish. Beyond these junctions, the
PCT heads north-northeast.

Now we contour around a knob to drop to
nearby Deception Creek, a small stream in a
deep and eroding drainage. This gully is cutting
along the Straight Creek fault, a major crustal
weakness traceable from near Yakima well into
British Columbia. In the past land to its west was
shifted north, displaced 100–200 miles over the
millenia. We continue out of the gully on a level
track, getting a glimpse back to the glimmering
heights of Mt. Daniel and its massive Lynch
Glacier. Next we round a ridge and jump one
stream and then, near a campsite (4400–1.9),
we jump another as we continue through cedar-
and-fir forest. The PCT starts a long, gradually
rising traverse above the valley of Deception
Creek, passing through the skeletons of an old
forest fire, and eventually rounding a ridge to
meet Deception Creek Trail 1059A, which

Mt. Stuart, from Cathedral Pass

J6, J7

Cathedral Rock, from the east

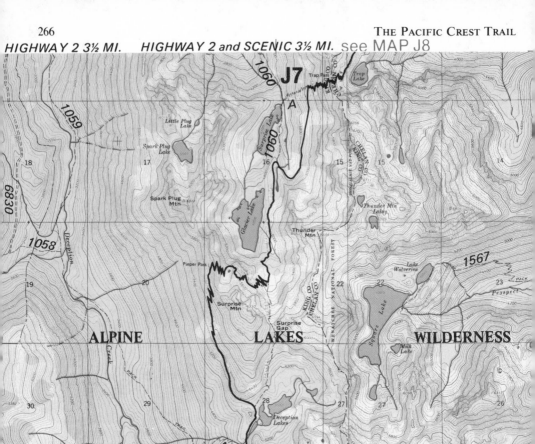

see MAP J6

Cathedral Rock and Mt. Daniel rising above Deception Creek valley

Pika

Glacier Lake, Surprise Lake and Glacier Peak

drops west. About 0.1 mile east of this junction we cross the outlet (5040–1.5) of Deception Lakes and then follow the west shoreline of the narrow lower lake. Although these lakes offer fine swimming and a pleasant rest, their accessibility has lured hordes who have beaten their campsites and much of their shorelines to dust.

Just as it nears the large upper lake, the PCT climbs northwest and enters a draw, at the end of which an unsigned and unmaintained trail drops off to the west. We, on the other hand, angle northwest uphill and around a ridge to resume the ascending traverse high above Deception Creek. Now, however, we can see northwest beyond a checkerboard of clearcuts to the jagged teeth of Mt. Index, Mt. Baring and Three Fingers, as well as across the valley, where Lake Clarice nestles against Terrace Mountain. We

J7

J7

Glacier Lake and Pieper Pass

see MAP K1

J8

see MAP J7

turn up a steep slope and with a few switchbacks surmount it at Pieper Pass (5920–2.0). From here the abandoned Cascade Crest Trail follows the ridgecrest north, but we turn east toward inviting Glacier Lake, and then drop off the pass for a braking descent.

Steep switchbacks take us down to a small bench with a tarn and a view of distant Glacier Peak, and then we wind among the granite boulders of a lower bench before descending a talus slope to the cirque floor. From here we descend into the forest past a campsite (5000–2.0) that is above the southeast shore of Glacier Lake. Beyond this we cross a creek and hike around the bottom of a talus slope as we parallel Glacier Lake's glistening east shore 50–100 feet above it. We then continue away from the lake past a narrow pond, with another campsite, and

J7   **J7**

shortly meet Surprise Lake Trail 1060 (4840–0.8), which heads north for about four miles to meet Highway 2 eight miles east of Skykomish. At the junction the route pivots southeast to arc around the head of a ravine and start a rising traverse north.

This traverse takes us through forests and rocky fields, ever higher above Surprise Lake, ever closer to gnarly crags atop the crest. It ends where we join Trap Pass Trail 1060A (5080–1.0), in the middle of a bank of steep switchbacks, and we grind up the rest of these to the Cascade divide at Trap Pass (5800–0.9). With the blue disc of Trap Lake seemingly a straight drop below us, we switchback and traverse down and across its steep cirque wall to a sharply descending access trail (5350–0.8) to the lake. After leaving the lake's bowl, the PCT keeps to flowery avalanche slopes and shady forested slopes high above Trapper Creek. At a small bench it passes a campsite beside a seasonal creek (4970–1.2), and then climbs briefly to a notch (5210–0.7). From here we slant and switchback down through steep forest and across another bench, dropping before long to a gentle terrain at overused Hope Lake (4400–1.1). From here, at a curiously low spot in the Cascade crest, Tunnel Creek Trail 1061 drops 1.4 miles northwest to Road 6095, which descends 1.2 miles to Highway 2.

North from the turbid waters of Hope Lake we climb through fir-and-hemlock forest onto a somewhat swampy parkland plateau, on which we turn east to the north end of Mig Lake (4670–0.7). By midsummer this shallow lake warms to a pleasant swimming temperature. East from it, we drop to a crest saddle, round a knob, and curve around a swampy pond. Onward, we climb around a forested ridge, and confront steeper climbing beneath cliffbands, topping out at an unnamed crest saddle (5190–1.8). Here a slice of Swimming Deer Lake tempts one to drop 300 feet through very steep forest, but more accessible water is just down the trail, which contours east to a spur ridge, beyond which it drops along a rill in a grassy swale to the rim of Josephine Lake's cirque (4980–0.8). From here Icicle Trail 1551 descends around the cirque to the turquoise lake's outlet.

Swimmers at Mig Lake

From the Icicle Trail junction the PCT proceeds northwest down a ravine, then down a talus slope to the north shore of Lake Susan Jane (4600–0.5). With powerlines and the crest of Stevens Pass Ski Area in sight, and probably a number of overnighters at this pretty and accessible lake, a wilderness-accustomed PCT hiker strongly senses re-entry into civilization. Next the trail traverses west under steep but well-flowered bluffs, where snow lingers across the track into August. Soon after crossing a tumbling stream it passes a campsite near the edge of the swath cut for the immense powerlines overhead. These buzzing cables carry hydroelectricity from the rural Columbia basin east of the Cascades to the cities of the coast. A couple of rough roads run through the logged swath, and we depend on trail signs to follow our climbing, switchbacking path across the eroding roadbeds.

North of the powerlines our trail continues climbing, taking long, meadowy switchbacks up to the Cascade crest at a saddle (5160–2.2) near the top of a chairlift. Steeper, tighter switchbacks then take us down beneath this and other chairlifts to lower-angled slopes, from which we make a long descending traverse north, crossing a creek on our way to four-lane Highway 2. The trail empties onto a parking area (4060–2.1) a couple hundred yards northeast of the Stevens Pass Ski Area village, which in 1985 lacked summer services.

J7, J8   J8

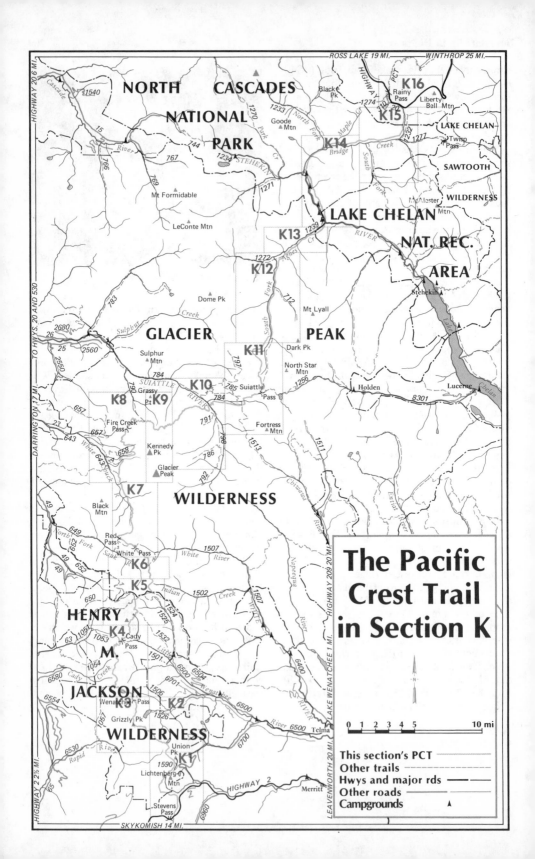

Section K: Highway 2 at Stevens Pass to Highway 20 at Rainy Pass

Introduction: In this section you will traverse along a very rugged section of the North Cascades. This hike ranks second only to Volume 1's John Muir Trail section in difficulty. Traversing around Glacier Peak, the hiker brakes down to, then labors up from, a number of deep-floored canyons that radiate from the peak. Unfortunately, a nice, contouring trail, such as the one around Mt. Adams, is impossible to route around Glacier Peak proper, for such a trail would be too snowbound and too avalanche-prone.

Not only does this section have rugged topography, but it sometimes has dangerous fords, cold, threatening weather and persistent insects. Why then do thousands of back-packers flock to the Glacier Peak Wilderness? Well, perhaps because it is a *real* wilderness and not, like so many others, a wilderness in name only. It provides a definite challenge to modern-day man, who is so protected from the elements. This area's intimidating, snowy terrain, which is contrasted with lovely, fragile wildflower gardens, will draw you back time and time again.

Declination: 19¾°E

Mileages:

	South to North	Distances between Points	North to South
Highway 2 at Stevens Pass	0.0		117.7
		5.5	
Lake Valhalla	5.5		112.2
		4.0	
Janice Cabin	9.5		108.2
		7.1	
Wenatchee Pass	16.6		101.1
		1.6	
Pear Lake	18.2		99.5
		9.9	
Lake Sally Ann	28.1		89.6
		4.7	
Indian Pass	32.8		84.9
		3.9	
White Pass	36.7		81.0
		1.9	
Red Pass	38.6		79.1
		7.3	
White Chuck Trail	45.9		71.8
		1.6	
Kennedy Ridge Trail	47.5		70.2
		7.2	
Fire Creek Pass	54.7		63.0
		4.0	
Milk Creek Trail	58.7		59.0
		5.3	
Dolly Vista campsite	64.0		53.7
		7.5	
Suiattle River access trail	71.5		46.2
		4.9	

Mileages:

	South to North	Distance between Points	North to South
Miners Creek.....................................	76.4		41.3
		3.0	
Railroad Creek Trail to Holden...................	79.4		38.3
		6.5	
Hemlock Camp	85.9		31.8
		7.0	
Five Mile Camp	92.9		24.8
		5.0	
Agnes Creek trailhead on Stehekin River road	97.9		19.8
		5.3	
Bridge Creek trailhead on Stehekin River road	103.2		14.5
		6.2	
Six Mile Camp	109.4		8.3
		8.3	
Highway 20 at Rainy Pass	117.7		0.0

Supplies: See "Supplies" in Section J for the facilities at Stevens Pass, our section's starting point. There are no other on-route supply points. However, upon reaching the Stehekin River near the end of the section, you can take a Park Service shuttle bus, $1.00 in 1985, over to Stehekin, which has a resort, post office, hiker-oriented store and information center. If you need new boots, clothes, or other special items, you can take a ferry from Stehekin to Chelan, then return again. In 1978 this round trip cost $10; in 1985 it cost $17.

Wilderness Permits: These permits are only required for overnight trips in North Cascades National Park. Write them at Skagit District Office, Marblemount, WA 98267.

About 200 yards northeast from Stevens Pass on Highway 2, our route starts as a closed road that contours north across granitic terrain. On this open, bushy stretch, we pass an assortment of aster, bleeding heart, bluebells, columbine, fireweed, lupine, monkey flower, paintbrush, parsnip and Sitka valerian before curving west into a forested environment. We reach a 3-yard-wide tributary (3850–2.5) of Nason Creek, beside which one could camp, but elect to continue up to a meadow (4220–1.0), through which Nason Creek flows. Here among the cinquefoil, shooting stars, red heather and grass are good campsites. Mosquitoes and several species of biting flies, common in northern Washington through midsummer, will not bother you if the day is cold or misty.

Now within Henry M. Jackson Wilderness we climb up the trail to a second meadow, where one could camp, then switchback up to a saddle (5030–1.7), from which we can look down at beautiful Lake Valhalla and across it at the challenging west face of dark gray Lichtenberg Mountain (5844). Descending north from the saddle, we reach meadow campsites and a spur trail (4900–0.3) that descends southeast 200 yards to the northwest shore of deep, cool, sparkling Lake Valhalla (4830).

Lake Valhalla and Lichtenberg Mountain

K1

Our trail now climbs east to a saddle, snowbound through late July, then steadily descends northeast to Union Gap and a junction with Smithbrook Trail 1590 (4700–1.8), which descends eastward 0.7 mile to Road 6700. From the gap, our trail descends northwest along a lower slope of Union Peak (5696) before turning north and ascending to a delightful, singing cascade (4200–1.8). Tree frogs and evening grosbeaks join in a dusky chorus as we approach the large Janice Cabin (4150–0.4) beside shallow Lake Janus (4146), which is somewhat disappointing after Lake Valhalla. The warmer temperatures of this semiclear lake, however, do allow you a comfortable dip. Just northwest of the shelter is the clear outlet creek, but, judging by all the horse manure around the lake—despite the posted 200-foot restriction against horses—we feel you should treat the water before drinking it.

Beyond this creek, the PCT switchbacks west up to a gully, on your left, in which you could camp. In ¼ mile the trail reaches the crest (5180–1.6), traverses a short, northeast slope with a view due north of distant, regal Glacier Peak (10,541), and then reaches a saddle. A moderate descent northwest takes us to a meadow (5070–0.8), from which a faint trail leads 40 yards northeast, then descends a

moderately steep gully toward Glasses Lake (4626). At the west end of the meadow, our trail passes a good, designated campsite, then follows a winding crest route up past outcrops of mica schist before it reaches the upper west shoulder (5580–2.1) of Grizzly Peak (5597).

From it we hike north along the ridge, round another summit, then come upon a designated but poor campsite on a saddle. Leaving it behind, we descend moderately across a west slope, pass well above shallow Grizzly Lake (4920), cross the crest (5120–1.4) and reach a good but shadeless campsite (5030–0.2) on a grassy flat. Descending north on a moderate-to-steep, sometimes soggy trail, we reach the crest again, then switchback down it to broad, forested Wenatchee Pass (4230–1.0), where there is another good campsite. Climbing north to a flat, we reach a junction with Top Lake Trail 1506 (4570–0.6), which curves east one-half mile to that lake (4590). You can camp 50 yards southwest of this junction, but with Pear Lake next on the itinerary, you'd be foolish to stop here if you can still make it to that lake by dusk.

Your trail heads west to a gully whose west side is composed of large boulders. Gushing from them is the outlet of Pear Lake, which is dammed behind them. We climb several short

K1, K2

K3, K4

Glacier Peak, from atop Grizzly Peak

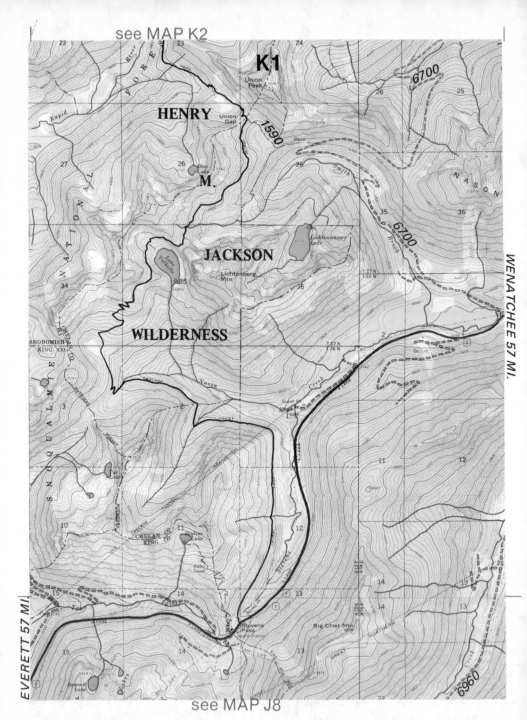

see MAP J8

switchbacks to a saddle, a few more to a ridge, and then descend west toward Pear Lake (4809). Following the trail to the lake's northwest corner, we reach the very good Pear Lake campsite (4830–1.0) by a few trees 35 yards from the shore. From this lake a new stretch of PCT, shown on Map K4, may be completed in 1987. Until then, our trail climbs above the west shore of this granite-lined lake, passes a good campsite beside a huge boulder, then soon switchbacks up to Frozen Finger Gap (5250–0.6). Looking back, we can see how Pear Lake got its name. Now we descend about 20 switchbacks on a slope rich in mica schist which con-

K4   **K4**

trasts with the cliff of granitic rocks across the gully. Arriving at lower Fortune Pond, we bridge its outlet creek and meet a junction with Meadow Creek Trail 1057 (4670–0.7), which bears west before descending south toward Rapid River. Above this junction are two very good campsites.

Our trail starts beside the outlet creek, curves north before crossing it, and then climbs steadily north to a large, subalpine meadow. Here, in addition to the flower species mentioned just north of Stevens Pass, this slope contains bistort, corn lily, pedicularis, heart-leaved arnica, ligusticum, spiraea, thistle and tiger lily, all living harmoniously within a community of ferns. On a misty day, this meadow becomes saturated with droplets, and you become soaked from the waist down.

We crest the west ridge (5220–1.3) of summit 5504, then make a steep northward descent past seasonal creeklets before the trail eases its gradient and crosses two permanent creeks. Thirty yards upstream from the second one (4700–0.7) is a small but good campsite. Beyond the crossing, the PCT makes a short climb, then contours north before its final climb to Saddle Gap (5060–1.3). We follow our northward-curving path down to a junction with West Cady Ridge Trail 1054 (4930–0.3), which climbs north-northwest. After descending north toward a prominent knob of metamorphic rock, we follow long switchbacks down to a fair campsite west of three-yard-wide Pass Creek. Immediately after crossing it on stepping stones, we meet Pass Creek Trail 1053 (4200–1.0), which descends north alongside the creek. Our trail climbs northeast and shortly arrives at Cady Pass, where Cady Creek Trail 1501 (4310–0.4) departs northeast before dropping to that creek. At this forested pass is a dumpy, dry campsite that we would recommend for emergency bivouac only.

A long ascent—a taste of what's to come—now begins as the PCT switchbacks north up to a metamorphic ridge and reaches an exposed campsite at its crest (5470–1.9). This strenuous ascent does reward us, near its top, with scenic views to the south and east. After descending slightly to a granitic saddle, our trail rounds the east slope of a knob (5642), then reaches another saddle. Beyond it, trailside snow patches last well into August. We contour across the east slope of rugged Skykomish Peak (6368), then descend to icebound Lake Sally Ann (5479–1.7). On the ridge just northeast of its outlet creek are several lovely campsites of

PCT below Skykomish Peak

excellent quality once the snow melts. If there is still snow or there are too many campers, continue northeast down to a junction with Cady Ridge Trail 1532 (5380–0.4), on which you can descend east 200 yards to suitable campsites on an open saddle.

Beyond this junction, our often-snowbound trail climbs northwest across a slope of greenish mica schist, glistening white-vein quartz and speckled adamellite before it switchbacks up to Wards Pass (5710–0.7). Turning north, we then hike along a crest route that takes us down to the soggy, volcanic soils of Dishpan Gap, where Bald Eagle Trail 650 (5600–0.6) veers left and contours northwest. Our route veers right and crosses the southeast slope of Peak 5892 to a ridge-crest campsite (5450–0.5) on an open slope of grass, cinquefoil and fawn lilies. Should you camp here or at a similar open site, don't be surprised to see deer come around and graze beside your tent.

Following the crest east across this glaciated country, we quickly arrive at a junction with Little Wenatchee River Trail 1525 (5440–0.3), which contours southeast. We diagonal up the northwest slope of a triangular summit, then reach a saddle where a spur trail (5500–0.2) contours south to Trail 1525. The PCT heads north toward Kodak Peak (6121), then climbs east across its flowery, picturesque south slope of metamorphic rocks to a ridge from where both Mt. Rainier and Glacier Peak are plainly visible on clear days. Along this ridge, a footpath called Little Wenatchee Ridge Trail 1524 (5660–0.7) strikes east-southeast across a long saddle. Along this ridge crest runs the southern boundary of Glacier Peak Wilderness and the northern boundary of Henry M. Jackson Wilderness.

Our trail turns northwest and descends across waning snowfields before it curves north, enters forest and arrives at a fenced-in pasture at

Indian Pass (5020–1.3). From it you can follow a spur trail 0.1 mile west to a good campsite with water. Ascending to the PCT from the southeast is Indian Creek Trail 1502. From its junction, we are northwest up to a southwest spur of Indian Head Peak (7442), then climb northward to an adequate campsite at the north end of shallow, semi-clear Kid Pond (5320–1.0). The location of this pond and the nature of its surrounding rocks of garnet-graphite-mica schist both indicate that it fills a slight depression behind avalanche deposits.

Our trail proceeds north to a ridge and is joined by an older trail, then it descends to Lower White Pass (5378–0.7), from which the old Cascade Crest Trail once descended northeast. Nowadays, the trail is called White River

K5

K5, K6

see MAP K4

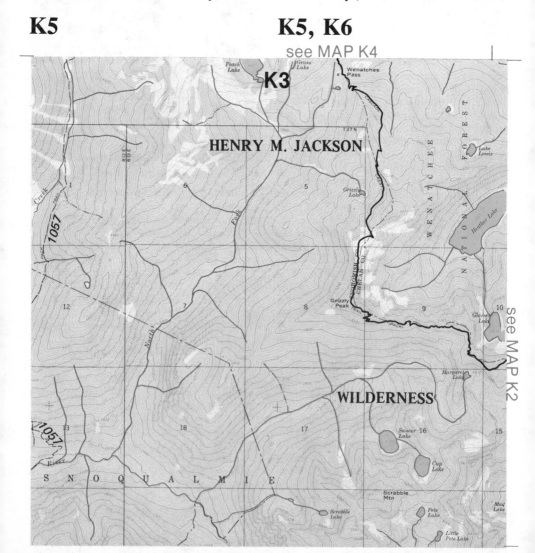

see MAP K2

Lake Sally Ann

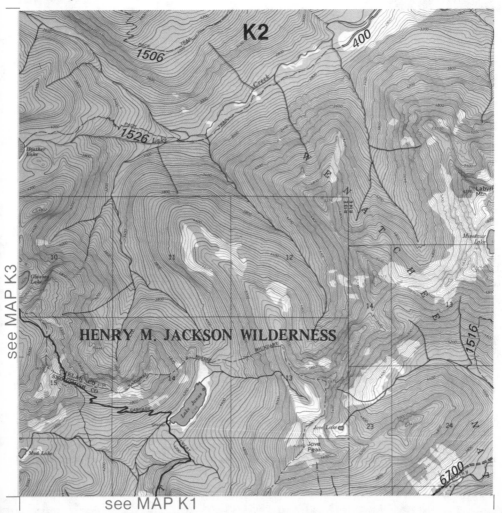

see MAP K3

see MAP K1

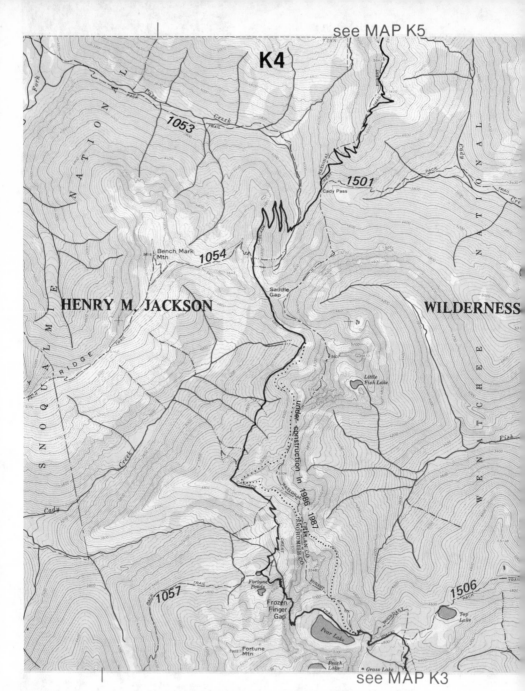

see MAP K3

Trail 1507. An adequate campsite lies 30 yards east of this junction. Our trail climbs a ridge north to good campsites on the west and southwest shores of pensive Reflection Pond (5560–0.3), then traverses across snowbound northeast slopes up to a junction at White Pass (5904–1.9). Here, a trail begins a curving traverse northeast to Foam Basin, with a campsite, about ¼ mile away.

K6, K7

Continuing along the PCT, we follow its contouring path west-northwest to a fork where North Fork Sauk Trail 649 (5950–0.6) descends steeply westward. The meadow here has such an abundance of flowers and insects, it's no wonder that birds fly north to feast on them. Flycatchers hover and snatch insects from midair as we start a steady climb west-northwest. The trail becomes dusty as we approach a small summit

K7

The Black Mountain glacier, from north of Baekos Creek

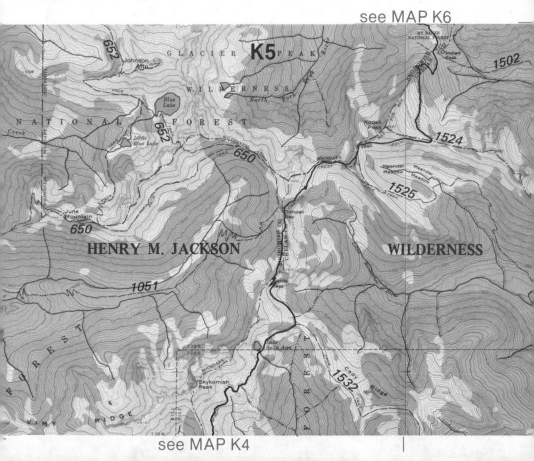

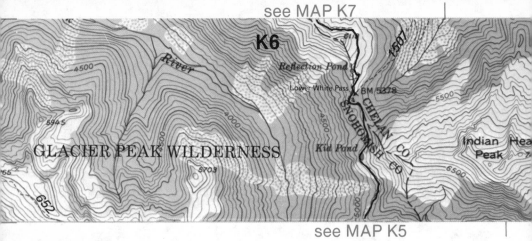

K6

River

Reflection Pond

Lower White Pass · BM 5378

4500

4000

5500

6945

GLACIER PEAK WILDERNESS

Kid Pond

Indian Hea
Peak

5703

6500

652

see MAP K5

(6650), then turns north and shortly reaches the gray, garnet-biotite gneiss rocks of marmot-inhabited Red Pass (6500–1.3).

The view from here is nothing short of spectacular. Above us and five miles to the northeast is a towering volcano, Glacier Peak (10,541), which last erupted about 12,500 years ago. Below us is the perennially snowclad upper canyon of the White Chuck River. To the distant south is lofty, glistening Mt. Rainier (14,410), cloaked in snow, giving it the appearance of a giant stationary cloud that reigns eternally over the distant forest. If you're heading south, you'll definitely remember your climb up to this pass.

Our trail first switchbacks, then descends along the base of the east ridge of Portal Peak (6999). Since this trail is usually snowbound, most hikers slide directly down the steep, but safe, upper snowfield, then head east down-canyon until they reach the visible trail. Keeping north of the headwaters, the PCT descends toward a lone, three-foot-high cairn (5700–1.4) on a low knoll, turns northward, and then descends to campsites at a saddle (5500–0.3) between a 20-foot-high hill to the east and a high

K7

K7

PCT traversing southeast from slopes of Peak 6203

slope to the west. Better sites are on the hill. Just 230 yards north, we pass another campsite; then, farther down, we can see numerous campsites along the banks of the rumbling White Chuck River, below and east of us.

We may spot a blue grouse and its chicks as we descend alongside a swelling creek that we cross three times via log bridges. Hikers have camped beside each crossing. Leaving the last crossing (4700–1.5), our trail switchbacks down toward the White Chuck River, parallels it above its west bank, and then crosses it (4000–1.0) eastward via a wide, planked horse bridge. We leave the river's side, follow an undulating

K7   **K7**

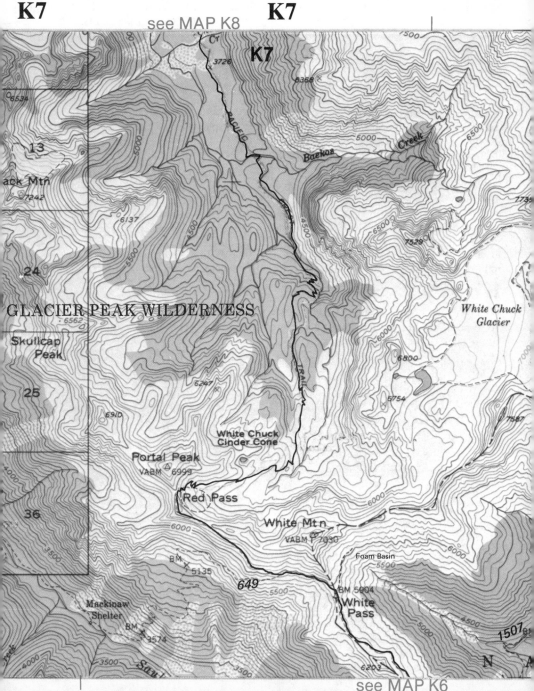

see MAP K8

see MAP K6

route north, then descend to a good campsite just before a log crossing of cold, roaring Baekos Creek (3990–1.0), whose north bank contains much green mica schist. We follow the base of its high north bank downstream a short way, switchback over it, then descend to level ground and a number of log crossings over small creeks. Mountaineers intent on climbing Glacier Peak (10,541) usually leave the PCT between Baekos and Kennedy creeks. Should you try, bring rope, crampons and ice ax.

Near a campsite beside the north bank of Chetwot Creek (3730–1.3), the vegetation opens enough to give us views southwest to broad Black Mountain glacier, which spreads across the upper rim of a deeply glaciated side canyon. Continuing northward, we reach Sitkum Creek, make a precarious log crossing of it, then find ourselves at an excellent campsite (3852–0.8), with a raised fire ring and an isolated pit toilet.

*   *   *   *

From a junction by this creekside campsite you can take a 3¼-mile alternate route that goes by inviting Kennedy Hot Spring. To take it, follow White Chuck Trail 643 as it first tra-verses northwest, then switchbacks down a crest to a junction beside Kennedy Creek. Here, on a spur trail, you curve southwest immediately over to the White Chuck River and, near a ranger station, bridge the river and hike 80 yards upstream to Kennedy Hot Spring (3275), a cubical, neck-deep hole in the ground. Many hikers used to skinny-dip at this 94°F soda spring, but its increasing popularity in the 1960s led to a ban of this fun in the early '70s. From the bridge, you can follow the river's west bank a short way down to campsites on a gentle slope. When you are ready to leave—if ever, considering what's ahead—retrace your steps to the Kennedy Creek junction, cross the creek, follow Trail 643 ¼ mile downstream, then climb 1¼ miles up Kennedy Ridge Trail 643A to the PCT.

*   *   *   *

From Sitkum Creek a long climb lies ahead of us. After an initial 250-yard climb north, we reach an adequate campsite. One-quarter mile later, we reach a better one beside Sitkum Creek, and then we cross an unmapped creek just before reaching a moraine ridge. Enjoying a short-lasting descent northeast, we pass by small outcrops above us that are quartz-and-

K7, K8   K8

Glacier Peak, from slopes above Pumice Creek; Glacier Ridge is in the mid-ground, Kennedy Peak on the left skyline; Kennedy Glacier (left) and Scimitar Glacier (right) descend the flanks of Glacier Peak.

Too often, clouds roll in and obscure views; Glacier Peak, to the south, is the pointed peak left of center.

biotite-rich, Miocene-age granitic intrusions. The slopes above them are composed of andesitic lava flows from Glacier Peak. We reach chilly, glacier-fed Kennedy Creek (4050–1.2), a 10-yard-wide torrent that sometimes has to be forded, since bridges built across it have a tendency to be wiped out by avalanches. Without a bridge, the ford can be treacherous. Around July 11, 1975, one such avalanche tore down this creek and nearly overwhelmed the Kennedy Hot Spring area, 1½ miles downstream.

After crossing the creek, we climb southwest up a path cut through unstable morainal material that is in turn being undercut by the creek. Soon we reach a junction with Kennedy Ridge Trail 643A (4300–0.4), down which you can head west toward Kennedy Hot Spring. Its warm water indicates that molten magma is relatively close to the surface.

Now the real climb begins as we ascend six short, steep switchbacks past huge andesite blocks to the lower crest of Kennedy Ridge. This we struggle upward, stopping several times to catch our breath and to admire the scenery around us. In spots, this crest is no wider than the trail. The gradient eases off and we eventually reach an excellent campsite by Glacier Creek (5640–1.9), which occasionally has an

avalanche roar down its canyon, destroying all the trees in its path. Nevertheless, mountaineers and hikers alike camp in its track. For mountaineers, the shortest climb to Glacier Peak's summit begins here.

Leaving the creek, we switchback north, then climb northwest past adamellite boulders to a junction with Glacier Ridge Trail 658 (6050–0.7), which is a six-inch wide footpath that descends that ridge westward. After a short, steep descent northeast, we contour in that direction to jump-across Pumice Creek (5900–0.5), whose bed contains metamorphic, granitic and volcanic rocks. You might try to identify all three types and decipher their stories. A fair campsite is beside the north bank. Our trail descends west, then contours over to a ridge (5770–1.6). North of it, we descend even more, then cross a branch of Fire Creek (5370–0.8) just below its fork upstream. On an open meadow atop a bluff 20 yards north of it is your last good campsite this side of Fire Creek Pass. Now we make one final effort, and *voila!* a magnificent panorama of the North Cascades unfolds around us as we gain access to Fire Creek Pass (6350–1.7).

The North Cascades of Washington contain 756 glaciers, which account for about half of all the glacier area existing within the conterminus

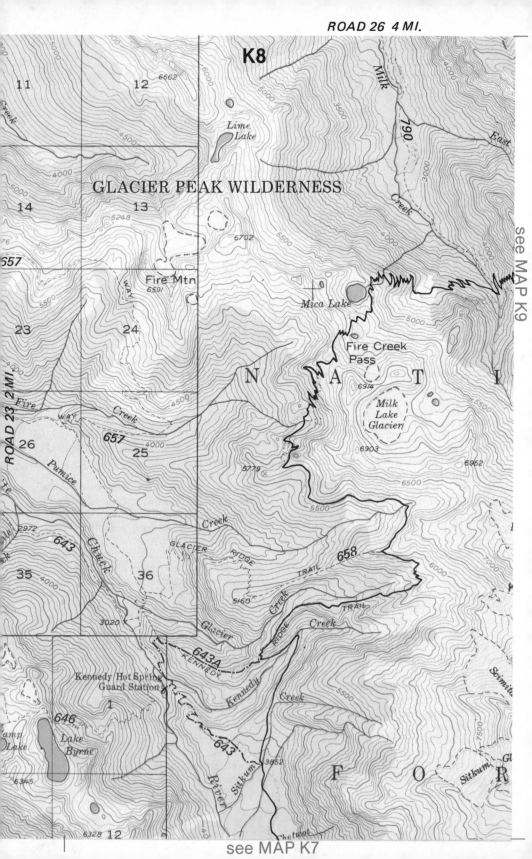

K8

11 12 6662

Lime
Lake

GLACIER PEAK WILDERNESS

14 13 6248

6702

6657

Fire Mtn
6591

Mica Lake

23 24

Fire Creek
Pass

N A T I

6914

Milk
Lake
Glacier

ROAD 23 2 MI.

Fire Creek

4500

Pumice

657

26 25

6903

6952

6500

5779

5500

5500

5500

Chuck

2972

643

GLACIER RIDGE

658 6000

7000

35 36

5460

TRAIL

5500

3020

Creek TRAIL

Creek

Glacier RIDGE Creek

643A
KENNEDY

Kennedy Hot Spring
Guard Station

1

Kennedy Creek

5500

7500

Scimit

646

Camp
Lake

Lake
Byrne

643

River Sitkum

3852

F O R

Sitkum Gl

6345

6328 12

Chetwot

Milk 790 East 4000

3500 3000

4000

5000

5500

see MAP K9

see MAP K8

see MAP K10

K8, K9

United States. The range's great number of fairly high summits coupled with a year-round barrage from storms accounts for its vast accumulation of ice and snow. Chances are that you'll encounter at least one storm, lasting only a few days if you're lucky, before you reach the Canadian border.

At Fire Creek Pass, the trail goes between two large cairns 30 yards northwest of an emergency campsite. Our usually snowbound route switchbacks down a ridge north-northeast to a ford of the outlet of perpetually frozen Mica Lake (5430–1.1), whose cirque wall of dark metamorphic schist is intruded by light pegmatite dikes. From its shore, you can see dozens of unappealing switchbacks you'll have to climb to surmount the next ridge. As we descend farther, we must boulder-hop across wide, shallow Mica Creek, just east of which is a good, but open, campsite (5110–0.5) on a small bench. We continue to switchback eastward and reach a basin, another creek and a good, obvious campsite (4400–1.1). From it our unrelenting descent takes us down to deep, 5-yard-wide Milk Creek. A log crossing existed in 1973, but was replaced with a $40,000 "permanent" bridge in 1974. This, however, was wiped out by an early-summer avalanche in 1975. Another bridge was built and was still standing in 1977, but there's no guarantee a bridge will be there when you reach the creek.

Immediately beyond this crossing, we meet Milk Creek Trail 790 (3800–1.3), descending north, which the old Cascade Crest route used to follow before the train of switchbacks to the east of us was constructed. Snowfields and avalanche hazards probably prevented the construction of a trail that would contour around Glacier Peak at the 6000-foot level.

When you leave the creek and an adjacent campsite, take your time switchbacking up the east wall of this canyon. If the day is drizzly, you'll find that the "fog drip" on the flowers of this heavily vegetated slope will saturate you from the thighs down. Ahead of you grow miles of this inconsiderate vegetation that you must switchback through. Rationalizing your fate, you can observe that in this weather there are no flies or mosquitoes around to bother you. When you finally finish your creekless ascent and reach the ridgecrest (5750–2.5), you may be greeted by a marmot. If not, at least you can expect a rest at an open campsite.

After a short, negligible climb, we contour the east slope of our ridge and leave behind its outcrops of densely clustered, light-colored

Miocene dikes, sills and irregular masses. As we enter the deeply glaciated East Fork Milk Creek basin, these outcrops give way to ancient, metamorphic rocks. Along the south wall of this basin, our trail passes just below a small knoll (5860–1.5), 100 yards below which is an adequate campsite. Beyond this point, we shortly cross a hundred-yard-wide boulder field that is laced with creeklets. Our route now climbs gently northeast to another ridge (6010–0.6), from which we can see an open campsite at the base of a ridge knoll 10 feet below and 100 yards north of us. The trail switchbacks slightly up the ridge, contours southeast across it, then starts the first of 59 switchbacks down to Vista Creek. After a few of these, we reach the Dolly Vista campsite (5830–0.7) beneath a few, protective mountain hemlocks. A pit toilet is immediately north; water is found by traversing about 100 yards southeast.

From the campsite, our path switchbacks northeast down through open forest to a saddle (5380–0.5) on Vista Ridge, where we reach a dry, open campsite. Northeast of us this resistant ridge is composed of Miocene intrusive rocks that are capped with remnant Quaternary

andesite flows from Glacier Peak. Starting down into deep, glaciated Vista Creek canyon, we're grateful that we're descending the last 38 switchbacks rather than ascending them. By the time we reach the last one, 50 yards from the creek, we've left most of the "rain forest" behind, and we hike 100 yards northeast to a large, signed campsite (3650–2.6) beside Vista Creek. From it, our trail descends into a Douglas-fir forest that has an understory of huckleberry, ferns and Oregon grape.

The trail curves east and the gradient eases as we approach a log crossing of wide, silty Vista Creek (2877–2.1). On its southeast bank is a good campsite with a fire ring and pit toilet. Now we contour east across a gentle slope to a crossing of Gamma Creek (2910–0.8). Part of its flow is derived from the 140°F., sodium-chloride-bicarbonate-rich waters of Gamma Hot Springs (5000), about three miles upstream. Our trail gradually curves southeast and arrives at a junction with Suiattle River Trail 798 (3028–0.7), which first bears southeast before climbing south up-river. The PCT descends north, switchbacks down to a 50-yard-long horse bridge across the silty-gray Suiattle

K9

K9, K10

The Ermine Glacier spreads out across Glacier Peak's lower flanks; viewed from switchbacks just below Vista Ridge

ROAD 26 6 MI.

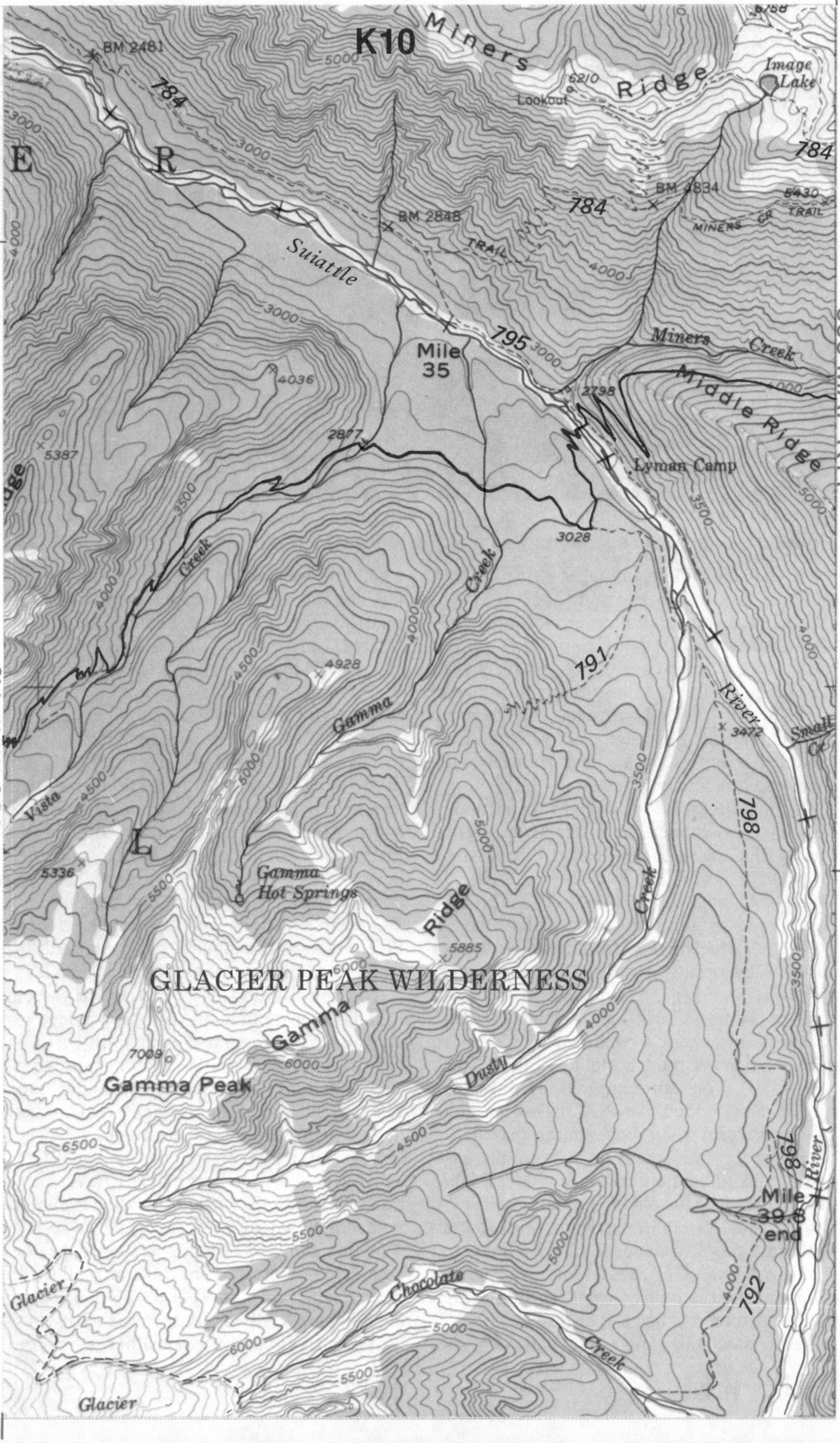

see MAP K9

see MAP K11

View northeast from upper Vista Creek canyon: Plummer Mountain and Fortress Mountain stand above smooth, dropping Middle Ridge

River, then immediately reaches a junction with the Suiattle River access trail (2860–0.8).

From here you can follow a trail southeast ⅓ mile upstream to Lyman Camp. Its large, flat site is a nice place to camp, once you get used to the horse manure. If you turn left (northwest) and follow this trail downstream, you'll pass by some campsites, then after 330 yards reach a good shelter and a separate toilet both above the south bank of Miners Creek.

Our next trail segment, straight ahead, makes long, easy switchbacks up to the lower edge of Middle Ridge, then climbs east up its north slope to a junction with the Buck Creek Pass trail (4580–4.4), which climbs five miles south to the pass. From this junction you can follow the old PCT route, which makes an initial steep descent north, bridges a sluggish creek, and then quickly arrives at a very good campsite on the south bank of Miners Creek—a 0.4-mile side trip. However, the new PCT continues ¼ mile east to a creek, then ¼ mile north to Miners Creek (4490–0.5). You can camp nearby. From the creek's horse bridge, the PCT makes an initial jog downstream, then passes more than half a dozen creeks and creeklets as it climbs east. Switchbacks ultimately take you 400 feet higher to a junction with the old PCT route (5280–1.5). You continue to climb eastward, soon getting southwest views of majestic Glacier Peak and southern views of Fortress Mountain and the deep, glaciated canyon below it. The route turns north and soon reaches a spur trail (5790–0.7) that goes about 150 yards east to a two-tent site.

Climbing, we reach a second trail in 0.1 mile, this one a footpath northeast over to the Railroad Creek Trail, which vaults Cloudy Pass. Immediately before Suiattle Pass, we meet a minor trail that climbs to the crest above the PCT. On the crest (5990–0.3), we meet an abandoned trail that starts east across the pass.

Switchbacks, often accompanied by snow patches, take us down to a creeklet (5730–0.3), from which a spur trail climbs north-northwest to a hemlock/meadow campsite. More switchbacks take us down to a junction with the Railroad Creek Trail (5550–0.2). If you've been having snow problems, you may want to start down this trail, which forks in about 0.1 mile. The north banch, down Agnes Creek, is the old PCT route, and although it is supposedly unmaintained, it was very hikeable in 1982.

The new PCT takes you on a fairly scenic rollercoaster route in and out of two deep side canyons. Your route is downhill all the way to the first of these (4980–1.3), which in August 1982, had a signed campsite—under snow! Leaving this cirque and its giant, rockfall boulders, which have buried the creek, we switchback (needlessly?) high up on the Agnes Creek canyon wall. After a northward traverse, our trail bends into the second side canyon, and we immediately encounter a spur trail (5450–1.4). This one climbs 110 yards to a poor, heatherbound, one-tent site. In 100 yards, the PCT gives rise to two more spur trails, one descending 60 yards to a two-tent site. The other climbs 90 yards to another poor, heather-bound, one-

K10, K11   **K11**

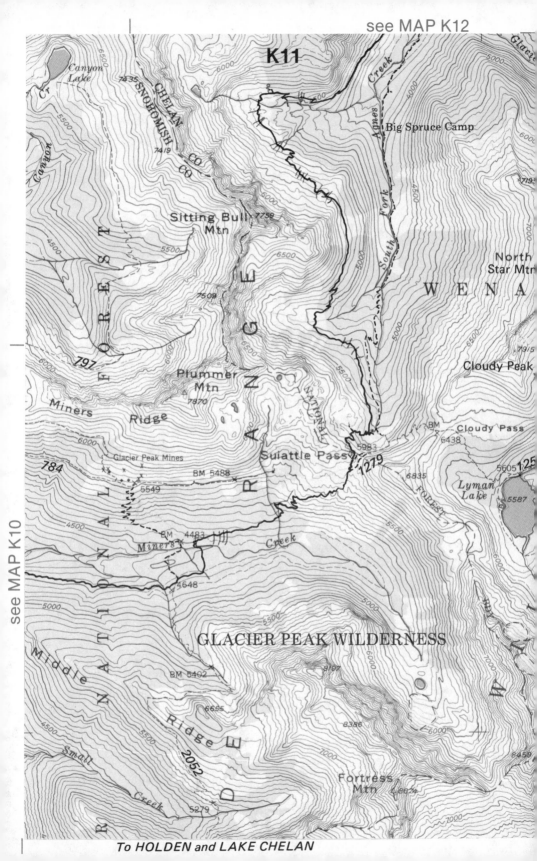

K11

Canyon Lake

Cr

Canyon

74 35

74 19

CHELAN CO

SNOHOMISH CO

Sitting Bull Mtn 7759

7509

N A T I O N A L   F O R E S T

797

Plummer Mtn 7870

Miners Ridge

784

Glacier Peak Mines

BM 5488

5549

BM 4483

Miners

4648

GLACIER PEAK WILDERNESS

BM 5402

6695

Middle

Small

Creek

5000

4500

5500

5279

Ridge 2052

R A N G E R

N A T I O N A L

Suiattle Pass

Creek

Agnes Creek

Big Spruce Camp

719

South Fork

7000

North Star Mtn

W E N A

Cloudy Peak

79 5

BM 6438

Cloudy Pass

5983

1279

6835

Lyman Lake

5587

5605

125

F O R E S T

W

8386

9197

Fortress Mtn 8674

8459

see MAP K10

see MAP K13

K12

1272

WENATCHEE

Agnes
Mtn

NATIONAL   FOREST

GLACIER   PEAK

712

Spruce Creek Camp

WILDERNESS

Needle
Peak

Mount
Blankenship

Hemlock
Camp

see MAP K11

tent site. A trickling creeklet flows between these three exposed sites.

Up to a dozen more creeklets are passed as we descend to a bridged creek on the floor of the second side canyon. About 300 yards past it, we meet yet another spur trail (4810–1.6), this one climbing 140 yards to a sheltered, two-tent site, with view and spring-fed creeklet. The PCT then drops east, briefly switchbacks west, turns east again and in 60 yards reaches the last spur trail (4680–0.2). This crosses the adjacent creek and ends at some small sites among firs of a nearby ridge.

Now we have a generally moderate descent to Agnes Creek, the forested route being punctuated with some bushy, wildflowered patches that present views. At last we bridge Agnes Creek and in about 150 yards reach Hemlock Camp (3560–2.0). If you've taken the old PCT route, which is considerably shorter, you'll meet the new route here. The camp comes equipped with benches, a table and a fire ring.

Continuing north along our near-the-creek route through a forest of western hemlock, Engelmann spruce, western redcedar, Douglas-fir and western white pine, we descend past Mt. Blankenship (5926) to the west and Needle Peak (7885) to the east before reaching Spruce Creek Camp (2900–2.7). At this site, you'll find only log stumps around a fire pit, but it's still quite a nice camp.

Our canyon grows ever deeper as we trek northward, catch a glimpse of the blue-green waters of the South Fork, and then contour over to well-equipped Swamp Creek Camp (2780–

1.3). Here, beside the seven-yard-wide torrent, Swamp Creek Trail 712 begins a three-mile climb up the creek toward Dark Glacier, which is tucked in a deep amphitheater below Dark Peak. Leaving this very good campsite, we cross the creek on a sturdy horse bridge, progress north to the rim of the inner gorge of the South Fork (2570–1.6), then gradually curve down to a junction with West Fork Agnes Creek Trail 1272 (2160–1.4), which descends west-northwest to that creek. Several fair campsites are just west of this junction, but much better ones are at Five Mile Camp, about 100 yards east, above the west bank of Pass Creek. These are the last campsites we'll see within Glacier Peak Wilderness. Hiking northeast, we'll soon leave the granitic rocks of the Cloudy Pass batholith behind and walk upon schist and gneiss that date back to Jurassic times or earlier.

The overpowering canyon which we hike through bears a strong resemblance to deep Kings Canyon in the Sierra Nevada of California, except that this one supports a much denser growth of flowers, shrubs and trees. We pass by seasonal Trapper Creek (2070–1.2), then approach Agnes Creek which, like its South Fork, possesses an inner gorge. Our undulating trail goes right out to its brink at several spots, then descends to switchbacks that take us down to a massive bridge 40 feet above roaring Agnes Creek (1550–3.6), which, at this point, is larger than most rivers we've seen along the Pacific Crest Trail. Now within the Lake Chelan National Recreation Area, we cross the 27-yard-long bridge, climb a low ridge, then contour

K11, K12   K12, K13, K14

Glacier Peak, viewed from near Suiattle Pass

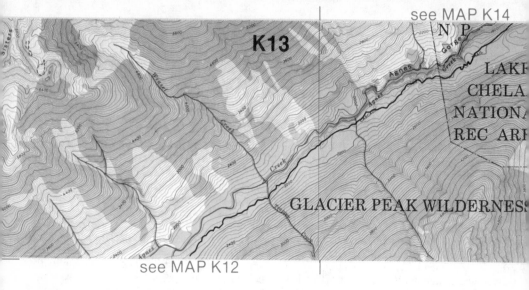

K13

N P

LAKE
CHELA
NATIONA
REC AR

GLACIER PEAK WILDERNES

see MAP K12

northwest to a trailhead at a bend in the Stehekin River Road (1650–0.2). Just 35 yards up the road is High Bridge Campground, with a shelter and outside tables. Water can be obtained by walking back down the road to the high bridge and then descending steep, short switchbacks northward to the west bank of the Stehekin River.

You can descend the road 200 yards to the High Bridge Ranger Station, which is immediately northeast of a bend in the Stehekin River. During the 1985 summer, shuttle buses from the

K14

Five Mile Camp

Stehekin resort area, 10.6 miles downstream, departed daily at 7:30 A.M., 9:00 A.M., and 2 P.M., arriving at the High Bridge Ranger Station about an hour later. The buses continued from this station north to Cottonwood Camp, 11.4 miles up-river, before returning to Stehekin. From the High Bridge Ranger Station, the buses in summer 1985 left for Stehekin at 10:45 A.M., 12:30 P.M., and 5:45 P.M. However, these departure times, like those from Stehekin, have changed in the past and could change in the future. In 1985 the bus fare was $2 per person, each way, so you could leisurely ride up and down 22 miles of the Stehekin River canyon and decide which of its nine campgrounds was best for you. A one-way trip from High Bridge to Stehekin was $1.

If you're like most hikers, you'll be weary by the time the PCT reaches the Agnes Creek trailhead, and you'll welcome the opportunity to relax overnight in Stehekin. The North Cascades Lodge dominates the Stehekin complex, providing good meals and accommodations. The old Golden West Lodge has been transformed into the National Park Service Information Center, at which you can get wilderness permits as well as information. There are also a gift shop, a photo shop, a packer station, and—very important—a post office and small, limited general store.

You'll find camping ¼ mile north of the complex at Purple Point Campground. It is possible, though very unlikely, that you'll encounter western rattlesnakes here, for they are quite common in the Stehekin area though become less common up-canyon. More likely, however, you'll meet black bears, which have become an increasing nuisance as they've grown bolder in recent years. You can expect to see them at any of the nine roadside campgrounds. Be sure you know how to "bearbag" your food.

Many backpackers hiking from Stevens Pass through the Glacier Peak Wilderness to High Bridge end their hike there and take the shuttle bus to Stehekin. They then take the Lady of the Lake ferry ($9.50, one way in 1985) along 50-mile-long Lake Chelan to the city of Chelan, at the lake's far end. (In its deepest spot, this huge lake is 1586 feet deep, or in other words, its deepest point is 488 feet *below* sea level and is therefore the lowest land surface in western North America. Glaciers certainly performed an impressive excavation!) The advantage of ending at Chelan rather than at Rainy Pass is that you are much closer to Stevens Pass, your starting point. The drive from Stevens Pass to Chelan is 90 miles, but it is an *additional* 103 miles to Rainy Pass. For non-through PCT Hikers, that additional shuttle is not worth the generally viewless hike along the last stretch of Section K.

To complete this stretch from the Agnes Creek trailhead, you walk down to the nearby bridge over the Stehekin River, immediately beyond which you'll find another trailhead by

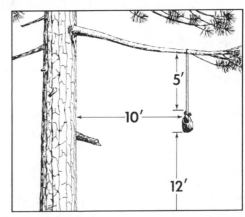

Recommended minimum distances for bearbagging your food

the High Bridge Ranger Station (1600–0.1). Take this trail, which starts initially east, then switchbacks up to a granitic bench with a trail junction (1860–0.4). The trail southeast descends to the Cascade Corral, on the Stehekin River Road. The PCT climbs northward, topping a low, bedrock ridge and reaching a junction at the west arm of swampy Coon Lake (2180–0.7). From it, a rigorously switchbacking

K14

K14

View up Lake Chelan, from Stehekin resort

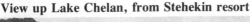

NORTH CASCADES

1233

NATIONAL PARK

Waddell Lake

McGregor Mtn

LAKE CHE

NATIONAL RECREAT

Coon Lake

STEHEKIN RIVER

trail climbs about 7 miles to the top of McGregor Mountain. The PCT heads northwest, passing two seasonal creeklets on a mostly descending grade to yet another junction (1940–0.8). Here we meet the Old Wagon Trail, which winds 200 yards west down to the Stehekin River Road. Dolly Varden Campground, with two sites, lies 0.4 mile up it.

The PCT coincides with a stretch of the Old Wagon Trail, and we cross two seasonal creeklets before climbing to McGregor Creek (2195–0.6). Our ascent abates, then soon we ford Buzzard Creek (2260–0.4), and later, two-branched Canim Creek (2160–0.7). In about ⅓ mile we leave the Old Wagon Trail and make an undulating traverse that ends about 50 yards

K14

K14

before Clear Creek, roughly opposite the Bridge Creek Ranger Station (2105–1.3), and just beyond it pass Bridge Creek Campground with its shelter. After a few more minutes of walking, we arrive at the PCT Bridge Creek trailhead (2180–0.3), located 240 yards southeast of Road 3505's crossing of Bridge Creek.

Back on a trail again, we climb up a wandering path that takes us past a small lily-pad pond, on a bench, then winds to the edge of the Bridge Creek gorge and climbs its slopes to jump-across Berry Creek (2720–1.7). Watching out for western toads, we climb a little higher on the slope before we descend to a sideplanked horse bridge above wild, roaring Bridge Creek (2540–1.0). Climbing a few yards north of the bridge, we reach the dusty, rustic North Fork Camp atop a rocky bluff that overlooks the junction of the North Fork with Bridge Creek. The camp's resident landlords—golden-mantled ground squirrels—may exact "rent" from your backpack while you're not looking.

From this site we switchback east up to a junction with North Fork Bridge Creek Trail 1233 (2810–0.3), which climbs northward. We climb east up a bushy, aromatic slope, reach a point several hundred feet above Bridge Creek, and take in gorgeous views below us as we descend slightly to a small, stonewall campsite imme-

K14

Inner Gorge of Agnes Creek

View up South Fork Bridge Creek canyon

diately before a saddle. Beyond it, we descend north to wide, alder-lined Maple Creek (3070–1.5), which has a suspension bridge crossing it 25 yards upstream. Be careful climbing the talus boulders to and from the bridge. We then follow our level, relaxing path east and come to a 250-yard-long spur trail (3130–1.7) that descends southeast, steeply at first, through a meadow of tall cow parsnips, to Six Mile Camp, a well-furnished site designed with horseback riders in mind.

Not far beyond this spur trail, the Rainbow Lake Trail (3240–0.7) peels off from the PCT, descends southeast, and climbs up South Fork Canyon to Pass 6230, immediately west of domineering Bowan Mountain (7895), and Rainbow Lake south of the pass. Just 330 yards down this trail is South Fork Camp, beside Bridge Creek. From the junction, our route continues east through alternating forest and brush

K14, K15

see MAP L1

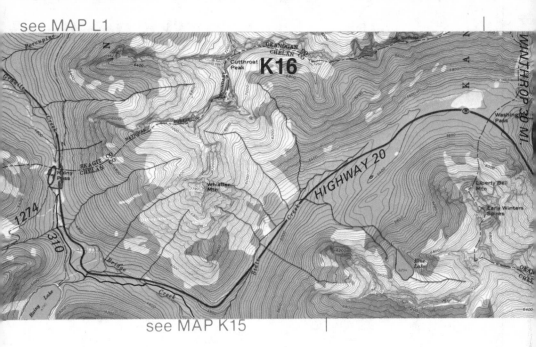

see MAP K15

cover, then reaches a junction with a 110-yard-long spur trail (3510–1.5) that descends first southwest, then southeast to the loveliest Bridge Creek campsite: Hide-Away Camp. Strictly for backpackers, this shady, creekside campsite has a table, log stumps and a fire ring.

Continuing east within hearing distance of the creek, we leave this campsite and eventually turn northeast just before reaching a junction with Twisp Pass Trail 1277 (3635–0.9), which curves east and bridges Bridge Creek after 70 yards. Forty yards east-northeast from this crossing, a right fork veers southeast 30 yards to the large, flat, dusty, but well-furnished Fire-weed Camp.

Our trail climbs moderately northeast and in ⅔ mile passes an old log cabin with good camping, then leaves North Cascades National Park just before a series of creeks, *not* just after them. Our trail then reaches a shallow, wide ford of Bridge Creek (4145–2.2), but a foot-trail bypass route begins about 100 yards before the ford. From where the foot and horse paths reunite, we climb to the nearby Crocker Cabin Historical Site, with a campsite, and immediately past it reach Stiletto Peak Trail 1232 (4250–0.2), which leads east-northeast. After a few minutes' walk, we make a log crossing of State Creek, pass an adequate campsite on its west bank, and then continue north toward the traffic we hear on the highway above us. We quickly encounter abandoned Washington Pass Trail 1275 (4420–0.5), on our right (east), which was desecrated when the North Cascades Highway (State 20) was paved over it. This new road, completed in 1972, lessened the wilderness experience at least to the same extent that the new Tioga Road in Yosemite National Park diminished that park's High Sierra wilderness character.

Our trail arcs northwest up to a spur trail (4510–0.5) that forks right (west) 50 yards to a parking lot beside the highway at a point 0.1 mile below its crossing of Bridge Creek. Our trail, also called Bridge Creek Trail 419, bears west-southwest 35 yards to a bridge across Bridge Creek, then parallels the highway west up to the outlet creek (4705–0.7) of Rainy Lake. From it, our path climbs gently north, levels off and strikes a course through the soggy headwaters of Bridge Creek before reaching a junction with Rainy Lake Trail 310 only 20 yards before our trail reaches a large trailhead parking lot. No camping is allowed at Rainy Lake. Immediately past the lot we cross a road, built in 1978, which cuts across Highway 20's Rainy Pass (4855–1.1), and bends north to nearby rest areas, one on each side of the highway.

K15   K16

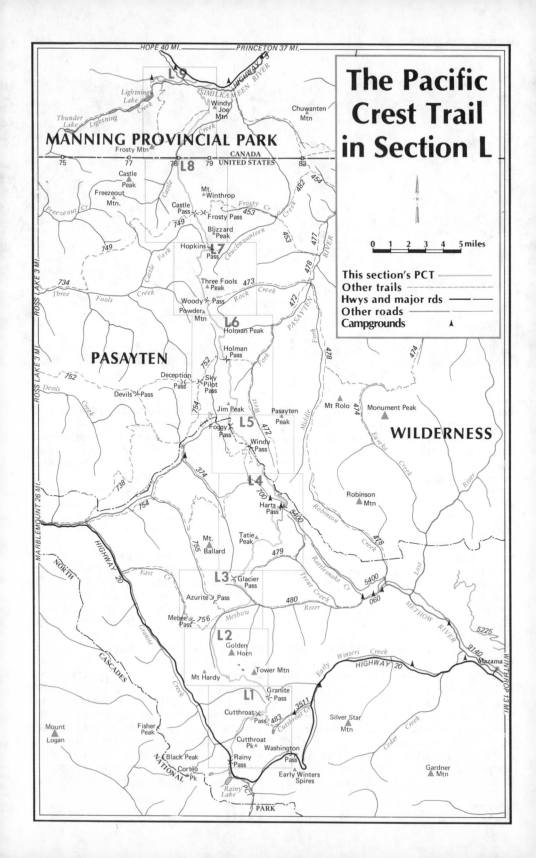

Section L: Highway 20 at Rainy Pass to Highway 3 in Manning Park

Introduction: The final leg of the Pacific Crest Trail leads from the North Cascades Highway (Washington 20) at Rainy Pass to Manning Provincial Park, British Columbia. In this relatively short trek, there is vehicle access only at Harts Pass (30 miles north), where gravel Road 5400 crosses the crest to serve a turn-of-the-century mining district.

In this entire section, the Pacific Crest Trail is well east of much of the Cascade Range. To the west, Mt. Baker, Mt. Shuksan and the Picket Range receive the brunt of any bad weather. Overall snow accumulation along the PCT route here is much less than it is at Mt. Baker, and PCT hikers may enjoy sunshine when Puget Sound and the western mountains are cloud- and rain-bound. Nonetheless, until midsummer, hikers should be prepared for a snow-covered and icy trail. After the snow melts, the mosquitoes have a heyday, so the most pleasant month to hike this section is, usually, September. Typically the winter snows do not start in earnest until at least October (but beware the exception!).

Near Rainy Pass the scenery is spectacular, and many mountains are crowned with craggy spires of Golden Horn granodiorite. Consequently the PCT only occasionally follows the crest of the Cascades exactly: much of the mileage is in long traverses and river valleys. Even if backpackers were as surefooted and agile as mountain goats, they would not choose a route true to the divide. Then, as the intrusive rocks give way to lower Cretaceous graywackes, the terrain becomes hilly, so the PCT can follow the crest more closely than before.

North of Harts Pass the PCT offers a variety of scenery and terrains. High meadows, wooded slopes and valleys, as well as rugged, precipitous ridges make up the bulk of this section, which traverses the backbone of the 790-square-mile Pasayten Wilderness. In good weather the views are frequently spectacular, particularly in the fall when larch, spruce and scrub maple splash gold, green and red across the slopes.

Declination: 20°E

Mileages:

	South to North	Distances between Points	North to South
Highway 20 at Rainy Pass	0.0	5.1	69.1
Cutthroat Pass................................	5.1	5.5	64.0
Methow Pass	10.6	10.6	58.5
Glacier Pass..................................	21.2	9.3	47.9
Harts Pass	30.5	5.2	38.6
Windy Pass	35.7	8.6	33.4
Holman Pass	44.3	5.9	24.8
Woody Pass...................................	50.2	5.1	18.9
Hopkins Pass.................................	55.3	6.6	13.8
U.S.-Canadian border at Monument 78	61.9	7.2	7.2
Highway 3 in Manning Park	69.1		0.0

Supplies: No supply points are found until northbound hikers reach trail's end, in Manning Provincial Park. In it, just west of the trailhead, you'll find Manning Park Lodge, with food and lodging, and the park headquarters, where you can get information. Greyhound Bus service is available to and from Vancouver, B.C.

Problems: Very early and very late season hikers should be ready for treacherous, precipitous snow slopes, avalanche hazards and dangerously exposed hiking along parts of this PCT section. It is also wise to acquaint yourself with the border-crossing information on page 21 of this book to avoid unpleasant hassles associated with customs and immigration regulations of both the United States and Canada.

Black Peak (right) stands high above Granite Creek canyon   *Hartline*

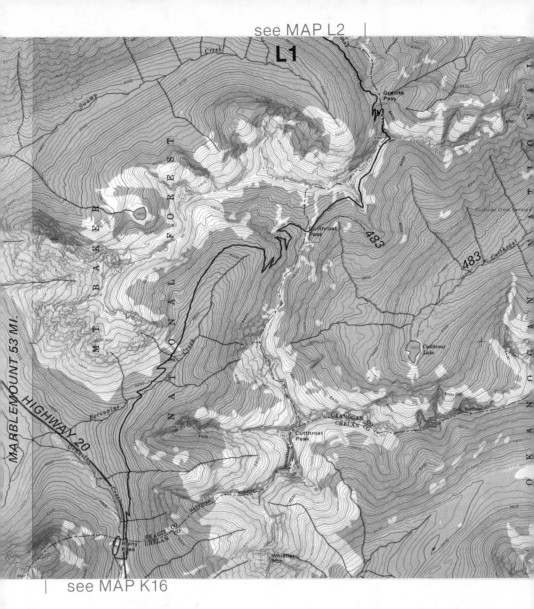

see MAP K16

A large, off-road rest area, equipped with "plush" toilet facilities has been built west of the North Cascades Highway. Ample trailhead parking for horse packers and hikers parallels the shoulder of the road. Nearby outhouses are smaller than those in the rest area. Our north-bound path bisects the narrow peninsula of wilderness between the highway and an eastern parking lot. At the north end of the parking lot we enter Douglas-fir forest to begin a climbing, northward traverse. One creek, draining Cut-throat Peak (7865) cascades across our path even in September and October. Numerous other streams are of nuisance value early in the season, but typically dry up by late August. The grade levels as we near Porcupine Creek (5080–1.5), which we bridge. Then we turn northeast to parallel it and resume our ascent. A pair of switchbacks lift the path away from the stream bed and guide us onto a steep, open slope where avalanches sweeping down from Peaks 7004 and 7762 may threaten May and June hikers. After traversing higher to contour around the headwaters bowl of Porcupine Creek, we switchback up the steep, glacier-formed basin wall. Deciduous larches, the poetic tamaracks, add foreground to the rugged panorama un-folding before us. Black Peak (8970) and Corteo

L1   L1

Peak (8100), across the highway, front the more distant North Cascades. Scrub huckleberry and heather compose the basic ground cover which "springtime" (July) flowers eloquently embroider.

We pass campsites which are inviting, though lacking late-season water, as the PCT levels to the west of grassy, granitic Cutthroat Pass (6820–3.6). Here Cutthroat Lake Trail 483 forks east to begin its traversing descent to Cutthroat Lake (4935), visible in the valley below. Liberty Bell Mountain (7720), a favorite rock climb, peaks above the ridge across the lake. We head northeast to arc around two bowls, contouring across steep scree slopes beneath precipitous cliffs. Before leaving the second cirque we choose the upper and more traveled of two trails. The lower trail dead-ends on the ridge 100 yards ahead. Climbing slightly, we reach a crest and pause to enjoy a picturesque view of Tower Mountain (8444).

Our route continues northward, balancing precariously across a precipice before executing several short, tight switchbacks down the rugged north ridge. Avoiding the rock walls above Granite Pass, we descend south to zigzag above beautiful, glacier-carved Swamp Creek valley. Then, at Granite Pass (6290–2.4), we reach "terra flata" and are welcomed into a sheltered camp. Don't expect convenient late-season water here.

From the camp our route to Methow Pass makes a long traverse of the open lower slopes of Tower Mountain. Scrub subalpine fir, western white pine, mountain ash and heather provide little protection for sun-beaten or windswept walkers. Outcrops of the Golden Horn granodiorite are clearly exposed by the trail cut. Upon reaching the bowl below Snowy Lakes, we lose some precious elevation as we drop into an idyllic park, where a bubbling stream, grassy flowerlands, larch and spruce all recommend a large campsite (6300–2.2). Shedding our packs and donning our sweaters, we settle in. Firewood in this delicate alpine valley is in limited supply, and is better left unburned. A cross trail from the campsite heads north, up-valley, to Upper and Lower Snowy Lakes in a higher cirque.

From the camp a pair of switchbacks help us climb out of the bowl to set up the approach to Methow Pass (6600–0.9) (pronounced METhow). Views of Mt. Arriva (8215) and Fisher Peak (8050) are the last we'll have of the mountains west of Granite Creek. Mt. Hardy (7197), just west of the pass, and Golden Horn (8366), to the north, will stay with us during our trek down the valley of the Methow River's West Fork. Like most high-elevation "campsites," Methow Pass is waterless when it is not swampy.

Leaving Methow Pass on a northward traverse, we spy below us a backpackers' campsite on a level bench with an uncertain water supply. Now zigzagging into the valley, the PCT crosses a few infant streams, then straightens to parallel the West Fork of the Methow. From here, at sunset, Golden Horn glows spectacularly against the deep blue-black of the eastern sky. A long,

L1

View southeast from Cutthroat Pass

L2

Hartline

slight but steady downgrade brings us to Golden Creek and Willis Camp (4570–4.2). Nimbly rock-hopping the stream, we have only a short stint before bridging the West Fork Methow River (4390–0.7). A small camp by the bridge on the east bank is the best trailside camp between here and Brush Creek. Within 200 yards the level path enters the first of several avalanche paths.

At a PCT mileage sign we merge onto the route of the old Cascade Crest Trail (now Trail 756) (4380–0.8). Westbound, this overgrown trail climbs out of the Methow Valley via Mebee Pass to descend along East Creek, pass the Gold Hill Mine, and meet Granite Creek and Washington Highway 20. This trail also extends diagonally 0.2 mile downhill to riverside Horse Heaven Camp. The PCT, bending east and crossing what the map calls Jet Creek, reaches a junction with Mill Creek Trail 755 (4380–0.2), which looks like a rocky stream bed in the grass of the clearing. Almost immediately we cross signed Jet Creek, dry in late season.

The scree fields change in character and composition as we head east out of the granodiorite body and into a zone of lower Cretaceous graywackes ("muddy" sandstones), conglomerates, argillites and shales. Then our trail turns northeast to enter the mouth of Brush Creek's canyon. After passing a small campsite, we cross Brush Creek on a bridge and in 50 yards meet West Fork Methow Trail 480 (4280–1.9). Here we zig once and start climbing in earnest along steep, brushy Brush Creek. A few small campsites line the trail in this fairly hospitable and picturesque valley, and high in the west some small glaciers cling between the rugged upper cliffs of Azurite Peak (8400). A few switchbacks ease the grade of the final climb to Glacier Pass (5520–2.8), where campsites without nearby late-season water are found in the forest-sheltered gap. Two trails, the first heading north, the second trending west, are separated by 100 PCT trail yards.

Ambling on, we gear down for a long, zigzagging climb to a grassy pass. Dwindling scrub subalpine fir, spruce and larch accompany us up the slope. Pausing for breath, we appreciate the view of three little lakes nestled near the head of South Fork Slate Creek's

L2, L3   L3

see MAP L3

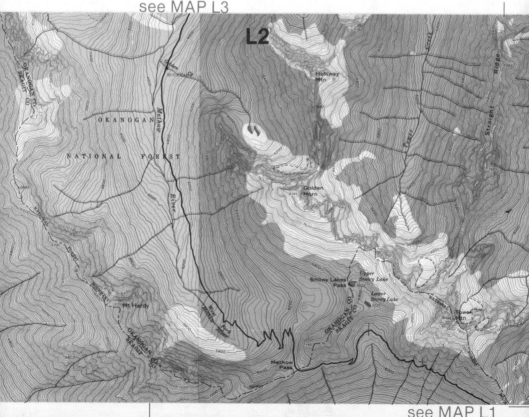

see MAP L1

Tower Mountain, from above Tower Pass

glacial valley, as well as the broadening pan-orama of the North Cascades. At last we top off the climb and descend slightly along the ridge into an alpine-garden pass (6750–2.6) above South Fork Trout Creek. Here the trail begins a long traverse north-eastward. Beyond the first ridge we round is a pleasant trailside campsite with water (6600–1.0). Continuing, we climb to a windy, viewful pass (6900–0.9) on the southwest shoulder of Tatie Peak (7386). As our trail contours around the peak we pass stratified outcrops of alternating shale and conglomerate, then approach a knife-edge saddle above Ninetynine Basin, beyond which the Slate Peak Lookout Tower (7440) is prominent. A de-scending traverse guides us around Peak 7405 through a gap in a side ridge. Both the Harts Pass Road and the Brown Bear Mine house remains can be seen from here.

Angling down, we pass below the sites of the mine tunnels, not obvious from the trail, and approach dirt Road 500. Twenty yards short of the road (6440–2.8), PCT emblems guide us onto a newer stretch of trail that avoids it. In 150 yards we cross the jeep-trail access to the Brown

L3, L4

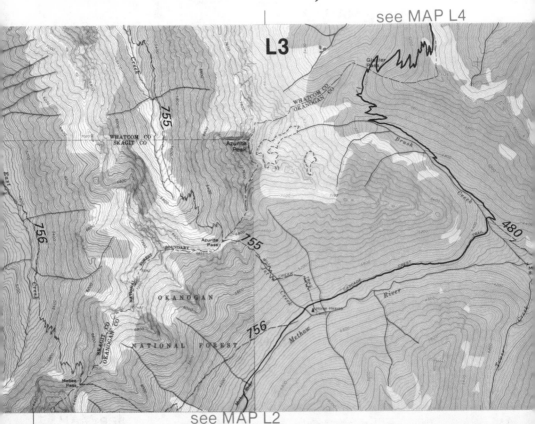

see MAP L3

Bear tunnels, and then continue to traverse above Road 500. A trail from the road joins us as we approach and then thread a minor gap (6390–0.7). Beneath exposed outcrops of banded argillite and gray sandstone, we traverse north along a steep hillside before our trail turns to traverse down to Harts Pass (6198–1.3). An infrequently manned Forest Service Guard Station, on the east side of Harts Pass Road 5400 across from a parking lot and car-camping area, sometimes has a backcountry register for hikers to sign. The small community of Mazama is

Climbing toward Glacier Pass   *Hartline*

Hartline

Tatie Peak, from Slate Peak area

18.7 miles east on Road 5400. Also at the pass, a road branches east-northeast from Road 5400 to parallel the PCT for 1.3 miles before switchbacking up to Slate Peak Lookout.

The Slate Creek mining district was a relatively rich mining area in the State of Washington. Boom camps were fairly populated in the early 1890s until word of the Klondike bonanza lured all the miners away. Del Hart, who owned some mines near Slate Creek, commissioned Charles H. Ballard in 1895 to survey a road from Mazama to the mining area. The pass through which the road was routed now bears Hart's name. The road today is a favorite summer-recreation route and one to the best access roads to the Pasayten Wilderness, which we will soon enter. Gold, silver, copper, lead and zinc are among the metals whose ores were mined in the Slate Creek District. An interesting sidelight to the history of this area is that the first hydro-electric power plant in the high Cascades was installed here. O. B. Brown designed, paid for and supervised construction of the 350-kilowatt plant that he located on the South Fork of Slate Creek.

From the PCT crossing of Road 5400, a scant 35 yards north-northwest of the pass proper, we proceed east-northeast through partly open

L4

spruce-fir woods parallel to a Forest Service road and about 100 feet below it. Beyond a meadow our trail switchbacks up onto a small shoulder with an adequate camp, where we come to a junction (6880–1.4) with a spur trail to the road. It is about 0.1 mile east-southeast down this spur to parking spaces.

Continuing west-northwest on the PCT, we ascend gradually past scattered Lyall larches, common on this small shoulder. Soon the shoulder gives out, leaving the trail hanging on the side of Slate Peak, with spectacular views down the Slate Creek valley, dominated by Mt. Baker (10,778) and other peaks to the west. Mt. Baker is a living volcano, and in March 1975 it increased its thermal activity, which lead many to suspect it would soon erupt. Since the end of the Ice Age, about 10,000 years ago, it has erupted violently at least four times, and on at least four other occasions it has produced enough steam to melt glaciers and trigger large mudflows. Some future PCT hikers may just witness a full-scale eruption.

Passing occasional outcrops of gray and green slate, we descend gradually to the pass (6700–2.2) just above Benson Creek Camp. Still on the west side of the divide, we climb up around an arm and descend past Buffalo Pass (6550–0.7) to Windy Pass (6257–0.9), from where a trail crosses ours to descend south-southwest to Indiana Basin. In about 35 yards we pass a sign heralding our entrance into the Pasayten Wilderness.

The PCT continues north-northwest, leading us out of true-to-its-name Windy Pass and around to the northeast cirque of Tamarack Peak (7290)—clad in tamarack, or larch. After crossing a small basin with water and an adequate camp, the trail switchbacks up to and over an arm of Tamarack Peak, descends the open north cirque, and finally traverses the northwest arm of the mountain to Foggy Pass (6180–2.2). From this pass we cross to the west side of the divide for a brief wooded hike to Jim Pass (6270–0.7). Then, back on the east side of the divide, we traverse around Jim Peak (7033) to

L4

L4, L5, L6

Silver Star Mountain, viewed from Harts Pass area   *Hartline*

Windy Pass   *Hartline*

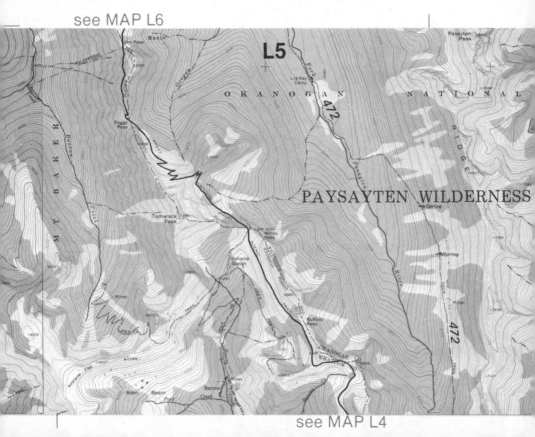

see MAP L6

see MAP L4

the rocky shoulder called Devils Backbone (6180–1.3). Descending into the north cirque of Jim Peak, the PCT crosses the head of Shaw Creek and ascends gradually for about a mile before plunging down switchbacks to a junction with Trail 752 at Holman Pass (5050–4.4). This

pass is heavily wooded and not particularly nice for camping, although wildlife abounds in the vicinity.

We climb northwest out of Holman Pass, crossing the outlet stream from Goat Lakes in about a mile, and switchback up a grassy knoll to

L6

see MAP L7

L6

see MAP L5

a never failing spring (6200–2.4) and a good but much used camp. From here the trail traverses up the steep, grassy slopes bounding Canyon Creek to Rock Pass (6491–1.2). Our trail bypasses the precipitous east-wall traverse of Powder Mountain (7714), climbs over the divide about 300 yards southeast of Rock Pass and descends southeast out of Rock Pass to switchback into the avalanche-swept valley of Rock Creek. The PCT next traverses northwestward, crossing an unreliable creek (and/or snowfield) draining the northeast cirque of Powder Mountain. We then climb the beautiful garden slopes of a small ridge, past nestled camps and a trail leading northeast via Coney Basin down to the Pasayten River, as we follow the PCT into misnamed, rock-strewn Woody Pass (6624–2.3).

From here our trail traverses open slopes with a few wooded fingers, the least spectacular side of Three Fools Peak (7930), until it rounds the south arm of the cirque that cradles Mountain Home Camp, a flat, grassy bench with good camping. Beyond, the trail begins to climb steadily as it traverses the grassy headwall of the cirque. Shortly after we arc to the north, climbing through occasional stands of scrub conifers, a faint trail (6800–2.5) takes off down a more or less open gully to the flat bench of Mountain Home Camp, now 400 feet directly below us.

Continuing on the PCT, a short switchback brings us to the crest of Lakeview Ridge, on which a short spur trail takes us to an enticing view of a nestled lake 1000 feet below, and the valley of Chuchuwanteen Creek beyond. The PCT continues along the crest for a short

L6, L7

L7

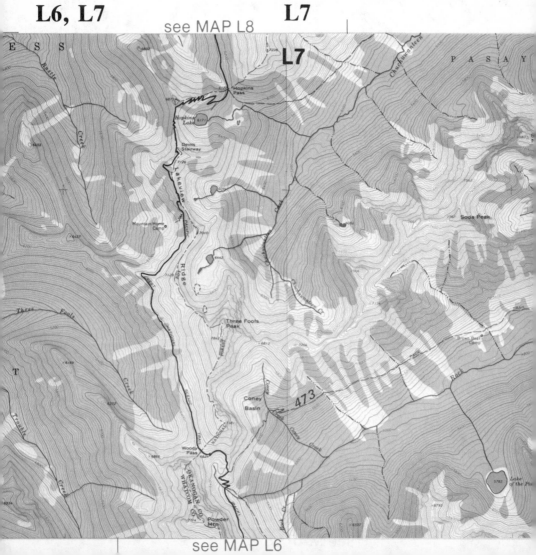

see MAP L8

see MAP L6

distance before it is forced to the west just long enough to switchback once more before climbing to an unnamed summit (7126–0.7) on Lakeview Ridge. From here we have views on all sides, weather permitting: to the south, the very rugged Three Fools Peak; to the north our first glimpse of Hopkins Lake; and farther north and west, the rugged Cascades of Washington and Canada.

Now heading down toward Hopkins Pass, we stick to the ridge crest most of the time until we are forced by Peak 6873 on the ridge to pass east of it. Then our route switchbacks around the north side of the amphitheater for which

Hopkins Lake is the "stage." Several short switchbacks and two longer ones bring us down nearly to the level of the lake, to where a trail (6220–1.7) to dependable campsites at Hopkins Lake (6171) takes off to the southwest. We continue almost eastward for a few hundred yards to Hopkins Pass (6122–0.2), where the old trail down Chuchuwanteen Creek linking up with the Boundary Trail is marked ABANDONED.

The Pacific Crest Trail continues north-northwest from Hopkins Pass, traversing the mostly wooded west slopes of Blizzard Peak (7622). After a mile we reach a stream and its clearing, then re-enter woods and continue our

L7

L7, L8

see MAP L9

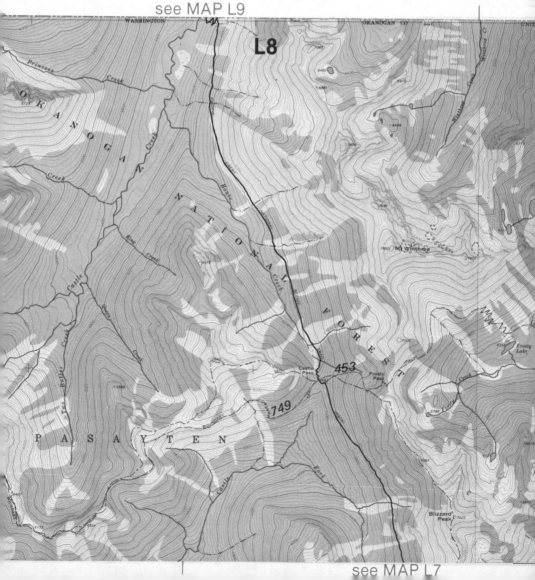

see MAP L7

see MAP L8

traverse about 0.4 mile before starting a gradual descent toward Castle Pass. Shortly before the pass we join Boundary Trail 749, turn sharply left and follow it around a small hummock to Castle Pass (5451–2.5), where we might lunch in the sunshine of a small open area. Then, after meandering northward down a quarter mile of lush alpine gardens, the trail becomes firmly established on the east slope of the Route Creek watershed. We cross two seasonal streams and two avalanche paths, one from the east and one from the west. A reasonable camp lies 200 yards off the trail on the edge of one avalanche track; don't stay there if there is still much snow on the slopes above. Continuing the traverse, we come to two reliable streams in about a mile, then leave the woods for more-open slopes with rounded granite outcrops.

L8

L8

Monument 78 on U.S.-Canada border

After passing two more streams and a stock gate across the trail, we finally pound down the last four switchbacks to Monument 78, on the United States-Canada border (4240–4.1). After shooting several pictures of the scaled-down, 4⅔-foot-high, bronze "Washington Monument" (with a lift-off top for notes within), we leave the Pasayten Wilderness for the final leg of our trip. Welcome to Canada! (See the section on border crossing on page 21).

Plunging into the dense, wet, valley-bottom woods, we emerge only briefly ¼ mile later to cross Castle Creek's seasonally raging torrent. In 1978 the rustic bridge spanning the creek was on the verge of collapse, and without the bridge, the creek's ford could be a major challenge in early season. Near the ford, you'll find one small campsite on the west bank and four others on the east bank.

Back in the woods, we wind through a dense spruce-fir forest and soon climb steadily but gently northeast. The ascent is mostly a viewless one, but on weekdays hikers may hear the inroads made against the forest by civilization's demands: loggers are stripping the slopes on the canyon's opposite wall. As the path climbs, we cross from granite to slate and back again, plod up a short switchback leg, cross a few ravines, jump a few creeklets, get some views of the clearcutting south of us, and arrive at the

L8, L9

A long-sought goal: trail's end in Manning Park

Playground by Manning Park Lodge

southwest base (5070–3.7) of Windy Joe Mountain. Here, by a spring, a spur trail starts a curve southeast to a nearby campsite complete with outhouse. Immediately beyond this spur trail, the PCT turns north and climbs briefly to a saddle and a junction with the Mt. Frosty Trail (5120–0.1), which starts to climb southwest.

From here the PCT makes an undulating traverse north across Windy Joe Mountain's west slopes. We soon hear the traffic on Canada's main east-west thoroughfare, Route 3, cutting a swath through the dense forest on the unseen, deep canyon floor below us. Our trail ends at a hairpin turn on the closed Windy Joe fire access road (5220–0.7), and we follow the road, first north and then south, down to a creek crossing. We immediately recross the creek, descend ½ mile, and then cross it for the last time (4500–1.2).

The moderately descending road soon winds down gentler, still viewless slopes to a bridge over the major branch of the Similkameen River, then in 200 yards crosses a smaller branch (3780–1.1). Here the fire access road curves left and climbs 250 yards up to Highway 3.

From the bridge, two trails start down-canyon, and we take the one that climbs east up a 20-foot-high bluff. It then winds northeast, almost touching Highway 3 near a sewage plant,

then parallels the highway east to the Beaver Pond parking lot (3800–0.4), which marks the end of the long trail—or the beginning, if you are going south. (If you are going south, you'll find the spur road leading to this lot begins about 0.3 mile east from the park headquarters road, or, 0.9 mile east from the east entrance to Manning Park Lodge.)

If you've hiked a good portion of the Pacific Crest Trail, or perhaps just one rainy day's worth, you'll want to stop at the lodge to shower and get a warm meal. It also has tempting accommodations, but they are beyond the budget of most backpackers. From the Lodge the economy-minded backpacker can trek one mile west on Highway 3 to Coldspring Campground, then later catch a bus from Manning Park Lodge west to Vancouver, B.C.

We hope you arrived in good spirits and in good health. And we also hope that your hike through Section L was, despite the odds, warm, dry and insect-free. If you have hiked all or most of the way from Mexico to Canada, won't you please write us and tell us about your experiences and about the usefullness of this guidebook. The letters we received from your predecessors helped make this edition more useful for PCT trekkers, and we'd like to see the tradition continued.

Recommended Reading and Source Materials

Pacific Crest Trail

Clarke, Clinton C., *The Pacific Crest Trailway*. Pasadena: The Pacific Crest Trail System Conference, 1945.

Gray, William R., *The Pacific Crest Trail*. Washington, D.C.: National Geographic Society, 1975.

Green, David, *A Pacific Crest Odyssey*. Berkeley: Wilderness Press, 1979.

Long, Chuck, ed., *Pacific Crest Trail Hike Planning Guide*. Lynnwood, WA: Signpost Publications, 1976.

Schaffer, Jeffrey P., and Ben Schifrin, Thomas Winnett, J.C. Jenkins, *The Pacific Crest Trail, Volume 1: California*, 3rd ed. Berkeley: Wilderness Press, 1982.

Sutton, Ann, and Myron Sutton. *The Pacific Crest Trail: Escape to the Wilderness*. Philadelphia: Lippincott, 1975.

Backpacking and Mountaineering

Beckey, Fred, *Cascade Alpine Guide, Climbing & High Routes, Volume 1: Columbia River to Stevens Pass*. Seattle: The Mountaineers, 1974.

Beckey, Fred, *Cascade Alpine Guide, Climbing & High Routes, Volume 2: Stevens Pass to Rainy Pass*. Seattle: The Mountaineers, 1978.

Beckey, Fred, *Cascade Alpine Guide, Climbing & High Routes, Volume 3: Rainy Pass to Fraser River*. Seattle: The Mountaineers, 1981.

Darvill, Fred T., M.D., *Mountaineering Medicine*, 11th ed. Berkeley: Wilderness Press, 1985.

Fletcher, Colin, *The Complete Walker III*, New York: Knopf, 1984.

Hargrove, Penny, and Noelle Liebrenz, *Backpackers' Sourcebook*, 3rd ed. Berkeley: Wilderness Press, 1986.

Manning, Harvey, *Backpacking: One Step at a Time*, 3rd ed. New York: Knopf, 1980.

Molenaar, Dee, *The Challenge of Rainier*, 3rd ed. Seattle: The Mountaineers, 1979.

Peters, Ed, ed., *Mountaineering, the Freedom of the Hills*. Seattle: The Mountaineers, 1982.

Schaffer, Jeffrey P., *Crater Lake National Park and Vicinity*. Berkeley: Wilderness Press, 1983.

Thomas, Jeff, *Oregon Rock: A Climber's Guide*. Seattle: The Mountaineers, 1983.

Wilkerson, James A., M.D., ed., *Medicine for Mountaineering*, 3rd ed. Seattle: The Mountaineers, 1985.

Winnett, Thomas, *Backpacking Basics*. Berkeley: Wilderness Press, 1979.

Geology

American Geological Institute, *Dictionary of Geological Terms*, rev. ed. Garden City, New York: Doubleday, 1976.

Bacon, Charles R., "Eruptive History of Mount Mazama and Crater Lake Caldera, Cascade Range, U.S.A." *Journal of Volcanology and Geothermal Research*, vol. 18, pp. 57–115; 1983.

Baldwin, Ewart M., *Geology of Oregon*, 3rd ed. Dubuque: Kendall/Hunt, 1981.

Crandell, Dwight R., *Surficial Geology of Mount Rainier National Park, Washington* (U.S. Geological Survey Bulletin 1288). Washington, D.C.: U.S. Government Printing Office, 1969.

Crandell, Dwight R., *The Geologic Story of Mount Rainier* (U.S. Geological Survey Bulletin 1292). Washington, D.C.: U.S. Government Printing Office, 1969.

Crandell, Dwight R., *Recent Eruptive History of Mount Hood, Oregon, and Potential Hazards from Future Eruptions* (U.S. Geological Survey Bulletin 1492). Washington, D.C.: U.S. Government Printing Office, 1980.

Dole, Hollis M., ed., *Andesite Conference Guidebook* (Oregon Department of Geology and Mineral Industries Bulletin 62). Portland: Oregon Department of Geology, 1968.

Harris, Stephen L., *Fire and Ice: The Cascade Volcanoes*, Seattle: The Mountaineers, 1976.

Howell, David G., "Terranes." *Scientific American*, vol. 253, no. 5; November 1985.

Jones, David L., *et al*, "The Growth of Western North America." *Scientific American*, vol. 247, no. 5; November 1982.

Luedke, Robert G., and Robert L. Smith, *Map Showing Distribution, Composition, and Age of Late Cenozoic Volcanic Centers in Oregon and Washington* (U.S. Geogical Survey Miscellaneous Investigations Series Map I-1091-D). Washington, D.C.: U.S. Government Printing Office, 1982.

McKee, Bates, *Cascadia: The Geologic Evolution of the Pacific Northwest*. New York: McGraw-Hill, 1972.

Pough, Frederick H., *A Field Guide to Rocks and Minerals*, 4th ed. Boston: Houghton Mifflin, 1976.

Staatz, Mortimer H., *et al*, *Geology and Mineral Resources of the Northern Part of the North Cascades National Park, Washington* (U.S. Geological Survey Bulletin 1359). Washington, D.C.: U.S. Government Printing Office, 1972.

Tabor, R.W., and D.F. Crowder, *On Batholiths and Volcanoes . . . North Cascades, Washington* (U.S. Geological Survey Professional Paper 604). Washington, D.C.: U.S. Government Printing Office, 1969.

Wells, Francis G., and Dallas L. Peck, *Geologic Map of Oregon West of the 121st Meridian* (U.S. Geological Survey Misc. Geol. Investig. Map I-325, 1:500,000). Washington, D.C.: U.S. Government Printing Office, 1961.

Biology

Arno, Stephen F., and Ramona P. Hammerly, *Northwest Trees*. Seattle: The Mountaineers, 1977.

Burt, William H., and Richard P. Grossenheider, *A Field Guide to the Mammals*, 3rd ed. Boston: Houghton Mifflin, 1976.

Franklin, Jerry F., and C.T. Dyrness, *Natural Vegetation of Oregon and Washington* (USDA Forest Service General Technical Report PNW-8). Washington, D.C.: U.S. Government Printing Office, 1973.

Hitchcock, C. Leo, and Arthur Cronquist, *Flora of the Pacific Northwest; an Illustrated Manual*. Seattle: University of Washington Press, 1973.

Horn, Elizabeth L., *Wildflowers 1: The Cascades*. Beaverton, OR: Touchstone Press, 1972.

Ingles, Lloyd G., *Mammals of the Pacific States*. Stanford: Stanford University Press, 1965.

Keator, Glenn, *Pacific Coast Berry Finder*. Berkeley: Nature Study Guild, 1978.

Larrison, Earl J., and Grace W. Patrick, William H. Baker, James A. Yaich, *Washington Wildflowers*. Seattle: Seattle Audubon Society, 1974.

Murie, Olaus J., *A Field Guide to Animal Tracks*, 2nd ed. Boston: Houghton Mifflin, 1975.

National Geographic Society, *Field Guide to the Birds of North America*. Washington, D.C.: National Geographic Society, 1983.

Niehaus, Theodore F., and Charles L. Ripper, *A Field Guide to Pacific States Wildflowers*. Boston: Houghton Mifflin, 1976.

Peterson, Roger T., *A Field Guide to Western Birds*. Boston: Houghton Mifflin, 1972.

Stebbins, Robert C., *A Field Guide to Western Reptiles and Amphibians*. Boston: Houghton Mifflin, 1966.

Sudworth, George B., *Forest Trees of the Pacific Slope*. New York: Dover, 1967 (1908 reprint with new Foreword and Table of Changes in Nomenclature).

Watts, Tom, *Pacific Coast Tree Finder*. Berkeley: Nature Study Guild, 1973.

Whitney, Stephen R., *A Field Guide to the Cascades & Olympics*. Seattle: The Mountaineers, 1983 (published simultaneously in Canada by Douglas & McIntyre, Ltd., Vancouver, B.C. under the title of *A Field Guide to the West Coast Mountains*).

Index

The italic letter-number combinations (*A1*, *B1*, etc.) refer to this book's topographic maps.

Use these next four pages for hitchhiking.

NORTH

SOUTH

EAST

WEST

THE FORSAKEN

THE SIXTH ORDER BOOK TWO

BY JARRET MADDEN

JARRET MADDEN

Cover design by Rebecacovers
Map by Jarret Madden

ISBN 978-1-9992005-1-0

Published by Jarret Madden

THE FORSAKEN

CONTENTS

MAP OF TERRENIA

CHAPTER 1

Moonlight washed over slate roofs and stone chimneys. The call of a raven split the night as wings blotted out the pale white of the moon. The bird alighted on the edge of a building; its frame outlined starkly against the half-circle in the sky behind it.

For a moment, all was silent. The air above the sleeping city was still, no wind rustled the awnings left open or creaked the wooden signs outside the taverns.

Unseen eyes watched the raven from the shadows of a house across the street. Lying flat on the slight slope of the roof, the onlooker shifted.

The raven's head snapped around, beady eyes searching for the source of the noise. The onlooker froze, staying absolutely still. For a long couple seconds, the raven stared directly at the hidden figure. Then, it turned away, deciding there was no threat.

The shadowed figure let out a long, silent breath, his muscles relaxing. He had nearly blown his cover.

The raven spread its wings and took off from the roof, gliding down to the cobblestones below.

The figure slid to the edge of the roof, moving while the raven flew so the flapping of the wings would cover any sound he made.

Two feet above the ground, the raven began to writhe, stretching and growing, feathers fading away. In seconds, the raven had transformed into a man in dark clothes. He hit the street at a run, slowing himself with quick strides.

The man made sure he was alone. He pulled a black hood over his head, hiding his face and leaned against the wall of a nearby building, disappearing in the shadows.

The one on the roof had been watching this spot for hours, relying on the word of an informant, who had told him that a courier sent from the king was coming to Forenfall. And although the watcher's informant had said nothing about the courier being a raven, this could very well be him. The watcher knew that if this person was met by another, he would have what he was looking for. No one had met the man yet, but the night was only half-spent. The watcher would have to wait.

Ten minutes turned into twenty, then thirty. The watcher on the roof slowly brought his hand up and rubbed his bleary, tired eyes. He couldn't afford to let his focus slip, but his sleep-deprived body fought him, begging for rest.

A sound disturbed the calm ambiance of the night. Footsteps. Someone was coming. The onlooker blinked hard to clear his eyes and peered down into the street.

The hooded man had noticed the sound as well. He turned his head to look, barely visible in his dark attire.

Soon, another person entered the watcher's field of view. They were also wearing a black hood, masking their identity. But the identity didn't matter. What mattered was that they had met the informant; this was the one he had been waiting for. He watched as the two on the street neared each other and whispered. Then, they exchanged slips of paper.

The watcher nodded. That was proof enough. He reached into his bag and pulled out a small vial of dull red, peering at the liquid. Once he pulled the cork, his cover would be blown. The ones on the street would know he was there and flee. But, the watcher knew he couldn't take them alone, he needed backup. And his backup was stationed on rooftops all over the city, watching for the very people that stood fifteen feet below him.

Readying himself for whatever was to happen next, the onlooker carefully got to his feet, making as little noise as possible. Then, as he crouched on the peak of the roof, he pulled the stopper from the vial and turned his face away.

The liquid began to glow and in an instant, it shot out of the bottle, illuminating the sky in a thin pillar of scarlet light.

Reaching high above the city, the pillar exploded outward into a shower of sparks that floated down like blood-red fireflies.

Below, the two meeting in secret yelled in surprise. The courier morphed back into a raven and took off into the night, leaving the other alone. The accomplice began to run back the way they came, making no effort at stealth.

The onlooker bolted after the runner, leaping over the gap between the houses. He slipped on the slate and bashed his knee, but was up in a half-second, sprinting across the roof.

The fleeing figure looked back at the watcher and sped up, cloak billowing behind them. They were fast, but the watcher was slightly faster. He gained step by step, drawing even with his quarry.

The watcher jumped across another gap, stumbling. He pulled back with a sharp inhale. He had reached the end of the street and the row of houses. In front of him was a steep drop. He cursed as the mystery figure turned right and sprinted away.

The onlooker slid to the low edge of the roof and turned around. His fingers grasped the lip of the overhang and he lowered himself down. The ground was several feet below, but he couldn't play it safe now. He dropped to the ground, absorbing the impact with his knees. Still, his left ankle twinged painfully.

Growling, he pushed off the cobbles and raced after the figure. His eyes darted around the new street, but he couldn't see his quarry. He stopped and listened, hearing boots pounding against paving stones up ahead. More than one person. They were coming toward him.

His head shot up as the cloaked person ran out of an alley back onto the main street. They saw the watcher standing there and darted the opposite direction. Moments later, another person came flying out of the alley.

The watcher smiled. Backup had arrived.

He pumped his legs, eating up the distance between him and his prey. The other person chasing glanced back and flashed a grin. Their steps synchronized as they closed the gap.

The cloaked figure suddenly skidded to a stop and veered off into another alley.

The onlooker saw a smaller person running toward them; another one of the watchers. She joined up with the other two as they entered the alley at full speed.

Ahead, a stack of crates was pulled over, crashing down in an explosion of splinters. The pursuers didn't slow. They leapt over the boxes, snapping thin, weathered wood under their feet.

Their quarry stopped again, having reached the solid wall at the end of the alley. The watcher's eyes gleamed. Their prey was trapped.

The unknown figure looked for an escape, but saw none. They let out a frustrated growl, putting their hands together in a clawed position. A deep purplish energy began to build up between their hands, throwing off dark sparks.

The watcher pulled up, halting his allies. He didn't know what was coming but he knew it wouldn't be good. He shouted a warning. The cloaked figure let out a bloodcurdling yell and released the magic.

The man beside the watcher barked a short word and twisted his hand. A translucent wall of energy encircled the three pursuers as the dark magic swept over them. It swirled and stabbed at the shield, but couldn't break through.

The watchers breathed heavily as the malevolent magic expended itself and faded away. Beyond was only an empty alley.

The man beside the watcher released his magic and the air cleared. He looked at the watcher. "He got away."

Letting out a long, frustrated sigh, Cody stared up at the moon and said, "I know, Guy, I know."

~~~

Levi hurried down the stairs of the grand entrance, taking them two at a time. He bumped into one of the third-years, Marshall. Muttering a rushed apology, he jumped down the last of the stairs and sidestepped a couple of first-years before racing to the front doors and slipping outside. A nod of greeting was exchanged with Osiris from yellow camp as the third-year entered the main building.

A cool breeze ruffled Levi's hair and he shivered. The winds of winter were on their way, pushing away the last days of autumn, which were clinging on with a faltering grip.

Levi jogged to the left side of the building, ducking around the corner to where Cody and Guy were waiting. Myron was off walking toward the south tower, much too far to overhear anything. No students were coming from the white or yellow camps. They were alone.

"How'd it go?" Levi asked, desperate to hear everything.

"Not great," Cody admitted. The bags under his eyes betrayed how tired he was. "We didn't catch them."

"Got damn close, though," Guy said. "Had them trapped in an alley. Then they did some crazy magic."

Cody ran a hand through his light brown hair. "We would have been goners, but Guy threw up a shield in time, saved us and Ember."

Guy shifted his stance. "Good thing Balak taught me that spell last week."

Cody nodded.

Levi made a face, disappointed. "So, no leads on who it is?"

"Nope," Cody said. "They were cloaked and hooded. I'm not even sure if it's a guy or a girl."

Levi punched his palm. "That was the perfect opportunity!"

"We know," Guy said. "We're not thrilled we botched it."

Levi let his head flop backward. "Ugh. I hate that we still haven't found this spy! It's been over a year!"

Cody lightly kicked his shin. "Hey, not so loud. Besides, we'll get another chance sometime. Now, you'd better get back to class. We don't want you looking suspicious."

Levi sighed, but he knew Cody was right. "Yeah. Thanks for trying."

The two older guys dipped their heads as Levi raced back inside the main school building. He slowed once he neared the Magic classroom. He didn't even bother trying to sneak in, he was only a minute or two late.

Everyone glanced his way as he slipped inside and he felt a flash of warmth in his cheeks, before pushing his embarrassment away. He walked over to where Miri and Kana were standing.

Miri moved her thin fingers in her silent language that Levi had learned to interpret with ease. "Good news?"

He shook his head and Miri's brows drew together.

"Now that we're all here, we can begin."

Levi shook himself and faced the front of the class where the Magic instructor stood.

His name was Karl Linae. He was a fair-skinned man of average build, blond, well-built and rather handsome. His nose was a bit hooked and his green eyes shone with intelligence. His dress was simple: dark pants and boots, and a beige shirt secured by a cummerbund. On his right arm, he wore a leather bracer inscribed with several runes.

"Now, today, we are learning about more advanced summoning. You Arcanes learned the basics in your first year, but there is much more to learn."

To Levi's left, Bram leaned over to Dante and muttered, "This is gonna be boring."

"Mr. Wick, must I say this again?" Linae asked dryly. "Even though most of you are not Arcanes and will never be able to do what I am about to explain, it is still important that you learn it. Once you become knights of the realm, you will be expected to keep it safe. And if you come across someone skilled in an order of magic that you haven't learned about, how are you going to stop them?"

"I know, sir," Bram said, sounding slightly apologetic. "I know it's important. But that doesn't mean it won't be boring."

A small smirk crossed Linae's face and he shook his head. Levi noticed a cut on his chin. Probably an accident in one of the other classes. He remembered a few months ago when one of his classmates, Coraline, had accidentally set Linae's hair on fire. He had burns on his face for weeks.

"Now!" Linae lifted a finger. "Who can tell me the principles of summoning?"

Someone raised a tentative hand. Christian.

"Yes?" Linae asked.

Christian cleared his throat, brow wrinkled. "Um, you have to picture the item exactly."

Linae pointed at him. "Exactly! Any more?"

"No, that's the only one I remember," Christian said.

Duncan raised his hand. "You also have to feel the item. The texture and weight. And you also need to open a channel through the magical plane, keeping it open until the item has been fully summoned."

14

"Correct," Linae said. "Anything else?"

"You need to keep your eyes closed while doing it," Kana said.

Linae nodded. "Yes. Most people do simply because it helps them focus and control their magic, but in the instance of summoning, it is actually vital. As you are opening a channel into the magical plane, you must defend yourself from stray magic. Most times when summoning, the only stray magic that will attempt to jump realms is very weak and its only way in is through your eyes, because..."

"The eyes are conduits for magic," the whole class chorused, having heard the phrase many times.

The instructor nodded. "Right. Now, what I want to discuss today, is the other types of stray magic. They will only come to you when you are summoning something larger than this." He pointed to where Balak stood holding a round shield. It was slightly smaller than the one Cody used, Levi noticed.

Linae took the shield from the assistant instructor. "This is the exact size something has to be before the stray magic comes. No one is quite sure why."

Duncan held up his hand. "What exactly is stray magic?"

Linae handed the shield back to Balak. "Now, that is a subject of much debate among the scholars. What we do know of it is that the stray magic does not belong to any of the five orders. It cannot be controlled by anyone. It can, however, be released into the world by a Chaotic. They cannot control it, only set it loose. There is not much else we know of it."

Kindrelle raised her hand. "Can the stray magic affect us in the other orders?"

It was Balak who answered. "Yes. Spellcasters can attract it if they do not understand the incantations or rituals they are performing. That is why we teach the basic principles and work our way up."

"Indeed," Linae said. "If a first-year student attempted to, say, cast the mind control spell, most likely they would be attacked by the stray magic, on top of possibly burning up their energy stores permanently. It can happen to all the orders, but it is most common in the Second and Fifth Orders."

"What does the wild magic do?" Kinzo asked. "Will it kill you?"

"In large doses, yes," Linae said. "Smaller amounts affect people in various ways. The most common side effects are lacerations, blindness and insanity."

Levi glanced at Kana. She was paying close attention, but her jaw was clenched. She was unnerved. And she wasn't the only one.

Linae noticed the nervous looks as well. "Fear not. There are ways to defend yourself against stray magic, such as keeping your eyes closed while summoning." He motioned to Balak.

The big man nodded and stepped forward. He fished under his collar and pulled out a bronze necklace on a chain. "This is a simple protective charm. Now, obviously only Spellcasters can create them, but anyone can use it. It casts a shield spell directly against your body, almost like a second skin and it will only activate when one is using magic. Now, it won't protect against all stray magic, but it helps." He hid away his necklace and stepped back.

Linae folded his hands together. "Now, not everyone has access to such defences. But there is a method that everyone can do. You see, when you are channelling your magic, it comes from inside you, but it can also come from beyond; the magical plane, which we discussed a few weeks ago. Now, when dealing with simple, easy magic, the doorway between our plane and the magical one, if opened, is very small and nothing harmful can cross over. It's once you start dealing with more powerful energies that you need to be careful, especially Arcanes. Now the way to defend yourself is to basically push some of your own magic, your own energy, back through the doorway. It will act as a barrier against the stray magic."

Holly lifted her arm. "If it makes a barrier, how can the summoning or other stuff work? Won't that be blocked too?"

"Good question," Linae said. "Since the energy you are pulling from the magical plane is the same energy that you carry inside you, the magic of your particular order, the barrier won't stop it. But it will stop the magic of any other order, as well as the stray energy."

"Man, this is confusing," Niles said.

His buddy, Christian, nodded. "Yeah, I'm so lost."

Levi had to admit that he wasn't sure he understood either.

"Don't worry," Linae said. "This is a tricky subject, but it is one that you need to learn before we can progress much further with your magic. Especially with advanced summoning for the Arcanes and complex spells for the Spellcasters. We will be spending the next several classes making sure you all learn this."

"Hey! Look!" Romeo called from his spot by the window. "The fourth-years are back!"

Everyone rushed to the window, trying to get a glimpse of the returning adventurers, the lesson completely forgotten. Linae sighed, but made no move to stop them.

"Let's go greet them!" someone called. That was received with an approving cheer and everyone rushed to exit the door. Levi was bumped and jostled as everyone hustled down the hallway. He ended up next to Evander.

"They're a couple of days early," Evander stated.

"I guess they are," Levi said. "Must have had some good luck."

The whole class spilled out of the building onto the grass outside. Walking up the path towards them was a group of fifteen or so people. At the head of the column was a tall man in a scarlet cape; Zoan Konalt, the instructor in charge of the fourth-year missions.

People from both groups began waving as they recognized their friends. Cries of welcome echoed throughout the academy. Soon, the first and third-year classes joined Levi's second-years outside as a reception for the returnees.

The two groups met, and Levi was immediately lost in the commotion. He waved and smiled at people he hadn't seen for months. They looked tired and worn, but they all had broad smiles on their faces.

Through the crowd, Levi caught a glimpse of a familiar face. He shouldered his way through the throng, ending up next to his friend. "Kaito! Hi!"

Kaito turned and nodded to Levi, a slight grin on his face. "Hello, Levi. It has been some time since we shared each other's company."

"Yeah, no kidding," Levi said. "We lost blue camp's voice of reason for three months. Things kinda got out of hand."

Kaito smiled knowingly.

"How was the trip?" Levi asked, excited to hear about it.

"It was very informative."

"That's good, I guess," Levi said.

"Good? Ha! Informative is boring!" Levi and Kaito turned to see Coral marching toward them, her classmates at her back. "What about the adventure? The fights! The chases! The barely escaping with your life! What about those?"

Kaito shrugged. "There wasn't a high element of danger."

"Oh, pfft, that's stupid," Coral said. "What kind of establishment are we running that doesn't put kids in mortal danger?"

"A responsible one," Ember said, cutting in.

"Responsible is stupid." Coral crossed her arms.

Cody and Guy walked up to Kaito. Cody slapped his back and Guy gave him a shot to the shoulder. "Welcome back."

Naomi came bursting through the crowd and wrapped Kaito in a large hug, surprising everyone. She let go and smiled. "Alright! The gang's all back together!"

"So it is," Ember said. "Good to have you back, Kaito."

"Good to be back," Kaito responded.

"Good timing, too," Guy said. "We were right in the middle of a really boring Politics class."

"I was almost asleep," Cody said, glancing at Levi. He still looked tired.

"I fall asleep in every one of those classes," Coral said proudly.

"Coral!" Ember scolded. "Those classes are an important part of our training! We need to pay close attention in them. Although, I will admit that after last night, my eyes were drooping."

"What happened last night?" Kaito asked.

"The you-know-what," Guy said. "We'll fill you in later."

Kaito nodded, understanding the secrecy.

"So, Kaito," Levi asked, trying to steer the conversation back to non-sensitive topics. "What was the actual mission?"

Kaito unslung his pack from over his shoulder and set it down. "Well, you see, there were actually multiple assignments. The first one I helped with was a simple search and rescue for a young girl who had become lost in the woods up north."

"Did you find her?" Naomi asked, concerned.

"Of course," Kaito assured her. "She was not far from her house. She had just gotten turned around."

"That's a relief," Naomi said.

"What else did you do?" Cody asked.

18

Kaito leaned on his spear. "Next, I and several others helped Konalt drive off a bear that had wandered into a nearby village."

"Did you fight it?" Coral asked.

"No. We simply waved our arms and made lots of noise to scare it off."

"You made lots of noise?" Guy's eyes widened. "I don't believe it."

Kaito rolled his eyes. "I can be loud, if the situation calls for it."

Guy crossed his arms. "Well, what about that time when we were trying to corral the horses after they escaped?"

"You mean after you set them loose?" Ember reminded him.

"Yeah, that," Guy grinned.

Kaito smiled. "I've learned that when Coral is around, she is more than loud enough for everyone."

"That is true," Coral said.

"So, after the bear, what happened next?" Levi wondered.

Kaito wove a tale of many deeds he and the other fourth-years had accomplished in their time out in the real world. The incidents ranged from helping build a schoolhouse to defeating a band of roving bandits that had been terrorizing a few towns.

After Kaito finished speaking, Ember spoke up before any more questions could be asked. "Alright, people. Kaito's had a long day and we should let him rest."

"But I want to-" Coral began, only to be cut off by Ember's harsh shush.

"No more pestering," she said firmly. Kaito looked at her gratefully.

Levi glanced around as Kaito picked up his bag and moved away. The crowd had diminished significantly. There were only a handful of people still talking. Most of the fourth years had already retired to their camp houses.

Kana caught Levi's eye and motioned for him to come over. He did so, dodging around Aster and Adelle, the twins. They glared at him and he glared back. They had sort of an ongoing feud ever since Levi had given Aster a black eye during a match.

"What's up?" Levi asked Kana. She was wearing brown pants and a black shirt along with the silver jacket she had won from a travelling salesman in a game of sailor's dice.

"I wanted to ask how Kaito was," she said.

"Why didn't you ask him yourself?" Levi asked.

19

Kana shifted her weight from one foot to the other. "I don't know him all that well and besides, I don't really want to be near Guy."

"Ah, right," Levi snickered. A week ago, Guy had asked Kana on a date and she had refused. Ever since, Guy kept harassing her by asking her out repeatedly. Most people, Levi included, thought it was hilarious, but Kana was annoyed by it and tried to avoid Guy at all costs.

"Kaito's fine," Levi said. "Still the same old guy. He does have a new scar on his leg from almost falling off a mountain."

Kana raised an eyebrow. "Exciting." She shook a stray strand of hair out of her face. She had let it grow out into long black waves, which she usually tied back in a ponytail. Today was no different.

"What about your friends?" Levi asked. "How are they?"

"They're good, although 'friends' is a loose term. I don't exactly have many of those." It was true. Kana tended to stay by herself, unless she was hanging out with Miri, Evander, Kinzo or Levi. The only other friend she had was Holly.

"Maybe you should try to make more," Levi suggested.

"I don't think so," Kana said. "I'm not sure I'm happy with the current group."

"Hey, now," Levi said.

Kana laughed. Suddenly, her eyes widened. "Quick! Pretend you're talking to me!"

"I am," Levi said with confusion. "What's wrong?"

Kana clenched her teeth. "Guy's looking this way."

Levi peeked over his shoulder. "I'm sure it was just a glance. He won't come over... oh, wait, here he comes."

"Hey there, Kana," Guy said with a charm that would have made most girls swoon. "How's it going?"

"It's going great," Kana said, a fake smile plastered on her face. "Just great."

Levi couldn't help but giggle. Kana shot him a menacing glare.

Guy flashed his charming smile. "So, I was thinking, maybe you and me could, you know, hang out. What do you think, gorgeous?"

"You know, I'm pretty busy," Kana said, feigning remorse. "I've just got a lot of work. Maybe another time."

"Sure thing, lovely. I'm always free for you." Guy turned to leave, but not before winking at Kana.

As soon as he was gone, Kana let out a massive sigh. "What am I gonna do?"

With a goofy smile, Levi replied, "Maybe you should accept."

"Are you serious?"

"Yeah. What's wrong with him?"

Kana groaned. "I don't know... He's just so, so... so *something*."

"Ah, yes. That," Levi said. "Also, there's the fact that you've fallen for someone else. Someone whose name starts with an E."

"Oh, shut up," Kana said, turning away with arms crossed.

Levi snickered.

Desperate to change the subject, Kana spoke up. "Do you think they'll cancel the rest of the classes?"

"Probably," Levi said. "Nobody will show up, at any rate."

"So, what are we going to do?" Kana asked.

Levi shrugged.

"Do you want to spar?"

"We did just have combat class a little while ago, you know," he said. He rubbed his wrist where a staff had whacked him.

"I know." Kana looked disappointed.

"Ah, what the heck. Let's do it."

Kana glanced up, her features brightening. "Great!"

The two left together for the training grounds behind the main academy building. It was a simple yard enclosed by a fence near which were racks of weapons, covered by a roof to protect them from the elements. The grass had been worn down to bare dirt from the constant beating it received from countless footfalls. Whenever it rained, the whole yard was transformed into a colossal mud pit that made fighting near impossible.

When they arrived at their destination, they were surprised to see a pair of students sparring with thin rapiers. Apparently, Kana hadn't been the only one with the idea.

"Corvin and Vonn," Kana said, recognizing the duo. Both were from red camp and they weren't the friendliest. In fact, they had well-known reputations for being bullies.

"Oh, great," Levi groaned. "This isn't going to end well." He placed a hand on the hilt of his sabre. Ever since the incident with Rorien Stern last year, all students went around armed, as to not be defenceless. It was fine for those who fought with swords or knives, but it was a pain for those who used heavy, two-handed weapons, such as an axe or a mattock.

As they approached, Levi saw a squirrel sitting high up on the wooden wall behind the duelling field. It had a distinct black and white pattern on its fur. Levi smiled. Paco. Levi often saw him around, keeping his word to Levi's mom and watching over Levi.

Paco flicked his tail and scampered along the top of the fence, disappearing from view.

Corvin and Vonn continued to duel until Kana and Levi were within twenty feet of them. They pulled apart and faced the newcomers.

"What do you think you're doing?" Corvin asked, putting a hand on his hip.

"We're coming to spar," Levi replied, keeping his voice neutral. He wanted to avoid a confrontation if that was at all possible.

"Well, I'm afraid you can't do that," Vonn said, crossing his arms.

"And why not?" Kana asked. The note of defiance and the tilt of her head suggested that she was not pleased.

"Because we're sparring right now," Vonn said. "You'll just have to wait your turn."

"Ok, as if," Kana scoffed. "This place is big enough for twenty people to duel at once. It can certainly handle four."

"I'm afraid that you don't understand," Corvin said in a mocking tone. "We are here, and that means you can't be. So begone."

"No," Kana said firmly.

"No?" Vonn looked at Corvin. "Did she just say no?"

"I do believe she did," Corvin replied.

Levi tried to intervene. "Look, guys. There's more than enough room for all of us. Let's just take a second to calm down and then we can go to opposite ends of the yard to spar."

The two guys looked at each other and by silent agreement, brandished their weapons. "If you want to spar, you'll have to get by us first," Corvin said.

"You've got to be kidding," Levi groaned. "Kana, we can just go... Oh. You're already fighting." She had leapt ahead and was taking them on, two on one.

"Are you gonna help me?" she called.

Levi sighed deeply, but he drew his sabre. "I knew this wasn't going to end well." He ran ahead and Vonn spun away from Kana to face him. Vonn swung his rapier in a flashing pattern to try to intimidate Levi. To be honest, Levi was intimidated. Vonn was one of the best fighters at the academy, able to hold his own against even Griswold, for a few moments. And while Levi had improved over the last year, he still wasn't on Vonn's level.

Swords clanged and clashed as Levi tried desperately to fend off Vonn's attacks. He hadn't managed a single offensive strike yet, which was a bad sign.

Vonn swiped at Levi's head. He ducked under the blade, but then immediately had to roll to the side to avoid a downward blow. His eyes bulged. *How can he possibly move so fast?*

Levi scrambled back and pushed himself to his feet, slicing his palm on a rock in the process. A thin line of crimson appeared, making him hiss in pain.

Looking to his left, he saw Kana and Corvin duelling. She was doing a much better job than Levi, managing to back Corvin up a few paces before Levi's attention was brought back to his immediate vicinity. He brought his sabre up and batted away three quick blows before jumping back a pace or two.

"What's the matter, Levi?" Vonn taunted. "A little outclassed, are we?"

Levi gave him a fake smile. "Oh, shut up."

Vonn laughed. "Careful, you might scar me for life with those insults."

Levi stuck out his tongue, enjoying the immature gesture. His brain spun, trying to come up with some way to end the fight that didn't involve him spending the night in the infirmary.

Vonn lunged forward, intending to skewer him. Instead of deflecting the blade to the side as he normally would have, Levi maneuvered his body so that Vonn's blade was in between his left arm and his torso. He quickly pulled his arm in tight, pinning Vonn's rapier. Then, with the sabre in his right hand, he smacked Vonn on the wrist, turning the blade so as not to cut him. Vonn cursed and let go of the rapier.

Levi released Vonn's sword and caught it with his free hand before it hit the ground. He levelled both swords at Vonn. "I win."

Vonn's eyes hardened and he growled. "You stupid little... I'm gonna kill you!" He took a step toward Levi and suddenly pitched forward and fell on his face. Behind him stood Kana, holding her sword high, having clubbed Vonn over the head.

"You're welcome."

Levi spread his hands. "I had two swords. He had none. I think I would have been fine." Kana simply sheathed her sabre and shrugged.

Levi leaned to his left to see Corvin lying on his back, spread-eagle. He scratched his head. "So, you still wanna spar?"

"You know, I think I'm good," Kana said. "I had fun and plus, I got to club a couple of idiots over the head."

"Yeah, you wouldn't have done that to me, right?" Levi said. Kana smirked mysteriously. "Right?"

"You never know," Kana said. "I might try it sometime."

"Please don't," Levi pleaded.

Kana laughed. "C'mon. Let's go find the others."

CHAPTER 2

Fingers drummed against the beautifully carved acacia table. A golden ring depicting a winged horse adorned the right index finger of the man at the front of the room. He waited patiently for the door at the end of the chamber to open and admit his messenger.

He was not alone in the room. High-backed chairs surrounded the table, four of them occupied.

"Excuse me, sire," the man to his left said. "Perhaps he has been beset by our enemies."

Turning to look at the tall, thin man, Farren Mistral, King of Terrenia, rumbled, "No, Dravin. He is coming."

Moments later, the door swung open and two guards in gold and red armour admitted a man in a black cloak. As the door was closed behind him, the courier dropped to a knee, bowing deeply.

"Stand and report," Farren ordered.

The man straightened. "Yes, sire." He reached under his cloak and produced a scrap of parchment, crumpled from the journey. "I received this from our contact inside Blackthrush Academy."

The woman at the end of the table took the parchment. She handed it to the king.

Farren nodded to the woman who had been his loyal servant for years. His eyes moved back and forth as he read the few lines scrawled on the paper. Finished, he looked back to the messenger. "Have you anything else to report?"

25

The man inclined his head. "Yes. There was someone there, waiting for us as we met. I do not know who. We both ran; I was not followed. I do not expect that our contact was apprehended, but I do know that someone is aware of the presence of the contact, even if they do not know who it is."

Farren carefully folded the parchment and set it on the table. "That is unfortunate, but we were not blind to this possibility. Our contact is well-trained and knows how to remain unseen. I have the utmost faith that they will remain unknown and provide proof that Aldus Calanol is plotting against us."

The man sitting beside Dravin, a shorter, bearded fellow spoke up. "Why wait for proof, your majesty? We certainly have the strength to take the Academy."

Farren folded his hands together. "Yes, Minos, we do. But, without proof, there is always the chance that we may be wrong. There may not be any traitors at Blackthrush, no matter how much we may think there are. And if I descend upon the Academy with my army and burn it to the ground without proof, it will send a message to the people of my realm. One that I do not want sent."

To Farren's right, a huge, broad man in black armour nodded. "The citizens have much love for the Academy and Aldus Calanol is respected by many. We need concrete evidence."

"Malroth is right," the woman said. "If we destroy it, it could drive more to join the Giala. We must wait and hope our contact proves they deserve the faith we put in them."

"Excellently put, Avelyn," Farren said. "I sense that someday soon, Blackthrush will fall. But not yet. For now, we must wait."

~ ~ ~

"Check," Evander said.

Levi groaned. He studied the checkered board in front of him and the pieces scattered about it. He and Evander were playing chess and Levi was losing. He counted the captured pieces on both sides; Evander had captured ten, whereas Levi had only managed to take two, both pawns.

"You're in trouble," Kana said to Levi. She and Miri were sitting across from each other, watching the game.

"Yeah, I noticed, thanks," Levi said. He made up his mind and moved his only surviving bishop three spaces up the board, putting one of Evander's rooks in danger.

Evander looked surprised. "That's your move?"

"Yes. Why? Is that bad?"

"Not for me," Evander laughed, "But for you..." He took his queen and slid her all the way to Levi's bishop, capturing it. "Checkmate."

Levi stared at the board for a long moment. Then, he slumped down and smacked his head on the board, knocking over several pieces. The girls couldn't help but giggle.

Evander sat back in his chair and crossed his hands behind his head. "I know you're just learning, but you are terrible."

"Really terrible," Kinzo said, leaning on the wall.

His face still on the board, Levi mumbled, "I know."

Kinzo picked at his teeth. "I mean you're actually good at strategy. That's literally all this game is. How can you be bad at it?"

Without lifting his head, Levi spread his hands helplessly.

"Ah, don't mind him," Kana said. "You'll get the hang of it."

"In a couple years, maybe," Evander said.

Levi lifted his head to see the taller guy grinning down at him. Levi made a face.

"What should we play now?" Miri asked, signing with her hands what she couldn't communicate with her voice.

"Don't know," Kana said. "Let's see what we've got here." She got up and went over to the shelf that was stocked with all sorts of games.

They were in a room in the southern tower of the academy, one that was used by students to relax and have fun. There was one in each of the four towers.

Kana picked up a small box from off the shelf. It was a simple pine box, but on the lid, there was a strange symbol of intersecting circles. "Should we play this?"

"Uh uh, I don't like that one."

Kana rolled her eyes. "Kinzo, you don't like any of these games."

Kinzo held up a finger. "Um, not true. I like some games."

"Like what?"

Miri propped her head up with an arm as the two argued. She was both amused and annoyed that they were bickering. Again.

Evander began placing the black and white chess pieces back in the box. Levi helped him, grabbing a handful of pawns, bishops and rooks. One slipped from his fingers and bounced across the floor, coming to a stop near the door. Grunting, Levi stood to retrieve it. As he bent down, the door opened and slammed into his forehead, knocking him flat.

"Oh, Levi, I'm sorry! What are you doing right behind the door?"

Looking up with a hand on his head, Levi saw Kavik looking down at him. Behind him, he could hear Evander and Kinzo laughing and the girls trying to get them to stop.

"Getting hit apparently," he grumbled.

Kavik had the grace to look sheepish. "Sorry. Um, Aldus wants to see you in his office."

Levi stood. "Aldus? What for?"

"Didn't say."

Levi exchanged glances with the others. He had no idea why Aldus would want to see him. Maybe something was up, something with the king and the Giala. Hopefully, nothing was wrong. "Hmm. Ok. I'll see you later." They all waved goodbye as he exited the room with Kavik.

They walked down the spiral staircase that rose the height of the tower, Kavik in front. Upon reaching the bottom, they opened the door and walked out onto the Academy grounds.

"So, Kavik," Levi said. "What have you been up to today, since, you know, no classes?"

"Bit of everything. I spent a while trying to catch Taro after he filled my boots with ants."

Levi laughed. "He actually did it? He's been collecting ants for days, ever since you dyed his shirt pink."

Kavik frowned, but his eyes betrayed his good humour. "Yeah, well now it's war. I just made a deal with Dante and Bram to help me get back at him."

"Oh boy, he's in for it now," Levi said. "Those two are masters."

Kavik grinned. "I know. Last week they nailed Corvin to the ceiling while he was asleep. No idea how."

Levi shook his head. Pranks ran rampant around Blackthrush. Even the instructors weren't safe. A month or so ago, Miss Nordstrom had been given a box that screamed each time she let go of it. It took her and Linae three hours to get rid of it.

Kavik pointed at Levi as they arrived at the main building. "Hey, there's a bunch of us going to play kicks, if you want to come. After you're done with Aldus, of course." Kicks was a popular game in which players used their feet to kick a ball into the opposing team's net.

"Yeah, I think I might do that," Levi said.

"Sweet," Kavik said. "See you then." Kavik peeled away from Levi, heading for the north side of the Academy.

Levi threw open one of the large double doors and entered the foyer. No matter how many times Levi went through there, it still brought a smile to his face. There was just something about the décor, the lighting, the statue of the Academy's founding father, Namor Linae, and the two staircases that joined in a balcony overlooking the entrance that made it so majestic.

Levi took the right staircase, hopping the steps two at a time. He reached the top and moved to the side as Taro came the other way. The redhead was carrying a leather bag. It seemed to be moving. Levi smirked and nodded as Taro passed by.

He strolled down the hallway, passing by a few other people who were wandering around, until he reached the end and Aldus' study.

Knuckles rapped lightly on the door. "Hey, Aldus, it's me, Levi. I heard you wanted to see me."

There was some shuffling and creaking, the sound of someone getting out of one of the comfy chairs that took up the centre of Aldus' study. A few moments later, the headmaster opened the door. "Ah, yes, come in, Levi, come in."

Levi smiled at the kindly face of the older man, the lower half of which was lost in the greying strands of his pointed beard. His blue eyes sparkled with good humour, as they always did.

Aldus stepped aside to let Levi in the room. It was as eye-catching as ever, with the collage of art on the domed ceiling, the landscape portraits interspersed between the pillars that held up the second level and the row of bookshelves up on said level.

Aldus closed the door behind him. "There's tea on the table."

"I'm good, but thanks," Levi said. "I never really liked tea and especially since the witch tried to poison me."

Aldus smiled. "But of course."

Levi looked expectantly at the headmaster. "So, what's up? Why did you ask for me? Is something up with the," he lowered his voice. "The Giala and stuff?"

"No, not presently," Aldus said. "At least, nothing that immediately concerns you. And you are no doubt well aware of the operation from last night, so there's nothing new you need to know. No, the reason I asked for you is that there is someone here who I imagine you would like to see."

"Who? Is it Marcus?" Levi asked. Levi's friend and protector occasionally stopped by the Academy to check in on Levi, whenever Giala business had him up on the island.

Aldus smirked. "No, it's not Marcus. But it is someone you are very familiar with."

"Who? Is it..."

"It's me."

Levi spun around at the sound of a voice he hadn't heard in ages. "Dad!"

Ramsey Sheppard stood in the doorway and laughed as he spread his arms. Levi jumped up and ran into the embrace. Moisture prickled his eyes. The familiar scent of woodsmoke and pine needles washed over him.

Ramsey pulled away after a time and held Levi at arms' length. "My goodness. You've grown. Why, you're almost a man now!"

Levi couldn't believe it. He grasped his father's forearm. "I can't believe you're here!"

Ramsey laughed again, but there was a slight huskiness to it. "It's true, Levi. I really am here."

"This is amazing," Levi said. "Why are you here?"

Ramsey finally released his son. "Well, I was delivering a message to a lord in Saken. All the nobles take a few days to conjure up a reply, so I thought I'd come on over for a quick visit."

"How long will you be here for?" Levi asked.

"Just until noon tomorrow," Ramsey said

Levi's face fell for a second, but it brightened a moment later. "At least you're here for a day. I'm so glad to see you."

"And I, you," Ramsey said. He went over to the chairs, motioning for Levi to join him. "So, tell me, what's happened to you? What sort of adventures have befallen you?"

Levi smiled. "Plenty." His mind flashed back to the year prior and his journey to Blackthrush.

"I'd love to hear about them," Ramsey said. He pointed to the tea set on the table and looked to Aldus for permission. Aldus nodded and Ramsey poured himself a cup.

"Where to even begin?" Levi wondered.

"Preferably at the beginning," Ramsey smirked. "Right after you left Stagrun. Your mother told me what happened before that."

Levi chuckled. "Alright. I'll start with meeting Marcus..." He launched into his grand tale of chases and escapes, fights and flights, near-death experiences and everything else in between. Ramsey made the odd comment or asked the odd question, but for the most part, he just listened.

When Levi had finished, Ramsey sat back in his chair and folded his hands behind his head. A smile tugged at the corner of his mouth. "So, basically, you managed to get on the bad side of an ex-Watch member, a legendary witch, the most dangerous bounty hunters in the realm, one of the king's lackeys and a pair of bloodsucking monsters."

"That about sums it up, yeah," Levi said, a wry smile on his face.

"You don't do things halfway, do you?" Ramsey laughed.

"No, I don't," Levi said. "What about you and mom? How are things back home?"

Ramsey's smile slipped a fraction. "I wish I could say it was going well, but that would be a lie. To be perfectly honest, the king has cracked down hard on the Giala in Stagrun, probably because he knew the Elder Gem had been there. Many members have been arrested and executed. Akira's on the run."

"Oh no! That's terrible!" Levi said.

"It's not ideal, that's for sure, but, at least for now, the king's men are only arresting those they can prove are part of the Giala. Those of us left have learned to be even more careful."

"So, you and mom are safe?"

Ramsey nodded. "Relatively."

"Keep it that way,"

Ramsey smirked. "We'll try." He took a sip of tea.

While they had been talking, Aldus had slipped away to his desk and had written a note which he put in an envelope and sealed. He came down and held it out to Ramsey. "Since you're here, could you do me a favour and deliver this to Jadon Liack in Saken?"

"Certainly," Ramsey said, taking the letter from Aldus. "I take it this is sensitive?"

"It is," Aldus said. "I did write it in code, but it would not do if it were to fall into the wrong hands."

"I will guard it as best I can," Ramsey vowed.

"That's all I ever expect," Aldus said.

"How often do you handle secret Giala messages?" Levi asked. He had never asked before because he had had no idea his father belonged to the Giala until after everything had kicked off.

"Quite regularly," Ramsey said. "Although I only ever deliver them if I have a non-secretive letter or two to deliver along with them, in case I ever get stopped."

"That's neat," Levi said. "Your job must make you an important member of the Giala."

"In some ways, yes," Ramsey said. "I provide communication for the Giala, which is crucial, but me, as an individual, I'm not a very high priority. I don't know what the plans and ideas are, I just get them to whoever needs to see them."

"So, your job is important, then," Levi surmised.

"Exactly. And besides, no one is more important to the Giala than you."

Levi rolled his eyes. "Yeah, yeah, I know. Me and the Elder Gem, the dynamic duo. I'm only reminded of that fact all the time by my friends."

"I do hope they don't say such things when others are around," Aldus said.

"No, they only do it when it's just us," Levi assured him. "They may be dumb, but they're not that dumb."

"Good. But perhaps I should talk to them again," Aldus said. "We can never be too careful."

"I guess not," Levi said.

A silence ensued.

Ramsey slapped his knees. "Well, Levi, are you going to show me around?"

"Oh, yeah! I can totally do that," Levi said. He got up quickly, but then looked at Aldus. "You didn't need to talk to me about anything else, did you?"

"No," Aldus waved him away. "Go and spend time with your father."

Ramsey stood and followed his son out of the study. Levi gave him a quick tour of all the classrooms, telling him who taught what.

"What's your favourite class?" Ramsey asked.

Levi rubbed his chin. "Hmm. I'd have to say Strategy and Tactics. That one is always fun. Plus, it helps that I'm decent at it."

"Are you now?" Ramsey was impressed.

Levi smiled, a bit embarrassed. "Yeah. Silverton says I have a natural eye for strategy. It irks Kinzo because he's terrible at it."

"Kinzo. That's one of your friends, right?"

"That's right," Levi said. "The grumpy, sarcastic one."

"Am I gonna meet him?"

"Of course," Levi said. "I'll introduce you to all my friends."

"Let's do that, then," Ramsey said.

"Sure thing."

Levi led his father out of the main building and into the Academy grounds. He pointed out the blue camp house. "That's where I live."

"Who do you live with?" Ramsey asked.

"A bunch of people. Everyone here is separated into one of six camps. So, a sixth of them live with me."

"That include girls?" Ramsey asked with a smirk.

"Yeah." Levi felt his face grow warm. "Oh, it's nothing like that!"

Ramsey tossed his head back and laughed.

They walked around back to the duelling yard. There was a large crowd sitting on the lawn. About twenty people were in the middle of a game of kicks.

"Been a while since I've seen this played," Ramsey remarked.

They stood back for a minute or two, watching the game. Eventually, Naomi noticed them and ambled over.

"Hey, Levi." She had a quizzical expression on her face. "Who's this?"

"Naomi," Levi said. "I want you to meet my father, Ramsey Sheppard."

Naomi's eyes widened. "Whoa! Mr. Sheppard! A pleasure to meet you!" She held out a hand.

Ramsey smiled at her and shook it. "Hello, Naomi."

"Wow," she said. "I didn't think you'd be so tall!" She had to crane her neck to look Ramsey in the eye.

Ramsey laughed. "I tend to get that reaction a lot. It's a shame I didn't pass any of it on to Levi."

"Hey now!" It was true. Whereas Levi was of average height for his age, Ramsey was nearly a foot taller than him.

"What brings you to the Academy, Mr. Sheppard?" Naomi asked.

"Please, call me Ramsey. I'm here because I'm a courier and I had a letter to deliver to Saken. So, I came up here while waiting for the reply."

"Oh, cool," Naomi said. "I'm glad I got to meet you."

"The pleasure's all mine," Ramsey said. "Levi's told me about you. The others as well. You all need to be thanked for saving my son."

Naomi blushed. "Well, Mr., uh, Ramsey, I didn't actually do all that much."

"But you did help," Ramsey said. "And that's all that I care about."

"Oh, well thanks. And you're welcome, too."

Just then, Cody and Guy walked over.

"Hello. Who are you?" Guy asked.

"I'm Levi's dad."

Both boys were surprised, but they composed themselves quickly.

"Pleased to meet you," Cody said. Guy repeated the words.

"And I, you," Ramsey replied. "I want to thank the both of you for saving Levi.

Cody shot Levi a look saying, *Does he know?*

"'Course he knows," Levi said. "He knew before I did."

Cody bit his lip. "Oh. Well, in that case, you're welcome."

"I suppose you'll want to thank the rest of them?" Guy asked. Ramsey nodded. Guy sighed. "Alright. I'll go get them." He jogged away.

"Let me guess," Ramsey said, pointing at Cody. "You're Cody."

"Yeah. How'd you know?"

"Levi described all of you." He looked at his son. "The other one was Guy, right?"

"Correct."

They made small talk until Guy returned with all the others. Ramsey introduced himself and again offered his gratitude to them all.

"No need to thank us," Kana said. "We'd do it again in a heartbeat."

"We would?" Kinzo asked. Kana punched him. "I mean, we would, yes."

Ramsey laughed. "That's a relief. I imagine you will all need to do so many more times before the world is set aright."

"Yay," Evander said, prompting a ripple of laughter.

Ramsey's face turned serious. "If any of you ever need anything, don't hesitate to ask. If it is within my power, I'll help."

Everyone thanked him for his generosity. "You're too kind," Ember said.

"Anything for Levi's friends," Ramsey said. He smiled. "Now, who's ready for a game of kicks?"

CHAPTER 3

Something large and soft smacked into Cody's face. He jerked awake and bolted upright, the pillow falling into his lap. "Aw, come on. Who threw that?"

The only two up were Kaito and Coral. Cody glared at Coral.

She spread her arms. "Why do you assume it was me?"

Cody raised an eyebrow.

"Alright, you got me," Coral said. "But we were going to go to breakfast."

Cody had to give her that. He flung back the covers and swung his legs out onto the floor. He quickly got dressed and went to the back room to wash his face in the basin.

When he returned, Coral had dragged Naomi out of bed and was working on Guy. He was breathing through his nose, so Coral pinched his nostrils together. For a few seconds, he couldn't breathe. Then, he flailed awake and gasped. Coral fell over, laughing.

"That's not funny, Coral!" Guy yelled, waking everyone else up.

Cody chuckled as he sat down to lace up his boots. He looked across the room at Levi. He was all dressed and ready to go. He kept looking at the door, as if he were expecting someone. Cody figured he wanted to see his dad again. After all, Levi hadn't seen his parents in over a year and a half.

Cody thought of his own father, Erik. He wondered what he was doing nowadays. It had been almost three years since he had seen his father. Then again, he didn't really care. His dad wasn't that important to him. Cody had been born eleven years after his siblings and his sister had been the one who had raised him, especially after his brother... He stopped himself from thinking about that painful memory. He had repressed the thoughts of his brother in order to cope. His sister, he could think of, though. She was the only one he wanted to see again. He hoped she was having a good life.

"Hey, Cody. You coming?" Ember asked.

Cody shook himself out of his ruminations. "Yep." He pushed off his bed and followed everyone else to breakfast in the mess hall.

When they arrived, blue camp's table was nearly full. There was quite a crop of first years that had come, blue camp receiving six of them. They had formed their own little group and had arrived before the others.

"Guess someone's standing," Guy said, counting the remaining chairs.

"Last one there!" Coral yelled. Everyone took off, wrestling to get a seat. Cody was caught flat-footed and arrived last.

"Guess I'll stand," he muttered. The others chuckled.

One of the first years, Walt, stood and offered Cody his chair. "You can take my spot."

Cody smiled at him. "Thanks, buddy, but I think you can keep it." The kid nodded and sat back down.

"How noble of you," Guy snorted.

"It was," Ember said. She turned to Cody. "I think that was well done. Very polite."

"Joke, Ember. It was a joke," Guy said.

Ember rolled her eyes. "I know. Everything's a joke with you."

Guy flashed a smile. "Mostly. But not everything." He discretely pointed at Levi and lowered his voice. "That whole business isn't a joke."

"I'm glad you think so," Ember said. "Because that is perhaps the most serious thing to happen in decades."

Levi leaned over and whispered, "Keep it down, guys."

"Yes," Kaito agreed. "It is unwise to discuss this with so many people around."

"Ah, you guys are just paranoid," Coral scoffed. "Nobody here would turn Levi in. Except maybe the twins. And maybe Corvin. And Vonn. And maybe..."

"We get the picture," Cody cut her off.

The dinner bell rang, signalling that the meal was ready. Everyone lined up to fill their plates with the day's menu. Today it was bacon, eggs and toast. When Cody arrived back at the table, he set his plate on the corner and proceeded to make a sandwich out of the meal.

Guy frowned. "What are you doing?"

"Making a sandwich," Cody replied.

"I can see that. But why?"

"Because I want to."

Guy rolled his eyes. "I hate when people say that."

"You use that one all the time," Cody said.

Guy conceded. "Ok. I hate when other people say that."

Cody snorted as he dug in, taking a large bite. Flavour filled his mouth as he chewed; the bacon was especially good, hearty and smoky.

"So," Naomi asked. "What does your schedule look like today?"

"Beats me," Coral said with a full mouth. "I just go wherever the others go."

"We have Combat," Ember said. She always knew the schedule. "Then Politics, Survival and Riding."

"Riding!" Cody said. "Nice. Today we're learning how to joust!"

Guy's mouth dropped open, an egg yolk falling out. "I totally forgot about that."

"That's gonna be so awesome!" Coral exclaimed. "I'm gonna knock you all off your horses so hard you'll land in next week!"

"That is impossible," Kaito stated.

Coral groaned. "Ugh, Kaito. Must you ruin everything?"

To his credit, Kaito didn't take offence. He smiled. "Not quite everything."

"Like, eighty percent," Coral said.

"That's quite a bit," Kaito said. "And isn't it usually Ember who ruins your fun?"

"Hey! Leave me out of this!" Ember protested.

It was too late. Coral turned to Ember, her eyes narrowing. "You're right! Ember does ruin all my fun!"

"Only when it's foolish, irresponsible and dangerous," Ember said.

"That's everything I do!" Coral said.

"Exactly," Ember said.

"Exactly," Coral said. "Wait, are we agreeing?"

"I think we are," Ember said. "Why are we agreeing? We were just arguing."

"We could continue, if you want," Coral offered.

"No, no, that's ok," Ember said hastily.

Cody chuckled at the exchange. He was actually glad Ember was arguing with Coral. It showed that she was loosening up. At first, Ember had just stuck her nose in the air and pretended that she was better than everyone else. That still happened occasionally, but far less often.

Over at the instructors' table, Aldus stood and called for silence. When the crowd had settled, he began. "Good morning, everyone. I have an announcement. As I'm sure you have all heard, the Midarra Festival is being held in Saken in two weeks' time. It is no secret that the Festival is one of the biggest events in the land. And seeing as it only occurs once every eleven years, we have decided to take this opportunity to bring you all to Saken. We will be attending the festivities, with all classes cancelled until we return."

The mess hall erupted into cheers at the news. People yelled and celebrated, jumping up from their seats.

Aldus waited until the commotion died down. "Of course, that is still two weeks away. That means we will still be having classes until then. I expect no slacking, as you will have two months off. Now, off to class!"

Cody laughed and discussed the upcoming vacation with his friends as everyone filed out of the hall. He couldn't believe Aldus was actually letting them skip classes for two months. He was prepared to have a great time.

"Can you believe it?" Bear crowed. "We're going to the Festival!" The third-year class cheered as they exited the building.

They arrived at the sparring yard to find Griswold waiting for them.

"You are all two minutes late," Griswold growled.

A chorus of 'sorrys' followed.

Griswold grunted. "You all heard Aldus. No goofing off for the next two weeks."

Cody started drawing his sword.

"Apolinar!" Griswold yelled, using Cody's last name. "What do you think you're doing?"

Cody froze. "Uh, I'm getting out my weapon."

"Did I tell you to do that?" Griswold asked angrily.

"Well, no, but-"

"But nothing!" Griswold thundered. "Nobody's touching any weapons until everyone does fifty push-ups!"

Everyone groaned. "Fifty?" Oliver cried.

"Make that sixty!" Griswold yelled.

Everyone, including Cody, dropped to the ground and began doing push-ups. In no time, Cody's arms and chest burned, but he wasn't about to give up in front of an angry Griswold. Finally, sweat dripping into his eyes, Cody finished the sixtieth push-up. He sat back on his knees and exhaled, muscles burning. He was pleased to notice that he was one of the first to finish.

Griswold stood with arms crossed as he waited for the slowest students to finish. Ember was among that group. She was fit, but small, having not much muscle mass. Still, she managed to finish the task.

At last, everyone completed the punishment. Griswold immediately had everyone grab their weapons and do three laps of the yard.

Cody hated running with a sword and shield. He tried to keep the sword up, so the point didn't catch in the dirt, but it was difficult, especially when pumping his arms. And the shield was so cumbersome that it just made everything awkward.

He finished the laps and leaned over, hands on his knees. Others stopped beside him and did the same. Guy complained about a stitch in his side. Ellis tried to suck in his breath and ended up coughing.

"Break into pairs with similar weapons!" Griswold called as the last students were finishing.

Cody looked around. He locked eyes with Marshall Reaver from green camp. Cody pointed at him. Marshall nodded and they broke away from the main group.

"Practice forms twenty to thirty!" Griswold called. Griswold taught in sets of forms, which he numbered and had the students memorize. They were different for each weapon type, hence why Griswold had them go with a partner who had a similar weapon.

Cody and Marshall began to go through the forms, exaggerating them so their muscles would remember the movements. They had already done these specific forms so many times before that Cody could do them without thinking. Still, not everyone could and that's why they were practicing them.

Marshall was decent. He could do the forms, but occasionally he would mix up which was which and Cody would have to remind him. Cody could also do them faster and with more precision. He would beat Marshall in a duel.

As they performed a double high parry, Marshall asked, "Why do you think Griswold is in such a bad mood?"

"Beats me," Cody said. "Maybe someone let an angry cat into his room again."

Marshall snickered. Someone had done that a few months ago. Griswold had gone ballistic. No one was sure who had done it, but there was a rumour that it had been Dante. Of course, he denied it, as any sane person would.

Griswold had them go through all ten forms fifty times. By the end, Cody could barely move his sword to the correct spot, and he wasn't even trying with his shield. Autumn and Corvin just stopped entirely.

Griswold finally called a halt and let everyone go, telling them to be on time for the next class.

Everyone dragged their feet as they left the training field behind. Cody wiped the sweat from his brow. He was exhausted.

Even Coral had lost her usual abundance of energy. "That was... a lot of work."

Guy nodded wearily. "I think I'm just going to sleep during Politics."

Ember was too tired to berate him. She simply shook her head.

They made their way into the main building and entered the third room on the right. The instructor, Vashi Terrant, waited for the class to assemble. He was a small man, but he made up for that by the way he dressed. Today, he wore a peach coloured suit with a frilled collar and puffy cuffs.

Once everyone had taken their seats, Terrant stood up. "Welcome everyone!"

No one responded.

Terrant put a finger on his chin. "Hmm. Quiet today. What class did you come from?"

"Combat," Taro said.

Terrant nodded knowingly. "Griswold pushed you hard, did he?" The looks on everyone's faces told him that he was correct.

"Well, I hope none of you fall asleep during the class."

"No promises," Guy said, making a few people chuckle.

"Alright," Terrant said, opening a huge leather-bound book on his desk. "Where did we leave off last time? Ah, yes, the Knight's Code of Conduct. Now, you'll remember that we learned about this in first year."

"So, we're learning it again?" Ellis asked.

"Not exactly," Terrant said. "You see, you have learned the basic, generic rules of conduct. To each of these rules, there are three sub-rules. This is what we will be learning."

There were some poorly concealed groans.

"Now, let's begin with the first rule," Terrant began.

A knock at the door forestalled him. He went over and opened it. "Aldus! Good morning. What brings you down here?"

"A new student," Aldus said. "You don't mind if I come in, do you?"

"Not at all!" Terrant said. He stepped aside to let Aldus in. Another person followed him. He was a tall, muscular, handsome guy with red-brown hair that was shaved on the sides. He stood with his hands clasped behind his back.

Aldus raised a hand in greeting to the class. "Good day, third-years. May I introduce Adam Lianon?" He pointed at the young man.

A few people waved or called a greeting.

"He's a new kid?" Corvin said. "Then why isn't he with the first-years?"

"Adam is a special case," Aldus said. "You see, his father is El Fen, the Lord Protector of Blackmere. Adam has been trained by him and so he has the adequate knowledge and skill to be placed with you."

Now there was some interest. Everyone knew who El Fen was. He single-handedly defended Tion's Pass against the wildlings from up north when they invaded Blackmere ten years ago.

Aldus smiled. "El Fen brought him up to attend the last few years at the Academy."

"Wait, El Fen is here?" Ember asked.

"Why, yes he is," Aldus said. "He will be staying until after the Festival."

"I can't believe El Fen is here!" Ember whispered.

42

Guy grunted. "I don't know what's so great about him."

Ember gaped at him. "He's a legend! One of the greatest fighters of our century."

Guy raised his eyebrows. "Ok, whatever."

"Which camp will he be in?" Aybrin from yellow camp asked.

"He will be joining blue camp," Aldus said. There was an uproar as everyone except blue camp complained. Aldus held up his hand for silence. "Please. It's where he fits best."

There was still some grumbling and muttering, but that was all.

"Now, I have some matters to attend to, so if Cody could show Adam around, that would be ideal."

Cody's eyes widened. He hadn't been expecting to be called on.

"Is that a problem?" Aldus asked, seeing Cody's expression.

"No, not at all," Cody said. "I just wasn't expecting to be asked, that's all." He stood.

Terrant cleared his throat. "I trust you'll talk to your camp-mates to get caught up."

Cody nodded. "Sure." He walked up to Adam and extended his hand. Adam gave it a firm shake.

"Come on," Cody said. "Let me give you the grand tour."

"That would be nice," Adam said. His voice was higher than Cody had been expecting.

Cody led Adam out of the room and quickly showed him around the building. Then, as they exited the building, Cody asked, "So, you're from Blackmere, huh?"

"I lived a half-league outside the city," Adam replied.

"Cool. What's Blackmere like?" Cody asked. "I've never been there."

"It is rather regular," Adam said. "Nothing sets it apart except the fact that nothing sets it apart."

"So, it's basically special for not being special," Cody said.

"Correct."

"Ok," Cody said. "These are blue and green camps." He pointed them out.

"Because that is what colour the trim is painted," Adam said as more of a statement than a question.

"Yeah, I guess so," Cody said. "Um, yellow and white are on the east side and black and red are on the west."

"What about the north side?" Adam asked.

"The instructors and staff," Cody replied.

"Ah, yes. I should have known."

"The gate's there." Cody pointed.

Adam raised an eyebrow. "I know where the gate is. I had to enter through it, you know."

"Oh right," Cody said. "Um... yeah."

"You are not sure what to say," Adam stated.

Cody glanced over at him. His face showed no sign of mockery. "Not really. I'm not great at talking to strangers."

"Fair enough," Adam said. "Although I do hope we do not remain strangers for long."

Cody smiled. "Well said. Let's go check out the towers."

~~~

Adam's tour took until partway through their Survival class. They arrived after Duncan Dunning had already explained how to start a fire with a shard of glass by angling it in the sunlight the proper way. Dunning helped the two of them understand while the rest of the class practiced.

After a few minutes, there was a shout. Oliver had managed to set his pile of kindling on fire, if only just. A thin finger of smoke curled up from the slivers of wood.

"Well done, Oliver," Dunning congratulated. He raised his voice. "The rest of you have ten more minutes to complete the task before class is finished."

As the time went by, more and more people set their wood alight, but not everyone managed to do it in the allotted time, Cody and Adam included. Dunning told those that didn't finish that they would try again next class.

After that, it was time for Riding class. Everyone was excited to learn how to joust and they were all talking about how good they were all going to be.

"This is Able Hejeck," Cody said to Adam, pointing out the short instructor when they arrived.

Hejeck whistled to get everyone's attention. "Alright! Alright! Settle down!" His gaze swept over the crowd and settled on Adam. "New kid. I was told about you. What's your name?"

"Adam, sir."

"Hmm. Polite. I hope you're actually good enough to be in this class. We are jousting today."

"I can already joust, sir," Adam said. "My father taught me."

"Oh, you can, can you?" Hejeck asked with no small amount of skepticism. "Well, in that case, show me what you've got."

"Sir?" Adam asked, unsure.

"I want you to joust me. We'll see if you're as good as you claim."

Adam looked at Cody, who shrugged.

"C'mon, boy," Hejeck said roughly. "Choose your horse."

Adam examined the selection of steeds and picked a medium-sized roan named Coin. He was already saddled, so Adam led him outside to where a jousting field had been set up. Everyone followed them out of the stables.

Hejeck was on his massive battle-charger. He looked tiny on the black beast. A couple of students handed both Hejeck and Adam shields and lances.

Adam picked up the lance and frowned. He adjusted it in his grip to find the right balance. He finally shrugged and turned Coin around and walked him to the end of the jousting field, a pitch three hundred feet long with a five-foot-high rail splitting it in two.

The horses stamped the ground and shook their manes as the riders readied themselves.

"Go!" Hejeck called.

Both riders dug their heels into their mounts, causing them to charge ahead, Hejeck's horse rushed ahead at full speed. Adam's galloped, but not full out. Both kept their lances trained on the other rider. Cody noticed that Adam seemed to hold his slightly steadier.

They swiftly closed the gap between them. Fifty yards, thirty yards, ten yards.

Just before they met, Adam dug his heels into Coin and leaned ahead, raising himself up a fraction.

The air resounded with the sound of cracking wood.

Hejeck flew off his horse and landed heavily on the ground with a grunt.

Adam wheeled his horse around and dismounted. He tossed the broken stub of his lance aside.

Hejeck struggled to his feet. His shield was cracked in two, only held together by the leather straps that went around his arm.

"Are you alright?" Adam asked.

Hejeck began to laugh as he discarded the shield. "Son, you are very skilled. I haven't been bested in a jousting match in eleven years."

"You are not upset?" Adam asked.

"My pride is a little bruised, but I'm mostly impressed."

Cody couldn't believe it. He had expected Hejeck to blow his top. Instead, he was shaking Adam's hand.

"I think you can help me teach this sorry group how to properly joust. What do you say?" Hejeck asked.

"I would be happy to."

"Great," Hejeck said. Then, to the class. "Mount up!"

There was a mad scramble as everyone rushed to get the best horses. Cody was shoved and jostled as people ran by. When Cody finally arrived, there were only two horses left. Only he and Gwen from green camp didn't have mounts.

They exchanged glances. "Well," Gwen said. "Levi can ride Banqo, so maybe she's not as bad as she used to be." Banqo was the horse that no one wanted to ride because she tended to buck everyone off.

"Go ahead," Cody said. "I don't feel like dying today."

Gwen smirked and went to saddle Banqo.

That left Cody to ride Copper. Copper was an old stallion, well past his prime. He walked with a limp and never managed more than a canter. Cody sighed as he entered Copper's stall. "Looks like it's you and me."

Copper turned to look at him with droopy eyes. Then, he sneezed, showering Cody with mucus.

"Thanks."

Once he got Copper saddled, he led him out of the stables. Naturally, he was the last one out.

"How kind of you to join us," Hejeck said dryly.

"Sorry," Cody apologized.

"Yeah, whatever. Pay attention, everyone!" Hejeck called. "First thing you need to learn. Stay on your horse. That's the most important thing."

Vonn held up his hand. "Isn't winning the most important thing?"

"I like where you're coming from," Hejeck said. "But you can't exactly win without staying on your horse, now can you?"

"I guess not," Vonn muttered.

"Pair up!" Hejeck called. "Grab a lance and shield." Everyone hustled to grab a buddy. Cody locked eyes with Coral. She nodded.

Cody led Copper over to the pile of weapons that had been taken from the combat yard. First, he set his own shield aside. He didn't want to risk breaking it, having seen Adam split Hejeck's shield in one blow. He grabbed a different shield and slipped it over his arm. It was heavier than his and more awkward, basically a convex wooden disk with a metal lip riveted around the edge and a metal boss in the centre. It weighed about thirty pounds.

The lance was hardwood, about twelve feet long. There was a round handguard about a foot from one end. Cody picked it up; it was ten pounds, somewhat lighter than he had been expecting. Gear in hand, he strode back to Copper.

Coral took her equipment and led her horse away. Cody followed her. Soon, everyone was split into pairs, spread out around the field.

"Alright!" Hejeck yelled, making sure he was heard. "Now, at half-speed, take turns ramming your lances into the other's shield."

Cody looked at Coral. She was grinning. "I'll go first."

Cody didn't like her enthusiasm. He expected he would be headed for the infirmary after all was said and done.

Coral backed her horse up a ways and then trotted toward Cody. As she neared, Cody hefted the shield and readied himself for impact. Coral's lance contacted Cody's shield and he jolted back, almost falling off Copper's back. He just managed to stay on.

"Geez! He said half-speed!" Cody cried.

"That was half-speed," Coral replied. "You're just a wimp."

Cody grumbled as he righted himself. "Well, let's see how you handle it, then." He wheeled Copper around and trotted until he was thirty feet away. Then he kicked his heels lightly, making the horse go. Copper went at a light canter, which was almost his full speed, but everyone else's half-speed.

As he closed in on Coral, he tightened his grip on the lance. The blunted tip wavered in a three-foot circle. He wasn't even sure he would hit Coral's shield.

Right before impact, Coral tilted her shield. Cody's lance hit and deflected off, throwing him off-balance. The tip of the lance jammed into the ground and catapulted Cody off his horse. He landed with a thud, knocking the air out of his lungs.

He opened his eyes to see Hejeck standing over him. "Sad, Cody, sad. She wasn't even moving, and she knocked you off."

"That was great!" Coral exclaimed.

Hejeck nodded approvingly. "Well done, turning the shield. That was an advanced move."

Coral beamed.

Hejeck looked down at Cody. "Do it again!"

Cody groaned. This was going to be a long class.

CHAPTER 4

"How'd you get so good at jousting?" Guy asked as the third-years from blue camp walked away from the jousting field.

"As I said before, my father taught me many things," Adam said.

"He did a terrific job," Ember said. "I can barely hold the lance steady, much less beat the instructor on the first try."

Adam had the grace to smile. "It did take a considerable amount of practice and much failure."

"What else can you do?" Coral asked.

Adam raised a brow. "What do you mean?"

"Like, can you do any other cool things?"

"Hmm. I am a decent shot with a bow," he said.

"No way!" Ember exclaimed. "You're an archer too?" It was a rare skill, one not taught to the students at Blackthrush.

Cody was impressed, but he was also a bit jealous. He was used to being the cool one. Now it seemed that Adam was taking that place. Also, Cody's pride stung from being embarrassed while jousting. Still, he wasn't petty, and he wanted to like Adam, so he pushed his envy down.

"Do you think you could show us?" Cody asked.

Adam nodded. "I could. My father has a bow with his possessions. I will have to ask him."

"Well, let's go," Guy said.

Ember squealed. "You mean, we actually get to meet El Fen?"

Guy rolled his eyes. "Oh, puh-lease."

49

"Yes, you can meet him," Adam said. "We will have to find him, though. I am unsure of where he is presently."

"Where should we start?" Coral asked.

"How about right there," Guy said, pointing in front of him where an unfamiliar man was walking. "That's him, right?"

"Yes," Adam said. "That is El Fen."

Ember grabbed Guy's arm and wheezed. "Oh my gosh. It's really him. Quick, how do I look?"

"Pathetic." Guy peeled Ember's hand off his arm.

"Never mind him," Cody said. "You look fine, as always."

"Fine won't cut it," Ember said. "I need to look great! Quick, I need to go before he sees me!"

"Too late," Coral said. "Adam's already got his attention."

Ember seemed to wilt, her knees buckling, but Cody caught her and held her up as El Fen approached.

He was an impressive figure. Over six feet of tanned muscle, he simply oozed confidence. A sculpted moustache and goatee framed his mouth, sleek black hair was pulled back in a ponytail. His clothes were simple and practical, coloured with earth tones, but a scarlet cloak that looked as if it cost a fortune was slung over his broad shoulders. A broadsword was strapped to his back.

He smiled easily at Adam. His face was kindly, full of good humour. To Cody, he seemed to be a pleasant man, unless one was his enemy. Then, Cody figured he would be a right terror.

"Hello, son," El Fen said in a smooth baritone. Ember let out a quiet moan.

"Hello, father," Adam said. "These are my new friends."

El Fen took his time studying each of them, still with a smile on his lips. "Pleased to meet you. May I have the pleasure of knowing your names?"

"Coral."

"Guyaramilliro, Guy for short."

"Cody."

"E... Ember."

"I trust you know who I am?" El Fen said. The four nodded.

"So, Adam, did you want something?" he asked.

"I do," Adam said. "I want to show my friends my archery skills."

El Fen nodded. "You'll need the bow then."

"Indeed."

"Come on, then. We don't want to keep them waiting," El Fen said. He led them over to the north side of the Academy, where he was staying in one of the guest rooms. It was sparsely furnished, only having a single bed and a small table with a washbasin. El Fen's belongings were packed in a bundle. An unstrung bow was tied to the side of the bag, the accompanying quiver of arrows rested beside the pack.

"Uh, your bow's broken," Coral said.

El Fen laughed heartily. "No, young Coral. It is merely unstrung."

"How come?" Coral asked.

"You see, if you aren't using your bow and you leave it strung, the string will lose tension over time, making it ineffective. Also, it could damage the arms if they are bent back all the time."

"Oh..." Coral said.

El Fen looked at Adam. "Try not to break any arrows. I don't fancy a trip to the fletcher."

"I will try my hardest not to," Adam said.

"Say, Mr. El Fen," Cody said. "Why don't you come with us? You two can have a little competition." He could feel Ember gaping at him.

El Fen rubbed his goatee. "I suppose that could be amusing. I was going to talk to a local blacksmith about repairing my left pauldron, but that can wait until tomorrow." He grabbed the bow and quiver and all six left the building.

As they headed for the gate, the groundskeeper, Myron, came to meet them. "What are you up to?"

El Fen lifted the bow and quiver. "We are off to have a competition."

"Oh ho ho. Archery." Myron glanced at the blue campers. "You guys enjoy this. We don't often get to show students bow work."

"Why not?" Guy asked. "That seems like a useful skill."

"Indeed, it is," Myron said. "But, Blackthrush is a public institution and as such, it has to follow a budget. And unfortunately, we couldn't afford to pay an archery instructor. We used to, but the job was cut thirty years ago."

"Meh, that's dumb," Guy said. "I want to learn."

Myron smiled. "Once you graduate, you'll have time to learn on your own. Now have fun. I have to go fix the ceiling in the east tower. Apparently, someone tried to create a portal and ended up just, well, I'm not exactly sure what they did."

Cody snickered. They all knew who had done it. Niles. He was always trying to create portals and had never once succeeded. He had, however, almost destroyed every room in the Academy trying.

Ember shook her head. "Honestly, he needs to stop."

"There's always someone who plays around with portals," El Fen said with a grin. "In my day, it was Chaelin Evicklan. Nearly swallowed up the stables once."

"You went to Blackthrush?" Cody asked.

El Fen nodded. "All knights come from here, or the school in Arathia."

"Yeah, I guess I should have figured," Cody said.

"Which camp were you in?" Coral asked.

El Fen smiled wider. "Black camp. We were the camp to be in, back then. Got into all sorts of trouble."

Coral made a gagging sound. "Black camp? Ew! They're the worst."

El Fen chuckled. "Funny. When I attended, blue camp was the worst. Now come on, let's go." He waved to Myron and started off down the path to Forenfall as Coral tried to think of something clever to say.

They stopped next to a large pine near the riverbank. El Fen set about carving a target in the tree trunk with his knife while Adam strung the bow.

"How long did it take you to learn how to shoot?" Guy asked.

Adam cocked his head. "Perhaps a year. Although I was busy with other tasks during that time."

"Do you think you could teach me? In our spare time, of course," Guy said.

"Certainly. It would be my pleasure."

El Fen walked over, having finished carving the target.

"How will the competition work?" Coral asked.

"Ten arrows each," El Fen said. "Most points wins. There are three rings. Outer ring is five, second is ten and middle is fifteen."

"Who will shoot first?" Adam asked.

"I will," El Fen said, plucking the bow from his son's hands. He tested the string. Satisfied that it was taught, he took an arrow from the quiver and nocked it on the string. He drew back, holding the arrow between his index and middle fingers.

Cody noticed that. He turned to Adam. "Is that the normal way to hold it?"

"There are a few different variations, but yes, that is most common."

El Fen sighted up the target, took a steady breath and released the arrow once he blew out. It shot off the string with a loud *twang* and zipped through the air. A second later, it struck the tree on the upper left of the second ring. He grunted. "Didn't think the wind would affect it that much."

"It was still a good shot," Ember said.

"It was decent," El Fen said.

Adam reached for the bow. "My turn."

Cody noticed he took it with his left hand. "You're left-handed."

"I am. My father discovered this when I could not learn how to fence."

"But, didn't you joust right-handed?" Coral asked.

"I did," Adam said. "But that is because jousting left-handed is ill-advised. The shield is on the wrong side of the body and is practically useless."

Coral tipped her head. "I guess that makes sense."

Adam grabbed an arrow, twirled it around his fingers, then nocked it and drew all in one smooth motion. He aimed for a moment and then let the arrow fly. It also struck the second ring, but much nearer to the centre than his father's had.

"Good shot," El Fen said. "I'm really going to have to try if I want to beat you."

"Have you challenged each other lately?" Guy asked.

"Not for a good while," El Fen replied. "And he's had much more practice than I since then." He took the bow again and loosed another shot. This one was a little better, but not much.

Adam took his second shot and struck the inner circle. He passed the bow back to his father.

They used up twenty arrows and at last, they tallied up the points. El Fen ended up with a hundred and twenty and Adam with a hundred and forty-five.

El Fen laughed and clapped his son on the shoulder. "I guess we know who the better archer is now."

"I owe it all to you," Adam said humbly. "You were a great teacher."

El Fen grinned. "Why, thank you."

"That was some brilliant shooting," Guy said. "I would love to learn that."

Adam held out the bow. "Would you like to give it a shot?"

"Was that a pun?" Coral asked with a smirk.

Adam looked at her blankly.

"Never mind."

"I would love to," Guy said.

Adam handed him the bow. "Alright. Hold it like this..."

Cody turned to look at the sun. It was the sixth hour of the afternoon. "I'm gonna head for the mess hall."

"Ooh, yeah. It's food time," Coral said. "I'll come with."

Cody glanced over. "Ember?"

She tore her gaze away from El Fen. "Uh, yeah, sure. I'll come." The three left the others behind as they walked back to the Academy.

"Adam's pretty skilled," Coral said.

Once again, Cody felt a flare of jealousy. "Yeah, he is."

"That's because he had such a great teacher," Ember said.

Cody wrinkled his brow. "What's with you and El Fen?"

"He's just so legendary," Ember said. "If only he were twenty years younger..."

Cody raised an eyebrow.

"Ok, maybe thirty."

"You are ridiculous," Cody said.

"I am not!" Ember huffed.

"Yeah, kinda," Coral said.

Ember stuck her nose in the air. "Hmph. You just don't know how to recognize true talent when you see it."

They walked through the gate and made their way to the mess hall inside the main building. Most everyone was already there, talking and laughing. Taro was the centre of attention, his clothes and hair singed and his face covered in soot. The unpleasant aroma of skunk wafted off him. Apparently, Kavik's joint operation with Bram and Dante had been successful.

With a chuckle, Cody slid onto a chair beside Levi, who was seated next to his dad.

"Hey," Levi said.

"Hey, how were your classes?" Cody responded.

"Actually decent. Griswold was in a bad mood, but he took it out on Holly and Duncan. Magic was pretty interesting. We learned about unexplainable magical phenomena."

"Oh yeah, like the Floating Cliffs and the Endless Well?" Cody asked, recalling learning of that the year prior.

"Exactly. Hey, where's the new guy?" Levi asked. He had already met Adam, briefly, at noon.

Cody jabbed a thumb over his shoulder. "He's teaching Guy how to shoot a bow."

"Huh. Cool," Levi said.

"Hello, Ramsey," Coral said as she sat across from him. "You're still here."

Ramsey smiled. "Hello, Coral. I'm just going to eat supper and then I'm going to leave."

"I thought you were leaving at noon," Cody said.

"So did I," Ramsey said. "But Aldus heard some news that he wished to send out as a letter, so I had to wait around for him to write it."

"It was nice," Levi said. "I got to spend a little more time with him before he leaves."

"I got to see him duel," Ramsey said with pride in his voice. "He's not too bad."

"Not anymore, you mean," Coral said. "He used to suck."

Ramsey looked at Levi. "Really?"

"Oh yeah, I was terrible. I basically survived out of sheer-luck."

"We should have taught you some self-defence," Ramsey said.

Levi shrugged. "Can't change it now."

"I know," Ramsey said. "But we should have better prepared you."

"Well, I survived. That's all that matters."

"And let's hope you continue to," Ramsey said.

"It's looking pretty good, so far," Cody said.

Naomi joined the conversation. "Yeah, now that all that business with Stern and the Kar-Sang is over, it seems pretty safe."

"As long as no one finds out," Ember said, hinting at the spy that they knew was somewhere in their midst.

Ramsey's face turned serious. "Yes. I am trusting that none of you ever reveal the truth to someone untrustworthy."

"We won't, sir," Cody said.

"Yeah, we haven't told anyone yet," Coral said.

"Good. Keep it that way," Ramsey admonished them.

The meal was served, and everyone got to fill their plates with potatoes, roast and carrots. Cody took extra; he was hungry after the physically taxing day he'd had. He sat down with his campmates and dug in. The roast was excellent. It was spiced in a way Cody hadn't tasted before and he loved it.

A couple minutes later, Guy and Adam wandered in. As they were walking toward Cody's table, Guy caught Kana's eye across the room and winked at her. She rolled her eyes.

Cody grinned as Guy sat down. "How'd it go?"

"Not very well," Guy said. "All I managed to do was break two arrows and cut my palm." He held up his hand to reveal a thin red line.

"Why would you do that?" Ember asked.

"Oh, because I meant to do this. Of course."

Ember frowned. "You don't have to be rude about it."

Guy crossed his arms. "You don't have to be dumb about it."

"Excuse me?"

Guy stuck out his tongue.

Adam caught Cody's eye, looking mildly concerned.

"They do it all the time. Just go with it," Cody told him.

"If you say so."

Cody stabbed a chunk of potato and popped it in his mouth. It was good, perhaps a tad dry, but he enjoyed it nevertheless. And, besides, the roast was more than moist enough to compensate.

Cody turned to Adam. "Where's your dad at?"

Adam pointed to the table where the instructors ate. "He is dining with Aldus. They are old friends, you know."

"I didn't know that," Cody said. "Did they grow up together?"

A smile touched Adam's lips. "No. But they shared an adventure as young adults."

"Really?" Cody said. "What did they do?"

"They were searching for treasure."

Coral leaned over. "Ooh. What kind of treasure?"

"They were searching for the fabled Runestones of Haldholm," Adam said.

"What are those?" Levi asked.

"They're runestones, idiot," Guy said.

Levi glared at him. "I know that. I mean, what is so special about those exact ones?"

"They are very powerful," Adam said. "They are rumoured to have been made by the last of the Il'Ka." The Il'Ka had been the race who lived in Terrenia before humans. They were immensely powerful in the magical arts, but a feud among them caused the species to lose the ability to reproduce. Eventually, they all died out. That had been a thousand years before the first humans had sailed to Terrenia from across the Sevian Sea.

"So, did they find them?" Cody asked.

"I could tell you all the story," Adam said.

Ember propped her elbows on the table. "That would be lovely."

"Very well. First, I must tell you the tale of how Aldus and my father met."

Ramsey leaned in. "Now this sounds interesting."

Adam laced his fingers together. "My father was travelling through the realm and passed through the city of Corina. He was flipping a coin absent-mindedly when someone bumped into him. He dropped the coin and it rolled to the feet of a man standing nearby. Aldus. He picked it up and recognized it, for it was no ordinary coin. It was a token bearing the mark of the Watch, denoting my father as an honorary member. That is another story, in which my father had done a great deed in the service of King Harold."

"Amazing," Ember whispered breathlessly.

Adam continued. "Now, because of the token, Aldus knew my father was a man of trustworthy nature and he struck up a conversation. My father mentioned that he was looking for an adventure and Aldus was looking for someone to accompany him on his own adventure. The two went back to Aldus' room at a nearby inn, the Rusted Hammer."

"They serve excellent soup," Ramsey interrupted. "But the barkeep tends to water down the ale."

"You've been there?" Levi was surprised.

"Eight times," Ramsey said, reminding Levi he travelled for his job. "But continue, Adam."

Adam nodded. "Aldus told my father that he believed he had discovered the location of the Runestones of Haldholm. My father was instantly on board. He had a chance to find a legendary artifact. There was no thought of refusal."

"And did he refuse?" Coral asked, her mouth full of food.

"No!" Guy said. "He literally just said that he wasn't going to refuse. How dumb are you?"

Coral swallowed. "Is that a trick question? Because, I feel like it is. I want to answer seven."

Guy rubbed his eyes. "Why do you want to answer seven?"

"Dunno, it's a good number."

Cody saw Adam looking at Coral with confusion. "Don't pay her any attention," he said. "You won't go insane that way."

Adam moistened his lips. "Very well." He composed himself and continued the tale. "They set out with plans to arrive in Seawall, where Aldus believed the Runestones to be. Little did they know that a third person had overheard their conversation and decided to follow them in secret. Aldus and my father made it through the Bearclaw Mountains with little trouble. Aldus was a great companion and a fascinating person. Just when my father thought he had figured his companion out; Aldus would surprise him once more."

"That sounds like Aldus, all right," Levi said.

"You know him that well?" Ramsey asked.

Levi smirked. "No. Which is exactly it. It's impossible to know everything about Aldus."

"True," Ramsey said.

Adam spoke. "While they were travelling along the pass, they were stopped by a knight in black armour, Sir Gonley of Sudrak."

There were sounds of recognition. They all knew the name. Sir Gonley was one of the most renowned fighters of the generation prior. He had a mean streak a mile wide and was known for using his influence to bully the common folk.

"Sir Gonley was down on money and wished to take my father's coin. He challenged him to a duel and my father emerged victorious."

"He defeated Sir Gonley?" Ember said incredulously. "That's amazing!"

"Yes. My father does not boast of it, but thirty years ago, he was one of the finest swordsmen in the realm. He said that at his prime, there were only four men who could best him."

"What about now?" Cody asked.

"Well, age has slowed him some, but he is still within the top twenty swordsmen in Terrenia," Adam said.

"What about you?" Cody asked. "How do you compare to him?"

Adam smiled slightly. "I may be able to best him at archery, but I certainly cannot best him at fencing."

Cody glanced over at Ember. She was looking across the room, staring at El Fen with wide eyes. Cody shook his head.

"What happened after he defeated Sir Gonley?" Naomi was fascinated by the story.

Adam continued. "They carried on through the pass. They stopped in a small town on the other side and restocked their provisions. Then, they headed into the Great Northern Forest, not wanting to take the eastern road and detour to Altor.

"They travelled for a week with nothing to trouble them but the cold. Then, one day, they were ambushed by wildlings. There were too many for them to defeat and my father was knocked unconscious. He was taken to the wildlings' camp. Upon waking, he found that he was alone, Aldus was not with him. He assumed his friend had been slain. He was left alone by the wildlings as they prepared something. As far as he could tell, they were readying for some sort of celebration. He could see a large fire pit with a spit above it. He had a bad feeling that he was about to be a meal for the wildlings.

"That night, while the camp was asleep, Aldus snuck into camp and freed my father. They made their escape but were unfortunately discovered and the wildlings gave chase. It was a wild sprint in the dark that ended with my father and Aldus jumping off a cliff into the lake below."

"I've always wanted to do that," Coral said.

"It's not advisable," Ramsey said. "If it's shallow or if there are submerged rocks, chances are, it'll kill you."

Coral shrugged. "Still be fun, though."

Ramsey looked at her quizzically. She grinned.

"So, they escaped the wildlings, right?" Naomi asked.

"Indeed," Adam said. "But they had lost all their supplies and had no way of making a fire. They were in serious trouble."

"Freezing to death is a real threat up north," Ramsey said. "You must always be prepared up there."

"How did they survive?" Levi asked.

"Fortune smiled upon them. They stumbled upon a man's house. He was elderly, but he welcomed them in and gave them food to eat. He saved their lives. Aldus, however, contracted pneumonia and they were forced to stay with the man until he recovered. It took a month. At last, they were back on their way. The rest of the journey to Altor was fairly easy, aside from an encounter with a pack of wolves."

"Were the Runestones in Altor?" Guy asked.

"If you let him finish the story, you'd find out," Ember said. Guy shot her a look of annoyance.

Adam smiled. "They rested for a day, recovering from their journey. Aldus studied some old texts he had acquired from a local library, that contained clues to the whereabouts of the Runestones. The language was ancient and cryptic, but finally, Aldus believed he had discovered all the secrets."

"Where were the Runestones supposed to be?" Cody asked. He was quite caught up in the story.

"They supposedly rested in the crypts beneath the city," Adam said. "Unfortunately, the crypts were booby-trapped to prevent grave robbers from taking the valuables buried with the bodies. Aldus believed he knew how to disable or subvert the traps and so, on the second day, they descended into the catacombs.

"Unbeknownst to them, the person who had been following them since Corina had joined forces with Sir Gonley and they headed down into the crypts after them. Aldus and my father managed to get around all the traps and found themselves in an antechamber where the body of Perrick the Proud, Seawall's most renowned knight, rested. But, by disabling the traps, they had cleared the way for their pursuers.

"They fought then," Levi figured.

"Yes. Gonley and my father duelled for a second time and Aldus was beset by the other man."

"Who was the other man?" Ember asked.

Adam shrugged. "To this day, we do not know his identity. He wore a mask. All we know is that he had one brown eye and one blue eye."

Cody noticed that Ember's eyebrows rose at that. Then they furrowed as she thought.

"That is a rare trait," Ramsey said.

Adam continued. "The man defeated Aldus and helped Gonley beat my father. Then they opened the coffin and extracted a fine purple silk bag with a golden pullcord. With much jeering and gloating, they opened it finding the Runestones of Haldholm. They left Aldus and my father in despair.

"That sucks," Guy said. "So close and then someone else swoops in and steals the prize."

"They were devastated. They both wished to pursue the thieves, but both were injured. Aldus looked inside the coffin, and something caught his eye. He reached in and pulled out a small stone rectangle. It was one of the Runestones, the cirth, to be exact. It had apparently fallen out of the bag." Adam smiled oddly as he said that.

"So, their quest wasn't a complete failure," Naomi said. "They still found one Runestone."

"What did they do with it?" Cody asked.

Adam took a moment to respond. His mouth twitched as he spoke. "I believe they gave it to a collector who paid handsomely for it. Father never went into much detail after that."

"That was a fantastic story," Ramsey said. "I'm glad I got to hear it. Thank you."

Adam inclined his head. "You are welcome."

Cody looked over at the instructor's table. Aldus and El Fen smiled at him as if they knew exactly what was being discussed. He wouldn't have been surprised if they did.

CHAPTER 5

Levi waved at the rider receding into the distance as the orange light of dusk cast long shadows on the road to Saken.

Seeing his father go left a pang in his heart, but along with it came a relief that his parents were faring well and hadn't forgotten about him. He was glad he had been able to spend time with Ramsey, even if it was just for a day.

Before Ramsey had left, Levi had given him a letter he had written to his mother. His father would deliver it, letting Aurora know everything that had transpired over the past year and a half. Levi had also included some more personal notes that he knew she would appreciate.

Kinzo, Kana and Miri stood a few steps behind Levi. He turned back to them and sighed. Kana smiled sympathetically. Miri too. Kinzo just raised an eyebrow.

"I wonder when I'll see him again," Levi said.

"It'll come soon enough," Kana said encouragingly.

Kinzo kicked at a stone. "At least you have your parents. Some of us aren't so lucky." He and Miri were both orphans. Only Kana still had her parents, but she never talked about them. Levi figured that she had had a falling out with them. Perhaps it was the reason she had decided to come to Blackthrush.

"Good point," Levi said.

"Besides," Miri signed. "You have us now and blue camp and the rest of your friends."

"Yeah, I know. And I'm glad. I didn't think it was possible to make this many friends."

Kana smirked. "I always figured it was easier to make enemies."

"Though we all have a lot of those," Kinzo said.

Levi smirked, recalling all the people he had angered during his journey to Blackthrush. Most notable were Rorien Stern and the Kar-Sang, but there was also Cia Del Toro and the Witch of Westwall. Dekar too, though he wouldn't be bothering them again since he was dead. And, of course, Levi couldn't forget King Farren. And though he had never actually seen the king, Levi knew he was the most dangerous one of all.

He also had a few enemies at Blackthrush, Aster, Adelle, Corvin and Vonn, to name a few, but they were mostly a pain and no real threat. The only threat was the unknown spy that was still at large at Blackthrush. Levi had stayed out of trouble, making himself seem like nothing more than a knight-in-training and not the most wanted person in the realm.

"So, are we gonna keep standing here or..." Kinzo trailed off.

"We should head back," Miri signed. "There's a camp match starting right away."

Levi nodded. "Yeah. Let's go watch that. Staring after him isn't gonna bring him back."

They all walked back to the Academy as the sun reached the western horizon, dazzling rays of light setting the low clouds on fire.

"Who do you think is going to win?" Kana asked.

"Red," Kinzo said.

"Black," Levi and Miri answered.

Kinzo sniffed. "We'd better go see who's right..."

~~~

A week and a half passed and Levi found himself busy with classwork. The instructors were condensing some of their material, to try and teach it before the trip to Saken. Even with the extra work, Levi found plenty of time to have fun, joining in on the prank war that had grown to include half the Academy.

Levi also spent a fair bit of time forging his armour. He had been working on his pauldrons for months and was close to completing them. Once done, he would wear them for matches and any other event that required full armour. The bracers and greaves he had forged already, he wore nearly all the time, as they weren't terribly heavy.

During the week, Levi noticed that Adam was growing more comfortable with the Academy and the people who lived there. Levi did everything he could to help the newcomer, as he knew how hard it was to be the rookie. Still, Adam was a third-year, being more advanced than Levi in basically everything, so there actually wasn't much Levi could help with.

One day, while Levi was walking down the first-floor hall, Aldus stopped him. "Hello. What's the matter?"

"No matter," Aldus said. "I just wanted to give something to you."

Levi raised an eyebrow. "Give something to me? What?"

Aldus held out his hand. In it was a curved piece of metal with a rune in the centre, a bracer.

"My shield!" Levi snatched it from Aldus' hand. "How did you find it?"

"Finding it wasn't the hard part," Aldus said with a smile. "It was convincing the governor to give it to me. He had taken a liking to it."

Levi caressed the curved metal, letting his fingers brush over the rune engraved in the middle. Taking off his bracer, he buckled the enchanted one around his left forearm and flicked his hand up. The metal vibrated as it expanded into a rectangular shield with a click. Levi smiled broadly. He had forgotten how satisfying that was. "Thanks!"

Aldus inclined his head. "You are welcome. Such a handy item should not be so easily abandoned."

"Yeah, I should have gone looking for it," Levi said.

"No sense worrying over what you didn't do," Aldus said sagely.

"I guess not."

Aldus clapped Levi on the shoulder. "You'd best be off to your Magic class."

"Wait, you know what classes I have?" Levi asked.

Aldus smiled. "I know when everyone has each class, Levi. I make the schedule."

"Oh, right," Levi laughed. "Ok, I'll be off." As Aldus passed by, he headed for Karl Linae's room. Everyone else was already present and waiting when he slipped in.

Linae gave Levi a reproachful look. "What's your excuse this time?"

"Uh, Aldus needed to talk to me. You can ask him if you want."

Linae shrugged. "Ok, that's an actual excuse. Now, let's begin."

Balak handed Linae a vial of some dark liquid. He was still the assistant instructor, even though his old partner and friend was no longer around.

Linae took the vial. "Does anyone know what this is?"

Kindrelle's hand shot into the air.

Linae rolled his eyes, but he was smiling. "I know you know, Kindrelle. Does anyone else have a guess?"

There was a pause as the rest of the class tried to figure out what it was.

Beside Levi, Niles leaned over to Christian. "Do you think it's a soup?"

Christian cocked his head. "Um, I don't know. Maybe."

Niles nodded. "Must be a soup, then."

Levi chuckled silently. Those two were the dumbest guys he knew. But they were friendly and on good terms with Levi. He liked them.

"Is it a potion?" Duncan asked hesitantly.

"Correct!" Linae said. "What kind of potion?"

Duncan looked blankly at Linae and shrugged.

Kindrelle's hand remained in the air and waved a little.

Linae smirked. "Ok, Kindrelle. What is it?"

"It is a potion known as Darrai which grants the consumer the ability to jump twice as high as they normally can, until it wears off."

"Absolutely right, no surprise," Linae said. Kindrelle let herself have a self-satisfied smile.

"Can I try that?" Dante asked.

"No."

Dante grumbled under his breath.

Linae ignored him. "Now, does anyone know what the greatest aspect of a potion is?" He paused. "I thought not. You see, potions are not limited to any one single order of magic. Any order can create and use potions, since it is the ingredients and methods used and not the person that provides the power. It is the same principle as amulets. Anyone can use them because the power is stored in the amulet itself."

"Cool!" Bram said. "We can all make them?"

"You can all attempt it," Linae said. "Potions are fickle things. They require precise measurements. A slight error may not only ruin the potion, but it may well create something that can kill you."

Bram looked less enthused. "Oh."

"Don't worry," Linae said. "We'll be joining Nian Verrol, who will teach you some simple potions to begin with. Even you and your goofball of a sidekick can't screw them up too badly."

"Hey! I'm not a sidekick!" Dante complained.

"Shut up, yes you are," Bram said.

"I am not!" Dante replied with a little heat in his voice.

Linae held up his hand for silence. The two boys stopped arguing, but Dante still glared at his friend.

"Are we going to make a potion today?" Kana asked.

"Indeed, we are. The Mangilt potion to be precise. Although it will be diluted."

"Why's that?" Levi asked.

"Well," Linae said. "The Mangilt potion makes the consumer full. It gives all the sustenance required so one doesn't need to eat. The full potion works for two weeks, so it's especially useful on long journeys. But here at the Academy, it would not do well for you. So, we will dilute it to last a day."

Levi nodded. "I see."

"I'm sure you don't," Linae said. Before Levi could complain, he continued. "Now, let's move to the room next door where Verrol has everything set up." He led the class out of his room and down the hall to the left where he entered another room.

"Never been in here before," Levi said to Kinzo.

"Me neither," Levi's friend said. "Then again, we've never dealt with potions before."

"No, we have not," Levi agreed. "I wonder if I'll be any good at making them?"

Kinzo snorted. "You? Yeah right. You'll probably create an airborne poison and kill us all."

Levi looked at him, unamused.

Miri, who was nearby, lay a hand on Levi's arm. "You'll do fine, I'm sure."

"Thanks," Levi said. "Although I might purposefully make a poison and slip it into Kinzo's supper."

"Good thing I'm not gonna eat dinner," Kinzo said. "The Mangy-whatever-it's-called potion will take care of that."

Miri laughed.

When Levi passed through the door, his eyes widened. There were four long tables, on which rested flasks, tubes, measuring equipment, knives and tongs. Beside each table was a cauldron hanging over a fire. On the far wall was a large cabinet with hundreds of drawers, all labelled.

Levi squinted to read them. Pickled sheep livers. Newt tongues. Boiled cactus roots.

"This place is cool," Levi said.

Kinzo grinned at him.

Standing at the end of the cabinets, Niles laughed. "Ha! This one says boar pen-"

"Yes, thank you, Niles," Linae interrupted. "Please, choose a table." Levi ended up at a table with Kinzo, Miri, Naomi, Michael from red camp and Coraline from black camp.

Coraline picked up a flask and immediately dropped it. Shards of glass flew everywhere. She cringed. "Oops."

Linae pinched the bridge of his nose and sighed. "Please try not to break anything else."

"Sorry," Coraline apologized.

Kinzo reached over and nudged another flask so that it was positioned directly behind Coraline's elbow. When she brought her arm back, it knocked the flask onto the floor, where it shattered.

Linae groaned. "Coraline, really?"

Coraline stuttered, trying to apologize.

Kinzo bit his lip, trying to contain his laughter. Miri kicked him in the shin. Hard. He squeaked in pain and grabbed his throbbing leg.

Levi glared at Kinzo, although he did find it was slightly funny. He helped Coraline pick up the shards. "It's ok, accidents happen."

"I know," Coraline said. "They just seem to happen to me much more often than to others."

"I have quite a bit of bad luck myself," Levi said.

Coraline raised an eyebrow. "If you're referring to all your adventures last year, they're over now."

You have no idea how much I wish that were true, Levi thought.

They swept up all the fragments and disposed of them in the trash bin and returned to their table.

"Alright," Linae said. "Assuming there are no other accidents, we can begin." He motioned to the short, brown-skinned, black-haired man standing at the front of the room.

"Ahem, yes. Hello, students. I am Nian Verrol and this is the beginning of your Potions classes with me." He held up a paper. "Each table has a recipe, but I am going to go over the whole thing with you first, making sure that you understand all the instructions. The first step is to boil four cups of water. Normally, it would be one cup, but we're diluting the potion. Now, I took the liberty to fill all your cauldrons before class; it's heating as we speak. The second step is to add a teaspoon of crushed pinecone."

Romeo picked up a pinecone that was sitting on the table in front of him. "These pinecones aren't crushed."

"No, they're not," Linae said. "You're going to have to crush them yourselves."

"Oh, right," Romeo said. "That makes sense."

Verrol went on to explain the rest of the steps, going over anything that someone didn't understand or had questions about. A lot of people were confused when he said to use gareltoen, which he explained was the proper term for the weed everyone called knightgrass.

Once he was finished explaining the steps, it was time for the students to begin brewing.

Naomi picked up a pinecone and bounced it on her palm. "Guess we should crush this up." She squeezed her hand and squashed the pinecone, letting the flakes fall from her fingers into a small dish. "Ok, what was the next step?"

Levi read the sheet. "Um, slice three frog legs into thin strips."

"These things?" Kinzo asked, holding up a two-inch-long green leg.

"Yes, those," Michael said. He grabbed it from Kinzo's hand and took a knife. Then, he proceeded to slice the three legs into strips. "Next step?" he asked impatiently.

"We need to wait for the water to boil and then put the first ingredients in," Levi said. "How we looking on that?"

Miri checked the cauldron and then held up her thumb and index finger an inch apart. Close.

"Make it go faster," Michael said.

"We can't do that," Naomi said.

"What's your rush?" Kinzo asked.

Michael glared at him. "Never you mind."

"Boy, aren't you a ray of sunshine," Kinzo said. Michael scowled at him.

In a minute or two, the water boiled, and Michael wasted no time throwing the prepared ingredients in the cauldron.

"Now, while they cook, we're supposed to mash a beet," Levi said.

Miri grabbed a nearby mortar and pestle. She dropped the beet into it and picked up the small crushing instrument. The vegetable didn't stand a chance. Soon, it was a gooey, purple paste. "What do we do with it now?"

"The knightgrass," Kinzo said, reading over Levi's shoulder. "Chuck that in there."

"Can you pass it here?" Levi asked Coraline.

She pursed her lips. "Knightgrass. Which one is that?" She moved a finger over the remaining ingredients.

"It's the one that looks like grass," Kinzo said. "There's only one of those."

"Oh, right," Coraline said. Grabbing the thin, green-brown stalks, she walked around the table to the fire and the cauldron hanging over it. As she neared it, she caught her foot on the table leg and tripped. Her fall was broken by her face against the hot metal cauldron. It rang loudly.

Everyone flinched. "Ooh, that looked bad," Kinzo said.

"You ok?" Levi asked.

Coraline sat up, a hand on her forehead, which was turning red. "I think so. I did drop the knightgrass in the fire, though."

"Of course, you did," Michael scoffed. "Go get some more and try not to completely ruin that too."

"Oh, come on now, Michael," Naomi said. "Cut her some slack."

Michael crossed his arms and muttered under his breath.

"Dang, dude, you could give Griswold a run for his money with your attitude," Kinzo said.

Michael sneered at him.

At that very moment, the door to the classroom opened and in came Griswold, as if Kinzo had summoned him. Hejeck followed the combat instructor in. The two older men made for the other two instructors.

"Good day," Verrol greeted them.

"Gentlemen," Linae said. "What can I do for you?"

Hejeck answered in a low tone; Levi couldn't make out the words. He shrugged. It probably didn't concern him anyway.

"What's the next step?" Naomi asked.

"Uh, we gotta add the beet, but the knightgrass was supposed to go in first," Kinzo said.

"So, we have to wait for Coraline," Miri signed.

They didn't need to wait long, Coraline returned shortly with some brown stalks covered with short fibres.

"Wait, those don't seem right," Levi said. "Hey, Coraline, did you grab..." he trailed off as Coraline threw the stalks in the bubbling concoction. "Ok."

The cauldron began shaking and it belched a puff of dark purple smoke.

"Is it supposed to do that?" Kinzo asked.

Naomi stepped back. "I don't think so."

The cauldron began rattling vigorously and a low rumble reached Levi's ears. Everyone turned to their table.

"What's going on?" Linae demanded, sounding annoyed. He froze when he saw their cauldron. "What did you put in there?"

Everyone at Levi's table pointed at Coraline. "She did it."

"All I did was put in some brightgrass, just like you told me," she said.

Verrol's face went pale. "B...Brightgrass? Are you sure?"

Coraline nodded. Verrol shared a glance with the Magic instructor.

Linae pointed to the door. "Everyone out now!"

"What's going on?" Kana wondered.

"Is it going to explode?" Dante asked.

"Much worse," Verrol said. "Now go!"

Levi headed for the door. An earth-shaking roar rent the air and dark violet smoke billowed out, spreading quickly.

A voice spoke in Levi's head, one he had heard before. *Don't let it touch you!*

Levi didn't hesitate. He scrambled back and dove out the door, rolling to the side as the purple smoke filled the Potions room. He could hear everyone inside coughing and hacking.

"What is happening?"

Levi looked behind him to see Taro with an armful of books, staring at the smog coming out of the room.

"I honestly have no idea," Levi said. "Something exploded."

A figure staggered out the door. It was Kinzo.

"You ok?" Levi asked.

Kinzo stepped out of the smoke. His mouth hung open and his eyes glowed a bright violet. He lurched toward Levi.

Run! the familiar voice told him.

Levi backed up, pushing Taro with him. "What's wrong with him?" Levi's red-haired friend asked.

"I don't know!" Levi said, his voice cracking.

Beyond Kinzo, more people stumbled out of the room, all of them slack and limp, eyes blazing purple.

"Ok, time to go!" Levi said. He grabbed Taro's arm, pulling him around. The books fell to the carpet as they raced away.

Looking back over his shoulder, Levi saw all his classmates and the four instructors shambling down the hall in a mindless horde.

A door on the opposite side of the hall opened and one of the first-years stepped out. He stopped in his tracks and stared at the infected people. When they reached him, Naomi and Niles grabbed him. He yelled and struggled, but they held him fast.

Levi watched in horror as Niles leaned in close and opened his mouth. Purple smoke poured out and engulfed the kid's face. When it cleared, he opened his eyes to reveal that he had become just like them.

Taro let out a squeak. "Holy mother of-"

"Run!" Levi yelled. They both turned and sprinted down the hall. Racing out into the grand entrance, Levi collided with Aybrin from yellow camp. She fell, catching herself with a hand.

"Sorry, sorry!" Levi said, reaching down and pulling her up. "You gotta run!"

Aybrin furrowed her brow. "What? Why?"

"Because of that!" Levi shrieked, pointing back down the hall.

Aybrin leaned to peek around him. Her jaw dropped. "What's wrong with them?"

"No time to explain!" Levi pushed her toward the entrance. Taro was already there. All three of them ran outside and shut the doors behind them.

"Will that hold them?" Taro asked.

"How should I know?" Levi said. "I've never had to run from my zombified classmates before."

"Can we fix them?" Aybrin asked.

Levi clapped his hands together. "Look, both of you. I do not know the answer to any and all of your questions."

"Sorry," Aybrin said, annoyed.

Taro clicked his tongue. "If anyone will know how to fix them, it'll be Aldus."

"Yeah, yeah. He'll know what to do," Levi said. "Where is he?"

Taro scratched his neck. "Uh, in his study."

Levi silently rubbed the scar on his chin and then in a tense voice said, "In his study. Which is inside. With all them."

Taro shrugged helplessly.

A strained moan escaped Levi's mouth. Everything was going horribly wrong. They needed to find a way to save their friends. Levi wasn't going to stand aside and let Kinzo, Kana, Miri, Evander and the rest stay as mindless monsters. They needed to get to Aldus' study.

"Where's the rest of the third-years?" Levi asked.

"Inside," Aybrin said, motioning to the door. As she did so, they began to shake, as if something ran into them.

Levi gulped. They were coming out.

"Do you think they can't open the door?" Taro asked with unrealistic hopefulness. The doors swung open and out poured the horde of purple-eyed drones, controlled by who-knew-what. The three survivors jumped in surprise.

Levi began running sideways, beckoning to the others. "Go! Lead them away from the door!"

"Are you mental?" Aybrin yelled.

"Yes! Distract them!" Levi called back.

Taro gave Aybrin a shove to get going and they took off down the path between the blue and green camp houses. The horde began to shamble after them, tripping and getting in the way of each other. Levi flattened himself against the side of the main building, hoping none of his mindless friends would be smart enough to look back. He wasn't sure what had happened to them, but it had certainly made them dumb and slow.

72

Levi's luck held, for once, and they all followed after Taro and Aybrin, who he could still hear yelling and screaming. Levi blew out the breath he had been holding. "Oh yes. Good, good. I'll just sneak around to the front door and..." He stopped dead in his tracks on the front steps. Not all the zombified students had left. Eight wandered aimlessly around the front hall. "I am going to die, and I hate everything," Levi muttered. He took a deep breath and jumped ahead, knowing he needed to get to Aldus.

The students turned as soon as he began running. They started coming for him from all sides.

"Ah! Go away!" Levi screeched as one of the first-years tried to grab him. He danced out of the way, directly toward Romeo, whose eyes glowed an unnatural colour.

Levi scrambled back, tripping over himself and falling to the carpeted floor. They closed in on him.

Terror lent Levi speed and he rolled away from grasping hands. He hopped to his feet and raced for the stairs on the right side. He practically flew across the floor, his feet a blur as he dodged around the ones still in his way.

One of them, a kid he was pretty sure was named Darryl, flopped at his feet, in what Levi could only assume was a horrible attempt at a dive. Levi didn't slow but leapt over the tumbling body.

He landed at the bottom of the stairs, his momentum throwing him off-balance. He caught himself on the second step and clambered up, using his hands to help. Upon reaching the top of the stairs, Levi turned and grabbed the rail, looking back down at the entrance. The infected students trudged toward the stairs, set on catching Levi.

They tripped over themselves trying to climb. *I've got some time.* He pushed off the rail and ran down the hall, shouting warnings to anyone on the upper floors.

The third door on the right, the Interrogation class, which was only available to fourth and fifth-years, opened and Iaarra poked her head out. "Levi? What are you doing?"

He skidded to a stop. "Iaarra, hi. Uh, a bad thing happened, and you guys should lock your door and hide. Don't let any of the purple people in."

"Purple people?" Iaarra raised an eyebrow.

"Uh, yeah, all the second and first-years have gone crazy," Levi said. "Probably the third-years too. Potion went bad. So, um, I'mma go get Aldus and hopefully fix this and save Taro and Aybrin, who are likely down by the river by now. So, stay inside."

Caesar leaned out of the room. "What are you on about?"

Levi pointed. "Go look downstairs." There was a thump as one of the infected students fell up the last step. "Guess you don't have to now. Bye!" He took off toward Aldus' study. He heard Caesar and Iaarra scrambling back into their classroom behind him.

Reaching the far end of the hall, Levi pounded on the door furiously. After thirty or so knocks, Levi stopped and shook his hand, his knuckles burning.

Aldus opened the door. "I heard you the first time, Levi. What is it?"

Levi stepped to the side. "So, uh everyone is a purple zombie now. Help?"

Aldus looked at the students shambling down the hall and appeared genuinely surprised for the first time Levi had seen. He faced Levi. "What did you do?"

Levi placed a hand on his chest. "I'll have you know that, for once, I had nothing to do with it. It was Coraline."

Aldus stroked his beard. "That does make sense. Come inside. They won't breach the door and we can discuss what to do." Levi followed him into the study and the door was locked behind them.

"So, how bad is this?" Levi asked as Aldus marched up the stairs to his desk.

The headmaster sat and linked his fingers. "I don't know. Tell me exactly what happened."

Levi sat in the peach-coloured chair across from him. "Well, we were making the Mangilt potion, uh, and once we got to the step where we were supposed to add the knightgrass, Coraline threw in brightgrass instead. Then, it started smoking and blew up. I ran and everybody else got all weird and shambly. Their eyes glowed purple and I saw one of the first-years get infected when a bunch of smoke poured out of their mouths and covered the kid and then he went all purple."

"Intriguing," Aldus said. "Brightgrass, hmm?" He stood and browsed his collection of books, searching for a specific one. He pulled one off the shelf, read the title and put it back. "Not you."

74

"What book are you looking for?" Levi asked.

The headmaster bent down to look on the lower shelves. "I am looking for any text that might have the information about this. Anything about potions or herbology or the dangers thereof. Come help me."

"Uh, ok," Levi said. He licked his lips and scanned the bookshelves on his side of the desk. He read over title after title, most of them he had no idea what they were about. Every once in a while, one would grab his attention; The Compendium of Chronomancy, A Guide to Enchanting Tools, Fundamentals of Counter-Curses. "You sure have a lot of books."

"Indeed," Aldus said. "Many are of my own personal collection, but most have been here since before I was headmaster. I have read perhaps a quarter of them."

Levi did a quick count of bookshelves. Twenty-three. "That's still a couple hundred books."

Aldus flipped through a thick leather-bound tome. "Yes, well one has to be something of a scholar to be in charge of a school." He turned the page. "Interesting. Apparently one can summon a unicorn with a vortern apple."

"What's a vortern apple?"

Aldus closed the book and put it back in its place. "Oh, it's a whole other thing. Used in blood rituals and dark magic, the type we don't teach here."

The door shook. Something pounded against it. Levi jumped, dropping a small yellow book.

"They can't get in," Aldus reassured him. "Relax. The whole study is well-protected."

Levi blew out a breath and snatched up the small book. Flipping it over, he read the title: Kaeli Vind. His fingers flipped through the pages. "It's empty."

Aldus peered above the top of a red text with a rose on the cover. "Yes, it always has been."

"Who's Kaeli Vind?" Levi wondered, tracing the name engraved on the front cover.

"Who?"

"That's what I'm asking," Levi said. "The name on the front of this book."

Aldus set down his book. "Levi, the front is blank. There has never been a name on it."

"What? No way. I'm looking right at it," Levi said. He held it up to Aldus. "See?"

"No, I don't." Aldus stroked his beard. "Curious. I'll tell you what. You keep it and see if you can read any more. We'll figure out that mystery later. Right now, we have more pressing matters." The thumping at the door punctuated his statement.

"Right." Levi slipped the palm-sized book into his pocket.

Aldus came back to his desk with the rose book. "I think I may have found something. This is the account of a monk, whose name has long been forgotten. In this passage here, it mentions something similar." He passed the book over to Levi to read.

Levi moved his finger along as he read.

The village seemed the same, at first glance. Then the villagers appeared, shrouded in a violet haze that befuddled their minds and made them sluggish and dense. As a horde, they surrounded any who came too near, joining them to their throng. What could cause such mass spell work? A hex? A curse? The answer remains unknown. The remedy, it seemed was simply to douse them with hallowed water of the slope. It broke whatever foul magic had taken hold of the villagers, with no ill effect.

Levi looked up. "Well, this sounds right. And, even better, it tells us what the cure is."

"Indeed, it does," Aldus said. "However, I have no idea what hallowed water of the slope is."

Levi groaned. "You know, I was expecting to run up here and have you fix this right away."

Aldus raised an eyebrow. "I may be a headmaster and an accomplished Mind Mage, but that does not mean I am all-knowing or all-powerful. There is much I do not know. But, if it makes you feel better, I believe I know of someone who might be able to help us."

"That's good," Levi said. "Except for the part where we're trapped in here. Without said person."

A smile spread across Aldus' face. "Now here is where I show you the perks of being a headmaster." He descended the stairs and walked underneath the half-floor, behind the pillars, where the large landscape paintings hung.

"So, we're admiring art," Levi said.

Aldus slid his hourglass pendant over his head. "Levi, we live in a land of wonder. A land of magic. Do you really think this is just simple artwork?" He centred himself in front of the painting

76

depicting a cliff overlooking the sea and a sort of trail of partially submerged boulders leading out to a tall spire of rock offshore. He reached ahead and placed his pendant in the exact centre. It clicked into place.

Before Levi's suspicion could fully form into a thought, the painting rippled as if it were made of water and the hourglass fell back into Aldus' hand.

The older magician smiled at Levi. "Ready?" Without waiting for an answer, he grabbed Levi's arm and jumped into the painting.

Levi briefly felt like he was being pulled in a hundred directions before he stumbled out onto a field of grass strewn with stones. He caught himself with his hands and hurled. After emptying his stomach, he sat up and wiped his mouth. "What was that?"

Aldus chuckled. "Sorry for not warning you. I enjoy the reactions this gets."

"I didn't!" Levi said. He froze as he heard a low growl from behind him. He turned slowly to see a massive white animal. It was vaguely canine, but its face more closely resembled a bear's. Covering the white fur on its back and shoulders were dozens of black plates. They extended all the way down to its long tail, which ended in a barbed stinger.

The creature pawed the ground with a massive front leg. Claws slipped out from under its skin and it growled, revealing black teeth the length of Levi's forearm.

Levi shook in fear and slowly crept backward. "A...Aldus? Wh...What is that?"

"I am Galorolen," the creature rumbled in a voice so deep Levi's ears buzzed. It sheathed its claws. "Please, stop your panicking."

Levi shut his mouth and got to his feet. His heart still beat like a frightened bird in a cage.

Aldus strode ahead and bowed to the creature. "Hello, Galorolen. It is good to see you again."

"And you, Aldus," Galorolen said, dipping his own, massive head.

Levi dusted off his shirt. "Uh, you two know each other."

"Certainly, Levi," Aldus said. "We have been friends for years."

77

Levi rubbed his hands together. "Ok. So, Mister Galorolen, what exactly are you? I've never heard of anything like you."

A growl grew in Galorolen's chest, but when he spoke, there was a hint of humour. "That is not surprising. Very few know of my species. There are only twelve of us left and we have few encounters with humans. There are stories of us, but they are old and regarded as folktales. We are known as the Taronall."

"They are guardians," Aldus said.

"Guardians for what?"

Aldus shared a look with Galorolen. "For whatever needs to be guarded. He is guarding the portal."

Levi glanced behind him to see a rippling painting of Aldus' study hanging on an ancient tree. "Huh. Cool." He turned back. "I'm assuming not everyone can just ask one of you to guard something."

"No," Galorolen said. "We only ever agree to help those who prove themselves worthy."

Levi wrinkled his brow. "How do you do that?"

Aldus lay a hand on his shoulder. "A conversation for another day. We are in a slight hurry, remember?"

"Right, yeah. Bad things are happening," Levi said.

Aldus looked up into the Taronall's large, white face. "Galorolen, we have a situation that requires the use of the hallowed water of the slope. I have never heard of such a thing, but you, being much older than I, may have."

Galorolen sat down, his back legs folding under him. "Indeed, I do know of the water. It is not what you think. There is no special place where it resides. It can be anywhere. All you need is to perform the ritual, to imbue the water with the properties necessary."

Aldus rubbed his beard. "A ritual. Of what sort?"

"It is simple enough," Galorolen said. "Although it has mostly been forgotten by humans. One simply needs to draw a circle of Caliacirus. I trust you know how."

"Yes," Aldus said. "I do."

Galorolen continued. "However, it must be done at the base of a slope. Any slope will do. Then, a Spellcaster must recite the incantation *sanctificabor,* while the water is in the centre of the circle. That is all it takes."

"Thank you, Galorolen," Aldus said. "Your help is most appreciated. Now, we must return."

Galorolen dipped his head. "Farewell."

Levi waved. "Bye."

Galorolen cocked his head. "You have a strange spark, Levi. I will watch your progress with interest."

"Uh, thanks?" Levi said.

Aldus put a hand on his shoulder and steered him back toward the picture portal hanging on the tree. "Back to Blackthrush now, Levi. We have much to do."

Levi moaned.

Aldus held up a finger. "Oh and try not to vomit on my floor." He stepped through the portal and was gone.

Closing his eyes, Levi followed him through. Again, it felt like he was being torn apart. He burst out the other side and fell to the floor, gagging. Aldus helped him to his feet. He held his stomach. "Ugh, that is horrible."

"There is some discomfort," Aldus agreed. He fished out his pendant and placed it on the painting, closing the portal.

"So, now we gotta do a ritual?" Levi said.

"Yes. Unfortunately, neither of us are Spellcasters."

Levi wagged a finger. "Uh, Taro and Aybrin are."

"As are many others," Aldus said. "But in their current state, they will be of no help."

"But Taro and Aybrin aren't purple yet," Levi said. "They were running away last time I saw them. Although who knows if they are still themselves now."

"One way to find out." Aldus strode to the stairs and climbed up to his desk. He pulled a key from his pocket and unlocked a drawer. Inside was a scroll, bound with a leather strap.

"What's that?" Levi asked.

"Watch." Aldus unrolled the scroll and said, "Taro Voroza."

A dark spot appeared on the scroll and expanded, growing into an ink drawing of Taro and Aybrin in a tree.

"They are still themselves," Aldus said. "For now."

"Wait, that scroll lets you see where anybody is at any time?" Levi asked.

"Not anyone," Aldus said. "Only those you know quite well. A useful object, this." He locked the scroll away. "Now, before we can run to their aid, we need several things for the circle of Caliacirus: an orchid, a flute and a phoenix feather."

"Do we have those things?" Levi asked.

79

Aldus folded his hands together. "Not in my study. We will have to go get all of them."

"Oh good," Levi said. "We've also gotta get Taro and Aybrin out of a tree and perform a ritual without getting turned into mindless monsters."

"Sounds daunting," Aldus said with a smile.

"You're enjoying this, aren't you?" Levi asked.

Aldus had the grace to look a little embarrassed. "You know, it is nice to have some adventure once in a while. Especially one that has nothing to do with the Giala or the king or the Elder Gem. It'll be just like the old days."

He descended the stairs and opened the door. "Come, Levi. We have a school to save."

CHAPTER 6

The hall was empty. There was no sign of anyone, mindless or otherwise.

"Where do you think they went?" Levi whispered.

Aldus faced Levi. "I haven't the foggiest clue. But if they aren't here, then that means we have a clear path to the Potions room."

"Where the stuff for the circle thingy is?"

"Correct."

They neared the Interrogation class and Levi bit his lip. The door was barely hanging by the top hinge, swinging slightly. "Uh oh. Looks like they got the fourth-years."

"Yes, unfortunate," Aldus said. "That adds nearly twenty to their number. I'll have Myron fix the door once this is over."

Levi had a thought. "Why could they break down this door but not yours?"

Aldus raised an eyebrow. "I'll let you guess."

"Uh, yours is enchanted?"

"Yes. The whole study is. There are wards on that room from generations of headmasters. I doubt anyone could break them."

"That's pretty cool," Levi said.

Their footsteps, though muffled by the carpet, were loud in the silence of the empty building. No one barred their way as they stepped out onto the balcony, nor when they descended the curving staircase, nor when they walked down the hall and entered the room where it had all begun.

Levi waved a hand in front of his nose. "Ugh. Gross." The smoke was gone, but there was a residue coating everything in a thin layer of dark soot.

"Hmm. Quite the mess," Aldus commented. "Now, best not to linger, in case we contract whatever it is. Hurry along and fetch me a phoenix feather."

Levi nodded and scooted around the tables to the front of the room to where the rare, expensive ingredients were kept. He skimmed the labels on the drawers until he found the one he was looking for. He plucked out a long red feather that faded to orange as it extended down the black shaft. Levi raised a brow in wonder. It was the softest feather he had ever felt and the lightest.

As he turned to leave, something crunched beneath his sole. He bent down and picked up a bit of parchment, ripped from a larger sheet. Very clearly imprinted on the paper was a winged horse: the royal seal of King Farren.

"Aldus?"

The headmaster looked up from a box of dried flowers. He pulled out a light pink one and joined Levi. "Yes?"

Levi held out the scrap for Aldus to see. The older man's mouth formed a thin line. "Do you know who lost that?"

"No," Levi said. "But I do know that four instructors were standing about there when it all went crazy."

"Who?" Aldus asked quietly.

"Well, Verrol and Linae, they were teaching and Griswold and Hejeck came in to talk to them."

Aldus' eyes were full of disappointment. "Pity."

"What do we do?" Levi asked.

"For right now, nothing but fix everyone," Aldus said. "After, your friends will need to investigate. Not you," he said, forestalling Levi's complaint. "You must seem as if you aren't involved. And as for I, if I start looking into them, whichever one of them is the spy will surely flee. Until we know who it is for certain, we will do nothing. I will speak to your companions as soon as this is over."

Levi slumped his shoulders. Do nothing? He wanted to help catch the spy, not sit around helplessly. But he understood the wisdom in what Aldus said and accepted it. He held up his feather. "Are we ready?"

"We still need the flute," Aldus said.

"Where are we going to get that?"

"If I recall correctly, Miss Holly plays the flute."

Levi tapped his fist in his other hand, thinking about his classmate. "You're right! She does!" He followed Aldus out of the room, trying to forget about the revelation that one of the instructors was the spy for a moment.

As the two neared the open doors at the end of the grand entrance, they slowed. There could be any number of infected students just beyond their sight. Levi crept to the threshold and poked his head outside. He looked left and right, then back left again. The way was clear. He waved Aldus ahead.

Levi's shoes slapped against the stone steps leading down to the grass. Still wary he turned left and hurried along the front of the building. He came to the corner and peeked around. There was one person shambling by aimlessly: Ellis.

"Just the one," Aldus said. "Shouldn't be too difficult to avoid."

Levi agreed. Ellis was wandering away from them and white camp was only a hundred and twenty feet away. Together, they stealthily stole across the lawn to the building where white camp lived. Levi opened the door and they slipped inside.

Levi glanced around. It was the same as blue camp, except for the colour, which was obviously white. "Now, where's Holly's stuff?"

Down at the far end of the building, someone sat up in bed. Demeter. "What are you doing?" She sounded congested.

"Hello, Demeter," Aldus said. "We are looking for Holly's flute. Do you know where it is?"

Demeter coughed. "Why didn't you ask her?"

Levi scratched his temple. "That would be because she is in a mindless horde, probably trying to pull Taro and Aybrin out of the tree right now."

Demeter sat up straighter. "What now?"

"Just a small dilemma we are in," Aldus said. "Potion accident. Just, stay inside, stay quiet and you should be fine. Now, the flute?"

"Ok?" Demeter was confused, but she got out of bed, coughing. "Uh, why do you need the flute?"

"We gotta do some weird ritual with some stuff to save everyone," Levi said. He held up the feather. "That's why I have this. You sound terrible by the way."

"Thanks," Demeter croaked. "I got it from Romeo. But she keeps her flute in a small box under her bed." She crossed the width of the building and bent down next to the third bed from the far end. She reached underneath and pulled out an acacia box.

Aldus went to take it from her. He lay a hand on her shoulder. "Get some rest. I don't like to see my students sick. I may send a message to Cam for you."

"Thanks, Aldus," Demeter said. She handed him the box and crawled back into bed. "I hope you fix everyone."

"Me too," Levi said. He and Aldus turned and exited white camp. Levi looked for Ellis, but he had wandered off. The coast was clear.

"Now, to find Taro and Aybrin. They ran out of the Academy."

Aldus tucked the flute box under his arm. "Then, they are most likely near the river, as they are in a tree."

"C'mon," Levi said.

They only spotted two infected people as they ran to the Academy's gate: Lance and Miss Nordstrom. Levi and Aldus avoided them easily enough and exited Blackthrush. Levi took three steps down the beaten path leading to the bridge into Forenfall before stopping. To the left of the bridge was nearly everyone from Blackthrush in a writhing throng around a tree, in which Taro and Aybrin clung to the branches desperately.

"Well, I think we found them," Levi said. "Geez, that's a lot of people."

"All of Blackthrush," Aldus said. "Save for the three we passed earlier, Demeter and, of course, us."

Levi ran his tongue across his teeth as he surveyed the scene. "So, how are we gonna get past them?"

Aldus tapped his fingers on his wrist. "I believe they will simply choose to chase you once you get close enough."

"Me?"

"Yes. I need to set up the ritual circle and will need some time. You must be the distraction. Would you hand me the feather?"

Levi stared at him, mouth hanging open. "You're joking, right?"

"Not in the slightest," Aldus said, tapping Levi on the back. "Now, off you go. Try not to get caught."

"Unbelievable," Levi muttered under his breath as he handed Aldus the phoenix feather. Walking toward the horde, he groaned, "I'm gonna die."

"Levi!" Taro cried from up in the tree. "Help!"

"Hang on!" Levi yelled. "Aldus has a plan, but you guys need to help!" The mass of purple students and instructors turned at the sound of Levi's voice. He gulped. "Uh oh."

Kana, eyes glowing unnaturally, lurched ahead, arms outstretched. The rest followed her lead, prompted by the unintentional magic Coraline had created. Levi scrambled back and slipped on a stone, losing his balance. His hands tore at the grass as he tried to get back to his feet. Shadows fell over him as the horde closed in.

Fear struck him through his chest like a bolt of lightning. He didn't want to be turned into a mindless monster. He channelled his inner energy and rolled over, thrusting out his hands. The closest eight people flew backward, crashing into the close-packed ranks, bowling others over. He used the momentary respite to scramble to his feet and sprint away.

Feet pounding, heart pumping, he tore across the meadow outside of Blackthrush. A glance over his shoulder showed him that the throng was shambling after him slowly. Levi blew out a breath and slowed, realizing he didn't need to run as fast as he could. They weren't quick, and he needed to make sure they stayed after him, giving Aldus and the other two enough time to perform the ritual.

It only took a few moments for his heart to slow and his breathing to return to normal. His time at Blackthrush had strengthened him more than he would have thought. He was in the best shape of his life.

Hands on hips, he faced the mindless students. "They're not so scary. From this far." They drew closer, all unblinking eyes focused on Levi. "Ok, time to move again." He jogged for close to two hundred feet, leading the horde further from Aldus and the ritual. He continued the game of cat and mouse, keeping just close enough so the horde wouldn't lose interest. Once he figured he was far enough away, he turned and ran to the left, circling wide around the mass, and headed back to the bridge.

Breathing heavily, he slid to a stop next to where Aldus was drawing in the dirt with a stick. Taro and Aybrin glanced up.

"Hi," Levi said.

"Hi. Where'd they go?" Taro asked.

Levi motioned over his shoulder. "Back there somewhere. I lost 'em."

Aldus finished scribbling and stood. The circle was actually a large circle with three smaller ones around it, connected by straight lines. Two of the small circles were close and the other was opposite them and the lines converged in a sort of Y shape. "The items. Place them in the circles."

Taro and Aybrin did as Aldus directed, Aybrin placing the orchid and the flute in the two close circles and Taro setting the feather on the other side.

"Now, the water," Aldus said. No one moved.

"Uh, we don't have like a cup or anything, do we?" Levi asked.

Taro spread empty hands.

Aldus cleared his throat. "Bit of an oversight."

"You think?" Levi asked.

"We could use the flute box," Aybrin said. "It will hold water."

Aldus raised a finger. "Yes, excellent. That will do fine. Levi, if you would?"

"Yeah, sure." He scooped up the rectangular box and jogged down to the riverbank. Its water flowed smoothly, passing under the bridge as it made its way to the ocean. Levi knelt and dipped the box in the water. He carried the full box back to the circle, splashing a small amount on the way. The headmaster pointed to the center of the circle, where the lines met. Levi placed it directly on top of the junction.

Aldus waved Taro ahead. "Are you prepared?" Taro nodded. "Good. Now, the incantation is *sanctificabor*. You'll know the spell is complete when the lines of the circle glow."

Levi's neck itched. He turned and moaned. "Uh, how long will this take?"

Aldus looked up at the infected students trudging down the path toward them. "Longer than it will take them to reach us. We will have to hold them off. Levi, use your telekinesis. Aybrin, have you learned the stunning spell?"

"Yeah, you want me to use that?"

Aldus nodded. "And perhaps the wall spell as well. We don't want to hurt them."

Aybrin nodded and pushed up her sleeves. "Right."

Aldus turned to Taro. "Once it's complete, you must have the water touch every one of them. And don't use it all because there are still a few up in the Academy."

"You got it, boss," Taro said.

Levi faced the oncoming wave and licked his suddenly dry lips. For all the times he had faced death, there was something even more terrifying about facing his own friends, who had no control over what they were doing. He dearly hoped he wouldn't injure anyone. Except maybe Corvin and Vonn.

Hundreds of glowing eyes closed in on Levi. He looked into the faces he knew so well. Guy was right up front. Levi called forth his magic. "Sorry about this." The first blast sent Guy ten feet into the air. He crashed down somewhere in the crowd. Levi winced. "Not so high."

Behind him, he heard Taro say, "*Sanctificabor!*" The ritual had begun.

Levi stretched out his hands again, pushing the advancing crowd back a few steps. To his right, Aybrin barked, "*Bayok!*" and a flash of red struck Bear in the chest. He crashed into three others and they all fell to the ground. The other three got back to their feet, but Bear stayed down. Levi gathered his magic and channelled it into his right hand, which he straightened and swiped down horizontally, cutting the legs out from under the first rank of the infected. They toppled over, tripping up and stalling the ones behind them.

"Nice one, Levi," Aybrin said, stunning Hejeck back into Adelle.

Levi flashed a quick grin, before turning to his left and shoving away those who were getting too close. Further over, a knot of students fell over, Aldus having caused them to fall asleep.

The ones Levi had tripped had gotten back to their feet and closed in. Levi mentally pushed back a couple to his right before picking up Silverton and Kavik. It took significant effort, but Levi managed to lift them back over the crowd and toss them onto the grass. He shook his head, feeling his stores of energy draining.

"*Bayok!*" Aybrin yelled and a mindless Kaito was blasted away.

"Hey! Right side!" Levi called, warning her. She turned around to see the far edge of the horde flanking her and heading toward Taro.

"*Murikon ultas!*" Aybrin clapped her hands together. The ground rumbled and a second later, a stone wall eight feet tall and ten feet long shot up in front of the mass. Aybrin stumbled as the magic took its toll.

"Heads up!" Levi warned. Aybrin stepped back, not ready to cast another spell. Levi swept his arm, taking out four people by the chest so she could recuperate. Dante's head bounced off a rock, making Levi wince. That was going to leave a mark.

Another group of people tumbled to the ground, knocked off their feet by Aldus. Levi threw Michael into one of the first-years and stepped back, wiping his brow. He had never moved so much with his mind at one time before and it was wearing him down.

"Done!"

Levi risked a glance behind him to see the Caliacirus circle glowing a soft white.

"Spray them," Aldus said, sounding slightly weary himself.

Taro dipped his head. Holding his index and middle fingers on his right hand together, he said, "*Aguir fawl.*" The newly hallowed water rose from the box in a rippling, snake-like shape. Tongue out, Taro pointed at the far-left edge of the horde. Water rushed at them. As it struck, there was a sizzling sound and smoke poured out of their mouths, dissipating into the air. Taro waved his arm around, commanding the hallowed water to touch every one of the infected people.

Levi stood back and looked on as everyone vomited smoke, their eyes returning to normal, the purple glow gone. They came to their senses, looking incredibly confused.

Taro, having cleansed everyone present, returned the water to the flute box and cut off his spell. "Whew! That was exciting."

"That's one way to put it," Aybrin said, plopping down on the grass.

The cured crowd muttered and looked around, wondering what had happened to them.

Aldus clapped for attention. "Yes, hello, everyone! You all have no idea what happened. A potion went awry, and you were all under a form of mind control. Luckily, we found an antidote and you are no longer under the influence. No need to worry, no harm was done. Except to a few doors."

Dante rubbed the back of his head. His hands came away red. "No harm? Then what do you call this?"

Levi winced. "Uh, yeah sorry about that."

"What'd you do to me?" Dante asked.

Levi spread his hands. "Well, we had to keep you guys from ruining the ritual, so I kinda threw you guys around."

Hejeck dusted himself off. "Whoever hit me with a stunning spell, well done. I feel like I've been kicked by a horse. I haven't seen a student here manage one so well in years."

Aybrin grinned. "Cool. I need a nap."

Linae tapped the stone wall she'd conjured. "No kidding. This is impressive."

Silverton pointed to the Caliacirus circle. "Taro, you managed that?"

"Yep."

"They all performed admirably," Aldus said. "Thanks to their efforts, you are no longer mindless drones. However, there are still a few left in the Academy who have yet to be purified. Taro, if you would?"

"Yeah, right behind you." Taro picked up the box and followed Aldus back up the hill toward Blackthrush.

Kana walked over to Levi. He smiled at the confusion still on her face. "Quit your grinning."

"Sorry," Levi said. "Now that it's over, it's kinda funny."

Kana rubbed her neck. "How long were we...?"

"Dunno," Levi said. "I'd say no more than twenty-five minutes, but I had to teleport across the world to find the cure, so I really have no idea."

"Teleport?" Cody was suddenly beside them. "How?"

Levi lowered his voice. "In Aldus' study, you know the-"

He stopped talking as Griswold lumbered close, remembering that he was possibly the spy. Levi's gaze flitted to the other three suspects, then back to the duelling instructor.

"So, you're not totally useless after all," Griswold grunted. He jerked his head in his approximation of a thank you and walked off.

"Round up the others," Levi whispered to Kana and Cody, once Griswold was out of earshot. "There's something I need to tell you."

"Like, something about the you-know-what?" Cody asked, voice equally low.

Levi nodded. "Meet me in the south tower."

"Will do," Kana said. She and Cody turned away to fetch those trusted by Levi.

He took a moment to stretch his back and crack his neck. He looked back at Aybrin, whistled for her attention and gave her a thumbs up. She returned it with a tired, but proud smile. He pushed through the crowd, patting Dante on the back and apologizing for his goose egg.

A minute or two later, he entered the south tower and climbed the stairs to the lounge area. Taking a seat on the couch set against one of the walls, he waited for the others to arrive. A cockroach scuttling across the floorboards provided some entertainment until the door opened to admit Ember and Naomi.

"You guys ok?" Levi asked.

"Yeah, a little sore." Ember rubbed her left leg.

"Not to mention wholly weirded out," Naomi said. "I can't remember the last, well I don't know how long!" She pulled out one of the chairs around the table and sat.

"It is disconcerting," Ember agreed.

Levi made a face. "Yeah, it was pretty disturbing watching you guys come at me with glowing purple eyes."

"Our eyes were glowing?" Naomi asked. "Creepy."

Levi chuckled.

Footsteps on the stairs heralded the approach of the rest of his inner circle. He counted heads as they came in. Ten. Perfect.

Guy massaged his shoulder, a pained look on his face.

"Sorry," Levi said. "I tried not to hurt anyone."

"No matter," Guy said. "We owe you, I guess."

Cody grabbed a chair, spun it around and straddled it, crossing his arms on the backrest. "What's the deal?"

Levi took a moment to look at each person in the room, making sure they knew it was a serious matter. "The spy."

"You know who it is?" Kana gasped.

Levi shook his head. "Not exactly. We know it's one of four. And they're all instructors."

Kinzo muttered a curse from where he was leaning against the wall. "Which ones?"

"The four in the potions class when it went off," Levi answered.

"Who?" Kaito asked. Half of them hadn't been in the class with Levi.

"Verrol, Linae, Griswold and Hejeck," Evander answered.

The room fell silent as the revelation was processed. Levi knew the betrayal they were feeling. They trusted those men with their education and safety everyday and now, one of them was a traitor.

"What do we do?" Naomi asked quietly.

Levi spread his hands. "Not sure. Aldus is gonna talk to you guys. I can't get involved. If I'm snooping around, there's a much better chance he'll find out I'm the one. Aldus too. If he gets involved, the spy will take off and we won't catch him. You guys are gonna have to do it yourselves."

Guy shifted uncomfortably and Ember put a hand on her forehead. Miri frowned, her fingers twitching, like they did when she was distraught. Even Coral's signature smirk was gone. The news had disheartened everyone.

Cody picked at a sliver on the chair. "Hejeck does hate you."

Levi grunted. The riding instructor had disliked Levi from his arrival and the whole Rorien Stern fiasco had only worsened their relationship.

"And Griswold just hates everyone," Guy muttered. "Right awful git that one."

"It can't be Verrol," Miri signed. "He's too sweet. Have you ever seen him angry at anyone?"

"Could be an act," Evander said. "The best spies have to be great actors, right?"

Kinzo crossed his arms. "Still seems unlikely. But we can't just dismiss him totally."

Kana nodded. "Kinzo's right. We'll have to investigate all of them."

"Linae too," Naomi said. "He's a difficult person to read, but he seems nice enough."

Levi sighed. "It doesn't matter how nice, or not nice they seem. One of them is our enemy. Don't trust any of them." No one was happy about it, but Levi could see in their faces that they were prepared to do whatever it took to find the spy.

A short breath, almost a laugh came from Cody. "Well, this has certainly been a day."

Guy smirked. "At least we missed Politics." Ember didn't even bother to argue with him.

Levi pushed himself to his feet. "Alright. Good chat. Aldus'll see you guys soon, I'm sure. But I need to go eat something." He walked to the door, chairs and shoes scraping across the floor as everyone stood to follow him out of the tower.

Stepping out onto the lawn, Levi looked over the people wandering back into the Academy from the river. They walked in small groups, talking about what had just transpired. Levi's mouth curled up; today was going to be the topic of discussion for the next while.

Kinzo nudged Levi. "You think Aldus will cancel the rest of the classes?"

"I don't know; it's not like anything serious happened," Levi said.

"Yeah, I guess," Kinzo said. "But one can hope, right?"

Levi smirked. "Yeah, you can hope. Won't change anything, but you can do it."

The mess hall was practically empty when they arrived, only Quinn and Osiris from yellow camp were there, talking at their table. Quinn spread his hands when they arrived. "Food's not ready yet."

"Ok, thanks," Levi said, taking a seat at blue camp's table with the others.

"To think we wouldn't even be remotely hungry if the potion had worked properly," Naomi said.

"Yeah, well, you have Coraline to thank for that," Kinzo said.

"She made the purple smoke?" Guy asked. "Not surprising."

Ember flicked his arm.

"What? She's a klutz," Guy said.

"She is," Cody agreed.

Ember crossed her arms. "It's not like she can help it. You shouldn't be mean."

"Be mean? How am I being mean?" Guy asked. "I just said I wasn't surprised that it was her."

Ember rolled her eyes.

Guy scoffed. "Oh, come on now..."

Levi's attention was drawn to the door as a couple other students entered. Christian was telling a story, waving his arms for emphasis. His friends burst into laughter as they claimed a free table.

Balak came in behind them and approached Levi's table. "Could you all come with me? Except Levi."

"Of course," Kana said, pushing her chair back. Everyone stood and followed Balak out of the mess hall.

Miri squeezed Levi's shoulder as she passed. He smiled up at her.

When they were gone, he let out a long sigh. They were off on an adventure without him, placing themselves in danger for his sake. "They better not get hurt."

"What's that?"

Levi glanced up to see one of the first years from blue camp, Walt, standing next to him.

"Oh, hi. Um, it's nothing. Never mind."

Walt sat down across from Levi. His long curls framed a young, dark face that always seemed to be smiling. He couldn't have been more than fourteen. "Where did all your friends go?"

"Uh, they have something to do. Aldus wanted them," Levi answered, half-truthfully.

"And not you?" Walt asked. "But you're always involved."

Levi's heart skipped a beat. "What?"

Walt put his arms on the tabletop. "Well, I wasn't here last year, but I heard that you were right in the middle of all that crazy stuff that happened. And you do spend a lot of time with the headmaster, more than most others. Everyone knows that. I'm just surprised you aren't involved with whatever they are."

Everyone knows? I thought we were being discreet about meeting. Levi tugged on his bracer's straps. "What can I say? I guess Aldus likes me." The conversation was headed toward dangerous territory.

Walt nodded. "Some people think it's because you guys are related. Are you?"

"Uh, um, yes," Levi lied. "I am. My father is his, uh, cousin. He was just here visiting, you know."

"Yeah, I saw him," Walt said. "That's cool that you're related to Aldus."

Levi rubbed his left thumb. "Uh huh. Really cool."

"By the way, thanks for saving us," Walt said. "I don't remember much, but it must have been scary."

"Yeah, no problem," Levi said. "It was a little scary, but not too bad. I've faced worse."

"Like last year?" Walt asked, eyes gleaming.

Levi mentally cursed for steering the conversation back toward sensitive topics. "Yep. That whole business was a lot scarier than you guys turning purple."

Walt's smile grew wider. "Because of the Kar-Sang?"

"You've heard a lot," Levi said. Walt nodded enthusiastically. "Yeah, I hope I never cross paths with those two again. Or their master for that matter."

"I do want to see a Kar-Sang," Walt said.

Levi looked him in the eye. "No. You don't. Trust me."

Walt's smile shrank slightly. "Well, maybe once I'm a full knight."

Levi tilted his head. "Maybe."

"I think it's really cool that you've had a great adventure already," Walt said. "I'm sure most people here wouldn't have survived it."

Levi rested his chin in his hand. "It's not so cool when you have to run and fight for your life over and over. And I didn't do it alone, I wouldn't have made it alone. And I got damn lucky."

"I don't believe in luck," Walt said, matter-of-factly. "I think everyone is destined for something. And you're destined for something great, I'm sure."

Levi stared at Walt. The kid smiled broadly and turned as the cooks brought out the meal to the serving tables. Levi shook his head.

A steady stream of people entered the mess hall. Other blue campers joined Levi and Walt at the table, but it felt empty without his friends, who were off doing who-knows-what.

Autumn smiled at him as she sat down. "Thanks."

"You should thank Aybrin and Taro," Levi said.

"I did," Autumn replied. "And they said I should thank you."

Someone jostled Levi as they took a seat next to him. "My apologies, Levi," Adam said.

"No harm done," Levi said.

Adam inclined his head. "I wish to thank you. Your actions allowed the accident to be taken under control. You utilized your magic wonderfully, allowing the ritual to be completed."

"I guess."

"I was not aware you could move so much with your mind at once," Adam said.

Levi raised an eyebrow. "Well, uh, I guess adrenaline helps."

Adam paused. "Adrenaline. Yes. Of course." His eyebrows drew together as he thought.

"Uh, what you thinking, there?" Levi asked.

Adam held up a hand. "Nothing of importance."

94

Levi shrugged. Adam was a bit of an oddball, but he liked him and didn't press for answers.

After the meal, Levi wandered over to the north tower for History class after swinging by his camp house for his books. He arrived early. The class was empty, save for Kindrelle, who was always plenty ahead of schedule.

"Levi, why are you here so early?" Kindrelle asked.

"Had nothing else to do," Levi answered, taking his usual seat at the third desk on the right.

"Your friends aren't with you," Kindrelle noted.

"Nope."

"Where are they?"

Levi spread his hands. "Honestly, not sure. Aldus had something for them to do."

"Aldus has them doing something and you're not involved?" Kindrelle didn't hide her skepticism.

"Why does everyone find that hard to believe?" Levi asked.

"Because you're always off getting into all kinds of trouble," Kindrelle said.

"Oh, come on. When was the last time I got into trouble?" Levi asked.

Kindrelle tapped her cheek. "If I recall, you and your friends were out in Forenfall at night two weeks ago. And you know that's against the rules."

Levi squirmed in his seat. He had thought they had snuck in and out without anyone noticing. "You know about that?"

"Of course, I know," Kindrelle said. "Everyone knows."

"Well, I actually wasn't out that night. I was in my bunk."

Kindrelle's expression didn't change. "You still knew about it. You've all somehow become the headmaster's personal army. So, that's why I'm surprised you aren't up to something with the others."

"Hold on. Personal army?" Levi asked. "No, definitely not."

Kindrelle crossed her arms.

The door to the classroom creaked open, revealing the History instructor, Miss Holbrook. "Kindrelle." She frowned. "Levi? You're early."

"Just don't ask," Levi said.

Holbrook exchanged a look with Kindrelle and shrugged. "Very well. Your classmates should be along shortly."

"Not all of them," Kindrelle said. "Levi says his friends are off doing something for Aldus."

"And you aren't with them?" Holbrook asked.

Levi threw his hands in the air and yelled, "You too?"

Holbrook took a step back, surprised. The door banged open again and in tromped the rest of the class, sparing Levi from any more questions about him and Aldus. Talking and joking loudly, they grabbed spots at empty benches, most trying to get the seats at the back, furthest from Holbrook. Bram ended up losing a spot at the back and slid onto the bench beside Kindrelle. She groaned loudly, prompting a chuckle from the class. Bram turned and winked at Dante, who gave him a thumbs up.

Holbrook cleared her throat for attention. "Hello class. We had an interesting morning, but that does not excuse anyone from not paying attention today."

"But it excused all Levi's friends?" Holly asked.

Holbrook shifted her weight onto one foot. "Well, Aldus asked them for some help."

"And he didn't take Levi?" Niles asked.

Levi flopped his head down on the table with a moan.

"Apparently," Holbrook said. "And I'm sure he will gladly tell them exactly what they have missed."

Levi lifted his head just enough to glare at Holbrook.

She ignored him. "Now, everyone to page two hundred fifty-four."

Levi dragged himself up and opened his copy of Vyrgond's Complete History. The sound of flipping pages filled the room. Levi turned half the pages at once, ending up way past the intended spot. He leafed back to the right spot. The title at the top of the page read: The Fall of The Free Knights.

"Who here knows of the Free Knights?" Holbrook asked. Every hand was raised.

"Are all the stories real?" Coraline asked.

"Not all, but many," Holbrook said. "And, as you know, they are no longer around. The last one died over forty years ago."

"Murdered, more like," Levi muttered to himself.

Duncan, who was sitting in front of him, turned. "What's that?"

"Nothing," Levi said.

Holbrook gave them a withering look and continued. "The Free Knights were the protectors of the realm for over a century. They worked with, but not under the rule of the kings and queens of Terrenia. They answered to no one but themselves and ultimately, that is what caused their downfall."

Levi snorted, earning him another scowl from Holbrook.

The teacher composed herself. "Dante, could you read the first paragraph?"

Dante cursed. "Uh, I guess." He cleared his throat. "The members of King Harold's court were, uh, subjugated to a series of-"

"Dante, turn the page," Holbrook said.

He flipped the sheet. "Oh, this makes more sense. Ok, so... Finding proof of a conspiracy against him, King Harold asked to..."

"Parley," Romeo whispered to him.

"...parley with the Free Knights," Dante continued. "But the royal messenger never returned with an answer. He never returned at all. Furious, the king sent another. Again, the messenger was never heard from. The king readied a force to arrest the commandant of the Free Knights, Corydon, but the following night, an assassin sent by the Free Knights attempted to kill King Harold. His life was saved by Prince Farren, but Harold had still been poisoned. Unable to personally arrest Corydon, he charged Farren with the task, telling him to kill any who stood in his way."

Levi couldn't believe the utter nonsense he was hearing. The truth was radically different, but of course Farren would have changed the story to cover up his coup. He shook his head. So many people had been deceived by a simple lie.

Dante was still reading. "When Farren attempted to arrest Corydon, he was attacked and all his men were slain, with Farren barely escaping with his life. He returned to his father, whose condition had worsened and was commanded to destroy the Free Knights as they had proven themselves to be traitors. Taking a large force, they tracked the Knights down to Riverton where the battle broke out. Farren's forces were successful, killing nearly all the Free Knights. Those that escaped were hunted down and killed, but not before forming the terrorist group known as the Giala."

Levi scoffed aloud.

Everyone looked at Levi. "Is there something you would like to say?" Holbrook asked.

"Yeah," Levi said. "This is a load of rubbish."

Holbrook crossed her arms. "Why would you say that?"

Levi knew he had already said too much, but he couldn't help himself. He was angry at the way that everyone had been duped into believing the exact opposite of the truth. "Because, it's not true."

"Of course, it's true," Holbrook said. "This text has been the culmination of the most respected historians of all time. To consider what's inside as falsehood, that is an insult."

"This whole story is an insult," Levi snapped, his pulse rising. "It's all a lie!"

"How would you know?" Holbrook asked, clearly affronted. "You're a sixteen-year-old who barely knows anything."

Levi's bench clattered to the floor. "I know so much more than you think! You've all been tricked and none of you can see that! I've seen the truth and if you knew," he pointed at Holbrook. "You'd run as far as you could."

The stunned class watched silently as Levi snatched up his books and stormed to the doorway.

He turned back. "Don't believe everything you hear. The world is in much worse shape than you think." He stormed out, slamming the door behind him. His feet pounded against the stairs as he raged. How could Aldus allow this to be taught in his school? Reaching the exit and stomping onto the grass outside, the realization of what he had done crashed down on him.

Furious at Holbrook, himself and Farren's lies, he flung his textbook across the lawn with a yell. Levi grabbed his head. *What have I done? I've just given myself away. The spy will find out for sure now.*

His eyes rose to the sky. Dark clouds were rolling in from the west, casting a shadow over the Academy. He was no longer safe at Blackthrush.

CHAPTER 7

Cody pushed open the heavy doors and descended onto the path outside. The air was heavy with the scent of rain and the dark clouds above told him why.

Guy came up behind him. "You ready for this?"

"Not at all," Cody admitted. "If this doesn't go right..."

"It will," Guy nudged Cody's arm. "Let's go."

They walked through the empty yard, everyone else attending classes as they were supposed to be. As they neared the north end of the main building, Cody glanced up. Aldus was watching from the window of his study. Aldus dipped his head and backed away from the window.

Cody tried not to take it as an ominous sign. But between that and the darkening sky, he couldn't help but feel as if bad things were in store.

Guy beckoned him forward. "C'mon, we have four rooms to search."

They arrived at the building that housed the instructors and staff. It wasn't shaped like the camp houses; instead it was long, at least three times the length of the other buildings and its roof was steep.

"Do we know which rooms are theirs?" Cody wondered.

Guy pushed open the door. "Nope."

"Wonderful," Cody muttered.

The interior was simple: a long, straight hallway with rooms spaced evenly on both sides. It was quiet, Cody didn't think anyone was home and besides, all who lived here were busy teaching or keeping the Academy running.

"Guess we'll just start peeking in rooms," Cody said. He grabbed the handle of the nearest door and turned, but it remained in place. "And it's locked. Course it's locked."

Guy nudged him out of the way. "Oh, don't worry. I'll get us in, no problem." He held his index finger an inch away from the lock and said, "*Esky tastus.*" Cody heard a pop and the keyhole began smoking slightly. Guy stepped back and bowed.

Cody snorted and pushed open the door. Peeking inside, he saw a small, square room with a bed taking up most of the floor space. A nightstand sat next to the bed and there was a small table next to the door. Shelves ringed the room at chest height; resting on them were all sorts of figurines of soldiers and small globes containing miniature landscapes. Sheets of parchment were stacked on the table beside a small, locked black box with gold trim.

"Silverton's room," Guy figured.

Cody pointed to the bedpost. "Look, his special hat." Silverton's outfit was never complete without his signature red and blue tasselled cap, but he had a black and silver one for special occasions and it lived on his bedpost, apparently.

The two intruders backed out and Cody shut the door. "Guy, can you lock doors? If not, they're gonna know someone was snooping around."

"Uh, yeah, I know that one," Guy said, his brow wrinkling. He closed his eyes and twitched his fingers, the way he did when he was thinking hard. "Got it." He held out his right hand, palm out, fingers splayed and twisted it to the left as he said, "*Kibon pors.*" The door clicked.

Cody wiggled the handle, feeling it locked in place once more. "Nice."

The next room they checked was Nordstrom's room, judging by the diagrams of various creatures on the wall and the jars of insects and small animals on her desk.

They locked the door behind them and carried on.

The next three rooms also did not belong to any of the four suspected spies. Anxiousness began to grow in Cody's stomach. He knew that the longer they stayed, the more likely they would be discovered and that would only lead to bad things, for both themselves and Levi.

Guy popped the lock of the third room on the right. Taking in the bare walls, clean desk and the broadsword leaning against the foot of the bed, Cody knew it was Griswold's room. They slipped in and closed the door behind them.

"Ok, what are we looking for?" Guy asked.

"Anything connecting him to the king or anyone high up in his court," Cody said. He started pulling open the drawers of the desk. The first one contained a dozen knives of varying lengths and styles. Cody picked up a long, straight one with a bone handle wrapped in leather. The blade was tinged blue and seemed to shimmer. "What's this?"

Guy turned from where he was kneeling beside the bed. "Dunno. I've never seen a metal like that before."

Cody stared at the blade, his reflection moving slightly. He shrugged and set it back in its place.

The next drawer held a small stack of loose papers, tied with a strip of rawhide. Cody leafed through the pages, looking for anything of interest. Most of them pertained to someone called the Pariah and clues about where they were. There were maps and diagrams of spells, all with notes scribbled beside them. "He's on the island," Cody read aloud. "Lera is a dead-end. A guardian? Can't be in Ashen. Six, there are six." Cody glanced up. "Guy, what is this? Have you ever heard of the Pariah?"

Guy backed out from under the bed, holding something wrapped in a cloth. "Huh? No idea. Never heard of it." He sat cross-legged and unwrapped the item. It was a bronze telescope. Guy put it to his eye. "Just a normal telescope. Wonder why he kept it under his bed."

Cody turned back to the pages. One was a drawing of what appeared to be a man standing in front of a cave. The one after was taken from a book, its edge was jagged. It spoke of a woman who had seen a dark figure on the hilltops at night.

Cody was about to put the bundle back when his eye caught on the corner of a sheet sticking out. He turned to the page and gasped. It was a letter from King Farren, signed with his name and seal. Cody tried to read it, but the words were all scrambled and broken apart into an unintelligible mess.

"Guy. Look."

"So, is it him?"

Cody faced his friend. "I don't know. But we need to find out what this is all about." He held up the bundle of papers.

"We can't just take it though," Guy said. "He'd know it's missing."

Cody thought furiously. There had to be a way to get them out without Griswold noticing. He grabbed Guy's shoulder. "There's a spell. I heard Balak telling you about it a few months ago."

"What spell?" Guy asked.

"Uh, what did he call it? The Seridion Spell! That's it!"

Guy's mouth dropped open. "Oh no. No way. I'm not doing that!"

"Why not?" Cody asked. "It allows you to copy something instantly, right?"

Guy crossed his arms. "Yes. But do you know what you have to do to cast it?"

Cody shook his head.

"I'd have to cut off a finger!" Guy said. "I want to keep all my fingers! And besides, we have nothing to copy it on."

Cody raised his eyes to the ceiling, exasperated. "Come on, Guy! This is for the fate of the world! You don't need a pinky, anyway. And you can copy it on..." He looked around for anything. The room was bare and taking Griswold's sheets would be another giveaway that they had intruded. "...Me. Just put it on my back. The writing will be small, but that should work."

Guy raised an eyebrow. "On your back? That's gonna hurt. It basically burns the copy on."

"Then we'll both be sacrificing something," Cody said.

The door at the end of the hall opened and voices filtered down to them.

Cody grabbed Guy's shoulder. "Do it!"

Guy knocked his hand away. "Damn it! Fine! I'll do it. Give me the papers."

Cody handed them over and Guy set them on the floor. He motioned for Cody to take off his shirt and drew one of his swords. With a deep breath, he held out his left hand and chopped off his pinky. He opened his mouth, screaming silently, his face a mask of pain. Blood splattered on the ground and a strangled grunt escaped him.

"Do it," Cody said as the voices slowly drew nearer.

Holding his left hand close, Guy put his right hand over the stack of papers, forming it into a claw. Through clenched teeth, he whispered, "*Seridio akima.*" A ghostly copy of the pages floated up to Guy's hand and he turned and jammed it onto Cody's bare back.

Incredible pain erupted through Cody's body. He arched his spine, throwing his head back and clenching his fists, but he refused to cry out. After a few seconds, it was over. Cody slumped down, his back burning as each stroke of ink scarred itself into his skin.

"You ok?" Guy asked, still grimacing himself.

Cody dashed away a tear. "Yeah. We've got to get out of here." He put the stack of papers back in the drawer as Guy kicked everything back under the bed.

"Out the window," Cody whispered as the voices outside came closer.

Guy crossed the room and heaved open the narrow window. He slipped out.

Cody took a moment to snatch Guy's pinky and wipe the blood off the floor with his shirt before scrambling out the window behind his friend. He pulled it down just as the door opened and Griswold entered. Cody ducked and began to crawl away, following Guy. He pulled his shirt on as he did, hiding the secrets Griswold had been keeping.

The two raced back to the classroom that Aldus had given them as their headquarters while they were tracking the spies. Ember and Naomi were inside.

"What happened?" Naomi asked, springing to Guy's side, seeing blood. Guy didn't answer, just flopped into a chair and cradled his injury.

Ember came up to Cody. "You're covered in blood. Did you get found out?"

"No," Cody said, his voice still thick with pain. "It's Guy's. We did find something. I'm not sure what it is, but it seemed important."

"Where is it?" Ember asked. "You're not carrying anything.

Cody gritted his teeth and pulled off his shirt, tensing as the fabric brushed against his new scars. He turned and heard both girls gasp.

"What did you do?" Naomi sounded horrified. "Are those burns?"

"Yep."

"Seridion Spell," Guy muttered. "Had to cut off my pinky."

Naomi whirled on Guy. "You did this to yourselves? Are you insane?"

"It was his idea," Guy grumbled.

"Look, this could be important," Cody said. "There's one page that's a letter from Farren himself. That can't be nothing."

He flinched, feeling Ember's cool touch. "Yes, you're right. But, it's all scrambled. I can't read it. But the rest... who's the Pariah?"

"Don't know," Cody said. "We need to tell Aldus about this."

"Yes, but not now. He said he was meeting with one of the Forenfall nobles, remember?" Ember said.

"We've gotta get that bleeding stopped," Naomi was saying to Guy. She marched over to Cody and snatched his already bloody shirt. "Hold this against it."

"Well, I can't exactly walk around with this visible," Cody said.

"I'll get you a new shirt," Ember said. "Hang tight." She slipped out the door.

Cody sank down into a chair, careful not to let his tender skin touch the backrest. Despite himself, he smirked. Last year, he would have never believed anyone if they told him he would be spying and stealing from his teachers, potential informants for the king, to protect the bearer of the fabled Elder Gem. He wondered what his sister would think of him. Would she be proud of what he was doing, or would she be horrified that he was a traitor to the crown?

"What is all of this?"

Cody felt Naomi's fingertips flutter gently across his back.

"That's what we've got to find out," Cody said. "It's important somehow. I know it is."

"I believe you," Naomi said. She brushed across a symbol. "I feel like I've seen this before. Like it was a dream that I've now forgotten."

Cody twisted his neck to see her concentrating on the scars he had never thought he would have.

Guy grunted in pain. "That better be something important. If I chopped off a finger for nothing, you and I are gonna have a problem, Cody." There wasn't anything in his eyes to suggest he was joking.

Ember returned in a few moments and dropped a shirt on the table in front of Cody. "I brought actual bandages." She reached out for Guy's injured hand. He reluctantly allowed her to wrap the wound properly with white cloth.

Guy held up his bandaged hand and frowned. "People are gonna ask questions."

"Tell them to mind their own business," Ember said.

"You know they won't."

"Make them," Ember told him, lifting her chin. "And if you won't, I will."

Guy couldn't stop the smirk from spreading across his lips.

"What?" Ember asked.

"Nothing," Guy said.

Ember joined Naomi in puzzling over the information burned onto Cody. He leaned ahead, resting his arms on the table and his head on his arms, wishing he could see the notes and help decipher the mystery.

"Lera is a dead-end," Naomi muttered. "Who, or what is Lera?"

"Look here," Ember pointed. "It keeps saying six, the number, over and over. What does it mean?"

Cody shrugged, wincing as he stretched the sores. "Beats me." He laid his head down again and closed his eyes, listening to the girls mutter under their breath and Guy groan as his missing finger pained him.

The door opened sometime later, how much; Cody wasn't sure. In came Kana and Miri, who both stopped in their tracks, seeing Cody's back.

"What happened?"

Cody sighed. "Things that I somewhat regret now."

"So, do I," Guy grumbled.

Miri stepped closer to him. "You're missing a finger!"

"Well spotted," Guy said, venom in his voice.

Cody flinched. Guy was not happy about what they had to do.

Naomi explained to the two newcomers what was scarred into Cody's skin.

Kana shook her head. "I'll admit, I'm quite impressed, you two. I doubt many others would have done that, Kinzo, for one."

Guy managed to smile at Kana. "I've always told you I was impressive."

Kana groaned.

Miri sat next to Cody. "That was very brave of you."

"Thanks. So far, it hasn't proved to be of much use. Did you guys find out anything?"

"Unfortunately, no," Kana said. "We snuck into Linae's classroom easy enough, but there was nothing suspicious in his desk. He is a fan of poetry, though." She smiled as she said the last.

"Wouldn't have thought that," Guy said.

"Why not?" Ember asked. "Many people are interested in poetry."

Guy scoffed. "Like who?"

"Like me," Ember said, sounding put out.

"Ok, but you seem more like the type than Linae does."

Ember put her hands on her hips. "Oh, and what type am I, exactly?"

Guy cleared his throat. "Uh… the refined, cultured type."

For a heartbeat, Ember stood still. Then, she sniffed. "Hmph. Don't think flattering me will help you." She turned back to Cody's notes.

Miri's eyes sparkled with good humour and she signed to Cody, "He got lucky this time."

Cody grinned back. He jerked and yelped as someone pushed on his back.

"Oops, sorry, Cody," Kana said. "I wasn't sure how painful it was."

"Quite," Cody managed through clenched teeth.

Kana studied the symbols and runes and lines of text. "I have no idea what any of this means. Why did you take it?"

"The letter from the king," Naomi pointed out.

"I can't read it," Kana said.

"No one can," Ember said. "And we must find a way to read it. It could be the key to everything!"

Someone knocked at the door. Kana opened it, revealing Kaito and Coral.

"How'd it go?" Naomi asked.

"We found nothing incriminating," Kaito reported.

"What do you mean nothing incriminating?" Coral asked. "We found nothing that would prove he was the bad guy."

Kaito gave her a dry look. "That is what incriminating means."

"Oh."

The two had been investigating Verrol, following him around the Academy, seeing as he had no class. They explained that he had done very normal, if rather boring things on his break, nothing to even suggest he was up to something.

A few moments later, Kinzo and Evander barged in, both covered with hay and smelling of horse droppings. Kinzo bent over, wheezing. "We thought we'd check the stables; you know in case Hejeck was hiding something. Couldn't find anything, then he came in."

"We had to hide in a pile of hay," Evander said. He poked at a dark stain on his shirt. "It wasn't all hay."

Kinzo straightened and stared at Cody's back. "What the bloody hell did you do?"

Cody grunted and let the others explain, wanting to take something to stop the itching that was beginning to drive him crazy. He wanted to scratch but knew it would only aggravate the sores.

"You guys are nuts," Kinzo said. "I would never do that."

"Told you he wouldn't," Kana smirked.

Kaito clasped his hands behind his back. "After all that, we have no proof other than a letter from the king that we cannot read."

Cody pulled his mouth to one side. Put in perspective, he realized they had accomplished next to nothing and yet they had given up much for the little they had gained.

"There has to be some way to decipher the letter," Ember said. She moved toward the door.

"Where are you going?" Coral asked.

"The library," Ember replied, closing the door behind her.

Miri stood. "It's our best bet at figuring this out, I'll go too." She followed Ember to the library on the first floor.

"What do we do?" Kinzo asked. "I'm terrible at research."

"That's because you never actually do it," Kana said. "But, we all shouldn't miss too many classes in a row or people will grow suspicious."

"I agree," Kaito said. "I think we shouldn't have more than three off investigating at once."

"So, off to class?" Naomi surmised.

"Great," Guy groaned.

"Cody, you do have the information on you, so I suggest you join the girls in the library," Kaito said.

"Yeah, I suppose it won't do them much good to read up if they don't remember what they're looking for." Cody stood and carefully shrugged his clean shirt on. Grunting, he realized that his back was going to be sore for the next few days, maybe weeks.

He walked down the hall to the stairs, passing several students. The previous class must have just ended.

As he descended from the second floor, one of his classmates, Marshall, called to him. "Hey, where were you guys? Dunning didn't know where you were either."

"Uh, Aldus asked us to do something for him," Cody answered. "I'll be in the library with Ember, but the others should be joining you this class."

Marshall raised an eyebrow but didn't press for answers. Cody left him and turned around to head down the first-floor hall.

The library was the last room on the left side of the hall, opposite the door leading to the basement. The left corner was the only part of the room not filled with bookshelves, it instead housed two small, circular tables and a few padded chairs.

"Hey, you guys in here?" Cody called.

"Over here."

Cody followed Ember's voice to a small nook in the far corner, created by different sized shelves not fitting together properly. She sat cross-legged, a thick, dusty book on her lap. Miri came up and set down two more books and a scroll.

"Come to join us?" Miri asked.

"Well, we figured you guys might need to look at the notes again," Cody said with a wry smile. "And since they're burned into my back, I had to come."

Miri grinned and patted the floor beside her. Cody took a seat. He picked up the scroll that Miri had just brought. It wasn't terribly old and was in good shape; Cody guessed it to be no more than fifty years old, but he was no expert. He undid the leather strap and carefully let it unroll. It might not be old, but scrolls tore easily, especially if one didn't handle them with care. And he certainly didn't need Holbrook angry at him for ruining historical records.

"A Census of Tellock. Why did you grab this?"

"You know Tellock uses a different alphabet, right?" Miri asked.

"Uh... maybe?"

Miri rolled her eyes. "Do you pay attention in class at all?"

"When I want to," Cody answered.

Ember scoffed. "You boys really need to start trying. The instructors are harder the further along you are."

Cody spread his hands.

Ember shook her head and went back to reading as Miri explained to Cody the significance of the scroll. "The island used to belong to the Mizrea Tribe, right? And as Terrenia conquered it, they pushed the Tribe into the south part of the island. When the Terrenians settled in Tellock, they mingled with the Tribe and developed a sort of hybrid culture which includes their alphabet."

Cody remembered the story somewhat; Holbrook having taught it to him in his first year. "Ok, so why is the alphabet important?"

"I haven't checked it yet, but it does look awfully similar to the mess written in Farren's letter."

Cody's eyebrows rose. "You think he could have written it in their alphabet?"

Miri shrugged. "It's a possibility."

Cody handed her the scroll. Seeing her confusion, he said, "I can't exactly compare the two, now can I?"

Ember laughed.

Cody turned so his back was to Miri and pulled off his shirt, gritting his teeth against the sharp, biting pain.

Ember pushed one of the other books in front of him. "At least be useful while you're sitting there."

Picking up the blue tome, he ran his fingers across the title: Enchantments of Secrecy and Mystery. Beneath the title was a rune-like symbol that reminded Cody of a man sitting down and fishing.

He put his fingers under the lip of the front cover and flipped. Instead of opening, the entire book flipped over. Confused, Cody turned it over and tried to open it again, to the same result. Holding the book firmly, he attempted again, but the front cover wouldn't budge.

"I can't open it."

Ember looked up. "Hmm?"

Cody shook the text. "It won't open."

Ember's brows drew together.

Cody tugged on the book's covers, demonstrating that he could, in fact, not open it.

Ember set her book aside and held out a hand. Cody gave her the stubborn book and watched her study it for a few moments, turning it over in her hands.

"What are you looking for?" Cody asked.

"It's a book about secrets. I'm almost positive there's a strange way to open it, something clever and not obvious..."

"How can there be a clever way to open it?" Cody wondered. "It's a book."

"Maybe there's something specific I have to say," Ember mumbled, paying no attention to Cody. "A password of sorts. What would it be?"

"Guess I'll leave you to it," Cody said. "Hey, Miri, how's it going?"

She scooted around to his front so he could see her signing. "I don't think they match. Some of them are close, but they aren't the same." Her expression was one of mild disappointment.

"Too bad," Cody said. "Guess it can't be that easy, huh?"

Miri's mouth twitched upward.

Ember was muttering phrases to the book, hoping one would unlock it, but she was having no luck.

Someone threw open the library door, calling for Cody.

He exchanged a surprised glance with the girls and quickly threw his shirt back on. He was just pushing his right arm through the sleeve when Oliver rounded a bookshelf.

"Cody, there you are." He paused. "What are you guys doing?"

"Nothing that concerns you," Ember snapped.

Oliver leaned away. "Ok, take it easy. Cody, Griswold is looking for you."

Cody froze, a feeling of dread rising inside him. "What for?"

"Didn't say," Oliver replied. "Just told me to find you. He didn't seem too happy."

Cody's eyes met Miri's and he saw his own fear reflecting back. Had Griswold found out?

~ ~ ~

Someone knocked on the door to Farren's personal study. "Enter."

One of Farren's guards leaned in. "Captain Steele has reported in."

Farren nodded. "I'll see to him shortly."

The guard bowed and closed the door.

Farren dipped his quill into the ink and scratched the last of his message on the parchment in front of him. He wiped the tip of the quill and set it down before rolling the letter and tying it with a ribbon. Then, he sealed it with wax and pressed his ring into the maroon substance.

Finished, he stood and adjusted his robes. Picking up the letter, the king strode out of his study. His guards fell in line behind him as he walked down the hall of his castle at a measured pace.

A servant in red livery bowed as the king neared. Farren stopped in front of the young man. "You. Take this to the couriers. It is to go to our delegate in Wintenveil."

"Yes, sire." The servant took the letter from the king's hand without meeting his eyes.

Farren continued on as the servant headed for the chamber of couriers. The two guards behind him let the servant pass without a glance. They were well trained and utterly loyal. They would die for Farren in an instant, but to the King, they were simply pawns to be used.

Arriving in the dungeons beneath the castle, Farren stood in the guardroom and waited for his captain to come to him. He didn't need to wait long. Captain Steele marched out of the hall opposite the King, straight and severe.

He bowed at the waist. "My Lord."

"What do you have to report, Captain?"

"I have captured the leader of the Giala in Stagrun. Akira Bellona."

Farren allowed his brows to lift slightly. He had not been expecting this. "Excellent. Has he revealed anything useful?"

Captain Steele nodded. "Yes, sir. Your interrogators made short work of him. He provided a list of names."

"Let me see him," Farren said.

"Of course, sir," Steele said. "Cell eighty-four."

They walked down the dark maze of tunnels that was the dungeon, ending up at the cell where their newest captive was.

Farren peered through the iron bars at the thin man crumpled on the floor. "Akira Bellona."

The prisoner lifted his head to reveal a myriad of lacerations and burns. One eye was missing, as was his left hand. His jaw trembled as he beheld the King. "Have mercy."

Farren's expression didn't change. "You have been charged with treason and espionage. I sentence you to death."

"No..." Akira moaned. "Please."

Without pity or remorse, Farren flattened his right hand into a blade, whispered two words and swung. Akira's head fell to the ground in a spray of blood. His body toppled over a second later.

"Clean this up," Farren said to the captain. "And good work."

"Yes, sir," Steele said. "Thank you, your majesty."

Farren turned, his robes billowing behind him as he strode away from the growing pool of red in cell eighty-four.

CHAPTER 8

A bead of cold sweat traced a path down the side of Cody's face as he followed Oliver outside. A cold wind bit into his face as a few light drops fell from the heavy clouds above.

Griswold was waiting near green camp, his braid swaying in the wind. A scowl deeper than usual split his craggy face. He was fiddling with one of the many knives on his belt.

Cody swallowed nervously. He glanced around for Guy, but his friend wasn't around. Strange. If Griswold had found out, wouldn't he have summoned him as well?

"Cody," Griswold rumbled as they approached him.

"Griswold," Cody replied, managing to keep his voice from shaking, despite the fact that Griswold might be the traitor and may have just discovered that Cody was snooping through his private belongings.

Griswold gave Cody a once-over. "No shield?"

"Uh, what?"

Griswold grunted. "Where's your shield?"

Cody didn't know where this line of questioning was going. "It's by my bunk. I don't lug that around all day."

Griswold tossed his head in the direction of blue camp. "Go get it."

Bewildered, Cody did as the Combat instructor ordered. As he turned toward blue camp, he heard Griswold tell Oliver, "Go fetch Wes."

Maybe he doesn't know, Cody realized. *Maybe he just needs me for something totally unrelated.* Entering blue camp, he jogged to his bunk, where his round oak shield rested at the foot. He picked it up with both hands, examining the face. A strip of metal was riveted around the rim and the centre was reinforced by a metal boss, but the wood bore many scars; cuts and splinters from blocking countless blows.

"What are you up to?"

Cody spun to see the first year, Walt, smiling at him. He was picking up a book from his bunk.

"Uh, I'm getting my shield."

"What for?" The younger boy's eyes were full of bright curiosity.

Cody shrugged his shield around onto his arm. "Honestly, I have no idea. Griswold wants me for something."

"Sounds exciting!" Walt said. "But you'd better not keep him waiting." He lowered his voice. "He's not very friendly."

Cody grinned. "No, Walt, he's not. I'll get going."

As he pushed the door open, Walt called. "Cody, tell me how it goes, whatever it is, ok?"

Cody dipped his head. "Sure, Walt."

Returning to Griswold, the apprehension he had momentarily forgotten returned. The gruff instructor eyed Cody as he neared. He said nothing, turning his gaze to where Oliver was leading Wes toward them from the stables.

"Griswold," Wes said, dipping his head in greeting. "You wished to see me?" He glanced at Cody, who just shrugged.

"Come with me." Griswold marched out of the Academy, not waiting to see if any of the three followed him.

"Guess we follow him," Oliver said, clearly having no idea what was going on either. The three students followed their instructor out into the meadow beyond Blackthrush's gate. Griswold had stopped a hundred feet out and waited for them.

When they caught up, he scanned the area behind them, as if looking for someone.

"Sir, what's going on?" Wes asked.

"Yeah, what do you want with us three?" Oliver asked. Cody agreed with the question. Even though he and Oliver were in the same class, they rarely interacted outside of classwork. And as for Wes, Cody had only spoken directly to him a handful of times. They weren't exactly used to working together.

Griswold looked each of them in the eye, holding the contact for a long moment. "I brought you three because you are all good fighters. But more importantly, you all know when to keep your mouths shut."

Keep our mouths shut? Are we doing something outside the bounds of the Academy rules?

Apparently, Oliver was thinking the same thing as Cody. "Are we doing something illegal?"

"Possibly," Griswold grunted.

The three students exchanged glances as silence grew. Before anyone could ask what they were about to do, Griswold waved them ahead and stalked off toward the bridge, his braid swaying in time with his quick pace.

Cody couldn't believe his luck. *We've been spying on him and then he just asks me to come along while he does something illegal? This could be it. We could catch the spy in the act!* Trying not to show his excitement, Cody adjusted his shield and followed Griswold into Forenfall.

Boots thudding against the thick pine planks of the bridge, the unlikely group entered the city, mingling with the citizens going about their day. Griswold's head was visible over the crowd; the students followed it down the main street.

After walking three blocks, Griswold turned right next to a quaint bakery. Picking up the pace, Cody reached the corner and halted. Griswold was nowhere to be seen.

"Where'd he go?" Oliver asked, coming up beside Cody.

"He can't have gone far," Wes said.

The door of a house nearby opened and Griswold beckoned them inside. As soon as they entered, he slammed and locked the door. "Downstairs. Now."

The hair on Cody's neck prickled. The house was clearly abandoned, even if it was in decent shape. The carpet of dust covering the floor told Cody that no one had been inside for years, except for the trail leading to the basement stairs. And, as if that wasn't ominous enough, Cody thought he could hear a quiet moan coming from below.

"What is this place?" Oliver wondered.

"Down," Griswold growled in a tone that prompted no argument. The three students headed for the stairs and began to descend.

Reaching the bottom, Cody's feet scuffed against cold flagstones. His eyes flashed around. He wasn't in a basement, at least, not one like he had ever seen. Mortared stone formed the walls that extended far into the darkness ahead.

A cool draft fluttered across Cody's cheek. It smelled old and stale. "What are we doing here?" His optimism at possibly catching the spy was being quashed by his growing fear of where Griswold was leading them.

"It looks like a dungeon," Wes said in a small voice.

"Walk," Griswold ordered. He prodded Cody ahead.

Cody stifled a groan of pain as his wounds shrieked. He took a step, starting off into the unknown.

The darkness seemed to close in around him as he walked, the only light a dull glow from the stairwell leading back to the city streets. He couldn't see anything in front of him. Hopefully, he wouldn't walk into a wall, or something worse. He held his shield close. His hand strayed to his sword.

The only sounds were the footsteps echoing into the distance and the breathing of Cody's companions. No one spoke. The atmosphere forbade them to.

They walked for ten minutes, until all the light behind them had faded into gloom.

"Stop," Griswold said. As the students obeyed, Griswold took three more steps beyond them. Cody heard the jingling of keys on a ring and one being fit into a lock. A door creaked open and torchlight spilled into the black tunnel. Cody shielded his eyes from the flickering brightness.

As his eyes adjusted, he began to make out what lay beyond the door. Wes had been right. It was a dungeon. Dark cells barred by doors of iron lined the stone walls. Three other hallways coming from each direction joined in the centre of the dungeon.

From off down the right hall came another moan. Something clanged against the iron bars and a man yelled, "Shut up! You've only been in here a day."

"Who is-" Oliver began.

Griswold whirled around, slapping his hand over Oliver's mouth. He leaned close to the students and spoke in a voice barely audible, "I need to see to the prisoner. The guards won't let anyone near him, so we'll need to fight them. Don't kill them. And put these on." In his hand was a bundle of black cloth.

Cody grabbed it and discovered it was a handful of masks. Feeling even worse about the situation, Cody slipped the fabric over his face. It covered everything except his eyes.

Griswold crept ahead, slowly unsheathing his sword with barely a sound. Cody drew his weapon with a slight scraping noise that earned him a glare from the instructor.

"Why is this guy so important, anyway?" came a voice around the corner.

The man who had yelled at the prisoner answered. "I don't know. We aren't important enough to know. We're just getting paid to keep him here."

"Pretty easy job, if you ask me," a third person said. "Hardly anyone knows this place exists."

Griswold halted at the corner for a moment, allowing Cody and the other two to ready themselves. Then he stepped out into full view. "Gentlemen."

As the guards scrambled to arm themselves, Cody joined Griswold in the hall. There were five soldiers, who had been sitting around a low table.

"Who are you?" asked the soldier whose armour bore the rank of captain. He levelled his sword at the intruders. His four subordinates spread out and did the same.

Griswold spread his arms. "Get out of the way."

The captain swung his arm. "Take them!"

Cody gulped. He was about to fight royal soldiers. That was enough to land him in prison, or worse, if he accidentally killed one of them.

The guards crossed the space between them in a few strides and the battle was joined. Cody gave way under the attack, taking the blows on his shield. The soldier pushed ahead, backing Cody up, while trying to get around his defence. Cody let the guard tire himself before lashing out with his own sword.

The soldier parried and sliced back at Cody. Lifting his shield, he blocked the strike and lunged ahead with his right arm. His blade clanged off the soldier's pauldron, knocking him off-balance. Cody didn't waste the opportunity. He surged ahead, bashing his shield into the guard's chest. Knocked off his feet, he crashed into the wall hard. He struggled to get back to his feet, but Cody's boot connecting with the side of his head put a stop to that.

Cody rolled his shoulders as the man crumpled into an unconscious heap. That had gone a lot better than he had been expecting.

He looked over the rest of the skirmish. Wes had just disarmed his opponent and was holding him at sword-point. Oliver was still duelling his soldier, but as Cody watched, he managed to take him down. The other guard was already splayed out on the ground and Griswold was advancing on the captain.

"You are going to regret this!" the captain spat. "You'll all be imprisoned." He slashed at the instructor.

Griswold swung his right arm. Metal rang on metal and the top half of the captain's sword clattered to the stones below.

The captain yelled and charged Griswold with the stump of his weapon. The old veteran snagged the soldier's arm as he rushed by and twisted it so it ended up behind his back. The captain yelped in pain and then fell silent as Griswold brought the pommel of his sword down on his head. He let go and the man dropped, his armour clanging against the floor.

Oliver scratched his neck. "Huh. You'd think royal soldiers would put up more of a fight."

Wes sheathed his sword. "I imagine they would be better trained in the important cities. Forenfall is hardly an important city."

"Fair enough," Oliver said.

Griswold approached the cell where the prisoner was kept. "Come here."

Chains rattled as someone stepped up to the door. Hands wrapped around the bars. Old hands, wrinkled and veiny, scarred and dirty. "Who are you?"

"I must ask you the same thing," Griswold said. "I've heard a rumour and I came to see if that rumour was true."

The man looked up, revealing his eyes. One was blue and clear, the other golden and silver. "Aye. It is true."

A stone skittered across the floor behind Cody. He turned to glimpse a cloaked figure, shrouded in shadows.

Griswold had seen it too. "Stop him!" There was a note of anxiety in his voice. "Go!"

Cody raced to the spot where the figure had been spying from, but it was gone.

"Where'd it go?" Oliver asked as he and Wes slid to a stop next to him.

"There!" Wes pointed. A shadow, darker than the rest, fled down the hall opposite them.

Cody sprung into action, sprinting after the mysterious watcher. He still wasn't sure what to make of Griswold's mission, but he had directly attacked the King's men. That hardly seemed like a thing Farren's spy would do. Perhaps the fleeing figure was the real spy.

Cody's feet slapped against the hard stones as he raced after the figure. The hallway it was fleeing down didn't have a door to the dungeon like the one Cody and the others had entered by. Instead, the tunnel split off into several branches, lit by the occasional torch that gave off just enough light to avoid walls.

The stranger darted down a hall to the left. Cody reached the turn a dozen seconds later. The way ahead was pitch black, no torches to light the darkness. Still, Cody didn't hesitate. He charged ahead, following the sound of fleeing footsteps.

"Where does this even lead?" Oliver asked between breaths.

"Who knows," Cody replied. He realized the footsteps ahead had stopped and skidded to a halt.

"What is it?" Wes asked.

"He's stopped," Cody said. He strained his ears, listening for any hint of movement. Something scraped the ground a few feet in front of him. "Duck!" He dropped to the ground and heard something fly over his head. It bounced away into the darkness with a metallic clang; probably a knife.

There was a fleshy thump and Oliver grunted. Cody leapt to his feet and charged ahead, hands out. His right hand touched loose fabric and he grabbed a handful. Heaving back, he heard someone's feet scrambling for purchase and then his momentum stopped for a brief second before the fabric tore and spilled Cody to the floor. As he got up, he heard the mysterious figure running away.

Moments later, he heard the pounding of feet on wooden steps and then he was blinded by dull light as a door was thrown open. Eyes watering, Cody saw the person framed in brilliance for a second, his black cloak torn. Then, he was gone.

Cody raced to the stairs, tripping over the first one in his hurry to get to the door. He looked out into the Forenfall market.

Rain was coming down now and everyone in sight was huddled beneath dark cloaks. Their quarry had blended into the sea of unidentifiable citizens.

"He's disappeared," Wes said at Cody's shoulder.

Rain drummed down on Cody's head, giving substance to his disappointment. He had hoped to catch the person, find out if they were the spy. But Wes was right. They could be anywhere now, lost from view.

Oliver stomped up the stairs. He was holding a hand over his eye, which was already bruising shut. "Ow."

The three looked out from the doorway of the small shed that hid the entrance to the tunnels and dungeon beneath the city, the rain soaking into their clothes. A passing woman with a basket of fresh produce gave them a suspicious glance and Cody remembered that they were all armed and masked.

Wes glanced at Cody. "Do we go back to Griswold, or..."

"No," came Griswold's gruff voice from the left. He was unmasked and pulling a handcart covered by a tarp. "Throw your masks and weapons in."

The boys did as directed, striping off the hot fabric. Cody let the drops wash away the sweat from his eyes as he put his sword and shield in the cart. He jerked back in surprise as he saw the strange eyes of the prisoner peeking out from under the tarp.

"What?"

"Never mind and go back to Blackthrush," Griswold ordered. "I'll drop off your weapons in your camps. And don't tell a soul what you just did." Not waiting for their reply, he set off, making a lane through the crowd.

"I've gotta say, this has been a really weird day," Oliver muttered, brushing wet hair from his face.

Cody couldn't stop the chuckle from escaping. "Yeah, it really has."

Wes blew out a long breath. "Guess, we go home now."

"How am I gonna explain a black eye?" Oliver asked as they began walking.

Cody snorted. "Say you walked into a doorknob."

Oliver sneered. "Oh, ha ha."

~~~

Cody sat on the bench outside of Silverton's room as he waited for the class to start. He, Oliver and Wes had managed to get back to Blackthrush with no problems. Everyone had been in class the whole time they had been away and no one had seen them go into the city. Still, Cody couldn't help but feel like someone would march up to him and demand where he had gone.

He absent-mindedly watched a small brown spider climb the wall across from him. It toiled to scale the vertical surface, unconcerned with the events unfolding around it that impacted the entire realm.

The door beside him swung inward and the first-year class spilled out, chattering about the Strategy class they had just finished. The spider forgotten, Cody waited until they had all left the room before standing and stretching. The skirmish in the dungeon had left him a little sore and his back was still tender.

From down the hall, the rest of Cody's class came toward him, talking and laughing. Oliver slipped out of another room and joined them. Ember was also with them, apparently done researching.

She sidled up next to him and whispered, "What happened?"

"He didn't know," Cody said. "He needed me for something." Feeling eyes on him, he whispered. "I'll tell you all later."

At her nod, the two joined their classmates and entered Silverton's room. They joined a table with Ellis and Gwen halfway down the far side.

"Where'd you go last class?" Ellis asked.

"He was studying with me," Ember said. "We were doing something for Aldus."

Ellis looked skeptical, but he didn't ask anything else.

"Good afternoon, third-years." Silverton stood at the front of the class, dressed in his usual attire. He smiled easily. "We've had quite a day, haven't we?"

You have no idea, Cody thought wryly, making eye contact with Oliver.

Silverton took a sip from the glass of water on his desk. "It's the last class of the day, and quite honestly, I could do with a long nap. So, we shall skip the lecture and I'll let you each pick whichever scenario you want to do. Sound good?"

"That's awfully generous of you, sir," Marshall said.

Silverton shrugged. "Well, we're about to head to Saken for the Festival, so no point starting anything new."

Everyone broke into conversation about the relaxed class and the upcoming Festival, which had everyone excited. Silverton made no attempt to quell the talking.

The group at Cody's table eventually decided to pick a random scenario from the booklet. Ellis said, "This one," and dropped the booklet down to show the others.

"What do you think, Cody?" Gwen asked.

Cody shook himself out of the thoughts that had been occupying his mind. "Hmm, oh that's fine." He quickly read the scenario and his eyes widened as it spoke of two forces battling in underground tunnels. He took a better look at the table they were at and saw that it was the cityscape. A large portion of it was an underground system of tunnels, the top cut off so they could access them.

"A fight in the dungeons sounds awesome," Ellis said.

"Yeah, real awesome," Cody said, trying to compose himself. He saw Ember's questioning glance, but only shook his head. He wasn't about to discuss his secret mission with Griswold just because the scenario they had picked happened to be the same sort of situation he'd just been in.

Even though he tried to forget all his problems and focus on the class, they kept creeping into his mind, invading his thoughts. He barely noticed the time go by until Silverton came over to see if they were ready to see if their plan would work.

The dark-skinned instructor examined the model landscape and the figures they had set up, representing the opposing forces.

Cody hardly paid attention as Silverton animated the small figurines and had them act out the battle. His mind was elsewhere, thinking on the issues of the spies and Griswold's secretive undertaking.

Someone shook his arm. "Huh?" Silverton was looking at him expectantly. "Uh, sorry, what did you say?"

The instructor tipped his head. "Are you alright, Cody? You seem distracted."

"Um, I'm ok. Just got a lot on my mind right now."

Silverton nodded knowingly. "Well, a lot happened today. Several first-years were quite distracted in my last class as well. Don't worry. No harm done."

"Thanks," Cody muttered.

Silverton clapped his shoulder and left to grade the next group.

"You are distracted," Gwen said.

"Yeah, more than usual," Ellis agreed. "And you aren't even talking with Guy." He pointed over his shoulder to where the now nine-fingered student was placing bowmen onto the side of a hill. Guy fumbled one of the figurines and knocked over the few he had managed to set up, prompting him to groan loudly.

"Does this have to do with what Aldus is asking you to do?" Gwen asked.

Cody shot Ember a glance, alarmed. She sighed. "Yeah, everyone found out immediately that we're doing something for him. They don't know what, and we need to keep it that way." She looked at Gwen and Ellis pointedly.

Gwen ducked her head. "Right, sorry. I shouldn't ask. If Aldus wanted us to know, he would have told us all."

"Yeah, but instead he told you lot," Ellis said, a hint of jealousy in his words. "What makes you guys so special?"

Cody shrugged. "Honestly, I have no idea. He could have decided to like any group of friends and he chose us, I guess. Sometimes, I wish he hadn't."

The table fell silent. Cody could hear the rest of the class still working on their scenarios or chatting after having finished them, but he didn't process any of it.

He found himself looking at Guy and the bandage around his self-inflicted wound. His eyebrows drew together. If Griswold was sneaking around, attacking soldiers and wasn't the spy, which Cody was thinking was the case, then there had been no reason for Guy to cast the Seridion Spell and cut off his pinky. Guy was not going to be happy when Cody told him. He expected a punch in the face, at the very least.

The class ended and Cody headed directly for the meeting room Aldus had given them, along with Ember, Guy and Coral. They met the others inside.

Miri marched up to Cody. "Spill."

Cody sat down in one of the chairs as everyone gathered around. "I may have just helped Griswold bust someone out of a dungeon underneath Forenfall."

"You what?" Kana and Ember asked at the same time. Evander grinned and Guy snorted in laughter.

"That's actually awesome," Kinzo said. "I didn't even know there was a dungeon under the city."

"Me neither," Cody said. He told them the whole story, ending with the mysterious figure dashing off into the crowd.

Kaito folded his arms. "Griswold is acting quite strangely, but his actions are not that of a spy for the king."

"I agree," Cody said. "Griswold is not who we are looking for." He made eye contact with Guy.

His friend stood, jaw clenched. He approached Cody and bent close, a hand on each armrest. "Cody Apolinar. You are telling me that it was completely pointless for me to cut off my pinky."

Cody leaned back. "Uh... yeah."

Guy straightened and blew a breath out his nose. He glared down at Cody. "One day, I'm going to ask you for something and you are not going to refuse me."

Cody sighed. He wanted to remind Guy that he had gone through pain and a permanent change as well, but he doubted his friend wanted to hear it.

"So that stuff on your back?" Naomi asked.

"Nothing we need to know," Cody said. "It probably has to do with the guy he broke out."

Coral, who was sitting on the table, letting her legs dangle, spoke up. "You think the stranger in the tunnels was the spy?"

Cody faced the redhead. "I have a pretty strong feeling it was him, yes."

"Well, if it was," Coral continued. "Then it can't be Verrol. I saw him out the window at the same time you were off infiltrating the dungeon."

The group fell silent for a moment.

"That leaves Hejeck and Linae," Kana murmured. "One of them is the spy."

Cody shook his head. As much as he disliked the small, greasy Riding instructor, he couldn't imagine that he was reporting to Farren. And Linae, he was a nice person and a good teacher. He had helped Cody with his Chaos magic, improving what Cody was weakest at. He seemed so unlikely to be working against them. But, Cody looked at the facts again. One of them had to be the spy.

He cleared his throat. "There's something else. I don't think I should keep investigating too close." The others were taken aback and Cody hurried to explain. "If that was the spy, I'm sure he's trying hard to figure out who was with Griswold. And there aren't many who fight with a sword and a round shield."

Kinzo was nodding. "Yeah, only four. You, Bram, Iaarra and Kavik. And one's a girl."

"He'll be watching me," Cody said. "I'll try to help out, but I've got to keep a distance."

The others begrudgingly accepted that he was right. It was too much of a risk for Cody to keep nosing around while under such scrutiny.

Naomi spoke up. "I think it's good that you're a suspect now, Cody."

Cody stared at her.

"Why would that be a good thing?" Guy asked, bewildered.

Naomi ducked at the poor reception.

"What do you mean?" Ember asked gently.

Naomi cleared her throat. "Well, I was talking with Levi and he said he had an incident in History class. Um, he kinda challenged Holbrook about the demise of the Free Knights in front of the whole class."

There was a collective groan.

"He is such an idiot," Kinzo grumbled.

"Do you know what they did?" Kana asked, sounding both annoyed and concerned.

Naomi spread her hands. "I'm not sure. Levi stormed out. But people are whispering things."

Kaito spoke. "Then, the best thing we can do is to all act as suspicious as possible. We must mask the scent, so to speak."

Coral's head popped up. "Does that mean mischief?"

Kaito smiled. "Yes, I suppose it does mean mischief. But make sure the two in question are around to see it."

Coral rubbed her hands together gleefully. "And we're heading to the Festival right away. There'll be all kinds of things to destroy."

Ember put a hand to her forehead. "Please don't destroy too much. There'll be soldiers there."

Coral shrugged. "We're already neck-deep in this stuff. What's a few more soldiers?"

Cody couldn't help but smirk even though he didn't share her enthusiasm. They were all about to try and convince the spy that they were the king's most wanted criminal in a city filled with soldiers from all over the realm.

"This will be great." Kinzo rolled his eyes. "What could possibly go wrong?"

CHAPTER 9

At last, the column came around a bend in the road and the city of Saken came into view.

The whole of Blackthrush was stretched out in a long caravan of carts and people. The journey had taken them three days, as caravans of such size moved slowly.

Levi's friends had told him of their findings and suspicions from the other day. The desire to help was still there, but they had persuaded him to stay out of it, for his own safety. He couldn't believe that Guy and Cody had actually performed the Seridion Spell, leaving the former with one less finger and the latter with a back full of scars.

They're doing so much for me, he thought. *There has to be a way for me to help.* But he knew that the best way to help them, at least for now, was to do nothing.

He looked up from his thoughts. Nestled in its cove, Saken glittered in the sunlight. The segments of the city: the harbour, the main city and the Outskirts expanded out in rings, like ripples in a pond.

A smile touched Levi's lips. Memories came unbidden to his mind. He recalled the escapade in Rivera Farm with Snare and Ring, and wondered if he would see them again.

Another, more uncomfortable, thought occurred to him. What if he ran into Rorien Stern or his goons? The oath Marcus had placed on Stern didn't allow him to harm Levi while actively hunting him, but it didn't stop Stern from attacking if their paths crossed unintentionally. Levi decided to stay far away from Rivera Farm.

Evander kicked at a stone in his path. "Home, sweet home."

"Not thrilled to be back?" Levi asked.

Evander gave him a rueful smile. "Not particularly. I am looking forward to the Festival, I just wish it were happening somewhere else."

"You have bad memories here or what?" Guy asked. He was hitching a ride on one of the carts laden with tent poles, canvases and other things meant for setting up a camp. No one was supposed to ride on the horse-drawn carts, but that wasn't stopping Guy.

Evander nodded curtly. "Plenty. This is where my mother died."

Guy made a face. "Sorry to hear that."

"Yeah, me too," Evander said darkly.

Levi gave Guy a look that warned him to quit the line of questioning. Guy nodded.

They entered the city via one of the gates that lined the Outskirts. With many people coming from Forenfall and beyond, the guard at the gates had been doubled. Clearly, no one wanted any trouble for the people coming to attend the Festival.

The guards waved the Blackthrush column through, past the waiting line. Being a knight-in-training had its benefits, Levi had to admit. They had a certain freedom that many people did not. Levi just hoped that nothing with the secret side of his life would interfere with that freedom at the Festival.

The caravan made its way through the Outskirts with no problems and into the main city, where decorations and advertisements for the Festival hung everywhere. The city of Saken prospered greatly whenever the Festival was held, and the citizens loved it.

Levi couldn't wait to see what the Festival grounds looked like. He had imagined it several times, especially during the History classes, in which they had learned about the Festival and its origin. It had been created by the two ruling families of Saken, the Mid's and the Arra's, nearly four centuries ago and became known as the Midarra Festival. Knights from across the realm were invited to compete for a grand prize, and most accepted, seeing as it was a time of peace. People from everywhere began travelling to Saken to watch the great tournament. It lasted for two months, during which the population of Saken more than tripled with all the visitors.

The champion of the first tournament, Sir Ectam, declared that they would have a rematch in ten years. However, when the allotted time came, there was a famine on the island and the lord of Saken postponed the Festival for a year. The eleven-year gap became tradition from then on.

The large procession arrived at the edge of a large clearing on the southwest side of the city. Thousands of tents and shacks dotted the valley that stretched for five square kilometers. The temporary structures ranged in size from tattered one-man tents to massive pavilions that housed entire extended families.

In the centre of the valley there were fewer tents, the space instead reserved for the jousting pitch, the archery range and the duelling arena. Off to the right was a cluster of shacks from which smoke was rising. Presumably the cookhouses. Beyond them was a plethora of pens, in which milled thousands of animals, destined to be slaughtered and consumed.

To the left of the event setups was a massive building, almost a small castle, with two wings extending from a central tower. Levi knew that was where the nobility and important people would stay.

"This place is huge!" Kinzo exclaimed. "There's gotta be, well, how many tents do you think there are?"

"Ten," Levi said jokingly.

"Oh, come on. A realistic guess."

"There's probably over seven thousand," Kana figured.

"I'd guess closer to ten thousand," Evander said. "There are a lot of small ones."

Aldus stood on a cart and got everyone's attention. "People of Blackthrush. Please, help set up your camp's tent and equipment and then you are free to go."

"Blue camp, let's get set up!" Cody called, claiming one of the tent carts. "C'mon guys."

"Ugh, I don't want to set up a tent," Coral complained. "Why can't I just not do it?"

"You could," Cody said. "But, then you'd be sleeping outside."

Coral groaned. "Fine. Let's put this stupid thing up." Blue camp began unloading the poles that would form the structure of their tent.

"Lift on three," Cody said to Levi and Duncan. "One, two, three!"

Levi heaved upward and the pole shot up, being lighter than Levi had expected. They had it in place in no time. "Guess we didn't need three of us," Levi said.

"Guess not," Cody said.

The rest of the poles went up and they were staked to the ground for stability. After that was done, the boys manhandled the large canvas, stretching it over the frame. It was awkward, but they managed to get it into place. The girls and some of the first-years took the remaining stakes and pinned the canvas to the ground so it wouldn't fly off at the first wind. Then, Levi and the others quickly set about unpacking and laying out their bedrolls and blankets and such.

Levi dusted off his hands as he finished. Guy waltzed over and put his elbow on Levi's shoulder. "Lovely home, isn't it?"

Levi tapped a foot on his bedroll. "Oh yeah, I'm gonna love sleeping on these thin mats."

"You could do what I did," Guy said.

"What's that?"

Guy's eyes twinkled. "I stole a mattress from black camp's wagon. Now, I have two."

"Heh, nice," Coral said as she walked past.

Once all Levi's friends had finished unpacking, he pointed to the door of the tent, which was just a flap. "Y'all ready to go explore?"

"Heck yeah!" Cody said.

"Let's go!" Guy exclaimed.

"Behave yourselves," Ember said. "We don't want to cause a scene."

Guy winked at her. "We always behave, princess. Besides, we're supposed to act a bit suspicious." He shoved Cody toward the door and they ran out.

Ember sighed.

"Don't worry," Naomi said. "What could they possibly do that will ruin this?"

"Quite a few things, I imagine," Kaito said. "But I trust that they will be smart enough not to. Or at least, Cody might be."

"I feel like I should still keep an eye on them," Ember said.

"Well, let's go catch them," Coral said, grabbing Ember's hand and dragging her out of the tent. "See you guys later!"

130

Kaito chuckled and followed them out, hands clasped behind his back.

"Looks like we're stuck together," Naomi said.

"Looks like it," Levi said. He leaned to the side and called to Adam, who was neatly folding his blankets on his mat. "Hey, Adam! You coming?"

"Hmm? Oh, yes. I will accompany you." Adam rose to his feet and joined them.

Naomi and Levi exchanged a glance and Naomi headed for the door. "C'mon guys, let's see what the Festival has to offer." Levi followed behind, Adam beside him.

Outside the tent, the rest of the Blackthrush people were finishing up as well. Seven other tents were set up in a non-symmetrical way. Friends and acquaintances were milling about as they went off to explore.

Levi spotted Bram and Dante waltzing past. "Let's go meet some hot girls," Dante said.

"Now you're talking." Bram gave his best friend a high-five.

Naomi snorted as the two passed by. "No way any girls will give them the time of day."

"Why's that?" Levi asked.

"They're idiots," Naomi said.

"Is that a bad thing?" Levi asked. "Because, if it is, I'm in big trouble."

Naomi turned quickly. "Well, no, I didn't mean you."

"So, you're saying I'm not an idiot?" Levi asked, concealing a smile.

"Well, I wouldn't say idiot, but you aren't the brightest. But you do have moments."

Adam looked quizzical. "Is it normal for people to think of themselves as stupid?"

Levi grinned. "Not at all, Adam. Not at all." He strode ahead and scouted the area around the Blackthrush camp. "Where to?"

"Ooh, let's go there!" Naomi pointed. "Romeo's over at that stall that's selling pies!"

"I do enjoy pies," Adam said.

"Great," Levi said. "Let's go get some."

They wandered over to the stall that was nothing more than a countertop covered by a canvas roof. There was a portable oven behind the counter and bags full of fruit that would end up in the pies.

The vendor was a portly, balding man with a hooked nose. His eyes were bright and he smiled easily. "Hello, kids. Can I interest you in some pies?"

Romeo turned around. His mouth was full of hot pastry. He swallowed and said. "Guys, you have to get some. It is amazing!"

The vendor slapped his paunch and laughed heartily. "Why, thank you for your praise."

"That does look excellent," Adam said, eyeing Romeo's pie.

Levi's eye fell on the rack of fresh pies that were cooling, steam curling off them like stalks of grass in the wind. "What kinds do you have?"

"Let's see," the vendor said, stroking his chin and the stubble he had forgotten to shave off in the morning. "I have apple, raspberry, gooseberry, peach, cherry and blueberry."

"Those all sound wonderful," Naomi said. "But I want to try the peach."

"So do I," Levi said, smelling the rich aroma of the fruity filling and flaky crust.

"I will have the blueberry," Adam said.

The vendor smiled. "Three marks each, please."

"A reasonable price," Adam said, handing over three bronze coins. Levi and Naomi also gave the man his due.

The vendor put the coins in a locked box with several slots in the top. Then he leaned forward. "You know, I've learned that if you sell for a slightly lower price than your competitors, chances are, you'll get more customers."

"Well, you can bet that I'll be back," Romeo said. There was filling and crumbs all around his mouth.

"I look forward to serving you again," the vendor said with a slight bow of his head.

"Come on, guys," Levi said. "We have lots to see." He began walking away from the stall, pie in hand. He chomped down on the pastry, the sweetness of the peach flowing across his tongue. "Oh, that's heavenly."

"Mmm," Naomi moaned, her mouth too full to speak.

"Where are you guys headed?" Romeo asked, licking the last bit of filling off his fingers.

"I would like to see the tournament setup," Adam said.

"Yeah, sure, we can go check that out," Levi agreed. "Now, which way are they?" Romeo and Naomi both didn't know, but Adam seemed to have an idea as to where to go, so they let him lead.

It took them a half-hour to reach the site of the tournament. There were no paths or streets as all the camps were set up haphazardly. They were forced to detour around tents and shacks, never going in a straight line.

Eventually, they rounded a square marquee of brown fabric and the jousting field came into view. It was ringed by a five-foot fence, more ceremonial than practical, that wouldn't keep anyone out. Down the centre was the dividing rail, painted with alternating red and white stripes. Rows of raised benches surrounded the field, where the spectators would watch from. In the middle of each row was a covered box where the important people would sit.

"Fancy," Levi commented.

"And yet, practical," Adam said. "With these benches, hundreds of people can watch in comfort."

Naomi pointed across the field to a long, rectangular building with a flat roof and dozens of hay bales piled up against its outer walls. "That must be the stable, right?"

"Sure looks like it," Romeo said.

They walked along the jousting pitch. Levi ran his hand along the fence that encircled it. The wood was smooth and slid easily under his touch; someone had spent much time sanding off the rough patches. He let his gaze wander. Everywhere he looked, there were people of all shapes, sizes, skin tones and accents gathered together to celebrate the Festival.

Ahead of Levi was a family of four, the daughter riding on the father's shoulders while the son held the mother's hand. A sad smile touched Levi's lips as thoughts of his own family crossed his mind. He was glad that he had been able to see his dad, but he missed his mom dearly. He wished that she could come up to Saken and visit him, although he knew such a thing was unlikely.

Levi shook himself out of his thoughts as they came to the sword-fighting arena.

It was a raised platform, a square that was six feet in the air, with a railing around the edge. Bleachers ringed around it, the same as the jousting field. At all four corners were raised boxes from which the nobles would watch.

Two men in full armour were duelling lightly. It was nothing more than practice and exercise.

One of the men wore bronze armour and a white coat with a diagonal grey stripe. His helmet was conical and had no face mask, save for a thin piece of metal that extended to cover his nose. He fought with a simple, yet practical longsword. His shield was triangular with the top edge curved outward. The symbol emblazoned on the shield was the same as on his coat; a diagonal grey stripe.

The second fighter was taller and he wore heavier plate armour. The pauldrons were shaped to resemble snake heads, complete with eyes, fangs and forked tongues and his helmet also had a serpentine theme. His garb was green and brown, sporting two crossed snakes on his tunic and round shield. His sword was more decorative, but it was well made and rang true when crossed with the other blade.

"Sirs Cassius of the Fall and Teodric the Serpent," Adam said.

"Which one is which?" Levi asked. He felt the other three staring at him and suddenly felt very stupid. "You know, I could probably figure that out myself."

"I hope so," Romeo said.

"Oh, whatever," Levi said. He stepped up onto the third row of the benches to watch. He wasn't alone. Nearly twenty other people were watching.

Levi's friends joined him to spectate as Cassius and Teodric battled.

The knights fought at half speed, exchanging blows that had little force behind them. They were going through the forms.

"They have very different styles," Naomi noticed.

Levi watched closer and found that Naomi was right. Sir Cassius was more reserved, preferring to play mostly defence and throw in the odd offensive combo. He used his shield to take most all the blows on the left side of his body.

Sir Teodric, on the other hand, was all about quick strikes and wide, slicing motions, mixing a few jabs and thrusts. He preferred to take Cassius' attacks on his sword, saving his shield as a fallback.

Even though they were only practicing, Levi could tell that they were both professionals. Now, Levi was an adequate fighter, but he knew that neither one of them would have any problem besting him. He hoped he never had to cross swords with them, or any other proper knight.

The bout lasted a few minutes before they agreed to call an end. They sheathed their swords and shook hands as was protocol. A smattering of applause rose from the gathered crowd. Both knights waved before exiting the arena and walking off toward their tents, where they would have their squires remove their armour to be oiled and polished for when the festivities began the following day.

"If that was only half speed, I can't wait for the real competition!" Romeo said. The others all agreed.

"We should check out the archery range," Levi said. "See if anyone's shooting." The others thought that was a good idea, so they hopped off the bleachers and headed off for the range.

The archery range was built much the same way as the jousting pitch, with a fence encircling it and benches around the back half. There were no bleachers on the far end of the range, as no one wanted to be hit by a stray arrow.

A dozen small shacks stood at the back end of the range, barrels of arrows in front of them. There were white lines painted in the grass, separating the twelve lanes, as well as the line from which the archers would shoot from. Three targets were set up down each lane; one at seventy-five yards, one at one hundred and the last at one-hundred-fifty.

A lone figure was in the range, shooting from the lane closest to Levi and his friends. He was a handsome young man with high cheekbones and refined features. Wavy blond hair cascaded down his neck over a black jacket and a light blue tunic. There was a stag embroidered on the left breast of the tunic.

He nocked an arrow to the string of his bow and drew it back. It looked a little awkward, but he managed to get a full draw. His tongue protruded from the corner of his mouth as he concentrated. Sighting up his target for a moment, he waited and released.

The arrow took off with a slight warble before straightening out. It sailed through the air and buried itself in the ground short and to the left of the closest target.

The young man frowned and sighed, scratching his cheek as he considered his attempt. Then, he shrugged and picked out another arrow.

Levi leaned over to Naomi. "He doesn't seem to be very good."

"No," Naomi agreed. "But he is attractive."

Levi snorted.

They watched as the blond man drew back the string with the same awkward technique and fired the new arrow. This one was closer to the target, but still too far to the left. The man cursed and slumped his shoulders in defeat.

Movement in Levi's peripherals alerted him to Adam climbing over the fence. "What are you doing?"

"I am going to assist him," Adam said as he walked over to the man.

"Hullo," the man said, looking somewhat surprised. "Who are you?"

"I am Adam."

"Good day, Adam. My name is Lawson Barric."

Adam's eyebrow rose. "As in the grandson of Lord Barric of Vantan?"

"The same," Lawson said. "Um, what might you be doing on the range?"

"I was watching you shoot and I could not help but notice that you were missing the targets."

Lawson's face reddened. "Yes. I am no archer, but my father, Edric, made me enter the archery tournament, for the family name." He rolled his eyes as he said the last few words. "I've been practicing all I can, but I'm afraid I haven't progressed very much."

"I could give you some advice," Adam said. "I am an adequate archer, myself."

"Way more than adequate," Levi said to himself. He had seen Adam's prowess with the bow. He was a master.

"I suppose it couldn't hurt," Lawson said.

"Very well." Adam dipped his head. "Would you draw back the string?"

Lawson nodded and pulled back on the string, bending the limbs of the bow until his thumb touched the corner of his mouth.

"As I suspected," Adam said. "You are drawing all from the arms."

"That's bad? I thought that's how you did it."

"You do use your arms, certainly," Adam said. "But you must also use your back muscles. They are strong and make the drawing much easier and smoother. It also allows for a straighter shot."

"How do I use my back to pull the string?"

Adam attempted to explain. "You begin pulling with your arm, but you must also squeeze your shoulder blades together."

"Squeeze my shoulder blades together," Lawson repeated. "Like this?" He arched his back and pulled back his shoulders.

"Not quite. Your back must remain straight."

Lawson tried again and Adam helped him adjust his posture, so he was standing relatively right. Then, Adam had him shoot an arrow.

Lawson selected an arrow with white fletching and set it to the string. He took a deep breath and drew, making sure to use his back. He sighted up the shot and let it fly.

Levi watched as the arrow flew past him and sailed beyond the target. Already, Adam had improved Lawson's shooting.

"Wow," the nobleman said. "I didn't know I could shoot that far."

"Well done," Adam said. "However, I noticed several other things. First, you grip the bow too tightly. If you relax somewhat, you will find the shot to be smoother. Second, when you release the arrow, you twist your fingers slightly, resulting in a change of direction. That is why you are always shying to the left. If you fix both of those things, your arrows will fly truer."

Lawson nodded, accepting the corrections. "I'll try again." Once more, he lined up for the shot, made the few adjustments Adam had suggested and released.

To everyone's surprise, the arrow struck the target. Not near the centre, but on the outer ring, an inch in. Nevertheless, Lawson had hit the target and was ecstatic.

"I've done it! I can't believe it!" He turned to Adam and stuck out his hand. "Thank you, Adam."

Adam shook the offered hand and nodded, a satisfied smile on his lips.

"I can't wait for my father to hear about this," Lawson said. "He had no faith in me."

"Even though he signed you up?" Adam asked.

Lawson waved a hand dismissively. "Yes. He believes that the representation of the family is more important than my dignity."

"Well, I am glad I could be of some assistance."

For the first time, Lawson looked to his right to where Levi, Romeo and Naomi were standing. "Are those your friends?"

"Indeed, they are," Adam said. He proceeded to introduce them.

Levi raised a hand when his name was said.

"Where might you lot be from?" Lawson asked, putting down the bow and approaching the fence.

"Blackthrush," Levi said.

Lawson's eyes widened. "The Academy! You are training to become knights!"

"Yep," Romeo said.

"I always wanted to attend the Academy," Lawson said. "But my father wouldn't allow it. He said I need to learn the skills to become a baron one day."

"Too bad," Levi said. "It's a lot of fun."

"I can imagine," Lawson said wistfully.

"I only arrived at Blackthrush a few weeks ago. I am still new to it," Adam said. "But from what I have seen, it does seem to be a pleasurable place."

"I'll have to visit before heading home," Lawson said. He brightened up. "Hey! Do you have plans for the opening ceremonies?"

"Well, we were going to watch them," Levi said, a little confused.

"Were you meeting people for it?" Lawson asked.

Naomi shrugged.

"I don't think so," Romeo said.

Lawson grinned. "Well, how would you like to come to my spot. I have one reserved in the third row."

"Eh, why not?" Levi shrugged. "Might as well get to see it up close."

"Four of us won't be too many?" Adam asked.

"The seats to my left weren't reserved, but we can say they were."

"Cool," Levi said. He had been looking forward to the ceremonies. Now, he would be able to enjoy them from a good seat. "Lead the way."

"Wait," Adam said.

The others turned to him, quizzical.

"As an archer, you must take care of your equipment," Adam told Lawson. He pointed back at the target and the arrows spread around it.

"Oh, right," Lawson said. "I'll grab them."

"No need this time," Adam said. He stretched out his hand. "*Caet.*" The arrows pulled themselves out of the dirt and the wooden target, flying neatly into Adam's hand.

Lawson's jaw dropped as he stared at Adam. "Great Ivik! You can do magic!"

"Certainly," Adam said, handing the dumbfounded man the arrows. "We are from Blackthrush, if you recall."

Lawson turned to Levi and the others. "You too?"

Levi grinned and lifted a nearby stone with his mind. "Yes sir."

Lawson laughed. "What good luck! I've made friends with magicians!"

CHAPTER 10

Levi turned in his seat to watch the crowd grow as people streamed to the benches set up in front of the stage. Behind the stage sat the Aedon, the small castle residence for the nobles.

There were three sections of seats arranged in a half-circle. Each section had twenty rows of benches, each one a half-foot taller than the one in front of it. They were all full. People were now gathering in the spaces between the seats and beyond, trailing back to the duelling arena.

Levi had never seen so many people in one place before. It was loud and busy and all-around exciting. Levi caught glimpses of familiar people. Bear and Kavik were on the far left side and he saw Dunning's funny hat for a moment before it was swallowed in the crowd.

"This is great!" Naomi exclaimed.

Someone sat down in front of Levi. He was very fat, his red suit bulging at the seams. He was constantly wiping sweat from his brow with a handkerchief. Levi recoiled as the stench of bad fish wafted over him. "Yeah, real great." He looked over at Romeo and gave him his best smile. "Hey, wanna change seats?"

Romeo scoffed. "Ha! Fat chance."

Levi narrowed his eyes. "Was that a pun?"

Romeo grinned.

"It is about to begin," Adam said.

Levi forgot all about the fat man and fixed his attention on the stage and the door behind it.

Two pages in white livery stood on either side of the door. Another man stood nearby; the bugler. At a nod from one of the pages, he raised his brass bugle to his lips and blew out a long note, quieting the crowd.

The page on the left lifted his voice and shouted, "Introducing Lord Isaac Bohr, Baron of Saken!"

There was light applause from the crowd as the door opened and the Baron stepped onto the stage

So, this is the guy Evander hates so much, Levi thought. *He's not much to look at.* Lord Bohr was barely over five feet tall and rather pudgy. His grey hair was puffed up in a tall ball on his head, as if he thought it was fashionable. A piggish nose protruded from his flat face. Brown eyes sunk into his face were surrounded by globules of fat, hiding the bottom part of his eyes. He wore a baby blue suit with gold buttons and ridiculous, fringed shoulder pads.

From one look, Levi knew that he commanded the respect of no one.

"Thank you, people of Terrenia!" Bohr called.

Levi cringed. It sounded as if Bohr's throat was filled with phlegm. Bohr cleared his throat, proving Levi right.

He continued, but his voice was still thick. "Welcome to Saken. It is my pleasure to introduce our most esteemed and benevolent master, King Farren." The doors were thrown open and the crowd erupted into cheers.

Levi's heart leapt into his throat as a figure emerged from the doorway. Levi's sworn enemy, Bane of the Free Knights, Archnemesis of the Giala and Thief of the Throne, stood a scant hundred paces from where Levi sat.

Levi froze, his breaths coming quick and short. He hadn't thought that the king would be here and he was more the fool for thinking so. The Festival only happened every eleven years and was the biggest event in the realm. It made complete sense that Farren would make an appearance to open the Festival.

Levi's pulse raced. He hoped the king wouldn't spot him. *I shouldn't be here. I need to leave.* He felt a hand on his arm and jumped, but seeing it was Naomi, he relaxed a slight bit.

She leaned close and whispered, "Stay calm. He's never seen you before. He won't know who you are."

Levi closed his eyes and focused on his breathing, trying to ignore the racing of his mind. *She's right*, he realized. *There's no way Farren can know that I carry the Elder Gem just by seeing my face.* His breathing steadied, he opened his eyes and saw the concern in Naomi's. "Thanks."

Naomi squeezed his arm before letting go.

Somewhat calmed, Levi took the opportunity to study his adversary. Farren was an average-sized man, but broad across the shoulders and narrow in the hips; the build of a swordsman. His hair was black with a sprinkling of grey, resembling the night sky. It tumbled down to his shoulders and rested beneath a golden crown of simple design. His face was handsome; a dignified nose, strong jawline, sharp cheekbones. A groomed goatee framed his chin and a moustache covered his upper lip.

The king wore his formal attire consisting of a dark grey tunic and black leggings of the finest fabric, black boots studded with real silver, black gloves made of the renowned Tacorine leather and a black and red cape fastened with a gold brooch.

Farren smiled readily and waved to the crowd as the applause lingered. "My people!" His voice was a strong, melodic baritone. "Today is a great day. It marks the beginning of the fortieth Midarra Festival!"

The cheering grew louder.

Farren laughed merrily. "Yes, it is wonderful. We have much in store for you. Games, plays, entertainment, feasts and of course, the Tournament!"

Another great cheer.

Levi watched in wonder. The people loved Farren. He seemed like the kind, generous king the tales made him out to be. Levi wondered how this man could be the one who had murdered his own parents, who had destroyed the Free Knights, who had wiped whole towns off the map. Uncertainty flickered through his mind. *What if the Giala is wrong? What if Farren isn't evil?*

Farren's gaze swept over the crowd and for a moment, his eyes locked with Levi's. In that split-second, the humour and warmth were gone, replaced with blinding wrath and fury. Farren blinked and his eyes returned to normal, his gaze moving on.

Levi was suddenly very sure the Giala was right. He knew he was on the right side of the secret war.

Farren continued to address the crowd, stoking their excitement while seeming like a good and just leader. But, Levi wasn't paying attention. His gaze had fallen onto the three figures that had come through the door while Farren had been speaking.

Two of them were obviously noblemen with their fancy garments and condescending looks. One was tall, thin and blond while the other was short and stocky with dark hair and a beard.

The third person was one that Levi and everyone else recognized. He was feared by all. Malroth. The King's bodyguard, Commander of the Royal Forces, the Fist of Farren, Crimson Death. He was utterly loyal to the king and fear incarnate to Farren's enemies. The stories told of him were enough to frighten even the most hardened of warriors.

He wore plate armour, black as midnight on a new moon. The massive broadsword that hung at his hip was a deep red, the shade of blood. He wore no helmet, but his face was still a mask, devoid of emotion, clean-shaven and pale. The only things alive were his eyes. They were bright blue, intelligent, constantly scanning the crowd, looking for threats.

Levi sucked in his breath. He dearly hoped he would never have to cross Malroth, but the path he was on, it might very well lead to a confrontation with the fearsome knight.

Levi's attention was brought back to the king as Farren finished. "Let the Festival begin!"

The cheers were deafening, vibrating the bench beneath him.

Farren let the adulation go on for a few moments before raising his hand for silence. "Now, for the introductions." He looked to his advisors. "Dravin, the list."

"Certainly, my lord," Dravin, the blond said, coming forward and handing the king a scroll.

The king dismissed Dravin with a nod. He opened the scroll and read aloud the first name. "Sir Gerart of Redvale."

Sir Gerart stepped out onto the stage. Beside him was a young squire holding aloft a banner with Gerart's coat-of-arms emblazoned on it: a green cross over a black circle. The two made a circuit of the stage while the knight waved to the crowd and winked at the ladies. Then, they both exited off the side of the stage.

Farren read the second name. "Raolin the Red of Westwall." A massive man with a wild, bushy beard came out yelling. The crowd responded with a cheer of their own. Raolin was a popular figure among the commoners. His banner was simple; a white battle-axe on a red background.

After he exited the stage, the next knight followed: Clerenbald the Dragonheart of Rizzen. His coat-of-arms was a checkered flag of red and yellow. He gave the crowd a formal salute with a smile on his face.

Things fell into a pattern. Farren would announce a name, the knight would come out, do a quick lap while the audience applauded, they would leave and the cycle would repeat.

Levi soon began to tire of the seemingly unending line of knights. It was somewhat interesting to see the banners of the different men and women, but Levi couldn't remember them for long, much less who they belonged to.

Levi turned to say something to Adam, but as he did, Farren said a name he recognized.

"El Fen Lianon, Lord Protector of Blackmere."

The tall, tanned man strode out, flanked by a young girl who held his banner, a running stag beneath a four-sided star.

Levi, Naomi and Romeo stared at Adam.

"Your dad is participating?" Naomi asked, incredulous.

Adam was shocked. His mouth hung open and he stared at his father. "I had no idea..."

"Hold on," Lawson said. "Adam, you're the son of El Fen Lianon? The legend himself?"

Adam nodded, still looking at his dad up on the stage.

Lawson's eyes went wide and he slapped his hands to his cheeks in a surprised and joyful expression. "This is amazing! I've befriended the son of one of the most influential men in the realm!"

Adam ignored Lawson. He was still stuck on the fact that his father was participating in the Tournament.

Up on the stage, El Fen looked at Adam and winked.

"Guess we know who we're cheering for," Romeo said.

"Think he'll win?" Naomi asked.

Levi shrugged. "I've heard he's really good."

"Really good?" Lawson said. "Friend, I say, he's much more than 'really good'. He's a master of the sword. An artist, in fact. Oh, what I would give to learn from him..."

"Well, you did just make friends with his son," Levi said.

Lawson's face lit up. "I did, didn't I? This is excellent!"

Adam finally turned from the stage. "He will be busy with the Tournament."

"I don't need much time with him. I would just like a few pointers, you know, the same type as you gave me for archery."

Adam bit his lip. "I suppose he may be able to give you a few brief lessons. Assuming he agrees, of course."

"Yes, yes, of course," Lawson said. "Oh, how my fortunes have reversed!"

CHAPTER 11

"Is this place awesome or what?" Guy asked as he flopped down on his camping mats.

Cody and his friends had just returned from a hot breakfast and a show in which a pair of acrobats performed daring feats on a set of high bars.

"It's great!" Coral exclaimed, playing with the yo-yo she had bought. Cody watched her attempt to use it correctly and smiled. She hadn't actually bought it at first, she had stolen it while the merchant wasn't looking. Ember had made her go back and pay for it.

"What are we going to do today?" Levi asked. He was flipping through the blank pages of the small yellow book he carried around with him. Cody didn't know why he did, it was totally empty, but Levi seemed to think it was important.

"We should go watch the first duel," Cody suggested.

"Who's even fighting?" Guy asked.

Ember reached into her bag and pulled out a fifty-page schedule she had purchased the night before. "Sir Renaud the Bold of Vichen against Sir Izett of Bellock Harbour."

"I'm sure we saw them yesterday," Guy said. "But for the life of me, I can't remember either of them."

"There were a lot of knights," Naomi said.

"Four hundred and two," Kaito said.

"Huh?"

"The number of knights," Kaito clarified. "Four hundred and two."

Levi raised his eyebrows. "You counted?"

Kaito inclined his head.

"Nerd!" Coral called.

"Oh, come on, Coral, don't say that," Ember chastised.

"Why not?" Coral asked.

"Because it's rude."

"It's rude," Coral repeated in a mocking tone. Ember glared at her.

Guy looked around and lowered his voice so Autumn, Adam and a few of the first-years wouldn't hear. "Also, we saw Hejeck around, so I made a show of sneaking into a tent. He followed me, but some woman caught him and laid into him!"

"I watched from a nearby booth. It was hilarious," Cody smirked. The others chuckled.

Levi chewed absentmindedly on a stick of taffy. "Uh, when is the duel?"

"It says here that it is at ten," Ember read.

"It's gotta be close to that, right?" Guy figured.

"Probably," Cody said. "I suppose we could head over there. Get some good seats." He didn't want to be stuck way in the back, far from the action. He didn't want to stand either. He pushed himself up, signalling to the others that he was ready to go. Everyone but Adam followed.

"Hey, you coming?" Naomi asked.

Adam shook his head. "No. I am meeting with my father today. He wishes to speak with me."

"Ok," Naomi said. "Come find us later."

Adam nodded.

Cody pushed aside the door flap and walked out into the sunlight. He squinted his eyes against the glare before they adjusted.

At the open-walled cook tent, there was a large group of fellow Blackthrush students. Cody and the other blue campers joined the crowd.

"You all going to watch the first duel?" Coral asked.

"You bet," Marshall said.

Bear shouldered his way next to Marshall. "We've already taken bets on the winner."

"Real money?" Cody smirked.

"Course," Bear grinned. "What else would we bet with?"

Cody heard Ember sniff disdainfully and he faced her. "What?"

"It's such an irresponsible thing to do with your money," she said.

"It's only irresponsible if you don't win," Marshall said, holding up a finger.

"That is very wrong," Ember said. "But, I'm not going to get into an argument with you."

"Who'd you bet on?" Guy asked.

Kinzo and Kana joined the conversation. "Almost everyone bet on Renaud," Kinzo said. "No one's betting on the girl."

"What's that supposed to mean?" Kana crossed her arms.

"Nothing," Kinzo said. "I'm just saying that everyone thinks the guy will win."

Kana's eyes flashed dangerously.

Cody hid a smile behind his hand. Kinzo was on thin ice. If he went much further, he was going to end up flat on his back with a broken nose. Cody had seen it happen a few times.

Kinzo noticed too and tried to backtrack. "Well, that is to say, it's not so much to do with the gender in this particular instance, it's more about the skills of each individual fighter."

"Oh, right." Kana rolled her eyes. "Because you remember which two these are."

"Of course I know," Kinzo said, folding his arms.

"Really? Then which knight is Renaud?"

Kinzo's mouth worked without sound for a few seconds. Then, "Well, he is a knight... who was up on stage last night."

Cody snickered.

"Every knight was on the stage last night," Kana said.

"He had a young boy hold his banner," Kinzo said.

"Which was...?"

Kinzo swallowed. "Which was...ah...probably a colour or two with maybe a design on it."

"Honestly, Kinzo, you can't remember one thing about him?" Kana asked.

"Yes, I can!"

"I'll make you a deal," Kana said. "If you can tell me one thing, one detail about him, I won't punch you in the face."

"That's not fair," Kinzo complained.

Kana made a big show of making a fist.

"Ok, ok," Kinzo said, holding up his hands. "He had, uh, he had... hair."

The sound of Kana's fist connecting with Kinzo's cheek rang through the air.

Cody burst out laughing, as did the others. Kinzo moaned and held his face as he lay on the ground. Guy whistled.

"Do you want to end up next to him?" Kana demanded. "Honestly!"

The group laughed harder.

"Let's go watch the match!" someone called. The group cheered and raced out of the camp toward the arena, leaving Kinzo in the dust.

There was no one path to the arena; everyone just broke off into small groups and picked a lane that wound around and between the tents and other structures that had been set up for the Festival.

Cody caught a glimpse of Hejeck ducking into a small black tent. His eyes narrowed. *What could he be doing?* Part of his brain told him Hejeck was up to something, but the other part told him that they were at the Midarra Festival. Hejeck was likely visiting a friend. Also, he wasn't necessarily the spy, he was only a suspect.

Shaking his head, he decided to ignore the Riding instructor for now.

Cody arrived at the arena with Levi and Aybrin. They found three empty seats halfway up the southern section of bleachers, next to a pair of identical girls. Cody sat beside them and his friends took the seats to his right.

"Hey, look, there's Griswold," Aybrin said. Cody scanned the crowd and found the taciturn instructor standing across the way with arms crossed and expression grim. Ever since the day in the tunnels under Forenfall, Cody had wondered what he was up to. Every time he saw the instructor, he tried to figure out what he had wanted with the prisoner with the strange eyes.

"Think he's here to enjoy the match?" Levi asked, breaking Cody out of his thoughts.

"No way," Cody grinned. "He'll be grading the knights on their technique."

Levi snorted. "Yeah and then he'll go yell at them afterwards."

As Cody watched the instructor, Griswold spotted an empty seat and tried to squeeze through the crowd to get to it. Right before he arrived, a man wearing a black hat took the seat. Cody couldn't help but laugh at Griswold's expression. It looked as if he was struggling not to pitch the man headfirst off the stands.

A trumpet blast drew Cody's attention and he forgot all about Griswold.

A steward stood in the centre of the arena and waited for silence. Or partial silence. With a crowd so large, it was never truly quiet. "Welcome all to the first match of the day and the Tournament! Please welcome Sirs Renaud and Izett!"

The crowd roared as the two knights stepped into the arena.

Sir Renaud wore plain, unadorned armour. The only bit of flair he had was a green plume protruding from the crest of his helmet. His tunic and round shield were all black save for the green lightning bolt in the centre of each. As for his weapon, he didn't bear the typical straight-bladed longsword that most knights used. Instead, he brandished a single-edged falchion.

Cody eyed the weapon with anticipation. He had never seen one in action and was eager to learn how Renaud used it. Cody imagined more sweeps and slashes and fewer thrusts.

Across the arena was his challenger, Sir Izett. Her armour bore wave designs of blue and green, her helmet painted to look as if it was covered in scales. Which was ironic, Cody thought, because she wore plate armour, not scale armour. Izett's coat-of-arms was a blue fin cutting through a line of water. She wielded a regular longsword and a kite-shaped shield.

The steward called for silence and then began his practiced speech to the contestants. "You are both held to the code of honour as knights. There will be no intentional maiming or killing. If your opponent is injured, give them a chance to yield. If they do not, continue, but if they do, cease the fight. You will be disqualified if you falsely yield and proceed to attack your opponent. Do not attack a downed opponent. Each combatant is allowed one respite. If one is called, both fighters must cease the fight. If you are disarmed at any time, you have lost and must yield." The steward cleared his throat. "Breaking any of these rules will result in the offender forfeiting the match. Do you understand?"

Both knights raised their hands in acknowledgment.

The steward nodded. "Good luck, then. And may the best knight win." He exited the arena as the crowd cheered again.

The knights squared off and readied their weapons. There was a tense moment as everyone held their breath.

Then, the bugle.

Renaud immediately moved to his left, trying to put Izett's shield in a less favourable position. Izett was no novice and turned with him, keeping her opponent in front of her.

They circled for a few moments before Renaud initiated the first attack. It wasn't much, just a quick swing to test Izett's reactions. She calmly flicked her wrist and knocked away Renaud's falchion. She then cut at Renaud's neck on the right, reversed and swung to the left. Renaud parried both in one smooth motion.

Izett whipped her arm around and slashed at Renaud's right side. He took the blow on his shield, letting her sword bite into the reinforced wood and swinging at Izett's head at the same time. She lifted her shield and blocked the stroke and then shoved her arm ahead. The heavy shield slammed into Renaud's chest, sending him stumbling. She followed up with a cut at his exposed side. Renaud managed to put his blade in the way and deflect the attack. He regained his balance and took a stride back, composing himself.

The whole first encounter had taken only twenty seconds.

"Wow! They're amazing!" Levi exclaimed.

"Yeah, they are pretty good, aren't they?" Cody said. "But I think Sir Izett has a slight advantage so far."

"Could be that he wasn't expecting Izett to be quite as good as she is," Aybrin figured.

"That's possible," Cody said. Cody knew that Aybrin was great at assessing other people's skills and flaws, he'd seen it many times at Blackthrush.

"I imagine he'll be more careful from now on," Aybrin said.

She was right. Renaud approached Izett from the front, his shield held in a more defensive position than last time. The tip of his sword made small circles as he anticipated what was coming next.

Izett lunged ahead, but it was a feint. Renaud went to parry the blow, but it never came. Instead, Izett struck to the right, but Renaud's shield was ready, deflecting his opponent's blade away. He chopped hard three times on Izett's shield, sending chips of wood flying. Suddenly, he spun around to her left and slashed at her leg. Izett swiped her sword down and knocked the attack to the side and at the same time, slammed her shield into Renaud's helmet.

Falling to one knee, he held his shield over his head just in time to block another strike from Izett. From his position on one knee, he lashed out and his falchion connected with Izett's right greave with a loud clang, denting it.

The half of the crowd rooting for Renaud cheered as Izett hopped away, favouring her injured leg.

Renaud got to his feet and shook his head, clearing the fog from the blow he'd taken. Across from him, his opponent tested her weight on her right leg.

"It still looks like Izett has the advantage," Cody said.

Aybrin nodded. "Yeah, I think she's the better fighter."

"Although Renaud is the one who's actually connected with his sword," Levi put in.

"True," Cody said. "This will be a good fight right till the end."

"Psst! Levi!"

Levi glanced over at Cody. "Yeah?"

"Wasn't me," Cody replied.

"Who was it, then?"

"Me," the voice said.

Cody glanced all around. Everywhere he looked, he saw only people transfixed on the match going on. *Who is talking to us?*

"Down here, idiots," the voice said with a hint of annoyance.

Cody bent over and looked down by his feet. There was a space between the bench and the platform for their feet. In that space was a face. Cody raised an eyebrow. "Um, hi?"

The guy's eyes widened and anger flashed in them for a moment before he said, "Get Levi for me."

Cody frowned, but tapped Levi's leg. A second later, Levi's head appeared. His eyes lit up when he saw who it was. "Snare! Hey!"

Snare cracked a brief smile "Levi."

"So, you're Snare," Cody said. "I've heard about you."

"I'm sure you have," Snare said coolly. "Now, Levi, if you'd come with me..."

"Sure," Levi said.

"Great," Snare said. "Meet me by the archery range."

"I'll come too," Cody said, wanting to meet the people Levi had told him about.

Snare growled and rolled his eyes. "Fine, whatever." He climbed down the underside of the bleachers, his head disappearing from view.

Cody sat up. He grabbed onto the bench as his head spun from being upside down. The same went for Levi.

A great cheer rose from the crowd and Cody focused on the arena. Sir Renaud was lying on his back, his sword six feet away. Sir Izett had her hands in the air, celebrating her victory.

Aybrin clapped along with most everyone else. "That was brilliant fighting."

"Uh huh, it really was," Cody said.

Beside him, Levi began working his way to the stairs on the side of the bleachers. Cody followed.

"Where are you off to?" Aybrin asked.

"Oh, uh, we're meeting a friend of Levi's," Cody explained.

"Cool," Aybrin said. "Have fun."

"Thanks, see you," Cody waved.

They made their way off the bleachers and set out for the archery range. "So, that was Snare."

"Yup, that was him," Levi said.

Cody scrunched his eyebrows together. "Hmm, he seemed a little, uh…"

"A little what?"

"Oh nothing," Cody waved it aside. "Never mind."

Levi didn't push the matter and they walked in silence until they reached the meeting place. "Where is he?" Cody asked, not seeing Snare anywhere.

"Not sure," Levi said, scanning the place himself. There were plenty of people milling about the range, but Cody couldn't spot the short, olive-skinned guy.

Something flashed into Cody's peripheral vision and hit the ground with a thud. He turned to see Snare dusting himself off.

Cody glanced at Levi. "What the heck?"

"Did you really just jump off that shed?" Levi asked, eyebrow raised.

Snare smirked. "I like to make an entrance."

"I remember," Levi said.

Cody examined the shed Snare had leapt off of. It wasn't large, but still ten feet off the ground. Cody was impressed with how quickly Snare must have climbed it for them not to have seen him.

"What are you up to?" Levi asked.

Snare held up a finger. "Uh uh. Not yet. We'll wait till Ring and Latch get here."

"Ring's here?" Levi asked. "Cool. And I assume Latch is another one of your friends."

"Ring's friend," Snare said. "He's more of an acquaintance of mine. He's not very smart, but I'll admit, he is fast and an expert pickpocket. Watch your money around him."

Cody unconsciously put his hand to the pocket that contained his coins. Snare raised an eyebrow at him. "And definitely don't show him which pocket it's in."

Cody felt his face flush.

"When will they get here?" Levi asked.

Snare picked at something in his teeth. "As soon as they get your friends to come here."

Levi nodded. "Figured as much." He kicked at a clump of dirt. "So, what have you been up to lately?"

"Bit of this, bit of that," Snare said vaguely.

Levi smirked. "Look, I know almost everything you do is illegal. I don't care."

Snare motioned toward Cody. "Yeah, but what about him?"

"What about him? Levi asked.

"Yeah, what about me?" Cody repeated.

"Well, would he turn me in if he knew certain things?" Snare asked.

Levi stared blankly. "Uh..."

"I wouldn't," Cody said. "Unless, of course, you're like a serial killer or something. Then I might."

"Well, I'm not a 'serial' killer," Snare said.

"Why did you stress the serial so much?" Cody asked.

"Because I did."

Cody narrowed his eyes. "Does that mean you're a regular killer?"

"What do you mean by 'regular' exactly?" Snare asked.

"Well, just like a killer."

Snare sighed. "Then yes, I am. I have killed people before. What are you going to do about it?"

"Nothing," Cody said. "After all, Levi's killed before."

"Just one guy," Levi said, crossing his arms. "And you know I don't like when it's brought up."

"Sorry," Cody apologized.

Snare's interest had been piqued. "You killed someone? Who?"

"It's nobody," Levi said. "Not important."

"Was he trying to kill you?" Snare asked.

"Not exactly. He was trying to hand me over to someone who was going to kill me." Levi looked decidedly uncomfortable.

"That's acceptable," Snare said. "Self-defence."

Levi stared at the ground. "But he wasn't attacking. He had already been beaten and was lying helpless on the ground."

Snare rolled his eyes. "Would he have attacked if he had gotten back up?"

"Yes," Levi said quietly.

"Then, there's nothing to feel bad about," Snare told him. "The world's a dangerous place. It's kill or be killed. And it's much better to be alive than dead."

Levi's eyes came up. "Yeah, I guess you're right."

"Of course I am," Snare said. "Now, no more feeling sorry for yourself. The others are here."

Cody spun around. Kana, Miri, Kinzo and Evander were being led by a petite girl and a slender guy who he assumed were Ring and Latch.

"Snare, good to see you," Evander said, clapping his friend on the back.

"Yeah, yeah, whatever, you old rascal," Snare said, shoving him away with a slight smile.

"Who's this one?" Ring asked, pointing at Cody.

"Hmm?" Snare said. "Oh, he's just one of Levi's friends that wanted to tag along." His tone made it obvious that he wasn't too pleased with it.

"I'm Cody," he said, trying to ignore Snare and the feeling that he wasn't wanted.

"Cool. Ring," she said by way of introduction.

"I assumed that," Cody said.

"Well, now you know," Ring said with a saucy smile that made Cody's ears turn red.

"Now that we're all here, can you tell us what's the deal?" Levi asked in a brighter tone. Cody figured that he had pushed Dekar's death and all that away.

"Yeah, what's up?" Kinzo asked.

"It's that favour you owe us," Snare said.

"What about it?" Kana asked.

Ring smiled at them, but it was devoid of humour. "It's time you paid it."

~ ~ ~

Farren looked out the window, gazing over the Festival in front of him. People, his people, his subjects, enjoyed the festivities outside, unaware of the situation Farren was dealing with.

He turned away from the window, clasped his hands behind his back and paced the room. He was in his personal meeting chamber, waiting for his trusted generals to return. They had gone out upon hearing word that a certain group of Giala rebels had been spotted in the city.

Farren sat and placed his elbows on the table, his fingertips pressed together. This particular group had been a thorn in his side for some time now and he wanted them caught. Hopefully, Malroth, Avelyn and a squad of soldiers under Captain Steele would be enough to capture them.

His mind drifted to the day prior at the opening ceremony. Something out there in the crowd, perhaps someone, had caused Farren to lose control for a fraction of a second. He had masked it quickly, but he couldn't be sure that no one had seen. Seen the hate and rage and pain that boiled beneath the calm surface he presented to everyone every day. Only six people alive had ever seen that side of him, the side that wanted nothing more than to watch the world burn.

"What could have caused it?" he wondered aloud. "Yesterday was quiet. There was no rebel activity. What could it be?"

He heard voices outside and straightened, fixing his features into a serene mask. "Enter."

A guard opened the door to admit Malroth and Avelyn. Both were covered in blood and Avelyn was holding her left arm gingerly. They both bowed to their King.

"Malroth?" Farren asked.

The black knight stood and put a hand to his heart. "Your majesty, we were not able to apprehend the rebels. They wiped out nearly all of Captain Steele's men. I killed one of them, but the rest escaped with a box. We do not know what was inside it or where they got it from."

Farren inhaled slowly. He placed his hands flat on the table. "They continue to evade us. They are a force beyond what our men can handle. We need our own counterforce. Avelyn, I am putting you in charge of assembling a team that can take down these rebels."

"Yes, my lord," Avelyn said. "How should I recruit them?"

"However you can," Farren said. "I don't care if they demand a fortune or if you must take their children from their arms. Do what you must."

"Very well, my King," Avelyn bowed. Both warriors exited the room, leaving Farren alone again.

Farren bowed his head. There was much to handle, being a king.

CHAPTER 12

"Whoa, whoa, whoa. Hold up," Kinzo said. Snare, Ring and Latch had explained their situation to the gang, but they didn't understand it. "Let me get this straight. You guys think there is some kind of cult kidnapping street urchins like you and brainwashing them and you think that they're being supported by one, if not more of the nobles here at the Festival?"

"That's right," Snare said.

"And you want us to help you take down the entire organization?" Kana asked.

The three street kids nodded.

Miri nudged Cody and signed, "Crazy." Cody shared her opinion.

"How do you know this is true?" Evander wondered.

"We don't know all of it," Ring said. "But we have heard mutterings of a secret cult, we've seen people in hoods and white masks wandering around and dozens of street kids have disappeared only to return completely different than before."

"How bad is it?" Cody asked.

"It's like they're different people!" Latch exclaimed. "I had a buddy, Coin, who was a normal dude. Now, he acts all, I don't know, almost righteous. He talks different too."

"It's pretty strange," Ring added.

Levi scratched his cheek. "What exactly do you want us to do?"

"Before we can do anything," Snare said, "We need to find the cult, where they're based, how many of them there are and who they are, if possible."

"And the only way to do that..." Ring said.

"Is to have one of you kidnapped and then we'll follow the kidnappers to their hideout!" Snare finished.

Cody's mouth dropped open. That idea was insane.

"Are you serious?" Kana cried.

Kinzo threw up his hands. "That's ridiculous!"

"No way, we're doing that!" Kana said. Miri nodded, agreeing with her fully.

"Look," Snare said, his tone serious. "We helped you out last year and you owe us for it. This is what we need help with. If you refuse, well, then we'll have a problem." His words held a thinly veiled threat.

The others noticed it and their complaints died away.

After a moment, Evander sighed and said, "Fine, we'll do it. But why does it have to be one of us getting kidnapped? Why not one of you?"

Latch spread his hands. "Uh, duh, we don't want to."

"Yeah, basically," Snare agreed.

"Wow," Levi said, unimpressed.

Kinzo shook his head. "I ain't doing it. I've already been kidnapped! Twice! It's not fun!"

"The rest of us, once too," Evander said.

"Well, somebody has to do it," Ring said.

Cody sighed inwardly. All these people were too stubborn to do it themselves. Someone had to volunteer. "I'll do it."

Everyone faced him. Snare rolled his eyes.

"Cody, you sure?" Miri signed to him.

"No, but let's do it anyway," Cody said. He caught Ring's gaze and she gave him another smile. This time, he returned it.

"Awesome," Latch clapped. "Thanks for volunteering."

"It'll be dangerous," Ring said.

"I know," Cody said. "But, I'm training to be a knight. I'd better get used to some danger. And you guys will be there to rescue me if things go wrong."

"Absolutely, we will," Kana assured him. The others all agreed. All but Snare. She glared at him. "Right, Snare?"

"Sure, whatever," Snare said, offhandedly.

159

"Thanks," Cody said, sarcasm dripping off every word. "I am so reassured."

Snare snorted.

Kana translated Miri's question. "Will the cultists mistake Cody for one of you?".

"Not dressed like that, he'll need a full makeover." Ring looked at Cody critically. "Too bad you've recently had your hair cut. We'll just have to get it dirty and hope it isn't suspicious."

"Do you guys have spare clothes anywhere?" Levi asked.

"Does it look like we own more than one pair of clothes?" Snare asked.

Cody looked at their garments. They were stained and filthy, ripped and patched, fraying at the seams.

Levi examined them too. "I guess not."

"So, how are you going to get Cody new, er, old clothes?" Kinzo asked.

"We steal them," Latch said, matter-of-factly.

"Oh," Cody said. "Are you sure we couldn't borrow some? Stealing seems a little harsh."

Ring laughed. "Relax, bud, We'll return them."

"That's not the part I have a problem with," Cody said. "It's the taking the clothes in the first place."

Snare crossed his arms. "Look, mister high and mighty, do you want to get kidnapped or not?"

"Not really, but I already agreed to, so yeah," Cody said.

"Then accept the fact that we're going to do a few things outside of the law," Snare said. "If you can't, then get lost. It's not like we wanted you along anyway."

"Ouch," Kinzo muttered. "Harsh."

"Well, if that's how you feel, maybe I won't be the volunteer." Cody stuck his nose in the air.

"No, no, it's ok," Kinzo said. "Snare doesn't know what he's talking about. We are all thrilled that you've volunteered." He glared at Snare.

Cody grumbled, but said nothing more about backing out. Still, he glowered at Snare. He had no idea why the short urchin had such a dislike for him. After all, Cody had never done anything to him.

Snare, on his part, sighed, but did nothing more to annoy Cody.

160

There was an awkward silence as everyone waited for someone else to speak.

Finally, Levi broke the silence. "So, where do we start?"

Latch began to answer, but Ring cut him off. "I just thought of something."

"What's that?" Evander asked.

"There's nine of us, right? Ring said. "Well, if Cody is being kidnapped, that leaves eight of us to follow. That's a lot of people to try and keep hidden while we tail them. Too many. I think we should leave at least three people back here, to reduce our chances of discovery."

"Makes sense," Snare said. "And those three could start the next part of the plan."

"What's the next part?" Cody asked.

"The part where we infiltrate the Aedon and spy on the nobles to discover who is funding the cult."

Evander rubbed his chin. "You know there are nobles funding them?"

"We aren't totally sure," Ring said. "But we've seen the cultists interacting with a few pages, you know, the ones with grey tunics and red patches on their shoulders?"

"And their clothes are nice," Latch piped up. "Expensive clothes that you can't get around here without spending a fortune."

Kana nodded. "Ok, sounds like it's worth checking into. Who should do that?"

Ring answered. "I was thinking that Latch could be part of that team, with you and Levi."

Levi and Kana exchanged a look and shrugged. "That works."

"Great!" Ring said. "You three can disguise yourselves as servants. That way you should have access to almost all areas and you can keep a low profile."

"Cool, how long will we have?" Levi asked.

"It shouldn't be too long, right?" Kinzo said. "I can't imagine the kidnapping and rescue will take very long."

"Hopefully not," Cody said. "I don't want to become part of a cult."

"Don't worry," Miri told him. "We won't let that happen."

Cody smiled thankfully.

Snare clapped his hands together. "Alright, if we're all set, let's go."

"We'll head over to the Aedon right away," Kana said.

"Yeah, good luck guys," Levi said. He looked pointedly at Cody. "Don't die."

Cody smirked. "I will try my hardest not to."

Latch, Kana and Levi waved goodbye and turned away to begin their phase of the plan.

Ring put a hand on Cody's shoulder and steered him away. "Come on. Let's get you an outfit."

~ ~ ~

Cody held a hand over his throbbing eye and plopped down on an overturned barrel.

Ring sat next to him. "Sorry about the eye." She was winded. They had just sprinted for the last five minutes, trying to escape an angry gang.

"You said they'd all be asleep!" Kinzo complained, holding a hand to his side.

"They were," Snare said. "Then we woke them up."

They had snuck into the hideout of a gang that operated by night and slept by day, in order to procure an outfit for Cody. Unfortunately, Miri had knocked over a crate, waking the thugs. They had managed to escape, but not before one of the goons had punched Cody in the face.

"You sure we lost them?" Evander asked.

"For sure," Snare said confidently. "I've been losing people in the back alleys since I was six. We lost 'em."

"Hopefully, they don't interfere with our plans," Ring said.

Cody agreed. "If I'm just hanging around outside, there's a chance they'll run into me."

Snare waved a hand. "Small chance. They rarely come out in the day. After we lost them, they probably skulked back to their hideout to sleep."

"One minus his clothes," Kinzo said with a snicker. The others chuckled.

Cody glanced down at the bundle of filthy, stinking rags in his hands. He really didn't want to put them on, but it was the only way to get their plan to work.

"Well, go on, get dressed," Snare said.

"Right here?" Cody looked around. They were in an alley between a tannery and a two-story house.

"Yeah, right here," Snare said.

"But, what about the girls?" Cody protested.

Ring laughed as Snare rolled his eyes. "Oh, come on. How old are you? So what if they see you without clothes on?"

Cody looked to Evander and Kinzo for help. They were both trying and failing to conceal their grins.

"Wow, thanks," Cody muttered. He swung his gaze over to Miri. She had a small smile and a slight pink tinge to her cheeks. Cody exhaled through his nose. "Fine. Whatever." He began stripping off his clothes and throwing them in a pile.

When he stood in nothing but his undergarments, Ring said, "Hmm. Not bad. Not bad at all." Cody's body was well built and toned from the training that he was put through every day at Blackthrush. His physique was rather pleasing to the eye. She circled him and stopped when she got to his back. "What are those?"

Cody spun around. "Nothing! Nothing important."

"Um, yeah right," Ring said. "That seems pretty important. Did you burn that on yourself?"

"My friend did, but it's none of your concern. So just leave it alone."

Ring spread her hands. "Ok, fine. You keep your secrets."

"I will," Cody said. He hurriedly slipped on the stolen pants. They were a tad large, but he pulled the drawstring tight so they wouldn't slip off. He then pulled on the dirty tunic. As the stench reached his nose, he coughed in disgust. "I can feel the dust mites crawling on me."

"Ew," Kinzo said. "At least you look great." He was kidding, of course. Cody looked homeless, which was exactly the point.

"Perfect," Ring said. "Now, let's get into position."

"And where's that?" Cody asked.

"Not sure yet," Ring admitted. "Somewhere fairly secluded and yet not too secluded that you won't be found by the cult."

"Do you have any ideas as to where we could go?" Evander asked.

"I do," Snare said before Ring could answer.

Ring was surprised. "Really? Where?"

Snare began walking. "Come on. I'll show you."

Everyone followed, Cody pausing to scoop up his clothes. He tossed them to Kinzo. "Don't lose those."

"You got it, boss," Kinzo said.

They walked down the alley to the main street and made a left. The pedestrians going about their business paid them no mind. They had more important things to worry about than a group of street urchins.

Snare led the group down the street until they came to a statue of some old man at the corner, probably a founder of something or other. His head was missing, broken off just above the chin. They turned right onto another narrow street, bordered by ramshackle houses and derelict businesses. They made a left and shortly after cut right into an alley.

"Um, Snare?" Ring asked, uncertainty in her voice. "Are we going into Bull's territory?"

Snare tipped his head. "Yeah, we've gotta go through his stomping grounds."

Ring's shoulders slumped. "Why? You know what he'll do if he catches us."

"Relax, he won't even know we're here," Snare said. Despite the confident words, Cody heard a hint of apprehension in his voice.

"Who's Bull?" Kinzo asked.

Ring and Snare exchanged a glance.

"I know who Bull is," Evander said. "He's basically the kingpin of the underworld here in the Outskirts. He has half the gangs under his control and he is a scary guy when provoked." He looked at the street kids. "But we were on decent terms when I left. What happened?"

Ring looked at her feet and mumbled something.

"What was that?" Cody asked, not hearing her.

"She doesn't want to talk about it!" Snare snapped at him.

Cody held up his hands. "Ok, sorry. Geez."

"No, no, it's ok," Ring said in a weary voice. "Bull approached me and asked to marry me. I said no."

"He didn't take it well," Evander surmised.

Ring nodded. "We had to jump into the river to escape his henchmen. We hid outside the city for three days until it was safe for us to come back."

"That's terrible," Miri said via Cody.

"It did suck," Snare said. "And to make matters worse, we've lost a ton of contacts since then, who are unwilling to risk Bull's wrath and keep us informed."

"No wonder you need our help with this cult," Evander said. "You need allies."

Ring made a face. "Mm hmm. And those still with us are slowly being picked off and brainwashed."

"We have some more friends back at the Festival who would be willing to help out," Cody said. He was certain Guy, Coral and the others would be on board to take down a cult.

Ring shook her head. "Thanks, but we don't want too many people involved, at least, at this stage."

"Ok," Kinzo said. "Just tell us when you need backup."

"For sure," Ring said. "Now, we should get going. If we're going to cross Bull's territory, we might as well get it over with."

"Right, let's go!" Kinzo said.

Snare dipped his head and took off, his pace quicker than before. They snaked down alleys and back streets until they came to a tavern named The Yellow Tortoise.

Snare paused. "This is the beginning of Bull's area. Be careful."

"You know," Ring said. "It would be better if they stayed back a bit in case we're caught. That way they could make it away."

"I like that idea," Kinzo said. "Best chance of escape? I'm all for it." Evander, Miri and Cody agreed as well.

Snare and Ring started off again. Cody waited until they were three hundred feet ahead before following. As soon as he passed the tavern, the hair on the back of his neck prickled, as if he was being watched.

Probably being paranoid, he thought. Still, he couldn't shake the feeling.

"Do you think they'll get caught?" Miri asked.

"There's a chance," Evander said. "But Bull's people aren't actively looking for them, which gives them an advantage."

"Let's hope for the best and prepare for the worst," Cody said. "If they're spotted, it'll be up to us to rescue them."

"What?" Kinzo exclaimed. "I thought we were supposed to run away if that happened?"

"We can't just leave them if they're caught!" Miri signed.

"Well, we can," Kinzo said. "It's physically possible."

Miri frowned at him. "We won't."

Kinzo spread his hands. "Ok, fine. So, say they are caught. What do we do?"

"We fight," Evander said simply. "After all, we do all know a little magic."

"Emphasis on little," Kinzo said. "Especially you, Evander. You can barely make a flame, much less throw a fireball."

Evander frowned. "Hey now, no need to be rude. I can move wind fairly well. Besides, any magic is more than they'll have."

"Hopefully," Miri said.

"Whaddya mean?" Evander asked.

"We can't know for sure that any of the attackers won't know magic. There's a possibility they will."

"She's right," Cody said. "It's a small chance, cause most commoners don't know magic, but it's still a chance nonetheless."

Kinzo sighed. "Fine. Maybe there will be a magic-user. What then?"

"Then we can run," Cody conceded.

"Then I'm hoping for a magic-user," Kinzo said. "I want to run away."

"You are a pathetic coward," Miri told him.

Kinzo crossed his arms. "Yes. Yes I am. But I'll outlive all of you being a pathetic coward."

"Doubt it," Evander said.

Kinzo raised an eyebrow. "Honestly, yeah. Miri's definitely gonna die first."

An outraged expression crossed Miri's face. "What? Why me?"

"Because you rush into dangerous situations too much. One of these times, you won't come out of it alive."

For a second, Cody thought he glimpsed a look of guilt on Miri's face. Then, she turned away and pouted.

"Really, Kinzo?" Cody asked. Kinzo shrugged, uncaring.

Up ahead, Snare and Ring turned left and disappeared.

"We'd better not lose them," Evander said. They picked up the pace until they reached the corner. They were just in time to see the pair make another turn."

"Hurry up!" Cody called as he led the others in a jog to the next alley. Cody turned the corner and froze.

Kinzo cursed.

"Guess they got caught," Evander said with a sigh.

A quartet of goons in filthy clothes and armed with knives and clubs surrounded Ring and Snare. Snare tried to resist and one of the assailants clubbed him in the back of the head. He dropped to his hands and knees.

Kinzo faced Miri. "Didn't you learn how to magically knock someone out?"

Miri grimaced. "Yeah, but that was only one time. And there was no pressure. I don't know if I can do it again."

"Well, try!" Kinzo snapped.

Miri shut her eyes and began to concentrate, her lips pressed together in a thin line.

"Is it working?" Cody asked.

"No idea," Evander said. "But we should go save them."

"Right. C'mon, Kinzo," Cody said. He ran at the attackers, his friends flanking him. One of the goons saw them coming and warned his buddies. "Stop right there!"

In response, Kinzo summoned a fireball in his free hand and lobbed it at the enemy. It was weak and fizzled out partway there, but it had spooked the bad guys.

As he closed in, Cody singled out one that he would attack first. He sized him up and decided that the man would probably try to brain him with his club right away. They met and the fight began.

Cody's opponent swung a mighty arm, the stout club whistling toward Cody's head. Cody, expecting such a move, sidestepped. He jabbed his sword ahead. The man tried to dodge the blow, but he wasn't fast enough and Cody's blade opened up a gash on his left arm. The man cursed and recoiled, flailing his weapon wildly.

Cody waited for the perfect moment to strike. The moment came and Cody reacted, stopping the club with a brilliantly timed swing. He stepped into his follow through and smashed his pommel into the man's face, just above the left eye. The man's gaze unfocused and he wobbled. Cody hooked his leg behind the man's ankle and kicked back, knocking the man over. Stunned, he was out of the fight.

Cody scanned the scene around him. Kinzo and Evander were both engaged in separate battles. The final assailant was trying to fend off both Ring and Snare.

The man fighting Evander suddenly went limp and fell to the ground. Cody knew that Miri had successfully knocked him out. Snare and Ring overpowered their goon. That left just the one facing Kinzo.

Everyone gathered around. "Want help?" Cody asked.

Kinzo, who was fighting with a sabre in one hand and a long dagger in the other, deflected a jab with ease. "Nah, I've got this."

The man snarled. "You will rue the day you crossed Bull and his men!"

"Yeah, yeah, shut up," Kinzo said. He charged the man, put a shoulder into him and knocked him flat. Then, before the man could react, Kinzo punched him in the face five times until his eyes rolled back into his head.

Kinzo sheathed his blades and dusted himself off. "There. All done."

"Nice work," Evander said.

Kinzo gave an embellished bow.

"You guys were supposed to run," Snare said.

"Yeah, well, there were more of us than there were of them," Kinzo said.

"Besides," Cody said, "If we had let them take you, we would have had to rescue you later."

Snare looked at Cody with annoyance, but before he could say something to make the situation worse, Ring intervened.

"Thanks for saving us. It was brave of you." She batted her eyelashes at him.

He smiled back. There was a snort of derision behind him. He turned to see Miri rolling her eyes. "What?"

She just shook her head.

"We should get a move on," Evander said. "Bull will find out about us soon."

"And now all of you are on his bad side too," Snare said. "Well done."

"Wow," Kinzo said. "And I thought I was an ungrateful douchebag."

Snare glared at him.

"Seriously," Kinzo said, spreading his hands. "You are actually, really annoying today. What's your deal?"

Snare rounded on Cody and pointed an accusing finger. "It's him!"

"What did I do?" Cody raised his voice.

Snare's hands balled into fists, but he managed to stay under control. "It's not you, exactly."

"What now?" Kinzo asked.

Snare ran a hand over his face. "It's one of the cultists. One that I've actually seen. He looks almost exactly like you. Only he has an X-shaped scar on his right cheekbone."

Cody felt the blood drain from his face. "It can't be."

"You know him?" Snare asked.

"Know him? He's my brother!" Cody exclaimed.

CHAPTER 13

Levi smoothed out his grey tunic for the tenth time.

"Will you stop that?" Kana asked. "It's annoying. Plus, no real page would be doing that."

"Sorry. It just doesn't fit right." He tugged on the collar.

"Suck it up. It's only for a little while," Kana said.

Latch, who was a few steps ahead of them, reached the door at the end of the hallway. "Ok. It's showtime."

They had signed up as pages for the various nobles that temporarily resided in the Aedon and had been given plain clothes with only a red patch on the shoulder to break up the grey. Their personal belongings they left back at camp, although Levi still carried the Elder Gem. He wasn't about to leave that lying around.

Latch opened the door and slipped through. Kana and Levi followed.

Levi let out a low whistle. The corridor on the other side of the door was a sight to see. A plush red carpet covered the floor and dark oak panels inlaid with gold-lined the walls. Bronze lanterns in intricate brackets provided light, illuminating various paintings and statues along the hall.

"This is nice," Levi commented.

"It's ridiculous," Kana said. "If even half the money used in this building could have gone to the common folk, it could have eliminated poverty in the entire city."

"Really?"

"Not quite, but it would certainly improve a lot of people's lives."

Levi took another look at the décor. "Yeah, they probably could have done without the inlaid gold."

Up ahead, Latch took the place of another page who was standing ready outside the chambers of some noble.

"We should get to our places," Levi said.

Kana nodded. "Let's spread out, hear as much gossip as possible."

"Each take a floor?" Levi suggested.

"I'll take the top floor," Kana said.

"Leaves me with the second, I guess."

They headed for the nearest staircase. It was at the end of the right wing, where it joined up with the central tower and the rooms used not as residences, but as dining areas and private meeting chambers.

When they reached the second floor Kana waved to Levi and continued on to the top.

Levi waited behind the door to the right wing and took a breath to compose himself before he entered. The second floor was nearly identical to the first, the only real difference being the metal inlaid in the walls was silver, not gold.

There was another grey garbed page standing outside the nearest room on the left. He raised a hand. "Are you a replacement?"

"Yep."

"Great," the page said. "Take my place, please."

"Sure," Levi said. "Whose room is this?"

"Oh, it's, um, Baron Silva and his wife."

Levi nodded. "Ok, thanks."

"No, thank you," the page said. "Now, I get to go enjoy the Festival." He jogged down the hall and exited out the door into the stairwell.

Alright, time to stand around for six hours, Levi thought.

He managed to stand still for two minutes before he became incredibly bored. He let his gaze wander around. There was a page standing near every door, all of them looking bored as well. Levi swivelled his head and noticed a small bell hanging beside him. The rope to ring it ran through a small hole in the wall, into the room beyond.

Must be for when the baron summons me, Levi figured. *I hope it rings soon, or I might die of boredom.*

As if hearing him, the bell rang.

Levi smiled. "Nice." He grasped the latch and opened the door.

His jaw hit the floor.

The room was magnificent. Tiled mosaics for a floor, golden lampstands, the finest furniture, satin drapes, expensive paintings on every wall and a glass chandelier hanging from the ceiling. The room was split in two, the main living area and the bedroom. Levi noticed a fine, bejewelled sword resting against the wall, two crystal goblets resting on the mahogany table and a white mask on the arm of a sculpted, purple couch.

"Page! Where are you?" a voice called.

Levi entered the room and saw a portly man in a red vest and a thin lady with her hair piled up in a lavish style near the window.

"Sorry, sir." Levi bowed.

The man, Baron Silva, waved his hand. "All fine, young man. My wife has a message she wants delivered to Count Ridu's wife. Will you deliver it?"

"Certainly," Levi said.

"Splendid." The baron clapped his hands. His long, thin moustache quivered.

His wife held out her hand and gave Levi a scroll wrapped with a red ribbon.

Levi bowed to the Silva's and backed out of the room, closing the door.

"Now, to find Count Ridu." He decided to ask a nearby page.

He meandered over to the next room. The waiting page was a girl with blonde hair, probably fourteen years old.

"Hello," Levi said.

The girl eyed him. "Hello."

"Can you tell me where Count Ridu is?"

"He'll be on the top floor," the girl said. "Other than that, I don't know."

"How do you know he'll be up there?" Seeing her expression, he added, "I'm new."

The girl rolled her eyes. "Floors are divided by rank. The lower you are in nobility, the further up you stay."

"Ok, thanks," Levi said to the page before walking to the stairwell.

On the way up to the top floor, he met two pages on assignment and someone who looked like a chamberlain or something of the sort. They paid Levi no heed.

Levi pulled open the heavy door and walked out onto the top floor. He spotted a page at the nearest room and went over to him. He was an older guy, twenty-five or so. His hair was brown and tied back in a ponytail and he had one blue eye and one green eye.

He smiled as Levi approached. "Hello there."

"Hi," Levi said. "I need to find Count Ridu. Could you tell me where he is?"

"I certainly can," the man said. "Name's Randall. But, first, you must do me a favour."

"Ok, I'm Levi. What's the favour?"

"Don't know yet," Randall said. "I'll let you know when you get back from the third room on the right."

"The third room on... that's where it is?" Levi asked.

Randal wiggled his eyebrows. "Yessiree."

"Thanks," Levi said. He made his way over to the door Randall had indicated. There was no page standing outside. "Must be off on an errand." He knocked on the door.

It opened after a half minute. A man with thinning, grey hair poked his head out. "Yes?"

"Hi, I'm here to deliver a message from Baroness Silva to Countess Ridu."

"Oh, thank you," the count said. "I'll take that." Levi handed the man the message and the door was closed, dismissing him.

Levi returned to Randall. "Did you think of that favour yet?"

Randall's smile gave Levi pause. "Yes, I did. I want you to steal something for me."

Levi froze. "St...steal something? No way!"

Randall's smile vanished in an instant, replaced by a mask of fury. He grabbed Levi by the collar and shoved him up against the wall. Levi struggled, but Randall was very strong.

"You'd better do as I say, Levi," Randall hissed. "No one who crosses me lives long."

Levi kicked him in the shin in an attempt to escape. Randall flicked his wrist and a shiv slid out from under his sleeve into his hand. He held it to Levi's throat.

Levi stopped struggling. "Fine, fine, I'll do it! What do you want?"

Randall let go of Levi and slid the shiv back. He smiled easily again, all traces of wrath gone. "Now, that's more like it. I want you to steal a signet ring from Lord Durst."

Levi sighed deeply. He was in trouble. "Where do I find him?"

"Last room on the left of the bottom floor," Randall said. "Oh and one more thing. The ring will most likely be on his hand. Now, skedaddle!"

Levi groaned. "Are you kidding me?"

Randall didn't respond. He stared past Levi, as if he didn't exist.

Levi rubbed his face and clenched his teeth. He was in a predicament. He had no desire to steal from Lord Durst, but Randall was a loose cannon, Levi didn't want to get on his bad side. He doubted he could beat Randall in a fight. Maybe if he had his own weapons, but he had left them at his tent, halfway across the festival grounds.

He did know some magic, mostly telekinesis, but all he could do is push Randall around, throw him into a wall. A fight would also bring guards and that was the last thing Levi wanted.

Levi groaned aloud and stomped away down the hall. On the way down the stairs, another page met him and smiled kindly. Levi glowered and the guy hurried past. Levi descended to the bottom floor, still grumbling. He watched the pages running to and fro, doing the nobles' bidding.

As Levi stood there, a pompous-looking man in a canary yellow suit came out of a nearby room. His bulging gut attested to his love for fine dining. He saw Levi looking and an expression of disgust and contempt crossed his unattractive features. Head held high, he turned and marched away.

Levi made a face at the noble's retreating form, enjoying the immature gesture. "Now, where's Lord Durst's room?" A guard in red and grey turned the corner and Levi asked him for directions. The guard indicated where Durst resided and went on his way.

Following the guard's directions, Levi crossed the central foyer area of the Aedon and entered the right wing. He began counting doors as he went down the hall.

"Hey, Levi."

Levi took a second to remember which number he was on and then faced the speaker. It was Latch. "Hi."

"How's it going?" Latch asked.

Levi's sigh turned into a strangled groan.

"Not good, huh?"

Levi checked over his shoulder to make sure no one was eavesdropping. "I accidentally got tangled up with a crazy dude named Randall. He's making me steal a ring from one of the nobles."

"Ooh, sounds like you're in some trouble," Latch said.

"Yes, I am."

"And you don't think you can beat him in a fight?" Latch asked.

"Not without my weapons," Levi said, spreading his hands in defeat. "What do I do?"

Latch scratched behind his ear. "I'd steal the ring."

"But what if I get caught?"

"Don't get caught," Latch said simply.

"Ugh, that's the best advice you have?" Levi moaned.

"Look, my expertise is in breaking the law. I'm not going to tell you how to stay within it."

Levi put his head in his hands and closed his eyes for a moment. "Ok, whatever. I guess I'll do it."

Latch nodded. "Yep. The faster you're in, the faster you're out."

"Alright," Levi said with no enthusiasm. "But, if I get caught, you're bailing me out."

"I'll just get Kana to do it," Latch said.

Levi tipped his head. "Probably a better idea." He made fists and put them on his hips. "Time to rob a noble in broad daylight."

"Good luck," Latch smirked.

Levi's feet began taking him down the hall once more and he resumed the counting of doors until he came to stand in front of the seventeenth room. His gut felt like it was tying itself in ever-tighter knots and a bead of sweat trickled down the nape of his neck.

The page standing in front of the door, a brunette girl of middling height, gave him a curious look.

Stay calm, Levi told himself. *You belong here. Act natural.* "H...Hi. Uh, I'm your replacement."

The girl raised an eyebrow. "A bit early, aren't you?"

Levi nervously licked his lips. "Uh, yeah. I was out watching the fights and, um, I had a fight with my cousin. It kinda soured the atmosphere and I didn't want to hang out with him anymore, so I came here." He found the story partway and it ended up sounding somewhat reasonable, at least to Levi. He hoped the girl thought so as well.

"I don't care why you're here," she said. "Just means I get to enjoy more of the festival. So thanks." She patted his arm and waltzed away, her mood improved.

Levi stood alone in front of Lord Durst's door. His knees were practically knocking together, which until up to that moment, Levi had thought was a ridiculous notion. He wrung his hands together as he attempted to calm himself. Finding no comfort, Levi reached beneath his tunic and took out the golden bird talisman, his most sacred possession. He stared at it for a good moment, letting the intricate details of the carving soothe his mind.

"You know, now would be a great time for you to work some of your magic," Levi whispered to the Gem. Then, he snorted and put it away. "What am I doing, talking to a piece of metal. It's not like it can answer me." A breath of air tickled his ears and for a split-second, Levi thought he heard the voice of a woman. Then it was gone and Levi shook his head, clearing it.

"Let's get this over with," he muttered. He took a deep breath and reached out his hand, knuckles an inch from the door. The pause lasted but for a moment before Levi rapped against the wood.

"Come in," a voice answered a moment later.

Levi pulled open the door and entered. He barely even noticed how extravagant the room was, with the finest craftsmanship going into the furniture and the décor. He was inwardly trembling, but managed to keep himself from showing it, if only just.

"Hello?" Levi called tentatively.

"Yes! Hello!" A tall, thin man appeared from the left side of the room. Clean-shaven, his receding hair was salt and pepper black. His nose was rather small for his face, which seemed a bit long to Levi, but was rather handsome, nonetheless. His garb consisted of black trousers and jacket over a blue chemise with red trim. On his left index finger sat Levi's prize, a round, silver ring.

Privately, Levi groaned. It was going to be impossible to steal it.

"Hello, son," Durst said. "What is it you want?"

A cold sweat broke out on Levi's forehead. "Uh, I uh, need to..."

Durst smiled kindly, eyes crinkling. "First day, huh?"

Levi nodded. "Yes, sir."

"It's ok, no need to be afraid. I won't bite." Durst chuckled at his own joke. "As long as you do as you're told, everything will be perfectly smooth. Trust me, I used to do similar work for my uncle when I was just a lad."

Levi was torn. Lord Durst seemed so nice and caring, fatherly, even. But, on the other hand, he didn't want to have to face Randall's wrath again.

Apparently, Durst could see the struggle going on in Levi's head. "Are you alright?"

"No," Levi said in a strangled whisper. Then, as if the dam had burst, the whole story came out in a rush of words. Durst listened intently, with a look of concern.

When Levi had finished, the lord stood straight and rubbed his chin. "Well, it appears you have a dilemma."

"I really do," Levi said. He glanced out the window. Sitting on the ledge outside was a black and white squirrel. Levi blinked and it was gone.

"It is unfortunate that you ran afoul of Randall on your first day," Durst said.

"You know of Randall?" Levi asked.

Durst nodded. "Everyone knows of Randall. He is a scoundrel and a bully and fully insane to boot, but no one can do anything to him as he is King Farren's cousin."

The blood drained from Levi's face. "That is so much worse than I thought."

"Fear not, um, what's your name, son?" Durst asked.

"Levi, sir."

"Fear not, Levi. All we have to do is give Randall my ring."

Levi's brows shot up in surprise. "You're going to give Randall the ring?"

"No," Durst said. "You're going to give the ring to Randall. Then, I am going to sound the alarm, saying I have been robbed.

We shall catch Randall red-handed and perhaps, Farren will finally do something about him."

"You'd really do this for me?" Levi asked.

Durst smiled and real warmth showed in his eyes. "Certainly. Not all us nobles are cold-hearted, you know. Most, but not all."

"Thank you, so, so much," Levi said, expressing his relief and gratitude.

"You are so very welcome," Durst replied. He slid the silver ring off his finger and dropped into Levi's open hand.

Levi examined the piece of jewelry. The face was circular and engraved on it was a bear paw symbol surrounding the letter D.

"I hope you get this back quickly," Levi said.

"As do I," Durst said. "Now, hurry and return to Randall."

"Yes, sir!" Levi gave an informal salute as he exited the room, the ring clutched in his left hand.

He made his way back down the hall quickly, waving to Latch as he strode on by. He came out of the left wing into the central tower and crossed to the stairwell, throwing open the door and taking the stairs two at a time.

Upon reaching the top floor, Levi waited in the stairwell, giving time for Lord Durst to call the guards. Figuring he had waited long enough, Levi walked back to Randall.

He smiled, looking surprised. "Back so soon?"

"Mm hmm." Levi held the ring in between two fingers and waved it back and forth.

Randall clapped his hands together. "I didn't have much faith you'd do it, much less this fast, but hey, here we are. Well done, Louis."

"Levi. What are you going to do with it?"

Randal's smile turned mischievous. "Need to know. And you don't need." He looked past Levi at something behind him. His eyes widened.

"What is it?" Levi asked. He held out his hand. "Here, take it."

Randall waved his arms and shouted, "Hey! Hey! Over here! He's got the ring!"

"No! What?" Levi spun to see three armed guards running at him. Levi tried to give Randall the ring, but Randall backed away.

"Right here!" Randall yelled.

"No!" Levi yelled, realizing he'd been set up. He tried to run, but something hard, probably the shaft of a spear, cracked across his shoulders and upper back. He dropped to one knee.

Instantly, the three guards were on him, restraining him. He struggled, but only ended up taking a fist over the eye.

One of the guards snatched the ring out of Levi's hand. "He has it!"

"No! You don't understand!" Levi cried. "It was Randall! He-"

"Shut up, thief!" A guard's fist smacked him across the mouth. Levi tasted blood.

"Throw him in the dungeon!" another guard said as they began to drag Levi away.

Levi looked back at Randall to see him smiling evilly, holding something silver in his hand. Levi struggled and yelled curses at Randall until something knocked him over the head and everything faded.

When he came to, he was in a cold, dark, damp, cell of stone bricks. The door was solid oak with a small barred window two-thirds of the way up.

Levi pushed himself to his feet, straw and filth on his hands and he charged at the door, slamming his fists into it, yelling to be released. It accomplished nothing except for splitting the skin on his knuckles.

Levi sank to his knees, a choked sob escaping his lips. Blood dripped from his hands onto the stained floor.

"It's no use," said a voice from the shadows.

Levi turned and could just make out the outline of a person in the left corner.

"What do you mean?" Levi asked, his voice broken.

"I mean," the voice said. "The only way you're getting out of here is through the gallows."

CHAPTER 14

"The gallows are the only way?" Levi asked.

The outline shifted, revealing a gaunt, pale face mostly hidden beneath a tangled mess of hair and beard. "In eleven years, I've never seen one person released. Only executed."

Levi bent forward. "How can this be? Surely there are people here in for minor crimes."

"If this were a normal prison, yes," the man said. "But, this is Felgath Prison. It's only for those whose crimes were against the highest of the noble class."

Levi's hand covered his mouth. Things had gone horribly wrong. He wondered if perhaps Lord Durst would come free him, but then he realized that, while Durst was a nice person, he wouldn't put his position in jeopardy to save a servant he had just met. Levi was on his own. There was no way Latch or Kana would find him now.

"If you don't mind me asking, what did you do?" the man asked.

"It's a long story," Levi said.

The man threw his head back and laughed. Then, his head jerked back to face Levi. "We have nothing but time here."

"I suppose you're right," Levi said. "Get comfy."

"Kid, we're in prison. There is no comfy." He picked up a handful of damp, moulding straw. "This is what they give us for comfort." He tossed it aside with a snort.

Levi began his tale, leaving out everything that might give his cellmate an inkling of who he really was. He finished ten minutes later.

"Sounds far-fetched," the man said.

"It's true!" Levi protested.

The man held up a hand. "Ok, I believe you. No reason to lie to me."

"Thank you," Levi said, dipping his head. They fell into silence and Levi examined the cell some more. It wasn't large, about eight feet by eight feet by seven feet. There was a tiny slit in the wall, near the ceiling where light filtered in. In the corner opposite of the man, was a hole in the floor. Levi assumed it was where he was to relieve himself. The only other thing in the cell was a small, dirty bowl that held a bit of scummy water.

Levi knew he needed to get out of the prison. He stepped up to the door and examined it. The lock on the outside was a simple bolt held in place by a loop of thick metal. It would be easy to slide the bolt out with his mind. Levi stretched out his hand and called for his magic. After a moment he frowned. He could feel the energy he needed inside him, but it was as if there was a barrier between it and his mind.

"Not gonna work, kid," the man said. "Magic is useless in here. There are wards all over this place. Over all prisons actually."

Levi rested his head against the door and sighed deeply. He was trapped with no way out. For a long time, he let himself mope about his situation.

He looked back at the man. His left arm ended in a stump. "What happened?"

"I crossed an angry man with a battle-axe. Not a good career move on my part." He looked down at the scarred stump as if remembering.

"What's your name? I'm Levi."

"Kyner Sinnas. Lost prince of Wintenveil."

Levi's mouth dropped open. In class, he had learned of Wintenveil, the land across the Sevian Sea, and how the heir to the throne had disappeared. "Seriously?"

Kyner nodded. "Yep. Brother to Queen Saya. Nobody ever seems to believe me, though. And even if they did, it wouldn't matter. Everyone back home thinks I'm dead."

"That's terrible," Levi said.

Kyner picked at something in his teeth with his good hand. Three identical red marks covered the inside of his wrist. "Eh, it's not that bad. Well, I mean, being in prison sucks, but for a few years, I got to run around Terrenia, doing whatever my heart desired. It was so much better than living in a royal court with a bunch of clodpolls."

"Why do they think you're dead?" Levi wondered.

"Oh, you know, the usual," Kyner said. "I had an affair with a duke's daughter, got her pregnant out of wedlock, she died in childbirth, the duke declared a blood feud, chased me to a cliff where we duelled and I fell into the sea, got picked up by pirates, sold as a slave in Altor, escaped and roamed free for a few years before ending up here. So, naturally, no one at home knows I'm alive."

"Wow, that is quite the story."

"It happens more than you think," Kyner said. "My grandpa and cousin both had similar experiences."

"You Wintenveilers are a strange lot."

"Quite true," Kyner said.

Levi's hand slipped into his pocket. He froze; something was wrong. The Elder Gem was missing. "Where is it?" He frantically searched his other pockets, not finding it. His eyes darted from side to side, looking for any hint of the medallion on the floor. It was nowhere to be found.

"What have you lost?" Kyner asked.

"My medallion," Levi said, searching along the walls.

"What does it look like?"

"Uh, it's a golden bird."

"Like a raptor?" Kyner assumed.

"Yes, definitely a raptor," Levi said.

"About two inches long?"

"Yes."

Kyner continued. "It has a spot for a chain, but no chain."

Levi glanced at Kyner. "How do you know?" He inhaled sharply. Kyner was holding the Elder Gem between his thumb and index finger.

"How do you have it?"

Kyner shrugged. "Fell out of your pocket when the guards threw you in here."

Levi took a step toward Kyner. "Give it here."

Kyner flipped the medallion over, examining it. "Special, is it?"

"You have no idea," Levi growled. "Now, give it here!"

Kyner cocked his head. "You know, I could use this to bribe a guard to let me out. It's gold, so it's gotta be worth a good amount."

"No!" Levi lunged ahead. His breath exploded from his lungs as he ran into Kyner's outstretched leg. He fell to the floor, coughing.

Kyner stood. "You really want this, don't you?"

Levi surged to his feet, only to be brought down by an elbow to the head.

"It could just have sentimental value, but I doubt it," Kyner said, walking to the door. "It must have a secret. Maybe I have to say the right word to get it to work. Hmm... Cabbage! Nope."

Levi struggled to his feet, holding a hand to his head. Everything was out of focus. "Give it to me!"

"Not until you tell me what it does."

"Not a chance, scumbag," Levi snarled.

"That's too bad, guess I'll have to call the guard over. He'll be happy to take this little treasure."

Levi stared daggers at his cellmate and swiped at the Gem. Kyner jabbed Levi in the sternum with the stump of his arm, which hit like a club.

"Guard!" Kyner called.

"No! I'll tell you! You win!"

Kyner smiled.

A grumpy looking guard appeared in the window. "Whaddya want?"

"Never mind, false alarm," Kyner said.

The guard grunted, said something unflattering and walked off.

Kyner turned to Levi. "Well?"

Levi screwed his eyes shut for a moment, hating everything. "The medallion, it...it answers any question you ask."

Kyner narrowed his eyes. He was silent for a moment, then, "I don't believe you."

"What do you mean?" Levi asked. "It's the truth."

"No, it's not," Kyner said.

A bead of sweat dripped down Levi's temple. "I swear it's the truth!"

Kyner shook his head. "I'm calling the guard."

Levi's shoulders slumped. If the guard got a hold of it, Levi would never see it again. He hated to let another person in on his secret, especially one like Kyner, who he didn't trust in the least, but he had no other alternative. He pinched the bridge of his nose and began to talk. "This pendant, it's really the Elder Gem."

Kyner burst out laughing. "The Elder Gem! You're crazy! That's insane!" He widened his eyes. "Wait, you're serious?"

Levi nodded glumly.

Kyner's mouth hung open. "Truly?"

"I'm afraid so. You can't tell anyone! Promise me!"

"Promise you?" Kyner scoffed. "Levi, you've just bought my ticket out of here! I'll tell Farren where his greatest prize is in exchange for my freedom."

Levi's heart fell. His face grew cold as the blood drained away. "You wouldn't."

"I would and I will," Kyner said. "I've got nothing against you, kid, but after eleven years in this hell-hole, I'll do anything to get out."

"I won't let you!" Levi yelled, charging the prisoner. His fist connected with Kyner's shoulder, knocking the older man back.

Kyner swung at Levi, forcing him to block. Levi readied himself for the next punch, but instead, his leg took the blow from Kyner's foot. Levi stumbled, but caught his balance and ran at Kyner, putting all he had in a right hook. Kyner caught Levi by the wrist with his good hand and hammered his club-like arm into Levi's ribs three times. Levi gasped in pain, but he managed to bring his free arm down on the side of Kyner's head.

Kyner growled and headbutted Levi in the nose. Levi felt a snap and bright spots appeared in his vision. He was overwhelmed by pain and lashed out wildly. His hand struck flesh and Kyner grunted.

The two separated and circled each other. Levi wiped blood off his mouth, his broken nose throbbing. Suddenly, Kyner attacked, leaping through the air, his foot aimed at Levi's head. Levi put his palms together and caught the kick, pushing Kyner's leg past his head. Kyner stumbled past, but Levi caught his wrist and twisted, putting his opponent in an armbar. Kyner yelled in pain and Levi jammed his elbow into Kyner's spine.

Pain erupted in Levi's toes as Kyner's heel stomped down on his foot, causing his grip to loosen. Kyner spun out of the armbar. He kneed Levi in the stomach, making Levi bend over in reflex.

Kyner slammed both arms into Levi's shoulders, driving him to the ground. Then, before Levi could get up, Kyner's boot concussed against the side of his head and he knew no more.

~ ~ ~

When Levi came to, he was alone in the cell. Kyner was nowhere to be found. He struggled to his knees, everything hurting. Through the spinning of his head, Levi realized that blood was still leaking from his nose, albeit slower than before. That meant that Kyner couldn't be far ahead of him.

Unsteadily, he got to his feet, cursing Kyner and his own foolishness. He staggered to the cell door. To his surprise, it was unlocked and partially open. The guard must not have cared about Levi after hearing what Kyner had.

Levi pushed open the door and ran out into the hall. Everything swam and he pressed his hands against the far wall to balance himself. He looked both directions, but they were identical; dark, low-ceilinged corridors lined with cells and few torches.

He moved to the closest cell and peered through the window. "Excuse me! Hey!"

The person inside swore explosively and told him to leave, so Levi did.

"You aren't going to get him to help you," a female voice said.

Levi turned to see a woman looking at him through the bars of another cell.

"Huh?"

"He hates everyone. He'd kill you if he was able to," the woman said.

"Will you help me?"

The woman chuckled. "It depends."

"Depends on..." Levi trailed off as he recognized the black shape of a swooping bird poking above the woman's collar. "You're Giala."

The woman jerked back. "I don't know what you're talking about!"

Levi leaned in close. "I can see your tattoo right there."

The woman blew out a breath, realizing Levi could in fact see her symbol, meaning he couldn't wish her any harm. "Quietly. What do you want?"

"A guard took a man out just a little while ago. Which way did he go?"

"Why?"

Levi put his lips between the bars and breathed, "He just stole the Elder Gem from me."

A flood of emotions crossed her face, but in the end, she simply said, "He what?"

"He stole the Elder Gem. I messed up, I know. That's why I need to go after him."

"Let me out," the woman said. "I can help."

Levi slid the heavy-duty bolt out from its resting place and opened the door.

"Thanks," the woman said with a huge grin. "I was beginning to think I wasn't going to get out of here."

"Let's go! We have no time to waste!" Levi said.

"Right," the woman said both as a reply and direction. She took off down the corridor. Levi followed, groaning as his head spun and his bruised ribs throbbed. The woman noticed he was lagging behind and slowed to accommodate.

"May I have the pleasure of knowing my rescuer's name?" the woman asked.

"Levi."

"Charmed. I'm Charlotte." She eyed him. "So, you're the special guy, huh?"

"Unfortunately," Levi grunted.

"Shorter than I imagined."

"Hey now," Levi said. He was a little sensitive about his less than average height.

Charlotte smirked. "Sorry. I've gotta ask, how did you lose the Gem?"

Levi sighed. "A string of rotten luck." He told her about the day's events, pausing to take enough breath to keep jogging.

When he finished, Charlotte clicked her tongue. "You're right. That is some rotten luck."

Levi grunted in response.

186

They neared the end of the corridor. Torchlight lit up the doorway to a room to the right. They burst in, startling three guards sitting around a short table, playing dice.

One of the guards began to rise, coming out of his surprise sooner than the others. Charlotte didn't hesitate. She tackled him into the table, sending dice in every direction. She wrestled the knife out of the guard's hand and slashed open his throat. Jumping to her feet, she faced the other two, who had both retrieved their spears. The rightmost guard jabbed at her, but Charlotte spun to the side, grabbed the shaft and cracked her elbow into his face, knocking him down. She whirled around, slashing the spear at the last guard. As he moved to deflect it, Charlotte threw the knife with deadly accuracy. It plunged into the man's neck. His hands went to his throat and he gurgled as blood spilled from the wound. Charlotte turned and finished off the second guard by running him through with his own spear.

She turned to Levi and smiled, not a scratch to show for being outnumbered and unarmed.

Levi gaped at her. He had never seen someone kill with such skill and ease and dare he say, grace.

Charlotte swiped her long black hair out of her face. "Professional assassin. Let's go." She went over to the door and opened it, letting sunlight spill into the room that was beginning to stink of fresh blood.

As she exited, Levi muttered, "I'm certainly glad she's on my side."

Coming out of the prison, Levi shaded his eyes against the sun. "Where are we?"

"Not sure."

They were standing in a stone-walled courtyard with a few ramshackle buildings scattered around. To the left, curving behind them was a crumbling cliff face, which the prison had been dug into. At the far end of the courtyard was an archway. The door had long since rotted away.

Exchanging a glance, the two escaped prisoners headed toward it. Levi was surprised to see no more guards around. He expected to see a couple more lounging in a barracks or posted near the exit, and yet the place was empty.

Coming out of the archway, Levi and Charlotte found themselves in a small gorge between two hills. There was a path leading up the one on the right. They climbed the hill, using the low shrubs to pull themselves up.

Levi reached the crest and halted in shock. In front of them, down the hill was a beach. And beyond that was the ocean.

Charlotte laughed in frustrated annoyance. "Well, I know one thing. We are royally screwed."

CHAPTER 15

"First of all," Kinzo said. "What? And second, you have a brother?"

Cody crossed his arms, uncomfortable, as everyone stared at him. "Look, I don't like to talk about him."

"Why not?" Snare asked.

A muscle in Cody's jaw twitched. "Because he ruined my life."

"What did he do?" Ring asked.

Cody closed his eyes and tried to calm the whirlwind of emotions that had been brought up by the mention of his brother. "He killed my mother. My dad sank into a depression and turned into an abusive alcoholic."

The others were silent.

"Huh. That sucks," Kinzo said awkwardly.

Miri turned on him. "That's all you can say! You're terrible!"

Kinzo looked apologetic.

Miri lay a hand on Cody's arm. He glanced down at her. She signed, "I'm so sorry."

Cody shrugged sadly. "Yeah, well, whatever. It's in the past now. Nothing I can do about it."

"Yeah, get over it," Snare said. "We've all lost people. No sense crying about it now."

Anger flared up inside Cody and he glared at Snare. He clenched his fists and breathed out, releasing the emotion. Snare was right, no matter how rudely put. "Are you sure he's in the cult?"

"I saw the guy I just described kidnapping a kid. He was with others who wore the cult masks."

"Why wasn't he wearing a mask?" Kinzo wondered.

"Not his style," Cody said. "Marek isn't one to hide his face. He wants people to know it's him."

"Hmm, he sounds like a real treat," Kinzo said. Miri rolled her eyes at him.

Evander asked, "What are we going to do?"

"Do?" Snare said. "We're going to do what we planned. This doesn't affect anything."

"What if he recognizes me?" Cody asked.

Snare spread his hands. "So what? He'll see it's you. Big deal. He won't think that you're part of a plot to take down the cult."

"I guess not," Cody acknowledged.

"Let's not stay here any longer," Ring said, glancing over her shoulder. "We're still in Bull's territory and more footpads could be on us any second."

"You're right," Snare said. "We'd best get out of here."

Cody knocked his fist against his leg. He was about to see his brother for the first time in twelve years. Nervous didn't even begin to cover what he was feeling. With a shrug that was more like a jerk, he followed the others down the street.

Cody paid no attention to where they were going. He trusted that the others would lead him to the right place. He was wrapped deeply in his thoughts. Although he hardly thought them, so much as they whipped themselves against his mind, beating emotions and memories into him so he could almost see them with his waking eyes.

Bumping into someone broke Cody out of the hurricane inside his head. He blinked a few times. "Where are we?"

"At the place," Snare said. "And watch where you're going."

"Sorry." Cody took a moment to check out his surroundings. It was a small square, one that would normally be at the crux of important streets. But this one was the junction of four back alleys, ringed by the corners of four houses; only one seemed to be in liveable condition. In the centre of the square was a broken fountain depicting a pegasus. Both front hooves and the left wing lay cracked and in pieces on the cobblestone below. There were several crates and boards stacked against two of the buildings, cluttering the space.

Even though it was a backwater kind of place, it still received foot traffic. There were five people in and around the square as Cody surveyed the scene. An old, dark-skinned man with a patchy beard sat against the wall of the house across the way. He appeared to be asleep. Two younger guys, obviously homeless, hung around the fountain. A woman and her daughter walked across the square and down the alley to their left.

The young ragamuffins saw Cody looking and scampered away, giving him rude hand gestures. The old man didn't move, save for his chest as it rose and fell with his breath.

"This will work," Ring said. "It's out of the way, but still gets enough traffic for the cult to take an interest in it."

"It should, but you never know," Snare said.

Miri signed, "Where are we going to hide?" Evander acted as her translator for the street kids.

Snare pointed to one of the rundown houses. The windows were boarded up and part of the roof was caved in. "There. That'll do nicely."

"We should get out of sight," Ring said.

Kinzo bowed deep, embellishing the movement. "Here is where we part ways, my good sir."

Cody rolled his eyes.

Miri touched Cody's shoulder. "Don't worry. We won't let them brainwash you."

The corners of Cody's mouth lifted a fraction. "I know you won't." He unbuckled his sword belt and handed her his weapon. He felt vulnerable, but it would ruin the disguise if he had a sword belted to his waist. Miri turned away and joined the others as they crawled through a space in the window of the decrepit house.

Apart from the old man, Cody was alone in the square. He watched the man for a few moments; he turned over and muttered something in his sleep.

Cody chewed his lip while he waited. He wasn't sure what to do. *Do I act inconspicuous or shifty? How should I act to get them to take me?* He wondered what they would do to him once they found him. Would they knock him out and take him through the streets or would they spirit him away magically?

He sighed and sat down on the edge of the fountain. His eyes fell on the thin layer of scummy water covering the bottom and the mottled brown frog splashing around. It crawled onto a jagged piece of rubble poking out of the water and ribbited.

191

"I kinda wish I were you," Cody muttered to the frog. "Your life is so simple. So minor. You don't care what others do, you just live your life. You survive, that's it. I envy that right now." He rubbed a hand over his face. "Marek. What are you doing here? I hoped I'd never see you again. And now I'm walking right toward you."

The frog croaked and leapt off the rock, swimming to the other side of the fountain.

"Sounds like you've gotten yourself into a predicament."

Cody swivelled to see the old man sitting up with legs crossed. "Yeah, you could say that."

"Who is Marek?" the man asked.

Cody chewed his lip. "He's my brother."

"Ah." The old man rose to his feet. He was short, under five feet. "Family trouble. I know of that." He hobbled over, coming to sit next to Cody. Cody caught a whiff of stale urine, mould and body odour. He wrinkled his nose, but the man seemed not to notice.

"What's your name, son?" the elderly fellow asked. He was missing most of his teeth, but his eyes twinkled with a kind humour.

"Cody."

"Well, Cody, family can be a blessing or a curse. And sometimes both." His voice held the promise of a story spanning a long life.

Well, I'm just waiting anyway. Might as well pass the time.

"Sounds like you know from experience," Cody said.

The man nodded. "Aye, that I do. And, while our stories may not be the same, I still can offer you some advice. You aren't your family. Who they are doesn't determine who you are. That is up to you and you alone."

A small laugh escaped Cody's mouth. The man had managed to speak directly to the fears Cody hadn't even fully formed in his mind. He glanced back at the man with a new respect.

Cody's visitor looked off into the distance. "I don't know what your problem with your brother is, but I expect that he isn't your entire family. Am I right?"

Cody nodded. "No, he's not."

"Hmm. By your tone, I would guess that he is the worst of them. Then, take comfort knowing that the others care for you, in their own way."

"How can you know that?"

"Because, if your family all hates you, either you are a horrible person or you have the worst luck in the world. I can tell you aren't a terrible person. And I doubt you're that unlucky."

"You're very perceptive," Cody said.

"Hmm. It comes with age." The man folded his arms. "And I've lived a long, long time."

Something caught Cody's eye. He looked down the alley in front of him. Four people walked toward the square. They wore long hooded cloaks of a dark grey material and white masks that covered the top half of their faces.

Cody swallowed, his throat suddenly dry. *They're here. They've come for me.* Everything was going to plan, but that didn't stop the fear rising in Cody's chest.

"You should get out of here..." Cody stopped as he looked into the empty space where the old man had just been sitting. He turned around, brows furrowed, but the man was nowhere to be found in the square or down the alleys. There was no way he could have run away that fast.

Cody had no time to ponder what happened to the old man as the four masked cultists closed in on him.

"Uh, hi," Cody said. "Can I help you?"

The four figures stopped in front of Cody, arraying themselves in a semi-circle. Their hands were hidden in the long sleeves of their cloaks. They stared for a half minute before the one on the far right said, "Yes, him."

"Whoa, whoa," Cody said. "Hold on a sec." He rose from the fountain, preparing to fight, as he couldn't let them know he wanted to be taken.

One of the cultists pulled his hand out of his cloak and threw a cloud of dust at Cody. He coughed and spluttered as the particles lodged in his nose and mouth. The edge of his vision began to darken and his balance betrayed him. He fell to one knee, a hand on the ground. His sight narrowed until all he saw was his hand. Then, he fell over and the darkness took him.

~~~

Consciousness slowly returned to Cody. With it came a throbbing headache. For a few minutes, the pounding in his head was all he was aware of. He couldn't form coherent thoughts other than he wanted the pain to stop.

He slowly came to realize that he was lying on a stone floor. The scars on his back protested, demanding he take the pressure off them. It was cold; his ratty clothes barely doing anything to warm him. He shivered.

Opening his eyes, he saw a broken coatrack a foot in front of him. It was listing heavily to one side. Beyond it was the wall. Bare stone, old and cracked, mortar crumbling away.

With a groan, Cody rolled onto his side. He blinked a few times to clear his head and get his bearings. There was no ceiling, just the beams supporting the floor above and a few of them were cracked. But it wasn't sagging, so he figured he was safe enough.

"He's awake," an unfamiliar voice said.

"Yeah, we noticed."

Cody propped himself up on one elbow, facing toward the voices. Three unkempt, bruised people were sitting against the far wall. "Hi." He winced as a fresh wave of pain rocked his head.

"Hi," a young boy with wild, curly, black hair said.

"Shut up," said a man with a shaved head and a thin moustache. "Don't be friendly."

The third person scoffed.

Cody got to his knees. "Where am I?"

"Hell," the bald guy answered.

"Actually, I think this used to be a bed and breakfast," the curly-haired boy said.

The bald guy rolled his eyes.

"But, where in the city?" Cody asked.

"Still in the Outskirts," the boy said. "Definitely still there." The other two offered no answer.

"How'd they get you?" the kid asked.

"One of them threw some kind of dust at me. I breathed it in and just passed out. Gave me a wicked headache."

The kid nodded. "Hmm. That's how they got Clovis here." He motioned to the bald guy. "They got Rick with the offer of food and led him into a building. They got me cause I was sleeping outside."

194

"Shut up, Teddy," Clovis said. Teddy ignored him.

"How long have you guys been here?" Cody asked. "I'm Cody, by the way."

"Hi, Cody," Teddy said. "I've only been here for a day."

"Felt like longer," Clovis muttered.

Teddy continued. "Clovis has been here for three days and Rick for four."

"No one ever stays longer than five days," Rick said in a flat voice. "My time is almost up."

"Almost up? What do you mean?" Cody asked.

"Don't you know?" Teddy looked surprised.

Cody shook his head.

Teddy turned to the others. "He doesn't know!"

"I've heard rumours," Cody said. "But I don't know if they're true."

"They are!" Teddy said.

Rick stood. He placed his hand on the wall and ran his fingers along the groove between the stones. "Everyone that ends up in this room leaves one time and when they return, they are not the same person. They are gone, replaced with a mindless drone."

"Some dark magic crap," Clovis muttered.

"They say it's brain swapping," Teddy said, his voice shrill.

Nervousness was growing in the pit of Cody's stomach. He hoped the others would come rescue him soon. He didn't want to have his brain swapped.

"Is there no way out?" Cody asked.

"Not while you are still yourself," Rick said.

"We're doomed," Clovis said, matter-of-factly.

Cody gulped and looked at Teddy. "Have you seen any of the kidnappers?"

Teddy nodded. "A couple of them. But they wear white masks, so I can only see their mouths and chins. They call themselves the Forsaken."

Cody worked his jaw. He had been hoping to hear about his brother. Though he wasn't sure why. He wasn't sure what he would do if he came face to face with his brother. Definitely punch him in the face. Maybe run him through with a sword.

He stood and walked over to the other wall where his fellow prisoners sat. Clovis eyed him with near hostility.

"Do they ever let us out of this room?" Cody asked.

Teddy nodded. "Yep. Twice a day for food and to relieve ourselves."

"That's good news," Cody said.

Clovis grunted. "Not really."

Cody considered the bald man. He seemed to be a real downer, but Cody figured it was his way of dealing with the fact that he was probably about to be killed; brainwashed at least.

Cody sat down against the wall next to Rick. He closed his eyes and let his head rest against the cool stone. He tried to ignore the thumping in his skull. He stayed that way for a while, waiting for his friends to break him out while Teddy talked and Clovis told him to shut up.

He was afraid of what the cult might do to him, but he knew he couldn't try to escape yet. He needed to let the others find the cult's headquarters first.

Some time later, the door rattled and opened to reveal a cultist wearing a mask identical to the other ones Cody had seen. "Up you get."

All four prisoners stood and were escorted out of the room, down a hall out into a central courtyard exposed to the air. It was an octagon, each side a wall pockmarked with doors, windows and arched walkways. There were three sheds spaced randomly. The courtyard was divided into sections by rows of small, neatly pruned trees of a species Cody didn't recognize.

The sky was a reddish-purple. Dusk.

At least forty cultists milled about in the yard, going about their business. They paid the prisoners no attention.

The man escorting Cody and the others prodded them toward a low table off to one side near the walkway they had come out of. A large metal pot sat upon it, its surface scourged by countless cookfires. There was a stew of some kind inside. Next to the pot rested a half loaf of rye bread and a pitcher of water.

Next to the table was a small shack that Cody assumed was the restroom. Rick headed there first, closing the door behind him.

The cultist motioned the other three to the food. "Eat."

"Stew again?" Teddy complained. "But we had that yesterday."

"It's stew every day," Clovis muttered before grabbing a spoon and helping himself right out of the pot. Apparently, they were sharing.

196

Cody shrugged and grabbed a spoon. He was about to take a scoop when Rick tapped his arm.

"Your turn."

Cody set down the spoon and turned. As he passed Rick, the other prisoner whispered, "Bottom left, upside down." Then, he continued on as if nothing had happened.

Cody had no idea what Rick was on about. He entered the outhouse and shut the door. There was a low bench with a hole cut in the centre. A stack of tissue sat on the right end of the bench.

Cody dropped his trousers and sat down to do his business. He let his gaze wander. Rick's words came back to him and he found his sight drifting down to the bottom left. There was something scratched into the wooden planks, a message of some kind. Cody couldn't make it out; it was gibberish.

"Upside down. I wonder..." Cody tilted his head and the words became clear. *Don't eat the stew.*

"Must be a warning," Cody said under his breath. Someone here was trying to help the captives.

The door shook as someone rapped their fist against it.

"Yeah! Coming!" Cody called. He glanced at the message one last time, hiked up his pants and opened the door.

The masked man stood on the other side, arms crossed. "Much too long."

"Sorry," Cody said. He hugged his stomach. "I'm not feeling well. I don't think I'll eat."

The cultist shrugged. "Your loss."

Cody walked over to the table and took a big drink of water, so he would at least have something in his stomach. He didn't touch the stew. Rick gave a barely perceptible nod.

When everyone was finished, the captives were led back into the same room as before. The door was locked behind them and they resumed their positions from earlier.

No one talked. Silence reigned until Cody dropped off to sleep.

Hunger woke Cody sooner than he would have liked. The room was dark, next to no light shone through the window near the door. It was quiet; the only sound was the occasional snore from Clovis.

Cody's stomach growled, reminding him of how he had skipped last night's meal. Part of him wished he had eaten the stew, while the other part told him he had done the right thing listening to the message's warning.

He also wished his friends would hurry up and rescue him. It had been a half-day already. Something must have gone wrong.

They have to know where I am, right? I mean, they were right there when the Forsaken took me. They should have just followed the cultists back here. What happened? He became convinced that his friends had no idea where he was and weren't coming to rescue him. He was on his own.

That thought echoed around his mind, keeping him awake until the sun rose two hours later. Cody rubbed his tired eyes as the others slowly woke and stretched.

A few minutes later, the door scraped open. In came not one, but three cultists, armed with short cudgels. They quickly surrounded Rick, blocking him off from the others.

"It's time," the tallest man said.

Rick bowed his head for a moment before straightening up. He nodded to Cody in a very final way and allowed the cultists to escort him out of the room.

The door closed with a loud bang that echoed in the room for a moment but in Cody's head for much longer.

"That will be all of us soon," Clovis said after a prolonged silence.

Teddy gulped, trembling slightly. Cody felt terrible for him. He was young, no more than thirteen. He deserved so much more. He didn't deserve to be taken away and experimented on until he was no longer himself.

I need to escape, Cody thought. *But how?* His Chaotic power wasn't strong enough to disintegrate the doors and he was nowhere near good enough to create a portal. He allowed his gaze to sweep around the room. It settled on the broken coatrack. A small smile touched his lips; it would make a perfect makeshift weapon. He walked over to it and pulled the beam out of the broken stand. The spokes on which jackets would have been hung he got rid of and was left with a round club about four and a half feet tall. He swung it around. It had good weight; a blow with this could easily down a man.

"What are you doing?" Teddy asked.

Cody looked him in the eye. "I'm breaking out. You guys want to come with me?"

Clovis shook his head. "No way we'd make it. You're gonna die trying. I'll take my chances with the brainwashing. They'll find I'm not easily broken."

Cody glanced at Teddy. The kid kneaded his hands together. "Will you make it?"

"I have no idea," Cody said. "But I have to try."

"No way you'll make it," Clovis said.

Cody rolled his eyes. "Try to be positive, will you?"

"Ok, I'm positive there's no way you'll make it."

"Should have seen that one coming," Cody muttered. "What about you, Teddy?"

Teddy chewed on his bottom lip. "I, uh, I don't want to... I can't. I think I'll stay."

Poor kid, Cody thought. *He's too scared to even try and escape.* He put his hands on his hips. "Well, I'm not gonna wait around while they plot my end. I have to fight back."

"When will you try it?" Teddy asked.

"Not yet, not till supper. I want to get another look at the compound first."

Cody began making a plan. His feet carried him around the room as he thought of the best way to escape. The only weapons he had seen on the Forsaken were the cudgels and small knives each one had belted to their waist. With his makeshift club, Cody believed he could beat his way through several of them if they got in his way. He was a half-trained knight after all.

But, there were many more of them than there was of him. He couldn't afford to get trapped in a long fight or their numbers would overwhelm him. He was going to have to sprint for the door, although he had no idea which one led out. That was why the recon was so important.

He recalled Silverton's lessons, hearing the smooth, deep voice in his head. *Go into a fight without any knowledge of your enemy and you'll be as blind as if you had your eyes gouged out.*

The wait until the same guard as before came back was short. The three remaining prisoners were led out into the yard once again and sent to the table. It was set the exact same way as yesterday. A pot of stew, a half loaf of bread and a pitcher of water.

Cody followed a very similar pattern to yesterday. He entered the outhouse and looked for any new messages, but there were none. He came out and feigned being sick to his stomach. The guard barely even glanced at him. Cody took a long pull from the pitcher and tore off a small chunk of bread. He wanted more as his stomach was growling, but he couldn't risk breaking the illusion that he was sick.

While the others ate, Cody furtively scanned the courtyard, marking the position of every archway and door. He noted which exits received the most and least traffic and whether or not there were any more weapons. There were none.

The meal ended and they were led back across the yard. A group of cultists walked in front of them. One of them was unmasked. Cody was taken aback when he realized that it was Rick.

The others noticed too. "Rick!" Teddy called. "Are you ok?"

Rick looked down at Teddy and sneered. "Stupid boy. Rick is no more." He continued on, head held high.

Teddy's breath trembled.

Cody shook his head. It was true. They were not the same. That was not Rick. Rick was gone. He silently vowed that after he escaped, he would return with an army and take down the Forsaken once and for all.

They were put back in their cell and the door was locked.

Clovis cursed. "They really do change people."

"You can still come with me if you want," Cody offered.

"I'll wait and see how well you're doing before I do anything," Clovis said.

"Fair," Cody said. He figured he had better rest up for the escape. He needed all the strength he could muster. Laying on the uneven stone, he shifted until he found a somewhat comfortable spot and closed his eyes. He had ten hours to wait. He could afford to drift off, he wouldn't sleep that long.

After a two-hour rest, Cody spent the remaining time going over his plan and thinking about how he had gotten himself into this mess.

Man, I wish someone else had come with me. Keep me company. Miri, or Evander would have been good. Kinzo too, although he would just complain the whole time.

He dug his fingers into a knot in the back of his neck that had formed while lying on the hard floor. He wondered how Levi and the others were faring. Much better, he hoped.

Eventually, the time for action came. Cody stood, stretched and picked up his wooden weapon, twirling it around his head. The guard was soon going to come and fetch them for the evening meal and when he did, he was going to brain the cultist, steal his cloak and mask and make his escape.

Teddy glanced his way every few seconds. He seemed like he wanted to join Cody, but fear was holding him back. Clovis on the other hand, watched impassively. He doubted it was going to work and wasn't about to get his hopes up.

Cody looked to the ceiling and clicked his tongue. He really wished his friends had come and broken him out before he had to resort to such drastic measures, but that wasn't the case. Cody had no other alternative.

He realized his lips were dry and licked them. He was nervous, more nervous than he had ever been. If he failed, he would be turned into a mindless servant of the diabolical cult. There was no room for error.

The sound of footsteps drawing close echoed in his ears like the hammering of a battering ram against a castle gate. He drummed his fingers on the coatrack in anticipation.

The door opened and Cody launched ahead, bringing the club down as hard as he could. It crashed over the man's head and he tumbled to the ground.

Cody's eyes widened as he saw the two other cultists behind the first man. They must have been coming for Clovis.

Cody swung up at the man on the left, but he knocked it aside with his forearm.

"Forget the other one! Take him!"

A cudgel slammed into his right shoulder and he lost his grip on the coatrack. Cody threw a punch at him, hitting the man in the chin but the other guard's club cracked against his head. He staggered back, seeing stars. He didn't even see the blow that dropped him to his knees.

Semi-conscious, he saw Teddy's horrified face as he was dragged out of the room.

He blacked out, but felt himself bumping across the courtyard, down some stairs, through a corridor and into a room. He was lifted onto a table and restraints were fastened around his wrists, ankles and forehead.

"Why this one?"

"He tried to escape."

"Ah. I see. Very well then. We shall proceed. Marek, bring the talisman."

Marek? The name acted like a lightning rod, shocking him back into wakefulness. He stared up into a familiar face. Marek's face. For a split-second, it registered shock, but was replaced by a cruel smile.

"Hello, brother. Who would have thought that I would be the last thing you see before you die?" He smirked, the scar on the corner of his eye wrinkling.

Cody struggled against the restraints, but they held fast.

"Tsk, tsk, Cody. Don't resist. It'll be fine," Marek said.

An older man entered Cody's field of vision. He barely looked at Cody. "Marek, place the talisman on his forehead."

Marek complied and cool, smooth stone touched his skin, just above his eyes. The older man began chanting in an otherworldly dialect and the stone grew uncomfortably hot.

Cody yelled and squirmed and the stone stopped feeling hot. In fact, Cody stopped feeling altogether. He couldn't feel the straps holding him in place, or the clothes against his skin. His voice became faint and his vision began to shrink.

The next thing he knew, he was floating in darkness with Marek's final words echoing in his mind. "Goodbye, brother."

CHAPTER 16

Cody had no idea how long he existed in the darkness. There was no space or time or anything, really. Just blackness. He couldn't see or feel his own body. He simply was.

He wondered if he was dead. If all there was afterlife was the void. Nothingness. He had always believed that there was something after death, even if he had never known what.

He wished he had lived a longer, better life. Nineteen was too young. He wished he had become a full knight and gone on quests, slaying monsters and saving people. He wished he had married a beautiful woman and had kids of his own. He wished he could have seen his sister one more time, told her how thankful he was to her. And above all, he wished he was still alive so he could stab Marek through the chest.

After a period of regret, Cody resigned himself to an eternity existing in emptiness. *I guess this is it. Definitely not the way I thought I would die.*

A speck, a tiny pinprick of light appeared. The darkness tried to snuff out the spark, but it grew and grew until dazzling bright white enveloped Cody. His thoughts wouldn't form, he was so enthralled.

Then, the light dimmed, its radiance diminishing only a little. Cody realized that he could see his hands. He glanced down and saw the rest of his body. It was his body, but yet, it was somehow different. The outline of his form was blurred, indistinct. When he moved, a hazy trail followed behind. It was almost as if he was a shadow. A wraith. A ghost.

Small spheres of colour began popping into existence all around Cody. There were cloudy wisps swirling inside the orbs. They floated around aimlessly, but gracefully. Occasionally, one would bump into another and change directions.

Cody stared in wonder. He had no earthly idea what they were, but he was mesmerized.

A light purple sphere floated near Cody. He reached out and felt it. It was rubbery under his touch and rippled at the point of contact, his fingers began to slide inside. For a second, Cody thought he could see shapes moving about in the swirling clouds within the ball. He blinked and they were gone.

More orbs appeared, each one a different colour. They stretched off into the light as far as Cody could see.

"What are these?"

Cody moved his arm as a green ball bumped into his left elbow. He stopped it and peered inside. The indistinct shapes clarified. Cody gasped. There was a scene playing inside. A man planting a garden near a brook, streaks of dirt on his brow from when he wiped away the sweat.

Cody let go of the pale sphere and grabbed another, a red one. Inside, a person was walking down an alley in the rain, hood up. A pair of men appeared further down the alley and the hooded man ducked into a nearby building.

"What...?" Cody looked at the other orbs. They all had scenes playing out within them. "Are these... memories?"

A brown sphere floated near him. He took hold of it and his hands began slowly sinking in. An idea came to his mind. He brought the orb up to his head and pressed his face into it.

Suddenly, Cody was inside the memory, in a bookstore, standing in a carpeted aisle between two rows of shelved tomes. A man stood in front of him. He was clearly the bookkeeper; a sweater vest, thin, wild hair and a book in his hand.

"I'm sorry, sir," the bookkeeper said in a high, thin voice. "But I have no books on the subject."

Cody shifted without him meaning to. Then, he spoke, scaring Cody. But the voice was not his own. "What about books on reincarnation?" Cody realized he must be in the place of the man who's memory this was.

The librarian nodded. "Yes, yes, I have several of those. Follow me." He walked down the aisle.

Cody began to follow, his legs moving without his consent. It was very disorienting.

They entered a back room lit by three brass lanterns. The books in this section appeared much older, the covers well-worn. The bookkeeper pulled three books off the shelves and handed them to Cody, or whoever he was in the place of.

"Thank you," Cody said. The voice was deeper and raspier than Cody's normally was.

"I'll leave you to your research." The bookkeeper exited the room.

Cody began examining the books. The first read, 'Reincarnation and Other Impossibilities'. Cody, or the other person, rather, set it aside. The other two were both simply titled 'Reincarnation'.

Cody opened one and began reading, following along with a finger, on which the nail needed to be trimmed desperately. It was written in the Old Tongue, which was similar to Common Speech when spoken aloud but written much differently. Cody struggled to follow along. What he did decipher made no sense to him anyway. It spoke of binding the mind and soul together and a bunch of other nonsense.

The man who Cody was replacing continued reading, skimming over some sections until he finished the book. Then, he opened the next and dove in.

Again, it was more nonsense that flew over Cody's head, but the other man seemed to understand, nodding from time to time. Eventually, he read a passage that meant something to him. He jammed his finger against the line of text and shouted, "Ha! I knew it! Host bodies!"

The memory ended abruptly and Cody blinked against the bright white. He shook his head. "Host body? Is that what I am?"

A noise, a murmur, caused Cody to spin around. In the distance, the whiteness was replaced with an opening through which Cody could see the real world. A window. Marek and the old man stood in the dark room beyond.

The murmur became louder until it formed into voices. "Antoth! Are you there?" It was the old man. The words sounded as if they were being spoken through a wall.

Cody was astonished to hear his own voice answer. "Yes." His heart dropped into his stomach. It was true. His body had been stolen from him.

"Welcome back, Antoth," the old man smiled.

"Jedar, is that you?" the thief named Antoth answered in Cody's voice.

"Yes, my old friend, it is me."

"By Solisk, you've gotten old!" Antoth said.

Jedar shrugged. "Yes. Someone had to stick around and make sure we all came back."

"How long did you wait?"

"Sixty-four years. It took a long time to find all the Gier root. It's becoming increasingly rare."

"Well done, brother. How many of our brethren have you raised?"

"Thirty-one, but we also have thirty acolytes, like Marek here. They have been a great help." Jedar put a hand on Marek's shoulder.

Cody couldn't believe it. Thirty-one people had been mind-swapped? He had expected perhaps a dozen, not almost three times that amount. And thirty acolytes? This cult was much bigger than Cody had expected.

"How does the body feel?" Jedar asked.

"Incredible. Whoever he was, he was in spectacular shape. I am sore, though. Why?"

"That would be because he tried to escape and the guards beat him," Marek said.

"Ah," Antoth sounded as if he had partially expected such an answer. "I am quite hungry. Do you not feed the prisoners?"

"We do," Jedar said.

"Not much," Marek added. "Just some stew. That's where we put the concoction."

Antoth asked, "Concoction?"

"It's something new I discovered," Jedar said, a note of pride in his voice. "You recall how before, occasionally, the host's mind wouldn't be killed, but would stay inside their body, locked away?"

"Yes."

Jedar smiled. "Well, this concoction of Gier root and other ingredients, makes sure their mind dies."

That's why I'm around, Cody figured. *I didn't eat the stew. Whoever wrote that message was telling the truth.*

Antoth sighed. "Well, this person must not have been eating your stew because he is still in here." He tapped his head.

Jedar looked startled. Marek's expression flickered through a range of emotions, although surprise wasn't one of them.

"Impossible!" Jedar said.

"I can feel his presence," Antoth said.

Cody's heart beat faster. They knew he was here. Hopefully, they couldn't do anything to him.

"He was supposed to be dead!" Marek said, sounding annoyed. "You can kill him, right?"

Jedar looked into Antoth's eyes, but Cody knew he was looking at him. "Of course, I can."

~ ~ ~

A small, rat-like man stood in front of Farren, his eyes fixed on the floor. He rubbed his hands together nervously. "You called for me, my lord?"

Farren sat tall in his chair. "Yes, I did. You have been keeping an eye on Aldus Calanol since he arrived, correct?"

"That is correct, my lord," the man said, dipping his head even lower. "H... have I done something wrong, my lord?"

Farren held up a hand. "No. No, you have not. I am simply reassigning you. Your skills are needed elsewhere."

The rat-faced man looked up. "Your majesty?"

"Aldus is not a threat presently," Farren said. "I would like to keep him under surveillance, but right now, the rebel insurgents are a bigger threat." He clasped his hands, a slight flexing the only sign of his stress. "They have been disrupting my agenda since I arrived in Saken, but no one has been able to find them yet. You are one of the best. I want you to track them down."

"Of course, my king," the man bowed. "I will not fail you."

Farren dismissed him. As the man left the room, the king said, "I hope you don't. I will not tolerate any more failures."

Shortly after, Malroth and Minos entered and bowed.

"What is it?" the king asked.

Minos held out a letter. "This is from the garrison at the Foghead River. The wildling attacks have increased and they need more men if they are to stop them from attacking Perrian and Seawall."

Farren sighed. He was growing tired of the wildlings, but every attempt to invade their forest had failed. "Send a company from Fabuller. Giala activity there is low, the men will not be needed there."

"Right away, your highness," Minos bowed. In a moment, he was gone.

Malroth stayed.

Farren motioned for his trusted general to speak. "I have received word that the Corsair's Guild has begun to prey upon royal ships again. There have been three confirmed accounts of our ships being boarded."

"What happened to our delegate in the Guild?" Farren asked.

Malroth tipped his head. "No word from him in two months."

Farren closed his eyes and gritted his teeth as his frustration allowed the storm inside him to flare up momentarily. Malroth said nothing as the king fought back the control. He smoothed his hair and exhaled. "Send another delegate. But I want him protected. Well-protected."

"I have several bounty hunters who would be willing to accompany the delegate," Malroth said.

"How much would they ask for?" Farren inquired.

"Their usual fee is ten thousand marks," the black knight said. "However, if it is an extended job, they may ask for more."

Farren nodded. "Hefty, but not unaffordable. Write up the contracts."

"Yes, sire," Malroth said, dipping his head as he left.

Farren stared at the spot he had disappeared long after the knight was gone.

CHAPTER 17

Though he was loath to admit it, Levi freaked out. He ran down to the beach, screaming incoherently about the end of the world now that he had lost the Elder Gem. A hundred meters out in the water, a small rowboat was carrying Kyner and the guard. It moved slowly, the guard struggling with the oars, but Levi didn't realize it. All he knew was that they were escaping with the Gem.

After a few moments, Charlotte had had enough. She walked up to Levi and kicked him over. "Shut up!"

Levi spat sand and sat up, staring at her in shock. "But-"

"Nope! No talking for you!" Charlotte ordered. "Just follow me. We're going to find a boat."

"Where are we going to find a boat?"

"Shh!" Charlotte began stomping away, sand spraying up the back of her legs. "There'll be a boat here. Trust me."

Levi followed behind her, still berating himself for losing the most prized possession in the world. He felt like a complete failure. He had let everyone down. He should never have been chosen to carry the Gem.

He was so wrapped up in his own self-misery that he didn't notice Charlotte had stopped walking and ran into her.

"Gah! Watch where you're going!"

"Sorry," he muttered.

"Whatever. Look. There was a boat here recently."

"Yeah, the one Kyner and the guard took," Levi said glumly. "There are no more boats left."

Charlotte rolled her eyes. "Yes, there are, idiot. There are, er, were still guards on the island. There's no way they wouldn't have a second boat stashed somewhere. We'll find it."

"It could take forever!" Levi wailed.

"It'll take a lot longer if you stand there crying." Charlotte marched to the edge of the beach, where a small forest of mostly tall shrubs grew. "It'll likely be in here."

They searched for ten minutes before Levi stumbled onto something. Literally. He tripped over a wooden plank. "Over here!"

Charlotte hurried over. "Well. It's not exactly a boat."

It was a crudely made raft, a ten-foot square of planks tied together with rope. A log served as the mast on which a tattered canvas hung. There were two paddles, one cracked down the middle.

"It'll work!" Levi said, putting his hands on one edge and pushing. It moved five feet, before Levi stopped. "It's heavy."

Charlotte lent a hand and together they pushed it down to the water's edge.

Charlotte straightened and looked at the raft with a doubtful expression. "Is this thing even waterproof?"

"Doesn't matter!" Levi hopped on. "We can't let them get more than a kilometre away!"

"Why not?"

"Because otherwise it'll explode and sink to the bottom of the sea!" Levi cried.

Charlotte sighed and stepped onto the raft. It bobbed, the near side dipping into the water. "Fine. We'll use this piece of crap. We'll be lucky if we make twenty meters."

Levi ignored the assassin's cynicism and shoved off with the paddle. Charlotte unfurled the sail and tied it off to two hooks set in the planks. It was small and the wind was weak, but it was in the right direction and every bit helped.

As he paddled, Levi squinted. He could see a thin line in the distance that was the mainland. Much closer was their quarry, the boat on which Kyner was escaping. The guard still hadn't improved his rowing.

"I can't believe this thing floats," Charlotte said.

"Hey! Help paddle!" Levi called. "We've got to catch up!"

"Alright, alright, keep your shirt on." Charlotte went to the other edge and began to take long strokes with the paddle.

Levi shrugged and returned to attacking the water with his paddle. Water splashed everywhere, soaking him quickly.

"Dig your paddle in deeper," Charlotte advised. "Take longer, more powerful strokes, rather than quick ones."

Levi heeded her advice and had to admit that the raft moved a bit faster. But still not fast enough. "Ugh! We're so slow!"

"It's a big wooden square," Charlotte snipped. "What did you expect? Besides, we're still gaining on them."

Levi peered ahead. They did seem to be closer. "Will we catch them before they reach land?"

"Do I look like a sailor? I have no idea!"

"Just asking," Levi said. "I'm a little stressed out right now."

Charlotte didn't answer, she was concentrating on paddling. Levi did the same. He gritted his teeth and pulled harder, willing the raft to go faster.

Soon, Levi's shoulders and arms began to burn. He took a three-second break to shake them out and continued. He couldn't give up. He upped the rhythm, going faster and faster.

"Levi! Cut it out!" Charlotte called.

Levi didn't stop.

"Hey! You're going to burn yourself out!"

Levi threw his paddle down in anger and flopped down on the planks. "Ah! I hate this! We're never gonna catch them!"

There was a long silence.

Charlotte sat next to him. "Look, kid. Levi. You can't help what happened. The past is the past. You can't change that. All the magic in the world can't change that. But you can change the future, it isn't over yet. So don't give up. The world is counting on you." She stood. "And besides, I hate quitters."

Levi glanced sideways at her. "For an assassin, you aren't half bad at speeches."

She snorted. "Shut up. Let's keep going. But at a reasonable pace."

Levi nodded and picked up his paddle. He returned to his place and they set a rhythm that wouldn't tire them out but would still move them at a decent speed.

"Charlotte?"

"Hmm?"

"Why are you in the Giala?"

"They hired me," Charlotte answered. "Being an assassin is just a job. They offered me good money."

"So, you have no loyalty to them?"

"Not at first, beyond the loyalty that can be bought. I even tried to betray them at one point. The tattoo stopped me. Burned like hell." She smirked. "But after a while, I, uh, met someone. A high ranking Giala official. And, well, we had a kid. I'd do anything to keep her safe."

Levi nodded. "So, you don't care that Farren is trying to rule the world with unlimited power?"

"Well, at first, I didn't know, and then I didn't believe, but now, I've seen enough to know it's true and yeah, I don't think that would be a fun world to live in."

"Hmm. Why were you in prison?"

"Oh, my team was hired to assassinate one of the nobles at the Festival. They caught me. Kinda embarrassing, actually."

The festival had only begun a few days ago. "You weren't in there long."

"Nope," she said. "But, long enough for me. I hate being cooped up."

"Me too. Although it has happened a few times in the last while." Levi stared down into the water, a deep blue that rippled as the raft moved through the currents. As he looked, a huge, long shape raced under the raft and sped off toward the mainland.

"Whoa! Did you see that?"

"See what?" Charlotte swung her head from side to side.

"That huge, snakey thing in the water!"

Charlotte raised a skeptical eyebrow.

Levi remembered Captain Haynes telling him about mythical sea beasts a year ago while travelling to the island. "It must be a sea serpent!"

"No offence, Levi, but that's stupid," Charlotte said. "There are no sea serpents."

"No, no! I saw it!" Levi insisted.

"They're myths," Charlotte said. "If they ever were real, they're extinct now."

Five hundred yards ahead of them, the water around Kyner's boat erupted as a massive serpent breached. Its head was the size of two horses side by side, with dark brown scales as big as dinner plates covering everything but its huge, green eyes.

"I stand corrected," Charlotte said in a small voice. "Good Lord, that's huge!"

Levi watched in horror as the serpent opened its mouth and chomped down on the boat, splintering it in two. Both figures were spilled into the sea with loud screams.

"No!" Levi yelled. The Elder Gem couldn't be gone.

The serpent's head had gone back under, but its massive coils still rippled above the water.

"We have to save Kyner!" Levi cried. He began to paddle closer.

"Get closer to that thing!" Charlotte yelled. "Are you insane?"

"You're an assassin! You shouldn't be scared of-"

"Of a huge freaking snake that could eat us both whole! Why wouldn't I be terrified of that?"

Levi growled and focused on moving the cumbersome vessel toward the wreckage. He could see a man swimming toward him wildly, water splashing all around him.

The snake circled back toward them, trying to cut off the fleeing figure.

It was going to be close.

"Hurry!" Levi screamed.

The man in the water flailed, kicking as hard as he could. Levi reached out his paddle. The man grabbed it and Levi hauled him out of the water. The serpent's mouth snapped shut just behind him, taking off a piece of the raft.

Levi grabbed Kyner by the shoulders and shook him. "Tell me you have it!"

Kyner opened his mouth and out flooded a torrent of water and something golden. The Elder Gem.

Levi snatched it up before it could slip through the cracks in the floor. A wave of pure relief washed over him. He had it. The king wasn't going to get it.

"It's coming back!" Charlotte yelled.

Levi followed her pointing finger to where the snake was racing for them, the water in front of it pushed up into a small wave. It was closing fast. If it hit the raft, they were all goners.

Levi knew what he needed to do. He stood and looked at the golden bird in his hand. He had the most powerful magical artifact in the realm. He could do it.

He closed his eyes and felt the familiar flow of power deep within him. He heard the water rushing as the serpent arched out of the water, felt the raft shifting beneath his feet, smelled the rancid breath of the monster.

The Elder Gem grew hot and Levi thrust out his hand as his eyes flew open. For a split second, all he saw was the pink maw of the beast, rows of teeth and a pulsing gullet. Then, with a loud whoosh, the serpent flew fifty feet into the air, its head snapping back with the disgusting, wet sound of bones cracking. It hung in the air for a moment and then came crashing down. Dead.

The splash was colossal.

"Look out!" Charlotte called.

Levi braced himself as the wall of water hit him. It was so much more powerful than he had expected. He was ripped from the deck and tossed into the sea, the Elder Gem torn from his grip. The golden talisman began sinking into the inky depths.

Levi's eyes bugged out and a gasp of bubbles escaped his mouth. He dove after it, swimming furiously. They both went deeper and deeper, the light growing dim. Levi reached out and snagged the Gem.

He spun around and looked up. The surface was far away, the sun a blurry dot. His chest began to tighten as his stores of oxygen ran low. Pushing his hands up and pulling down, he ascended, kicking as hard as he could. He repeated the motion again and again.

His chest burned and his vision began to darken as his brain stopped receiving the air it so desperately needed. He was still too far away. He was not going to make it.

A blurry figure dove into the water and grabbed Levi's wrist. He felt himself being pulled up and suddenly, his head broke the surface. He gasped, gulping in huge lungfuls of sweet, sweet air.

He swam over to the raft and a hand pulled him up. Charlotte.

"Wait, what?" Levi looked back and saw Kyner swimming behind him. He hauled himself up, water pouring out of his long hair and beard.

"You helped me. Why?" Levi croaked.

Kyner swept hair out of his face. "You saved me. Now we're even."

"Um, no," Levi said. "You beat me up and robbed me. You still owe me one."

"True," Kyner admitted, flopping down on his back. "But, now that the guard is dead. I won't be forced to turn you over to the king. And I still could. But I won't. So, we're even."

Levi's eyes narrowed. "Why should I believe you?"

Kyner took a moment to wring out his filthy beard. "Alright, Levi, I'll swear a *sareeva*."

"What's that?"

The waterlogged prince folded his fingers together. "It's a Wintenveil custom. An oath basically. To break one is to, well let's just say that even after all the laws I've broken, that's still one line I don't dare cross."

Levi looked into Kyner's eyes and saw sincerity for the first time. He felt strongly that the prince was telling the truth. With a sigh, Levi said, "Ok, Kyner. Swear a *sareeva*."

"Give me your hand."

Levi extended his hand and let Kyner grab onto his wrist with his good hand.

"Normally we use the opposite arms, but that's not really an option." Kyner grinned. "Ok. Now, just keep eye contact while I'm talking. Don't blink."

Levi nodded and took a second to blink rapidly before Kyner began.

The prince licked his lips and began. "Witness me, *sareeva*, as I swear to Levi that I will never reveal the secret of the Elder Gem to anyone. If I fail to uphold my word, *sareeva*, administer justice."

Kyner released Levi's wrist just as Levi's eyes began to itch. He rubbed them vigorously and heard a slight sizzle. A sharp pain shot up his arm and he looked at his wrist. A small red mark identical to the ones marring Kyner's wrist had burnt itself into his skin.

"Yeah, I forgot to mention it does that." Kyner held up his arm to show that a fourth mark had appeared. "If it turns black that means I've broken my word. But I won't. Your secret is safe."

Levi massaged the new scar, but he felt a bit better than he had. He believed that Kyner would keep his oath.

Charlotte coughed. "So, do I not kill him, or..."

Levi let out a long breath. "No, I think we're ok."

"Totally ok," Kyner said. "There doesn't need to be any killing of me."

Charlotte narrowed her eyes. "Ok, but I'm not trusting you just because you did some weird magic bond. I'm keeping my eye on you until we get back to civilization."

"Hey, yeah how did you do that?" Levi asked. "Are you an Arcane?"

"Nope, I'm First Order. No one knows why, but all us born in Wintenveil can perform a *sareeva*. Been that way through our entire history."

Levi got to his feet and watched the shoreline far away. "That's actually pretty neat, but we need to get going. People are going to be worried sick about me."

The others agreed as they both had their own reasons for wanting to be back on land.

The guys took turns on the paddles first and went for fifteen minutes before Levi switched out with Charlotte. They continued to rotate the person resting until, at last, the raft hit bottom on the shore's edge.

Levi and Charlotte dropped the paddles, exhausted beyond exhaustion and they plodded through the surf until their boots became caked with sand. They all dropped to the ground and rested.

Ten minutes passed before Kyner said, "Question is, where are we?"

Levi glanced around. All he could see was a grassy hill in front of them with some trees up on the crest.

"No idea," Charlotte said.

"So, we're lost," Levi muttered. "Great."

"We should climb the hill and see if we can see anything," Charlotte said. She stood and dusted herself off. Then, she began to scale the hill.

"Oh, that rest was not long enough," Levi said as he got up.

The hill was steeper than it had looked. With Levi already tired, he was reduced to a slow climb, using his hands as much as his legs. His breath came in ragged gasps and by the time he made it to the top, he had a stitch in his side. He sat back on his knees and hung his head in exhaustion.

"Good news and bad news," Charlotte said.

"Good first, please," Levi said.

"I think I know where Saken is." She pointed at the range of small mountains that ran parallel with the coast. "I'm pretty sure it's just beyond that peak there." The mountain in question was at the end of the range, perhaps forty kilometres away.

Levi groaned. "That's the good news? What's the bad news?"

Charlotte pointed down the hill. "We have to cross that." A barren field of erupting geysers five kilometres across stood between them and the path to their destination.

Levi's face fell. "Uh, bad."

"Very bad."

Levi turned to see that Kyner had finally scaled the hill. His hair and beard were now matted with wet sand.

"We're gonna have to cross it," Charlotte said. "Can't go right, there's a cliff and left is the mountains, where we'll definitely get lost."

"You know, I almost wish I'd stayed in my cell," Kyner said.

Charlotte checked the position of the sun in the sky. "Let's go. We might make it through before dark if we hurry."

"Oh, that's comforting," Levi said. "I certainly want to be wandering through that after dark."

Charlotte didn't respond. Instead, she set off down the hill.

Levi sighed. *Why does everything have to be so difficult?*

The slope on the landward side of the hill was much flatter and made walking down significantly easier. Levi was glad for the respite after all the physical exertion of the past hour.

Kyner was enjoying it as well. He whistled a tune as he walked. It was a jaunty little tune, and Levi soon found himself bobbing his head to the melody. "What song is that?"

Kyner glanced back. "Oh, just an old Wintenveil tune my mother used to sing to me. Would you like to hear the lyrics?"

"Sure."

Kyner cleared his throat and began singing. His voice was strong and clear.

> *Where do you find the old grey fox?*
> *Where do you find the scoundrel?*
> *Where do you find the old grey fox?*
> *Why, you look over yonder hill.*
> *He comes in the night to steal your sheep.*
> *He comes in the dusk to steal your flocks.*

He robs you of all your sleep.
Then, he'll sneak back home to the rocks.
Where do you find the old grey fox?
You don't, oh he finds you.

He finished and grinned at Levi, spreading his arms. "Well?"

"That was great! What's it called?"

Kyner shrugged. "Dunno. I assume 'The Old Grey Fox' but I've never heard its name."

"I like it," Levi said.

Up ahead, Charlotte chortled to herself.

"What?" Kyner asked. "Don't you have a song your parents used to sing to you?"

"I was an orphan," Charlotte replied. "Never had any parents."

Kyner paused for a moment. Then, "I guess that way they couldn't be disappointed with your career decisions."

Charlotte laughed. "Like yours probably are?"

Kyner held up a finger. "You don't even know who my parents are."

"Does it matter? Spending years in prison doesn't seem like the type of thing that would impress anyone."

Kyner attempted to retort, but shut his mouth when he realized she was right. He instead scratched under his long tangles of facial hair.

The ground at the bottom of the hill flattened out into a plain. Even the trees grew shorter and shorter until they were completely replaced by shrubs. They trekked across the landscape, weaving around the scraggly bushes until they came to a small stream, just a trickle of water over a bed of stones. They stopped for a drink, lapping up the water thirstily.

Levi glanced up from the stream, water dripping from his chin. The geyser field was close, the grass turning to brown a scant two hundred yards away. The shrubs were dead, nothing more than leafless skeletons.

"This is going to be such fun," Levi muttered.

"As long as we don't walk into a geyser, we'll be fine," Charlotte said.

Levi looked at the dozen water spouts he could see before the steam and fog blanketed everything beyond. "Oh yeah. That'll be easy."

Charlotte stood and headed for the edge of the field. Levi grumbled, but followed her. Kyner was right behind him.

They stopped ten feet from the first hole. The exploding jets of water were deafening, a constant sound that hammered against Levi's ears.

"At least being boiled to death is a unique way to go," Levi said.

"That's how a cousin of mine died," Kyner said.

"You guys are so very weird," Levi said.

Kyner spread his hands. "What can I say? We like to keep things interesting. Makes life more entertaining."

"And shorter," Charlotte added.

"So do you, assassin," Kyner replied.

Charlotte smirked. "And these geysers might very well make our lives much shorter."

"You think we'll survive?" Levi asked.

"Honestly, kid, I'm not sure we will." She pulled her mouth to one side. "Then again, I wasn't expecting to escape from prison or fight a sea serpent. With you, I'm not quite sure what to expect."

"Aw, thanks," Levi said.

"That wasn't a compliment."

"I'm going to take it as one."

"Hey, either of you have any food?" Kyner asked. "I'm starving."

"No, neither of us have food," Charlotte said. "We were all just in jail!"

"Just thought I'd ask," Kyner said.

Levi was suddenly conscious of his growling, empty stomach. "I'm hungry too. All the more reason to get back to Saken."

"Just need to walk into this foggy death field," Kyner said.

They all stared into the mist.

A nearby geyser exploded, startling them and showering them with tiny droplets.

"And I was just starting to get dry," Kyner complained.

"You wanted things to get interesting," Charlotte said. "Well, now it is. Let's go."

She plunged ahead into the fog.

"Here goes nothing." Levi rubbed the new burn mark and followed the assassin into the unknown.

CHAPTER 18

Levi lost Charlotte immediately. He tried to follow her as she wound around pits of bubbling liquid. The fog proved to be too dense and she was swallowed up by the mist.

"Charlotte!" Levi called over the sound of erupting geysers. There was no response.

"Is she gone?" Kyner came up beside Levi.

"Yeah. I looked up and she had just vanished."

Kyner cupped his hands around his mouth and bellowed Charlotte's name. Nothing. He shrugged. "Oh well."

Levi turned on him. "Oh well? Oh well? That's all you can say?"

"Whoa! What's with all the venom?" Kyner asked.

"She's gone! What if we never find her again?"

"Good!" Kyner said. "I don't trust her not to kill me!"

Levi glared at him, open-mouthed. "How can you say that? She helped save your sorry life!"

"Did she?" A bit of heat was creeping into Kyner's voice. "She wasn't tagging along to rescue me. She was coming to kill me and give you your stupid medallion. And when things turned around, she didn't rescue me, you did!"

Levi grabbed fistfuls of hair. He couldn't believe this. The rational part of his brain told him that Kyner was making sense, but he was so flustered at losing Charlotte that he was taking it all out on the lost prince.

He cursed and stormed away.

"Where are you going?" Kyner called.

"To find Charlotte!"

Kyner threw his hands in the air. "You're not gonna find her!" But he followed Levi, not wanting to be left alone.

It was impossible for Levi to know where he was going. He could only see ten feet ahead of him, just far enough to avoid the geysers. Jets would erupt next to him or Kyner and hot water and steam would splash over them, stinging their skin and eyes.

At one point, Levi stepped back to avoid one geyser and backed into another one as it blew. He yelled, the back of his neck and arms burning. He jumped ahead and rubbed his arms.

"We're never going to find her!" Kyner called over the blasting of the hot water.

Levi knew he was right. They stood no chance of finding her unless it was completely on accident.

"We need to concentrate on getting out of here!" Kyner said.

Levi nodded.

"Besides," Kyner said. "That's what she'll be doing." A nearby geyser went off, punctuating his statement.

"Alright, fine," Levi relented. "You lead the way."

Kyner pointed at himself. "Me? No way! I want to be able to avoid them if you blow up. You go first."

Levi groaned, but he was done arguing. "Coward." He tucked his head down and began walking again.

It was difficult to predict where the geysers would appear. There were no straight paths between them and yet they weren't in any sort of pattern or order. There would be a group of them close together, maybe ten or more that forced the guys to go around. Then, there were stretches where there were fewer spouts, but due to the fog and lack of visibility, they couldn't travel any faster.

They wandered for two hours, or so Levi figured. He didn't know how long they had been in there or how far they had come. With no point of reference, he couldn't gauge how far they had to go.

Kyner tripped on a rock and fell face-first toward a boiling pit. He managed to turn his head away as it went off, but when he stood, his hair was steaming.

"You ok?" Levi asked.

Kyner grunted. "I guess. That's gonna hurt for a while."

Levi touched the back of his neck. Kyner was right. The burns were going to be a pain.

They kept moving forward.

Soon, Levi began to hear sounds in the fog, and not the sounds of geysers. Unnatural sounds. Whispers. He looked around for the source, but all he saw was drifting shadows in the mist.

After a few minutes of listening to the murmurs, Levi turned to Kyner. "Do you hear anything?"

"Oh good, I thought I was going crazy," Kyner said. "It's like a strange whispering, right?"

"Yeah, but, I can't make out any words."

"What do you suppose it is?" Kyner glanced over his shoulder.

"I have no idea," Levi admitted. "Maybe it's the wind."

"But the fog is moving so slowly, it can't be the wind." Kyner went silent for a moment. "You don't think it's some kind of mythical creature that devours people, do you?"

"I doubt it," Levi said.

"But, we all doubted that sea serpents were a thing and we just got attacked by one."

Levi licked his lips nervously. "I suppose it's possible." Now, he saw all the shadows as the outline of some sort of wraith ready to pounce. He shuddered.

"We don't even have anything to defend ourselves with," Kyner said. "Unless you can do that neat trick again."

"I don't know, maybe I- Look there!" Levi yelled, pointing to the right.

"What?" Kyner swung around, fists balled. "I don't see anything!"

Levi blinked. The thing he had just seen was gone. "I swear I saw something."

"Over there!" Kyner cried.

Levi spun but saw nothing. "Where?"

"Right in front of you! How do you not see it?"

Something caught the corner of Levi's eye. He whirled around. "No! There it is!"

"What? It's still right there!" Kyner said.

"What does it look like?"

"It looks like... like..." Kyner trailed off.

"Kyner?"

"It looks like me," he said softly.

Levi swung his head back and forth but couldn't see it. Then, a shape materialized in front of him, but it didn't look like Kyner. It looked like him.

"What sorcery is this?" Kyner whispered, echoing Levi's thoughts.

The figure in front of Levi moved, lifting its arm. It began to fade, but before it was completely gone, another image began to form.

When it clarified, Levi gasped. He recognized it. It was the first time he had met Kinzo, Kana and Miri. He watched in awe as the scene played out exactly as he remembered; him fleeing Kalipo, stopping in the woods, the other three coming up behind him and drawing their weapons.

That scene began to fade as well and a new one appeared. The time when Levi and his friends were escaping the safe house in Cabalk with Alexander and Nat. The scene ran its course, ending with the tunnel collapsing with Kana and Alexander still inside.

A new scene came into existence and a second one. Levi looked back and forth between visions of him being attacked by the Kar-Sang in the grove outside of Blackthrush and he and his friends arriving in Saken on the Nomad's Darling.

Levi closed his eyes and shook his head, thinking it must be some strange hallucination. But, when he opened his eyes, the visions were still there, except now there were more. They kept coming. His last birthday with his parents, the fight with the kathauk, the arrival in Blackthrush, sneaking into Rivera Farm and more.

Levi's eyes darted to and fro, trying to take it all in.

Suddenly, the scenes changed. Levi didn't recognize what was in them.

He saw people fleeing from soldiers on horseback while smoke rose behind them, obscuring whatever was on fire.

He saw himself talking with an old man with a great grey beard and eyes of bright silver. The man made a complex motion with his hands and a strange symbol floated in the air. It resembled an S with a circle in the centre and a vertical line running through it.

Levi looked to his right where he saw people walking down a dark corridor. They reached the end and came out into a courtyard. A hooded figure was waiting on the far side with a bow and they loosed an arrow at the lead person. One of the others, a woman, dove in front of them, taking the arrow.

He saw himself fighting Malroth on a cliff in a circle of scorched earth. Bodies of soldiers and others lay around them and beyond stood a man, holding something glowing in his hand.

He saw someone on a farm, opening a barn door. A sword appeared in their hands with a flash. They fell to their knees, clutching the blade until blood dripped from their hands.

A different vision showed a person standing on the foredeck of a massive ship. There was a massive army of corsairs behind him. The person spread their arms and opened their hands. Green light flared and the boat exploded into flames.

Next, he saw someone in full black and orange armour fighting through an army. They mowed through the soldiers, taking blow after blow until they reached Malroth on a massive battle charger. They fought and both fell over a cliff into a gorge below.

A different scene showed a battlefield filled with soldiers from various armies. A dark bolt ripped through the sky and a portion of them simply vanished.

All of the visions vanished but one. It grew until it filled all of Levi's sight. It was him, dirty and injured, lying on the ground in full golden armour that was rent and battered. His helmet was broken in two next to him. There was a pool of blood growing beneath him. Another person in golden armour, holding a round shield that glowed white knelt beside him. The injured Levi reached up and grabbed the other person's helmet and threw back his head, eyes blazing gold.

The scene went dark and Levi was left staring at whitish-grey mist. His mind raced. What did those visions mean? Were they real or was he just imagining them?

He slowly turned to face Kyner. The prince was kneeling on the ground with his head bowed. "Kyner?"

Kyner shuddered. "I saw things. Terrible things."

"Me too," Levi said, squatting beside him. "Some were from my past, others weren't."

Kyner swallowed and nodded. "I saw the last time I talked to my mother before she died."

"I'm sorry."

Kyner ran his hands through his hair, sweeping it out of his face. "Do you think the other ones were... were our future?"

"I really hope not," Levi said quietly. "I saw myself dying. I wasn't very old."

Kyner looked down at his stump and then at the other hand, as if comparing them. "I saw things worse than death. It can't be the future. It just can't be."

Levi had nothing to say. They stayed there in silence, between erupting geysers for a long time. He didn't know what had caused them to see such things, but he guessed it was one of the unexplained magical occurrences Linae had taught him about. That seemed to be the only explanation.

At last, Kyner stood. "Let's get out of this wretched place."

"I agree," Levi said.

Kyner walked off, shoulders hunched.

Levi stared after him. He wondered what the prince had seen in his visions. Whatever they had been, they had shaken him, badly. Levi shrugged. He would probably never find out. He followed Kyner as he trekked through the geyser field.

They didn't speak as they walked. They were both too wrapped up in their own thoughts. Levi was trying to comprehend what the scenes meant. He thought perhaps they could be metaphorical, not literal, but he couldn't think of what the metaphors might be.

An hour later, Levi glanced up and could see bright light ahead. A minute after that, they broke out of the fog into the afternoon sunlight. Beyond was green grass and trees and further, the mountain behind which lay Saken.

Levi breathed in the cool, crisp air. "We made it."

"We did," Kyner said evenly.

Levi tried to judge the distance from them to the peak. "Still a ways to go. We won't make it today."

Kyner began walking.

"Oh, you want to keep going. Good idea."

They travelled along, reaching the green meadow and walking through it until the sun went down. Finding a little grotto with an overhanging shrub, they bedded down for the night. A lot of ground had been covered, but there was still a long trek back to the city.

Before Levi closed his eyes, he glanced up at the starry sky and hoped that Charlotte had made it out alive. He drifted off to sleep.

~ ~ ~

Levi had expected that he would wake with the rising of the sun, but to his surprise, when he opened his eyes, the sun was already well above the horizon. He stretched and let out a huge yawn. He must have been really tired.

He looked around. Something was wrong. It took him a moment. "I'm alone."

Kyner was nowhere to be found. Instead, there was a note scratched into the dirt.

Levi, sorry to take off on you like this, but I need to sort some things out without anyone around. I am eternally grateful for you helping me escape prison and I feel like I owe you another favour. Good luck with your whole thing with the Gem and whatnot.
Yours cordially, Kyner Sinnas.

Levi reached into his pocket, fearing the worst, but the Elder Gem was still there. Kyner had been true to his word about not turning Levi in. He had figured Kyner wouldn't double-cross him, but he still blew out a breath of relief.

"I hope you figure out whatever it is you need to," Levi said, feeling his mark that connected him to the prince. He kind of liked Kyner, even if they had gotten off on the wrong foot. Kind of. He also did hate him for beating him and stealing the Elder Gem. His feelings were very mixed.

Levi used his foot to wipe out the message. It was way out in the middle of nowhere, but he still didn't want to risk anyone finding something that said both his name and the Gem.

Levi's stomach gurgled loudly. "I need some food." He hadn't eaten in almost a day. "Guess the only way to get food is to get back to the city."

He rubbed his burnt arms and neck, wincing at the discomfort. Then, he set his sights on the mountain and started out.

He walked for hours. A blister developed on his left heel. He stubbed his toes several times and rolled his ankles twice.

Once, as he was passing a bush, a fox darted out, scared the living daylights out of Levi and ran off. Levi remembered the song about the fox Kyner had sung and tried to sing it himself. He couldn't quite remember the words, but he knew the tune and hummed it when he forgot the lyrics.

The bushes shook again. Levi waited for the red fur of the fox to appear, but instead, a familiar black and white squirrel came out. "Paco?"

"Levi," the squirrel said, sounding unimpressed and out of breath. "You are a damn pain to look out for. Why did you have to go and get thrown in prison?"

Levi shrugged. "Sorry. I couldn't do much about it. I take it you couldn't exactly find me."

Paco crossed his thin arms. "Nope. I had to call in a favour to find out where they'd taken you. It was so much nicer when you were just at Blackthrush, not getting into any trouble." The squirrel was quite annoyed. "As soon as you leave, you decide to get wrapped up in the most ridiculous things and send me all over the city looking for your sorry hide!"

Levi couldn't help but grin at the ill-tempered rodent. "Oops."

"Oops? Oops? That's all you have to say? Paco flopped his head back. "Oh, you are the worst! When I agreed to Aurora's request, I expected to follow a kid around for a bit, that's it! I didn't sign up to get dragged into this damn war and tangled up with some of the most dangerous people in Terrenia!" He blew out a long breath.

"Needed to get that out?"

"Yeah. I feel better now. But I still wish you'd stay out of trouble."

"I'm trying, Paco," Levi said sincerely. "But sometimes, it can't be helped."

The squirrel grumbled.

"Well, thanks for coming and finding me. I'm not actually sure where I am."

"I know," Paco said. "There's actually a pass in the mountain that would have taken hours off the trip, but you missed it."

"Good thing you're here," Levi said. "Lead the way."

Levi continued on, Paco keeping pace with him. They didn't talk much, as Levi knew Paco was still annoyed. But it was nice to have some company, even if said company was twelve inches tall and mostly tail.

Eventually, the two climbed a hill overlooking the southern end of the city. From his vantage point, Levi could easily see the divide between the main city and the Outskirts. He could also see the Festival grounds and knew that people would be worrying about him.

He hurried down the hill, tripping only twice.

Paco led him through the Outskirts, since Levi had no idea which way to go. He still got lost once and Paco had to backtrack to find him.

Forty minutes later, Levi arrived at the grounds. Music and laughter mingled with wood smoke and the scent of cooking food to create a lovely atmosphere.

Levi exhaled. He had made it. There had been a few times, well, a lot of times, when he hadn't been sure he would.

He made his way to the Blackthrush camp. A group of people was standing around someone who was talking loudly and animatedly. Kana.

He turned to thank Paco, but the squirrel had already gone. Levi just caught a glimpse of black and white darting back into the maze of tents. He shrugged and looked back.

"We have to get him back! If we act quickly, we can bust him out of prison before the soldiers know we're there."

"Kana, be reasonable," Hejeck said. "We can't just go breaking into prisons, much less Felgath Prison."

"Breaking in there would require quite the explanation," Myron agreed.

"But he's been framed!" Kana cried. "I have intel that says he's innocent!"

"And how did you come by this information?" Silverton asked, stroking his groomed goatee.

Kana bit her lip. "Er, well, it doesn't really matter how I know, I just do know!"

"Kana, that's a little suspicious," Silverton said. "You didn't threaten anyone for this, did you?"

"Well, maybe, but that doesn't matter!" Kana said. "We need to get Levi back!"

Aldus began to chuckle. Everyone stared at him. "I don't believe we need to do anything at all."

"What?" Kana yelled. "How can you say that?"

Aldus pointed at Levi. "Because, he is standing right there."

Everyone turned and chorused, "Levi!"

"Uh oh," Levi said as he was swarmed by his fellow students, who clapped him on the back and tousled his hair.

"You're back!" Walt said with a grin.

Caesar laughed. "Good to see you, bud."

"Told you he'd be back," Taro smirked.

"Out of my way!" Kana yelled and the crowd cleared. She stormed up and punched him square in the mouth.

"Ow! What the heck!" He was cut off by a massive bear hug.

"Don't ever do that again!" Kana ordered.

"It was not my fault," Levi defended himself.

"Doesn't matter. Never again." Kana realized everyone was watching them hug and quickly let go. She cleared her throat.

"Were you actually in prison?" Bram asked.

Levi glanced down at his red mark. "Yep. It sucked. I got robbed, beaten, attacked by a monster, nearly drowned, nearly boiled and almost driven insane." He paused. "Does anyone have any food? I'm starved!"

CHAPTER 19

Cody began to panic. The cult leader was about to kill him and he had absolutely no way of defending himself.

"There has to be something I can do!" Cody cried. The only things in the whiteness were the window into the real world and the thousands of colourful memory spheres. What good were memories going to do in this hopeless situation?

"I can't believe that bastard survived," Cody heard Marek say. "How do we kill him?"

"Patience, Marek," Jedar said soothingly. "Your brother will be dead soon enough. I just need to assemble some items for the exorcism."

"Exorcism!" Cody yelled. "I'm not a demon! You can't exorcise me from my own body!" He felt better after yelling even though he knew there was no way he could be heard outside.

The voices echoed around the white space, speaking of how they would remove Cody from existence. It sounded like a horrible experience. Cody wanted no part of it, but unfortunately, he had no say in the matter.

He clenched his hands as he tried to think of something, anything to help him out.

Outside, Jedar was holding an ancient book inscribed with runes and a spiral wand. "Not good," Cody gulped.

"What are those?" Marek wondered.

Jedar held the book up. "This is the Tome of Laruel."

Marek's brows went up as he recognized the name.

Cody recognized it as well. Everyone had heard of the Tome of Laruel. Its author, Laruel, had been one of the most powerful and respected Arcanes in his time and well, in all times. He single-handedly saved the residents of Corina when they were possessed by malevolent spirits. But, the book, the tome, was said to have been lost five centuries ago. Twenty knights had set out to find it and only three returned, telling the court of their failure. And yet, somehow, Jedar was in possession of the legendary book.

"I'm so dead now," Cody moaned. If it truly was the Tome of Laruel, and Jedar read it properly, it certainly would have the knowledge necessary to exorcize Cody.

Outside, Marek was having the same thoughts as his brother. "How did you find it?"

"I didn't," Jedar said.

"Then who-"

"I did," Antoth said in Cody's voice. "But that is a tale for another day. First, we must rid this body of its mind."

"Certainly," Marek said, clasping his hands behind his back. "Carry on."

Jedar stepped in front of Antoth and leaned in until he was all Cody could see. He opened the Tome to a marked page and scanned it until he found what he was looking for. He placed the tip of the wand on Antoth's forehead and began to mutter in an unknown language. The wand began to glow with a dark red light.

An incredible pain ripped through Cody's chest, right where his heart was. A split-second later, an identical pain started in his head. It felt like someone was stabbing him with red-hot knives from all sides.

He screamed, grabbing at his chest and head as the pain worsened. Through squinted eyes, he could see that he was glowing the same colour as the wand. Pain engulfed him and he crumpled into a ball. He had never experienced agony so horrible before. He didn't care if he died. He just wanted the pain to end.

Through the agony, Cody heard a loud crash, the splintering of wood and shouting. The pain vanished and Cody gasped. He lay, shuddering and panting.

Yells, the clashing of weapons and combat echoed through the mind space, but Cody couldn't make himself look up. He was too weak.

Suddenly, there was a sickening thud and everything went dark.

"What just happened?" Cody wondered. His voice sounded small in the crushing darkness.

Slowly, the coloured memory orbs came back to life, illuminating the mind space.

Cody uncurled, rubbing his chest where the incredible pain had been a few moments before. Grimacing, he hoped never to endure such agony again.

"What do I do now?" Cody wondered aloud.

"Whatever you like."

Cody whipped around and found himself face to face with a strange man and yet he knew exactly who it was. "Antoth."

"In the flesh," he said with a bow. "Or, in the mind, rather." He had a thin, angular face and a prominent, hooked nose under black hair that hung down to his chin.

Cody gaped. "How are you here?"

"The same way you are here," Antoth replied. "These bodies you see are not physical, they are subconscious constructs of ourselves we project into the mindscape."

"We're not real?" Cody looked down at his hands. With the glow and blurred edges trailing off, he could see how Antoth's explanation made sense.

"Oh, we are real, simply intangible," Antoth said.

"So, I can't punch you in the face?" Cody asked.

"I'm afraid not," Antoth said with a slight smile.

"Better make sure." Cody stepped ahead and threw a powerful right hook. His fist passed through Antoth's head as if it were made of mist.

"But of course." Antoth's smile was devoid of warmth.

Cody rolled his eyes and crossed his arms.

"You must have questions," Antoth said. "And, since we have nothing but time and you will die shortly, I would be happy to answer any questions you have."

A muscle in Cody's jaw jumped. He didn't want to indulge this body-snatching cultist, but he was curious. Also, he seemed to be the leader of the Forsaken, so who better to ask?

Cody groaned. "Ugh, fine, yes I have questions! Who are you, what's this cult about, why steal bodies and how the heck did you find the Tome of Laruel?"

"All good questions," Antoth said, folding his hands together. "As for who I am, my name is Antoth Remy Lokar. I come from a family of spice merchants who travelled up and down the east coast. I am something of a scholar and a philosopher."

"Not to mention a body-snatching cult leader," Cody said snidely.

"Yes, that too."

Cody spread his hands. "And you're just fine with that?"

"Of course," Antoth said. "It is my life's work. I discovered a way to achieve immortality."

That gave Cody pause. "You've done this before."

Antoth nodded. "Five times. This will be my seventh body, counting my original one, which you now see. I am four hundred and six years old."

Cody's jaw dropped. "Four hundred and six? How?"

"Simple," Antoth said. "I transfer my mind and soul into a new host body once the previous one grows too old."

"I can't believe that this is possible," Cody whispered.

"It is the truth. I long ago discovered how one could transfer their essence into another person."

"I think I saw that memory," Cody said. "In a bookstore, right?"

"Yes," Antoth said. "That was it. I knew it was possible, but I also knew there would be a period of trial and error. Not wanting to test it on myself-"

"Because of course you wouldn't."

Antoth cleared his throat and continued. "I created this brotherhood you call a cult so I had test subjects. After several failures, I succeeded in placing the mind of a man into another body. It was, in fact, Jedar, the one outside. He became my partner and friend as we grew our group little by little. Unfortunately, as we grew, so did our notoriety. People began to shun us and run us out of towns. We were soon ousted from most settlements on the eastern coast and we earned our name: The Forsaken."

"I'll admit, that's a cool name," Cody said, "But, still, I don't like you. You steal innocent people's bodies!"

"Hardly innocent," Antoth said. "We choose our hosts from the underground, where all make their living through thievery, cheating and killing. We are actually cleaning up the city."

"Oh, come on!" Cody cried. "You guys are doing the exact same things as they are! You're no better!"

"I respect your opinion, but don't expect it to change mine."

"Wasn't expecting it to," Cody grumbled. "You also still haven't explained how you found the Tome."

"Ah, yes, the fabled Tome." Antoth gazed past Cody, returning to a past adventure. "Back when I was in my original body, over four hundred years ago. As you know, every attempt to find it failed."

Cody nodded. "We've all heard the stories."

"And do you know why they all failed?"

"Uh, no."

Antoth clasped his hands behind his back. "It is because everyone who attempted to recover the Tome followed the clues left in a letter Laruel left to his brother before his death. And those clues led nowhere good. The real Tome was buried with Laruel in an unmarked grave near Rizzen, his birthplace."

"Really?" Cody said, unimpressed. "No one thought to look in his grave?"

"Not before me," Antoth said. "Now, I believe I have answered all your questions."

"I guess so."

"Good timing. I feel that I'm about to come to."

Cody glanced around. The mindscape was beginning to gradually lighten, turning grey. He looked back at Antoth, who was starting to fade away.

The old cultist raised a hand. "This will be the last time you see anyone. Farewell, and thank you."

"No, no, no!" Cody raced toward Antoth and leapt at him, trying to tackle him. He passed through the fading body, flailing wildly. He scrambled to turn around but when he did, Antoth was gone.

The mindscape was now back to white, the brightness still increasing. The window appeared, allowing Cody to see out into the real world.

His body was staring up at a wooden ceiling. It wasn't in great shape, cracked and chipped, mould and cobwebs in the corners.

Antoth sat up and Cody could see that he was on a straw mattress, stalks poking out of a busted seam.

"He's awake!" a familiar voice said.

Antoth turned his gaze and the faces of Kinzo, Miri, Evander, Snare and Ring came into focus.

Cody whooped. His friends had done it. They had rescued him.

"Cody! How are you feeling?" Evander asked.

"Sorry we took so long," Ring said. "The cultists were very good at losing us. Took a long time to track them down, even with a tip from a contact."

Kinzo laughed nervously. "Yeah, I didn't accidentally hit you in the head with a table leg."

"Who are you?" Antoth asked, sounding unsure of himself for the first time.

Miri's mouth dropped open and she smacked Kinzo's arm. "Kinzo! You've given him amnesia!"

"Ow! Sorry!" Kinzo yelped. "I didn't try to."

"Where have you taken me?" Antoth asked angrily.

"He's really confused," Ring said.

Inside his head, Cody groaned. "Oh, this is bad! I need to let them know it's not me! But how?" He bounced a fist off his leg as he thought.

Ring leaned close to Antoth and squinted her eyes. "Do you know your name?"

"I am Antoth."

"Uh, what now?" Kinzo asked.

Snare swore. Everyone turned to look at him.

"What is it?" Evander asked.

Snare licked his lips. "Uh, Cody may have been brainwashed. They got him."

There was a moment of profound silence and then everyone began yelling at Snare, saying how stupid his idea had been in the first place and how he should have been the one to get kidnapped. During the commotion, Antoth stood up and slowly began sneaking toward the door. He was nearly there when Evander noticed.

"He's escaping! Stop him!"

Antoth tried to run, but he was still woozy from the blow to his head and he stumbled. Kinzo slammed into him and tackled him to the ground. For a few seconds, all Cody could see out of the window was a cockroach scuttling across the floorboards. Then, Antoth was flipped over to see five angry faces.

"What have you done with him?" Evander demanded.

Antoth didn't reply, instead, he sniffed disdainfully.

Miri kicked him in the side. Fury blazed in her eyes.

"Hey!" Cody called. "That's still my body!" He knew they couldn't hear him, but yelling made him feel better. A sudden revelation struck him. Miri was a Mind Mage. She'd been learning telepathy. Maybe she could hear his thoughts. He began trying to project his thoughts, hoping that Miri would be able to hear them.

Outside, Evander and Kinzo hauled Antoth back onto the bed. Then, they stood between him and the door with his arms crossed.

"Give him back!" Kinzo said.

"I will tell you nothing," Antoth said. "This body is mine now."

Miri lunged ahead, intending to deck Antoth again, but Evander caught her arm. "No, don't."

C'mon, Miri. Hear me. I'm still alive, he thought.

Miri flinched and glanced around with confusion.

Yes! Yes, Cody thought. *It's me! I'm here!*

Miri squinted one eye and put a hand to her temple as if she had a headache. Cody heard a voice in his head say a tentative hello.

Miri! It's me! I'm here!

Cody?

Yeah!

Where are you?

I'm in my own head! This Antoth guy stole my body but didn't get rid of me completely.

You're inside your head, but there's another guy in control of you? She sounded confused.

Yes! That's it exactly, Cody thought.

I'm so glad you're alive, Miri said. *But how do we get you out?*

No idea. Also, it's very strange to hear you. Cody could actually hear Miri, a voice he had never heard before. It was high and soft with a flowing lilt to it.

It is pretty strange, Miri said. *Though, I gotta admit, it's hurting my head. I'm not very good at this telepathy stuff.*

Oh, sorry. We can stop now. You go tell the others.

I will, Miri said. *Bye.*

Cody felt her presence depart and he suddenly felt very lonely, trapped in the mindscape. He saw Miri jerk and blink a few times. She immediately turned to Kinzo and began signing rapidly, her hands a blur.

Kinzo held up his hands. "Whoa, whoa, slow down, Miri. All I got out of that was trash dumplings, and I know you aren't trying to tell me that."

Miri rolled her eyes in exasperation, but repeated the signs slower.

Kinzo's brows rose and his lips parted slightly. "He's...alive?" He pointed at Antoth. "Cody's in there? In his head?"

Miri nodded vigorously.

"You've got to be kidding!" Evander said.

"No!" Miri signed. "I just talked to him!"

"You can't talk, though," Kinzo said.

"Telepathically, stupid," Miri said.

"Oh, you actually managed it?"

"Yeah, surprising, right?" Miri replied.

Evander cut in. "Hey, focus."

"Right." Kinzo spun toward Antoth and jabbed a finger at him. "You. Buddy Guy. Give Cody back his body this very second, or so help me, I will not hesitate to nail your knees and elbows to the underside of a wagon and roll it off a cliff!"

"Dang," Ring smirked. "That escalated."

Antoth didn't flinch. He calmly looked past Kinzo's finger and said, "I can't."

"Whaddya mean you can't?" Kinzo asked, raising his voice.

"I have neither the knowledge, nor the ability to do so," Antoth said. "It cannot be undone. It would take someone to use three of the orders of magic at once to do it."

Kinzo's hand dropped to his side. "Oh... Three orders? But that's..."

"Impossible," Evander said. "No one can do that."

Cody felt like he had been punched in the stomach. He felt empty, drained. There was no way to undo what had been done. It would take three orders. Three. Cody truly felt all hope abandon him. He was doomed.

Outside, Miri covered her mouth with a hand and steadied herself against the wall. Evander rubbed his thumb and forefinger across his forehead. Kinzo and Ring stared at the floor and Snare crossed his arms, looking mildly put out.

Cody punched his palm. "No. No. Nope. I am not giving up. There has to be some other way." He glanced around at the thousands of memory orbs. "Antoth is really old. He's bound to have seen something over the centuries that can help me out. I've gotta investigate." He stood straight and wrung his hands together. Part of his brain told him that there was no chance of him finding anything that could help, but he didn't listen. He couldn't. If he did, he would totally give up and that was something he wasn't willing to do. Cody hated giving up. Especially when his life was at stake.

He corralled the nearest memory sphere and pushed his head inside. In an instant, he was transported to somewhere else. He was once again in Antoth's place, sitting on a tree stump on top of a green hill overlooking a forested valley. A narrow river wound lazily through the landscape as birds chirped and the breeze blew gently. In his hand were a scroll and a pen. An inkwell rested on the stump beside him.

What's he writing? Cody wondered. The scroll was covered in runes and symbols and pictograms that made no sense to him. He did know that they were channelling magic of some sort, but nothing like he had ever seen.

His arm, or Antoth's past arm moved, dipping the pen in the ink and scratching a symbol in the very centre of the scroll; two parallel lines on a diagonal slant from the upper left crossing over a triangle with the top corner left open and a small circle in its place. As Antoth lifted the pen from the final stroke, the symbol blazed a dark red and began to burn away the scroll until all that remained was the symbol floating in the air. It remained there for a moment before breaking apart and fading away.

The memory ended and Cody stumbled out into the mindscape once more.

"That was weird. I wonder what that had to do with anything? It wasn't any type of magic I've ever seen."

He glanced back at the window to the outside world. His friends were discussing how to rescue him, without much luck. They had no realistic idea of how to do so. The best idea was Ring's suggestion that they could sacrifice a goat.

Leaving them to their discussion, Cody entered another memory, a brown one. He found himself in a dimly lit room in what he assumed was an inn. The door and the shutters were closed and there were no items suggesting that he was staying in the room. Cody figured that Antoth was trying not to be found.

There was a knock at the door. Memory Antoth walked quickly to the door and opened it, revealing a small, slender figure in a cowled cloak.

Antoth waved the figure in. "Were you followed?"

"I don't believe so," answered a female voice. She threw back her hood.

"Whoa," Cody said.

She was a raven-haired beauty. Cody had never seen anyone whose looks rivalled hers. High cheekbones, sculpted eyebrows, full lips, a graceful neck and mesmerizing blue eyes, she had it all.

Antoth and through him, Cody, wrapped the woman in an embrace. They stayed locked for a long moment and then they brought their lips together in a tender kiss.

"Whaaa...?" Cody was helpless to do anything as the memory versions of the people shared this lovely moment. "This is not how I pictured my first kiss. I certainly didn't expect it to be in the place of a man in whose memory the immaterial construct of myself is in while trying to escape the mindscape of my own body, which the man whose memory I am in now controls." He paused. "This is bloody confusing."

The two finally broke away, although their hands remained clasped together.

"Layla, I must warn you, you are not safe," Antoth said.

"This I know," Layla said. "It is why I came here cloaked as I am."

"No, you don't understand," Antoth said. "You aren't safe from my brethren. They grow jealous of you."

"Of me? Why?"

Antoth let go of Layla's hand and clasped them behind his back. "They fear that I have given you the gift many of them wait for."

Confusion crossed Layla's face. "What gift?"

Antoth reached out and brushed her cheek, staring into her striking eyes. "The gift of immortality."

A gasp escaped Layla's lips. "Immortality? Truly?"

"Yes. Long did I search for it and at last, I found it. It is possible."

"And you would give to me this gift?"

Antoth nodded. "I would. But not yet. It is for when one is nearing death."

The sound of footsteps echoed down the corridor. Antoth turned to face the door, changing Cody's view. "Get behind me."

Seconds later, the door crashed open and smashed against the wall. Six armed men entered the room. They fanned out in a semi-circle, pointing their weapons at Antoth. A seventh man entered the room behind them.

Antoth sighed. "Jedar."

"Antoth," Jedar replied evenly.

Whoa! That's Jedar! Cody thought. *"But wait, I thought they were partners.*

"What's the meaning of this?" Antoth asked.

"You know very well," Jedar said. He pointed at Layla.

"What about her?"

Jedar raised his voice. "You know why we're here. Now hand her over!"

"I will not," Antoth said.

Jedar frowned. "I won't ask again."

"I know you won't," Antoth said.

"This doesn't have to end violently, as long as you didn't tell her. Did you tell her, Antoth?"

Antoth met Jedar's gaze but remained silent.

"Oh, Antoth. I'm sorry, but now this only ends one way." Jedar looked to the man to his right and gave a curt nod.

The six armed men began to advance.

"Out of the way," one of the men said to Antoth.

Antoth sighed deeply. He launched himself at the man and caught his cheek with a vicious right hook that sent the man stumbling. He spun around and punched another man in the chest.

No use, Cody thought. *You're unarmed and outnumbered badly.*

Layla's scream pierced the air. Antoth immediately turned to run to her, seeing two attackers pin her against the wall. Before he could reach her, something hard cracked down on his head, knocking him to the floor. His vision blurred and he tried to get to his feet, but strong arms grabbed him and held him fast. He struggled and yelled, but was unable to break free.

He could only watch as the men drove their swords through Layla's chest without remorse. Antoth's scream of anguish filled the room as his lover's body crumpled to the floor.

The room faded out and the whiteness faded in as the memory ended.

"That was… something," Cody said. "It's a wonder Antoth doesn't hate Jedar."

He glanced around at all the memory orbs. There were at least thirty within arms reach. "There's gotta be one that shows Antoth learning how to undo this magical mind-swapping. I just have to find it. In a sea of thousands upon thousands of memories." His shoulders slumped. "Yeah right."

He felt an itch on the back of his neck, right at the base of his skull. He turned around, but there was nothing but more memory spheres. The itch increased extending down his spine and up into his brain.

"Ah, what is that?" He rubbed his neck.

The feeling intensified and Cody finally figured out what was happening. He opened his mind. *Um, Miri, is that you?*

Of course it's me, Stone Ears, Miri said, annoyed. *I've been trying to reach you forever.*

Sorry, Cody said.

Whatever, Miri said. *We've come up with a plan. But you're not going to like it.*

Why not?

Miri hesitated. *Well, we'll need someone's help.*

Whose?

There was a pause before Miri answered. The name she said sank Cody's hope like a ship with a hole in its hull.

Rorien Stern.

CHAPTER 20

Hang on. Hold up, Cody thought. *You're suggesting that we should kidnap Rorien Stern's sister, give her to the Forsaken, then tell Stern they have her and help him get her back in exchange for having the Kar-Sang get me back in control of my body?*

That's about right, yeah, Miri said.

Are you out of your mind? Cody cried.

No, this is serious. We have no other ideas. We need someone who can use more than one order of magic. And we don't know anybody who can do that. But we do know that Kar-Sang can. So, unless you know where we can find some other ones, we're going through Stern.

We are talking about the same Rorien Stern, right? Cody asked. *The one that tried to kill you and the others multiple times, actually killed Rosalyn and terrorized Blackthrush for weeks?*

Yep, that Rorien Stern, Miri said.

Cody shook his head. *No. No way. Not happening. This is a terrible idea. We are not doing it.*

Miri's mental voice took on a hard edge. *Well, it's a good thing you can't actually do anything about it, being stuck in here. You have no say in the matter.*

Cody tried to protest, but Miri withdrew her mind, leaving Cody alone again. He growled and looked out the window.

"Did he like the plan?" Kinzo asked, once he realized that Miri had stopped talking to Cody.

Miri signed her answer. "Not exactly. But he can't do anything to stop us, so let's go ahead and do this."

"Great," Snare said in a tone that didn't agree with what he said. "The sooner we get this over with, the sooner we can get rid of this cult and get on with our lives."

"Also, we want to help Cody," Ring said.

Snare rolled his eyes.

Evander clapped his hands. "No time to waste, then. On to Rivera Farm."

Kinzo walked up to the bedside and looked down at Antoth. "Are you gonna come quietly?"

"I should think not," Antoth said haughtily.

"Shame, I like Cody's face." Kinzo drew back his fist and jammed it into Antoth's cheek.

"Oh, come on!" Cody yelled inside his own head. "You're gonna break something!"

Antoth shrugged off the blow. "Pitiful attempt."

Kinzo growled from the back of his throat, a very animal sound that he was known for. "Shut up." He punched him again.

"Stop!" Cody cried. "That's my face!"

Antoth spit bloody saliva at Kinzo.

Kinzo swore and grabbed Antoth's hair in one hand and began hitting him over and over. "Just go to sleep already!"

Cody moaned in self-pity as the window blacked out and the mindscape began to darken. Antoth was finally unconscious. "Kinzo, when I get out of here, you are going to regret that." He crossed his arms as he waited for Antoth's construct to appear. He didn't have to wait long.

"Greetings, Cody," Antoth said as his glowing, indistinct form solidified. "My, my. That grey-haired fellow certainly did a number on our face."

"My face, not yours," Cody grumbled.

"And yet, it was I who felt the pain and not you," Antoth said.

"That part doesn't bother me."

Antoth smiled. "It is good to see that you retained your sense of humour."

"Why, did you think you stole it from me along with my body?" Cody asked with a huff.

"No. That is not possible. One cannot steal any aspect of another's mind or personality. Well, they can, but they cannot take it for themselves."

244

Cody muttered something and crossed his arms even harder.

"I am curious," Antoth said, ignoring Cody's anger and annoyance. "What is the plan your friends have concocted?"

"Didn't you hear?" Cody asked.

"No, they whispered to one another."

"At least they had that much sense," Cody said. "And no, I'm not going to tell you what it is."

"Even though you don't agree with it?"

Cody's brows rose until he remembered that that had been said aloud. "No, I don't agree with it, but I can't do anything about it and so, it'll happen. Or, at least, they'll try to make it happen and fail miserably."

"Will you tell me why you don't approve of the plan?"

Cody ran his tongue along his teeth. "Because the people involved are more likely to kill them rather than help them."

"Ah. That does seem rather foolhardy on their part."

"Very much so," Cody agreed.

They lapsed into silence. Cody was in a bad mood and wasn't keen on talking. After a time, Antoth said, "I suppose you've been browsing my memories."

Cody didn't bother denying it. He nodded sharply.

"I would have done the same thing, in your position," Antoth said. "What did you see?"

"Uh, you on a hill writing something on a scroll and then it burned up."

A flash of concern appeared in Antoth's eyes for a split-second before he composed himself. "Do you know what it said."

"Not at all. It was a bunch of runes and symbols that I've never seen before."

Again, a quick expression from Antoth, this one of relief.

There's something important about that scroll and that last symbol, Cody figured. He raised an eyebrow. "Is there something special about it?"

Antoth chewed his cheek. "Aye, there is. But if you are expecting me to tell you what it is, you are in for a disappointment."

Cody inclined his head, trying to feign indifference. "Fair enough."

"What else did you see?"

"Something, I doubt you like to remember," Cody said. "Layla's death."

Antoth sighed and his eyes grew sad and distant. "Oh, my sweet Layla."

"You must hate Jedar," Cody said.

"I did for a time. I wanted him dead. But we had signed a blood pact not easily broken. And, in time, I grew to realize that he was right. She had not been part of the brotherhood and yet I told her our most sacred secret. Her death was necessary to keep the brotherhood alive."

"Good lord, you are really fanatical," Cody said with a sort of disappointed awe.

"Some call us that," Antoth said. "I prefer the term enlightened."

Cody tipped his head and put on a condescending face. "You're enlightened because you realized that your friend was helping you by murdering your girlfriend who had done nothing wrong except trust you?"

"In a way, yes."

"God, you're horrible," Cody said with disgust.

"You are simply too young to understand," Antoth said.

"No, you're just a nutcase, who is scared of death."

Antoth sniffed. "And you're not?"

"Well, I mean, yeah, a bit," Cody said. "I certainly don't want to die, especially because I haven't even lived two decades. I haven't lived enough yet. But I know that everyone has their time. Everyone dies. And that's just how it is. I hope my time isn't for a while, but I'm not going to cower from it by killing young people who have their whole lives ahead of them. You are a selfish, cowardly leech that the world would be much better off without."

"Hmm," Antoth said. "Well, that may be so, but I don't care. The world turned its back on me over four hundred years ago. What the world thinks is none of my concern. I will continue to survive, like I always have while everyone else lays down and dies."

Cody scoffed and turned away. "Just leave me alone. I'm done with all this for now." He walked away until Antoth was lost behind the floating spheres. He sat down and crossed his legs, resting his elbows on his thighs and cupping his hands around his chin. "This is the worst day of my life."

~~~

Cody watched out the window of the mindscape as his friends stopped at the gate leading to Rivera Farm. Antoth had come to partway through the journey and had tried to make a scene, but Kinzo and Evander had subdued him. Now, he was bound and gagged, wearing a hooded cloak to conceal his restraints.

"Never thought I'd be back here," Kinzo muttered. Miri nodded her wholehearted agreement.

"So, how are we planning on doing the kidnapping?" Evander asked.

Kinzo held up a finger. "Um, I am not hanging under a sheep again. Just putting that out there.

"Yeah, well, I don't think Stern would fall for that twice," Snare said.

"How can we get in without anyone noticing?" Miri asked.

"Well, Ring could do it," Evander said.

Ring bobbed her head, and wiggled her fingers, drawing attention to the ring on her left hand.

"But she'd be alone, and that's not gonna cut it," Snare said.

Ring turned to him. "Why, you don't think I can do it myself?" There was a hint of challenge in her voice.

"You could get in and probably knock her out, but there's no way you could drag her unconscious body out on your own."

Ring crossed her arms and pouted, although she didn't argue any further.

"How are we going to do this then?" Miri asked. Kinzo translated. Everybody shrugged, having no ideas.

"Uh oh, here comes somebody," Evander said. All heads turned to see a middle-aged man with greying hair walking down the path toward them. He was clearly a farmhand, wearing dirty working clothes and leather gloves. He chewed on a stalk of wheat. "I say, hello there! What are you younguns doing here?"

"Uhh, we're looking for Mr. Stern's sister," Snare said, trying to seem innocent.

"You mean, Ara?" the man asked.

"Yessss," Kinzo said. "That would be the name of the person we are looking for."

Cody blew out a noisy breath. They really needed to stop letting Kinzo talk when they were lying to people. He was horrible at it.

The farmhand raised a hand in a sort of shrug. "Well, sorry folks, but she's not here. She left with Master Stern to go to the Festival."

"Should have seen that coming," Kinzo muttered.

"They're staying in the Aedon," the farmhand said. "Haven't been home for a few days and we aren't expecting them for another two."

"Thank you for the information," Ring said sweetly, batting her eyelashes. "You've been such a help. We'll be on our way now."

The man dipped his head. "You're welcome."

The group turned away. Evander had to give Antoth a little extra shove to get him going. Cody's field of view changed as Antoth swivelled around and followed behind Ring as they headed back into the city. Antoth occasionally gazed to the left or right, but for the most part, he stared at the back of Ring's head, not giving Cody much to look at.

"I can't believe we didn't think to check at the Festival," Miri said, turning around so the others could see her hands.

"Yeah, we're pretty dumb," Kinzo said.

"This might actually make the whole thing easier," Snare said. "Lots of crowded areas, plenty of cover, plus not Stern's home turf. We'll just have to separate them somehow."

"Yeah, it'll be a real piece of cake," Evander said sarcastically.

"We might need more help," Ring said.

"We've still got the other three in the Aedon," Miri said. "I wonder if they've found who's behind the cult."

"We should keep this as secret as possible," Snare said.

"So, you're saying we shouldn't get our headmaster involved," Kinzo said.

Snare shook his head. "Absolutely not."

"Ok, well, there goes my plan," Kinzo muttered.

Ring tipped her head. "What was your plan?"

"Doesn't matter," Kinzo said.

"C'mon, what is it?" Evander prodded.

Kinzo tilted his head up. "Nope. Doesn't matter." He walked away, withholding his secret, prompting the others to follow behind and bug him. He refused to answer despite all of their cajoling and coaxing and threatening. The others finally gave up and talked of other things as they crossed the fence at one of the secret access points and made their way across the city and entered back into the festival grounds.

"The Midarra Festival," Antoth said, apparently having worked the gag loose. Cody could hear his smile, despite not being able to see it. "The memories I have of this place, well, there's a lot from each time I've visited."

"We don't care," Snare snapped, stuffing the cloth back in his mouth. "Let's just go get the other team and get on with this mess."

Evander pointed to the clump of tents that belonged to Blackthrush. "We'll have the best luck there, I think."

I hope Aldus finds out about this, Cody thought. *They need all the help they can get. I really need my body back!*

The group wound their way through the cramped, confusing labyrinth of tents and booths. Miri had to pull Kinzo away from a stall serving fresh venison. They finally arrived and Cody spotted several familiar faces.

Kindrelle jumped up from the barrel she was sitting on and ran up to them. "There you are! Where have you been? Half the instructors are out looking for you!"

"We had an adventure," Kinzo said. "Don't ask any questions, because we won't tell you, ok?"

Kindrelle's eyebrows rose. "What?" She looked at Snare and Ring. "And who are they?"

"Just some friends," Evander said. "Do you know where Levi and Kana are?"

"Well, Levi just got back from escaping prison," Kindrelle said.

"What?"

"You weren't the only ones with an unauthorized adventure," she said, hands on hips.

Evander couldn't believe it. "He went to prison?"

"Leave him alone for five minutes and this happens," Kinzo muttered.

"Is he alright?" Miri asked, signing to Kindrelle.

249

It took the other girl a few moments to decipher the signs, but she finally said, "Yes, he is ok. He's in his tent." She was still talking as everyone took off, Evander hauling Antoth away by the arm. "You guys are gonna get in trouble one of these times!" Kindrelle called after them.

They raced over to blue camp's tent and threw back the flap. Levi was on the other side, about to do the same.

"Oh, hey guys."

"You went to jail!" Miri signed, practically screaming with her hands.

"What went wrong?" Evander asked.

"You are so, incredibly, impossibly stupid," Kinzo said.

Levi scratched his cheek, then answered them in order. "Yes, I did, there was a douchebag in the Aedon who sold me out and thanks, Kinzo."

"What'd you do?" Ring asked.

Levi tapped his wrist. "Basically, I got framed for stealing a signet ring from a noble."

"And how'd you manage to escape?" Snare asked. "If I recall, you're pathetic."

Levi smiled falsely. "You guys are too nice. It's a long story that involves lost princes, professional assassins, sea serpents and a raft. Oh, also there was the boiling hallucination death field." He rubbed several raised blisters on the back of his neck.

Everyone stood silently for a good while.

Inside the mindscape, Cody had a chuckle. When Levi did something, it always ended, usually through fluke, with him being wrapped up in the most ridiculous things ever. And yet, he always came out unharmed.

Everyone moved inside the tent, which had been empty before.

"Well, it's good to see you guys again," Levi said. "How did your half of the plan go?"

Miri crossed her arms and didn't answer.

"Not good," Evander said.

"Bad," Ring added.

"Horrible, really," Kinzo said. "Pretty much couldn't have been worse."

Snare spread his hands. "We could have died."

"True," Kinzo said. "It technically could have been worse."

Levi looked from one to the other. "What happened?"

Another long silence.

Kinzo groaned. "Uh, fine. Basically, Cody went in as bait so we could find the headquarters and we couldn't find it, uh, so they, uh kinda, I don't know, summoned their stupid leader guy inside of Cody's body and tried to kill him, except something went wrong and now Cody is trapped inside his own head and the cult guy is in his body." He pointed at the cloaked person.

Antoth managed to push the hood back with his bound hands and take out the gag.

Levi approached, his mouth hanging open. "You're not Cody?"

"No, I am Antoth."

Levi spun around, alarmed and yelled. "Well, get him back!"

"We're working on it," Evander said. "Uh, but the only way it can be undone, is if we get the help of a Kar-Sang."

Levi's face fell. "Oh no. Please tell me this has nothing to do with Rorien Stern." The following silence answered him. Levi groaned as he dragged his hands down his face.

"Don't worry," Ring said. "We have part of a plan."

Levi glanced up. "How much of a plan?"

Ring stuck out her bottom lip. "Uh, like maybe half."

"That's actually better than I was expecting," Levi said. "What's the half of the plan?"

"Well," Ring said, fiddling with her namesake. "We kidnap Stern's sister, give her to the cult, then tell Stern they have her but only after he agrees to have his Kar-Sang get Cody back. Then, we help Stern take down the Forsaken, solving all our problems."

"That sounds like every part of that is going to go wrong," Levi said.

"Oh, it definitely will," Kinzo said. "You're involved, remember?"

Levi made a rude gesture at him.

"You are in quite the situation, aren't you?"

Everyone turned around to see Aldus standing at the front of the tent. Snare swore and put his hands on his head.

"Oh, hi, Aldus," Evander said. "You heard all that, huh?"

Aldus nodded, a wry smile on his lips.

"Well, yeah, we're in a predicament," Evander said.

Antoth took a step toward Aldus.

What's he doing? Cody wondered.

251

"Aldus Calanol!" Antoth yelled.

Aldus looked at Cody's body quizzically. His eyes went wide and he whispered, "Antoth."

"You backstabbing son of-" Antoth began. Aldus snapped his fingers and Antoth stopped talking. He still moved his mouth, but no sound came out. Antoth touched his throat, shocked.

Everyone shared the emotion. They stared at the headmaster. "What just happened?" Levi asked.

"That is none of your concern," Aldus said.

Cody was astounded. Aldus and Antoth clearly knew each other and from the anger in Antoth's voice, they hadn't left on good terms. Cody wanted to know what Aldus could possibly have done to anger Antoth so.

Aldus gave his head a shake and composed himself. "Well now, you kids best tell me everything that has happened."

"No way," Snare said, arms crossed. "Why would we do that?"

"Because I can help you," Aldus said simply.

"Why would you help us?" Ring asked, sounding more curious than hostile. "It's our problem, not your students'."

"That may have been true," Aldus said. "Originally. But now, they are involved and in some danger and I am sworn to protect them."

"We should accept his help," Miri signed. "This is too big of a problem to deal with on our own."

"I agree," Evander said. "Plus, if we are successfully gonna kidnap Ara Stern, we're gonna need a big crew."

"So, bring in the rest of blue camp?" Levi figured.

"Why not," Kinzo said. "It's their buddy stuck in there anyway." He pointed at Antoth.

Aldus held up a hand. "Levi, remember, the oath you had Stern swear only prevents him from coming after you. If you go to him, he is free to retaliate."

"Yeah, I know," Levi said. "That's why we need a big team."

Aldus nodded. "Very well. I just wanted you to understand the repercussions."

"I do."

Snare sighed and then walked up to Aldus. "So, you'll help us?"

Aldus placed a hand on his shoulder. "Of course, son."

"Sweet," Kinzo said. "Let's go plan a human heist."

CHAPTER 21

"Is everyone clear on the plan?" Aldus swung his gaze around the table. Levi, his nine friends and the three urchins all nodded.

Butterflies fluttered in Levi's stomach, the kind one got when about to do something risky. And what they were about to do was very risky. His fingers brushed over Kyner's mark on his wrist.

"We've got to do this carefully and precisely," Kana said, hands spread on the table. "If anyone messes up, we'll all be in serious trouble."

"You can count on us," Ember said. The five others from blue camp had been eager to help once they knew Cody was in trouble.

"Yes, you can," Guy said, making Kana scoff.

"We will all do our part," Kaito said.

"Great. Now the fun part," Kinzo said. "Prep work. Yay."

Miri scolded him. "It's important."

"I know, I know," Kinzo said. "Alright, go team, let's get em, yeah."

Levi shook his head. Kinzo always had the worst attitude. At least he always came through in the end. All his friends did, in fact. Levi glanced at all their faces. Each one had helped him in a time of trouble.

"Get going," Aldus said, shooing them away. Everyone broke away from the table and rushed out of the tent. The group split up as each person went to do a specific task that would assist them in their mission.

Levi's job was overwatch. He was to be their eye in the sky when the heist went off. He needed a high vantage point from where he could see everything. The plan was to take Ara at the ring where the knights duelled, so that's where Levi headed.

As he walked past the tents, dodging carts, people and wagons, he felt like everyone was about to find out what he was up to and put a stop to it. Each person that made eye contact felt like the one to blow the whistle. He wiped his forehead, telling himself that he was being foolish. No one knew what he was up to. Still, he couldn't convince himself and kept looking over his shoulder.

He arrived at the event setup. The crowd in the stands was cheering on the two knights in the midst of a bout. Levi could hear the clanging of sword on sword as they fought. A pompous-looking noble in a frilly red suit walked by with a silver cane. Levi wondered if perhaps he was the one funding the Forsaken.

After he had returned from his little escapade in prison, Kana had informed him that they had found no signs of the benefactor while he was gone, meaning he had pretty much been jailed for nothing. He shrugged. Right now, he had other things to worry about. They were about to tangle with Rorien Stern. Everything needed to go exactly right, or Levi would end up on the wrong side of a Kar-Sang again.

"Where's a good lookout point?" Levi asked himself. He scanned the area, looking for a tall structure he could get into without raising suspicion. His eyes landed upon a watchtower of sorts that overlooked both the duelling ring and the archery range to the south. "That'll do nicely."

As he strode around the knights' service tents and the bleachers on the near side, he picked at his blisters and the dead skin that was beginning to flake off. Arriving at the base of the tower, he estimated it to be about forty feet to the platform and ten to the roof. There were a few people up there.

"You want up, son?"

Turning, Levi saw a rather tall man with a thin, curling moustache standing near the ladder. His tunic was striped with red and grey and he wore a satchel over his shoulder.

"Uh, yeah, that'd be great."

"Well, in that case, you're going to need one of these." The man produced a little metal token from his bag. It was an inch by inch square with a yellow star stamped on it.

"How do I get that?" Levi asked.

"You must win it," the man said. "At the commoner's range."

"Like, shooting?"

"Exactly like that. Each bullseye wins you a token which is good for a one-time entry to the observation tower."

"Ok, I'll try that. Thanks," he said. The man waved as Levi headed for the archery range. He sighed. He was no good at archery and was never going to hit the bullseye. If only there was some way to get really good. "Wait! What if I get someone to do it for me? I could get Adam to do it. He's a great shot! Now, where to find him?"

He figured that his best bet would be back at the Blackthrush camp. Even if Adam wasn't there, Levi could still ask others who might know his whereabouts. He turned back east and set off for his temporary home. Halfway back, he ran into Gwen from green camp.

"Hey, Gwen!"

"Oh, hey, Levi," Gwen said, carrying a basket of apples.

Levi pointed at the basket.

She smiled. "Oh, this is for Taro. I don't know what he wants with it, but he got me to pick it up. You know how he is."

Levi smirked, figuring Taro was up to another prank. "Yeah. Hey, have you seen Adam around?"

Gwen pursed her lips. "Um, I saw him at lunch, but not since. Why?"

"Oh, I just need his help," Levi said.

"Well, sorry, I can't help you," Gwen apologized.

"That's alright," Levi said. "Have fun with whatever Taro's planning."

"I will," Gwen said. "Bye."

"Bye." Levi left her and continued back to camp. He sped to a jog, but it still took him another five minutes.

The first person he saw was El Fen. "Perfect."

The knight saw Levi coming and raised a hand. "Levi, how are you?"

"Not bad, not bad," Levi said.

"Good to hear, considering you were recently in prison," El Fen said with a smile.

Levi laughed. "That was, uh, quite something. Glad it's over. What about you? How are things going?"

"Quite well. I've had three matches and won all of them. Also, I had a marvellous luncheon with Countess Kerra of Redvale. I haven't seen her in several years. We had much to talk about."

"That's great. When's your next match?"

"Soon," El Fen replied. "It's against Turner the Bold. He's quite the scrapper. Going to give me a real run for my money, I think."

"I hope you beat him," Levi said. "Uh, I need to find your son. Do you know where he is?"

"I do," El Fen said. "Or, I did, rather. He was meeting with that Lawson fellow. Teaching him some archery tips, I think. That was a half-hour ago, so I'm not certain he will still be there."

"At the archery range," Levi sighed. "Of course. I was right next to it. Now I gotta go back."

El Fen chuckled.

"Thanks. Good luck with your match." Levi started heading away.

"Thank you and farewell," El Fen called after him. Levi waved over his shoulder without turning.

On his way back to the archery range, he caught a glimpse of Kana and Miri as they hurried to complete their part of the plan. He wondered if anyone was done or if they were all having setbacks like he was.

He finally came out into the clearing around the range where no one was allowed to pitch a tent. He scanned the crowd for Adam and spotted him in the farthest lane.

Closer to him, he saw a quartet walking toward him; Corvin, Vonn, Aster and Adelle, the bullies of Blackthrush.

"Uh oh," Levi said. He looked for an escape, but they were fixated on him. In a few seconds, he was surrounded. "Hi," Levi said, trying to seem unfazed.

"Well, if it isn't Mr. Special, Levi Sheppard," Corvin said.

"Always getting into messes," Aster said.

"And never getting in trouble," Vonn added.

Corvin crossed his arms. "Just escaped prison, eh? What were you doing that got you there?"

"Uh, I messed with the wrong people," Levi said.

"Looks like that's about to happen again," Adelle said.

Levi's shoulders drooped. "Oh, come on, guys. Do we really have to do this? I'm in a hurry!"

"Oh, little baby's in a hurry," Corvin mocked. "What, you gotta mess with more Kar-Sang?"

"Actually, yeah, I do," Levi said.

Corvin snarled. "Shut up!" He gave him a shove.

Levi stepped backward near Adelle, who shoved him in the back. He stumbled ahead. All four of them took turns shoving him. Then, Corvin moved out of the way and stuck his leg out, tripping Levi. He hit the ground hard and bit his lip. Hot blood sprayed across his mouth, filling it with a coppery taste.

Growling in annoyance, Levi pushed himself to his knees. A boot nailed him in the ribs, knocking him over. He saw a fist coming down and leaned aside. The blow glanced off his left cheekbone.

The four attackers began insulting him as they rained down blows on him. He blocked as many as he could but it didn't do much. He was pummeled from all sides, acquiring bruise after bruise.

There was a loud *twang* and a yell of pain. The beating stopped and Levi looked up at Vonn, who was holding a hand to a bloody ear.

Everyone turned to see Adam standing twenty feet away with a drawn bow. "The next one I will put through your knee, crippling you." His voice was devoid of emotion.

"You'll regret that!" Corvin yelled as he rushed him. Adam calmly sighted up his shot and released the arrow, sending it into the front of Corvin's knee. With a cry, the bully collapsed, the joint ruined. By the time everyone looked from Corvin back to Adam, he already had another arrow nocked and aimed at Aster.

"Let's get out of here!" Adelle cried. She and Vonn took off. Aster stayed just long enough to help Corvin hobble off.

Adam walked over and offered Levi a hand up. Levi gratefully accepted. He groaned. Everything was sore. The bruises were already colouring and a few places blood had been drawn. His left eye was swelling.

"Are you alright?" Adam asked.

"Not really," Levi said, holding a hand to his ribs. "I just got the ever-living crap beaten out of me. Thanks for getting rid of them."

"You are welcome," Adam said. "I could not allow a friend to be attacked. I put an end to it."

"I'm glad you did," Levi said. He grimaced in pain. "I'm going to be a walking bruise tomorrow."

"Ooh, you look terrible."

Levi glanced up to see Lawson looking on. "Thanks."

"Do you want me to have those four arrested?" Lawson asked. "I certainly could."

"No," Levi said. "It'd be too much of a hassle. Besides, I'm on a schedule and I need your help, Adam."

"My help? For what purpose?"

Levi explained that he needed Adam to win him a token so he could get into the observation tower.

"I will certainly help you," Adam agreed.

Levi paused. "You will? Just like that? No persuading?"

"Indeed. I will do it," Adam said.

"I had a whole thing planned to say."

"You do not need to say anymore. Let us go." Adam looked back at Lawson. "I will see you at a later time to continue your practice."

"Of course." Lawson dipped his head. "I look forward to it."

Adam and Levi headed over to the commoner's range, beyond the main one. It took some time as Levi was still quite sore. He was disappointed to see only two lanes and long lines for each.

"We will have to wait," Adam stated.

"Mm hmm." Levi wasn't pleased with yet another setback. They got in line and waited for fifteen minutes before it was Adam's turn to shoot. The man running the range gave him five arrows and explained that each time he hit the bullseye, he would get a token.

Adam nodded, accepted the arrows and prepared to fire. Levi watched as he drew back the bow smoothly and evenly. He made tiny, minute adjustments as he aimed, compensating for the crosswind. When he was ready, he simply released the arrow. It careened ahead, striking the target just outside the centre ring.

"Very close!" the man supervising said. "Well done."

Adam didn't reply, just cocked his head slightly as he considered the shot. He nocked, drew, aimed and fired in two seconds. This time, his aim was true and the arrow hit dead centre.

"Yes!" Levi cheered.

Adam allowed himself a small smile. He shot the remaining three arrows, each one striking the bullseye.

"Incredible!" the man said, hands in the air. "Four out of five! Well done!" The crowd lined up cheered as he handed Adam four tokens.

Levi and Adam exited the range. Levi clapped him on the shoulder. "Way to go! That was great!" Then he winced at the movement.

"Thank you," Adam said, looking satisfied. He tried to hand Levi all the tokens, but Levi only took one, explaining that he only needed one and Adam deserved the rest.

"What are you going to do now?" Adam asked.

"I've gotta meet some people," Levi said.

Adam nodded. "I do need something to eat. I shall have something sweet, I think. Sweet for victory." He smiled to himself and his joke.

Levi snorted. "Ok, see ya later."

"Yes, farewell."

Levi headed back to the Blackthrush camp again, taking longer as he limped along, nursing his injuries. Upon arrival, he entered Aldus' tent, the prearranged meeting spot. He was the last to arrive, except for Ring, who was on lookout.

"Whoa! You look awful!" Guy said as he entered.

"What happened?" Kana stepped close to him and looked him over.

"Just a little incident," Levi said. "It's taken care of. All good."

Naomi looked concerned. "Are you sure? You look pretty beat up."

"I'll manage," Levi said. "Is everyone ready?"

"Indeed," Aldus said. "Now, all we have to do is wait for the go-ahead from Ring."

Levi nodded. They had decided that, since Aldus was a very proficient Mind Mage, he would be used to communicate with everyone. They had all allowed him access to their minds and Aldus had left the channels open. That way, he could talk to each of them and relay the information to others.

While they waited for Ring's signal, they all went over their parts of the plan again, making sure that they had everything right. It would not do for something to go awry halfway through.

Now that the time was almost upon them, the butterflies in Levi's stomach returned with a vengeance. He couldn't stay still, he kicked at the ground and tapped his fingers nervously.

He could tell the others were anxious as well. Latch chewed on his nails, Kinzo constantly licked his lips, Guy massaged the knuckle of his missing finger and Ember fiddled with the hilt of her rapier. The only ones who seemed calm were Aldus, Kaito and Snare.

At last, Aldus, who had been resting on his mat with his eyes closed, stood and said, "It's time."

There was a collective deep breath.

"Let's do this," Evander said. Everyone nodded in agreement.

Coral led the way out of the tent. Levi was the last to leave. He looked back at Naomi, who was staying behind to make sure the sleeping Antoth didn't wake up.

"Good luck," she said.

"Thanks," Levi replied as he ducked out of the tent.

The twelve walked to the area assigned for the heist. The closer they got, the faster Levi's heart beat. He barely noticed the bruises covering him. When they arrived, Levi swallowed past the lump in his throat.

Aldus stopped and turned to the group. "Everyone does their part and this goes off smoothly. No mistakes."

"For Cody," Miri signed. Everyone repeated the two words. Then, they all dispersed.

Levi went as fast as he could to the tower. The moustached man was still there.

"Here you go," Levi said, handing the man his token. He stepped aside to allow Levi to climb the ladder. His limbs shook as he climbed the many rungs, but he made it to the platform.

Exhaling forcefully, he stood up and stretched. There was one other person in the tower. Levi's eyes grew wide. "Adam? What are you doing up here?"

Adam turned. "Levi. I am watching my father's match. Is that not what you came up here to do?"

"No, yeah, of course," Levi lied. "That's exactly why I'm up here."

"Come have a seat," Adam offered, patting the chair next to him.

"Oh, no thanks, I think I'd rather stand. You know, bruises and stuff." He rubbed his sore ribs.

"Very well." Adam turned his attention back to the ring.

Cheers went up from the crowd as the knights were introduced.

Are you all set, Levi? Aldus' voice resonated in Levi's head.

Yes, Levi thought. *I can see Stern and his entourage. They're all sitting where we predicted.*

Good, Aldus said. *Let us begin.*

Wait, did Ring get in position on the flag? He was referring to the large flagpole on the edge of the bleachers. It flew the king's banner.

Yes, she's there. Everyone is ready, Aldus said.

Ok, Levi said with a long breath. *Let's go.* He leaned over the side of the platform, trying to see everything at once. He held his breath until Coral stood up in the stands. She was right in front of Stern and his goons. She began yelling and jeering at one of the knights as a distraction. Hopefully, it wasn't El Fen.

As soon as Coral started, Levi glanced up at the flagpole. Partway up, he could make out a faint shimmering where Ring was busy sawing through the pole. With a loud crack, it fell right where it was supposed to, narrowly missing a large bearded man. The flag landed on top of Stern's section of the bleachers, causing a panic as people were trapped under fifty square feet of fabric.

Go! Go now! Levi mentally yelled at Aldus. He couldn't see under the bleachers, but he knew that Aldus would be opening the specially prepared bench seat under Ara and putting her to sleep.

She's unconscious, Aldus reported.

A few seconds later, Levi watched Kinzo and Evander in cook outfits emerge from under the benches with a cart of food, covered with a sheet. Ara was hidden in a compartment underneath. They hustled away from the tent to a tent they had cleared out before.

Something caught Levi's eye. The flag went flying in the air with a gust of summoned air. Rorien Stern began moving animatedly, motioning at the seat.

Sten knows she's gone, Levi said.

I'm out of sight, Aldus said.

Levi swung his gaze back to the tent. Snare and Latch were now pushing the cart back toward the bleachers in costumes of their own. Kinzo and Evander were headed the other direction with a different coloured cart.

Levi watched Stern and the Kar-Sang surround Snare and Latch. They yanked off the sheet to reveal a platter of food and not Ara.

They fell for it, Levi said as Latch and Snare made a show of being insulted.

"What is happening down there?" Adam asked.

"Uh, no idea," Levi said.

Stern and his lackeys looked around. They headed off in the direction that Kinzo and Evander had gone.

Tell Guy and Kaito it's their turn, Levi said.

Certainly, Aldus replied.

A few moments later, Guy and Kaito walked in front of the Kar-Sang and Stern from opposite directions, each pushing a wheelbarrow of round logs. They bumped into each other and spilled their wheelbarrows, sending logs rolling all over. They began an animated argument, trying to stay in the way of Stern and the Kar-Sang. They managed to stall them for a few seconds before being pushed aside.

Levi waited until the pursuers were two hundred feet down the path. *Ok, get Kana and Miri on it,* he thought.

A loud thundering reached Levi's ears as he watched a small herd of cattle stampede down the path. The girls were behind them, driving the six cows but making it seem like they were trying to stop them. People everywhere began to panic and run, adding to the chaos.

Aldus' voice reached Levi's mind. *They have loaded her into the cart. Ember is driving her off to the safe house.*

"Yes!" Levi celebrated.

Adam stared at Levi with suspicion.

"Um, I'm going to go down now," Levi said.

"Alright," Adam said.

Levi climbed down the ladder and raced out of the festival grounds where he met with the rest of the crew. "We did it!" Levi cried.

"Yeah, we did!" Guy smiled.

Kana and Miri came running up, laughing. "That was awesome," Kana said. "We made such a mess."

Aldus came strolling up, a bemused expression on his face. "Well done, everyone. But let's move to the safe house to celebrate." The troop set off for the house they had secured earlier.

Upon arrival, Coral performed the arranged knock.

Ember opened the door. "Come in."

Everyone filed in and the door was closed behind them.

"Where is she?" Kana asked.

"In the back room," Ember said.

Levi peeked into the room. Ara Stern slept peacefully on the bed. "Atta be, guys."

"Does this make anyone else want to become a professional criminal?" Kinzo asked. After a few stares, he said, "Just me? Ok."

"What are you doing?"

Everyone spun around to see Adam standing behind them.

Levi sucked in his breath. This could ruin things.

Coral spread her hands. "Hey, didn't we lock the door?"

~ ~ ~

A guard ran up to Farren. A regular guard, not one of the King's highly-trained, highly-dangerous protectors. He bowed to the King.

"Yes, soldier?" Farren said.

"Sir, there has been a kidnapping. Ara Stern was taken fifteen minutes ago."

Farren tapped his cheek. "Ara Stern. That name is familiar. Is she related to the Taskmaster?"

The guard nodded. "Yes, my lord. She's his sister."

"Intriguing," Farren said. "Why would someone kidnap her? It must be those Giala fighters." He turned to the two red and gold armoured men standing exactly three paces behind him. "You, tell Captain Steele to ready four squads. You, inform the generals of this. I wish to speak with them."

"At once, your Excellency," the guards chorused and marched off.

Farren dismissed the other soldier and made his way to the meeting room. His war leaders would meet him there. As he walked, he wondered what this latest move by the rebel cell meant. Farren and his advisors had yet to discover what the rebels' end goal was in Saken and this kidnapping brought them no closer to figuring it out.

Malroth and Avelyn had arrived before Farren and waited for him with straight backs. Farren waved them inside and told them of the recent news.

"The Giala, sire?" Avelyn asked.

Farren nodded. "I am certain. Who else could have pulled off a kidnapping in such a crowded place, but the ones who have been one step ahead of us for days?"

"What is the plan?" Malroth asked, his blue eyes meeting Farren's.

"You two are to each take two squads and go to the most likely places they are hiding," the king said. "Do not hesitate. Break-in and arrest everyone in each building. I don't care if it's a brothel or a church. Do it. I need them found."

"Yes, sire," both generals said.

"Also," Farren said as they were about to leave. "Send out extra patrols, send them all out. When the rebels make their move, I want to know about it immediately."

The two nodded and left to bring their King's wishes to fruition.

Farren looked out the window at the darkening sky. They would catch these rebels one day. He hoped it would be today.

CHAPTER 22

"It was you who kidnapped that woman," Adam said.

No one said a word.

"Why?" Adam asked.

Aldus stepped forward and put an arm around Adam's shoulder. "Let's take a walk." He led Adam outside.

"Do you think he'll sell us out?" Ember asked with a quaver.

"Aldus will convince him not to," Kaito said. "He is an expert orator."

"And if he doesn't..." Snare said ominously.

Levi faced him. "Ok, no. We are not hurting Adam. Or Ara for that matter. We're not gonna hurt anybody."

Snare scoffed. "You're all too soft. You need to be hard to survive in this world."

"We're not hurting them," Kana said, backing Levi up and ending the conversation.

Silence ensued as they waited. Levi grew bored and pulled out the yellow book. He examined the title that only he could read, the two words that he knew not the meaning of: Kaeli Vind. His fingers flipped through the thin pages, each one as blank as if the book had just been bound. It seemed useless, but a feeling in Levi's gut that told him he should hang onto it.

Looking around, he saw others entertaining themselves silently. Latch was peeling paint off the walls and dropping it on the floor. Coral was trying to balance her axe on her foot. Ember wasn't even trying to stop her. She had found a pencil and a sheet of paper and was drawing something. Kinzo was rolling a coin over his fingers as he sat against the far wall. Kana and Miri sat at the table, saying nothing. Ring was trying to get something off her shoe, to no avail. Snare and Guy were both snooping around the house while Evander lay on the floor by the table. Kaito was taking the time to meditate. He sat cross-legged at the foot of the bed, eyes closed, hands on knees.

Levi smiled, remembering the first time he had seen Kaito meditate. He had thought it was incredibly strange. Now, he was so accustomed to it that usually he didn't notice it.

Ring noticed, however. "What are you doing?"

"Meditating," Kaito said, eyes still closed.

"Why?" Ring banged her shoe against the floor.

"It helps me remain centred throughout the day."

"Centred? What does that mean?"

With a sigh, Kaito opened his eyes. "It means, calm, in control, mentally balanced. It allows me to do what I need to do without emotion clouding my judgment."

"Huh, weird," Ring said.

"I suppose it is weird," Kaito said. "But it has improved my life since I began. I have no desire to stop."

"Well, you do you, buddy," Ring said.

"I shall," Kaito replied.

Ember looked up from her drawing. "What about you, Ring? Do you have anything you do to help you wind down?"

"Not really," Ring said. "I'll smoke a pipe every once in a while, if that counts."

"Yes, lots of people smoke to relax," Ember said, "Despite it not being terribly healthy."

"What do you do?" Ring asked Ember.

"I draw. And paint," Ember said.

Levi rubbed his black eye. "I didn't know that."

"Well, you're not very observant usually," Ember said dryly. "I do it during my free classes."

"What do you draw?" Kana asked, tuning in to the conversation.

"Mostly landscapes," Ember said. "Of places I've been. I have a fairly good memory for things like that. This one is from a trip I took three years ago." She held up the page she'd been working on. It was a boulder resting on a hill above a forest. It was quite impressive, despite being incomplete.

"That's really good," Levi said.

Ember smiled. "Thank you."

"Ha! Drawing!" Coral scoffed. "Snore!"

Ember crossed her arms. "Excuse me? It's a productive pastime. And very calming."

"Who wants to be calm?" Coral asked.

"Most normal people," Guy said as he came back into the main room.

"Bah! Normal people suck!" Coral said.

Guy raised an eyebrow and leaned against the doorframe. "Are you saying we suck?"

"Ha! You guys aren't normal at all!" Coral exclaimed.

"Is that good or bad?" Kinzo asked.

The door creaked open and everyone jumped to their feet. It was Aldus and Adam. They relaxed, but only slightly.

"He good?" Evander asked.

"If by that, you mean he will assist us, then yes," Aldus said. "He good. I informed him of the incident with Rorien Stern last year and your issue with the Forsaken."

"I do not approve of kidnapping an innocent woman," Adam said. "But I understand that it seems to be the only way to save Cody. But we must not let Ms. Stern come to any harm."

"I agree," Aldus said. Everyone else also voiced their agreement, except for Snare, who snorted.

"Now, is it time for phase two?" Miri asked, fluttering her fingers.

Aldus glanced out the window at the lengthening shadows. "I believe it is, for those of us transporting Ara. Now, where did you say the Forsaken headquarters were?"

Ring explained where it was, using names and locations that meant nothing to Levi, but Aldus seemed to understand. He bobbed his head in comprehension.

"Shall we go?" Kaito asked, standing. Aldus nodded. It had been decided that they, along with Miri and Latch, would bring Ara to the Forsaken. The others would head back to Naomi and Cody and prepare for phase three, which they would begin tomorrow.

Kaito and Latch picked up Ara and took her outside to the waiting wagon, where they disguised her under a few bags of potatoes. The woman began to stir, perhaps about to wake soon.

The two hopped on board as Aldus and Miri took the front seat. Miri waved as they headed toward the Outskirts.

The rest waited until the wagon was gone from view before heading back to the Festival.

As they walked, their footsteps echoing off the cobblestones, Levi glanced up at the sun nearing the horizon. About time for a meal.

Quick, marching footsteps rang in the near-empty street. Levi looked at Kinzo, who shrugged.

From around a tall, three-story marble house with a wrap-around balcony came a troop of soldiers in full gear.

Levi's heart stopped. Pretty much everybody cursed and looked for a way to escape.

"Do we run?" Guy asked fearfully.

"No," Snare said. "Then they'll know we're up to something. Just stay calm and let me do the talking."

The troop marched down the street and crashed to a stop in front of Levi and his friends. The lead soldier held up a hand to stop them. "We are looking for Ara Stern, who was kidnapped this afternoon. Have any of you seen anything suspicious? Anyone who might seem like rebels?"

"No sir!" Snare said. Levi shook his head too, just in case. A bead of cold sweat worked its way down the side of his face as he looked into the eyes of twenty-five soldiers.

"I was showing my friends around town," Snare said, motioning to the others. "They're from out of town, you see-"

"I don't care," the soldier said rudely. "If you don't have anything of importance to say, move along."

"Yes, sir," Snare said, dipping his head. "Come on, guys." He led Levi and the others out of the way as the lead soldier barked an order and the troop began marching again. Soon, their clanking footsteps faded into the distance.

"Whew, that was close," Kinzo said.

"Yeah," Ember agreed. "I thought I was about to be caught doing something wrong."

"Because you've never done anything wrong," Guy said sarcastically.

Ember folded her arms. "Not never. Just very few times."

"Honestly, I was surprised you agreed to help us," Kana said.

Ember exhaled through her nose. "It's to help Cody. And we're not hurting anybody. It's just a little kidnapping."

"Kidnapping, eh? So, it was you lot."

Everyone froze.

From out of the shadowed alley stepped a familiar man. Last time Levi had seen him, he had been filthy and hairy, but he recognized the cleaned up, shaved version.

"Kyner?" Levi asked.

Kyner smiled. "Hello again, Levi."

"You two know each other?" Evander asked.

Levi nodded. "Last time we saw each other, he beat me, stole my medallion and tried to get me killed. What do you want?"

"Not to be a fugitive," Kyner said as he glanced down at his wrist. "They're still after me, you know. But, actually, I'm here for Evander, not you, Levi."

"Me?" Evander was shocked.

"Yes, you," Kyner said. His face grew serious. "I know who your father is."

Evander's jaw dropped open.

"Am I the only one who's really lost?" Coral asked. No one answered her. "Guess I am."

Evander stepped toward Kyner. "How? How do you know?"

"Your father has the same birthmark as you." Kyner pointed at Evander's neck where there was a patch of darker skin.

Evander's hand went to his neck. "Tell me!"

"Not here," Kyner said. "Not in front of all these others."

"Where?" Evander asked.

Kyner extended a hand. "Come with me and I'll change your life."

Evander crossed over to him.

"Evander!" Levi called. "Don't trust him!"

"Don't go, Evander!" Kana cried.

"I have to," Evander said. There was a strange hunger in his eyes. "I need to know who my father is."

And with that, he and Kyner disappeared into the dark alley.

Levi stared after them.

"What just happened?" Guy asked.

"I don't know, but I doubt it's good," Levi scowled. "This won't end well for anybody."

"Are you sure?" Kana asked. "Maybe he's actually trying to help Evander."

Levi cocked his head. "Well, with Kyner, he's always got his own agenda. He doesn't help people unless it benefits him more. Something's in this for him."

Kana's lower lip trembled, as if she was trying not to cry. With an obvious effort, she managed to calm herself. Miri put her arm around her.

"We should still go ahead with phase three, right?" Ring asked after a moment.

Levi glanced at his mark. Still red. "I guess so. Nothing we can do about Evander now." He hoped that Evander wasn't getting into anything over his head, but he knew it was a vain hope.

They trudged back to the festival grounds, feeling much worse than they had before. When they got back to camp, they headed straight for Aldus' tent. Before they could get there, Able Hejeck stopped them. "Any of you kids seen Aldus?"

"A while ago," Ember said. "He was going into the city. Said he had some business."

"Huh, he didn't tell me about it," Hejeck said. "You know there's been a kidnapping, right?"

The kids nodded.

Hejeck narrowed his eyes. "Say, you wouldn't happen to know anything about that would you?"

"Nope, not a thing," Coral said.

"Uh uh," Kinzo said.

Guy shook his head. "Definitely not."

Hejeck looked at them for a long minute. Then, he shook his head. "Ok, well, run along." He moved off grumbling to himself. Levi heard him say, "... think a bunch of kids did it? Really, Able? No way they could..."

Everyone ducked into Aldus' tent.

"You're back!" Naomi exclaimed. "Did it work? I heard rumours of a kidnapping!"

"It worked," Kinzo said. "Phase three is a go."

"Great!" Naomi said. She noticed that Kana was looking distraught. "What's wrong?"

Levi saved Kana from having to explain by doing it himself.

When he finished, Naomi said, "But nothing bad has happened yet, right? So, don't worry about it."

Kana took a deep breath. "You're right. We should just focus on saving Cody. We have a mission to do."

"That's the spirit!" Ring said. "Now, what do we have to do?"

"Nothing tonight," Levi said. "We're waiting until tomorrow."

Naomi nodded. "Well then, we had best get some rest."

Ember pointed at Snare and Ring. "You two stay here and watch Antoth."

"Where are you going?" Snare asked.

"Back to our tent," Ember said. "We mustn't look any more suspicious."

Everyone agreed and the Blackthrush students left Aldus' tent and headed for their own. As he was ducking into blue camp's temporary home, Levi saw Linae watching them from a table across the camp. Levi shivered and slipped inside.

The rest of blue camp, the ones not involved, greeted them as they headed to bed. Duncan asked where Kaito and Cody were, seeing as they weren't there. Levi was caught off-guard, but Naomi came up with a plausible explanation of them still being out at one of the late-night plays that were performed every other day. The suspicion averted, Levi and his friends headed to bed. They needed to be rested for the following day.

Morning came faster than Levi had expected. He must have been more tired than he realized. As he sat up, his body groaned in protest. He put a hand to his black eye, his bruises reminding him of his encounter with Corvin, Vonn and the twins. After stretching for a minute, he decided that his soreness wouldn't hinder anything. He stood and woke the others. They took a few moments to shake the sleep from their heads before they all snuck back into Aldus' tent.

The urchins woke at the sound of the tent flap moving.

"Morning," Ring said.

"Morning," Levi replied. "So, what do we have to do?"

"We've got to bring Cody to the safe house," Guy said.

Kinzo motioned to Levi and Kana. "That's us."

"So Stern doesn't see you and try to kill you right away," Ring recalled.

"Right," Levi said.

"Then, Guy and I find Stern and tell him we know where his sister is," Ember said.

"While the rest of us follow silently in case something goes wrong," Coral said, patting her axe.

Snare grumbled. "Which it will."

"Hey now, we're half done. We can do this," Ember said.

271

"What do you want my assistance with?" Adam asked.

Levi was taken by surprise. He had forgotten that Adam didn't have an assigned job. "Oh, uh I guess you can just come with us back to the safe house. Evander was supposed to come with us anyway."

"I will do that, then," Adam said.

"Well, ok then." Levi clapped his hands. "Let's go. Give us some time to get there."

"Will do," Guy nodded.

Levi and Kinzo went to Aldus' bed and threw back the covers. Cody, or Antoth, rather, was bound and gagged. He glared daggers at them as they hauled him up and draped the cloak back over him to disguise his bonds.

They led him out of the festival grounds with no problems and headed to the safe house.

"You know," Kinzo said as they walked. "We could have just stayed there. Had someone else bring him. Then we wouldn't have to walk there three times."

"Too late now," Levi said.

"Well, yeah, I know," Kinzo said. "I was just saying we should have."

"We'll do it next time," Levi said.

"You are planning to do this again?" Adam asked.

"No, I was joking," Levi said. "I hope I don't ever have to kidnap someone again."

"Well, I certainly hope you do not make a profession out of it," Adam said. Levi raised an eyebrow. Adam smiled. "Now, I am joking."

Levi chuckled. Adam was a very strange person.

They arrived at the safe house and put Antoth in the back room, tying him to the bed frame. Then, they waited for the others to arrive with Stern.

"You know," Levi said. "This could go sideways real fast."

"As I have stated before," Kinzo said. "I hate sideways. But if it does go that way..." He patted the sabre at his hip.

Levi flicked his left wrist up. The shield popped into position. Levi looked it over for knicks and dents, but there was nothing too major.

"That is a fascinating piece of armour," Adam said.

"Hmm? Oh, yeah." Levi flicked his wrist down and it collapsed into bracer form.

"Where did you get it?"

A smile touched Levi's lips. "A friend gave it to me."

"That friend almost killed us," Kinzo muttered.

"But he didn't," Levi said. "He changed his mind."

Kinzo grumbled something that Levi didn't catch.

"I would love to have a shield such as that," Adam said.

"You know what?" Levi said. "If I ever come across another one, I'll give it to you."

Kinzo walked over to where Kana was sitting at the table, staring at the wall. "You just gonna mope or what?"

Kana glared at him until he backed off, hands raised. "Sorry. Evander'll be fine. Worry about us when Stern gets here with his two freaks of nature."

Someone knocked on the door. Levi's stomach tightened into a knot. He looked to the door as it opened and locked eyes with Rorien Stern.

"You!" Stern said in a deathly quiet voice.

"Me," Levi said.

Stern turned to Guy and grabbed him by the shoulder. "You said you'd bring me to my sister!"

"I will!" Guy said, knocking Stern's hand away. "As soon as you help us out."

"No, I am going to kill all of you," Stern said. The Kar-Sang behind him both growled menacingly.

"I don't think so."

Stern turned to see Coral, Naomi, Ring and Snare standing behind them, weapons drawn.

Stern pinched the bridge of his large nose. "What do you want?"

"We want to help you rescue your sister," Levi said. "And we want you to help our friend who we rescued from the people that took her."

"What's wrong with him?" Stern asked, coming in the house. Levi noticed that he had taken to wearing a sword. And his fingers were twitching on the hilt.

Levi walked over next to the bed. "His body's been stolen."

"Dude named Antoth took over," Kinzo said. "But Cody's mind is still stuck inside his head."

Stern's only reaction was to raise his left eyebrow.

273

"We learned that the only way to reverse the process is to have a Kar-Sang do it, because it requires multiple orders of magic," Levi explained.

"So, you want me to save your friend and then you'll help me get my sister back?" Stern asked.

"Actually, we want to totally destroy the cult that took her," Guy said. "But, yeah."

"What's to prevent me from just killing you all?" Stern asked in a grave tone.

"Uh, the fact that it's ten against three, we've beaten you three times before and we've all grown stronger since then," Levi said. "You might kill some of us, but you'd be dead before you're halfway through us."

One of the Kar-Sang whispered something to Stern in its guttural language. Stern's cheek twitched.

"What'll it be?" Kinzo asked.

Stern glared at Levi for a long time.

He's not going to go for it, Levi thought.

"Fine!" Stern snapped. "For Ara. But once this is all over, I will not hesitate to kill you all."

"Of course," Levi said. "I wouldn't expect anything less."

"Now, fix Cody!" Kinzo said.

Stern nodded to the right-most Kar-Sang. It moved next to the bed, passing Levi as it did so. Levi coughed. The stench coming off it was repugnant.

The Kar-Sang put a hand on Cody's forehead. Antoth began to shake his head and struggle against his bonds. It pained Levi to see Cody's face in distress as the Kar-Sang began to chant. The air grew cold and still. Everyone clapped their hands over their ears against a high-pitched whine.

Levi's eyes widened. It was actually happening.

The Kar-Sang summoned a black talisman in his free hand as he chanted. A light began to pull away from Cody's body toward the amulet. Levi blinked. The light seemed to have a face. And it was screaming in agony.

The chanting and whining grew louder as the light grew brighter. Everyone was forced to turn from the brightness until the light snapped away from Cody's body and slammed into the talisman. The Kar-Sang stopped chanting and the whine stopped, the air returning to normal.

Everyone held their breath.

Cody didn't move.

Levi began to fear that something had gone horribly wrong.

"Is he-" Naomi began. She was cut off when Cody's eyes shot open and he gasped.

"Is that you, Cody?" Ember asked cautiously.

In response, Cody cracked a huge grin and yelled, "I'm back!"

CHAPTER 23

Cody couldn't stop smiling. He was back. He was in control. "Oh, it's so good to feel again!" he said as Kinzo untied him. "And I can talk too! This is amazing!"

"Glad to have you back, Cody." Levi slapped him on the back.

"Glad to be back," Cody said. "Oh, if I see another floating ball..." He ignored the strange glances and instead marvelled at the air on his face, the clothes against his skin, the discomfort from being tied up, the dull pain from being punched in the face, the slight soreness of the nearly-healed scars on his back. He had never been happier to be in pain.

"A touching reunion," Stern said. "But it's time for you to show me where my sister is being kept."

Cody stood unsteadily as he wasn't used to his body yet. "Hey, creepy vampire guy. Can I have that?" He pointed at the amulet where Antoth was trapped.

The Kar-Sang growled something, but handed Cody the black triangle.

"Thanks."

"Hurry!" Stern urged. "Who knows what they'll be doing to Ara right now?"

"I didn't know you had feelings at all," Kinzo said. "Much less feelings for someone else."

Stern glared at him. "You know nothing of me."

"Wrong," Kinzo said. "I know you have a big nose and you're an utter crapsack."

"Oh, I would love to kill you," Stern seethed.

Kinzo laughed. "Let's go get your sister."

"Get a move on, people!" Coral called. "I wanna hit something." Everyone exited out onto the street.

Cody fell in line beside Guy. His friend punched him in the shoulder and grinned. Cody grinned back.

Stern glared at the kids. "Which way?"

"I'll take you there," Snare said. He pushed past the Kar-Sang to the head of the group. They growled as he passed, remembering him from the fight at Rivera Farm. Snare ignored them and started off to the west.

Stern soon figured out where they were headed. "The Outskirts, eh?"

"Yep," Snare said without looking over his shoulder.

"If anything happens to her…" Stern growled.

"Yeah, yeah, save it, Taskmaster," Snare said.

Stern tapped the hilt of his sword. "Oh, how I do want to kill you all." The Kar-Sang hissed in agreement.

"So, you keep saying," Kinzo said. "We know you hate us. Trust me, the feeling's mutual, but we're actually here to help you."

"Yeah," Levi said. "I mean, if you want, we could just leave and let you deal with the cult all on your own."

"And if you do that," Kana said, "Ara is a lot less likely to make it out unharmed."

Stern sighed and rubbed the side of his nose. "Yes, I do realize all of this. But be warned, the second we've destroyed this cult, I will give you one chance to run before I kill you."

"Fair enough," Kana said.

They continued on in silence. Or most of them. Coral was singing a jaunty little tune about a cat who fell in love with a dolphin and ended up drowning itself. Cody soon found himself humming along. He was in a great mood, still on the high of being practically resurrected. His smile refused to shrink.

A good half-hour passed before they arrived at the fence and gate that led to the Outskirts. There were three bored-looking guards leaning against the side of a small shack. The gate was nothing more than two wooden poles mounted horizontally on hinges so they could swing out of the way.

One of the guards, a redhead, strolled out in front of the gate. "You've got an awfully big crowd here. What's your business in the Outskirts?"

Stern pushed his way to the front. "They're with me, unfortunately."

The guard, recognizing Stern, hurried to open the gate. "Mr. Stern. Apologies for the holdup. Please, go right through."

"Yes, I will," Stern said. "Don't hold me up again."

"Of course not, sir." The guard bowed his head. "It won't happen again."

"It better not," Stern said. "For your sake."

The guard tugged on his collar nervously.

Stern waved the Kar-Sang ahead and they strode through the gate.

"Why is he taking the lead?" Cody asked. "He doesn't know where he's going."

"He probably wants to show the guards that he's in charge, because if they saw that he was following kids, it would undermine his reputation and authority," Coral said.

Cody raised an eyebrow at her. "Since when do you make well-thought-out assessments of people?"

Coral shrugged. "Dunno. Just seems obvious."

Cody glanced at Guy who shrugged.

Once everyone was a good hundred yards past the gate, Stern looked back at Snare and spread his hands. "Well, where to?"

"End of the block, turn left," Snare replied.

Without any further words, Stern turned and marched away, the Kar-Sang at his heels.

As the rest followed, Levi dropped back next to Cody. "Hey, so this cult place, what's it like?"

Cody wrinkled his brow. "From what I could tell, it was a bunch of interconnected buildings surrounding a central courtyard."

"Ok, how many entrances?"

Cody smirked. "I wasn't exactly conscious when I got there or when I left, so I really have no idea."

"Oh, right," Levi grinned.

"Go ask Ring or Kinzo," Guy suggested. "They helped rescue him."

Levi took his advice and left to talk to them so he would know what he was walking into.

"I'm a bit confused," Cody said. "We used Stern and the Kar-Sang to rescue me, so why are we still helping them?"

Naomi spun around and walked backward. "Well, Levi and the others still have to help the urchins take down the cult."

"Right. That's why I got into the mess in the first place." Cody tapped his forehead. "Guess I forgot what we were originally doing while I was trapped in there."

"So, yeah," Naomi said. "Stern will help us take down the cult. Plus, we don't want Ara to get hurt."

Guy nodded. "Good point. We should never let hot women come to harm."

"She was hot?" Cody asked, never having seen her.

Guy touched his thumb and index finger together. "Oh yeah. She was real fine, my friend. Real fine."

Naomi rolled her eyes.

Cody chuckled. "We also don't want her to get hurt because we're good people."

"Are we though?" Guy asked. He lowered his voice. "I mean, we are the ones who kidnapped her. Just saying."

Cody bit his lip. "True. We did. Well, actually, you guys did."

"But it was for you," Guy pointed out.

"I know, I know," Cody said. "And thanks for that."

"As long as we rescue Ara, it will be worth it," Naomi whispered.

"Also, if we don't rescue her," Guy said. "Stern will definitely blame us and try to kill us. And that'll be after fighting an entire cult."

The corners of Cody's mouth lifted. "I think I might have a way to deal with the cultists."

"How?"

Cody opened his hand and let the amulet where Antoth was trapped dangle from his fingers by the string.

Guy cracked a smile. "That could work. They'll want him back."

"Exactly," Cody said, eyes flashing.

Naomi clasped her hands. "We could potentially avoid all conflict with that."

"Potentially. But, for some reason, I don't think that's gonna happen," Guy said.

"You never know," Naomi said. "Good things do happen, you know."

Guy smiled wryly. "Just not to us. At least, not without a lot of bad stuff happening first."

"Well, then, we'd best appreciate the good when it comes around," Naomi said.

Cody smirked. "Guess so."

The group walked for another twenty minutes until Stern finally let Snare lead the way, unsure of where to go. Ten more minutes passed before Snare stopped.

"Are we there?" Stern asked impatiently.

"Yep," Snare said. "The building at the end of the street."

Stern drew his sword and flashed it about. "Mig, Frel, it's time to kill some wretches." The Kar-Sang made strange, staccato hissing noises. It took Cody a second to realize they were laughing. It was a chilling sound.

"Wait!" Kana called. "You're just going to rush in without a plan?"

Stern brushed his hair out of his face. "We have no time to scheme. We must act quickly!" He took off toward the building with the bloodsuckers right behind him.

"He really wants his sister back," Cody muttered as everyone else hurried to follow.

Cody expected someone to see them coming and shout a warning, but he was wrong. They reached the front door without an alarm being raised.

"Let's do this," Coral said, spinning her axe.

Stern snapped his fingers and pointed at the door. One of the Kar-Sang placed its pale, veiny hand on the door.

"What's he doing?" Guy asked. The door exploded into smithereens and Guy leapt back with a yelp.

There were cries of surprise from inside the building as the Kar-Sang rushed in. The sound of flesh being torn reached Cody's ears and the cries stopped.

Everyone began piling in the door.

Cody was the last one to enter. He took in everything as he rushed by; the crudely decorated entrance, the halls leading off in different directions and the three bodies of masked cultists lying on the floor in crimson pools.

"Split up!" Levi called. "Don't let them band together!"

"Well, go, then!" Stern yelled. "I'm not doing anything until Ara is safe."

Levi, Naomi and Ember headed down a hall to the left. Kana and the urchins took off to the right. The sounds of combat followed them.

"I'll take you to her," Cody volunteered.

Guy tapped his arm. "Want backup?"

Cody nodded.

"Where to?" Stern asked, patience gone.

"We need to get to the central courtyard," Cody said. "But they'll be a lot of them. We'll need a distraction."

"Did someone say distraction?" Coral asked, twirling her axe.

"Ack! Watch where you swing that thing!" Kinzo ducked out of the way.

Coral snorted. "Oh, don't be a baby."

"You swung a battle axe at my head!" Kinzo snapped. "I think I have a right to be upset."

"Silence, you fools!" Stern yelled. "Where is she?"

Cody held up his hands in a calming gesture. "Ok, calm down. You two grab Adam and go cause a scene so we can go get Whats-her-name."

"Her name is Ara!" Stern growled.

"Oh, I don't care," Cody yelled. "Just go!"

Coral, Kinzo and Adam took off down the hallway. Cody raced after them, hearing Stern and the others behind him.

"Hey, Carl! I told you no running inside!" a voice said from a room up ahead. A masked head poked out. "You're not Carl."

"Nope." Coral smashed the butt end of her axe into his face. He collapsed to the floor. Nobody broke stride.

The door at the far end of the hall stood between them and the central courtyard. One of the Kar-Sang growled and the wooden door disintegrated into a fine powder. Coral and her two companions raced out and attacked the unsuspecting cultists. Cody waited a few moments until all the Forsaken were busy paying attention to the distraction team.

"Let's move," Guy said.

Cody took off, making a beeline across the courtyard to where the captives were held.

"There's more of 'em!" someone cried.

Cody saw something flash in front of him and instinctively ducked. A throwing knife whizzed over his head, parting his hair.

There were seven armed cultists barring their path. One of them held out a hand. "Stop!"

Stern barked an order and Cody heard a loud whine. Something flew by him and landed amongst the cultists, exploding on impact. They were tossed aside as a fireball flared up. Cody could feel the heat from twenty-five feet away.

Cody ran through the scorched stones. A few of the Forsaken were still alive. Stern ordered the Kar-Sang to kill them and they obeyed, summoning long daggers and plunging them into the hearts of the cultists.

Cody groaned. "That was not necessary. Half of these people were innocents, stolen like your sister and possessed!"

"They were. Now, they are my enemies," Stern said. "I have my enemies killed. Now take me to my sister."

Cody cursed under his breath. Stern was out of control. But he led him across the compound to the hallway that led to the room where the prisoners were kept.

A panicked cultist tried to run past, but Stern cut her down without pausing.

Cody gritted his teeth, but ran to the end of the hall. Two guards barred the door.

"Intruders!" one yelled and rushed ahead with a spear.

Cody waited for the right moment and spun to the side, chopping down and cleaving the spear in two. The guard tried to stop his momentum, but he got too close to one of the Kar-Sang. It grabbed his head with one hand and jammed a dagger into his left eye. The man screamed, limbs flailing for a second before going limp. The Kar-Sang tossed him against the far wall.

The second guard clutched his spiked cudgel close. His eyes were wide, his breaths quick and panicked.

Cody lowered his sword. "Just let us in the room and we'll let you live."

"You give your word?" the guard asked fearfully.

"Yes," Cody said. Guy said the same. When Stern didn't answer, Cody glared at him.

"Fine." Stern rolled his eyes. "We won't kill you."

The guard swallowed and slid the bolt out of the latch and opened the door, letting everyone in.

Cody scanned the room, looking not for Ara, but for Clovis and Teddy. He had hoped they would still be here, but they weren't. In fact, no one was. It was empty.

"Where is she?" Stern's voice cracked. His jaw jumped and a vein throbbed in his temple.

"Wait, wait!" Cody said. "If she's not here, she'll be in the operating room! They could be stealing her body right now!"

Stern stood stock still for a moment. His cheek twitched. Then, before anyone could react, he spun and lunged, taking the cultist through the throat. He yanked out his sword and blood spilled from the wound. The guard clawed at his throat as his eyes became glassy.

"Oh, come on!" Cody yelled. "We gave him our word!"

"I don't care," Stern said. The body crashed to the ground. "Now, take me to the operating room. If she isn't there, you two are dead."

Guy put a hand to his throat.

"She'll be there," Cody said.

Stern's eyes blazed with barely controlled fury. "She'd better be."

Cody stormed out of the room, growling. Stern was a monster. Why were they helping him? They should have found some other way.

He rushed out into the courtyard, Guy on his flank. It was chaos. There were bodies everywhere, all Forsaken, their white masks broken and bloodied. A stack of boxes was on fire, smoke billowing up into the sky. Coral, Kinzo and Adam were still fighting, leaving behind a trail of destruction. To Cody's relief, they only attacked the cultists who tried to fight. They left the unarmed ones alone.

"Where to, boy?" Stern growled.

"Look, I'm not fully sure where it is," Cody said, his frustration coming through. "I was only semi-conscious when they took me there. But I remember being dragged across the courtyard and down some stairs."

"There's stairs over there," Guy pointed.

"That'll be it," Cody said. He took off before Stern could decide to just kill him. He and Guy ended up a few paces in front of Stern and his goons. Cody leaned over and whispered. "Guy, we need to make sure we're close to the door in case she's not there, or worse."

Guy nodded and shifted his grip on his left-hand sword, still not totally used to only four fingers.

They had no problems crossing the compound. There were few cultists left, and the ones that were left were dealing with the distraction team. Cody vowed to thank them after. He also wondered how the others were faring as they went through the buildings. He hoped everyone was ok.

They reached the far side and stairwell leading down. The right doorpost was covered in blood. Halfway down the steps was the body that had left the stain. Cody stepped over it and descended down.

The hallway below was dark, only three torches lit the space, leaving most of it wreathed in shadows.

"Is this the right place?" Stern asked, coming up behind him.

"Yes, definitely," Cody said. "I just don't know which door it is."

"Well, check them all!" Stern said.

"Ok, fine!" Cody yelled. "You start at the far end, we'll start here."

Stern grunted and moved past him, waving his henchmen ahead.

"Good move," Guy whispered.

Cody shook his head and sighed. "Let's check some rooms." He yanked open the first door and stuck his head inside; it was dark and empty. He moved on. The next room was the same.

"Any luck?" he called to Guy.

"Nope."

Cody reached out to open the next door. It slammed open before he could and four armed cultists ran through. Cody didn't think, he simply reacted. His sword lodged itself in the first man's side. The cultist cried out in pain and staggered to the far wall, Cody's sword slithering out of the wound.

"No! Cody!" a familiar voice cried. "What have you done?"

The cultists tore off their masks, revealing themselves to be Aldus, Miri and Kaito. Their faces were slack with horror.

Aldus knelt and helped the injured man sit up against the wall. He moaned in pain as he pulled off his mask. Latch.

Cody's sword dropped from his numb fingers and clattered to the stones. He stared at Latch in shock.

Guy muttered a soft curse.

Cody tore his gaze away from Latch. Miri was staring at him, eyes filled with fear, shock and sadness. "I... I didn't mean to..."

The only response was Latch's strangled cry of agony. "Why are you dressed like them?"

"It was the plan to get Ara in here," Kaito said quietly.

"Well, no one told me!" Cody yelled. Miri took a step back. Cody dropped to a knee, hands covering his face. "No one told me."

Guy knelt next to Latch. "Is he gonna make it?"

"No, I'm afraid he won't," Aldus said wearily. He placed his hand on Latch's forehead and his moans quieted. "But I can make him more comfortable."

Cody crawled over to Latch, pants soaking up blood. He grabbed the dying urchin's leg. "I'm so sorry."

Latch managed a pained smile. He coughed and doubled over, chest spasming. "It's ok. I... I didn't have a great life anyway."

"I want to take it back," Cody said.

"Not possible. Here." Latch reached in his pocket and pulled out a smooth oval stone with a star carved in it. "You take this. I don't need it anymore."

Cody took the stone from Latch's outstretched fingers. They were cold. "I'll keep it safe."

Latch coughed again, weaker this time. He blinked back tears. "Say goodbye to Ring and Snare for me."

"Of course," Cody said, gripping his shoulder.

Latch's head drooped till his chin rested on his chest. His breathing grew shallower and shallower until at last, it stopped.

Miri let out a shuddering breath as Aldus pulled his hand away.

Cody closed his eyes and whispered a prayer to a childhood god he had long forgotten. He begged that Latch's soul would find rest.

Aldus stood with a sigh. "An unfortunate turn of events."

"It is a pity," Kaito said. "He was a good person."

"With some rotten luck," Guy added.

Cody still knelt by Latch's body. A hand touched his shoulder. Miri's. He looked up into her tear-filled eyes and saw compassion. She pulled him to his feet.

"I'm glad you're back in your own body," she signed.

Cody didn't say anything, he just wrapped her in a hug. Miri let out a strange squeak. Cody let go. "Let's go find Ara and get out of this wretched place." He headed down the hall, trying to leave behind the black cloud that filled his mind.

Kaito walked next to Cody. "I'm glad to see you."

Cody scoffed in disgust. "But how can you be glad to see me? I just killed Latch!"

"That was completely accidental," Kaito said. "You should not feel accountable."

"Well, I do!" Cody cried. "And I always will." He opened his hand. The smooth stone felt heavy, weighed down with the burden of Latch's death.

"The best thing to do right now is to finish what we came here to do," Aldus said. "I'm sure Latch would want us to see it through."

"Yes," Kaito said. "Latch was vocal about wanting the Forsaken destroyed, to give the people of the Outskirts a better life."

One that he'll never see, Cody thought miserably.

Shouts and the sound of combat echoed down the hall.

"Stern's found them!" Guy said. They raced to the room where the commotion was coming from.

As he ran, Cody berated himself, cursing his stupidity and poor judgment. He was so wrapped up in his thoughts that he barely noticed when everyone turned off into a room on the right. He almost overshot the door and grabbed onto the doorframe to swing himself in.

It was the same room where Antoth had stolen his body. Stern and the Kar-Sang stood on the close side of the operating table. On the other side stood Jedar, Marek and another masked cultist. There were two others dead on the floor. Marek was holding a dagger against the throat of an attractive young woman who Cody could only assume was Ara Stern. She was bound and gagged and absolutely terrified.

It was a standoff. Neither side wanted to make the next move.

"Well, this is a bit of a pickle," Guy said.

Everyone looked to the door.

Seeing Cody, Jedar's eyes lit up. "Antoth! You've returned!"

Cody glared at him. "Guess again."

Shock crossed his face.

Marek groaned. "You survived?"

"But how?" Jedar asked. "What happened to Antoth?"

Cody lifted the black pendant. "Here he is."

Jedar's mouth dropped open. "But that's impossible!"

"Clearly not," Guy said.

"You are outnumbered," Aldus said in a commanding tone. "So, if you'd kindly return Mr. Stern's sister to him, we can all go home happy."

"Yes!" Stern said, flecks of spit flying from his mouth. "Give her to me and I might spare some of you."

The masked cultist leaned over to Marek. "We need to get out of here. But I can only take three, not four."

Marek narrowed his eyes, the way he did when he was thinking. He mused aloud, "Only three, eh? Well, with Antoth out of the way…" He turned to Jedar with an evil gleam in his eye.

"What are you doing?" Jedar's voice quavered.

Before anyone could react, Marek swung the dagger and slashed open Jedar's throat. The old cultist grabbed at the crimson fountain gushing from his neck and sank to the floor.

"What are you doing?" Cody yelled.

"Taking over this cult!" Marek called. He nodded to the masked man, who grabbed him and Ara.

"No!" Stern screamed. He charged Marek, vaulting over the table. He reached for his sister, but there was a loud pop and Marek, the masked man and Ara all disappeared.

Stern crashed into the far wall. He got to his knees and screamed into the air. Turning to the Kar-Sang, he yelled, "Kill them."

Cody inhaled sharply. Everyone raised their weapons.

"Stop!" Aldus cried. "I know where they went!"

The Kar-Sang halted and looked at their master.

Stern got to his feet. "How can you know?" His eyes were dangerously mad.

"I am a Mind Mage," Aldus said. "I looked into the man's mind and saw their destination as he left."

"Where?" Stern staggered toward him. "Tell me!"

"Swear not to kill us," Aldus said. "And I will."

Stern growled and buried his sword into Jedar's chest, spraying blood. "Yes! I won't! Now tell me!"

"They are back at the Festival. In the Aedon. I believe they will be meeting with whichever noble is funding them. We will have a fight on our hands."

"I don't care if I have to kill every noble in the city," Stern seethed. "Nothing short of death will stop me from saving my sister!"

CHAPTER 24

Although Aldus tried to persuade Stern to wait, the Taskmaster and his lackeys immediately left for the Festival grounds, leaving the others to deal with the aftermath.

Aldus had Cody and Kaito carry Jedar's body out of the room before Guy set fire to it with a simple spell.

"No one will be using this knowledge again," Aldus said as he watched the shelves of ancient writings catch fire.

Cody tried not to think of anything as he and Kaito carried the dead Forsaken leader down the hall. But as he passed Latch's body, the dark cloud returned to his mind. He forced himself to look away, not wanting to see the irreparable damage he had caused with one bad decision.

He and Kaito ascended the stairs to the courtyard above. It was quiet. Dead cultists lay all around on stones painted with scarlet. Kinzo, Coral and Adam rested at the table where the prisoners were fed.

"Did we win?" Kinzo asked, as they came close.

"Not exactly," Kaito said. He and Cody set down Jedar's body none too gently. Cody looked down in disgust at the blood covering his arms and chest.

"Who's that?" Coral asked.

"One of the leaders," Cody said. "My brother killed him so he could escape with Ara."

Adam looked past them to where Aldus, Guy and Miri were coming up the stairs. "And who are they carrying?"

Cody looked at the ground, avoiding eye contact.

Kinzo straightened. "That's Latch. What happened?"

Another wave of guilt crashed over Cody. He felt like a traitor, just like his brother.

"He was cut down as we rounded a corner," Kaito explained. "There was nothing we could do."

Cody glanced at him. He hadn't mentioned that it had been Cody who had killed him. Kaito nodded ever so slightly.

Miri came up beside Cody and signed, "It was no one's fault." She was telling the distraction team, but it was obviously meant for Cody. It didn't make him feel any better.

Kinzo scratched his neck and blew out a breath. "The urchins aren't gonna be happy."

"What about the urchins?" Ring asked. She, Snare and Kana came out of the building to the south. Ember, Naomi and Levi exited a different door right behind them.

Aldus and Guy gently lay Latch down. Aldus walked over to Ring. "I am very sorry, but your friend lost his life."

Cody watched the colour drain out of Ring's face. Shame swept through him as she ran past Aldus and dropped to her knees beside the body of her friend.

"No! Latch!" She touched his cheek lightly as tears dropped from her eyes.

Snare came to stand beside Ring. As he looked down at his friend, a muscle in his jaw jumped. He breathed forcefully out his nose. Angry. Furious. And he had every right to be.

"Tell me the bastards who did this are dead," Snare said, voice strained.

"The people responsible were dealt with," Aldus said. "But we aren't done yet. Several of the Forsaken escaped with Ara. We must get her back."

"No," Snare said.

Everyone stared. "Why not?" Coral asked.

Snare clenched his hands. "We've done what we set out to do. We've destroyed the Forsaken. We don't need to rescue the sister of that maniac!"

"We can't let her come to harm," Ember said.

"Oh, but you're all ok with Latch being dead!" he yelled.

"No one's ok with that, you idiot!" Guy yelled back. "It's awful. But we can't do anything about it now."

"Also, two of their leaders escaped," Kaito said. "If they are still abroad, the Forsaken may yet rise again."

Snare grumbled under his breath and kicked Jedar's body violently.

Ring finally stood and wiped her eyes. "Snare, they're right. We have to save her. Latch would have wanted us to." She touched his arm.

He ran his hands through his hair and swore. "Fine. We'll get this stupid girl back."

"Shouldn't we do something with the body?" Levi asked.

"Like what? Have a funeral?" Snare asked rudely. "We're street kids. We don't have funerals. When one of us dies, we leave them for the rats."

"That's horrible," Naomi said, putting a hand to her mouth.

"Yeah, it is. That's our life," Snare snapped. "Now, are we gonna go, or what?"

"If you insist," Aldus said.

"I do," Snare said. "I want this over with. Done for good."

"Very well," Aldus said. He led the group out of the courtyard. Cody was the last to leave. He paused to touch Latch's forehead. "I'm so sorry." He turned away and cursed himself as he followed the others into the building they had entered in by.

As Cody stepped inside, there was a commotion ahead; someone was attacking. Kana and Adam ended up knocking the man down and restraining him. Cody recognized him as the cultist Coral had clubbed when they had first arrived.

Snare drew his knife and stepped toward the man.

"Stop! We can use him!" Aldus called.

Snare swung at the man, but Kaito caught his arm. "Let go!" He yanked his arm away from Kaito.

Aldus stepped in front of the cultist, blocking Snare from him. The man spit in his face. "I curse you all!"

Aldus wiped spittle from his face. "How thoughtful of you. Now, I want you to pass on a message to all your friends. Your leaders are gone. Your acolytes are dead or have fled. Your secrets are burned, there is nothing left. The Forsaken are finished. Tell them that. Tell them it will never rise again."

The man's eyes were wide, but he refused to be cowed. "I don't believe you!"

"Go check the courtyard, buddy," Kinzo said. "You'll find all the proof you need lying in blood."

"No! You're lying!" the man yelled, straining against Kana and Adam.

"I can assure you we are not," Aldus said. He nodded to his restrainers. "Let him go." Kana and Adam stepped back.

The man rubbed his arms and stood. "You will all rue the day you ruined my life," he glowered. "I, Garold Ansen, will hunt you down. You hear me? I will come after all of you!"

"Great," Kinzo said. "Something to look forward to. Now, go on, get! Deliver our message, Garold."

Garold cast a glare of hatred at the group and ran out into the courtyard. Cody watched him go, heard his wail of despair when he saw the carnage.

"Let's move," Kana called. "We've got to save Ara."

They exited the compound, stepping over bodies and the shattered fragments of the door. Miri, Kaito and Aldus all stripped off their Forsaken disguises and threw them in the ruined entrance.

"I never want to touch anything that has to do with them again," Miri said.

"Let's hope we never have to," Kaito said.

Snare was already walking down the street, not waiting for anyone.

"Hey, wait up!" Levi called.

Ring grabbed his arm and stopped him.

"Huh?"

She shook her head. There was still moisture in her eyes. "Let him go. He needs space right now." She sniffed.

"Yeah, I guess," Levi said. "What do you need right now?"

Ring's face crumbled and she broke down crying again. Naomi hurried over and put an arm around her, steering her away.

"Way to go, Levi," Kinzo snorted.

Levi spread his hands. "What did I do wrong?"

"Just start walking, dummy," Kana said, shoving him ahead.

Cody fell in line, walking in silence, watching the stones below his feet. He paid no attention to where they were going, or to what anyone was saying. His mind was a hurricane of emotion. Digging in his pocket, he took out Latch's stone, squeezing it with all his strength, venting his anger until the pain forced him to stop. He opened his hand to see a bruise already forming in his palm. He cursed and slipped it back in his pocket.

"You ok, Cody?" Ember asked gently.

Cody clenched his jaw, refusing to look at her.

"Cody?"

"Not now, Ember," Cody growled.

She stepped back, respecting his wish.

When they arrived back at the gate to the main city, Cody's mood hadn't improved. He had simply gone from being horrified to being angry. Very angry.

There were three different guards at the gate when the fourteen stopped in front of their little shack.

Two of the guards stepped in the way and crossed their spears. "What business do you have coming into the city?"

"We are headed to the Festival," Aldus said.

The guards looked them over skeptically. "Right. That's why you're all armed and half of you covered in blood. No, you can't pass."

"No, we can explain," Levi said.

"We really need to get through," Naomi pleaded.

The guards were unmoved. "No passage."

"Come on, let us through," Kinzo said.

The guards shook their heads. "No. Now leave before we arrest you."

Cody growled. They were interfering with the mission. He pushed his way to the front of the group. He must have looked like a madman, his sword and clothes bloody, his eyes hard and flinty. "We're going to pass through and you won't stop us. I don't want to hurt you, but I will if you stay in our way."

The guards looked at each other and scoffed. "What are you going to do with your little sword? We're professionally trained soldiers. There's nothing you can... hey! What's happening?" The guards looked down at their feet. They were beginning to sink into the stones.

"What is this sorcery?" the second guard asked.

Cody didn't reply. He knelt on the ground, his left hand pressed flat against the stones. He gritted his teeth as his anger fueled the magic changing the natural state of the ground beneath the guards' feet. They continued to yell and struggle until he at last released the magic and looked up. Both men had sunk up to their armpits in the ground, which had again solidified around them. They yelled for help and tried vainly to break free.

Cody blew out a long breath, some of his anger leaving with it.

"Damn, Cody," Guy said. "Where'd that come from?"

Cody glanced back to see everyone staring at him.

Aldus smiled. "That was some fine matter manipulation, Cody. Very impressive, for your first time."

Cody nodded. Normally, he would have been ecstatic over such a leap in his magical abilities, but his mood wouldn't allow him to even smile. Also, it had taken a fair deal of energy from him.

"Let us out!" one of the guards yelled as they made futile attempts to break out of their stone prisons. "Dirk! Call for reinforcements!"

Dirk, the third guard who had stayed out of the confrontation, stood up. Fourteen weapons pointed at him. Dirk held up his hands. "I think I'll just let them through."

"Dirk! Don't you dare!" one of the guards yelled. "You are in such trouble when I get out of here!"

"Oh, shut up," Kinzo said, kicking dirt in the guards' faces as he passed by.

Once through the gate, everyone congratulated Cody on his quick thinking.

"I had no idea you could do that," Levi said.

"That was amazing," Ember said.

"About time you did something useful with your magic, not just disintegrating pinecones," Guy said.

Everyone congratulating him made Cody feel much worse, because half of them didn't know what a horrible thing he had just done.

Luckily, Miri came to his rescue. "Enough dawdling, have to hurry." She set the pace to a quick march, taking few breaks until they arrived at the festival grounds.

Kaito scanned the grounds. "We must hurry. I do not wish to see Ara come to harm. She is simply a victim in all this, scared and confused."

"How do you know that?" Levi asked.

"She woke as we took her to the Forsaken," Kaito said. "She was quite terrified."

"Yes, she was, until I put her back to sleep," Aldus said. "She is very much a victim in this scenario. We must get her out of Marek's hands." The group agreed silently with the headmaster.

Naomi put a hand above her eyes. "Right. So, they're in the Aedon? Where all the nobles are?"

"Yes," Aldus said. "At least, that was their original destination. They may have left by now."

"They're not just gonna let us in, are they?" Levi asked. "And for sure not with our weapons."

"That'd be a problem," Guy said.

Snare folded his arms. "I'm not going anywhere without a weapon."

Aldus stroked his beard. "You raise a good point."

"What are we going to do?" Ember asked.

"I'm not entirely certain," Aldus said.

He was interrupted by a low rumble. A pillar of smoke arose from the centre of the grounds, near the duelling arena.

"I wonder what that is?" Levi asked.

"Not our problem," Snare said.

Cody narrowed his eyes at the smoke. He thought he could glimpse flames among the billows. "What if it is our problem? There's a good chance they already left the Aedon and that," he pointed. "That only comes from a fight."

"They are duelling in that vicinity," Adam said.

Cody shook his head. "No. I mean a real fight. With magic. Life and death."

"You could be right," Kaito said. "We should investigate."

"You two go," Aldus said, looking at Cody and Kaito. "Take a few others and make sure it's not them. The rest of us shall continue on to the Aedon."

"Any volunteers?" Cody asked.

Kinzo and Naomi lifted their hands.

"I will also come along," Adam said. "Even if we do not find our quarry, I may see my father and inquire about how he is faring in the tournament."

"Yeah, yeah, save it," Kinzo said, grabbing his wrist. "Let's go!"

Guy slapped Cody on the back as he turned to leave. "Good luck."

"You too," Cody replied. He followed Kinzo into the maze of tents. Their destination was clear; the smoke rose above everything. It could probably be seen from outside the walls of the harbour.

People milled about, doing whatever they desired on their holidays. Most of them didn't pay attention to the rising smoke, but they did take notice of Cody and his friends. They hastily made a way for the five armed and bloodstained knights-in-training. Whispers, pointing fingers and poorly concealed gasps followed them.

Cody tried his best to ignore them. He knew that there was no way they could know, but he felt like each person who saw him knew the truth. That he killed Latch. He sped up, taking the lead.

"Hey, Cody?" Kinzo asked, as they jogged. "How'd your brother get mixed up with the Forsaken?"

"No idea," Cody said. "I haven't seen him since I was seven."

"Right..." Kinzo said. "When he killed your mom."

Cody's face darkened. "Yeah. Apparently, he visited my sister two years later, but she never told me what happened."

"Huh," was all Kinzo said.

"All I know is that Marek is a terrible person and he found some people just as bad as him," Cody glowered. He recalled Marek laying open Jedar's throat. "Or, almost as bad."

"I'm sorry to hear that," Naomi said. "I always knew Ember had family issues, but I didn't know you did."

"I don't like to talk about it," Cody grunted.

Naomi wisely decided she had said enough.

"Listen," Kaito said. Over the general cacophony of the festival, they could hear screams. People were in trouble.

They broke into a run. Rounding a large red pavilion, they found themselves in absolute chaos. People ran and screamed, trying to escape the roaring bonfire that used to be the arena and the bleachers. A troop of soldiers battled with Stern and his Kar-Sang, defending the last cultist and Marek, who held Ara captive behind them. The bodies were already piling up.

"Whoa," Kinzo said. "This is a mess."

"Whose soldiers are those?" Naomi asked.

Cody drew his sword. "Who knows. But they're defending the wrong people."

"So, we fight?" Kinzo asked.

Cody nodded. He turned to Kaito. "Can you sneak around and get Ara if we distract the others?"

Kaito inclined his head. "I will do my best."

"With this much commotion, it shouldn't be a problem," Kinzo said, twirling his sabre.

Kaito sprinted back the way they came, turning left around the red tent.

"You guys ready?" Cody asked.

Kinzo grinned. "Oh yeah."

"Yep," Naomi said.

"I am," Adam replied.

"Then, here we go," Cody said. He hefted his shield, raised his sword, let out a war cry and charged. The others lent their voices to his.

A few of the soldiers turned to face the new threat. Most of them were too busy with the Kar-Sang, who were tossing them aside like nothing.

Cody slammed his shield into the nearest soldier, bowling him over. He slashed wildly, his blade bouncing off armour. In his peripherals, he saw Naomi sweep a man off his feet with her longsword, Kinzo darting between soldiers, Adam backing up his opponents with methodical forms.

A soldier leapt at Cody, snarling. Cody caught the sword on his shield and swung up at the man's exposed side. His blade crunched into the breastplate, crumpling the metal. The man yelled, grabbing at his broken ribs. Cody brought his sword down on the man's helm. It rang like a bell and he toppled over sideways.

Cody swivelled to face the next opponent, a man with a spiked mace. He didn't want to block that weapon with his shield; it could easily break his arm. As the soldier swung at him, Cody rolled away from the crushing blow.

Unfortunately, he rolled into the legs of another soldier, who stomped on Cody's left shoulder. Something crunched and he cried in pain. His sword slashed across the back of the soldier's knee, where there was no protection. Tendons severed, the man collapsed directly on top of Cody's sword arm. Pinned, Cody raised his other arm, ignoring the spike of pain and jammed the rim of his shield into the man's throat. The soldier gagged and coughed, both hands going to his neck and Cody managed to pull his arm out from under him.

He got to his feet, shoulder throbbing. He didn't have time to assess the pain as the mace-wielding soldier came at him again.

Cody lifted his shield. He couldn't afford to take a heavy blow with his arm already injured.

The man swiped at Cody, who danced out of the way. He risked a quick jab, but the man deflected it with his bracer, putting Cody out of position. The soldier swung at his unprotected back. Cody leapt ahead, almost out of range. The mace ran across his upper back, cutting his tunic and opening a bloody line. Cody spun to see the mace heading for his face. He dropped backward, catching himself with his good arm and the mace sailed high. Cody scrambled back, trying to escape the next blow, but the soldier was right on top of him. He managed to get his shield in the way as the mace smashed into the reinforced wood. A scream tore itself from Cody's lips as his shoulder grated in its socket, his shield falling to his side.

The soldier lifted his mace to end the fight, but a fireball soared above Cody's head and slammed into his chest, throwing him ten feet.

Cody twisted his head.

"Thank me later," Kinzo said, sword locked with another soldier. Blood ran down his left cheek. He dropped his left hand to his belt and his dagger. Swiftly, he plunged it under the soldier's arm and threw him to the ground.

Cody hauled himself to his feet. No one was after him, he glanced around. Naomi was getting off the ground, her sword buried deep in the side of an unmoving soldier. Two other soldiers were fighting Adam, who was fending them off brilliantly with both blade and spell. The rest of the soldiers were busy with Stern and the Kar-Sang.

Cody looked the other way. Marek stood watching, knife still at Ara's throat. He smiled at Cody and pushed the knife harder against Ara's neck. A scarlet drop of blood ran down her skin.

Cody started for his brother. He saw Kaito appear over Marek's shoulder and tried to keep his expression neutral, but something on his face alerted Marek.

As Kaito attacked, Marek spun and shoved Ara in the way of Kaito's strike. Kaito pulled his spear back, the tip stopping an inch from Ara's chest.

The masked cultist beside Marek drew a long dagger and attacked Kaito, who blocked the knife easily and swung his spear, cracking it across the man's shoulder. As he stumbled back, Kaito switched his grip and threw his weapon, the razor-sharp point impaling the man's heart. The cultist's mouth fell open and he grabbed at the spear with numb hands. He fell to the ground, dead.

However, Kaito was now weaponless and Marek seized the opportunity. He knocked Ara on the head, dropping her to the ground, and charged Kaito. He lashed out with powerful, strategic strikes forcing Kaito to nimbly dodge out of the way. Marek jumped in close and slashed upward. Kaito caught his wrist and swung himself around so he was behind Marek. He attempted to put him in an armbar, but Marek dropped the knife to his other hand and struck the opposite way.

Letting go of Marek, Kaito managed to block the blow, but Marek's elbow caught him in the mouth. Kaito stumbled back and Marek lunged, aiming for the throat. Kaito threw himself into a backward somersault, avoiding the blow and came to rest on his knees.

Cody raced to Ara's side and checked her vitals. She was breathing. A bloody lump was forming on her head from where Marek had clubbed her. "Don't die, ok?"

He took a second to rub his shoulder as he stood. Something clicked as he moved his fingers over it. "Ah! Not good."

Marek was now using elemental magic against Kaito, who was knocking away rocks that Marek was launching at him. As Cody looked on, one got past Kaito's defences and crashed into his hip. He doubled over for a second, but that was all Marek needed to close in and jab his knife into Kaito's side.

"No!" Cody yelled. His friend staggered back and dropped to a knee, holding a hand to the gash on his right.

Cody raced at Marek, intending to cut his head off.

Marek flashed Cody an evil grin. He held out his left hand and a flame appeared on his palm, growing to a melon-sized ball. Marek whipped his arm and the fireball was flung at Cody. Without pausing, Cody dropped and slid across the dirt under the fiery projectile, popping to his feet on the other side.

Cody leapt at Marek, swinging for his head. Marek stepped to the side and Cody tumbled past, landing in a crouch. He spun around to face his brother.

Marek's smile was devoid of warmth. "Well, brother. Show me what they've taught you."

Anger welled up within Cody and he cursed Marek. "I will kill you."

"Good luck with that." Marek spun his dagger around his fingers.

Cody closed in on Marek, moving slower. He attacked horizontally at Marek's neck, but the older man bent backward and the blade sliced above his face. Grunting, Cody brought the sword back the other way, but Marek danced out of its path.

"What's the matter, little brother?" Marek taunted. "Can't hit me?"

"Stand still!" Cody yelled as he stabbed at Marek's chest. Marek spun to the left and Cody's sword pierced only air. Cody yelled in frustration.

Marek laughed. "Fine, brother, if it's a fight you want, I'll oblige, But I must warn you, you must do better, or you won't stand a chance."

Cody jabbed his shield ahead into Marek's face, breaking his nose. Both brothers yelled in pain. Cody grimaced as his shoulder tensed. "That better?"

Marek's smile was gone. He wiped his nose and glowered at the sight of his own blood. "Now you've done it."

Cody glanced past Marek at the battle raging behind him. Kinzo and Adam were side by side, protecting Naomi, who was nursing a leg wound. On the opposite side of the wall of soldiers, Rorien Stern and one Kar-Sang were still fighting. The other bloodsucker was lying face down. Cody wondered if it was dead.

He flicked his eyes back after a split-second. Marek was testing his knife against his fingertips. "You know, I'm going to enjoy killing you almost as much as enjoyed killing mom."

Cody's eyes widened. A deep fury rose from within him. "You bastard!"

Marek spread his hands.

Cody attacked, cutting down on an angle and then reversing to cut the other way. Marek deflected both strikes with ease. With his smaller weapon, he directed Cody's sword away from him instead of trying to stop the blade.

Marek kicked out and connected with Cody's left shin, causing him to stumble. Cody brought his shield up to take the next blow meant for his chest, fighting through the agony.

Marek's fist slammed into Cody's jaw and he saw stars. Staggering backward for room, he ducked behind his shield.

After a second, he looked out, but still saw a bright light. He realized it was another ball of fire. It slammed into his shield, sending him flying and searing his skin around the shield. He landed hard, banging his head. Groaning, he checked himself. Smoke rose from his blackened shield and part of his tunic had burned away.

He struggled to his feet and assumed a ready position.

Marek ambled over, that infuriating smirk on his lips. "How'd that feel?"

Cody seethed. He ran at Marek, who sidestepped and sliced his dagger across Cody's back. He yelled as a ribbon of fire tore across his shoulder blades. He turned to face Marek, chest heaving.

Marek waved his arm and air swept Cody off his feet. He tried to get up, but another gust shoved him back down. Then, the earth beneath him erupted upward, flinging him forward. He smashed his chin on a rock and his vision blacked out. When he could see again, Marek was squatting beside him, picking his teeth with his dagger.

"You are a disappointment." He sounded genuinely sorry. "I was expecting much from you. I guess you'll die a pathetic excuse for a human. Oh well. It was nice knowing you, brother." He raised his knife.

Cody tried to defend himself, but he was so thick-headed from all the blows that he could barely move. Everything hurt.

Marek cried out in pain as a spearhead ripped through his chest. Wide-eyed, Cody's brother stared at the spear and then toppled over.

Standing behind him was Kaito, bloodied and bruised. He pulled out his spear and leaned on it heavily. "Are you alright?"

"I'll... I'll survive," Cody said. "Thanks."

Kaito nodded and shuddered as a wave of pain passed through him.

"Are you ok?" Cody asked.

Kaito took his hand away from his wound. Blood still flowed freely, but it didn't look too deep. "I think I will be fine, as long as I stop the bleeding.

Cody looked over at his brother. He was moving slightly, tiny gasps escaping his mouth. "He's still alive."

"He will bleed out in minutes," Kaito said. The growing pool of red agreed with him.

Cody sighed. "It's for the best."

"Hey! You two dead or what?" Kinzo called. He and Adam were helping Naomi limp over. All the soldiers were dead or too injured to fight.

"We're still alive," Cody said. "Somehow."

"I see you're injured, Naomi," Kaito said.

She shrugged, but couldn't keep the pain off her face. "Nothing that won't heal."

"Me and Adam are fine," Kinzo said. "No injuries here."

Adam pointed at Kinzo's cheekbone, where blood still oozed. "You are wrong."

"What? That doesn't count," Kinzo said. "It's barely a scratch."

"It is bleeding a lot for a scratch," Adam said.

"No, it isn't."

Cody looked beyond them to where Stern was kneeling beside Ara. "Ara! Speak to me!" She didn't respond. He turned to the remaining Kar-Sang. "Wake her up!"

The Kar-Sang grabbed her wrist and a second later, she sat up, gasping. "Rorien?"

"Yes, it's me. You are safe."

Ara lay her head down, looking in the direction of Cody and his friends. She stiffened, eyes fixed on Kaito. "They're still here!"

Stern frowned. "I know."

Ara scrambled back. "No! They'll take me again!"

"What?" Stern asked.

"They are the ones who took me!"

Stern slowly turned, murder in his eyes.

"Uh, we have a problem," Cody said, getting up unsteadily.

Stern drew his sword and levelled it at Cody's chest. "You are all dead!"

CHAPTER 25

The Aedon stood tall among the sea of temporary shelters. With its stone walls, heavy oak doors, observation decks and troops of guards, it looked more like a fortress than the glorified inn that it was.

Levi pulled his mouth to one side. Last time he had been inside, he had been thrown in prison off the coast of the island. He ducked back behind the tent they were using for cover.

"They aren't going to let us in, are they?" Ring stated more than asked.

"Nope," Guy said. "We have no business going in there and we are literally the definition of a threat." He held up a cutlass for effect.

"We've got to find another way in," Miri signed.

"Well, we won't get in through the back door," Levi said. "They'll recognize me for sure."

Snare squinted at the Aedon. "The ground floor windows are pretty low. We could find an empty one and break-in."

"I like the sound of that," Coral grinned.

Ember wrinkled her nose. "I'd rather not break-in."

Guy gave her a dry look. "Look, darling, breaking and entering is hardly the worst thing you've done today."

Ember frowned. "Didn't need to remind me."

Aldus tapped his chin. "That is a possibility. However, if we choose to go that route and are caught, we won't be given a chance to explain ourselves. They will throw us directly in prison."

Levi recalled his brief time in jail. "That's not something I'm eager to do again."

Kana turned to the headmaster. "Are you sure there's no legal way to get in?"

"There certainly is," Aldus said. "But, unfortunately, I would only be able to bring one, maybe two with me. Not all of you."

Kana wrinkled her brow.

"I'm not staying behind," Snare said. "I have a score to settle."

Coral looked up from chopping the dirt with her axe. "I don't want to stay either. Not doing stuff is boring."

"Breaking in sounds like our best option," Guy said.

"Some of us are used to doing it," Ring said, the barest of smiles below red eyes.

"If only Evander was here with his amulet," Kana sighed.

Snare snorted. "Well, he's not here."

"And besides, we're going through a window, not a door," Levi said. "The amulet would be useless."

Kana crossed her arms. "It would still be better if he were here."

Guy scoffed. Ember elbowed him.

Levi peeked his head back around the tent. At the main entrance to the Aedon, four guards armed with halberds stood at attention. There would be at least two more on the other side of the doors and two at each stairwell. Plus, there was the attached guardhouse which held a thousand soldiers from the combined retinues of the nobles. That was a lot of people to avoid.

Levi scooted back behind the tent. "Hey, Aldus?"

The headmaster turned to Levi. "Yes?"

"You can create illusions, right?"

"Indeed," Aldus said.

"Could you make us look like carpenters repairing a broken window?" Levi suggested. "That way, at first glance, we'll seem innocent."

"That could work," Kana said. "It's bound to happen from time to time."

Aldus nodded. "Yes, yes. A good idea."

"What are we waiting for?" Snare said. "Let's infiltrate one of the most heavily guarded buildings in the realm.

"We are going to get caught," Ember said. "I hope my family will be willing to pay bail."

Guy nudged her. "C'mon, princess, be optimistic."

"Yeah," Coral said. "What's the worst that can happen?"

Ember opened her mouth to reply, but Guy cut her off. "Don't answer that."

Aldus steepled his fingers. "I will provide the illusion for you, but once you are in, I won't follow immediately."

Everyone stared at him.

"Why not?" Miri asked.

A wry smile crossed his face. "There is a high chance we will be caught. I am simply going to, how shall I put this, interfere with the guards' ability to come after us."

Levi grinned. "Not gonna tell us what you're going to do?"

Aldus put on a serious face. "Some things you aren't ready to know. I'll tell you one day."

Coral jabbed a finger at him. "You'd better. I wanna know how to stop a whole garrison of guards."

"Well, it only works if they don't know it's coming. So, we'd better hope they don't see me coming." Aldus stretched his back. "Now, hop to. We can't allow our quarry any more time to make plans and escape." He stretched out his left hand and closed his eyes for a brief moment. "There. Now we appear to be craftsmen." He motioned for the others to follow and stepped out from behind the tent.

"You sure?" Coral asked, looking down at her clothes. "I look the same."

Aldus strode toward the Aedon. "The illusion is for those looking at us from a distance. Up close, we appear as we are."

Some of the guards gave them a once-over as they neared, but no one paid them any special attention.

"Guess it is working," Coral said.

The group made it to the north wall with no trouble. There were only three windows on the narrow end of the building.

"Better hope at least one of these is empty," Kana muttered.

"I'll check," Ring volunteered. At Aldus' nod, she twisted her ring and vanished. Well, vanished was not quite true. Levi could still see a faint, shimmering outline, but unless one was looking closely, they would have no idea she was there.

Levi grew impatient after a minute. "Well?"

305

"Shut up, I'm looking," Ring answered from near the first window. "I can't see in the whole room. I'm waiting to see if anyone comes."

"Well, go faster," Levi grumbled.

Kana gave him a shot in the arm. "Cut it out. She can't decide if the people in there are gonna move in front of the window."

"Oh, hey!" Levi whacked her hand away. "Don't."

"Then don't be annoying," Kana replied.

Coral snorted. "You guys argue so much."

Miri raised an eyebrow and pointed at Guy and Ember.

Coral laughed.

"I think it's all clear," Ring said. "Wait! Here comes someone. Never mind."

"Next window?" Ember asked.

"Next window," Ring agreed.

As they moved to the next room, a woman walked around the corner. Levi sucked in his breath. This could blow their cover and bring the guards down on them. He ducked his head as the woman passed by. She glanced over with a questioning look.

"Maintenance," Guy said.

The woman nodded and continued on her way.

Levi released his breath. "Too close."

Ring snuck up to the second window and peered inside for a minute. "All the lamps are out. I don't think anyone's in here."

Levi pumped his fist. Good news.

"Let's hurry before someone comes in," Guy said, drawing one of his swords.

"Hold up," Levi said. "Aldus, we look like carpenters, right? But does it look like we are fixing the window?"

"Not yet," Aldus said. "I shall alter the illusion. Levi, Miri, come here. This is a prime teaching moment and I am an instructor, after all." He continued as Levi and Miri came to stand next to him. "Creating an illusion is all about picturing a specific image in your mind and projecting it in the same way that you do to communicate with others' minds."

"Doing that always gives me a headache," Miri signed.

"And I can barely even do that at all," Levi said.

"You will both improve," Aldus said. "The headaches will lessen the more you practice. Now, you must take care to not forget any details, such as which way the sun is casting shadows, or how hair and fabric moves in the wind. If you do, it will become more obvious to onlookers that it is nothing more than a mirage."

"Sounds complicated," Levi said.

Aldus gestured with his hand. "Again, practice." He began to explain the nuances of how to cast a believable illusion. Levi soon lost focus and let his gaze wander. He watched random people walk past as they went about their day, enjoying the festival. A trio of kids ambled away, arms full of prizes they'd won. A father carried his toddler girl on his shoulders. A middle-aged lady guided her elderly mother along by the hand.

His eyes caught on a patch of black and white. His guardian squirrel was sitting on a wagon, looking directly at him. Levi waved his fingers and Paco shook his head. Levi looked beyond him, eyes widening as he recognized two men walking past. Kyner and Evander. They walked fast, heads down, as if not wanting to be noticed.

"Hey, look!" Levi called, prompting everyone to look where he was pointing.

Kana's eyes lit up. "Evander!"

Hearing his name, he turned. Recognizing who was calling him, his face went white. Kyner grabbed his shoulder and broke into a run, the two slipping behind a shack.

"Wait! Where are you going? Come back!" Kana took off after them.

"What are you doing?" Ember tried to stop her.

"Going after them!" Kana yelled, knocking her hands away.

"Don't be ridiculous!" Ember said, but Kana didn't listen. She was already halfway to where they had disappeared. She melted into the crowd.

"Why'd he run?" Ring asked.

"Beats me," Guy said. "I'm sure he'll tell us when he's done with that other guy."

Levi narrowed his eyes. "Hmm. I'm not so sure."

"Never mind him," Snare said impatiently. "Let's get inside and get this over with."

"We're down one," Guy said.

"Leaving us with eight," Aldus said. "Enough to do what we've come for. Kana will be fine." He waved his hand. "The illusion is done."

307

Guy blew out a breath. "Alright. We can break the window now?"

Aldus nodded.

"Let me!" Coral said, shoving Guy aside. She swung her axe at the pane of glass, shattering it into thousands of razor-sharp shards.

"Oh, so many people heard that," Ember groaned.

"Definitely," Snare said as he climbed through the window with the grace of someone who had done so many times before.

Coral's grin was massive. "Awesome."

Guy slumped his shoulders. "I wanted to do that."

"Shoulda been faster," Coral taunted.

"I was there first!"

Coral stuck her tongue out and jumped through the window. Guy followed behind, still grumbling.

Levi went next. As he hauled himself up, his hand slipped, slicing his palm on the broken glass. He sucked in his breath and clenched his hand as warm blood seeped through his fingers.

"You ok?" Ring asked.

"Yeah, just a scratch," Levi said as he landed on the floor inside.

"Lot of blood for a scratch," Guy noted.

Levi grimaced. "Mm hmm. Get me something to bind it with."

Guy walked over to the four-poster bed and tapped the sheets that could be closed for privacy. "They don't really need these, do they?"

"Nah," Coral said. "Plus, we already smashed the window."

Guy smirked. His cutlass slashed through the light blue fabric as if it weren't there. He balled up a thin strip and tossed it to Levi. It fell short and hit the ground.

"Thanks," Levi muttered as he picked it up. He wrapped it around his palm, the fabric soaking up the blood quickly. He grunted as he tied it tight and the flow stopped.

"Are we clear?" Miri asked as she entered the room.

"So far," Ember said. "But we haven't gone into the hall yet."

Levi's eyes fell on the door on the opposite side of the room. On this side, they were safe, no one around to call them out. But on the other side, there were servants and nobles and guards, hundreds of people who knew they weren't supposed to be there.

"Can we make another illusion?" Guy asked.

Levi and Miri exchanged a glance. "Nope. We aren't good enough."

"And Aldus went to deal with the guardhouse," Ember said.

Levi scrunched up his eyebrows. They needed some way to move around undetected. *But how?*

"What if we actually get disguised?" Coral was standing in front of a walk-in closet stocked with dozens of outfits.

"That could work," Ring said.

Levi went over to the closet and peeked inside. The clothes hanging up probably cost more than his family's house back in Stagrun. Wide-eyed, he touched a silver dress that seemed to be made of pure starlight. It was soft and light, making Levi's own clothes seem like rawhide.

"Great," Snare said. "Let's play dress up."

Five minutes later, everyone was dolled up. Guy wore a dark green and brown suit with a waistcoat. The four girls wore blue dresses of varying styles. Snare had chosen white pants and a red jacket with golden shoulder pads and cuffs.

Only Levi was left. He was trying to figure out how to put on a jacket with an attached vest. There were just too many armholes. "Help," he pleaded.

"Levi, you are pathetic." Ember assisted him in getting his arms through the proper places.

"Thanks."

Ember raised an eyebrow. "That outfit does you no favours."

Levi looked down at himself. "What do you mean?"

"Never mind," Ember said. "We've wasted enough time already."

"Right," Levi said. Decked out in their new outfits, everyone readied themselves behind the door.

"Be careful," Miri advised. "Anyone could sound the alarm."

"They probably will," Snare said. "We're all armed."

Ember pursed her lips. "Many nobles do carry weapons..." She trailed off, looking at Miri and Coral. "Just the ladies don't usually have axes or longswords."

"Guess we're exceptions," Coral said as she picked at her dress, obviously not impressed by it.

"We're gonna die," Guy groaned.

"We'll be fine," Miri signed. She pointed at the door.

Levi dipped his head and opened the door. His pulse quickened as he stuck his head out and looked both ways. Grey robed servants stood near a few of the doors. None of them looked at Levi. He waved everyone out into the hallway.

"Where do we look?" Miri signed.

"I don't know," Levi said. She looked good in the dress, almost like a real noble. The scar on her cheek ruined the disguise a bit, but nothing was to be done about that. "We should check the private meeting chambers in the centre of the building. It would be a good place for whichever noble is paying to meet with what's his name."

"Marek," Ember said.

"Yeah, him," Levi said. "Is he actually Cody's brother?"

"Apparently," Snare said. "They look very similar, though they are clearly different people. Cody is a better person."

"That was mature of you," Ring said.

Snare made a face. "Shut up."

Levi took the lead, having a better idea of the building's layout than the others thanks to his brief stint undercover. He shook his head, remembering how disastrous his last visit had been. He hoped he wouldn't run into Randall. That would cause a scene.

His mind drifted to his imprisonment and fight with Kyner and then his escape thanks to Charlotte. He wondered if she had survived the geyser field. He hoped she had, he hadn't even had a chance to thank her for her help.

"I feel like one of these guys in grey is gonna rat us out," Guy whispered out of the side of his mouth.

Levi discreetly glanced left and right. On both sides, faces watched with mild curiosity and confusion.

"I doubt they will," Ember said. "It isn't their place to question the nobility."

Guy tipped his head. "But what if they notice we aren't nobility?"

"They won't as long as you act the part," Ember said.

"How?"

Ember rolled her eyes. "Walk with intent, head held high, posture straight, measured steps."

Guy gave her a look.

She sighed. "Just try it."

"Ok." Guy squared his shoulders, puffed out his chest and took exaggerated, swaying steps.

Ember covered her face with her hands. "Oh no. Stop. Just stop."

Guy stopped and turned, annoyed.

"Just walk normally," Ember said. "You look ridiculous."

"Make up your mind, woman."

"I have," Ember said. "Ignore what I said."

Guy held up his hands. "Alright. Fine."

Levi chuckled. Guy may have come from a well-off family with a distinguished heritage, but he was a far cry from Ember's upbringing, all prim and proper.

They neared the centre of the Aedon. Two guards were posted at the base of the close stairwell. Levi bit his lip. They would stop them for sure as soon as they noticed their weapons. And Coral was dragging along a battle-axe, which wasn't exactly subtle.

He leaned close to Miri. "Get ready for things to go bad."

She nodded. "I'll be ready, but this stupid dress will make it hard to move around."

"Just try your best," Levi said.

One of the guards turned to look at them, but a loud thumping echoed down the stairwell. It sounded like someone had fallen.

"What was that?" one of the guards asked.

"I don't know," the other replied. "But we best check it out." They threw open the doors and entered the stairwell.

"Now's our chance!" Levi said. He rushed past the guards' empty post into the central hall. The others hurried behind him.

"That was timely," Ember said.

"It was, wasn't it?"

Levi looked to his right. Aldus was sitting on a padded bench, one leg crossed over the other. He looked rather pleased with himself.

"That was you?" Snare asked.

Aldus bowed his head with a smile.

"Huh. Nice."

Around the corner, the guards came out of the stairwell. "Strange, very strange."

"I could have sworn something fell down..."

Levi chuckled. A perfect distraction that caused no suspicion.

"It was interesting," Aldus mused. "The guardhouse was nearly empty. There were only two squads inside."

"A stroke of luck, for once," Levi said. "But let's enjoy that after we're done."

He scanned the hall. It was thirty feet wide, the floor a beautiful carpet depicting the first festival. Tapestries on the walls rose all the way to the ceiling high above, golden chandeliers hanging from sturdy chains. Doors lined the far wall with more padded benches between each.

There were several people in the hall; mostly servants, but a few ladies in green and yellow dresses and an old gentleman, whose bald head shone in the light from the chandeliers above.

"Are those the private chambers?" Ring asked, motioning at the doors.

"Yeah. But I don't know which one to pick."

Snare pointed at the third door from the left. "How about the one with blood on the doorpost?"

Levi squinted and made out a red smear against the tan wood. "Good eye." He crossed the hall. As he neared, he began to make out muffled voices inside. They seemed to be in the midst of an argument.

"Can you tell what they're saying?" Miri asked.

Levi shook his head and pressed his ear up against the door. The voices became clearer.

"What do you mean, they've lost?" a man's voice said.

Another man answered. "I mean, some meddling kids got involved and beat all our men. Also, Marek and Rell are dead."

The first man spluttered. "What? Impossible! How can this be?"

"We should get out of here before anyone comes for us," a third, much deeper voice said.

"Yes, I agree," the second man said.

The first man growled. "All of this for naught! I will kill these meddling kids!"

The third man sighed. "You'll need more men. All of yours are dead."

Levi had heard enough. He pulled away from the door. "These are definitely the guys behind the Forsaken. Sounds like Cody and the others caught up with Marek and killed him."

"Good," Snare said.

Levi heard chairs being pushed back. "They're coming!"

"What do we do?" Ember asked.

"We fight," Ring said with a hard edge to her voice. She drew her dagger and sliced through the bottom of her gown, freeing her legs.

Aldus smoothed out his robe. "I would prefer a more diplomatic approach. But I fear they will give us little choice."

The handle turned. Levi wrapped his hand around the hilt of his sabre.

The door opened and Levi's eyes widened. "Baron Silva?"

The portly, moustached baron gasped in surprise. "You! You're supposed to be in prison!"

Levi couldn't believe it. "You're the bad guy?"

Silva was confused for a moment as he took in the rest of the group. Then, "You are the ones who ruined my plans!"

"Well, only half of us," Guy said. "But yeah."

Levi took a second to glance at the men with Baron Silva. One was obviously a knight in full armour with a serpent emblazoned on his chest plate. Levi recognized him as Teodric the Serpent. The other man was a guard, but the coloured band on his arm denoted him as a captain. His left hand was bandaged.

Aldus stepped in front of the students. "Greetings, gentlemen. We have matters to discuss."

"We have nothing to discuss!" Silva yelled, face red with rage. "You must be executed! Guards!"

"That's harsh," Guy muttered as he drew his cutlass. He fumbled it before assuming a defensive stance.

Silva turned to his companions. "Take them!"

The captain looked at Levi and his friends dubiously. "They have us outnumbered."

"Not for long," Silva said as four guards came running into the hall.

"Right. Let's get this over with." Teodric drew his sword. The honed edge caught the light, reflecting it into Levi's eyes. The pommel was also shaped as a snake, with rubies for eyes.

The captain drew a plain, utilitarian, but still very deadly sword and took a defensive stance. The four other guards closed in.

"Attack!" Silva yelled.

Teodric lunged, swinging his sword in a horizontal arc. Everyone leapt back, giving the bad guys more room.

Coral yelled and charged ahead, only to trip over her dress and stumble out of the way as a knife flung by the captain whizzed by. Levi saw him run at Ring before one of the guards demanded all his attention. Levi was put on the defensive, blocking a series of high sword strokes. He managed to slip in a strike of his own, but the guard leaned out of the way.

They broke apart and circled for a moment before re-engaging. Levi struck first, angling up at the man's neck. Their blades rang as the blow was blocked. The guard's free fist connected hard with Levi's jaw and his head snapped back. Out of reflex, Levi swung his left arm, whipping up his wrist. The shield hidden in his bracer sprang open, catching the guard under the chin and knocking him flat.

Levi cleared his head and waited to see if the guard would get up. He remained still. "Huh. That worked." He spun, looking for the next threat. Aldus, Snare and Miri were dealing with the other three guards while Coral and Ring battled the captain. Teodric, meanwhile, took on Guy and Ember. He spun and twisted like, well, like a snake.

Guy deflected a blow and yelled, "*Cindarior!*" Flames leapt at Teodric, who spun out of the way and doubled his attacks.

Ember was having a tough time defending against his attacks. Guy was faring better with his two swords, but Teodric had them both on their heels, not giving Guy the time to cast another spell.

Levi raced to help them, but was too far to help as Teodric's sword slammed into Ember's side. By sheer luck, the blade was turned and didn't cut her, but she still went flying, losing her rapier.

"Ember!" Guy cried. Teodric took advantage of his distraction. His sword flashed and Guy went down, left leg bleeding. He tried to get up, but the knight planted an armoured boot in the middle of his chest and kicked. Guy ended up on his back near Ember, who was coughing violently.

Teodric turned to Levi. "If you run, I won't chase you."

Levi swallowed. "Thanks, but you already hurt my friends. Now I have to fight you."

"Very well," Teodric rumbled. Levi barely saw him move before his sword was racing toward his head. Levi backpedalled, parrying furiously. Teodric pressed the advantage, allowing Levi no respite. He hammered on Levi's defences until his arm went numb and his sword was batted away. Levi lifted his shield.

Teodric wound up and punched the shield squarely in the centre. It slammed back into Levi's chin, stunning him.

A moment passed before Levi could see clearly. He was surprised to find himself still standing. Then, he saw Aldus battling Teodric. The headmaster held a curved sickle in each hand, attacking with smooth, graceful movements that were deceptively fast. There was a scowl on the knight's face as he tried his hardest to break through Aldus' intricate pattern of attacks and blocks and feints.

Levi stared in awe. He had never seen Aldus in combat before, except for when he had fought Stern in the Forenfall cathedral, but Aldus had conjured some strange magic that had concealed him from view. No wonder he was the headmaster of Blackthrush. He was a blur, always moving, seeming to attack from all sides at once. Teodric, a renowned fighter, was strictly on the defensive against him.

A yelp of pain brought Levi's attention to the others. All four guards were down, dead or not, he couldn't tell. Ring was backing up, shaking her left hand. The captain was now facing Coral alone, but as Levi looked on, Snare and Miri joined the fight, Miri having taken Ring's idea and cut open her restricting garments.

The captain fought admirably, but he couldn't last in a three on one. Miri knocked the sword from his hand and he sunk to the ground, bleeding from several wounds. Snare hit him in the face with the hilt of his dagger and he dropped.

"Where's Silva?" Snare asked, searching.

Levi glanced around. The baron was nowhere in sight. "He must have taken off!"

"We have to find him!" Coral exclaimed.

Levi looked at Guy and Ember. "You two ok?"

Guy gritted his teeth. "We'll survive. Go get that bastard."

Ember held a hand to her ribs and nodded.

"Right." Levi took off, leaving Aldus to deal with Teodric.

"I'm not letting him escape!" Snare growled as he limped to the hallway. Blood dripped down his left leg.

"There he is!" Coral cried, pointing down the hall on the right. He was making for the exit. She and Ring raced after him, Snare hobbling behind them. Servants scattered out of their way and noblewomen screamed.

Levi got a funny feeling in the back of his neck and a strange female voice spoke in his mind, one that he had heard before. *Turn around.*

He did as directed and froze. Karl Linae was walking purposefully down the hall. Levi tapped Miri.

"Linae? What's he doing here?"

"I think we both know," Levi said with a sinking feeling. "C'mon. We need to follow him and make sure we're right."

Miri nodded, her face serious. "The others can deal with Silva."

They raced to follow Linae, who was heading for a room on the left side of the left hallway.

"If he really is the spy, what's he up to?" Miri signed.

"Not sure," Levi said. "But we need to stop him before he tells anyone anything."

"Do you think he knows it's you?"

Levi shook his head. "If he did, I'd be captured already and probably dead."

Miri nodded grimly.

Linae held a hand against the door and a light flared from his palm. The door opened and he disappeared into the room. The door began to close, but Levi accessed his power and stopped it just before it shut. They jogged silently, not wanting Linae to hear them coming. Levi peeked through the doorway to see that the room beyond was actually another staircase, this one leading down in a spiral.

"Didn't know this was here," he whispered.

Miri pointed down, saying all she needed to. They began to creep down the stairs after closing the door behind them. They moved as quietly as possible, but the stairs still creaked slightly. Luckily, Linae was making enough noise to cover it as he descended.

They came to a railed landing that extended a few feet beyond the stairs. Levi peeked over the edge. About thirty feet below was a long chamber lined with pillars and flickering torches. There was nothing else in the room except a locked chest.

A few moments later, Linae stepped off the stairs and walked down the chamber. "Hello? Sire?"

At the far end of the chamber, two figures appeared from out of the shadows. Levi's stomach tightened as he recognized King Farren and Dravin.

Miri squeezed Levi's arm. He looked into her eyes and saw his fear reflecting back. "This is bad."

Levi swallowed, his throat suddenly dry. He looked back at the most powerful man in Terrenia, the one who above all wanted Levi dead. "Yeah. This is really bad."

CHAPTER 26

Torchlight flickered across rough-hewn stones lining the passage. Cobwebs clung to the ceiling, their weavers scuttling into the cracks in the mortar as the torch drew close.

Farren ignored the spiders as he descended the sloped path behind Dravin, who held their light source.

Every sound was amplified in the small passage, each footstep a slamming door.

No one had used this tunnel in years. The dust on the floor was thick, undisturbed. Farren needed to meet with a contact and it was crucial that no one saw them together. This tunnel led to a place where they could meet in total secrecy.

Dravin held the torch higher. "Sire, I believe we have arrived."

Farren didn't answer. He walked up to a closed door. The king closed his eyes, feeling the magical energy coming off the barrier. This was the right place.

"The password?" the king prompted.

"It is *shien nars*, sire," Dravin said.

Farren held his hand against the door and repeated the words. He felt a sharp stab in his palm and a light shone out from under his hand. There was a click as the lock released and the door opened. Farren glanced down at the small cut oozing blood in the centre of his palm. He clenched his fist and entered the room beyond.

It was dark, Dravin's torch barely illuminated anything. Air caressed Farren's face; the chamber was large. In the sparse light, he could make out thick pillars on each side of the room. Set partway up each of them were unlit cressets.

Farren whispered, *"Cindaria,"* and snapped his fingers. The cressets flared to life, illuminating the next set of pillars. A second later, the oil in the containers on the further supports caught fire as well, sparking a chain reaction until the entire chamber was lit. The light revealed a spiral staircase at the far end and closer, a locked chest.

Farren's eyes narrowed. "What is in that chest?"

"No one knows, your Majesty," Dravin said. "Everyone who has attempted to open it has died. It is a mystery."

Footsteps echoed down the stairs.

"Someone comes." Farren motioned for Dravin to step behind a pillar. "We will wait until we know if it is our informant."

Karl Linae stepped off the staircase and tugged on his bracer. "Hello? Sire?"

Farren stepped into the light and crossed his arms. "Well?"

Linae dropped to a knee. "My Lord."

"Stand and report," Farren said.

"Yes, sire." Linae ducked his head. "As you know, I have been observing Blackthrush for a long time."

Farren raised an eyebrow.

"Yes, yes, of course you know that," Linae said hurriedly. "And in that time, I have come to believe that there is a great chance that Aldus Calanol and several other instructors are working with the Giala and have persuaded some students as well. There are those who are always off on missions for Aldus, things that most students would not be allowed to do. Also, I have heard whispers that one of them may have what you are looking for, although of that, I am less sure."

"Do you have evidence?" Farren asked. He was glad that Linae believed his enemies were at Blackthrush, but he needed to be sure.

"Only circumstantial evidence, sire," Linae said. "But it is beginning to add up. I know that you want this resolved, so I am here to ask if I can openly question several of the students."

Farren shifted. This was a bold move. "What is your plan?"

Linae swallowed. "Well, they trust me. I can easily convince two or three of them to follow me to a location where your men are waiting. Then, I can question them."

"And what if they know nothing?" Dravin asked. "We can't let them go back, they would reveal you as the informant."

Linae looked uncomfortable. "I am aware. They would need to be imprisoned. It would be unfortunate, but the loss of a couple kids is well worth finding our enemies."

"Quite right," Farren said. "You have my permission. I will send a patrol to the Baron's second house as soon as they return. You will lead them there for questioning."

"Thank you, my Lord," Linae said.

"Linae," Farren said. "If anything is revealed, you are to report it immediately."

"Of course, sire."

Farren dismissed him. He rubbed his goatee as the spy began to climb the stairs. This could be a great opportunity. He hoped Linae proved there to be traitors at Blackthrush, the good news would be welcome. Every attempt to deal with the band of rebels here in Saken had been thwarted and left Farren frustrated. All his patrols had come back empty. Perhaps executing some traitors would soothe his worries. And if one of them was the bearer of the Elder Gem, all his problems would be solved.

"If Aldus is a traitor," Dravin said, "How will we deal with it?"

"We won't deal with it here," Farren said. "Not in this place, with tens of thousands of citizens to witness it." He tapped his cheek. "Not to mention all the knights, many of whom may not be loyal to me. No, we must draw them back to Blackthrush, get them alone. Then, we will crush them and I will kill Aldus Calanol myself."

The king found himself staring at the locked chest as he thought, *If Linae is successful, Blackthrush will fall.*

~ ~ ~

Levi's heart pounded. Aldus, the other Giala members, his friends, they were all on the verge of being discovered. And if they were, everyone at Blackthrush was in terrible danger.

Linae's footsteps drummed against the stairs. Coming close. Toward their hiding spot.

"We need to go," Miri signed. Levi had never seen her so scared.

"Yeah." They stole quietly across the landing and up the stairs. Miri opened the door and slipped out into the hall. Levi tried to follow, but something held him back. His fancy jacket was snagged on the latch. He pulled away, to no avail. He was stuck. "Help!"

Miri raced back and worked him loose and they silently closed the door.

Linae was only a few steps away.

"He'll recognize us," Miri warned.

"I know," Levi whispered in a panic. There was nowhere close enough for them to hide in time.

Linae was at the door.

Levi grabbed Miri, spun her around against the wall, leaned in and kissed her, his back to the door. Miri was too stunned to move.

Linae exited the room and snorted as he saw the two embracing. "Huh. Young nobles." He walked away purposefully.

Levi pulled away. "Whew."

Miri stared at him, mouth open.

"What?" Levi said. He felt heat rushing to his face. "It worked. He has no idea!"

Miri punched him in the chest.

"Ow!" Levi stepped back. "Hey!"

Miri's face was bright red. "Let's just go after him." She turned on her heel and marched away. Levi followed.

Levi's head was all over the place. He couldn't help but think about the kiss, even though there had been no romantic intentions behind it. It was his first kiss after all. Not how he thought it was going to be. He pushed the thought aside to deal with the more serious matter. Blackthrush was in grave danger and by extension, his friends and the Giala and, well, Terrenia as a whole. They needed to silence Linae. For good.

Up ahead, Linae exited the Aedon. Levi picked up the pace, not wanting to lose him in the crowd outside.

He turned to Miri. "Can you call Aldus? Tell him about Linae?"

Miri dipped her head.

They raced outside. There should have been guards on the steps leading up to the doors, but there were none. Patches of blood led Levi to guess that Coral, Snare and Ring had taken care of them. Levi scanned the crowd and spotted Linae heading in the direction of the Blackthrush camp. Further on, the pillar of smoke was still billowing into the sky.

"That must be where the others fought Marek," Miri said.

"Probably."

"Hopefully, they're ok," Miri said.

"They'll be fine," Levi said. "But not for much longer, if we don't catch Linae."

Miri caught his meaning and her brow furrowed. She took off after Linae.

Unaware that he was being followed, Linae was in no rush. They caught up to him quickly, next to one of the few permanent buildings, a two-story grocery store. Levi didn't come up with a plan or discuss anything with Miri. As soon as he reached Linae, he tackled him into the building.

Linae cried in surprise and pushed Levi off. He scrambled to his feet. "Levi?" His face registered shock that morphed into suspicion.

"I'm going to kill you," Levi growled. "Spy!"

Linae glanced behind Levi to where Miri was standing with Evenfell pointed at him. He chuckled. "I guess I won't have to question anyone. You've given yourselves away. Farren will be pleased."

Levi yelled and thrust out his hand, blasting Linae across the store with magic. He was so angry, he hardly noticed he was buzzing with magical energy. "You'll never betray Blackthrush! You won't turn against Aldus! And you won't get the Gem!"

Linae picked himself up off the ruins of a table and dozens of potatoes. He stared at Levi for a moment, smirked and whipped both arms down, long dirks sliding out of hidden sheaths into his hands. "So, you do have the Gem. I should have known it was you. Everything changed the minute you arrived."

"Good thing you were too dumb to realize it," Levi said, leaping ahead mid-sentence. His sabre was easily blocked by Linae, who returned the attack. Levi parried and lashed out. Linae jumped back and to the left, out of the sword's deadly path.

Miri joined the fray, kicking Linae in the chest. He crashed into a row of shelves, knocking them over. Miri followed up with a downward stroke, which Linae dodged. Evenfell bit into the overturned shelf and stuck fast.

Linae stabbed at Miri, who let go of her sword to leap out of harm's way.

Levi charged ahead, flicking open his shield and ramming into the spy. Both tumbled across the floor, landing at the base of a staircase. Linae got to his feet first and kicked Levi in the chest as he tried to get up. Levi slammed back, air rushing from his lungs.

Linae swooped down for the kill, but Evenfell's long, straight blade flashed to intercept. Linae's left dagger was knocked from his hand and stabbed into the wall.

Miri hacked left and right, backing the spy up the stairs. They slipped out of view on the second floor. Levi could hear them battling as he pushed himself to his feet and climbed the steps. He grabbed the end of the banister and swung himself around.

Miri and Linae played a game of cat and mouse, Linae trying to avoid the long reach of Evenfell by running behind shelves and tables. Miri didn't let up. She soon backed him against the far wall, an open window behind him.

Levi ran over as Miri struck out at Linae. His dirk took the hit, but he lost his grip on it and it spun away into the store. Linae didn't try to move out of the way as Miri prepared to finish him. He closed his eyes, touched his ring fingers to his thumbs and crossed his arms at the wrist. The air rippled like a wave, washing over Levi.

He slowed. "What?" He was still running, but at a fraction of the speed he had been. He strained vainly to move faster.

Linae let out a breath. He stepped out of the path of Miri's blade, which was slowed the same way Levi was. He circled her and shook his head. "Pity. I liked you." He gave her back a hard shove and then waved his hand.

Levi stumbled ahead, suddenly released from the magic. Miri tumbled forward and pitched out the window, her gasp as fearful as any scream.

"Miri!" Levi propelled himself across the store toward the window. He heard the dull thump and leaned over the ledge. Miri lay unmoving in an awkward position. "What have you done?" Levi yelled, turning to face the spy. He saw the wooden plank for a split-second before he was struck in the forehead and tumbled backward out the window.

He must have blacked out for a few moments. He opened his eyes and groaned mightily. His chest burned with each breath; broken ribs for sure. His head throbbed and everything else felt bruised. He turned his head, fighting through the spinning of the earth and looked at Miri. She hadn't moved, but her chest rose and fell. Her sword lay a few feet away.

Levi heard someone coming. He managed to look up into Linae's hard eyes. He had retrieved his daggers. His fingers twitched on their hilts, anticipating the killing blows.

Levi strained to get up, but Linae's boot knocked him down, sending a shock of pain through his broken ribs.

The spy knelt down between the two and touched his dirk to Levi's throat. "I would like to, but you're spoken for. Her, on the other hand..." He moved his other knife over her chest.

"No..." Levi croaked. He pushed himself up with an elbow, only to be shoved back to the ground.

"Goodbye, Miri," Linae said as he raised his dirk.

Levi watched in open-mouthed horror as his former teacher prepared to kill his friend. Something inside of Levi shifted, like a gear clicking into place. His back arched as a flood of power raced through him. He couldn't contain it, it was too much. He thrust out his hand and a bolt of blue lightning flew from his fingertips and slammed into Linae's back.

The spy screamed as he was launched through the air, smashing through tents, flattening them. A trail of smoke followed him to where he landed, a hundred feet away.

Levi stared down at his hands. Sparks jumped as electricity crackled between his fingers. "What?" He sat up in wonder. He felt fine. Placing a hand on his chest, he took a deep breath but felt no pain. His head was clear. He felt great, better than he ever had. The power flowing through him made him feel unstoppable.

He sprang to his feet and glanced at Miri. She stirred slightly. *She'll be fine. I have to stop Linae!*

"Levi!"

Aldus, Guy and Ember were coming toward him, the students supporting each other. Leading them was Paco. The headmaster nodded to the squirrel as he knelt next to Levi.

"Dude, you're sparking!" Guy said.

324

"I know," Levi said. "Not sure how. But I've gotta catch Linae. He's the spy!"

"Karl Linae?" Ember asked.

"Yeah, I blasted him with lightning."

"How? You're a Mind Mage, not an Elemental," Ember said. "Is that possible?"

Aldus didn't answer. He was studying Levi intently.

"We can figure it out later!" Levi insisted. "Linae can't get away!"

"Of course. That is more pressing." Aldus turned to Ember and Guy. "Watch over Miri."

Guy tossed him a salute. "You got it."

Levi spun on his heel and raced toward the spot where Linae had crashed. He leapt through flattened tents, startling people who stared at his sparking form. There was a ten-meter long trench where Linae had impacted. He was still struggling to get up, one arm clearly broken.

He stared at Levi. "How are you doing that? It is not your order."

"No idea," Levi said. "But now, I'm going to kick your-"

"So, it is you, Karl," Aldus said.

Fear flickered in the spy's eyes for a second before they hardened. "Yeah. It's me. You're an old fool, Aldus. All this time, you had no idea it was me."

Aldus shook his head. His voice was sad. "I had hopes for you, Karl."

Linae scoffed. "What, to join the Giala? I would never join your pitiful band of revolutionaries."

"Can we just kill him already?" Levi asked. The electricity coursing through him had him twitching and fidgeting.

"You could," Linae said with a cough. "But are you really going to waste time chasing me when your friends are about to die?"

"What are you talking about?" Levi asked.

Linae pointed to Levi's left. Levi gasped. Cody and the others were battling Rorien Stern and one of the Kar-Sang. And there were already too many of his friends on the ground.

He took a step toward them. Aldus grabbed his wrist and stopped him. Levi's eyes flashed. "Hey!"

"Levi!" Aldus said, face grave. "Linae is more important! The fate of the world depends on stopping him. And if your friends have to die to make sure that happens, that is a sacrifice we must be willing to make."

Levi's heart dropped. "But..."

"Levi, this is bigger than them. Now, we must stop him! He's gone!"

Linae had taken off. He was slow, injured from Levi's attack.

Levi looked between his friends and the spy he needed to stop. He was torn. He desperately wanted to help his friends, but he knew Aldus was right. They couldn't let Linae escape. Tears of frustration sprang to his eyes and he dashed them away. "Let's get this bastard." He began to run.

Linae had a head start, but his injuries slowed him enough that Levi and Aldus closed the gap quickly.

Linae turned right around a green tent and when Levi and Aldus reached the spot, they halted in their tracks. Four guards were running at them, weapons drawn.

"Halt!" one of them called.

Levi glared at Aldus. "I thought you dealt with the guards."

"All of the ones who were in the barracks, yes," Aldus said. "Not every guard was."

Levi growled. "We don't have time for this." He opened his hands, letting the electricity leap from his fingertips to the guards in front of him. Two of them screamed as they were thrown back. One of the other guards dropped down, unconscious: Aldus' doing.

The last guard backed up, disconcerted at how quickly his companions had been taken care of. "St... Stop!" he stammered.

Levi charged and threw his sabre. It spun end over end until the hilt slammed into the man's head. His helmet rang, his eyes glazed over and he toppled to the ground. The sabre bounced off the helmet and Levi snatched it out of the air as he raced by.

Bystanders scurried out of their way, seeing at how they had dismantled the guards in an instant.

Linae checked over his shoulder and grimaced. He hadn't gained much ground at all. He couldn't evade them for long. While he was looking behind him, his ankle turned on a loose stone and he pitched forward. Unable to keep his balance, he flailed and landed heavily on his chest.

Levi and Aldus were on him in a moment. Levi punched him in the back of the head as he tried to get up, driving him to the ground.

Linae flipped over and swung his legs, taking out Levi's ankles. He landed on his rear. Linae's boot rammed into his right cheek. Levi's head jerked back as his eyes filled with reflex tears. It took him a moment to clear his head.

Linae was trying to fight Aldus, but it was one-sided. Linae had a broken arm and Aldus was a master. Levi sat and watched as Aldus disarmed Linae. The spy looked at his empty hands, then at Aldus and his bloodstained sickles. "Please," he whimpered.

"I'm sorry, Karl," Aldus said, truly meaning it. Then, he slashed open Linae's throat. The spy didn't even try to stem the blood. He stared into Aldus' eyes as he faded away, finally dropping to the ground.

Aldus bowed his head and whispered something.

Levi stood. "Guess it's over."

"Yes, it is," Aldus agreed.

Levi's eyes drifted down to Linae's lifeless body. He remembered him as the instructor teaching magic at Blackthrush, doing a fine job of replacing Korlec. He sighed. "Pity." Suddenly, a wave of exhaustion crashed over Levi as the flow of power stopped. It felt like someone had put a stopper in a tap. He stumbled and bent over, breathing heavily.

"You burned through your stores of energy," Aldus said. "You won't be able to use magic until they replenish."

"That sucks." Levi held his hands close. They were no longer sparking. His head shot up. "We've got to save the others!" He saw images of Rorien Stern standing with a bloodied sword over the bodies of his friends. He couldn't let that happen.

"Yes, now that this is done, we should help them," Aldus said.

Levi didn't wait for him. He took off back the way they had come, but he could only manage a fast jog. He was out of energy, running on willpower alone.

Passing the place where they had beaten the guards, he saw the one he had knocked down tending to the one Aldus had dropped. When he saw Levi coming, he held up his hands. "Don't hurt me!"

Levi snorted and ran past, leaving the pathetic guards behind.

Up ahead, he could see the pillar of smoke still rising and the orange under glow from the flames that engulfed the duelling arena. He urged himself to go faster, ignoring his burning muscles and screaming lungs. Sweat dripped into his eyes. He stumbled and caught himself with his hands. With a growl, he pushed off the ground and kept running.

The battlefield came into view as he rounded a shack. He barely took in the bodies on the ground, his gaze drawn to Stern battling Cody. Cody was in rough shape and Stern beat through his defences. Cody was knocked down and Stern's sword began its descent.

"No!" Levi yelled. He could only hope he would make it in time.

CHAPTER 27

Cody struggled to his feet. "Whoa, whoa, Stern. Hold up."

"No!" Stern yelled. "You lot are done lying to me! All your lives are forfeit!"

"I don't even know what that means!" Kinzo shot back.

"It means he is about to kill us," Adam explained.

Kinzo nodded. "Probably coulda figured that out."

"Silence!" Stern yelled, his face red. He lowered his sword at them. "Attack, Mig!" The Kar-Sang at Ara's side flew at Cody, summoning a huge battle-axe.

"Scatter!" Cody shouted. Kinzo helped Naomi up and Kaito managed to drag himself away.

Adam exchanged his sword for his bow, letting an arrow fly at the Kar-Sang. Mig shifted and the projectile sped past. Adam fired again and the Kar-Sang dodged the second arrow, but Adam had learned. He sent another arrow directly after the first. It struck the bloodsucker in the upper left chest. With a screech, the Kar-Sang dropped out of the sky, landed on its feet and ripped the arrow out in a spray of black blood.

Cody turned away as Stern advanced on him. Bloodlust was in the Taskmaster's eyes.

"Just so we're clear," Cody said. "I had nothing to do with the kidnapping."

"You were the cause of it! You still die!"

Cody's shoulders drooped. "You are the worst."

329

In three quick strides, Stern closed the gap and attacked. Cody parried. The next blow he took on his shield, groaning in pain as his shoulder resisted. He needed to go on the attack. He side-stepped and launched a side cut, overhand slash combination. Stern batted both aside. Stern kicked at Cody's leg, but he spun out of the way and slashed at Stern's side. The Taskmaster saw it coming and ducked under the blade.

Cody stepped back for a brief respite, but Ara threw a rock at his chest, distracting him. Stern took the opportunity and lunged. Cody brought up his shield, but he was late and only deflected the sword. Stern's weapon sliced across Cody's ribs. He yelled in pain and swung blindly. Stern was so close that the crossguard of Cody's sword cracked against his head. Stern backed off, blood trickling from his forehead. Cody checked his side; the wound was shallow, but still stung.

Stern looked past Cody and began beckoning. "Get over here and help me, you fools!"

A group of ten soldiers had come from the east and were staring at the carnage. "What's going on here? We heard there was a fight."

"They kidnapped my sister!" Stern said. "Kill them!"

"Right, come on, men," the lead soldier said.

Cody groaned. This was getting worse and worse. The soldiers closed in on them.

A blur came from the right side and attacked the guards. Kaito. He spun like a whirlwind, striking with both ends of his spear, never staying still enough for the soldiers to attack back.

Cody watched in wonder. He had never seen Kaito fight like that before. And he was injured as well. *How is he doing that?*

Kaito retreated after thirty seconds. Three soldiers had fallen to the lightning attacks. He was bent over, leaning on his spear. He seemed utterly spent.

"Look out!"

Cody was tackled by Kinzo as Stern's sword missed both of them. Kinzo rolled off and said, "That's twice, you know."

"I know, I know." Cody accepted Kinzo's extended hand and stood. "Watch out!"

Kinzo turned to get a huge armoured fist in the face. He crumpled into an unconscious heap.

"I tried," Cody said. He glanced up and swore. Stern was encased in his massive, magical armour. "Aw, I thought that got broken."

"I repaired it, you dunce," Stern said, his voice amplified.

Cody backed up, looking at the other fight. Adam was fending off Mig, who seemed off-balance and clumsy. Naomi was sitting a few metres away, holding a hand to her temple. She was using telekinesis to keep the Kar-Sang off balance. She had never been great at it, but it was helping Adam and was all she could do with her injured leg.

Cody focused back on Stern and his giant suit of armour. The sword was massive, it would easily smash through his shield with a direct hit. And he couldn't hope to block with his own sword. He recalled Levi telling him how he and Miri had beaten him. They had tag-teamed, never fully engaging and had kept Stern moving. Of course, they had both been injured and hadn't actually won, simply escaped.

Stern lifted his gigantic blade and swung it at Cody. He dropped to the ground, let it pass overhead and scrambled back to his feet. Stern lunged ahead, intending to skewer Cody, but he jumped to the right. He then immediately had to fall backward as Stern swiped at him. He held himself up with his hands. The sword just missed.

He pushed himself up and thought, *I need to go on the attack.* He darted ahead and chopped at Stern's knee, but his sword just bounced off the metal with a loud clang. Cody had just enough time to realize he had made a mistake before Stern kicked him ten feet.

The impact tore the air from his lungs and popped his back in a strange way. His sword lay three feet away. He rolled over, ignoring the pain and went for his weapon. He could hear Stern's heavy footsteps approaching. His fingers wrapped around the sweaty hilt of his sword. Flipping over, he held his sword and shield over his head, bracing for the blow.

It never came.

Cody heard a yell and a metallic thunk. He peeked out from behind his shield. Stern was stumbling back. Between him and Cody was a fully armoured man; a knight.

He turned to Cody. His visor was up, revealing him to be El Fen. "Help Kaito. I'll deal with Stern."

Cody struggled to his feet. Every part of him groaned in protest. He had never been in so much pain, but he knew he couldn't stop yet. In his peripherals, he saw El Fen charge Stern, only to spin to the side when Stern attacked. The knight brought his sword down in a series of heavy blows before darting away from Stern's blade.

Cody jogged over to where Kaito was fighting the soldiers. One more had joined his companions on the ground, but it was six on one. Kaito was only avoiding their attacks now, having sustained several new wounds.

Cody hit the soldiers from the side, catching them off-guard. He rammed his shoulder into one, knocking him and the soldier behind him to the ground. He lashed out wildly, feeling his sword slice through flesh. Another soldier dropped, holding his side.

The rest of the soldiers backed off, regrouping.

Cody stood next to Kaito.

"Nice of you to join me." Kaito gritted his teeth and swayed. His tunic was soaked in blood, mostly from the wound Marek had given him.

"Yeah. How'd you manage that attack?" Cody asked.

"A Chaotic power," Kaito said. "For a short time, you can't feel anything. I have only used it once before."

"Cool. Teach me sometime."

Kaito grimaced. "Let's first finish this."

"Right." Cody pointed his sword at the five remaining soldiers. "You've lost. Surrender."

"Stupid kids," one of them snarled. "We'll kill you both."

Cody smirked. "Good luck. You couldn't even manage that with twice the men."

The soldiers shifted uncomfortably.

Cody continued to taunt them. "They must pick the worst candidates to become soldiers. You guys probably have never fought anybody more than street urchins weighing ninety pounds." He chuckled. "I mean, puh-lease. The king expects you to keep the realm in order? You can't even control a couple of kids!"

One of the soldiers had had enough. He yelled insults as he rushed Cody, lowering his spear. As he jabbed, Cody deflected the spearhead with his shield and held out his sword. Meeting no resistance, the man careened forward, Cody's sword slipping under his arm and into his heart, killing him instantly. Cody pushed him over and yanked his sword out. He shook off bits of gore and said, "Anybody else?"

"That's it, I'm out!" one of the soldiers said. "I'm not getting killed today."

"Yeah," another said. "Besides, it's just the Taskmaster. Nobody likes him anyway." The other two nodded. They all lowered their weapons and hustled away, leaving Kaito and Cody facing no one.

"That was well-handled," Kaito said. "Good job."

Cody let his shoulders droop. He had put on a show, knowing that he was too injured and exhausted to actually beat all five of them. "I wish we could solve all our problems by bluffing."

Kaito lowered himself to the ground and pointed over his shoulder. "They have that under control, right?"

Cody looked at his friend's injuries and the amount of blood still seeping out. "Yeah, they've got it." He put a hand on his shoulder. "Get those tied up."

Kaito nodded, already tearing his tunic into strips.

Cody left him and headed back to the others. He watched El Fen battle Stern for a moment. Adam's dad was a phenomenal fighter, quick on his feet and even quicker with his strikes.

Stern, on the other hand, was nowhere near as fast. While his armour made him incredibly strong, it also made him slower and clumsier than normal and El Fen was running rings around him.

"He doesn't need help," Cody said. He decided to help Adam and Naomi fight the Kar-Sang. Adam and Mig had moved away from Naomi and Cody slid to a stop next to her.

"Oh, Cody! You scared me!" She sounded drained.

Cody looked her over. Her leg wound was still weeping blood into a pool in the dirt and she was paler than normal. "You alright?"

"Uh, not really," Naomi said. "It's pretty deep and I'm starting to get dizzy."

Cody winced as he looked closer. He could see split muscle underneath and a hint of white. "Yeah, no kidding."

"I need to wrap it, but I was helping Adam."

"I'll wrap it," Cody said. "Although I don't really know what I'm doing." Blackthrush taught first-aid in first year, but Cody hadn't paid attention.

"I'll guide you," Naomi said. "We'll need a clean rag."

Cody looked down at his filthy, tattered, bloodstained clothes. "How bout we use yours?"

Naomi frowned. "I like this shirt."

"It's your leg."

"Fine, rip off a sleeve," Naomi sighed, holding out her arm. Cody grabbed the light blue fabric and tried to tear it. He was unable to.

Despite the situation, Naomi giggled. "You have a very sharp weapon with you."

Cody gave her the stink eye. "Yeah, yeah, whatever." His sword easily sliced through the fabric. "Don't say anything."

Naomi tried to keep a straight face as she zipped her lips. She moved her leg and grunted, her face a grimace.

Cody shuffled down to her leg and made a face of disgust at the sight of the cut. "Ok, so I just wrap it?"

"You need to clean it first," Naomi said.

"Clean it?"

Naomi nodded. "It would be good if we had alcohol, or at least some water."

"Fresh out."

"Then just wipe it with the rag. Get all the debris out."

Cody paused. "You want me to put my hand in the cut?"

Naomi nodded.

"Uh uh. That's gross."

Naomi rolled her eyes. "You have no problem inflicting these kinds of wounds and worse on other people."

"Yeah, but I never have to stick around to see, much less put my fingers inside."

"Just do it!" Naomi snapped.

"Ok, fine!" He clenched his teeth and slowly pushed the rag into the cut and gagged as he felt warm blood and twitching muscle.

"Clean it!" Naomi said in a pained voice. Both hands were digging into the dirt.

Cody took a deep breath and began to wipe the wound. Naomi grunted with each stroke. He hated to hurt her, but it was necessary and he kept going until there was no dirt in the cut.

"Now, wrap it," Naomi said.

Cody looked up to see tears clinging to her eyelashes. She glared at him. He took the rag and carefully wound it around her leg and began tying it loosely.

"No, idiot! Pull it tight!" Naomi said. "It has to stop the bleeding."

"Right. Here goes." Cody yanked it tight and tied it. Naomi screamed, arching her back. "Sorry,"

She shuddered. "No, it's ok. It's good." She looked down. "The bleeding's slowed. Good."

"Mm hmm. You good if I go help Adam?" Cody asked.

She waved him away. "Yeah. Go help him."

Cody snatched up his sword and took a moment to study the fight. Adam was doing a remarkable job against the Kar-Sang. Most of his friends wouldn't have lasted half as long as Adam had. And he had found his mark several times, judging from the dark blood dripping from the monster. There were also several torn ropes tangled around the Kar-Sang, a testament to Adam's spellcasting that hadn't proved to be as useful as Adam had hoped. But Adam was tiring. Cody could see it in his swings. They were beginning to become sloppy. Soon, he would make a mistake and Mig would drive the head of his axe into him.

"Not on my watch," Cody said. His eyes landed on a large stone near his feet. "Hey! Ugly!"

The Kar-Sang turned to get the rock directly above the left eye.

"Catch!" Cody ran at the recoiling monster. He drew back his arm and put everything he had into his swing. His blade chopped through the haft of the axe, the head falling to the ground with a dull thunk. Cody followed up with another swing, but the Kar-Sang ducked away.

Cody glanced at Adam. "How you holding up?"

Adam wiped his brow. "I am in an undesirable condition to continue the fight."

"Ok, how bout I fight and you watch my back?" Cody said.

"That would be ideal," Adam said.

Cody tossed him a thumbs up and faced the Kar-Sang. "You give up yet?"

Mig hissed at him. Then, it shimmered and disappeared.

"What the?" Cody's head swung from side to side. He couldn't find it.

"I believe it has gone invisible," Adam said.

"Uh, yeah, I gathered that." Cody backed up a step, holding his shield at the ready. He listened closely and heard the rustling of cloth nearby. He lunged to his right, slashing through empty air.

"Look for the blood drops!" Naomi called. "Over there!"

Cody scanned the ground and saw what she meant: little specks of black liquid. The trail came closer and closer. Cody attacked again, but still hit nothing. "Huh?"

From above came a screeching. Cody reacted too slowly. The Kar-Sang dropped from the sky, its foot slamming into Cody's jaw. His vision went black.

He came to sometime later. He rubbed his eyes and shook his head. It throbbed as if something inside was beating against his skull. The first thing he saw was Adam lying awkwardly on the ground. For a second, he feared the worst, but then Adam stirred. The sound of combat reached his ears. He looked beyond Adam to where Mig was beset by Coral, Ring and Snare. They were tag-teaming him perfectly, never staying in reach for long, giving him more injuries with each attack, even though Snare was limping slightly and Ring's hand was bleeding. Relief swept through him. They couldn't have arrived at a better time.

Cody heard grunting behind him. Naomi was dragging herself over.

"They showed up a minute ago," Naomi said, answering the question she knew Cody was about to ask. "They barely saved Adam, he was a goner if they had been two seconds later."

"I'll have to thank them after," Cody said. He rubbed his aching jaw. "Wow, he really got the drop on me."

Naomi pulled herself up beside him. "Yeah. If he had used a sword instead of his foot…"

"I'd be dead," Cody finished. "I know." He was tired of nearly getting killed and having to be rescued by his friends. He wanted to be the one doing the rescuing. He felt pathetic.

Naomi noticed he was feeling bad. "At least you are alive."

Cody's face fell even more as he remembered Latch. How he had looked into Cody's eyes as he lay dying in the hallway beneath the Forsaken compound. His hand slipped into his pocket, wrapping around the smooth stone Latch had given him with his dying breaths.

A cry of pain drew Cody's attention. Ring was staggering back, holding her left arm close to her chest.

"Ring! You ok?" Snare asked.

Ring gritted her teeth. "I don't know."

"Then fall back!" Snare said. "We've got this."

Coral jabbed the butt-end of her axe into the Kar-Sang's side. "Yeah, we're good."

Ring came over to where Cody and Naomi sat.

"How bad is it?" Cody asked. He could see a lot of blood running between the fingers of the hand covering the wound. She uncovered it, revealing a four-inch-long cut.

"Ouch," Cody commented.

Ring grimaced. "I can't move two of my fingers."

"It probably severed a tendon," Naomi said.

Ring moaned. "Can you fix it?"

Naomi's eyes widened. "Me? No. I have no idea how to repair a tendon."

Ring's face fell. "Stupid monster."

"Speaking of it, I should go help the other two." Cody swayed as he stood.

"You sure that's a good idea?" Naomi asked. "Plus, it looks like they have it handled."

Cody closed one eye against his throbbing headache and watched Coral and Snare work together to wear Mig down. Snare particularly was doing a great job. He used his speed and agility to avoid all the attacks and stick the Kar-Sang with his knives.

As Cody looked on, Snare jumped in, stuck Mig in the abdomen and did a backward somersault to evade the incoming strike. That allowed Coral to sneak up behind the bloodsucker and swing her axe into its head. The sound was horrible; a wet crunch like someone breaking a watermelon. Without a sound, the Kar-Sang dropped to the ground, blood pouring from the canyon in its skull.

"Whoo!" Coral yelled. "Take that, you mangy prick!'"

Snare managed a smile. "Good job."

Cody helped Naomi hobble over to the victorious duo. "Great work."

"Thanks," Coral beamed. "I always wanted to split a skull."

"Odd," Cody said. "But, ok."

"Where'd you guys come from?" Naomi asked. "Weren't you guys infiltrating the Aedon?"

"We did," Snare said. "And we found the filthy lord backing the Forsaken. We chased him down and I relieved him of his windpipe."

Ring shook her arm. "The others were fighting the guards and stuff."

"Then, we happened to be close enough to see you get kicked in the head," Coral said. "Came and saved the day."

"We're very thankful for that," Naomi said.

Cody put a hand to his head. "Yeah, I owe you guys."

"We'll just count it as all covered for helping us destroy the Forsaken," Ring said. She looked at Snare. "Right?"

"Yeah, sure," Snare said. He looked past Cody. "Who's that fighting Stern?"

"Oh, that's Adam's dad," Cody said. "He's a great knight."

"I can see that," Snare said.

Cody watched the seasoned warrior batter away at Stern's armour. "I'm actually surprised he hasn't beaten Stern yet."

"It shouldn't take him too long to-" Snare stopped mid-sentence, choking and gasping. Everyone turned to see a black blade sticking out of his chest.

Cody was frozen in place, too shocked to act.

Snare's tunic turned red. He grabbed the wound, his breathing rapid and shallow. The blade was torn out and Snare dropped to his knees. Behind him was the Kar-Sang, head still split wide-open.

Horrified, the words of the Creatures instructor at Blackthrush came back to Cody. "A Kar-Sang can only be killed by a thrust to the heart. All else will only injure it." His jaw jumped and he was suddenly able to move. He lunged forward, jamming his sword directly into the middle of the monster's chest. The Kar-Sang shook once, violently and began to smoke, dissolving into a black cloud. Its cloak fell to the ground as the wind dissipated the cloud into insignificant specks. He hardly dared to believe it was dead, that he had killed it.

He turned, his heart heavy.

Snare was resting in Ring's arms as she wept over him. His chest was soaked in red. No breath moved his chest.

Naomi sat nearby, hands over her mouth.

Coral swore explosively and chopped her axe into the earth with a yell.

Cody slowly knelt next to Snare's body. He let his sword fall from his hand and looked into the urchin's unseeing eyes. "I'm sorry."

Ring let out a sob. "Oh Snare. What am I going to do? First Latch and now you? I..." Her words crumbled as she lay her head on her friend's shoulder.

Cody stood and stalked away. He was angry, furious. He hated how unfair life was, how cruel the universe could be. He looked up at the sky and the billowing smoke.

A yell startled him. He saw El Fen trapped under a heap of giant armour and Stern racing toward him, a naked sword in hand.

He went to raise his own sword and realized he had left it beside Snare. Panic seized him as he raised his shield, his only means of defence.

Stern was on him in a heartbeat and rained blow after blow down on his shield. His arm went numb, but he managed to keep it up. He backed away, but Stern kept on him and the inevitable finally happened. After the many blows it had taken, Cody's oak shield cracked in two.

Cody gasped and tried to run, but Stern tripped him up. He fell on his back, the two halves of his shield falling uselessly beside him.

He looked into Stern's eyes. There was no mercy, no compassion. Only blind rage.

The sword began its downward descent.

CHAPTER 28

A flash of grey slammed into Stern with a heavy thump.

Cody yelled in surprise as a large grey wolf mauled Stern, ripping into him with vicious teeth. Stern fought back, but his sword had fallen out of reach and the wolf had him pinned.

Cody scrambled to his feet and put some distance between him and the wolf, but it seemed content to attack Stern.

"Cody!" Levi ran up. He was plastered in sweat and wearing a fancy gold jacket.

"Levi, hi," Cody breathed.

Levi stared at the large canine. There was a lot of blood around Stern. "Where did that come from?"

"No idea," Cody said. "Saved my life, though."

The wolf decided that it had ravaged Stern enough and turned to the two standing nearby.

Levi pointed his sabre at it.

"Hey, now," the wolf said.

Cody's jaw dropped open.

The wolf bared its bloody teeth in a horrifying approximation of a smile. "That's three times, Cody."

"K...Kinzo?"

"Yep," the wolf bobbed his head.

"How?" Levi and Cody asked at the same time.

Aldus walked up behind them and looked at Kinzo with a bemused expression. "He is an Anicrea."

Levi scrunched up his face. "A wassawha?"

The wolf, Kinzo, flicked his ears back. "It's a person who is sometimes a human and sometimes an animal."

Cody was incredulous. "That's a thing?"

"Well, you're looking at one, so yeah," Kinzo said.

"Why are you a wolf now?" Levi asked.

"Stern had Cody dead to rights," Kinzo said. "No one was gonna get there in time and neither was I, in human form. So, I changed."

"Just like that?" Cody asked.

"It only takes a second or two," Kinzo said. "Here, watch." He closed his yellow eyes and began to shimmer. He morphed back into his regular human self. "Ta da."

"Gonna be honest," Levi said. "This is kinda freaking me out."

Kinzo smiled, but it was a sad smile. "Yeah, that's usually the reaction I get when I show people. It's why I left my home." His eyes were faraway. "They were a superstitious lot and thought I was a demon. Blamed me for everything. Leaving was the best thing."

"If it makes you feel any better, I don't think you're a demon," Levi said.

"Even if you do act like one sometimes," Cody said.

Kinzo smirked. "Thanks."

Cody leaned around Kinzo to look at Stern. "Is he dead?"

Kinzo shrugged.

"We should check," Aldus said.

Cody wrinkled his nose at the sight of Stern's ravaged body. His face was a bloody ruin and his chest had been raked by claws over and over.

"You sure did a number on him," Levi said to Kinzo.

Aldus knelt and felt for a pulse. "He is alive, if only just."

Stern's eyes fluttered open. Full of fear and pain, they settled on Levi. "You bested me again. I don't know how, but you did." He coughed, spraying blood droplets. "And this is the last time. Is Ara alright?"

"She is," Levi said. "We never meant her any harm."

Stern swallowed with obvious effort. "I would like to speak with her privately."

"Certainly. I shall fetch her." Aldus walked over to where Stern's sister was sitting with her knees to her chest.

Stern coughed again, doubling over. "You... you were worthy opponents."

"Uh, thanks?" Cody said.

"Now, leave me be," he said, his words getting softer as the life drained out of him.

Levi nodded. "Goodbye, Rorien."

Cody took one last look at Stern's lacerated, pained face before turning away.

"Hey! A little help?" a voice called.

"Oh! El Fen!" Cody had forgotten about the knight. He jogged over to where Adam's father was pinned under Stern's massive suit of armour. "Looks like he got the best of you."

"Indeed, he did," El Fen said. "He is a crafty one. He knew I was about to beat him, so he did something I was not expecting."

"How heavy is that?" Kinzo asked. He was holding a hand to the lump on his forehead where Stern had clocked him earlier.

El Fen strained to push the metal off him, but only moved it an inch or so. "Quite heavy."

Cody motioned for Levi and Kinzo to each take hold of the armour. They heaved upward with all their strength, managing to lift it half a foot. El Fen squirmed his way out and the boys dropped the armour with a clang.

El Fen checked himself over. "Good thing I was armoured, or my legs would have been squashed. Thank you."

"No problem," Cody said. Kinzo gave a thumbs up.

Cody glanced back to where Stern lay. Ara was beside him, holding his hand. Aldus had gone over to help Kaito. They stood a respectful distance away as the siblings shared their final farewell. Ara bent forward and kissed Stern's forehead. Then, she threw back her head and let out a long, aching cry.

Rorien Stern was dead.

"Well," Levi said after a moment. "I guess that's that."

"Can't say anyone besides Ara will miss him," Kinzo said.

El Fen rubbed his chin. "In fact, life in the Outskirts may improve."

"That'll make Snare happy," Levi said.

Cody's face fell. For a short moment, he had forgotten the terrible news. "Levi?"

"Yeah?"

"Snare's dead. The Kar-Sang got him."

Levi and Kinzo stared in shock.

342

"Are you serious?" Kinzo asked. Cody's expression told them he was.

Levi shook his head and whispered a curse.

"So, all this was for nothing?" Kinzo threw up his hands.

Cody tapped his fingers on his leg. "Well, there's still Ring."

"She'll be devastated," Levi said.

Cody nodded to where the others were gathered around Snare's still form. "She is."

"Is that Adam lying over there?" El Fen asked, a note of concern in his voice.

"He's just unconscious," Cody said.

El Fen strode over to his son, kneeling down and placing a hand on his brow.

Levi sighed and kicked at a stone. Cody knew he was distraught by Snare's passing. Even though Snare may not have been the easiest to deal with, Levi had considered him a friend.

Kinzo blew out a breath. "So... what do we do now?"

Cody had no answer. His eyes wandered over the battlefield, the destruction and bodies splayed all over. He paused at a pool of blood where there was no body. "Where'd he go?"

"Huh?"

"Marek. He was almost dead. Kaito stabbed him from behind and he was bleeding out right there. But he's gone."

"Maybe someone took his body," Kinzo said.

"Who?" Cody asked. "All the Forsaken are dead or scattered. No one else would help him." He was baffled. He had already accepted his brother's death and now he was gone, maybe still alive. And if he was alive, he could recover and cause Cody more trouble. "Hopefully he dragged himself away and died."

"Harsh," Kinzo muttered.

"He deserves it," Cody said.

Aldus and Kaito were making their way toward the group gathered around Snare.

"We should go say our goodbyes," Levi said, his voice catching. The others agreed silently and trudged over.

Cody stood back a few feet and let the others say their farewells. He rubbed his chin in an attempt to contain all the emotions he was feeling. He saw Naomi looking at him. There was moisture in her eyes, but she was managing to hold herself together. She hadn't really known Snare, but seeing him killed had shaken her.

Coral was standing back, arms crossed. She muttered angrily under her breath.

A few minutes later, Miri, Guy and Ember came wandering in. Wide-eyed, they took in all the destruction.

Seeing Snare, Miri covered her mouth and stood in shock for a moment before going to kneel beside him.

Ember helped Guy stand next to Cody.

"You ok?" Guy asked.

Cody nodded. "You?"

"Nothing serious," Ember said. Guy didn't argue. Then again, it was not the time or place for such petty things.

"Glad to hear it," Cody said, his voice cracking.

Guy reached up and tapped him on the back, his equivalent of a hug. "At least we didn't lose anyone else."

"This is more than enough," Cody said.

"Way more," Ember agreed.

A deep silence fell over the group.

A few minutes later, Miri stood and walked away, shoulders trembling.

Cody walked over. "Hey."

Miri turned, her cheeks wet. Cody spread his arms and she stepped into his embrace. He held her for a while, letting her cry into his shoulder.

After a time, she stepped back and signed, "Thank you."

"You're welcome," Cody signed back, rather clumsily.

She smiled for a brief moment.

Aldus cleared his throat. "Students... as much as I know you are in pain, it is time to go. And not just back to camp. Back to Blackthrush. We've caused enough chaos here and once they break my spell, the soldiers will be on us. I would rather not be here when that happens."

Levi stood, dragging his hands over his face. "Right. Yeah. We should go."

Everyone slowly got up.

Ring grabbed Aldus' sleeve. "Take me with you. Please. I have nothing left here."

Aldus lightly touched her hand. "Of course. You will be welcomed."

"Thank you," Ring said. She stood, squared her shoulders and walked away from her lifelong friend. She didn't look back once.

~ ~ ~

"Whaddya mean, we're leaving?" Corvin asked, unimpressed.

"Yeah!" Kavik said. "The fights were getting good, until the arena blew up."

"Is that why we have to leave?" Iaarra asked.

"Partially, yes." Aldus stood outside his tent, addressing the whole of Blackthrush. Nobody seemed thrilled to leave, even the other instructors.

"What did you and those brats do this time?" Hejeck asked. Cody glanced at the small man without the fear that he was a spy for the first time in days.

"Please, Able, restrain yourself," Aldus said.

"But you did do something, right?" Hejeck said. He pointed to where Cody, Levi and the others stood at the back of the crowd. "I mean, look at them. Did they just return from war?"

Everyone looked back at them. There were a lot of angry faces, although a few showed some sympathy.

Aldus sighed. "Fine. I will tell you." Cody looked up sharply. Aldus fingered his hourglass pendant. "We accidentally ran afoul of a cult while doing someone a favour. We killed their leaders, but that won't stop them."

A stunned silence fell over the crowd.

Then, Bram exclaimed, "You fought a cult? Awesome!"

Silverton raised an eyebrow. "Truly?"

"Yes," Aldus said. "They were known as the Forsaken. It was not supposed to happen the way it did, but there is nothing to be done now, except leave. Unless of course, any of you would like to have your body stolen."

"Body stolen?" Romeo asked. "What?"

"I don't recommend it," Cody raised his voice. "I was stuck in my own head for two days. It sucked. But we got him out of my head." He held up the black triangular pendant, letting the crowd see it. He imagined that he could see Antoth's face leering out at him.

The crowd murmured at the news.

"When do we leave?" Lance asked.

"Immediately," Aldus said.

"What if we don't want to go?" Adelle challenged.

"I'll make you a deal," Aldus said. "If we go back now, we'll take a week off of classes and have a tournament of our own."

That got everyone's attention. People started placing bets and bragging about who would win.

"Now, go pack your things."

The crowd dispersed to take down camp.

"Huh," Guy said. "That actually went better than I thought."

Cody turned to pack his things. He spotted Kana sitting on the ground next to a cart. "What's with her?" he asked Levi.

"She couldn't catch Evander. Spent the whole time we were fighting looking for him. She'll be fine."

Guy started toward her. Cody grabbed him by the collar and swung him around. "Uh uh, not now."

Guy sighed. "Ok, fine."

Two hours later, everything was packed and the people of Blackthrush were ready to leave Saken and head back to the Academy. To home.

~~~

Farren stood out on one of the Aedon's balconies. Below, the final stages of the arena reconstruction were being completed. It had been five days since an unknown group of rebels had infiltrated the Aedon, killed Baron Silva, Rorien Stern and Karl Linae, along with thirty-one soldiers.

Farren gripped the railing tightly as the storm within threatened to burst out. He breathed deeply. This must have been the rebels' plan from the beginning. Cause enough trouble to draw out all of Farren's forces and then attack when he was most vulnerable. Still, something didn't add up. Why would the Giala kill the ones they had? They must have found out about Linae, that much was obvious. Rorien Stern, he had caused the

Giala in Saken problems, but he was hardly a major player in the conflict. And as for Baron Silva, Farren could see no connection that made sense. He was missing something.

The Festival had been postponed for a few days while repairs were made and many people had left, including everyone from Blackthrush. Farren wanted to confront Aldus about any involvement with the incident, but he had no proof and now his informant was dead.

He allowed a low growl to escape his lips. He had been made to look like a fool. The Giala was getting stronger. He needed something to go his way. Anything.

Someone knocked on the door behind the King. Farren turned to see Malroth and another man with brown hair and eyes.

"Who is this?" Farren asked.

Malroth dipped his head. "Sire, this man is Kyner Sinnas. The Lost Prince of Wintenveil."

Farren's eyebrows rose a fraction. "Weren't you in prison?"

Kyner cleared his throat. "Ahem, yes, well, I was. And before you get mad at me, there is something you should know."

"What is it?"

Malroth spoke. "He claims to know someone who has all the information you want on Blackthrush."

Farren looked at Kyner with a renewed interest. "Truly?"

Kyner nodded. "Yes, sir. I will tell you where to find him. All I ask, is that you grant me my freedom. Your men are still after me. I have been in prison for eleven years."

"Yes, you shall have your freedom," Farren said immediately. He needed the information. He didn't care for Kyner, but he was sure the prince would have some plan for if the king tried to take the information by force. "Malroth, tell the men Kyner Sinnas is a free man. Now, where is this person?"

Kyner glanced down at his wrist and smiled. "Thank you, your Majesty. I shall take you to him immediately."

Farren allowed himself a small smile as the prince turned away. His fortune had reversed. He was about to learn everything about Blackthrush.

CHAPTER 29

Six days had passed since they had left the Midarra Festival. The first few days, Levi had been on edge, expecting someone to show up and arrest them all for the trouble they had caused. But, as time wore on, Levi began to worry less and less. And now that the spy, Linae, was dead, the little knot of concern that had plagued Levi since arriving at Blackthrush dissolved. He felt safer than he ever had since the whole adventure had kicked off in Stagrun in what seemed to be an eternity ago.

True to his word, Aldus had planned a tournament. Everyone who wanted to join had been included. Once it had begun, everyone forgot to be annoyed about missing out on the Festival. Most everyone had entered, but a couple of Levi's friends were still too beaten up from the battle with the Forsaken and Rorien Stern. Cody, Guy, Ember, Adam and Naomi all decided to sit out and rest up.

It was the second last day of the tournament. The bracket was down to sixteen people, Kaito, Miri and Coral among those left. Levi had been surprised when Kaito had entered, seeing as he had been injured in Saken. Kaito had told him he knew a small secret for Chaotics. They could use time magic, chronomancy, to speed up the natural healing process. It was a dangerous practice and not taught at Blackthrush. When Levi asked where he learned it, Kaito smiled mysteriously.

Levi himself had been eliminated by Ellis from black camp, only managing to win one match, against Demeter from white camp.

Levi leaned against the back wall of the main building. He fiddled with the straps on his bracers.

"Nice day, huh?" Kinzo said, sliding along the wall next to him.

Levi glanced up at the sky. It was grey and overcast, wind blowing steadily. Snow was on the way. "Yeah, gorgeous."

Kinzo snorted. He was happy with himself, having made it to the round of thirty-two before Winchester, who was favoured to win the whole tournament, bested him. Aldus had banned betting, of course, but that hadn't stopped anyone.

"Who you got this match?" Kinzo asked.

Levi glanced at the two entering the sparring field: Wes and Bear. Wes was an expert swordsman, but Bear was huge and scarily strong. A solid hit from his mace would end the match. "Hmm. I think Wes will do it. He does have a year over Bear."

"It'll be close, but I'm thinking Bear," Kinzo said.

"Guess we'll see how it plays out," Levi said.

The referee, Adelaide Kross, pointed at Wes. "Are you ready?"

"Yes, ma'am."

Kross turned to Bear. "Are you ready?"

"You bet," Bear smiled.

"Visors down, gentlemen," Kross said. Both combatants, dressed in full armour, pulled their visors into place. "Begin!" The crowd erupted in cheers.

"Go get him, Wes!" Iarra yelled. Wes tossed her a quick salute before facing his opponent.

Bear tapped his mace against his palm as he waited for Wes to make the first move. He always waited; it was his style.

Wes took slow steps toward Bear, spinning his sword around his hand. Once in range, he brought it up into a defensive stance.

The two faced off for a long moment.

Wes darted to the right, only to spin back the other way and cut at Bear's side. The sword clanged into the head of the mace. Bear flicked his wrist, knocking the sword aside. Then, he jabbed straight ahead, an unconventional move with such a weapon. It slammed into Wes' breastplate and with all Bear's weight behind it, drove him back a few steps before Wes could catch his balance by digging his sword into the ground.

Wes stood straight, pulled his sword from the dirt and held it with both hands.

Bear closed the gap and swung at Wes' head. Wes ducked and slid to the left. He sliced down, but Bear held up his arm, deflecting the blade off his bracer with a grunt. Bear's other arm whipped around, intending to smash the mace into his opponent's back. Wes arched his back and put his arms behind his head, his sword blocking the blow. The crowd cheered as the weapons clashed.

"That was a brilliant move," Levi commented.

"It was alright, yep," Kinzo said. The two watched as the combatants duelled, the momentum shifting back and forth as one would do something incredible only to have the other do something equally as impressive.

The duel dragged on for ten minutes, much longer than any of the matches to date.

It finally ended when both fighters were so exhausted that their weapons only moved at a fraction of their original speed. The finishing blow was nothing more than Bear half-heartedly batting his mace into Wes' sword, but the blade dropped to the ground and Wes made no move to retrieve it.

He held up his hands. "You win. I'm done."

"That's the match!" Kross yelled. "Bear wins!"

Half the crowd cheered as their favourite won, the other half grumbled and handed over coins.

Wes extended his hand and Bear shook it, each acknowledging that they had both been taken to their limits and they were both formidable opponents.

"Update the board!" Kross called.

Everyone turned to look at a large corkboard on the back wall of the main building. It was covered with a giant sheet of parchment on which the bracket was drawn.

Kindrelle raised a hand to acknowledge Kross. She had been eliminated in the first round and since then had given herself the title of bracket master. She didn't let anyone else touch it. Taking a quill, she dipped it in ink and wrote Bear's name in the next tier. His name was the first to appear in the round of eight.

The crowd began to disperse. There was a twenty-minute break between matches. People took the time to do whatever they wanted, but most wandered over to the table of goodies and pastries that the cook staff had set up for the occasion.

Kinzo left to get a cherry pie, his third piece of the day. Levi wanted something, but felt like he should restrain himself. He decided to use the restroom, but he wasn't the only one with the idea and was forced to wait in line. He slipped in behind Caesar, who nodded to him.

"Quite the match, huh?" Levi said.

"Mm hmm," Caesar said. "Unfortunately, I bet on Wes."

"Did you lose much?"

Caesar frowned. "No money, but I have to do all of Osiris' homework for the next week."

Levi couldn't help but smirk at Caesar's predicament. He never bet on anything. He never had liked leaving things up to chance and he knew that his personal fortune tended to be on the bad side.

Five minutes later Levi exited the restroom and walked out into the grass. He watched as Walt ran by, still following Kavik around as he had been all week. The first-year caught up to the older guy and began chatting happily. Kavik flopped his head back as Niles and Christian walked by, laughing at his predicament.

Levi glanced to his right as someone called his name. Gwen. Marshall was with her. "What's up?"

The two students from green camp stopped in front of him. Marshall was holding a box under one arm.

"Whatcha got there?" Levi asked.

Marshall glanced down at the package. "Oh, just, you know, stuff."

Levi smirked. "Ok. Did you want something?"

"We were just wondering if you'd heard anything about Evander," Gwen said. "It's been almost a week."

Levi's eyebrows pressed together. "Unfortunately, no. I haven't heard a thing since Myron went to find him." Before they had left the Festival, Aldus had tasked Blackthrush's groundskeeper with finding Evander. So far, there had been no news. Plenty of people were concerned for Evander. He was a rather popular figure at the Academy, especially among his campmates, like Gwen and Marshall.

Marshall made a face. "Too bad. He's missing pretty much the best week we've ever had."

"I hope he's ok," Gwen said.

Levi scratched his mark as he thought of Kyner leading his friend away into the dark. "Yeah. Me too."

Marshall cleared his throat. "Well, we're off to, uh, do things that have nothing to do with what's in the box. Bye."

Levi grinned, his worry for Evander pushed aside. "Alright. You two have fun with whatever's not in the box."

The two laughed and walked off, waving to Levi. He shook his head, sure someone was about to get pranked.

Something small and white drifted into Levi's field of vision. A snowflake. He tilted his head back to see more flakes drifting down lazily as the sky released the first signs of winter.

Something else caught his eye. It was Ring, sitting with her back against the wall, all alone. He sighed and started over to her. Since Aldus had allowed her to come to Blackthrush, things hadn't improved much for her. She still acted like a street kid and had ostracized herself from most of the students. Several of them openly bullied her. Levi and his friends tried their best to help her out, but she was having a tough time fitting in.

"Hey," Levi said, plopping down beside her.

"Hi."

"Been watching the duels?" Levi asked.

"Not much else to do right now"

Levi smirked. "True."

Ring absentmindedly fiddled with her ring. Levi noticed a line of tiny runes inscribed on it. They probably gave it power.

"You doing ok?" Levi asked.

Ring worked her jaw as she mulled over the question. "Not really. My whole life was just turned upside down. And my friends, they're never coming back." She sniffed and blinked back a tear.

Levi sighed. "I've never lost anyone that close, so I don't know what you're going through, but I expect it'll get better eventually."

Ring eyed him. "It better. Or I'm blaming you."

Levi's mouth curled up. "You know, I don't have a say in how life goes."

"Good thing, that," Ring said, the ghost of a smile on her lips.

"Oh, there you are!"

Levi looked up to see Naomi limping toward them with a handful of treats. "I got you something." She held out a chocolate chip cookie.

"What is it?" Ring asked.

"A cookie. You'll like it," Naomi promised.

Levi sometimes forgot that Ring had grown up without the many luxuries that he and most other people took for granted.

Ring took the cookie with a skeptical expression. She sniffed it and took a small bite. Her eyes widened. "Whoa. That's good."

"Told you," Naomi said, looking satisfied.

Ring quickly gobbled up the cookie. "Thanks."

Someone walked up to them. Balak. "Levi."

"What's up?"

Balak pointed in the general direction of Aldus' study. "Aldus wants to see you."

Levi's brow furrowed. He wasn't sure what Aldus wanted him for. Perhaps it had something to do with Evander, but, if that were the case, the others would have been told too. *Must be about the Giala.*

Balak led Levi into the building, up the stairs, down the hall and into the study.

Aldus was sitting at his desk, writing something. He glanced up as they entered. "Ah, Balak. Good, you brought Levi. Thank you. Can you please shut the door?"

Balak nodded and pushed the heavy door closed.

Levi watched expectantly as Aldus descended from the upper floor of the study.

"You don't know why I summoned you," Aldus said.

"Nope."

"Can you not guess?" Aldus asked. "It is about something you have done."

"Something I've done?" Levi wracked his brain, trying to think of everything he'd done over the last few days. "Like, uh, a bad thing?"

Aldus sat down in one of the peach-coloured chairs and placed his palms together. "Bad? No. Quite the opposite, in fact. To put it lightly, I would say what you did was," he paused and smiled. "Shocking."

Balak snorted.

"Shocking. I don't..." Realization dawned in his eyes. "You mean when I shot lightning at Linae when he was about to kill Miri."

"Precisely," Aldus said.

Levi pulled his mouth to one side. "I kinda forgot about that, actually."

"How you manage that is a wonder," Balak said. "We have been thinking about it all week."

Levi scratched his cheek. "You know? But you weren't there."

"I told him," Aldus said. "I needed a second opinion and someone to help me research." For the first time, Levi noticed the dozens and dozens of books and scrolls piled on the coffee table.

"We haven't stopped reading for days," Balak said.

"Uh, sorry," Levi said.

"Don't be," Aldus said. "We finally believe we know what you are."

"What I am?" Levi asked. "What's that supposed to mean? Am I not a human? Am I one of those what-do-you-call-them things that Kinzo is? Can I turn into a wolf? Or another animal? I hope I'm a falcon or something."

"No, no," Aldus chuckled. "You are no Anicrea. I would have sensed that the moment we first met."

"You mean, you knew that Kinzo was a wolf this whole time? Why didn't you tell us?"

"It wasn't my secret to disclose," Aldus said. "But we digress. What I meant is what order you belong to."

"Well, we know that," Levi said. "I'm a Mind Mage. I can move stuff around and sorta barely talk with my mind."

"If that's all you are, how can you explain your sudden ability to harness lightning?" Balak asked.

Levi opened his mouth to answer and shut it again, frowning.

"Exactly," Balak said.

Aldus stood and ran his hand over the stacks of books. "After extensive research, we've pieced together enough stories and myths with known facts to have a plausible answer. We believe that you do not belong to the Third Order, but rather the order that can use all magic. The lost order. The Sixth Order."

Levi stared for a long time, mouth agape. He tried to work out what Aldus was saying. "This goes against everything we've been taught about magic. There are only five orders and nobody can use more than one. How can there be a sixth?"

"We don't have all the answers," Balak said. "But these legends and stories only make sense if there is a sixth order."

"But they're legends!" Levi said. "I mean, all the stories my mom told me as a kid can't be real."

Aldus tugged at his beard. "You'd be surprised at how many of those are based in fact, although most are greatly embellished."

"This is crazy!" Levi ran a hand through his hair. "There's no way."

"Something is different about you," Balak said. "No matter what you say, the fact remains that you have used two separate orders of magic. Now, either the rules that hold the fabric of this world are breaking, or there is another rule we don't know about."

Levi held a hand over his mouth. "This... this is a lot to take in."

"Yes, it is," Aldus said. "We know nothing about this development or the ramifications it brings with it. We are in the dark as much as you."

Levi thought for a while. Aldus and Balak were content to let him mull over the information. Then, "Um, do you think it's possible that me being this, um, in the Sixth Order has something to do with me bonding with the Elder Gem?"

Aldus raised his brows and glanced at Balak. "I hadn't even considered that. We don't know either way, but there certainly could be a connection."

Balak crossed his arms. "Honestly, we don't know much about the Elder Gem. The Free Knights guarded its secrets fiercely. But we do know that it has never bonded with anyone before, the way it has with you. It was always able to pass on from one leader of the Free Knights to the next without exploding anyone. Then again, none of them were part of the Sixth Order, as far as we know."

Aldus tapped his cheek. "The Free Knights disclosed little about themselves. There may have been some belonging to the Sixth Order. But there should be some evidence of it. The latest evidence we found regarding the Sixth Order was over a thousand years ago, before the founding of the Free Knights. We will need to investigate this deeply."

"So that means..." Levi said.

Balak pointed at him. "It means you and I are going to spend time seeing if you can access all the orders."

"Yay," Levi groaned.

"It should be done in secret," Aldus said. "Linae may be gone, but there may well be other spies here. And while we don't know what being a Sixth entails, it would not help matters if undue attention were drawn to you."

"Can I tell my friends at least?" Levi asked.

Aldus sighed. "They'll find out no matter if I forbid it or not. But only the ones who already know your other secret."

Levi accepted his decision.

"While you're here, we thought we should test you a bit," Balak said.

"You want me to do the lightning again?"

"I would actually rather not have my study blown up," Aldus said. "We were hoping you could make your hands spark, as they did before."

Levi puffed out his cheeks. "Ok, but I can't promise anything will happen. Or that I won't blow up the room."

"Fair enough," Aldus said. "But if you do shoot lightning, preferably point it at Balak."

"Very funny," Balak grumbled.

Aldus chuckled at his own joke. "Go ahead, Levi."

"Alright. Here goes nothing." He closed his eyes and focused inward on the power that resided in him. He breached it and felt energy fill him, but it felt like his normal magic that he used to move stuff with his mind. It wasn't the tingly, electric power. He screwed up his face as he released the magic and dug deeper, trying to find where the other magic was. After a minute and no results, he withdrew and opened his eyes. "I can't. It just feels like my normal magic."

"Try searching a different part of your mind," Balak said. "From descriptions people have given me, all the orders feel different and come from different places. Don't search in the same place as you normally do."

Levi grumbled. "Fine." He closed his eyes and began searching inward. He felt himself going toward the familiar magic, but forced himself away, moving off to a different place. He thought of how he felt when he had activated it the first time. He had been desperate, horrified, scared and angry. All strong emotions.

Hmm. I wonder.

He focused on his feelings, his emotions, his passions and hates, loves and fears. A shock of energy raced through his limbs. Searching closer, he discovered a pocket of energy, many times smaller than his other reserve of magic. He opened it and instantly felt electricity course through him. His eyes shot open and he stiffened.

"It worked!" Balak exclaimed.

Levi looked down and saw the blueish-white sparks dancing between his fingers.

"Well done," Aldus said.

"Um, I have a problem. I can't stop it." Levi tried to halt the rush of energy, but it was only increasing. He couldn't sever it the way he was used to.

"Just, relax, take deep breaths and let go." Aldus lay a reassuring hand on Levi's shoulder. The instant he made contact, all the energy raced out of Levi with a huge thunderclap. Aldus was sent flying across the room where he slammed into one of the support pillars.

Levi's mouth dropped open. "Oh, oh, oh. I'm sorry, I'm so sorry." He was barely aware that the electrical energy had disappeared. He was horrified at what he had done.

Aldus grunted and pushed himself to his feet. His hair was sticking in all directions and his robes were smoking, but a grin crossed his face. "There is no doubt about it now. Levi, you are a Sixth."

CHAPTER 30

Levi waited for the day's activities to end before breaking the news to his friends. He gathered them in an empty room at the far end of the first floor and told them of Aldus and Balak's theory that seemed to be true.

There were mixed reactions. Guy and Coral both thought it was awesome. Most of the others were confused and Kaito flat out refused to believe it.

"It is simply not possible," Kaito said. "There are five orders, no more, no less. That's the way it has always been."

"Well, something's up," Guy said. "I mean, I saw him all sparky back in Saken and you all heard the boom." The thunderclap had caused quite the stir in the crowd. No one had known what had happened and Silverton had gone to investigate. Aldus had told him some half-truth while not revealing Levi's new-found ability.

"But that's not how magic works!" Kana said.

"Yeah, you'd think we'd have heard rumours about a sixth order," Cody said. "This seems really out of the blue."

"My guess is that it's really rare," Levi said. "And I imagine being a Sixth would paint a large target on someone's back, so they probably kept low profiles."

"Why, though?" Coral asked. "Why wouldn't they use all the orders to dominate everyone and take over the world?"

Kinzo shook his head. "You do realize we're trying to stop the maniac who's doing exactly that?"

Coral froze for a moment. "Oh, right. Well, I assume they couldn't have been as evil and douchebag-y as old Fa... For... what's his name?"

"Farren," Ember said.

"She and Cody do make good points," Naomi said. "They should have made a bigger impact on history."

Ember linked her fingers. "Look, who knows why they didn't. But that doesn't change the fact that Levi can use two orders of magic. I've seen it myself. You can't argue that it's not possible, because it happened."

"Maybe Levi just broke magic," Cody said.

"He would be the one to do it," Guy agreed.

"Hey!" Levi protested. He looked around at his friends' faces. They were confused and some still unbelieving. Kaito was shaking his head. He wasn't sure what the truth was and it was making him uncomfortable. No matter which way the issue was looked at, it didn't make sense logically.

Miri appeared thoughtful. She hadn't contributed to the conversation, so Levi asked her what she thought. "Last year, when we fought the kathauk, you brought it down with lightning, right?"

Levi nodded. He hadn't even considered that, but it made sense. The chance that a stray bolt had struck exactly where and when he needed was astronomically low.

Miri smiled. "I don't know what this all means, but I think that if Levi can learn to use all five orders of magic, Farren's gonna be in for a nasty surprise."

Levi cracked a grin. He hadn't even thought of that.

Kinzo scuffed his foot against the floor. "Great. Now Levi's even more special. Fantastic."

"Oh, come on," Levi said. "You've got your own trick."

"Yeah, he does," Cody said. "Pretty sweet."

"What are you talking about?" Kana asked.

Everyone turned to Kinzo. His cheeks reddened. "Look, it's nothing."

"Nothing? Ha!" Cody scoffed. "He saved my life with it. Killed Stern too." He and Levi had been the only ones to witness Kinzo's transformation.

Coral leaned close to Kinzo. "Tell us."

"Perhaps we shouldn't press if he doesn't want to tell us," Ember said.

"Perhaps, shut up," Guy said. "Come on, tell us, Kinzo." He didn't see the daggers Ember was glaring at him.

Kinzo dragged his hands down his face. "Fine. You'll all find out eventually anyway. But I'd rather show you."

Everyone watched in anticipation. Levi tried to hide a smile, but couldn't.

Kinzo rolled his eyes. "Try not to freak out." A moment later, he was a wolf.

The silence was so profound, Levi fancied he could hear everyone's heartbeats.

Then, Coral screeched, "He's a fricking wolf!"

Everyone began talking at once, voicing their wonder and surprise. Miri began laughing uncontrollably and Cody had to grab her so she didn't fall over. Guy grinned from ear to ear and Kaito put a hand over his forehead with a smirk on his lips.

Kana's reaction was priceless. She pointed at Kinzo, swaying slightly as she worked her mouth without words coming out.

"You all done gawking?" Kinzo asked.

"Ah! He talks!" Coral shrieked.

"Of course, I talk!" Kinzo snapped, quite literally. "Hey, what?" He turned as he felt Naomi's hand running along his back.

"You're so soft!" she cooed.

Kinzo sighed, defeated. "Anyone else wanna pet me?" Everyone moved in to feel the thick, smooth grey coat covering him.

"You would make a lovely fur coat," Ember giggled.

Kinzo just groaned.

Miri couldn't stop laughing as she ran her hands around his neck.

"I can't believe you're a wolf," Guy said.

"I'm not a wolf," Kinzo explained. "I am an Anicrea who can turn into a wolf."

Kana finally managed to say something. "I can't believe it took you this long to tell us."

"It's not exactly something I'm proud of," Kinzo said. "It's only ever caused people to look down on me. It's why I was on the run in the first place."

"Look down on you?" Coral said. "Well, technically, since you now are the shortest, but come on! You're a wolf! How is that bad?"

Kana lay a hand on Kinzo's shoulder. "We'll never do that. You might be a colossal pain most times, but you're one of us. We'll accept you no matter what you look like."

"Unless you can also turn into a slug," Coral said. "Because I hate slugs."

Kaito nudged her. "This is no time for jokes."

"That wasn't a joke," Coral said. "I made it my personal mission to kill every slug I ever see, Hideous, ugly, little..."

Kinzo sighed. "Thanks, guys. But can you stop touching me? It's weird."

"Aw," Naomi said as Ember pulled her away. "But he's so fluffy."

"I think he's done being the centre of attention," Ember said.

"Yes, I am," Kinzo said. "Levi, how do you handle being so special all the time?"

Levi shrugged. "It was weird at first, but there's only a few people who know and it's not weird with them."

Kinzo harrumphed. "Well, I don't like it." He pushed himself onto his hind legs, transforming back into his human self.

"That is..." Kana began.

"Fascinating," Kaito said. "I would love to know how it works."

"Course you would," Kinzo muttered. "Well, sorry, but I have no idea how it works."

Levi pointed up. "You could ask Aldus. He knows about the Anicrea."

"He does?" Kinzo asked.

"Mm hmm," Levi nodded. "He knew about this right away."

Kinzo frowned. "How?"

"Probably when he examined your mind," Naomi said. "He had to know the basic facts about you to choose your camp, and this is obviously an important fact."

"Hmm." Kinzo didn't seem thrilled that Aldus had known all along.

Cody cleared his throat. "You know, this is great and all, but we got distracted from the bigger news about Levi being a, well, a..."

"A Sixth," Levi said. "That's what Aldus and Balak called it."

"Ok, he's a Sixth," Cody said. "This is game-changing. But we gotta keep it a secret, just like the other one. No telling anyone."

"Wasn't planning on it," Guy said.

"You never plan anything," Ember said. "You just impulsively do things. Make sure you don't spill this secret."

"Hey, princess, I've kept the first secret, haven't I?"

"It's a wonder you have," Ember said.

"What's that supposed to mean?" Guy asked, offended.

Ember turned away, but Levi saw the smile. She was pleased to have gotten under Guy's skin for once, instead of it being the other way around.

Kana got them back on track. "Cody's right. This secret, while maybe not as dangerous as the other, could lead to people taking an interest in Levi. And then, there's a better chance the other secret will get out."

"And that is mega bad," Coral said.

"That is one way of putting it," Kaito said. He looked at Levi. "I still don't see how this is possible."

Levi spread his hands. "No one does. But it's true, nonetheless."

Kaito pinched the bridge of his nose. Like it or not, he was going to have to accept that Levi could do things that shouldn't be possible.

Naomi yawned. "I think it's bedtime."

"It was a busy day," Ember agreed.

"Also, Miri and Kaito need rest," Cody said, patting Miri's shoulder. "They've still gotta fight tomorrow."

Coral crossed her arms. "Stupid Vonn." He had beaten her earlier in the day and she was not pleased.

Kinzo slapped her on the back. "Hey, cheer up. You did better than all but two of us."

"I should have been better than all of you," Coral said. "After all, I am undoubtedly the best."

Everyone scoffed and snorted.

"You go on thinking that, sister," Guy said.

Cody opened the door. "Let's get some rest."

~~~

A noise woke Levi. He rubbed his blurry eyes and groaned before looking around. The light of dawn was streaming in through the window set in the door.

Someone was sitting up in bed. They were breathing heavily.

Levi swung his legs over the side of his bed and dropped down from the top bunk.

The person started as he landed. It was Naomi.

"You ok?" Levi whispered.

"I... I don't know," Naomi said. She was shaken up, hugging her knees close.

"What happened?"

Naomi looked up at Levi. "I don't know that either. I saw things. In my sleep."

"What kind of things?" Levi sat on the end of her bunk.

Naomi looked past him, as if reliving whatever she had seen. "There was smoke and fire. And blood. I saw blood. So much blood. And there were people dying, but I couldn't tell who. It was like they were in a fog. I also saw a blue flag being ripped in half." Her eyes locked with Levi's. "What does it mean?"

"It wasn't just a dream, was it?" Levi asked.

Naomi shook her head. "It felt real. Like a warning. Was it a warning?"

"I don't know, Naomi," Levi said. "It could be. Mind Mages sometimes have visions and premonitions."

Naomi sniffed. "But a vision of what? What's going to happen? And who is it going to happen to?"

Levi shook his head. He didn't know. "I think I had a vision last year. Right before Stern kidnapped us. I saw many things that I don't understand, but if it was a vision of something to come, they haven't happened yet. Maybe they never will." He also thought about what he had seen in the mists of the geyser field outside of Saken, but he wasn't sure if that was the same thing as the vision of a Mind Mage.

Naomi nodded. "Yeah. Maybe it's not for now. Maybe it's showing me far into the future."

"I wouldn't worry about it too much," Levi said. "We've both been taught that visions are rarely what they seem and people have gone mad trying to understand them."

Naomi sighed and nodded.

Levi gave her a sympathetic smile. "Go back to sleep. We've still got an hour or two." He stood and walked back to his bunk.

"Levi?" Naomi said.

"Yeah?"

"Thanks."

Levi inclined his head and climbed back into bed. He wondered if her vision meant something important, but he wasn't about to worry about it. Life at Blackthrush was finally safe for him. He wasn't ready to get tangled up in something else yet.

He found a comfortable position and let himself drift off to sleep.

When he woke again, Levi found Adam sleeping in his bunk nearby. Cam had cleared him for everyday activities. The concussion he had sustained fighting the Kar-Sang hadn't been too serious.

He glanced at Naomi as everyone woke and readied themselves for the day. She seemed better and smiled at him when she saw him looking. Levi grinned back. Today was going to be a good day.

Levi and the rest of blue camp joked and laughed all the way to the mess hall where the cooks were serving up bacon and eggs and pancakes with syrup.

Everyone was in a great mood for the final day of the tournament. Someone would be crowned the winner today and everyone had their favourite to win.

After breakfast, the crowd tromped out to the duelling field for the first match: Oliver against Quinn. The match was a fantastic, crowd-pleasing affair, both competitors showing why they had made it to the quarter-finals, but eventually, Oliver's skill won out and he disarmed Quinn. He was a good sport and shook hands with Oliver after his defeat.

The second match was the one Levi was excited for. The way the bracket worked out, Miri and Kaito were facing each other. All of his friends had taken sides, but Levi couldn't decide who he thought would win. Miri was an excellent fighter, having proven herself in real life-or-death fights over and over, but Kaito was bigger, stronger and had two more years of Academy training.

Levi and his friends stood against the fence surrounding the match area as Miri and Kaito entered the ring.

"Go get him, Miri!" Kana cheered.

"You're not gonna let her beat you, are you?" Guy called to Kaito.

Kaito paid them no attention, completely focused on the impending duel. Miri, on the other hand, waved nervously to her friends and adjusted her armour.

Levi knew she desperately wanted to win, proving to everyone that just because she was mute didn't mean she was weak or helpless. Most people already knew this, but she wanted to reinforce it.

Someone jostled Levi. It was Taro, his hair as red and spiky as ever. "Heyo, Levi. This is gonna be interesting, huh?"

"Yep," Levi smiled. He liked Taro and the enthusiasm he always brought to whatever he was doing.

"Who you got?" Taro asked, grabbing Levi's shoulder and pointing him first at Miri then at Kinzo. "Spear or sword?"

"I'm really not sure," Levi said.

"Ah, come on, you've gotta have a suspicion of who'll win," Taro said.

Levi shook his head. "Honestly, I have no idea."

Taro eyed him suspiciously. "Hmm. You don't seem to be lying."

"Huh?"

"Oh, I can tell when you're lying. Your lips twitch and you rub your left thumb. I noticed it last year when you asked me to help with Stern, but I decided to help anyway."

Levi's mouth hung open. "What?"

Taro shrugged. "I can read you. Don't know why. You're hiding something big, I know. You'll tell me when you're ready."

Levi was flabbergasted. He didn't think he had done anything to arouse Taro's suspicion, but apparently, Taro knew. He might not know what it was that Levi was hiding, but Levi was suddenly wary. What if he was a spy too? He looked into Taro's broad smile and friendly eyes, devoid of anything but good humour. Levi couldn't make himself believe that Taro was a bad person. Still, he needed to be careful.

His thoughts were interrupted when Kross yelled, "Fight!" and the crowd began to cheer.

Kaito began to circle to his left, as he did at the beginning of any match.

Miri didn't turn, just followed with her eyes. When Kaito was level with Miri's right side, he stopped. They exchanged a glance and Kaito lunged. Miri leapt out of the way, doing a backward roll. That prompted a loud cheer.

Miri rushed Kaito and placed three exact strikes, which were deflected with ease. Still, Kaito stepped back and Miri pressed the advantage. Kaito dodged to the side and grabbed her wrist, pulling her past him.

She stumbled a few steps, swinging her arm behind her to block Kaito's strike. She spun at Kaito from the left, tossing Evenfell to her off hand and slashing at him. He leaned to the side, avoiding the blow and stuck the shaft of his spear in between her feet. She tripped, but turned it into a semi-graceful cartwheel, putting her out of range.

The crowd was going wild. This duel was the most exciting yet.

"I've never seen half these moves before!" Kinzo exclaimed.

"They're incredible!" Naomi said.

"Yeah, yeah, sure," Coral sulked. She was still put out about not making it to the round the two were currently battling in.

Cody gave her a playful shove. "C'mon, Coral. You've gotta be enjoying this somewhat."

Coral grumbled and pushed him away.

Inside the fence, the small respite had ended. Kaito closed the gap in a few quick strides. He swung his spear like a bat, but Miri ducked under it, pushing it up and away. She stabbed at Kaito's stomach, but he spun his spear and deflected her sword to the side. Letting herself go with the motion, she tried to catch Kaito's head with her elbow. He jerked back, only getting clipped.

Kaito put a hand on her back and shoved her away, sticking out his foot to trip her again. She lifted her knees and avoided the obstacle, facing him again. The tip of Evenfell made small circles. She brought her hands up and chopped down with all her strength. Kaito angled his spear and guided her sword away from him before swiping down and catching the tip of his spear on the inside of Miri's left leg. She buckled and fell to one knee. Without armour, it would have been a serious injury.

Kaito brought his spear around, intending to place the tip at her throat and gain the victory. Miri refused to give up and sprung ahead, tackling him around the knees and bringing him down. Both lost their weapons.

Miri scrambled on top of him and began to rain punches down on Kaito. He put his arms together to block the blows. He wasn't about to be beaten unarmed. He swung his legs up, hooked them around Miri's neck and pulled down, driving her to the ground violently.

There was a collective gasp from the crowd.

"That looked bad," Ember said.

Kaito staggered to his feet and retrieved his weapon. Miri still lay on the ground.

"I think she's unconscious," Cody said.

"She hit her head pretty hard," Naomi said.

Kaito shook his head and walked over to Miri. He lifted his spear, about to tap her with it and end the match, but suddenly, Miri shot to her feet, grabbed the spear, twirled it around and bashed him in the head so hard his helmet fell off.

He wobbled and Miri touched the point to his exposed throat.

"We have a winner!" Kross yelled.

The crowd erupted into cheers, at least, the ones who had bet on Miri.

Miri pulled off her helmet. Her hair was plastered to her face with sweat and she was gasping air, but she was beaming.

Kaito was kneeling on the ground. Miri walked over to him. He glanced up and nodded. "Well fought." He got to his feet and extended his hand. Miri ignored it and gave him a quick hug.

She let go and signed, "You almost had me."

Kaito smiled slightly. "Almost."

Levi shook his head. That had been the best duel he had ever seen. He could scarcely believe that his friends had put on such a great performance.

"That was extraordinary," Adam said, standing nearby. "Both sides performed admirably."

"I'll say," Taro grinned. "What a match!"

Guy chuckled. "I can't believe Miri won."

"Well, she did," Ember said. "And you'd best go congratulate her."

"Yeah, yeah, I will," Guy said, waving his hand.

Kaito and Miri both exited the ring and headed for the rooms where they would change out of their armour and be examined by Cam for any injuries. She had been at the Academy all week, at Aldus' request, helping all who were hurt during the tournament. She had also fixed up everyone who had been involved with the Forsaken.

"I want some cake," Taro decided. He walked away and was swallowed in the milling crowd.

Levi and Adam followed the others to the rooms where they would wait to congratulate Miri. As they walked, Levi asked, "Hey, Adam, has your dad written to you yet?"

"Indeed, he has," Adam said. "He reported that while he was questioned about the incident, he was not found guilty of anything and allowed to continue the tournament. It was postponed several days while the arena and stands were rebuilt. Since resuming, my father has won both his matches."

"Good news," Levi said. El Fen had elected to stay behind and cover for Levi and his friends, protecting them from the inquiry into the battle with Marek and Rorien Stern. After all, it would have been suspicious if one of the foremost knights in the realm just up and left such a prestigious tournament.

It was already suspicious that the whole of Blackthrush Academy had left early, but Aldus had managed to convince those inquiring that the students needed more time to focus on studies.

Levi and Adam joined the others who were standing in a circle.

"Quite the match, eh, Levi?" Cody said.

Levi smirked. "Best I've seen."

Kaito exited his changing room. He received lots of pats on the back as everyone told him what a great job he had done.

"Thank you," he said. "But Miri's win was well-deserved. I fought my hardest and she bested me fairly."

Another door opened to reveal Miri. "Well, that was something, huh?"

Everyone laughed.

~ ~ ~

Levi sat on a barrel next to the racks of weapons used in combat class. He sipped on a glass of sweetened lemon water.

Cody relaxed beside him, his elbow resting on the edge of the barrel. "A good week." The black amulet was dangling from his fingers as he absent-mindedly fiddled with it.

"Mm hmm," Levi said, mouth full.

"I mean, I thought we were gonna be in some real trouble after making such a mess at the Festival, but it turned out ok." Cody shook the pendant for emphasis.

Levi swallowed. "Yeah, I was expecting a troop of soldiers to come in and lock us up."

"Looks like Aldus took care of it," Cody said.

"He always does." Levi took a moment to adjust the small book in his pocket, as it had twisted sideways and was digging into his leg.

The two lapsed into silence.

Oliver and Winchester were heading for the field. They were the only ones left in the tournament aside from Bear and Vonn. Miri had been beaten by Winchester earlier, though she had put up a heck of a fight.

There were still a few minutes until the match began.

Levi's eyes followed Dante and Bram as they ambled by, carrying steaming pieces of pie and bickering like usual. Wes and Iaarra were sitting together on top of a wagon to their right. Elsewhere, Corvin and the twins were picking on a couple of first-years and Kindrelle was getting after Walt, who had drawn something on her bracket. Everything was back to normal.

"That pie looks amazing," Cody said, watching Dante gulp down his treat.

"You just had a slice," Levi said.

Cody pushed himself off the barrel. "And now I want another one. You coming?"

"Sure," Levi said, hopping down. The friends wandered around to the north side of the Academy, to where the goodies table was set up near red camp.

Most everyone was back at the field, ready for the match. Only Kana and Marshall were there.

Cody got a piece of blueberry pie and took a large bite of it. "Oh, that's good."

"You're gonna get fat, eating like that," Levi said.

Beside them, Marshall choked on his pastry.

"You ok?" Levi asked.

Marshall coughed and pointed. "Is that Evander?"

Looking to where he pointed, Levi saw their missing friend walking up the path toward them.

"Evander!" Kana cried and rushed out to meet him. "Where have you been?"

"Places," he said bruskly, brushing by her.

She frowned. "Are you ok?"

Evander ignored her and walked directly up to Levi. His face was deathly serious. "Levi. You need to run. Now."

"What? Why?" Levi had no idea what he was on about.

"Just run," Evander said. "Don't come back."

Levi glanced at Cody, who was just as confused as he was. Something was clearly wrong with Evander.

"Why does he have to leave?" Cody asked.

Evander took a deep breath, but didn't say anything.

Marshall cleared his throat. "Uh, guys? You might want to look at this."

Levi stepped around Evander and looked to the entrance to the Academy. His heart fell into his boots.

Row upon row of armed soldiers marched into Blackthrush, ten wide. They crashed to a stop when over three hundred had entered the Academy.

Cody lunged ahead and grabbed Evander by the collar. "What did you do?"

Evander broke free and stepped back. "I'm sorry. I didn't have a choice. Kyner tricked me."

Levi barely processed his words. He was drowning in terror. His worst fear had come true.

A trumpet rang out, loud and long. The soldiers parted to form a path. A woman in black and green armour came through and stood with her hand on her sword. Following behind her was the towering figure of Malroth, his onyx armour seeming to darken the air around him. He stood opposite the woman.

Then, to Levi's absolute horror, King Farren came down the ranks, dressed in full battle gear. He stopped next to his two lieutenants and in a magically enhanced voice that boomed across the Academy, called, "People of Blackthrush! Surrender Levi Sheppard or die!"

CHAPTER 31

For a moment, Cody's mind went blank as the situation overwhelmed him. Then, he drew back his arm and punched Evander in the face as hard as he could. Evander went down with a cry and didn't get back up.

Everyone came running to the front of the Academy after hearing the trumpet and Farren's order. Now, no one moved, unsure of what to do.

Cody scanned the crowd to see the rest of blue camp, Miri and Kinzo standing a hundred feet away, shocked and wide-eyed.

Farren called out again. "As your king, I command you to hand over Levi Sheppard! If you join me in the next ten seconds, we will spare your lives. If not-"

"No one move!" The doors of the main building burst open and Aldus stormed out, robes billowing behind him. "Begone, Farren! You have no power here!"

"I have all the power! I am King!"

"Not rightfully!" Aldus responded.

"Do not listen to your foolish headmaster, who has fallen to the lies of the Giala!" Farren said. "Come to me if you want to live."

People started going over to the enemy's side. Cody watched as people he had known for years turned their backs on Levi. Corvin, Vonn and the twins. Michael Long and Isabella Rain. Miss Holbrook. Lance. Cody felt like he had been punched in the chest, to be betrayed like this. In all, perhaps fifteen people chose to abandon Levi.

Everyone else was too scared to move.

"What did Levi do?" Christian asked timidly.

Farren straightened. "He stole the Elder Gem from me."

"It was never yours, you bastard!" Cody yelled before thinking it through. "You stole all the gems after murdering the Free Knights!"

Farren swung his gaze onto Cody. He felt the king marking him for death. "I see that some of you have also been led astray by the Giala's lies."

"The only lies are yours, Farren!" Aldus called, angrier than Cody had ever heard him.

"Enough!" Farren yelled. "Your life is forfeit, Aldus Calanol, along with all who side with you." He turned to the students who had joined him. "Now, where is Levi Sheppard?"

It was Lance who pointed him out. "There."

Levi staggered back as if struck.

Cody's rage was building up. He was going to kill everyone who changed sides.

The king's eyes narrowed on Levi. "At last. Men! Bring me Levi. I have a headmaster to kill."

Malroth raised his blood-red sword and said in a deep, grating voice, "Kill them."

The soldiers advanced, lowering swords and spears.

Cody spun and grabbed Levi, who was frozen in shock. "Run, Levi! You have to run!" He gave him a shove and Levi sprinted away, hyperventilating.

Cody turned to face the oncoming soldiers. He unsheathed his sword and went to shrug his shield around, but remembered that he didn't have it anymore. He cursed.

"Are... are they really gonna kill us?" Marshall asked in a small voice.

"Yes, they will," Kana said. Her eyes blazed with fury. "They're monsters."

A guttural roar erupted from the far side of the Academy as Griswold charged the line of soldiers. He crashed into them, dealing death blows with each stroke of his sword. So, he was on their side after all.

"Attack!" someone yelled. It was Taro, unarmoured and only carrying a sword.

Behind him, Guy and Kinzo yelled and charged ahead, prompting the rest to follow.

Cody growled and ran forward, determined not to let anyone at Levi. He met the line of soldiers and began hacking. They seemed surprised by his ferocity and gave ground before their numbers forced Cody back. His shoulder ached, but not enough to slow him down.

He faced three soldiers at once, two swordsmen and a spearman. The one with the spear jabbed at Cody, keeping him at bay while the other two tried to flank him. Cody needed to act fast. He spun to face the soldier on the right and brought his sword down on the man's helm. It wasn't a killing blow, but it put the man out of the fight for a time.

He began to turn the other way and saw a blade whistling toward him. He ducked just in time and stabbed ahead, now that he was under the soldier's guard. His sword slammed into the man's chest plate, denting it and sending him backward.

Cody rolled out of the way of the spear and came to his feet, parrying the next blow. The point still sliced his right forearm. It wasn't deep, but it bled profusely. The soldier jabbed again, aiming for Cody's stomach. Cody sidestepped and grabbed the shaft of the spear, pulling the man toward him. His sword intercepted the man under his arm, where there was no protection. The man died silently.

Cody's head swivelled left and right. Kana was slicing her sword across a soldier's throat. "Kana!"

She hacked at another man and raced over to him. "What?"

"We have to get Levi out of here!"

"I know!" Kana spun, blocking a sword meant for her head. She kicked the man in the front of the knee and slashed him across the chest.

"Protect him!" Cody cried, eyeing another soldier closing in. "I'll keep them off your back."

"Don't die," Kana said as she raced off to find Levi.

Cody yelled at the man in front of him. "Come on, then!"

The man snarled and attacked, sending powerful cuts at Cody, who held his ground, deflecting them all. He twisted his wrist, disengaging his sword and bringing it above the soldier's. He chopped down, severing his hand.

"My hand," the soldier said, dumbfounded. Cody finished him with a blow to the head.

Cody looked for the next opponent, but there were no more close by. Most of the battle was happening to his left, in the centre of the Academy. Soldiers were overwhelming the young, unprepared students. There were already too many of them on the ground.

Still, they were putting up a good fight. Bear was ploughing through the enemy, tossing men aside with powerful strokes. One of the fourth-years was lobbing crackling orbs of green energy at the soldiers, frying them where they stood. Someone else had summoned a small tornado that tore through Farren's men, flinging them into the air. Elsewhere there was a stone leopard on the loose, wreaking havoc.

But even with magic on their side, the fight was still tipping in Farren's favour.

Most of the instructors were taking on Malroth and his female companion. It wasn't going well. As Cody watched, the crimson blade of the king's enforcer flashed, cutting down Blackthrush's leaders. Cody gasped as he saw Dunning fall, holding his hand to his side as blood spilled out.

A cry for help drew Cody's attention. He spun and saw Marshall fighting desperately against two soldiers. He wasn't going to last long. Cody sprinted for them, but was too late. One of the soldiers slipped by his guard and plunged his sword into Marshall's chest.

"No!" Cody yelled. He took the soldiers by surprise and slashed through them, nothing restraining his blind rage. They were dead in seconds.

Cody knelt next to Marshall. He put a hand on his chest, but it was a fatal wound. There was nothing he could do. Marshall grabbed Cody's arm, terrified.

"It'll be ok," Cody said.

"Cody..." Marshall said, breaths coming in thin, ragged gasps. Cody bent close.

"Survive," Marshall whispered in his ear. His hand fell away from Cody's arm and his eyes drifted off.

Cody clenched his jaw and punched the ground. He slowly stood, anger growing in his chest. The sound of the battle faded away as a pounding in his ears took over.

There was no one close to Cody. He was on the far right of the battle and the only ones around were the dead and injured. He looked left, eyes locking on Farren, who was standing back and watching the carnage with a smile.

"I am going to kill you," Cody growled. "I swear it."

Someone was making their way toward the King. Aldus. He carved through the soldiers like nothing, his sickles stained red. A line of bodies followed in his wake. As he drew near, the king began to laugh. They exchanged words, but Cody was too far to hear. Then, Farren drew his sword.

Cody saw another friend fall and shook himself out of his stupor. "I can't just watch. I have to help!"

He was twenty metres from the nearest enemy, who was battering away at Demeter, slowly wearing her down. Cody raced to her aid, but could only watch as the soldier cut her down. As she crumpled to the ground, Cody ran her killer through.

He turned to face another soldier and blocked his sword. He battered it away and slashed across his chest. The man stumbled and Cody kicked him in the stomach. He fell and Cody plunged his sword between his collar bones.

He searched for his next opponent, but he only saw the bodies of those he had called his friends; Ellis, Samuel, Coraline, Shinzi. Moisture crept into his eyes. He dashed it away. He could mourn later. He needed to save as many as he could now.

Black lightning struck a nearby soldier, turning him to dust. He looked back at the King. In front of him was a glowing purple sphere. Aldus. To their right, he saw Silverton and Balak fighting back to back and a flash of grey race past them, taking out soldiers with claws and teeth: Kinzo. The spinning tornado broke apart, the caster either too tired to continue, or more likely, dead. Cody tore his gaze away, knowing he needed to fight.

The bulk of the battle was taking place directly in front of the main building. The Blackthrush fighters were outnumbered and being pushed back into a small semi-circle in front of the steps. He saw a spear take Verrol through the stomach and the small instructor went down.

Cody raced to get there before he was completely cut off by the king's men. Two soldiers stood in his way, backs to him. He scooped up a discarded spear, its head covered in gore. Cody hefted it into a throwing position and once in range, launched it at the left soldier. Fueled by his emotions, it struck the man in the back and pierced his armour. He yelled and threw up his arms before toppling over.

The other soldier began to turn but Cody's sword laid open his neck and he fell beside his comrade.

He entered the circle of survivors and took a second to catch his breath. Someone bumped him. Guy. He was bleeding from multiple cuts, though none seemed serious.

"You're alive," Cody said with relief.

"For now," Guy said grimly.

Cody touched the wound on his arm. "Where's Levi?"

"I saw him heading through the stables," Guy said. "Kaito, Naomi and Coral went after him."

"Good," Cody said.

"Look out!" Guy swung his cutlass in front of Cody, taking the blow that would have ended his life.

Cody flipped his sword around and jabbed backward. The thrust slowed as it encountered armour and flesh and the soldier screamed.

Guy stood shoulder to shoulder with Cody as they faced the incoming wave of soldiers. The next few minutes were a haze of chaos. Cody didn't think, he just fought. He feared that if he allowed himself to process what was happening, he would fall apart.

He acquired several injuries. First, a spear caught him on the inside of the left thigh, giving him a limp. After that, a soldier punched him in the forehead, opening a gash. Blood seeped down into his eye, making it hard to focus. Last, Cody blocked a blow from a large man and his bad shoulder popped again, renewing the agony that had been gone for the last few days.

Still, he didn't give up. The bodies began piling up around him. He lost count after nine. But, despite his efforts, there were just too many soldiers.

The sky darkened and lightning flashed, but Cody barely noticed it.

Around him, students and instructors fell beneath the unstoppable tide of Farren's forces. Cody saw Wes finally succumb to his wounds after taking out two spearmen. Above the din of the battle, Cody could hear Iaarra's cry of lament. Nearby, Walt was lying still on the ground, his shirt stained red.

We're not going to survive, Cody realized. They were trapped with their backs against the wall. A sudden idea popped into his head, as if someone had whispered it to him. A small spark of hope leapt to life. But for the idea to work, they would need a few moments respite and they weren't going to get one.

Cody shook his head as he deflected a spear and cut off its owner's arm. He was a Chaotic and he knew they were capable of chronomancy, manipulating time. Both Korlec and Linae had spoken of it. Of course, he had never done it before and had no idea how, but he had no choice but to do it now.

There was no time to stop fighting to compose himself. He would have to summon the magic while fighting for his life. He took a deep breath and forced himself to calm down. He parried a blow. Took a deep breath. Parry. Breath. Slash. Breath. Dodge. Breath. Stab. Breath.

Suddenly, his mind was clear, clearer than it had ever been. He could see, with his mind's eye, the magic he needed. He opened his mind to his magic and felt the cold, biting rush he always did. He twisted the power in a way that he never had before, certain this would work.

As he stepped back and reached out his left hand, a soldier stabbed at his chest, too close to block. A huge thunderclap boomed as a transparent wave of energy blasted out of Cody's hand and the soldier froze. Cody blinked. He looked around. All the soldiers were frozen. There was a rippling line between them and the Blackthrush fighters.

"What the hell?" Guy asked, out of breath.

"Hurry! We don't have much time!" Cody could already feel himself straining. "Get inside!"

Everyone still alive rushed into the building, limping and bleeding. Kinzo was back in his human form, his clothes a bloody ruin. Ember was helping Kindrelle to her feet. Griswold was pulling Iaarra away from Wes' body. Cody was the last to go. He saw those who hadn't made it; Osiris, Romeo, Kross, Terrant.

He ran inside and turned around, looking at the sea of frozen soldiers. His arm was burning, both from holding it up and from the massive amount of magic he was channelling. He dropped his hand and the soldiers jerked to life. For a moment, they looked around, thoroughly confused. Then, they raced for the door.

Quinn and Aybrin cast a spell together. A large knot of soldiers turned into spiders in a bright flash. The two ducked inside and Guy and Bear swung the doors shut.

The last thing Cody saw was Aldus looking at him, unarmed, as the king stood in front of him. Farren raised his sword and Aldus nodded to Cody.

The doors slammed closed and Balak cast a locking spell on them. Seconds later, the doors shook as the horde outside tried to break-in.

Cody turned to face the survivors. There were only twenty-four.

"What do we do?" Kindrelle cried. "We're trapped!" Others echoed her, saying they were doomed.

"Not quite," Cody said. "There's another way out of here."

Hope flared in Ember's eyes as she held a hand to a bloody gash in her side. "Of course! The tunnel!"

"What tunnel?" Silverton asked. "I know of no tunnel."

"We found it last year," Cody said. "Now let's move! Those doors won't hold long."

~ ~ ~

"This can't be happening!" Levi moaned for the tenth time.

The sounds of battle, metal on metal, screams and yells, energy crackling and feral growls echoed off the walls of the Academy that kept Levi contained.

"I need to find a way out of here!" He let his eyes slide over the back half of Blackthrush, searching for any way to escape. His gaze landed on the stables and the door leading into the countryside. "Perfect."

"There he is!"

Levi spun to see two soldiers running toward him. They closed quickly before Levi could run. Both swung their swords at Levi. He flicked open his shield, using it and his sabre to block the blows. Quickly accessing his magic, he telekinetically shoved one of the soldiers away, sending him crashing down.

The other soldier attacked, but Levi managed to parry his attack and put the man on the defensive. He struck out, but the soldier turned so Levi's blade glanced off his chest plate. The attacker whipped his sword around and cut at Levi's right side. Levi held his sabre in the way, his arm stung from the contact. Levi took a chance and swung his left arm. The man didn't see it coming and the edge of the shield clipped him in the side of the head. He collapsed on the spot.

Levi didn't stick around to see if he was going to get up or not. He needed to get away. He took two strides and scrambled back as a sword flashed in front of him.

"Stop right there!" the first soldier ordered.

"No way!" Levi said.

"Then, prepare to die!" The soldier pulled his sword back and dropped it as his throat exploded into a red shower as a blade pierced through.

Kana tossed him to the side, pulling out her sword. She grabbed Levi's arm. "Come on! We need to get you out of here!" She began to pull him toward the stables, obviously coming to the same conclusion he had. They sprinted for freedom.

With each step he took, Levi expected the king to appear in between him and his escape with a hundred men at his back. But the way remained clear of enemies. They reached the stable and Levi slammed his hands into the latch, hurrying to pull open the door. Kana lent her strength and the door slid open. Cold light spilled into the dim barn.

"People coming," Kana warned.

A bolt of fear shot through him, but he relaxed when he saw the group of eight weren't in armour. Levi recognized his friends: Kaito, Naomi, Coral, Adam, Taro, Gwen, Niles and Caesar. "What are you doing?"

"We're getting you out of here!" Naomi said, limping as fast as she could. "You need all the help you can get!"

"Who cares why they're here!" Kana said, shoving Levi into the stable. "Get going!"

Levi went right for Banqo's pen. He wasn't sure why, but he had a feeling he was supposed to take her. He threw open the gate and snatched the bridle and reins off the wall. He hastily put it on the horse, twisting straps and tangling the reins. She didn't struggle as she usually did, as if she knew this was of great importance.

In the next stall over, Caesar was lifting the saddle onto his horse.

"No! We don't have time!" Levi called. "Just grab the reins. We'll ride bareback."

Caesar nodded and dropped the saddle to the floor.

Levi led Banqo out of her stall and down the central aisle. "Come on! Hurry up!" He broke out into the light and snow, swinging himself up onto Banqo with some difficulty. He winced as the horse's hard backbone dug into his rear, but it was something he'd have to bear. Levi clicked his heel into her side and she shot ahead, past the corrals and the walls of the Academy.

As Banqo sped to a full gallop, Levi turned to look for the others. They were close behind, snapping the reins and holding on for dear life. Beyond them, Malroth and the armoured woman entered the stable, followed by ten soldiers.

"They're on us!" he yelled. A chill shot down his spine. They were going to race for survival. Banqo's hooves churned up snow and dirt as she strove to leave Blackthrush behind. The din of the battle faded away, replaced by pounding hoofbeats and heavy breathing.

Without a saddle, Levi struggled to keep his seat. He shifted constantly, squeezing with his calves to keep balanced. He grabbed Banqo's black mane and checked back. The Academy was already a half-kilometre behind them, but much closer were Malroth and his men, whipping their mounts to maximum speed.

"Faster!" Levi yelled, leaning over his steed's neck. He bit back a curse. The king's men were too close for them to hide somewhere. They would be run down. Underneath him, Banqo's flanks heaved. Her pace showed no signs of flagging and Levi hoped she could keep up the pace long enough to evade the pursuers. He doubted it.

A cry of surprise made Levi whip around. Gwen's horse had stumbled and pitched her off. She hit the ground hard and tumbled several feet before stopping with a groan.

"Whoa!" Levi yanked back on the reins, bringing Banqo to a stop.

"What are you doing?" Kana cried. "You need to go!"

Levi slid off his horse's back. "I'm not leaving her to be killed!"

The others pulled up beside him. "They will catch us now," Kaito said wearily.

"Then, we'll give them a good fight!" Taro said, drawing his sword. Blood still clung to the blade.

Levi slid to a stop next to Gwen. "Are you alright?" He helped her sit up.

"Ugh, I'll be ok." Red ran down her face from a gash on her right eyebrow. She blinked a few times, trying to clear the fog.

Levi pulled her to her feet. "We've got to go."

"Too late!" Kana yelled. Levi's head shot up as Adam's bowstring thrummed four times, loosing arrows. Two soldiers cried out and fell out of their saddles. The third arrow struck a horse. With a terrible scream, it pitched forward, crushing its rider. The last arrow missed.

The gap closed and the two sides met.

Levi yanked out his sabre as a horse barreled down on him. He shoved Gwen out of the way and leapt to the side. The soldier's sword sliced through his shirt, scratching his back.

Another soldier came at him, his horse rearing up. The man chopped down at him and Levi deflected it to the left, but with the speed of the horse behind the strike, it knocked Levi onto his back. A rock jammed into his left shoulder blade and he grunted. The horse reared up again about to stomp him to death. As the hooves came down, Levi twisted sideways, somehow ending up between the horse's legs. Grabbing the hock, he swung himself around and rolled to his feet.

The soldier urged his steed ahead. Levi darted to the left and as the man tried to bring his sword around to the opposite side, Levi stabbed his calf, tearing a bloody line. The soldier yelled in pain and reached down to cover the wound. Levi grabbed his arm and hauled him off the horse's back. He had no time to scream before Levi ran him through.

Levi straightened and caught a glimpse of Coral chopping off limbs and Caesar leaping from his horse to another, stabbing the soldier in the side. Adam was taking out his opponents with the stunning spell and finishing them with his blade.

A dismounted spearman approached Levi and jabbed at him. Levi stepped aside and chopped down on the shaft of the spear, levering the butt end into the man's chin. Dazed, he stepped back and Levi chopped at his chest until he dropped to the ground.

"Levi Sheppard!" Malroth boomed. He walked purposefully at Levi, scarlet blade in hand. "Surrender and your friends might survive."

"No! Run, Levi!" Naomi charged in on her horse, swinging down at the black knight. Malroth met her sword with a mighty swing that knocked her clean off her mount.

"Naomi!" Levi cried. He prepared to attack Malroth, but Niles swooped in.

"Get her and run!" he called. He reared his horse up to attack Malroth, but the black knight swung his sword and chopped off the horse's head. It flopped over and Niles jumped clear.

Levi ran to Naomi's side. She was unconscious. "C'mon, c'mon." He tapped her cheek until her eyelids fluttered open. Levi threw her arm over his shoulder and hauled her up. They staggered away from Malroth.

Levi glanced back to where Niles was fighting Malroth. Except he wasn't. He was sliding off the end of Malroth's sword, pierced through the heart.

A yell warned Levi and he brought up his shield just in time. He shook from the force, but before he could retaliate, the soldier dropped, skewered by Kaito.

"All the soldiers are defeated!" Kaito said. "We must escape!" He was right. All the men-at-arms were on the ground, some writing in pain, most still. But Malroth and the woman were still very much a threat.

"Surrender yourself, Sheppard!" the woman said.

"No thanks," Levi said. "Coral, blast them!"

"You got it!" Coral thrust out her hand and a torrent of wind blasted at the king's enforcers. They staggered back, the wind halting them. "Get going!" Coral yelled over the howling.

Levi helped Naomi onto her horse before he raced over to Banqo and climbed on. He checked to make sure everyone was mounted. They were. All but Niles.

Levi snapped the reins and took off, the others doing the same. Coral cut off the wind and followed.

Levi leaned over Banqo's neck and squeezed his heels, trying to go faster. They needed to escape. If not... his friends would all be executed. So would he, but only after days of torture.

"Are they after us?" Gwen asked.

"No," Kana said, confused. "They're just standing there."

"Huh?" Levi turned to look. Malroth was standing with both hands on the hilt of his sword, which was buried in the dirt. The woman was kneeling on the ground, a hand splayed on the snow.

"She's using magic," Adam said.

"Magic for what?" As soon as the words left Levi's mouth, the ground in front of them began to shake violently. A crack appeared in the earth and the horses stumbled. The ground dropped away as the crack widened into a fifteen-foot chasm.

Banqo tripped and fell, spilling Levi. He smacked his head and his vision went fuzzy. He could hear the others and their horses tumbling down around him, yelling and braying.

Levi pushed himself up. His head spun.

"Help!"

Levi shook his head as he got to his feet. He couldn't see who was calling.

"Help!" The voice came from in the crevasse. It was Caesar.

Levi raced to the edge. Dirt crumbled beneath his feet and he scrambled back. Twenty feet below, Caesar was hanging off a root sticking out of the newly formed canyon wall.

"Levi! It's not gonna hold much longer!"

"Hold on!" Levi yelled. His eyes darted around, looking for something to rescue him. There was nothing in sight. *I'll have to use magic.* He swallowed. He wasn't sure if he could lift Caesar all the way up, but he had to try.

He stretched out his hands and closed his eyes, letting the power inside him flood his body. He could feel Caesar's weight in his mind rather than in his hands.

"Let go!" Levi called.

"Are you crazy?" Caesar yelled, his voice cracking.

Levi nodded. "Trust me! I've got you."

"Hurry up!" Kana said, behind them. "They're coming!"

"We must hold them off," Kaito said.

The root Caesar was hanging from shifted, dropping him another foot. He yelled.

"Let go!" Levi began to lift Caesar slowly. Caesar let his hands fall away from the root as he floated upward, lifted by the power of Levi's mind.

Levi began to tremble as the effort grew. He gritted his teeth and kept going. He was not going to let him fall. He could hear yelling and the clashing of weapons behind him. Their enemies had arrived. He needed to get Caesar up now. Straining with every ounce of strength he had, Levi heaved him up. He was almost at the top of the chasm.

Pain erupted in Levi's back. His nerves fired bolts of agony into his brain. He howled as the flow of magic was cut off and dropped to his knees. Caesar disappeared into the earth, his scream echoing up the chasm. He was gone.

"No..." Levi croaked. The pain was unbearable. He could feel liquid running down his back. Something must have stabbed him. He couldn't move his right arm, so he lifted his left arm and found the knife that was buried in his back. He grasped the hilt and tore it out. His whole body spasmed and his vision blanked.

He panted as his sight returned. Managing to turn around, he could only watch as his friends were beaten by Farren's generals. Taro and Naomi were both on the ground already, Taro clutching his stomach and groaning, Naomi not moving at all.

The woman battled Kaito and Gwen while Malroth faced Kana, Coral and Adam. The woman spun around and flicked her wrist. A short knife sliced through the air and tore into Gwen's hip. She fell to one knee.

Levi looked the other way as a cry of pain reached him. Coral was staggering back, holding both hands to her side as red spilled over her fingers. Malroth kept pressing. He battered at Adam and Kana's defences, giving them no quarter. His great red sword flashed like a cobra, which his friends barely avoided. The knight shoved Kana aside and lunged at Adam. He blocked the strike, but Malroth grabbed his head with his free hand and slammed his face into his armoured knee. Adam dropped like a rock, his sword falling from his hand.

Levi swung back at the other fight. Kaito was holding his own for the moment, but a second later, he stepped back onto Gwen's foot and lost his balance. Lashing out, the woman caught Kaito's left eye. His cry of agony chilled Levi. He stumbled back, bent over and covered his face.

Another cry. Kana. Levi turned to see his friend holding the stump of her wrist. Her right hand lay on the ground, turning the snow around it red.

Malroth left her standing and strode toward Levi, as did his companion. They were splattered with blood, none of it their own.

"No!" Levi grabbed his sabre with his left hand and struggled to his feet. He let out a yell and attacked. Malroth knocked the sword from his hand. It landed on the edge of the crevasse, where it teetered for a moment before tumbling away into the darkness.

Levi flicked his shield open in a desperate last defence. Malroth simply snagged it and ripped the whole thing off his arm. He placed his sword under Levi's chin.

"It's over."

Despair and crushing defeat were the only things he could feel. Even the knife wound in his back paled in comparison to what had just happened. He had been caught. That was it.

Farren had won.

~ ~ ~

Farren watched as his soldiers crashed against the traitors in an unstoppable wave. They would be destroyed in no time.

To his right, he heard yells and screams as someone carved their way through his soldiers. Without seeing, he knew exactly who it was. The last few men between the king and Aldus fell beneath the headmaster's curved sickles.

Aldus' mouth was pressed into a hard line and his eyes shone with fury.

"Aldus Calanol," Farren said. "I have heard great things about you. I wish to see if they are true."

Aldus reached up and touched the pendant around his neck: a small hourglass. "You'll find that the stories do me no justice."

Farren tipped his head back and laughed. "Ah, dear headmaster, do not overestimate yourself. You are about to die."

"We'll see," Aldus said.

"Yes, we shall." Farren wrapped his hand around the hilt of his sword and pulled it out in a smooth motion. The golden blade refracted the sunlight into a rainbow. He stepped ahead into an offensive stance.

Aldus blew out a breath and attacked. The thin blades flashed rapidly, striking on all sides in a matter of seconds.

Farren stood firm, deflecting every blow. He was impressed with Aldus' speed and skill. Farren hadn't faced someone so powerful in years. He finally retreated a few steps under Aldus' relentless attack.

Farren had seen enough and struck out viciously. Aldus caught his sword in the crook of his blade and pushed it wide. His other sickle leapt at Farren's side. The king whipped his arm around quickly, blocking the strike.

The headmaster stepped back and vanished. Farren growled as he retreated. Reacting on instinct, he swung to his left and was met with a satisfying clang. He lunged ahead, hoping to clear away his invisible enemy.

He saw the fresh snow being kicked up by unseen feet and attacked. His sword jumped from one form to another seamlessly, but each one was blocked by Aldus.

Farren closed his eyes for a second and barked, "*Vewil!*"

Aldus appeared to his right, his sickles raised. For a moment, he was surprised that Farren could see him, but he recovered and attacked the King. As the headmaster slashed with his curved blades, he also attacked with another weapon, one unseen, yet equally as deadly.

A staggering force blasted against Farren's mind, seeking to break through his mental shield. Farren grimaced as he resisted the powerful attack. He could feel the immense strength coming from Aldus. This was magic of the most powerful kind, magic that would destroy all but the strongest. And Farren was the strongest.

The king lashed out with his sword, battering against Aldus's weapons, trying to break his concentration and the mental attack. Aldus parried the blows and renewed his invisible spear into Farren's mind. The king grunted aloud and stepped back, shaking his head. He could feel Aldus slipping past his armour, catching glimpses of what lay behind.

"No!" Farren growled, striding ahead and putting everything behind a series of forms. His golden blade rang against the sickles, but he managed to push Aldus back and the pressure in his mind lessened. Farren switched his grip and chopped downward. Aldus brought up both sickles, the blades curving around Farren's sword and pushed it up over his head. In the same movement, he swung his arms out, both weapons streaking for the king's head.

Farren knew he couldn't get his sword back in time. He barked a short word. A spell. "*Khyia!*" Aldus halted in place as blue shackles of light appeared around his wrists, ankles and neck. The magic dragged him back two feet into the air.

The king breathed out as the mental attack ceased. Aldus was using everything to break the spell holding him in place. The headmaster's face was frozen in a wordless grimace. The blue shackles began to glow brighter as Aldus fought. Farren averted his eyes as the spell shattered, the energy radiating into the air with a hiss.

"Impressive," Farren said, meaning it. There were very few people he knew who could have escaped such a spell.

Aldus wiped at his mouth and glowered at Farren. "You'll have to try harder than that."

Farren allowed a smirk to cross his lips. "Very well." Whispering several words and twisting his hands in a strange fashion, Farren directed another enchantment at Aldus. The space around the headmaster flared yellow, thin fingers of smoke curling up.

Aldus arched his back for a moment, before the magic passed. "You won't be ending the battle that way."

Farren shrugged. He hadn't expected a killing spell to break through Aldus' wards that he had no doubt been building up for years, just as Farren had. He manipulated his left hand and said, "*Lekion xera!*" His palm filled with red and black energy and he hurled it at Aldus.

The headmaster tried to avoid it, but it still struck his shoulder. He yelled in pain, but stayed on his feet.

Farren cast the spell twice more, but Aldus was ready. He crossed his sickles and the runes along the blades glowed purple. A shield of energy the same colour surrounded him and Farren's magic impacted against it, doing nothing.

Farren's eyes grew wide. Never had he seen such magic before. He stabbed his sword into the earth beside him and used both hands to channel black lightning. With a yell, he blasted the shield, but the lightning deflected off the energy and struck three nearby soldiers, who disintegrated into piles of ash.

Aldus came closer, backing Farren up. The king swore and cast a wall of fire. It washed over Aldus but did no damage. He

387

growled and cast the Breaking Spell. The shield flared brightly, but held strong.

A few soldiers ran at Aldus and struck at him, but when their blades touched the purple energy, they were launched into the air.

Breathing hard, Farren shook his head. He needed his power. He needed to let it out. Just for a moment. He threw his head back and let open the floodgates. His mind was filled with burning hatred and bloodlust, the desire to kill and destroy. Farren fought through it to cast a single, destructive spell.

High above them, the wind picked up and the clouds swirled together, darkening and thickening. Snow began to fall and lightning struck the towers of the Academy, lighting them ablaze. A shape grew in the clouds, something vaguely spherical. It grew larger and larger and dropped from the sky. A massive ball of ice broke free from the clouds, burning with an unnatural fire.

It struck Aldus' shield and a tremendous thunderclap split the air.

Farren wrestled to subdue the tempest and seal it back inside. He bent over, panting. Lying ahead of him was Aldus, his shield gone.

Farren straightened and held out his hand. "*Caet.*" His sword flew back into his hand. He approached Aldus, who was struggling to his feet. His sickles were smoking and blood was seeping from his nose.

The headmaster stepped forward and stumbled, utterly spent. He must have very nearly used up all his energy keeping the shield up.

"*Dissariarm!*" Farren twisted his left hand and the sickles were ripped from Aldus' grasp. He stood, unarmed before the King.

"Well fought," Farren said with sincere respect. "The stories did do you an injustice."

"Your stories didn't," Aldus replied. His voice was quiet and exhausted, but still remained strong, full of conviction. There was no fear, no despair. He wasn't afraid to die. Farren admired that, even envied it.

Farren nodded. He held Aldus' gaze until the headmaster looked beyond him and dipped his head. The king swung his sword. The headmaster fell to his knees, then to the ground. With his last breath, he whispered three words that Farren couldn't hear. Then, he was still.

Aldus Calanol was dead.

~ ~ ~

"The tunnel is in the basement?" Dante asked. He was limping badly and his left arm hung uselessly at his side.

Cody nodded, his whole body trembling with exhaustion.

"Remarkable," Silverton said. "A secret tunnel under the Academy this whole time." He too was limping and a bloody line was drawn across his right eye.

Cody led the survivors through the storage shelves to the back wall.

"Uh, I don't see the door," Guy whispered to Cody.

Cody sucked in his breath. "Me neither. But the other side had a door."

"It's gotta be there, right?" Guy said. "We just can't see it."

"So, you should still be able to open it," Cody said.

Guy tilted his head. "I hope so."

Cody looked over the twenty-four people crammed in the basement. Every one of them was injured in some way and in some degree of shock. Several people were openly crying and Aybrin was sitting in a corner with her knees to her chest, rocking back and forth with a blank stare.

"What's the holdup?" Kavik asked. The left side of his face was covered in deep gouges.

"You don't know where the tunnel is, do you?" Oliver asked.

Holly gasped. "You've led us into a trap!" People began panicking.

A loud crash boomed down through the ceiling.

"What was that?" Bram asked in a small voice.

"That," Griswold said. "Was the soldiers breaking down the doors." Before the students could panic again, Griswold held up a finger. "Shut up! They don't know where we are, but they will if you keep crying." He glared at Autumn, who was on the verge of a full-blown panic attack. Ember slipped an arm around her, trying to calm her.

Griswold faced Guy. "Get that door open."

Guy swallowed and began running his hands along the wall. After a moment, he shook his head.

"C'mon, man," Cody said. "Can't you just do the spell?"

"No. If I don't know where the lock is, I can't unlock it."

"He's right," Balak said. "He has to know exactly where it is."

Cody swore. This was not going how he had hoped. Tromping footsteps and doors being kicked down filtered down to the survivors.

"Help me, Balak," Guy said. The older man joined him at the wall.

"We'll never make it out alive," Kindrelle moaned, tears clinging to the corners of her eyes.

"Guess we'll go down fighting," Kinzo muttered, tracing a line in the dust on one of the shelves.

"We certainly will," Bear said. Cody didn't know how he was still moving. There were three long gashes across his torso and one on his left leg.

"But the door is right here! I know it is! I've walked through it!" Ember's voice quavered, but she refused to cry.

Cody sighed and ran a hand down his face. Defeated. He had led the survivors here on the wings of a false hope. This would be their tomb.

"They're getting close," Winchester said in a flat voice. Cody looked into his eyes. He had given up and he was right. The soldiers were nearly above them.

"It's no good," Balak said, letting his hands drop away from the wall. "I can't find it."

There was a dull smack. Guy groaned with his fist against the wall. "We're so close! I don't want to die here."

A deep silence fell over the survivors as they tried to make peace with their impending doom. Cody folded his hands together and leaned his chin against them. *I hope Levi got away. I hope this was all worth it.*

Footsteps grew louder as the soldiers closed in on them.

Miri bowed her head for a moment before walking up to the wall. She drew Evenfell and held it vertically with both hands in front of her face.

"What are you doing?" Cody asked. He flinched as Miri's consciousness touched his.

Don't worry. I'm getting you out of here.

How?

It doesn't matter how. Just, whatever happens, don't leave me behind.

Leave you behind? Never! Cody was hurt she would even think that he might do so.

Miri ran her left hand up the blade, slicing her palm.

"Miri, what are you doing?" Silverton asked, concerned.

Miri ignored him. She placed her bloody palm on the wall and closed her eyes.

Guy looked at Cody, just as confused as everyone else. Cody shrugged.

A bright light exploded into existence. Cody turned away, seeing spots. Squinting hard and shading his eyes with his hand, he turned back and gasped. The light was coming from Miri, radiating off her like a star. It grew brighter until Cody's eyes burned and watered, but he couldn't look away.

A resounding crack split the air and the wall exploded outward, revealing the tunnel behind in a cloud of dust.

The light vanished.

"You did it!" Cody exclaimed.

Miri turned to him, a trickle of blood coming from her nose. She smiled and collapsed. Cody's joy vanished as he raced to her side. "No! No!" He felt for a pulse, but there was none. "Miri!" He was barely aware of everyone rushing past him into the tunnel, or the sound of the soldiers racing toward the basement.

Someone grabbed his arm. Guy. "Cody! We have to go!"

Cody gulped in air, trying not to lose it.

"Cody!" Guy yelled.

Cody stood. "Help me with her. Please."

Guy grabbed Miri's limp form and put one arm around his shoulder. Cody did the same and they ran into the tunnel. Behind them, wood splintered as the soldiers broke down the basement door.

"Faster!" Guy yelled.

Cody groaned as he forced his legs to move quicker. But he knew that, as injured as he and Guy were and encumbered with Miri, they would never outrun the soldiers.

Cody and Guy caught up to three people who had stopped: Griswold, Winchester and Bear, three of the best fighters.

"Keep going," Bear said. "We'll hold them off."

A lump formed in Cody's throat. They were sacrificing themselves for him. There was no way they could survive.

He and Guy kept running. They didn't stop as the sound of combat echoed through the tunnel. They didn't stop as screams and yells reached their ears. They didn't stop as the tunnel began to shake and collapse behind them. They didn't stop until they reached the other end of the tunnel and climbed up the ladder into the bluff of trees.

They stumbled out into the gulley and collapsed on the ground. Survivors lay all around them, totally spent.

Cody hurt. His whole body hurt. But what hurt most was his heart. So many friends killed, slaughtered. He blinked back tears, but as soon as he looked at Miri's still form, they began to fall. "I'm so sorry," he whispered.

Kinzo and Ember joined them. Kinzo put a hand on Miri's shoulder, his face blank.

"Cody," Guy said, his voice thick.

Cody dashed away tears and raised his head. He followed Guy's finger to where a large plume of dark smoke rose into the air.

"It's gone," Cody whispered. "Blackthrush is gone."

END OF BOOK 2

ACKNOWLEDGMENTS

Look at that. I've finished the second book of my Sixth Order series. Sometimes, I still can't believe I wrote a book and yet here I am with two of them. Mind-blowing. I can't wait to continue this story that's been stuck in my mind for years and I'm glad I've at least been able to tell the amount I have already. I wouldn't have been able to get this far without lots of help. Thanks goes to my parents who have put up with my weird writer quirks and antics. Also, my siblings, Brendan and Chandal, deserve a huge shoutout. They pruned and scourged and polished my drafts until the story was much better than I could have ever made it myself. Thanks a ton. A final thank you goes to anyone who has read my stories. You guys are awesome.

ABOUT THE AUTHOR

Jarret Madden is a young author from Saskatchewan with a love of all things adventurous and magical. He grew up playing LEGO and going on quests with his brother, which helped expand his imagination, paving the way for his journey into authorhood. He started writing his debut novel when he was 18, just after graduating high school. His first novel was published in the summer of 2019 and he plans to release a new book each year.

Made in the USA
San Bernardino, CA
26 July 2020